Life, Death
& the Government

Life, Death & the Government

Edited by Melinda Maidens

Facts On File

119 West 57th Street, New York, N.Y. 10019

Life, Death & the Government

Published by Facts On File, Inc.
119 West 57th Street, New York, N.Y. 10019
Copyright © 1980 by Facts On File, Inc.

Library of Congress Cataloging in Publication Data

Maidens, Melinda.
  Life, death & the government.

  Includes index.
  1. Medical policy—United States—Addresses
essays, lecture.   2. Medical laws and legislation—
United States—Addresses, essays, lectures.
I. Title.
RA395.A3M35   363.1   80-29094
ISBN 0-87196-336-1

International Standard Book Number: 0-87196-336-1
Library of Congress Catalog Card Number: 80-29094
9 8 7 6 5 4 3 2 1
PRINTED IN THE UNITED STATES OF
AMERICA

Contents

Preface

"Get the government off our backs!" has become America's rallying cry for the 1980s. Individuals see themselves at the mercy of a huge, lumbering bureaucracy that threatens to take total control of their daily lives. Government regulations affect our places of work, our homes and the very food we eat. We cannot pick up a pack of cigarettes without reading a government warning; we cannot get into our cars without a government-required buzzer scolding us for not buckling our seat belts. Government-sponsored advertisements warn us against alcohol, overeating and a host of other things that endanger our health.

Naturally, we want to avoid obvious health hazards. We want protection from environmental poisoning, unsanitary food processing, dangerous drugs and unsafe automobiles. We see those dangers as forced upon us by unscrupulous or uncaring manufacturers. However, what are we doing about the dangers that we inflict upon ourselves? We expect the government to protect us from corporate enemies, but we resent it when the government tries to protect us from ourselves.

The regulatory agencies that were created to protect us were created in answer to real needs, when the public truly was the victim of gross corporate abuse. Those agencies have made American food and drug standards the highest in the world. However, as they continue their mission into the 1980s, they are faced with an increasingly skeptical public. We are so accustomed to high safety and health standards in manufacturing that we take them for granted and dismiss health warnings as the products of an overly fussy government that has nothing better to do. So many new cancer dangers are discovered every day that people are inclined to throw up their hands and agree with the editor who wrote: "Living causes cancer." This is the new public cynicism, which has created hostility to government efforts to improve our health habits.

The editorials in this book were drawn from newspapers around the country. No effort has been made to favor any particular point of view. Together, the editorials draw a picture of media sentiment, the most potent influence on public thought.

January, 1981   Melinda Maidens

Eating & Drinking

After *The Jungle,* Upton Sinclair's 1906 expose of the horrendous conditions in the meat-packing industry, few people argued against federal regulation of food processors. That year, Congress passed the Food and Drug Act, which created several agencies to police food processors and enforce health and sanitation standards. In 1930, the agencies were merged into the Food and Drug Administration. The FDA's purpose, in Washington's words, was "directed toward protecting the health of the nation against impure and unsafe foods, drugs and cosmetics and other potential hazards." Because of the FDA, every can, package or bottle in the supermarket must carry a label listing its contents. FDA regulations specify minimum percentages of ingredients in food products: ice cream must contain a certain percentage of butterfat, for example; otherwise, it must be labeled "ice milk."

Has the FDA become overenthusiastic in its mission? In recent years it has issued a stream of announcements that many of the staples in the American diet are health hazards. Americans use too much sugar, eat foods that are too fatty and practice poor nutrition in general, according to the FDA. Almost every food we eat has been linked to cancer and heart disease, the two leading causes of death in the country. The FDA has been supported in its zeal by the growth in public concern with "health" foods and "natural" foods. Preservatives and chemical additives have come under suspicion for causing a variety of health problems. FDA warnings about saccharin and nitrites find ready acceptance among the nutrition-minded, but many Americans are beginning to wonder where it all will end. They believe the FDA, but they question the need to ban the offending foods. Once a health hazard is identified, they say, it should be up to the individual to decide whether to eat it.

As if eating weren't dangerous enough, the perils of alcohol loom ever larger. Alcohol, unlike nitrites, is a proven health problem. Ten million adults, 7% of the U.S. population, have drinking problems. Alcohol is responsible for at least 10% of all deaths in the country: 50% of all traffic fatalities, 40% of fatal industrial accidents and 83% of fire-related deaths. Alcohol abuse costs the country more than $43 billion each year in terms of lost working time, medical care, automobile accidents and violent crime.

Given the weight of evidence, what should the government do? A drive to abolish alcohol entirely resulted in a well-known failure—the Prohibition era of the 1920s. However, Washington feels compelled to try. A 1977 proposal to issue health warnings on liquor bottles was quickly dismissed in Congress. Although it did not threaten anyone's freedom to drink, it was considered an unnecessary government intrusion into people's personal habits. It was also termed silly, since if government educational campaigns against drinking had failed, why should labels on liquor bottles succeed?

FDA Proposes Banning Saccharin; Canadian Study Finds Cancer Link

The Food and Drug Administration March 9 said it would propose a ban on the use of saccharin, the only artificial sweetener available in the U.S. The agency based its decision in part on laboratory tests conducted by Canadian scientists that showed rats fed high dosages of the sweetener developed malignant bladder tumors. The FDA, in announcing the ban, had admitted that a human would have to drink 800 12-ounce soft drinks sweetened with saccharin every day for a lifetime to match the doses given to the rats in the Canadian tests.

The saccharin ban would be made under the so-called Delaney clause contained in the food-additive amendments added by Congress in 1958 to the Food, Drug and Cosmetic Act. The clause, which was named for Rep. James J. Delaney (D, N.Y.), required the FDA to withdraw from the market any food additive that had been found to cause cancer in either humans or animals. Saccharin had been in use in the U.S. for about 80 years. Americans consumed about five million pounds of the substance each year, according to the government. Saccharin was a staple of the diet-food industry, with low-calorie soft drinks accounting for three-quarters of the yearly consumption. The FDA ban would apply to all foods and beverages with saccharin additives.

The Canadian government March 9 announced that a broad ban on saccharin would take effect in that country June 1, based largely on the results of tests conducted by Canadian scientists that linked saccharin to cancer. In Canada, saccharin would be forbidden in practically all its current applications. Beverages containing the substance would be outlawed after July 1. Drugs containing saccharin as a non medicinal ingredient would not be permitted after Dec. 31, 1978, with the exception of some "life-saving" drugs. Cosmetics, toothpaste and mouthwash containing saccharin would not be allowed after Dec. 31, 1979. Canada planned to make saccharin available in pharmacies Sept. 1.

The FDA's proposed ban on saccharin drew angry protests from consumers and representatives of the food industry March 9–10. William P. Inman, a vice president of Sherwin-Williams Co. of Cleveland, the only U.S. manufacturer of saccharin, March 9 said his firm had not "seen anything that even [came] close to conclusively proving that saccharin [was] a health hazard." Inman's contention was supported the same day by a spokesman for Abbott Laboratories in Chicago, maker of a popular saccharin-based sweetener, Sucaryl. The spokesman said that "a number of other well-controlled studies" in addition to the Canadian experiments had "shown no harmful effects from saccharin used in equally high doses."

The FDA defended its decision in congressional hearings March 21. Dr. Richard R. Bates, FDA associate commissioner for science, testified that "at the highest level of risk" for humans, four persons out of 10,000 would develop bladder cancer if they drank only one 12-ounce can of diet soda daily during their lifetimes. Dr. Guy R. Newell Jr., acting director of the National Cancer Institute, added that the NCI projected the possibility of an increase of 600 to 700 cases of bladder cancer in the U.S., based on the results of the Canadian study. Dr. Newell also said, "We have no evidence that saccharin causes cancer in humans."

Detroit Free Press

Detroit, Mich., March 14, 1977
"Sugar in the mornin', sugar in the evenin', sugar at suppertime. . ."
—The Maguire Sisters

IT HAS BEEN more than a decade since regular viewers of the Arthur Godfrey Hour listened to that ditty sung by the ever effusive Maguire Sisters trio.

Now, come July, it may be back to sugar three times a day for all the millions of Americans who have come to rely upon saccharin, the only allowable sugar substitute currently marketed in the states, to satisfy their sweettooth needs.

The federal Food and Drug Administration is preparing to ban saccharin because a test has shown it to cause cancer in rats. The FDA acted, as it was legally required to, under the terms of the Delaney Amendment to the basic FDA statute, which mandates the banning of any food additive that "is found to induce cancer when ingested by man or animal."

Complaints against the ban have reached a feverish pitch already, and more can probably be expected.

We can understand why people do not want to give up a low-calorie sweetener. We especially understand why diabetics, who must restrict their intake of sweets, would be upset with the saccharin embargo. And we agree with those people who point out that it is inconsistent for the government to permit the sale of cigarets, a known carcinogen, while preventing the sale of the sweetener.

But it is appropriate for the FDA to ban saccharin, and it is a move that should be applauded, not vilified.

There have been just too many cases where very suspect substances have been allowed to remain in the food supply and in the environment because no one was 100 percent certain they should be banned. Asbestos fibers are in some Great Lakes water supplies. Red Dye No. 2 was allowed to be sold for decades after initial indications of it possibly leading to cancer.

The American people should not be guinea pigs. Perhaps it is true that a person would have to drink 800 bottles of diet soft drink to consume the same proportion of saccharin as that fed to the laboratory rats that contracted cancer. But science has not progressed to the point that we know for certain that smaller amounts over a long period of time don't create problems.

It is better to not take a chance.

There will be differently formulated diet soft drinks available when the ban takes affect, according to spokespersons for both Coca-Cola and Pepsico, the two giants of the industry.

Other, as yet unmarketed sweeteners for use in coffee and on cereal are ready for testing now, and could be available as early as a year from now.

The needs of diabetics are to be considered, too. The FDA chairman will investigate the possibility of having saccharin available with a doctor's prescription—a move that would make perfect sense. If saccharin were available to the relatively few people who really do need it for medical reasons, the rest of us would learn to survive without it.

The key word is "survive."

The Providence Journal
Providence, R.I., March 13, 1977

In announcing its proposed national ban on use of the artificial sweetener saccharin, the Food and Drug Administration once again has dramatized the problem of dealing with public-health dangers that may be only dimly seen.

Saccharin, in use since about 1900 and now the only artificial sweetener permitted in the U.S. market, is the sugar substitute used for flavoring in diet soft drinks, diet fruits and ice cream, and as a coffee sweetener. Several years ago, suspicions were raised that saccharin might be a cancer-causing agent. A study sponsored by the Canadian government now has shown that large doses of the product indeed have caused malignant bladder tumors in laboratory animals.

The FDA, acting under a sweeping amendment requiring it to bar from the use in food of *any* product known to have caused cancer in animals or man, cited the Canadian tests in announcing its prohibition. The FDA acted in the only way it could. The law governing its action in such cases, known as the Delaney amendment, provides no latitude — no method for weighing the acknowledged benefits of saccharin against the possible risks.

There currently is no approved substitute for saccharin, and the FDA ban (if it goes through) will mean a phase-out of many popular diet foods and drinks, to the undoubted inconvenience of many dieters and the dismay of diabetics and others who for medical reasons must shun sugar. Yet even the critics of the FDA's move have to acknowledge that a substance known to cause cancers in rats could, over time, contribute to cancer in humans. The word "could" is used advisedly. There is no empirical evidence, and probably no way to obtain any, on whether X milligrams of saccharin ingested daily in the human body over a period of Y years will produce a Z risk of acquiring cancer. No human cancer has been traced to saccharin, and it is estimated that a person would have to drink 800 bottles of diet soda a day throughout his life for a saccharin intake comparable to that seen in the Canadian rats. However, no one can say with certainty that the accumulated effects of hundreds or thousands of doses in the human system, over several years, would *not* pose a serious risk.

The risk, though perhaps slight, seems real. In such situations the prudent approach is not to take unncessary chances — not to gamble with potentially dire aftereffects that may come to light only years into the future.

But let's be realistic about it. There is such a thing, after all, as overreacting to suspected dangers, which can be more harmful than the dangers themselves. The FDA is hardly a capricious agency, but its scientists can't always be locked into only a yes-or-no choice. They need to have somewhat more latitude to look at the problems of carcinogens from all angles

Perhaps pharmaceutical houses can devise some new sweetening agent that can be shown to carry no risks to the user. In the meantime, Congress ought to look again at the needlessly rigid Delaney amendment that forces the FDA into such sweeping actions.

THE LOUISVILLE TIMES
Louisville, Ky.,
March 16, 1977

By deciding to ban saccharin while continuing to encourage the production of tobacco, the federal government appears to be the sort of policeman who writes parking tickets while citizens are murdered nearby.

Cigarettes are almost certainly linked to the steadily increasing rate of lung cancer. Saccharin, an artificial sweetener, is charged only with causing tumors in a few rats. There is no proof that it hurts humans.

Indeed, a more persuasive case might be made for banning sugar, which is responsible for millions of Americans being toothless and fat.

It would be a mistake, however, to conclude that the Food and Drug Administration's action is merely an example of bureaucracy run amok.

The cancer plague is now believed to be largely man-made. Sixty to 90 per cent of all cases may be caused by chemicals or other substances in the air, the water, in our food, or in the places where we work. Saccharin is suspected of being one of those chemicals.

The tests that led to this finding cannot be taken lightly. Of 100 rats that were fed saccharin, three developed tumors. A more disturbing statistic shows that 14 per cent of their offspring got cancer.

It's irrelevant to argue that a person would have to drink 800 bottles of diet soft drinks a day for life to consume a comparable amount of the sweetener. Researchers long ago concluded that a minute amount of a carcinogen can be dangerous.

Unlike many chemicals added to our food, saccharin does have benefits. It is the only sugar substitute available to diabetics and the obese.

But under a law known as the Delaney Amendment, the FDA has no choice but to ban any food additive that induces cancer in people or animals, even if the risk is small. Many people now say that the law is too rigid, that the agency's judgments would be more rational if it were allowed to weigh costs against benefits before deciding what to do.

Wouldn't it be enough, for instance, for the government merely to publicize tests implicating certain foods or to require warning labels?

Perhaps so. But Congress should approach any such proposals with extreme caution. "Rational decisions" would by no means be assured if the agency had to weigh such values as a sweet taste in the morning coffee against a possible cost in human lives.

Saccharin may yet be proved innocent. Let's hope so. In the meantime, let's not forget that the FDA has good reason to be suspicious of the chemicals we so freely consume.

THE CINCINNATI ENQUIRER
Cincinnati, Ohio, March 17, 1977

WHEN THE CYCLAMATE ban was announced in 1969, Dr. Albert Sabin, the former Cincinnatian who fathered the oral antipolic vaccine, took the action with, as they say, a big grain of salt. He was unpersuaded that cyclamates threatened human life simply because massive dosages of them caused cancer in animals.

Other voices also were raised against the Food and Drug Administration (FDA) bar on the sweetener. But diabetics, weight watchers and others who must guard against sugar intake had saccharin as an option. Now the FDA has taken that from them (or will when the agency gets the appropriate new regulations ready and published in the Federal Register about midyear).

So barring perfection of some exotic African fruit source, or extraction of a suitable substitute from grapefruit peel, those requiring sugar options may simply have to surrender all sweets. For many that would be a cruel result of what is, at best, a suspicious system of federal banning of food additives and the like said to cause cancer in animals.

The Calorie Control Council, a private organization, was quick to denounce the ban, contending a human being would have to drink 1250 12-ounce diet drinks daily for life to consume the saccharin equivalency of the FDA's test rats' ingestion. In all fairness, the FDA's hands are tied, so to speak, by the law requiring it to ban any substance causing cancer in animals.

No matter that the amount pumped into the rat would be the equivalent of more than a human being could ingest in several lifetimes. No matter that in the case of saccharin, many Americans have been eating and drinking it for 40 years or more without apparent ill effect.

The whole subject of FDA bans would seem to merit a thorough congressional investigation. And fortunately, the House health subcommittee headed by Rep. Paul G. Rogers (D-Fla.) is making a start with saccharin. Might not sugar substitutes be sold the same as cigarettes, with a health-warning label? In any case, we hope the Rogers subcommittee produces recommendations under which those for whom sugar assuredly means peril or death may have a reasonable option.

Sentinel Star

Orlando, Fla., March 18, 1977

WHEN THE Food and Drug Administration banned cyclamates in 1969, saccharin survived — the only remaining artificial sweetener on the market. But it was a cancer-causing suspect even then and has since undergone extensive laboratory testing.

The other shoe fell this month when the FDA, acting on Canadian research, banned saccharin on the open market.

The fear and fury of diabetics is justified. No individual can consume all the saccharin which tests on rats indicate is necessary to induce cancer. But because the danger, however remote, exists, the FDA is required by law to act. Its authority is the Delaney Clause, a 1958 amendment to the Food, Drug and Cosmetic Act prohibiting use of any additive that causes cancer in people or animals.

The law has no loopholes. It makes no allowance for illness, allergy or the affliction of an excessive sweet tooth.

Indeed, the use of sugar, which is high in calories and has no food value, is discouraged by physicians, dentists and nutritionists. It probably is far more harmful to health than the insignificant amounts of saccharin used to replace it.

In effect, the Delaney Clause is driving saccharin into pharmacy prescription departments where its cost will be increased out of all proportion to its intrinsic worth.

Prescriptions, valid for one year at the most, are not easily or cheaply come by. To cover the cost of recording and filing, druggists add, on the average, $1 to the price of each prescription they fill. And the cost of saccharin itself can be expected to go up because of reduced production.

Let's give the Delaney Clause the benefit of the doubt. When it was written nearly 20 years ago legislative concern was for deadlier impurities than artificial sweeteners which never have been known to cause cancer in humans.

Congress has had enough experience putting loopholes in laws to relax the Delaney Clause until acceptable sugar substitutes can be marketed in quantity.

HERALD EXAMINER

Los Angeles, Calif., March 16, 1977

The decision by the Food and Drug Administration to ban the sugar-substitute saccharin has created a storm of controversy in Los Angeles and throughout the country. And no wonder!

Medical tests do not prove conclusively that saccharin causes cancer. The test rats in a Canadian laboratory were fed approximately 150 times the amount of saccharin found in a 12-ounce soft drink. A human being, by comparison, would have to drink more than 800 bottles of soft drinks each day to consume an equivalent amount. Saccharin has been in use more than 80 years with no evidence that it has produced cancer in human beings.

Diabetics and others who cannot use sugar have no available alternate.

Since making its ruling, the FDA has been bombarded with complaints from consumers. It has also been condemned by some government officials and the soft drink industry as being too hasty and based on skimpy evidence. Robert M. Kellen, president of the Calorie Control Council in Atlanta, has called the FDA ruling "an example of government overregulation in disregard of science and the needs and wants of consumers."

Under the Delaney clause (pertaining to all ingested food) in the basic FDA statute, the FDA had no choice but to ban saccharin after the medical tests were finished. This was done despite another saccharin study with monkeys which produced no cancer cases over a period of six and one-half years. No qualifications are allowed under this law. A bid to delete the Delaney clause is now before Congress. It commands immediate action.

Meanwhile, the order banning saccharin should be lifted until such time that medical science can prove conclusively that saccharin is a threat to human health.

RAPID CITY JOURNAL

Rapid City, S.D., March 21, 1977

Although federal officials see almost no danger in the use of saccharin, its days as a food and beverage sweetener are numbered.

That's a bitter dose for dieters and persons who depend on saccharin for medical purposes because they are left with no ready substitute.

The Food and Drug Administration is being scored for issuing the ban on saccharin after a Canadian test showed some rats fed a concentrated diet of the substance developed cancer of the bladder.

Actually the FDA had no choice in view of the evidence that saccharin does not meet the standards for food additives established by Congress.

The standards are stated in what is known as the "Delany clause" of a 1958 amendment to the Food, Drug and Cosmetic Act. It states that "no additive shall be deemed to be safe if it is found to induce cancer when ingested by man or animal."

That clause in the law allows no leeway for weighing the benefits of saccharin against the possible hazard revealed in laboratory tests. It makes no difference that the amount of the artificial sweetener fed to the laboratory rats constituted five per cent of their daily diet and that such doses represent more than a consumer would receive from drinking 800 12-ounce diet drinks daily for a lifetime.

Diabetics with a sweet tooth will be hardest hit by the saccharin ban. The loudest cries, however, will probably come from diet addicts. About three-quarters of the five million pounds of saccharin produced annually is used in diet soft drinks.

While the results of the Canadian tests shouldn't be ignored, they should be balanced against saccharin's record. It has been used for some 80 years without any link being established between its use and cancer in human beings. Two studies, one of cancer among diabetics in England and one of people with bladder tumors in New York, also failed to show a link between cancer and saccharin.

Thus it appears that the saccharin ban is based on a legal decision rather than a medical decision.

It is probable that the initiative and imagination of American industry will produce an alternative to saccharin as an artificial sweetener.

Nevertheless, the saccharin ban, based as it is on doses given to rats in amounts that ordinarily would never be ingested by humans, indicates the Delaney clause is too restrictive. Congress should take steps to bring the legal restriction on food additives into line with medical reality.

"We have (cough) determined (choke) that saccharin can (wheeze) be dangerous to your (hack) health."

Reprinted by permission of the Los Angeles Times Syndicate.

Amsterdam News
New York, N.Y., March 26, 1977

The Food and Drug Administration, as one of the watchdogs of the nation's health habits, has every right to bar a product off the market when it is clear that that product is detrimental to the nation's health.

Recently, the FDA arrived at the conclusion that saccharin, which we have been using for 80 years as a substitute for sugar, breeds cancer in rats, and therefore is dangerous for human consumption.

But some of our best medical authorities deny this and even the FDA admits that its study is inconclusive.

Nevertheless saccharin has been banned.

We think the FDA should reverse itself on this matter and wait until all facts are in before banning saccharin, or any other product.

THE ROANOKE TIMES
Roanoke, Va., March 16, 1977

Normally, the prospect of Congressmen rushing into the domains of science is not a cheery one. But Congress' interest in the Food and Drug Administration ban on saccharin is welcome and fitting. Science, it seems, played a rather limited role in the ban; the chief role was played by law enacted by Congress, and Congress alone can fix what it has set awry.

Characterizing the kind of laboratory experiments that indicated saccharin to be a carcinogen, food scientist Bernard L. Oser said: "The practice has been to administer the highest possible dose to the animal without killing it. It is a rather absurd situation—atypical and unrepresentative of conditions you'd have with hu-

mans." Dr. Oser should know; his lab test results led in 1969 to a questionable FDA ban of another artificial sweetener, cyclamates.

A 1958 amendment to federal law, the Delaney Clause, requires FDA to ban any food additive found to cause cancer in humans or animals, and never mind how unrealistic the test. The law is much too rigid. The saccharin uproar is leading toward new hearings and perhaps new legislation that could make FDA's authority more flexible. It would make better sense, as one saccharin manufacturer suggests, to let the product be sold with a health warning on the package, just as the government now allows the sale of cancer-causing cigarettes.

The News and Courier
Charleston, S.C., March 15, 1977

Going about its business of consumer protection, the Food and Drug Administration apparently has hit a sour note by banning saccharin, the artificial sweetener.

Saccharin safety has been studied in this country for five years. The FDA decided to impose its ban not on the basis of findings of those studies, but because Canadian scientists said they found rats develop cancer after being fed saccharin.

Applying conclusions from animal experiments to man is acceptable practice. However, skeptics among manufacturers and commercial users of saccharin are saying that to get a saccharin dosage equivalent to what the Canadian rats got, a person would have to drink 800 cans of low-calorie cola a day — somewhat above the median consumption level. If FDA has answered that criticism, we missed the response.

While recognizing that it doesn't pay to take chances where health is concerned, American citizens still are left to wonder at the inconsistency of a watchful government which requires only warnings of possible hazards on packages of cigarettes, but orders saccharin off the shelves.

The Houston Post
Houston, Tex., March 16, 1977

The Food and Drug Administration is taking flak that it does not deserve. In announcing its decision to ban the production and distribution of saccharin, it was only obeying the law under which it must operate. The Food, Drug and Cosmetic Act was amended in 1958 to include what is known as the Delaney clause, sponsored by Rep. James J. Delaney. The Delaney clause directs the FDA to pronounce any food or additive unsafe "if it is found" after "appropriate" testing "to induce cancer in man or animals."

The problem, therefore, is with the law rather than with the FDA. It can be argued, of course, that in the 80 years that saccharin has been used in America, there is no evidence that it has ever induced cancer in man. The American Cancer Society, which does not support the ban on saccharin, makes this point. But saccharin has caused cancer in the bladders of laboratory animals. It could next be argued that the testing was not exactly "appropriate" in that the animals were fed saccharin amounting to 5 per cent of their total daily diet. For a human to ingest that amount, he would have to drink 800 diet soft drinks a day for life. But the problem is still in the law—the Delaney amendment.

For the American who is merely trying to lose weight, the ban is bothersome but not a major problem. Those on reducing diets can simply count their calories more strictly. But for the nation's 10 million known diabetics, for the uncounted millions of hypoglycemics, the ban on saccharin greatly reduces their choices in an already sharply restricted diet. Honey and other natural sugars have much the same impact upon their body chemistry as cane sugar.

The trouble with the rigid rule is that, as the Wall Street Journal comments, "it forbids us to balance costs against benefits in the way that is necessary if we are to make reasonable decisions . . ." By the nature of his body chemistry, the diabetic runs fewer risks of death from cancer induced by saccharin than he does by an uncalculated use of sugar. The person who has any reason to fear cancer in the urinary tract, on the other hand, should appreciate the warning against any substance thought conducive to cancer, however slight the enhancement.

The protests against the FDA ban on saccharin are nationwide and swelling in number. But those protests should be aimed at the law and at congressmen who are in a position to modify the law. The FDA is doing what it was directed to do.

The Wichita Eagle

Wichita, Kans., March 14, 1977

If, as a Food and Drug Administration spokesman is quoted as saying, it would be necessary to drink 800 bottles of diet soda daily for a lifetime to approximate the cancer risk level found in tests on lab animals, then why is the FDA imposing a ban on the use of saccharin?

The FDA certainly is wise to make it a gradual shutdown. The order will not take full effect for several months since the lab test findings "do not indicate any immediate hazard to public health."

Almost anything ingested in sufficiently excessive quantity can cause harmful effects. There are those who contend that that applies even to good advice.

Philosophically, pure science is a search for truth — an effort to search out provable facts of the physical universe as it can be discerned. At least that's one way of putting it.

But there is a dangerous growing tendency for those who know better to seize fragments of information and use them out of context to create public alarms about whatever is being campaigned for or against. Keeping the public in a state of confused emotionalism is not good for public — or personal — health, either.

Probably people do use too many artificial sweeteners. Sugar provides energy (which saccharin does not) but can be bad for the teeth and even fattening if consumed in excess, particularly in rich foods. Maybe we need to change our dietary habits and preferences.

Press Herald

Portland, Me., March 12, 1977

The Food and Drug Administration apparently is prepared to fight the war of the cyclamates all over again.

Its ban on saccharin seems likely to be fully as controversial as the cyclamates issue. There is something about the ban on the artificial sweetener that is somewhat artificial itself.

FDA Commissioner Sherwin Gardner seems excessively dramatic in announcing the ban and the test on which he is acting can hardly be called exhaustive.

Gardner wants manufacturers to stop using saccharin immediately even though the departmental paper work ordering the prohibition will take until July.

The ban is based on a Canadian test in which 100 rats were fed a diet of five per cent pure saccharin from conception until death. Fourteen of the rats developed cancerous bladder tumors. That's significant. But it also means that 86 of the rats did not develop the tumors. That's significant. And two rats in the test group given no saccharin also developed tumors. That is significant.

And Gardner admits that for a human being to consume an equal amount of saccharin he would have to drink 800, 12-ounce bottles of diet soda a day for all the days of his life. That's significant, too.

There is no evidence to indicate what might have happened had the saccharin been discontinued when the presence of the tumors became known.

The government's concern about the public health would be more convincing if it were more consistent and less hypocritical. The case against tobacco smoke is documented much better than the case against saccharin. Yet we are only warned about tobacco.

The ravages of alcohol are undisputed. Yet there is not even a warning about that. State governments are in the business of selling it and at the same time spending millions to care for its victims.

But a substance much sweeter than sugar but without calories is banned because 14 rats out of 100 given massive, lifetime quantities of it developed cancer.

Somehow, it all just doesn't add up.

Democrat ⚡ Chronicle

Rochester, N.Y., March 23, 1977

NO ONE is sure whether or not saccharin is safe for people, yet it may be off the market within a few months unless a clause in the Food and Drug Act is amended.

According to the Delaney Amendment, the Food and Drug Administration must ban any food additive which causes cancer in humans or animals. Since recent tests showed that saccharin caused cancer in Canadian rats, the artificial sweetener must be dangerous to humans — so the logic goes — and therefore banned.

The trouble with this is that there's no scientific proof that something which is carcinogenic in animals is also dangerous to humans. And worse, the FDA has no choice in the matter.

The Delaney law undercuts the raison d'etre of government regulatory agencies: to protect the public interest. In effect, the FDA is reduced to a child playing "Simon Says," with Congress calling the shots.

The law directs a saccharin ban even though that action is based on tests in which Canadian rats ate the human equivalent of 140 pounds of saccharin a year.

Most — if not all — saccharin fans don't use that much in a lifetime. Indeed, it's even unlikely that most diabetics or dieters even exceed the daily 1-gram (60 small saccharin tablets) safety ceiling the FDA set five years ago.

But the saccharin controversy reaches beyond the Delaney Amendment's inflexibility and raises some pretty heady questions:

What makes a substance a public risk? Who should determine what's dangerous — scientists or Congress? How can the public be protected from both harmful substances and profit-oriented manufacturers of those substances? Why all the fuss over saccharin when tobacco, pesticides, and birth control pills aren't regulated under the same stiff standards? Will public demand be so great that a ban will only create a lucrative black market for the substance?

The Delaney law needs amending. Badly. In doing so, Congress should take a look at the precedent it set with the Toxic Substances Act, which gives the FDA discretionary regulatory powers beyond a flat ban. It should also ensure that any new chapter in food additive control won't be written without the public welfare at heart.

Oklahoma City Times

Oklahoma City, Okla., March 23, 1977

AMERICAN consumers would have considerably more confidence in the credibility of their federal government if the bureaucrats in Washington could get their act together and speak with a semblance of unanimity on major issues.

The mounting furor over the Food and Drug Administration's proposed ban on saccharin is a good case in point. Because some laboratory rats developed bladder tumors after ingesting heavy diets of the artificial sweetener, the FDA felt compelled to tell Americans they might get cancer from using saccharin in diet foods and beverages.

FDA officials acted under their interpretation of existing law, one section of which prohibits the use of any food or drink additive found to have induced cancer in either animals or humans. They contend they have no leeway in administering that law, even though a human would have to drink 800 cans of diet soda a day for life to absorb an equivalent amount of saccharin fed to the test rats.

The consumer rush that emptied supermarket and drug store shelves of saccharin attests to the fact that the FDA has a credibility problem with the public.

The case for the saccharin ban grew even weaker this week when the head of the National Cancer Institute told a House health subcommittee hearing that NCI doubts saccharin has any carcinogenic properties for humans. And while feeding inordinate amounts of saccharin to rats did indeed cause some tumors, it is also true that similar experiments with rhesus monkeys resulted in no ill effects.

Given this contradictory testimony, the lay public is quite likely to conclude that the NCI is a more competent source of what constitutes a hazardous cancer-causing agent than the FDA. In any event, the NCI testimony by itself is reason enough for Congress to tell the FDA to back up on saccharin.

The Montreal Star

Montreal, Que., March 11, 1977

DEPENDING on one's point of view, the decision to ban the use of saccharin as an artificial sweetner can be seen as extremely silly or profoundly sane.

Not unnaturally, soft drink manufacturers are upset because the decision could have serious financial repercussions. Diet drinks, banned from supermarkets and corner grocery stores after July 1, make up an estimated 10 per cent of their business.

As they rightly point out, doses used in the federal health department's $300,000 study far exceed normal human exposure. To consume the same proportionate dose, an individual would have to drink 800 12-ounce bottles of diet soft drink a day. Their argument is further buttressed by Dr. Alex Morrison, head of the federal department responsible for the study, pointing out that "no cases of human cancer attributable to saccharin have been identified."

Their argument breaks down, however, when compared to the safety standards set by the World Health Organization. That organization calls for a 5,000-fold difference between the amount of a substance shown to cause cancer in animals and the average amount of that same substance consumed by human beings. On that score, saccharin just doesn't measure up.

Perhaps the most overlooked aspect of the announced ban — it also applies to its use in foods, cosmetics and as a non-medical ingredient in drugs — has nothing to do with saccharin's possible side effects. Washington saw fit to announce a similar ban in the United States following a review by its own researchers of studies by Canadian scientists. The ban in the U.S. also will take place immediately.

The U.S. Food and Drug Administration has, in the past, with respect to food additives and drugs developed abroad, relied almost exclusively on the results of its own testing in formulating courses of action. Its decision to take at face value the results of Canadian research indicates, in some measure, the high regard with which our own health protection service is held. Both countries have chosen to play safe rather than sorry.

Winnipeg Free Press

Winnipeg, Man., March 11, 1977

Entirely aside from those people whose business it will harm — manufacturers of sugar-free soft drinks, food and cosmetics — the decision of the federal government to ban the use of saccharin in Canada because it is a potential cancer causing agent will strike many Canadians as a case of Big Brother being far too big brotherly. That the U.S. administration has taken similar, though more gradual, steps, merely adds millions of Americans to those disgruntled Canadians.

★　　★　　★

Health officials in Ottawa say that the step is being taken as a "prudent" measure. How prudent can you get? According to the same officials, there is no imminent danger to people who have been using saccharin in the past and there is no evidence so far that saccharin causes cancer in humans. Then why the ban? Because Canadian scientists found that male rats developed bladder stones and tumors if their mothers had been fed large amounts of saccharin. The rats in question were fed a diet of five per cent pure saccharin for their entire lives. For a person to consume the equivalent (and thereby, presumably, risk getting bladder stones) he or she would have to consume everyday 800 12-ounce diet drinks for life.

It is extremely difficult for the man or woman in the street — especially those who use diet foods — to understand the thinking of the Ottawa panjandrums. On the basis of logic, if Ottawa is so hell bent on saving human lives, the government should immediately ban the use of all motor vehicles. They take thousands of lives a year and saccharin has yet to take one.

Edmonton Journal

Edmonton, Alta., March 16, 1977

The case to support Ottawa's ban on saccharin is hardly overwhelming.

Health Minister Marc Lalonde noted it was strictly a precautionary measure when he announced the ban on the sweetener as an additive. There have been no known deaths from its use since it was invented in 1879.

Ottawa based its action on a three-year study which showed that rats fed large doses of saccharin developed malignant bladder tumors. Daily amounts of the chemical consumed by the rats were equivalent to those contained in 800 bottles of low-calorie soft drinks.

If one wants to match studies, a U.S. researcher says no ill effects from use of saccharin were found in monkeys fed large amounts of the sweetener over a six-year period. He also pointed out that saccharin may have different effects on experimental animals than on humans and said the rhesus monkeys used in his test "are as close as we can get in an experimental animal to man."

Mr. Lalonde did not help his case by making a rather curious distinction between smoking and use of saccharin. He said smoking is more dangerous than normal consumption of the sweetener but that the risks of smoking have been accepted by society. Tell that one to the legion of non-smokers!

The health minister added that saccharin is not essential and can be replaced. But, because it is only used in specially-labelled dietary foods — low-calorie and low-carbohydrate products — it seems unnecessary to ban it at all.

The government could have fulfilled its responsibility to guard public health by merely publicizing the possibility that saccharin might cause cancer. Or, it could have had the food industry label the relatively small range of products containing the sweetener as "possibly dangerous to health."

At least there will be some exceptions to the ban, as in the case of products for diabetics. But there hardly seems to be evidence to warrant a general move against saccharin, at a time when health scares related to hundreds of foods and food ingredients are rampant.

The London Free Press

London, Ont., March 17, 1977

The jokes are already going the rounds — people saying they'll have to give up their 800 bottles of diet pop a day. That's the wag's way of disagreeing with the decision last week to ban the use of saccharin as an artificial sweetener for all but those who need it as medicine.

But really, there was little else the federal health department could do. It's expected to look out for the public's interest and take normal precautions. While it does seem that everything we like is illegal, immoral, fattening or cancer-causing, the health protection people did their research and then acted on it.

The research was impressive enough to have the United States, for a change, following Canada's lead.

It was only three years ago that Dr. A. B. Morrison, assistant deputy minister of the health protection branch, was saying that studies proved saccharine "safe" for human consumption. So it would seem a bit odd that now he would be saying we're going to ban it forthwith. But in the plodding, meticulous specific world of scientific research, it all apparently makes sense.

Without going into any detail, the 1974 report showed that suspect impurities in saccharin did not cause bladder cancer in laboratory rats. The researchers were looking for a link between bladder cancer and an impurity caused in the saccharin manufacturing process. But the recent series of tests showed that it wasn't the impure chemical which caused bladder cancers, but the pure saccharin itself.

With those results, it was difficult for a responsible health official to act differently. It is possible that hardship to industry and saccharin users could have been eased by extending the period before the ban to a year or so. But everyone will eventually have to put up with the absence of diet soft drinks and other goods like sweetened toothpaste (although industry is almost surely busy finding a substitute).

The ban raises questions, however, about the food Canadians eat. It has become something of a chemical feast. Remember cyclamates? They were an artificial sweetener, too. They were banned eight years ago in Canada and the U.S. for the same reason that saccharin is being banished — under laboratory conditions massive doses of the chemical produced cancer in rats.

If saccharin has now been found to be a health risk, it's possible that other additives used as preservatives or to enhance the taste, texture, or appearance of food are potentially unsafe.

Consumers are entitled to wonder just how thoroughly food additives are tested for safety before they become a routine part of food production.

FDA Approves Selling Saccharin While Prohibiting Use as Additive

The Food and Drug Administration April 14 modified its proposed ban on saccharin to allow the artificial sweetener to remain on the market for limited use as a nonprescription drug. Under the new proposal, saccharin could be sold in tablet, powder or liquid form in pharmacies, food stores and restaurants, but its use still would be prohibited in commercially prepared foods and beverages. (Commercially prepared foods and beverages currently account for 90% of saccharin use.)

The new proposal would ban the use of saccharin in cosmetics likely to be ingested, such as lipstick, and in nonmedical additives used to make prescription drugs taste better. It also would allow the sweetener to be labeled as an over-the-counter drug. This would circumvent the legal ban on cancer-causing food additives—the so-called Delaney Clause of the 1958 Food, Drug and Cosmetic Act. The proposed drug classification would force manufacturers to show that saccharin was both safe and effective for the medical purpose for which it was intended, pursuant to the 1962 Harris-Kefauver amendments to the act. Finally, the FDA proposal would require that packages containing saccharin be labeled: "Warning: saccharin causes bladder cancer in animals. Use of saccharin may increase your risk of cancer. For use as a non-caloric sweetener when sugar-restricted diets are medically indicated, as in patients with diabetes."

THE STATES-ITEM
New Orleans, La., April 19, 1977

The federal Food and Drug Administration (FDA) has hit upon a practical solution to the saccharin controversy. The agency proposes to permit the marketing of the artificial sweetener over the counter as a non-prescription drug, thus satisfying the desires and needs of weight-watchers and diabetics.

The FDA proposed banning saccharin as an additive in food and drinks after Canadian laboratory tests showed the chemical sweetener caused cancer in rats when fed to them in large doses. The agency still intends to ban saccharin from such wholesale usage in products that are distributed widely. Packaged saccharin sold as a non-prescription drug would contain a warning that it might cause cancer, similar to the surgeon general's warning on cigarettes.

The FDA proposal is a step toward evaluating benefits against potential risks. In the case of overweight persons and diabetics, the benefits of saccharin might far outweigh the potential risk of cancer. This practical consideration would be welcome as an integral part of the deliberations of federal agencies on health issues involving chemicals. It should not be used, however, as a foot in the door to roll back federal efforts to protect the public from *involuntary* subjection to potentially dangerous chemicals, including industrial wastes, agricultural and horticultural pesticides and herbicides; and various fabric dyes and food additives which laboratory tests have demonstrated to be potentially carcinogenic.

While some would belittle laboratory tests with mice as being inconclusive where human health is concerned, the public should be reminded that such experiments are the best that science can do in the absence of experimenting with live human beings.

Ideally, chemical products should be tested and evaluated by the FDA and other agencies before they are marketed and become widely used. The Toxic Substances Control Act, enacted last year, is a beginning toward such advance testing.

Los Angeles Times
Los Angeles, Calif., April 15, 1977

In the end, the argument over a ban on saccharin comes down to weighing known risks against speculative risks. The known risks of a ban are to diabetics and others who must use the artificial sweetener in their diets because sugar is bad for their health. The possible risks are that saccharin could cause bladder cancer in some persons. Because of that possibility the Food and Drug Administration has ordered stringent reductions in overall saccharin use.

Stringent, but not total. For while saccharin is to be eliminated from beverages, foods, cosmetics and drugs, it can still be sold "for medical reasons" in pill or powder form as an over-the-counter drug. The FDA, in other words, is persuaded that saccharin is or at least may be dangerous, but it recognizes that for a lot of people doing completely without it could be more dangerous still. Since the ban on cyclamates in 1969—a ban many cancer scientists now feel was unnecessary—no other artificial sweetener has been available to those who cannot use sugar. This absence of alternatives was the practical if not strictly consistent cause for the FDA's dilution of the total ban on saccharin it was talking about a month ago.

If one accepts, as the FDA does, the human relevance of those Canadian laboratory tests on saccharin-fed rats, then its action makes sense. If saccharin is indeed a carcinogen, however weak, prohibiting its use in products that now consume up to 90% of what is produced each year should significantly reduce the risks of bladder cancer caused by this suspected agent, without doing serious harm to people who depend on the artificial sweetener.

We can see the FDA's point, but we are still bothered by what has happened. What remains troubling—and it is not the FDA's fault—is the lack of conclusive evidence that saccharin may do harm. Experiments in which massive doses of saccharin were fed to other laboratory animals have failed to confirm the Canadian tests with rats. More directly applicable have been two extensive British surveys involving diabetics—who plausibly would be expected to use more saccharin than nondiabetics—that failed to turn up any evidence that people with this disease suffered from any unusual incidence of bladder tumors.

Under the law, the FDA had no choice but to ban saccharin as a food additive, though it evaded a total ban by permitting saccharin to be relabeled as a nonprescription drug. That denial of discretionary choice, as we have said before, certainly means that this law needs reexamining by Congress. What is also needed, pretty clearly, is more extensive scientific study of saccharin's effects, to prove or disprove the Canadian rat study, and to clear up the confusion and contradictions that have caused so much controversy.

AKRON BEACON JOURNAL
Akron, Ohio, April 14, 1977

DESPITE all the fuss and furor over the Food and Drug Administration's announcement that it planned to ban saccharin from the food market, the FDA's new "compromise plan" on the sugarless sweetener probably makes sense.

The agency's solution: Ban saccharin from such uses as in diet drinks and other things sold basically as food, but allow its over-the-counter sale as a nonprescription drug, as freely available to the seeker as aspirin.

The basis for red-lining it altogether has perhaps not been as well understood as it should have been by us nonscientists. But we have been told repeatedly that the tests on which the prospective ban was based followed the normal procedures used in tagging potential cancer-causers, making the ban both a logical and a legal necessity.

And though questions have been raised about the law creating this necessity, who's ready to recommend passage of a new law saying, in substance, that it's all right to put cancer-causing substances in our foods?

This compromise answer will allow the diabetes sufferer who regards the benefit as more than offsetting the risk to go on using the synthetic sweetener — in the awareness that there is now evident more possible risk than was earlier known.

On the other hand, it may reduce the likelihood of cancer for those whose minds are on such other things as staying slim, which can be done in numerous ways other than through drinking diet colas.

Lincoln Evening Journal
Lincoln, Neb., April 15, 1977

To those for whom the good life includes swilling barrels of diet soft drinks, the Food and Drug Administration's compromise decision about saccharin probably is unacceptable.

The FDA's proposed ban of processed commodities containing the chemical sweetener will hit most everything saccharin is used in.

Nevertheless, the federal health agency is acting in concert with national law, and acting responsibly in recognizing special problems of diabetics.

Saccharin can continue to be sold as a non-prescription drug in pharmacies, and elsewhere. There must be warnings, however. Ingestion of the coal derivative might increase the risk of bladder cancer.

For the country's 10 million diabetics, the choice is a free one, and theirs exclusively. For the many additional millions of non-diabetic fatties, they'll have to fall back on other crutches, like water. Or self-control.

Initial media reporting of Canadian research findings of bladder cancer development in rats fed saccharin was about a D minus performance at best. Sensationalism catering to consumer preferences warped much of the early news stories. Those of us in the craft ought to offer apologies.

The Canadian tests were carefully, properly done. The evidence was conclusive — and reaffirmed previous research.

What wasn't underlined for the general public was the fact that in some cases — not all — chemical carcinogens are not converted through the metabolic process of our body into non-carcinogenic elements.

Maybe this is the situation with saccharin. Even the FDA isn't sure. But it does have a sufficient basis to think harshly about saccharin and do its duty protecting the public.

Which it seems to be doing with appropriate maturity.

The TENNESSEAN
Nashville, Tenn., April 20, 1977

THE FEDERAL Drug Administration has decided to go ahead with its ban on saccharin, but in an effort to ease the shock it decided to let the sweetener be sold as a non-prescription drug.

A slice of a loaf may be better than nothing, but it hasn't quieted those — including many medical experts — who are assertively opposed to the FDA action. They point out that it still penalizes a great number of people.

Rep. James G. Martin, R-N.C., is continuing to push his bill to relax a 19-year-old law known as the Delaney Amendment. That law requires the FDA to ban any substance that causes cancer in man or animals.

While it may be debatable whether the Canadian tests which led to the FDA action were sufficient proof that relatively small intakes of saccharin over a period of years would cause cancer, the law does not leave the FDA much leeway.

The intent of the law is certainly praiseworthy and the question is whether it ought to be repealed outright. That could be a case of throwing the baby out with the bathwater and leaving the government in a situation where it would have discretionary power only on cancer-causing substances.

Surely the law could be improved without wiping it off the books. And, there ought to be new tests carried out on a basis of moderate use of saccharin. With an improved law and new test data, perhaps the FDA could reconsider its ban on saccharin.

Rocky Mountain News
Denver, Colo., April 16, 1977

THE FOOD AND DRUG Administration (FDA) has made a wise decision in rescinding its previously planned complete ban on the use of the artificial sweetener, saccharin.

Instead, it will permit saccharin's sale as an over-the-counter drug for use by diabetics and in weight control, but will stand by its ban on use in commercially prepared foods, beverages and cosmetics.

Thus, the public will be able to buy and use saccharin in coffee and similar beverages, and in foods such as homemade cakes, pies and ice cream.

The FDA's original decision to lower the boom completely created a storm of protest from the public and many doctors who regard its use as an important factor in treatment of diabetes, obesity and high blood pressure.

The FDA had been moved to act on the basis of a Canadian study which indicated that high intake of saccharin caused bladder cancer in laboratory rats.

The new decision, however, is by no means an unlimited go-ahead.

Within the coming year, manufacturers of saccharin must prove to the satisfaction of the FDA that, used sparingly, the product does not represent a cancer menace. If they do not do so, the total ban will go into effect.

All told, the FDA has taken a responsible middle-of-the-road course that should satisfy most people – except, to be sure, those who are addicted to vast quantities of diet soft drinks.

The Miami Herald
Miami, Fla., April 14, 1977

BECAUSE the heat was becoming hazardous to its own health, the Food and Drug Administration is expected to announce today that it is toning down its proposal to ban the use of saccharin altogether.

Use of the artificial sweetener in foods — most generally in diet soda — will be prohibited, but sale of saccharin as a non-prescription drug, like aspirin, will be approved. There is a possibility FDA might want to make it a prescription item, but the heat would be turned back on high if it did so.

We suspect that FDA has done a bit of arabesque re-interpretation of the Delaney Amendment clause in the law which prohibits any amount of a cancer-causing substance in the food supply. As the FDA can see it now, but couldn't before, pure saccharin isn't in the food supply until somebody puts it there. So a consumer won't be able to get a diet pop but he will be able to, say, pop a tablet or two in his coffee or tea.

There will be appropriate warnings, of course, on saccharin containers pointing out that it is possible that saccharin may not be good for all of us. Which is fine. The FDA along with the surgeon general should keep us informed about these things, and then let us decide whether it is bad enough for us to stop using.

Surely anyone using saccharin, for whatever reason, now knows that it has caused cancer in some rats in Canada when administered in massive doses. Some will take their chances and some won't, but at least they'll have a choice.

We can recall when nobody had a choice, one Thanksgiving some years back, as to whether they would have cranberry sauce with their turkey.

Newsday

Garden City, N.Y., April 18, 1977

In dealing with the saccharin problem, the Food and Drug Administration may have found a solution worthy of Solomon. If the artificial sweetener is reclassified as a drug, the so-called Delaney clause won't apply. That law, enacted as an amendment to the Food Additive Act of 1968, bans any food ingredient that has been shown to give animals cancer, as saccharin has.

Allowing saccharin to be sold as an over-the-counter drug, like aspirin or vitamins, would enable people who need a sugar substitute to go on using this one. But saccharin still couldn't be used in ready-made products like diet soft drinks. And saccharin, like cigarettes, would carry a health warning.

The food and beverage industry isn't likely to be satisfied with the compromise. Neither are those who want an absolute ban on saccharin. But until some other substance is discovered that meets the needs of diabetics and the obese, the risk to their health from a ban on saccharin may well outweigh any risk of cancer. Besides, under the proposed FDA ruling the decision would be up to them and their physicians. For the time being at least, that seems a reasonable proposition.

The San Diego Union

San Diego, Calif., April 18, 1977

The Food and Drug Administration is trying to reconcile public policy with private choice on the issue of saccharin. Its proposed regulations for the artificial sweetener will satisfy some and displease others.

People who want to add saccharin to their food would be able to buy it at a pharmacy — in a package warning that its use carries a risk of cancer. But saccharin would be banned from the marketplace otherwise, no longer permitted as an ingredient of processed foods and drinks or cosmetics.

This is simply straddling the fence on the issue of the scientific evidence linking saccharin with cancer. FDA Commissioner Donald Kennedy acknowledges that the debate is not over, and it is by no means certain that the proposed regulations will survive the hearing process now beginning.

Can the government come up with anything better? The case against saccharin is not conclusive, but it cannot be ignored. The dilemma arises because federal law as it is now written makes no provision for weighing the risk of cancer in the use of a food-additive against the benefits that might justify taking that risk. The FDA is trying to leave the door open for personal decisions about the use of saccharin while heeding the law which requires a ban on incorporating it into food products and cosmetics.

That's an imperfect solution, but it may be the only fair one as long as imperfections remain in our understanding of the causes of cancer. The puzzles of that disease are creating puzzles for public health policy as various substances in our environment and the human diet come under suspicion as cancer-causing agents. Regardless of the fate of saccharin, the dialogue is far from over on where the line should be drawn between our freedom to risk damaging our health and the government's obligation to keep us from doing so.

WORCESTER TELEGRAM

Worcester, Mass., April 25, 1977

Bowing to public demand, the federal Food and Drug Administration has backed off a bit on its saccharin ban.

The FDA will now allow saccharin to be sold in drug stores, but it will still ban its use as a food additive in products found on supermarket shelves.

This indicates that the FDA feels saccharin may have a valid application as an artificial sweetener for those with medical problems such as diabetes and obesity. Or does it?

The FDA says it will allow the sale of saccharin over the counter, without a doctor's prescription. By doing that the agency has avoided the question of the safety of saccharin.

By its ban, the FDA has said that saccharin is unsafe. Tests on Canadian rats produced incidences of bladder cancer and the FDA is bound, so it says, by the Delaney Clause, which requires it to ban any cancer-causing product.

But there have been suggestions that the tests might not be reliable. To the lay person, at least, the huge quantities of saccharin fed to the rats was ridiculous. Humans would have to drink 800 cans of diet soda a day to achieve that intake. And other studies, including one at Johns Hopkins University and another in New York, have indicated that humans and monkeys might not develop bladder cancer from more normal saccharin consumption.

And now the FDA has clouded the picture even more by fooling around with its ban. If saccharin poses no danger, it should not be banned. If it does, that danger should be clearly spelled out to the public. Either way, the FDA has a lot more explaining to do.

St. Louis Globe-Democrat

St. Louis, Mo., April 18, 1977

Still pressing on, despite mounting public criticism of its proposed ban of saccharin, the federal Food and Drug Administration has issued another proposal saying that saccharin could be sold only in tablet, powder and liquid form as a nonprescription drug.

Saccharin could not be used in commercially prepared diet drinks and food that now account for about 90 per cent of its use.

Thus the FDA seems to be clinging to its contention that the widely-criticized Canadian study on rats is justification enough to wreck the saccharin industry.

And this autocratic action comes only days after a research group at Johns Hopkins University in Baltimore has concluded, after a four-year study on humans, that the consumption of saccharin does not have any significant effect on the development of bladder cancer in humans.

The fact that the FDA is moving ahead with its restriction on commercial soft drinks and food even though a human would have to drink more than 800 cans of diet soda to ingest the same amount of saccharin given the Canadian rats should spur Congress to repeal the Delaney amendment and to set up proper standards for testing substances by qualified research groups in this country.

The FDA, like other power-happy federal agencies, hates to admit a mistake. It will try to put in the saccharin ban no matter what evidence is revealed to dispute the Canadian rat study.

To allow the agency to destroy a $2 billion industry on such questionable evidence is bad economics, as well as bad from a public health point of view. When a move of this magnitude is contemplated, the nation must not rely on a study made in another country under dubious standards. It must determine beyond any reasonable question that it is taking the right move.

THE SAGINAW NEWS

Saginaw, Mich., April 17, 1977

The Food and Drug Administration's decision to soften its ban on the artificial sweetener saccharin makes the agency's action a somewhat less bitter pill for millions of diabetics and weight-watchers.

Whether the move by the FDA will be enough to call off congressional action against the Delaney clause, enacted in 1958 as an amendment to the Food, Drug and Cosmetic Act, remains to be seen.

Just now a number of congressmen, distressed by the FDA's original ban order early in March — and mountains of public protest mail — are determined to take after the Delaney clause. They want it less rigid, less prone to such arbitrary and sweeping action as that followed by the FDA.

But at least the FDA is taking some of the stress out of its original order. It would now propose saccharin be sold over-the-counter as a nonprescription drug. But bearing a label warning that it could cause cancer.

Considering the way we handle cigarettes, this would seem to make better sense. The public can take its own risk, but the sweetener is available at affordable prices to all who rely on it as a sugar substitute.

There is still a bit of inconvenience involved. The FDA will still insist saccharin be banned in the manufacture of diet soft drinks, as well as in toothpastes and cosmetics.

So there may be some home-mixing involved if the FDA's revised thinking stands. But this is better than being left without sweetener options. Not easy-sweet perhaps. But available-sweet anyway.

The Seattle Times

Seattle, Wash., April 15, 1977

HOPING, apparently, to cool off a hot potato with a patently political compromise, the Food and Drug Administration has modified its earlier intention to ban saccharin.

Instead of an outright ban effective this summer, the F.D.A. plans now to allow the sale of the artificial sweetener as a nonprescription drug.

There is, however, a "Catch 22." Saccharin still would be disallowed in diet soft drinks, lipsticks, mouthwash, toothpaste, and other commodities representing about 90 per cent of saccharin's present uses.

The average consumer might well ask: If saccharin is not a potential cancer-causing agent when sold over the counter like headache and stomach remedies, how come it's a health risk in diet pop or mouthwash?

The answer is that the beleaguered F.D.A. is looking desperately for a way out of the storm of protest generated by its invocation of the "Delaney clause."

The latter is the federal statute that requires a ban on any substance found in tests to "induce cancer when ingested by man or animal."

Congress is exploring modification of that law, to allow for common-sense management of laboratory findings like those that showed huge doses of saccharin caused cancer in rats. (Saccharin has not caused a known case of human cancer in nearly a century, or in more recent experiments involving saccharin consumption by laboratory monkeys.)

Meantime, the F.D.A. action has spurred a scramble among manufacturers to produce alternative sweeteners in the event that even the limited saccharin ban sticks. The alternatives are likely to cost consumers far more than saccharin.

Given public resentment toward the government's handling of the saccharin issue (while all but ignoring such health hazards as tobacco and liquor), the F.D.A.'s "Catch 22" announcement should not end the matter.

San Francisco Chronicle

San Francisco, Calif., April 15, 1977

THE FOOD AND DRUG administration yesterday eased somewhat its previous order banning the use of saccharin, issued last month on the basis of laboratory reports it could cause some forms of cancer. The new order bans the artificial sweetener in diet sodas, foods and cosmetics, but leaves open the option of marketing saccharin as a nonprescription drug.

Former Stanford University biologist Donald Kennedy, the newly appointed FDA commissioner, said, "our intention is to eliminate the risk of cancer from unnecessary uses of saccharin while continuing its availability for people who may need it for medical purposes." The FDA's suggestion is that saccharin containers, sold over-the-counter, bear a warning similar to those now seen on cigaret packages: "Warning: The Surgeon General Has Determined that Cigaret Smoking Is Dangerous to Your Health."

THE FDA'S ban on saccharin arose from the strictures of the so-called Delaney Amendment, 1958 legislation by which Congress required the FDA to prohibit from the market any food additive shown on the basis of conclusive laboratory tests to cause cancer in humans or animals. The "all-or-nothing" character of this law makes it increasingly difficult to apply and enforce at a time when detection methods are becoming more sophisticated.

We accordingly support legislation of Representative James G. Martin (Rep-N. C.), which would allow the Secretary of HEW to exempt a product from the reach of the Delaney Amendment if he found that public benefit in the distribution of the product outweighs the public risk. It is certainly arguable that the benefit to dieters and diabetics of saccharin does outweigh its risk. Congressman Martin's easing of Delaney's law acknowledges, moreover, a stubbornness in the American spirit that leads a citizen to balk at being told by government what he may smoke, eat or drink.

CASPER STAR-TRIBUNE

Casper, Wyo., April 22, 1977

The transition of saccharin from a widely used, easily obtained sugar substitute into an over-the-counter drug may take place as early as July unless the Food and Drug Administration is convinced otherwise in the few months ahead.

FDA banning of the drug came about through tests in Canada which indicated that saccharin caused cancer in rats. However, at the time that the Canadian tests were made public it was revealed that the rats used were fed massive doses of the sugar substitute. To achieve an equal intake of saccharin it was said that a human would have to drink 1,200 ordinary soft drinks daily for years.

Now, however, FDA is taking a different stance on it and is quoted as saying that if a person were to ingest one large diet soft drink daily by every American over a lifetime that it might lead to 1,200 cases of bladder cancer annually. Notice the use of the word "might."

Saccharin has been in use as a sugar substitute for 80 years. It has never previously been linked with cancer in humans. However, under the language of the so-called Delaney amendment, the FDA must ban any substance which has been shown to cause cancer, no matter how unusual the dosage, such as that given to the Canadian rats.

In 1969 cyclamates, another artificial sweetener, was barred from use by the FDA. Many scientists today think that action was premature and unnecessary.

Saccharin, which is used in a host of products such as drugs, soft drinks, diet drinks, tooth paste, etc. is the only substitute sweetener now available to those industries using it, except for sugar. And sugar cannot be used in some of these products.

The impending ban has caused great concern among diabetics who use it as a sugar substitute. It will still be avilable to them, but only as a drug.

Almost equal concern has been voiced by those with a tendency to obesity, who rely on saccharin as a substitute for fattening sugar. They will be unable to buy the dietary products which are sugar free.

The move is being opposed by pharmaceutical associations, many doctors and, of course, the industries using saccharin, because it will be absolutely disrupting to their normal operation.

We think the move premature The FDA might do well to engage a reputable testing laboratory in the U.S. to conduct its own tests and come to an independent conclusion. This action is far too hasty for the risks involved.

12 — Eating & Drinking

The Kansas City Times

Kansas City, Mo., April 18, 1977

The rationale of the Food and Drug Administration in allowing saccharin to be sold as an over-the-counter, non-prescription drug while maintaining the ban on its use as an additive in commercially prepared food and drink products is a little hard to follow. Obviously this latest announcement is intended to allay some of the outcry from dieters and diabetics which greeted last month's FDA statement of intention to ban the artificial sweetener later this summer.

The proposed ban was based on Canadian experiments in which rats fed massive saccharin doses developed some bladder cancers. The protesters noted that saccharin has been in use in this country for 70 years without ill effects and said that human beings would have to ingest inconceivable amounts of the substance to match the rats' laboratory dosage. But the FDA replied that under the Delaney amendment to the 1958 FDA law additives could be banned if considered a cancer threat to either animals or humans.

Redesignating saccharin as a drug would place it in a different technical category, where it could be sold with a health warning on the label. Nearly three-fourths of the 6 million pounds of saccharin now used yearly in this country, however, goes into diet soft drinks so the convenience of access to the product would be greatly reduced by a ban on other than bulk sales.

The proposed switch in tactics may neatly solve the FDA's legal problems in keeping this popular, useful artificial sweetener available to those who cannot or do not want to use sugar. But it raises a troubling question for the average layman: If saccharin truly is a cancer-causing agent on such a scale of risk that it should be withdrawn as an additive, it doesn't seem very prudent to sell it over the counter in bulk to anyone wanting it.

The Hartford Courant

Hartford, Conn., April 29, 1977

The Food and Drug Administration's decision to allow the purchase of saccharin powder or pills over the counter as a non-prescription drug is welcome news for diabetics and dieters who like to sweeten their beverages and make desserts now and then. But the directive, pending further tests, that is, is puzzling to say the least.

If saccharin is safe enough to be used in that way, why must it be banned from foods and soft drinks? It is either a cancer-causing substance or it isn't. If the Canadian tests, which took time to complete, are valid, and even scientists disagree about that, then how can a short-term, abbreviated follow-up make any difference?

Dr. Sidney Wolfe, research director for Ralph Nader, explains that the huge quantity of saccharin fed to rats, equal to 800 cans of soft drink a day for a human lifetime, was necessary. This is because rats live brief lives and the quantity had to be excessive for its effects to be seen.

Not everyone agreed about the harmfulness of cyclmates, either, but billions of cans were discarded, nevertheless when tests on laboratory rats showed the chemical to be carcinogenic when ingested in tremendous amounts by small animals.

Bewilderment and frustration are the principal by-products of FDA decisions. It has been more than a decade since the Surgeon General warned of a link between cigarette smoking and lung cancer, followed by firm proof of it.

Also, laboratory findings later indicated that heart disorders are likely to strike heavy smokers in greater numbers than nonsmokers.

With all that evidence piled against its use, tobacco is still sold in huge quantities and, not content with that, our government even encourages other nations to buy it, plant it, and use it.

THE PLAIN DEALER

Cleveland, Ohio, April 18, 1977

The Food and Drug Administration compromise allowing over-the-counter sale of saccharin as a drug but banning it as a food additive might blunt public anger over the issue, but it fails to resolve a central question. Does saccharin pose a real threat to human health?

The way to resolve widespread doubt is through further testing. As it is, millions of diabetic and overweight Americans who consume diet drinks and foods artifically sweetened with saccharin will continue to wonder about the wisdom of even a partial ban. The ban is based on a single Canadian test series that showed increased bladder cancers in laboratory rats fed massive saccharin doses.

If saccharin is a significant carcinogen, further testing should demonstrate that and vindicate the FDA ban on saccharin as a food additive. But if thorough testing showed no meaningful cancer threat from a reasonable consumption of saccharin, the artificial sweetener could be restored to its former useful role.

Meanwhile, classifying saccharin as a drug and permitting its over-the-counter sale as a nonprescription drug does enable it to escape the rigid requirements of the Delaney Amendment. That 1958 amendment to the basic FDA law compels the banning of any food additive shown to cause cancer in animals or humans.

Classifying saccharin as a drug permits the FDA to weigh the sweetener's potential benefits against any undesirable side effects. Judged in that light, federal officials might conclude that the benefits of saccharin use by the overweight and diabetic is a contribution to public health that outweighs its minimal harmful potential.

Finally, Congress and FDA officials might be wise to consider the feasibility of adding specific testing standards to the Delaney Amendment.

The Dispatch

Columbus, Ohio, April 18, 1977

IT IS DIFFICULT to follow the reasoning of the federal Food and Drug Administration (FDA) which perhaps acted with undue haste in banning saccharin.

Now, after being inundated with protests of more than 800 letters per day, FDA backed down but only a trifle.

The bureaucrats equivocated by placing saccharin in a gray area.

The sugar substitute can be sold as an over-the-counter drug, available to anyone. But it cannot be used in diet drinks and foods.

Explanation is limited usage will benefit diabetics and the obese but certainly they would benefit much more if all restrictions on saccharin were removed.

It is safe to predict a sizable outpouring of protesters next month when the FDA conducts hearings on the matter preparato-ry to implementing saccharin bans in July.

The modification order will require saccharin to be labeled as a cancer risk. But aren't some medicines suspect?

The saccharin ban resulted from a Canadian rat study. It concluded saccharin caused cancer in some rats and therefore could cause cancer in some humans.

Doubt that the test conclusions are accurate has been expressed by some medical authorities.

And, obviously, there remains doubt in the minds of FDA officials. Otherwise, why give manufacturers of saccharin six months to prove it is a safe and effective drug?

It seems the latter should have been determined prior to the FDA ruling. FDA surely has contributed to the doubt.

Chicago Tribune

Chicago, Ill., April 21, 1977

After weeks of standing up to a storm of public outrage protesting its ban on saccharin, the Food and Drug Administration has found a way to bend a little. The FDA is now proposing to open a little loophole for saccharin users by letting the no-calorie sweetener be sold as a non-prescription drug. It would continue to forbid its addition to diet drinks, foods, and cosmetics, which now account for about 90 per cent of saccharin consumption.

The FDA is hedging even that loophole, however, by ruling saccharin manufacturers will have to prove that the product meets standards imposed on drugs — that it is actually effective in helping diabetic and obese persons as claimed. The FDA is also ruling that saccharin must carry sterner warnings than do cigarets. [Smoking is known to cause bladder as well as other cancers in humans; action against saccharin is being taken by the FDA because it produced bladder cancer in a second generation of rats fed massive overdoses.]

The FDA originally claimed its initial ban on saccharin was based on the Delaney Clause, an amendment to FDA law with prohibits any food additive shown to cause cancer in humans and animals. The FDA had no choice, it said, but to ban saccharin. It did concede hazards seemed minimal to humans and so did not order saccharin-sweetened products off the market immediately.

But the FDA's shuffle of such terms as "food," "additive," and "drug" and its citing of other FDA laws to wiggle part way around the Delaney Clause has not calmed the controversy over saccharin. Spokespersons for groups of diabetics and for weight control organizations are still contending that banning saccharin-sweetened diet foods will cause unreasonable hardships and hazards for persons who should restrict use of sugar. Consumer groups are protesting any modification of the flat-out ban.

What is at issue is whether or not massive overdoses of a substance fed to a small number of experimental animals can predict risks when the same substance is consumed in much smaller amounts by large number of humans. A pragmatic question is whether or not the FDA should be permitted to weigh benefits and risks in evaluating substances like saccharin. A public health problem is how to reduce exposure to carcinogens in daily life [when even sunshine, in overabundance, can sometimes cause cancer]. A political question is whether or not individuals should be permitted to decide for themselves to use a product like saccharin, given information about possible risks.

"The decision-making process on saccharin is not over," says Dr. Donald Kennedy, new FDA commissioner. The FDA will hold hearings on saccharin before making its action final, possibly by sometime this summer. And several congressmen are considering revision of the Delaney Clause. By then, we can hope, we will have more light and less heat on the issue. Until we do know more, the FDA's current compromise seems logical.

Congress Delays Saccharin Ban, Calls for New Studies

Congress Nov. 4 passed legislation delaying the Food and Drug Administration's proposed ban on saccharin until 1979. The move was prompted by the general outcry against taking the artificial sweetener off the market. The law called for a new study of the effects of saccharin and for another study of food additives in general for cancer-causing properties. While saccharin could still be used as a substitute for sugar, Congress required foods containing the chemical to bear a label reading: "Use of this product may be hazardous to your health. This product contains saccharin, which has been determined to cause cancer in laboratory animals." The bill also required stores to post health warnings if they sold products containing saccharin.

The measure passed the House and Senate by voice vote Nov. 3 and 4, respectively. It was signed into law Nov. 23.

The Seattle Times

Seattle, Wash., September 21, 1977

WITH medical authorities still divided on the potential cancer risks to humans from saccharin, the Senate wisely has voted to delay a ban that would have taken the artificial sweetener off the market effective October 1.

Reasoning, as Senator Magnuson put it, that "we just don't know enough about this thing yet," the Senate voted, 87 to 7, to defer the ban sought by the Food and Drug Administration for 18 months.

During that time, government researchers are to make additional investigations weighing the cancer risks of the only artificial sweetener left on the market against its benefits. Millions of diabetics depend on saccharin and countless others use sugar-free products in hopes of controlling obesity and related health problems.

The Senate bill does bow to those favoring a saccharin ban, however, by requiring that labels carry warnings that the product contains saccharin, "which causes cancer in animals" and "may increase your risk of developing cancer."

(A majority of senators overrode an angry Senator Kennedy, who wanted the warning included in all advertising for saccharin products.)

Given the inconclusive laboratory verdict on saccharin (the F.D.A. based its attempted ban on Canadian research linking the sugar substitute to bladder cancer in rats), the Senate's action was prudent and responsive to furious public protest over the F.D.A.'s posture.

We believe the House should follow the Senate's lead.

Meantime, Congress would do well to give close attention to existing statutes under which federal regulatory agencies can issue bans against any food additive found in tests to "induce cancer when ingested by man or animal."

That language is so narrow as to preclude common sense and flexibility in evaluating research on food products, or so it would seem after the past eight months' furor over saccharin.

And many Americans remain puzzled at the inconsistency of government health policies, which focus on theoretical findings on such items as saccharin while doing little to discourage the marketing of such proven health hazards as liquor and tobacco products.

The Toronto Star

Toronto, Ont., Canada, September 23, 1977

The United States is showing much more caution and common sense than Canada on the subject of saccharin and its possible health dangers.

Last March, the Canadian government imposed a ban on this artificial sweetener — which is widely used as a sugar substitute in low-calorie foods and drinks — on the ground that it was a cancer hazard. This decision was based on experiments conducted by health department scientists in which laboratory rats were fed enormous doses of saccharin — far in excess, proportionally, of anything a human being would conceivably take — after which some of them developed cancer of the bladder.

These experiments have been widely criticized as inconclusive. The results conflict with similar tests performed on monkeys, and in addition no connection has even been shown between saccharin and cancer in humans. But the government went ahead and prohibited the use of saccharin in foodstuffs and drinks, the ban to become total by the end of the year.

The U.S. government has been under pressure from its own health department to impose a similar ban on the basis of the same experiments. But Congress has balked. The Senate last week voted 87-7 for an 18-month delay in banning saccharin, and this is likely to be concurred in by the House of Representatives and become law. The proposed legislation calls for further scientific study during the 18-month period, to determine more definitely whether saccharin really is a cancer hazard for human beings.

Ottawa would be wise to follow Washington's example in this matter and suspend its deadline on saccharin for the same period.

It should be emphasized that this is not a mere matter of medical theory. Foods and drinks (especially "diet pop") sweetened with saccharin are widely used by diabetics and others with health problems, who have to keep their sugar intake down, but who find unsweetened food unpalatable. If saccharin is eliminated, there is apparently no other safe artificial sweetener. The only substitute the industry has come up with is fructose, a fruit sugar, which behaves in the body much like ordinary cane sugar. If it is used in low calorie foods, many diabetics and others are likely to take, unsuspectingly, more sugar than they can safely handle.

In trying to eliminate a remote and speculative health hazard — which may not exist — our federal health department may thereby be creating a real and immediate danger for many Canadians. Surely it is only common prudence to do as the Americans are doing and postpone the saccharin ban until there is more solid evidence the substance does in fact cause cancer in human beings.

SYRACUSE
HERALD-JOURNAL
Syracuse, N.Y., November 11, 1977

Some months ago, the Food and Drug Administration warned that a ban on the use of saccharin, as a substitute sweetener, was in the works.

The agency, in response to immediate protests, cited the Delaney rule — named after legislation written by Rep. James D. Delaney, Democrat of Long Island City — which directs the agency to ban the consumption of anything found to create cancer, even in laboratory animals.

The agency's warning was based on tests in a Canadian laboratory which reported saccharin had produced bladder cancer in mice.

The soft drink industry, particularly, challenged the findings, maintaining a person had to drink at least 800 cans of diet soft drink a day to consume the same amount of saccharin fed to the rats in the Canadian test.

We recall voicing a protest, too, based chiefly on reasoning that U.S. decisions should be grounded in U.S. experience.

The U.S. should prescribe a standard procedure to determine product safety and the testing should be done in this country since we're dealing with the health and jobs of millions of Americans.

Congress, after weeks of pushing and pulling, agreed finally to direct the FDA to delay banning saccharin for 18 months.

During that time — within a 15-month span — the FDA's researchers are to round up more information about the impact of saccharin, good and bad, either to verify or to refute the Canadian findings.

At the same time, producers of foods and beverages using saccharin are being asked to inform purchasers, through labels, that the saccharin may be a hazard to health.

The compromise is reasonable and all that either producers or consumers could ask.

Let's find out whether a ban, or a limitation of intake, or no ban but a warning, or nothing should make up the content of the FDA's next order on saccharin.

THE BLADE
Toledo, Ohio, September 22, 1977

THE U. S. Senate passed the buck to American consumers last week along with a bill that would require a stern warning to be printed on the packages of all products that contain the controversial artificial sweetener, saccharin.

Under the bill, approved 87-7, the Food and Drug Administration's ban on saccharin — the only nonnutritive artificial sweetener now available to diet-conscious Americans — would be delayed for 18 months.

But meanwhile, diet soda pop and all other food products containing saccharin would have to carry this grave admonition:

Warning: This product contains saccharin which causes cancer in animals. Use of this product may increase your risk of developing cancer.

The Senate action, on the surface, may appear to be a commendable effort to protect the health and well-being of consumers. But on deeper inspection, it actually carries the appearance of a slick and even sleazy attempt by lawmakers to cover their own tracks on the saccharin issue, rather than honestly and forthrightly granting scientists additional time to clarify the findings about saccharin and human health.

Surely the Senate must be aware of how miserably previous warning statements have failed to achieve results. Witness, for example, the health-hazard warning that has been required for years now on all cigarette packages and in all cigarette advertising.

What has the impact of that been? Precious little. Despite the warning, and despite all other efforts at reasoning with smokers, cigarette consumption continues to grow. Americans now smoke 84 billion more cigarettes a year than they did in 1970.

And surely the senators must have realized that such a similar warning for saccharin would shift the burden for interpreting the complex and confusing scientific findings about the sweetener to consumers. They apparently are supposed to provide personal answers to the question that scientists need 18 more months to ponder: Are the benefits of saccharin worth the risks?

Such an expectation, when the scientific evidence is so preliminary and contradictory, amounts to a farce. The Senate knows it, and American consumers have grown sufficiently sophisticated to suspect it. Happily, the Senate decided against requiring the same health warning to appear in all advertising for products containing saccharin.

As the bill moves to the House, we trust that more courageous voices there will simply accept the need for additional months of scientific study of saccharin's health effects and benefits — without puffing up the acrid smokescreen of a "health" warning that in reality stands to protect little more than the political health of its originators.

St. Louis Globe-Democrat
St. Louis, Mo., November 7, 1977

It took awhile but the House and Senate finally have agreed on a bill to delay any ban on saccharin for 18 months.

The compromise bill requires a 15-month study of saccharin by the Food and Drug Administration to determine if the risks of banning it outweigh the benefits.

The curious part of the bill is that it will require this warning label be put on all products containing the artificial sweetener:

"Use of this product may be hazardous to your health. This product contains saccharin, which has been determined to cause cancer in laboratory animals."

A test, made in Canada, has been challenged by the soft drink industry and others. They maintain that a person would have to drink at least 800 cans of diet soft drink a day to get the same amount of saccharin fed to the rats in the Canadian test.

Whether this claim is true or not, the fact remains that the proposed ban was based on a test made in another country under conditions beyond the control of our government.

There should be standard testing procedures to determine the safety of products under question. And such tests should be carried out in this country.

When the health of millions of Americans and billions of dollars in revenues are at stake, it is irresponsible to try to make judgments based upon studies carried out in foreign countries using methods that are questionable, to say the least.

ARKANSAS DEMOCRAT
Little Rock, Ark., September 21, 1977

In a mild attack of common sense, the Senate voted 87 to seven last week to delay at least until spring 1979 the federal Food and Drug Administration's proposed ban on the last of the nutritive artificial sweeteners — saccharin. Canadian researchers had said massive doses of the sweet stuff force-fed in laboratories had induced cancer in white rats, whose bladders are cancer-prone, anyway.

Following the letter of the law (the Delaney clause of the federal Pure Food and Drug Act) FDA proposed to ignore the pleas of millions of diabetics and dieters who depend on the sweetener. The Senate wisely said nay.

Just as wise was the Senate's decision not to require saccharin manufacturers to put warning labels on their products, labels similar to those that the U. S. Surgeon General puts on cigarette packages with so little effect.

Sen. Edward Kennedy, D. Mass., who wants the federal government to dabble in everything possible, said he was appalled that the "warnings" provision was scrubbed. He said it destroyed the "careful balance" of the bill delaying ban imposition. And Sen. Gaylord Nelson, D-Wisc., said he was shocked by rejection of the warning statement provision, adding that "we should at least tell people about it, if we're going to feed them cancer."

We suspect that, contrary to Nelson's opinion, many more saccharin users will learn from the news media and by word-of-mouth about the possible carcinogenicity of saccharin than would ever do so from reading product labels. We also suspect that the comment of Sen. Richard Schweiker, the Pennsylvania Republican, is also valid, that the potential health benefits to be derived from use of saccharin by dieters and diabetics far outweigh any possible harm the substance could do as a carcinogen.

Among others who seem to agree are the Calorie Control Council (manufacturers), the American Diabetes Association, the Juvenile Diabetes Foundation and the American Heart Association, all of which have lobbied against the saccharin ban.

And the American public seems to feel that way, as well. The Calorie Council's poll last spring of almost 700 adults nationwide indicated that almost 70 per cent of Americans aged 18 to 59 were bone weary of the federal government's telling them that everything they eat is bad for their health.

The survey showed one-third of Americans thought saccharin was safe for consumption in any amounts, and more than half — 56 per cent — had concluded saccharin was safe when consumed in moderate amounts.

We'd accept their opinion over that of the Canadian white rats any time. And we're glad to see the senators did, too.

THE DALLAS TIMES HERALD

Dallas, Texas, September 19, 1977

THE ACTION of the Senate in voting to block for 18 months a government ban on saccharin will, if also approved in the House, provide time for additional tests on the possibility the sweetener causes cancer.

Under current law, the Food and Drug Administration had no option but to ban the use of saccharin, following the report of Canadian researchers that massive doses of saccharin had caused bladder cancer in laboratory animals.

The proposed ban drew strong protests from saccharin users, particularly those with diabetes, who pointed out that saccharin is the only artificial sweetener now on the market.

Various proposals were reviewed during the saccharin debate, including one which would have banned its use in manufactured products but would have left it on grocery shelves if warning labels were used. The Senate bill requires warnings be printed on products containing saccharin but the lawmakers decided against requiring the same warnings in printed ads or in radio and television commercials.

Given the wide attention concerning the saccharin controversy, most consumers now must know that there is a possibility, however remote, that the sweetener poses a risk. Consumers also remember, however, that another sweetener, cyclamate, was banned some years ago and latter was virtually cleared of being a cancer-causing substance.

Various research reports indicate that almost every thing man consumes has some potential as a health hazard. Given the years of saccharin use, it would appear that keeping it on the market for another 18 months — with adequate warnings — is an acceptable move. The time obviously should be spent in extended research into the sweetener's effect on human health.

The Philadelphia Inquirer

Philadelphia, Pa., September 18, 1977

Saccharin has a powerful lobby behind it and a broad constituency, as the Food and Drug Administration quickly learned when it proposed last March to ban the artificial sweetener from soft drinks and other products as a potential cause of cancer.

The outcry was enormous, and moves promptly were launched in Congress to force the FDA to back down. Still, the fact is that the scientific evidence did show that saccharin caused bladder cancer in rats. So the FDA was only following Congress's own mandate when it acted last March.

That is, the FDA has no choice but to ban any substance if "it is found to induce cancer when ingested by man or animal." And subsequent scientific evidence in a new Canadian study has provided even more compelling evidence that saccharin may cause cancer in human beings.

A congressional delay of the FDA ban, however, appears inevitable. The Senate has now voted 87-7 to suspend the FDA's mandate, where saccharin is concerned, for 18 months while further government studies are made to evaluate the substance's health hazards and benefits.

If such a moratorium is enacted, it will set an ominous precedent for further political decisions in areas where scientific judgments should prevail. But if Congress insists on going ahead, at least it should require (1) warning labels on products containing saccharin and (2) warnings in the advertising of such products.

Before clearing the bill, the Senate voted the first but rejected the second. That caused Sen. Edward Kennedy of Massachusetts, principal sponsor, to move to kill the bill by returning it to committee.

Unfortunately, he lost. But not irretrievably, since the House now has its whack. It may be expecting a lot, but Congress should be consistent. Cigarettes carry health hazard warnings on packages as well as advertising. The same should apply to saccharin.

CASPER STAR-TRIBUNE

Casper, Wyo., December 1, 1977

The Congress has acted sensibly in passing legislation which delays the Food and Drug Administration's ban on saccharin for an 18-month period. During this time the Department of Health, Education and Welfare will conduct tests to determine if the sugar substitute causes cancer when used in reasonable amounts.

The Food and Drug Administration had banned the product because of a Canadian test which claimed that it had produced cancer in rats. A later claim also was that it caused bladder cancer in men.

The FDA acted under the so-called Delaney amendment which made it mandatory for any foodstuff to be banned from use when it was known to have caused cancer. However, the results of the Canadian test were criticized by many on the grounds that the rats had been fed amounts of saccharin which were greatly larger than a human would ingest in normal living.

The proposed ban on saccharin dismayed millions of diabetics and people with weight problems who depended upon saccharin as a sugar substitute and used diet soft drinks.

The ban on saccharin followed closely on the heels of a similar ban on cyclamates, also a sugar substitute. We have never felt that the ban on cyclamates was justified or the danger clearly proved.

The legislation providing for the 18-month test period also makes it mandatory that warnings must be carried on the labels or packages of substances containing saccharin.

Undoubtedly the FDA moved too fast in this instance and we suspect in others. Saccharin had been in use for about eighty years and had never been considered carcinogenic.

The public has been subjected to cancer scares from many quarters with many of them based upon scanty research or insubstantial testing. And it is probable that cancer can be induced by many causes, if the exposure, as in the Canadian tests, are in gross amounts far beyond ordinary usage.

The effects upon diabetics and those with problems of obesity balanced off against the unknown effects of saccharin. The hastily imposed ban could have had effects much more harmful than what it was trying to prevent.

We believe that in this and other instances the FDA should use a temporary warning method, such as is in the new legislation, while an adequate testing program is pursued. If then it is found that a substance is harmful a ban could be imposed.

CHICAGO DAILY NEWS

Chicago, Ill., September 19, 1977

The U.S. Senate has initiated a temporary reprieve for the thousands of people plagued by diabetes or obesity who rely on saccharin to sweeten their food. It approved an 18-month delay in imposing a ban on the artificial sweetener to permit additional study of its health risks and benefits. The House is expected to concur. This unique approach to a food additive that has been shown to cause cancer in laboratory animals was prompted primarily because saccharin is the only artificial sweetener on the market.

Following the logic that consumers who benefit from saccharin should be able to weigh its risks and decide for themselves whether to continue using it, the Senate also mandated that a cancer warning appear on packages of food containing the sugar substitute and on grocery store displays. But it threw logic, and public safety, to the wind by exempting print and broadcast advertising from the requirement.

Giving people a choice is one thing. But limiting the information on which a choice can be made, particularly a choice involving the scourge of cancer, is irresponsible. Warnings on packages are easily overlooked, and warnings in stores are impossible to police. Warnings in advertising would have closed these gaps. They, too, should be required.

Congress Postpones Saccharin Ban Until 1981, Pending Further Study

BUFFALO EVENING NEWS

Buffalo, N.Y., July 27, 1979

Unable to decide on what to do about the use of saccharin as a sweetener, the House has voted to do nothing for another two years. Saccharin has been determined to be a moderate cause of cancer by a panel of the National Academy of Sciences, but the majority of the panel, considering the benefits of saccharin for diabetics and dieters, opposes an outright ban at this time.

Some restrictions, however, would make more sense than no restrictions — such as making saccharin a prescription or over-the-counter drug. At present, the lack of any curb raises the cancer risk significantly. The head of the latest scientific study was particularly concerned about the needless risk to pregnant women and to children who might be drinking a lot of diet pop this summer.

Many people nowadays have come to rely unduly on the government, and if the government hasn't banned saccharin they assume it's safe. The government has, however, put the following warning on every can of pop that uses saccharin. "Use of this product may be hazardous to your health. This product contains saccharin which has been determined to cause cancer in laboratory animals."

One scientific study estimates that the widespread use of saccharin would probably result in 2,000 cases of bladder cancer a year. Think about it.

The Philadelphia Inquirer

Philadelphia, Pa., July 28, 1979

The people who two years ago were thrown into a tizzy when the Food and Drug Administration announced its intention to ban saccharin needn't have worried. Congress blocked the ban with an 18-month moratorium, and may be about to do it again. This week the House voted overwhelmingly and without debate to allow the artificial sweetener to remain on the market for two more years. If the Senate follows suit, nothing is likely to be done about saccharin until after June 30, 1981. That would be unfortunate and, according to the preponderance of scientific evidence, even deadly.

The FDA proposed to ban saccharin as a food additive because it was shown to cause cancer in laboratory studies on animals. The first moratorium was supposed to allow time for further studies, which it did. They confirmed that saccharin is a carcinogen, albeit a "mild" one, and can aggravate the cancer-causing effects of other chemicals. Under federal food safety law, any substance found to cause cancer in animals must be taken off the market.

Then why is saccharin as readily available as ever, and why are so many congressmen willing to extend the moratorium? The answer is that the members of Congress are reacting to the outcry from the 50 to 70 million Americans who consume saccharin regularly in diet soft drinks and other beverages and foods. They also are responding to pressure from the diet food industry. The pro-saccharin forces assert that the substance really isn't all that dangerous, that it helps curb obesity and, besides, that people have a right to choose their poison.

Here the matter stands and will stand for two years more if the Senate extends the moratorium. Other alternatives are preferable: Don't extend the moratorium but let the FDA proceed with publishing a proposal to ban saccharin as a food additive. The administrative process for enacting that proposal, which includes public debate, would take at least 15 months and would itself amount to a moratorium. Let the FDA consider a compromise under which saccharin would no longer be "hidden" in many foods but would be available almost like a drug, probably as a table-top sweetener with a warning written on its package, as now.

If the Senate goes along with the moratorium on banning saccharin two years from now the same issues will be unresolved. The evidence says that such a delay would be dangerous.

WORCESTER TELEGRAM.

Worchester, Mass., August 16, 1979

A few weeks ago, the House of Representatives voted 394-22 to extend the moratorium preventing the Food and Drug Administration (FDA) from banning saccharin.

That followed reams of testimony favoring the continued use of saccharin and also continued study of it.

Saccharin is one of the FDA's hot potatoes. After it was shown to have caused cancer in rats (when given in huge doses), the FDA clamped down.

But the ban was strongly opposed by the American Diabetes Association, the Calorie Control Council and lots of ordinary citizens. Both the American Medical Association and the American Society of Internal Medicine say that saccharin should be kept on the market until it is proved to cause cancer in human beings.

That proof seems hard to come by. A study published recently in the Journal of the National Cancer Institute says that "present data provide virtually no support for an overall positive association of AS (artificial sweeteners) with cancer." A Norwegian study concludes that saccharin is neither carcinogenic nor mutagenic.

But if saccharin is safe for the moment, other artificial sweeteners are not. Both aspartame and cyclamates are under intense FDA scrutiny. FDA Commissioner Donald Kennedy says he will make a final decision on cyclamate before he leaves his post next summer.

Like saccharin, cyclamate has a question mark over it. Yet, as is the case with saccharin, the danger is not at all clear.

The FDA should give the public full information about saccharin, cyclamates and the other artificial sweeteners. People should pay attention and should conduct themselves accordingly.

But in a nation where tobacco is subsidized by the government, it seems outlandish to think of banning a sweet on the flimsy evidence available at this stage of the game.

New Studies Discount Serious Risk of Cancer from Saccharin

Three separate studies released March 6 discounted any link between saccharin and cancer of the bladder and urinary tract. The studies were conducted by the National Cancer Institute, the Harvard University School of Public Health and the American Health Foundation. They contradicted Canadian studies in 1977 that found a link between saccharin and bladder or urinary-tract cancer in laboratory rats.

The three studies agreed that saccharin was not a major factor in bladder and urinary-tract cancer, but they noted that there was no proof that the artificial sweetener was completely harmless. Some doctors involved in the studies cautioned that the long-term effects of saccharin in the human system could not yet be determined. Saccharin held some risks for those who used it excessively and for children, smokers and pregnant women. Heavy consumption of artifically sweetened soft drinks, which contained saccharin, posed the greatest threat to health, especially in children, according to the studies. Dr. Robert Hoover, director of the National Cancer Institute study, said "any use by nondiabetic children or pregnant women, heavy use by young women of childbearing age and excessive use by anyone are ill-advised and should be actively discouraged by the medical community."

THE RICHMOND NEWS LEADER

Richmond, Va., March 22, 1980

The great saccharin debate has reopened. When Congress voted to delay the Food and Drug Administration's proposed ban on saccharin in 1977, it recommended additional research into the safety of artificial sweeteners. The evidence has been mounting steadily for the past two years. And it suggests that saccharin is not harmful to health.

At least 12 scientific studies have failed to link cancer in humans to the consumption of saccharin. The current issue of *Science* magazine discusses an important saccharin study conducted by the American Health Foundation. A summary of the foundation's test, which was financed in part by a grant from the federal government's National Cancer Institute, states: ". . . There was no greater incidence of bladder cancer among the users of artificial sweeteners and diet beverages than would be expected in the general population."

While the FDA based its proposed ban on experiments with rats, the new saccharin tests were made on humans. (Even the FDA admits a human would have to quaff 600 diet sodas a day for a lifetime to equal the saccharin doses administered to the rats.) While it is theoretically impossible to prove something is perfectly safe, the saccharin tests involving humans apparently rebut the FDA's original claims.

The FDA isn't exactly our favorite federal agency, but it does not deserve all the blame for the saccharin imbroglio. The proposed ban was based on the so-called Delaney Amendment, which *requires* the banning of any food additive shown in laboratory tests to cause — possibly — the merest smidgen of cancer in man or beast. If reputable tests turn up traces of cancer in rats, for example, then the FDA has no choice but to ban the substance in question.

The elimination of carcinogens is a worthy goal, but the Delaney Amendment wields a messy meat-axe. Few things are risk-free. The FDA ought to have to authority to balance a substance's advantages against its risks. In the case of saccharin, the many clear advantages heavily outweigh the possible disadvantages. Given the increasing evidence that saccharin is not hazardous to humans, Congress should (1) permanently enjoin the FDA from imposing even a limited saccharin ban, and (2) rewrite the Delaney Amendment to maximize the discretion of the scientists employed by the FDA.

THE [ ] SUN

Baltimore, Md., March 7, 1980

Attacking federal regulatory agencies is all the rage nowadays, and there can be little doubt that the anti-regulators are going to have a field day soon with the Food and Drug Administration on the issue of saccharin. Three years ago the FDA attempted to ban saccharin after animal tests showed it may cause bladder cancer in humans. There was a great cry of outrage then from the anti-regulators, who insisted the FDA wanted to use flimsy evidence to deprive dieters and diabetics of an allegedly highly useful substance. Congress banned the ban.

This week, epidemiologists—who study the rates of occurrence of various diseases and attempt to relate susceptibility to factors in victims' lives—came forward with new studies which indicate that saccharin may not cause cancer in humans. The anti-regulators are certain to seize on these new findings with cries of "We told you so"— while at the same time, probably, calling for curbs on federal regulation of everything from insecticides to workplace safety.

They will have no grounds for doing so. The FDA's mandate is to protect the public against harmful foods and drugs, the harmfulness or lack thereof to be judged by the best available evidence *at the time the call is made.* In 1977 when the FDA tried to ban saccharin, it was following this mandate as it is enunciated in the Dulaney Amendment, which says that substances that are cancer-causing in animals are to be presumed to be cancer-causing in humans. Most scientists agree this approach is sound, for many substances that have been found to cause animal cancers indeed later are found to cause human cancers as well. Moreover, chemicals do not, like human defendants, deserve a presumption of innocence till proven guilty. On the contrary, if there are only suspicions that a chemical is guilty—provided the suspicions are based on the best available scientific evidence—simple prudence dictates ending human exposure till more definitive studies are done.

Most of the FDA's judgments turn out later to have been correct. One memorable call the agency made was on the tranquilizer Thalidomide. Because an FDA official suspected Thalidomide might cause severe birth defects in infants if pregnant women took it, the agency refused to approve it. Experience in Europe, where the drug was approved, later showed the FDA's suspicions to have been entirely correct. The FDA thus saved thousands of U.S. infants from severe deformities. Saccharin probably is not another Thalidomide, but for all the FDA knew in 1977 it might have been. Its action on saccharin was entirely correct.

The TENNESSEAN

Nashville, Tenn., March 10, 1980

SEVERAL recent studies seem to refute previous findings that saccharin, an artificial sweetener used in numerous diet foods and soft drinks, causes cancer.

The Food and Drug Administration proposed a ban on saccharin in 1977 after studies showed it caused cancer in rats.

Congress postponed the ban for 18 months and the FDA has not resumed steps leading to the ban. Now it appears that the ban may not come about at all.

A study of 1,118 people, conducted at the Harvard School of Public Health, failed to show a definite link between saccharin and bladder cancer.

A similar study of 367 bladder cancer patients by the American Health Foundation reached the same conclusion. The researchers found that the bladder cancer rate for men and women who use saccharin was actually 10% lower than that among other people.

However, some subgroups in the Harvard study showed the risk of cancer was double among men who drank more than two diet sodas a day and four times higher than normal among women who had been drinking diet beverages for more than five years.

Researchers speculated that these exceptions might be statistical flukes.

But a federal cancer expert urged that non-diabetic children and pregnant women avoid saccharin.

The latest findings are good news to people on diets. But it might be a good idea not to go overboard on the use of saccharin until there is a better resolution of the contradictory studies.

ST. LOUIS POST-DISPATCH

St. Louis, Mo., March 9, 1980

New studies by two well qualified scientific organizations have found that the link between saccharin and cancer is unfounded. The American Health Foundation found "no association between saccharin and bladder cancer," and Harvard University's School of Public Health's study showed that persons who use the artificial sweetener have little or no increased risk of cancer. Those reports — good news for saccharine users — corroborate an earlier study done by the National Cancer Institute. So what's to be done about saccharine?

Although the Food and Drug Administration favored restricting the sweetener in 1977 after research on rats showed a link with bladder cancer, Congress imposed an 18-month moratorium on any FDA action and has indicated that it will extend that moratorium through mid-1981. That would make it possible to collect more data on human research and is perhaps the best way to deal with the new evidence. If subsequent reports bear out the latest findings, then the sweetener ought to be declared safe.

The Seattle Times

Seattle, Wash., March 11, 1980

Now that two more prestigious studies have found little or no proof that saccharin has anything to do with bladder cancer in people, the Federal Food and Drug Administration can expect more brickbats.

The FDA has been under fire ever since it tried to ban the use of saccharin a couple of years ago. Congress quickly put a moratorium on the ban, once it began hearing from the people.

The two new studies differ slightly in some details of their findings but agree that saccharin is, at most, a weak carcinogen. Detailed study of bladder cancer statistics shows almost no correlation with saccharin use.

Nevertheless, the concern about saccharin is not wholly imaginary. The study by Alan S. Morrison and Julie E. Buring, reported in The New England Journal of Medicine, raises a cautionary finger: It is not wise to use too much saccharin.

While "The evidence is that little, if any, current bladder cancer is due to the consumption of artificial sweeteners," writes Robert Hoover of the National Cancer Institute, "There is also general agreement that these studies did not address the carcinogenicity of artificial sweeteners for organs other than the bladder, the effect of very heavy use of artificial sweeteners many decades ago, the effect of heavy use of artificial sweeteners by the young, or the effect of in utero exposure to artificial sweeteners."

Hoover goes on to note that "the general patterns of use of artificial sweeteners in this country are troublesome . . . When all the evidence of toxicity is weighed against the lack of objective evidence of benefit, any use by nondiabetic children or pregnant women, heavy use by young women of childbearing age, and excessive use by anyone are ill advised and should be actively discouraged by the medical community."

The FDA ban on saccharin was an over-reaction, not justified by the evidence. But that does not mean that anyone should go on a saccharin binge.

In saccharin use, moderation is still the best rule.

AKRON BEACON JOURNAL

Akron, Ohio, March 15, 1980

NEW MEDICAL studies haven't given saccharin, the artificial sweetener thought at one time to play a significant role in bladder cancers, a clean bill of health.

But they have taken a significant curse off the substance.

The studies provide no evidence that saccharin use plays a significant role in cancer of the urinary tract.

And to think that the U. S. Food and Drug Administration wanted in 1977 to ban the use of saccharin.

In honor of the new studies, how about a toast? With diet pop, of course.

The Knickerbocker News
Albany, N.Y., March 14, 1980

It now appears that saccharine, the artificial sweetener that causes bladder cancer in rats if they're stuffed with the equivalent of 800 soft drinks a day in everyday terms, isn't so bad for the human animal after all.

After all the hoopla and hubbub a few years ago, when the Food and Drug Administration attempted to ban the substance and the nation's diabetics, obese and perennial calorie-watchers virtually rioted in the grocery aisles, this cautious removal of the medical curse on saccharine is surprising, to say the least.

The chemical is still carcinogenic, but only if you take too much of it. No one is certain what small dosages over many years will do to us, but they do think that more than a couple diet soft drinks or a few packets of coffee-sweetener a day is excessive. And they're worried that the biggest consumers of saccharine appear to be women of child-bearing age and children, who will probably continue to consume it for many years.

So a few people will have health problems sometime in the future. But who really knows who? Or when?

That's a pretty hard risk to assess. But it's not really the saccharine risk that has us bothered right now.

We are worried that more Americans than ever will figure all government warnings are just so much hogwash — remember the little boy who cried "Wolf!" once too often? — and ignore anything inconvenient that comes from Washington in the future. The saccharine problem isn't exactly analogous, since there is a slight but true danger from the sweet wolf, but the effect is probably going to be the same.

It's difficult enough to judge what's good for us and what's bad for us in this complex world of ours. The government isn't helping by failing to put its warnings and caveats into proper perspective for the average consumer. We must be told how to judge the danger of saccharine against the danger from the nitrites in bacon, for instance. Is coffee worse for your heart than lack of exercise?

Is there a consumer agency that interprets the outflow of words from other consumer agencies?

DAILY NEWS
New York, N.Y., March 7, 1980

Remember those experiments with laboratory rats that indicated saccharin causes bladder cancer? Well, it ain't necessarily so, at least not for human beings, according to two newly completed scientific studies.

A lot of people with diabetes, high blood pressure or weight problems will want to hoist cans of artificially sweetened soda pop to toast that news, no doubt. But a word of caution. Not all of the evidence is in; saccharin hasn't been around long enough for any conclusive findings on its cancer-causing potential. The best bet for fans of the sweeteners still is to observe the wise old maxim: moderation in all things.

BUFFALO EVENING NEWS
Buffalo, N.Y., March 18, 1980

It is good news for diabetics and dieters that new scientific studies conclude that saccharin poses a lesser cancer threat than previously supposed. Users of saccharin should, however, study the latest reports with care, since there is still some risk

The latest finding of the National Cancer Institute is that, for most people, the moderate use of saccharin — for example, in coffee or one or two diet drinks a day — is nothing much to worry about. The risk, if any, is quite small.

However — and this should be emphasized — there are believed to be dangers in some cases. There was a 60 percent increase in cancer with heavy use — more than five packets of sweetener a day (in tea or coffee, etc.) or more than two diet drinks. There is increased risk among heavy smokers. Children and pregnant women should not use saccharin at all, the study said.

In addition, there may be hazards that have not shown up yet. Exposure to some chemicals sometimes produces cancer up to 50 years later. Saccharin has not been on the market long enough to properly assess all the long-term perils.

All the public can do is abide by the best scientific knowledge available, and perhaps the next saccharin study will find new dangers. Until then, however, those for whom saccharin is practically a necessity will be able to enjoy its use with much less anxiety.

The Dallas Morning News
Dallas, Texas, March 24, 1980

Results of two recent studies cast more doubt on warnings of the federal government that saccharin and similar artificial sweeteners might cause cancer in humans. They illustrate the tangle of uncertainty involving health and nutritional tests.

More significantly, these latest findings support the belief of many Americans: That the federal health control agencies have been crying "wolf" too many times and therefore are losing their credibility as public health protectors and advisors.

The saccharin studies were conducted by prestigious health groups — the Harvard School of Public Health and the American Health Foundation — and were made independently of each other. Unlike previous tests on rats (some of the rats died after consuming great amounts of the artificial sweetener), these latest studies were made on humans. No clear pattern developed from them, although at least one group that used saccharin actually had a lower bladder-cancer rate than those who shunned the sweetener.

The Harvard doctors admit they don't know why saccharin makes rats sick but not humans. But they speculated that perhaps rats simply are different from people.

Such a possibility deserves a little more consideration by the governmental regulators if they expect to be effective in future warnings against products that really do present hazards.

The Idaho STATESMAN
Boise, Idaho, March 9, 1980

While two recent studies failed to show any broad link between the use of saccharin and the occurrence of bladder cancer in humans, the results of the studies should be viewed as inconclusive.

In the studies — 1,118 persons examined by the Harvard School of Public Health and 367 bladder cancer patients examined by the American Health Foundation — researchers did not find alarming bladder cancer rates among users of saccharin or cyclamate, a sweetener that was banned 10 years ago.

The Harvard researchers, however, came up with some troubling findings. In some subgroups, the cancer risk was found to be four times higher than normal among women who had been drinking diet beverages, which are flavored with artificial sweetners, for more than five years. The researchers speculated the findings might have been statistical aberrations.

Medical science remains unable to explain why large doses of saccharin cause cancer in the bladders of rats, and after the studies came out last week the public was warned against heavy use of products that contain saccharin.

The jury is still out on saccharin.

THE PLAIN DEALER
Cleveland, Ohio, March 15, 1980

"Humans are not rats," went the emotional argument by heavy users of saccharin in 1977 when a Canadian study showed that some rats fed concentrated doses of the artificial sweetener developed cancer of the bladder.

Now, it turns out, that the sloganeers may have been right. Three studies of humans comparing diet with cancer cases would seem to indicate that the risk is slight. But "slight" means there still is some risk, according to the major study.

The 1977 slogan became a rallying cry to prevent the banning of saccharin as a carcinogen. Cyclamates were banned in 1970. In a nation of overweight dieters, the loss of the last acceptable artificial sweetener was seen as a threat to personal well-being.

It was especially seen this way when the rats' dosage was put in terms of the equivalent of 800 soft-drink servings a day instead of in terms of 5% of the rats' daily diet.

As a result of the protests, including a delaying act of Congress, saccharin was never banned. Instead, warnings were posted, such as those on soft-drink can labels, noting that the product could be hazardous to health.

The National Cancer Institute interviewed 3,000 bladder cancer patients and 6,000 healthy persons about their diet. The results indicated the risk was slight. The Harvard School of Public Health failed to find a pattern of saccharin use among 592 cancer patients. And the American Health Foundation found a similar lack of pattern among 367 patients.

While the institute said the risk was greater for heavy users, its definition of "heavy" use was not reassuring. It defined it as two or more eight-ounce diet soft drinks or seven packets of sugar substitutes a day.

That should give users pause. The threshold can easily be crossed. Soft-drink cans usually contain 12 ounces. And one or two packets are frequently used in each cup of coffee by dieters.

The failure to find heavy concentrations of bladder cancer among saccharin users may well be due to a physiological difference between rat and man which may cause a different degree of susceptibility.

However, it also may be that the period of heavy saccharin use has not been long enough, that there may be a long time lag between exposure and effect.

While the evidence so far does not indicate saccharin should be removed from the shelves, neither does it indicate that it should be sold without warning of possible health hazards as shown by animal studies.

SAN JOSE NEWS
San Jose, Cal., March 7, 1980

THE latest word in the saccharin-cancer controversy came out Thursday. Already the thundering chorus of I-told-you-so is starting to roll from Puget Sound to the Potomac.

Dr. Robert Hoover, environmental studies chief of the National Cancer Institute, says in the current issue of the New England Journal of Medicine that "there is no saccharin-induced epidemic of bladder cancer in this country" and that the cancer risk to moderate users of the artificial sweetener, "if present at all, is quite small and little cause for concern."

The latest research findings will provide reassurance for the estimated 44 million Americans who use saccharin, and probably will deliver the *coup de grace* to the U.S. Food and Drug Administration's three-year effort to ban it.

Unfortunately, they'll also have some pernicious effects on public attitudes.

First, they'll inspire a lot of people to jump to the comforting but simplistic conclusion that saccharin is safe. The studies suggest saccharin poses little danger for most people most of the time; they don't prove that saccharin is absolutely safe for everybody all of the time. Saccharin was linked to increased cancer risks for smokers, for children and young persons, for the unborn, and for people who consume more than about 160 milligrams a day — roughly the amount in two diet soft drinks.

Second, the new findings will provide ammunition for the campaign to repeal or severely weaken the Delaney Clause of the U.S. Food and Drug Act.

The Delaney Clause, which forbids the addition to foods of any substances found to cause cancer in human beings or animals, is based on the premise that there is at present no way of determining a "safe" threshold of exposure to a carcinogen. We think that's a sound principle, and we see nothing in the new research to alter our conviction.

A persuasive case can be made that the Delaney Clause should make allowance for chemicals like saccharin whose minimal cancer risks may be outweighed by enormous value in the prevention and control of other killer diseases. Congress might want to make Delaney more flexible, but until we develop reliable ways of setting safe tolerances for carcinogens, abolishing the clause would be playing Russian roulette with the nation's health.

Finally, the latest saccharin reports will increase public skepticism about all cancer warnings, and possibly jeopardize the whole national effort to identify and remove environmental carcinogens.

Two decades of news reports about cancer-causing agents cropping up seemingly everywhere have caused Americans to arm themselves with cynical defensive beliefs. Everything gives you cancer anyway, one belief goes, so why worry. A variation: If you eat or drink or breathe enough of anything, it's going to give you cancer. Or: Just because something gives rats cancer doesn't mean it will give people cancer.

As folklore, these ideas have a certain quaint appeal. As science, they have no more basis than Druidic fertility rituals.

It's just not true that everything gives you cancer, or that anything will give you cancer if you consume enough. Only a carcinogen will give you cancer. A non-carcinogen may give you heartburn or kidney stones or dandruff, but it won't give you cancer no matter how hard you try.

Laboratory rat studies, besides providing a rich vein of material for stand-up comedians, are one of the best techniques we have for spotting carcinogens quickly and reasonably accurately. Researchers administer high doses of suspected substances not because they're out to prove that everything causes cancer, but because they're trying to observe in an animal that lives two or three years the possible effects on human beings who live 60 or 70 years.

Most laymen don't understand such technicalities, of course, and the news media by and large have done a lamentably bad job of helping them understand. All too often the newspapers, wire services and television take a carefully researched, meticulously worded scientific report and boil it down to a simplistic 20-second spot or a six-inch article under a headline shrieking: "Shampoo Causes Cancer, FDA Warns." It's no wonder that a lot of Americans are in a state akin to shell-shock after 20 years of such bombardment.

The task is to increase public understanding, and the place to start is with more extensive, more knowledgeable and less strident news coverage.

It won't be a quick or easy job, but the end product — a society capable of making informed decisions about cancer hazards instead of reacting with irrational panic or equally irrational fatalism — will amply repay the effort.

The Honolulu Advertiser

Honolulu, Hawaii, March 9, 1980

Moderation in all things is the golden mean and it is especially applicable to saccharin, the sugar substitute which was thought by some to increase the risks of bladder cancer.

A pair of scientific studies — from the Harvard University School of Public Health and the American Health Foundation — have disproved the connection first observed in laboratory animals. That must be a relief to the nation's 10 million diabetics.

STILL, THE STUDIES have not found saccharin to be completely safe. They warn against "heavy" use, by which they mean the amount that would be consumed in more than two diet drinks a day.

Another finding is that women who are pregnant or at the age when they might be ought to be especially careful about saccharin.

And there is good reason for concern about the heavy use of saccharin in diet soft drinks by youngsters who may go on to consume large amounts during their lifetime.

Only one study found evidence to support an earlier warning that smoking further increased the risks of cancer for saccharin users. But there is already enough evidence against smoking to discourage anyone who would be convinced by scientific data.

THE CONTINUING studies of saccharin are the result of a "scare" that led the Food and Drug Administration to call for a ban in 1977. Congress moved to prevent the FDA from banning saccharin completely on the basis of insufficient evidence, although warning notices about possible risks were required.

There is every reason for prudence when dealing with scientific and technological advances that appear to offer risks that outweigh their convenience and usefulness. That the FDA's concern appears in retrospect to have been overzealous does not change that.

Caution — and even over-caution — is preferable to the alternative. It is better to be able to remove the cloud of suspicion from a new product even after heavy warnings than to find out years later that something thought quite safe was not. The FDA's concern was not groundless. Saccharin ought to be used prudently, by adults. The publicity that was attracted by this controversy should help to alert people to the dangers of excessive use of this artificial sweetener.

Recent studies indicating that artificial-sweetener warnings have been greatly overstated are a mixed blessing.

Although they show that there is no saccharin-caused bladder cancer epidemic in the country, they don't let that substance and other artificial sweeteners entirely off the hook.

For smokers, pregnant women and youths, the warning flag is still up: Cut back to two diet drinks a day, or the equivalent in sweetener packets (about five).

For the possessor of a sometimes sweet tooth and for diabetics, however, the news is good: Normal use of artificial sweeteners does not carry the threat of cancer implied in the warnings from the Food and Drug Administration in the Seventies.

The saccharin scare is one more indication of the limitations of what might be termed the FDA "early warning system." When it tests early, it too often operates on limited research: too little system, too much warning. The FDA at one point was gearing up to ban saccharin, a reaction that, in the light of studies in 1969 confirmed by the recent findings, appears to be a conspicuous case of overreaction.

THE LOUISVILLE TIMES

Louisville, Ky., March 12, 1980

All those who have to avoid sugar will of course be relieved by yet another finding that normal use of saccharin is unlikely to cause cancer in human beings.

The study, made by the Harvard School of Public Health, nonetheless indicates that pregnant women and youngsters who consume a lot of artificially sweetened soft drinks run some risk. Health officials worry especially about heavy use of diet drinks by teen-agers, although the actual effects on their health may not be known for many years.

What's more, the findings offer little consolation to cigarette smokers, who seldom find encouraging words in health studies these days.

A U.S. surgeon-general's report baldly stated last summer that "cigarette smoking is responsible for more cancer and more cancer deaths than any other known agent." Smokers are more susceptible to several varieties of the disease, including bladder cancer, which is also linked to saccharin.

Smoking also has a nasty way of multiplying "risks associated with other carcinogenic agents," and that seems to happen, though to a very small degree, when people use both saccharin and cigarettes.

These conclusions strengthen the view that cancer is less likely to be defeated by a miracle cure than by individual decisions to avoid disease-causing agents. While the report will take most of the worry out of consuming a one-calorie drink, its message should not be lost on Americans who are immoderate in their use of saccharin or cigarettes or, worst of all, both.

Roanoke Times & World-News

Roanoke, Va., March 8, 1980

The whole federal regulatory apparatus, costing some $100 billion a year, is under increasing criticism — not, it critics contend, because it is not needed, but because it is often over-zealous and its resuls are often minimal or non-existent.

The regulatory "industry" (and that is what it has become) was shaken by the thalidomide disaster in Europe and the United States, quite understandably. But what developed in the aftershock of that case of too little warning too late was the kind of regulatory mentality described by Sir Ernest Benn, British publisher and author, as "the art of looking for trouble, finding it everywhere, diagnosing it wrongly, and applying unsuitable remedies."

Barry Crickmer, in an essay in *Nation's Business,* has traced the efforts of economists like Sam Peltzman of the University of Chicago and toxicologists like William Wardell of the University of Rochester to evaluate federal regulations. Many have concluded that. more often than not, federal regulations do not prove worthwhile in a cost-analysis.

Where human life and well-being is obviously at stake, as in the case of thalidomide, any cost-analysis is cynical and misdirected. But on a far more familiar level, federal agencies too often seek to protect a butterfly with the regulatory equivalent of a Fort Knox.

As University of California geneticist William Havender puts it: "Why . . . do we find ourselves serenely contemplating a person's plan to climb a dangerous Himalayan peak at the same time that we propose making it illegal for [him] to buy a can of Tab?"

THE BLADE

Toledo, Ohio, March 20, 1980

Richmond Times-Dispatch

Richmond, Va., March 15, 1980

It is gratifying to read, for a change, that something does *not* cause cancer. Or, at least, even if it could cause cancer under certain conditions, the threat is not nearly so great as originally announced.

The new medical reports have to do with saccharin. Three years ago, on the basis of experiments showing that saccharin caused bladder cancer in rats, the U.S. Food and Drug Administration attempted to put a ban on saccharin, but Congress prevented it. So the FDA had to be satisfied with warning signs in stores that sell items that include saccharin, and with warning labels on the products themselves.

Now come reports of findings in two new studies which, when taken together, suggest that there are no discernible adverse health effects from the moderate use of saccharin by most people. One of the studies, made by the National Cancer Institute, did claim to find some increased cancer risk among "heavy" saccharin users, meaning persons who drink four or more eight-ounce

diet drinks or six or more servings a day of saccharin as a sugar substitute.

The National Cancer Institute does not give saccharin a totally clean bill of health. According to Dr. Robert Hoover, head of the institute's bladder cancer project, 'Any use by non-diabetic children or pregnant women, heavy use by women of childbearing age and excessive use by anyone are ill-advised and should be discouraged by the medical community."

One reason for the Institute's caution is the fact that diet drinks did not become popular until the 1960s, whereas medical science holds that the effects of a weak cancer-causing agent may not be manifested for 30 years or even longer.

On balance, however, the latest reports are good news for saccharin users, or would-be saccharin users. On the basis of what is known today, most adults can use saccharin in reasonable amounts without fear that they are doing any measurable damage to their bodies.

MILLIONS of Americans, concerned about the health effects of obesity, can breath a sigh of relief now that three separate scientific studies have affirmed the safety of saccharin, the only nonfattening sweetener on the market.

The new saccharin studies, however, provide reason for both optimism and caution.

Optimism is justified because of what the studies show about saccharin's effects in humans. Until stopped by Congress several years ago, the U.S. Food and Drug Administration was set to ban saccharin after it was found to cause urinarytract cancer in laboratory rats fed huge doses of the substance. Such studies were criticized because people do not consume the quantities of saccharin fed to the rats — the equivalent of 800 12-ounce cans of diet soda pop daily.

Scientists and laymen alike wondered: Would the much smaller amounts of saccharin consumed by humans also cause urinary cancer? So scientists went to persons who actually have urinary tract cancer — a total of 4,000 in all three studies — and matched them with 4,000 persons of similar background who did not have urinary cancer. Scientists checked the dietary histories of each group.

Here is how the New England Journal of Medicine summarized conclusions of the biggest studies: "The major finding is that there is no saccharin-induced epidemic of bladder cancer in this country. The evidence is that little, if any, current bladder cancer is due to the consumption of artificial sweet-

eners, at the doses and in the manner that sweeteners were commonly consumed in the past."

The final 15 words of the summary are important. For they establish the need for further caution about saccharin by emphasizing what the new studies did not show: the effects of saccharin at the doses and in the manner that it is consumed *in the present.*

For decades after saccharin's introduction as a food additive 69 years ago, it was used primarily on an occasional basis, with consistent, daily use being rare. But this pattern of usage has changed. Today, thanks primarily to diet soda pop, consistent, day-to-day use is common. And children and women in their childbearing years are among the heaviest users of diet soda.

Because of the health and social stigma attached to obesity and worry about the health hazards of sugar, Americans now are being exposed to high doses of saccharin throughout the entire human life cycle. Strikingly, in laboratory animals, saccharin is most effective in causing cancer when the mother is exposed to it before pregnancy, and the offspring are exposed to it as fetuses and throughout their lifetimes.

In addition, the largest of the new human studies did show some increased cancer risk among persons consuming the equivalent of four or more dietetic beverages per day, and among other "heavy" saccharin users who smoked cigarettes.

Because of such factors, it is wise to re-emphasize what the National Cancer Institute advised after publication of the new saccharin studies: Nondiabetic children and pregnant women still should avoid use of saccharin, and excessive use by anyone is "ill-advised."

But the person who uses an occasional packet of saccharin in his morning coffee or sips an occasional diet soda pop can now do so with some assurance that the risk, if present at all, is small and no reason for concern. Most importantly, the new human saccharin studies should add momentum to the legislative efforts now under way to modify federal food laws, eliminating the automatic ban on any food additive shown to cause cancer in laboratory animals.

For there now is evidence that an epidemic of cancer in laboratory rats does not automatically translate into an epidemic of cancer in people.

St. Louis Globe-Democrat

St. Louis, Mo., March 10, 1980

For years the federal government has been scaring saccharin users with the specter of cancer. It even proposed a ban on the use of the artificial sweetener on the ground that it had been determined dangerous to users' health.

Now it appears that saccharin has been given a bum rap. A series of new medical studies has concluded that the saccharin-cancer scare of the 1970s was largely overstated.

Except for certain special groups, such as children and women who are pregnant, it was found that people who use modest amounts of the artificial sweetener have "little cause for concern" about cancer.

"The studies' major finding is that there is no saccharin-induced epidemic of bladder cancer in this country," Dr. Robert Hoover, environmental studies chief of the National Cancer Institute, said in the New England Journal of Medicine.

The dieter who uses a packet or two of saccharin a day in coffee, or the diabetic who drinks diet drink, he added, "can be assured" that their risk of cancer, "if present at all, is quite small and little cause for concern."

The New England Journal summarized a new Harvard School of Public Health study that failed to find any general pattern of

artificial sweetener use in 592 Bostonians with bladder cancer. Similar results in a study of 367 patients in six cities, conducted by the American Health Foundation, are reported in Science magazine.

The latest studies confirm a largely similar finding in a December National Cancer Institute report on a study of more than 3,000 cancer patients.

It is pointed out that none of these studies proves saccharin to be completely safe. It should be pointed out further that even the proponents of saccharin never contended that it was completely safe, any more than sugar, salt or hundreds of other items are completely safe if used to excess.

The sin in the sad saccharin saga, it appears, is that federal regulators jumped the gun. They tried to impose a ban before all the facts were in. Subsequent findings have shown there was insufficient evidence to support their original case against saccharin.

The experience should not serve to diminish the importance of the regulatory role played by the Food and Drug Administration. There should be ongoing tests of products in the American marketplace. But before bans are proposed, the evidence should be conclusive. The saccharin lesson should have taught that.

Los ANGELES
HERALD EXAMINER

Los Angeles, Cal., March 11, 1980

With the results of the three saccharin studies released late last week, it seems unlikely that the federal Food and Drug Administration (FDA) will ever try to ban saccharin again. And therein lies a tale.

The FDA has been trying to ban the artificial sweetener for years, ever since tests on rats showed a strong link between saccharin consumption and bladder cancer.

But to yank saccharin from the market would deny it to diabetics, as well as the gravely overweight. And for that reason, Congress declared a moratorium on FDA attempts to ban the sweetener. Though the moratorium expired in May 1978, the FDA hasn't brought it up again for fear of being rebuffed.

The most recent tests ought to obviate any further FDA action. Especially interesting were the results of the National Cancer Institute's long-awaited study, which did not conclude that saccharin was "safe," but which refused to declare it harmful.

Epidemiological studies still haven't had sufficient time to offer absolutely convincing statistics. But the NCI's findings suggest that we can all use saccharin relatively fearlessly in moderate amounts, with the exception of: (1) heavy smokers, (2) pregnant women, and (3) people who consume both saccharin and diet drinks repeatedly each day.

But why would saccharin cause cancer in rats, and not in people?

That's something we probably won't know for sure for yet another 20 years, when all the epidemiological statistics are in. But the three most recent studies bring to 11 the number of surveys which have failed to link saccharin use to increased incidence of bladder cancer. Maybe all this isn't exactly good enough for the FDA, but we suspect it's good enough for most of us.

A final note: the FDA's concern with public health is obviously important and incontestable, but what is somewhat more arguable — and worrisome — is the sometimes panicky way it seems to blow the whistle on products that, in the end, seem harmful only to laboratory animals exposed to levels of consumption light-years beyond even the most obsessive use.

And therein, we think, is the moral of this story. ∎

The Cleveland Press

Cleveland, Ohio, March 12, 1980

Medical researchers have tried and tried again, but have failed to come up with any statistically significant evidence that saccharin causes bladder cancer.

So they've done what they should have done years ago — called off the "red alert" regarding the artificial sweetener.

Three separate studies involving several thousand saccharin users and nonusers found little or no additional risk of cancer among the users. The studies were conducted by the Harvard School of Public Health, the American Health Foundation and the National Cancer Institute.

Not only that, but whatever risk was detected was often contradictory.

For example, the NCI found some extra risk among heavy smokers, but Harvard doctors observed no such effect. The latter, however, found a "moderately high" risk among women who were long-term consumers of diet beverages. But a 1977 study in Canada, where the whole saccharin flap started, found an increased risk among men, not women.

To confuse things further, men in the Harvard study who used diet drinks only occasionally ran less risk of developing urinary cancer than men who didn't drink the beverages at all.

In the face of such conflicting findings, the researchers can only say that while saccharin doesn't do anybody any good — especially pop-guzzling kids and pregnant women — and while saccharin could yet be indicted in 20 or 30 years, most persons can safely consume it in moderation.

As it turned out then, Congress showed good judgment back in 1977 when it imposed a moratorium on any ban of saccharin by the Food and Drug Administration. A ban could have been a real threat to the well-being of persons like diabetics, who must use sugar substitutes.

The moratorium has since expired, however, and it probably wouldn't hurt anything if the lawmakers reinstated it.

But, now that it has been so abundantly shown that whatever health risk saccharin poses is extremely remote, we hope the FDA finally puts its ban in limbo and devotes its resources to investigating the multitude of chemicals and other substances we know far less about than we do saccharin.

The Hartford Courant

Hartford, Conn., May 3, 1980 Worchester

Weight-conscious Americans — that is, almost everyone — cheered when Congress overruled the Food and Drug Administration proposal to ban saccharin from processed foods in 1977.

They may have a chance to cheer anew now that the Senate seems about to again delay the ban, this time to June 30, 1981. The House has already passed legislation that would keep saccharin on the shelves.

A decision against the ban would certainly be popular, but not necessarily wise. It would suggest a misreading of scientific data, a capitulation to powerful lobbying groups and a failure to come to grips with a difficult regulatory problem.

Congress seems to be acting on the mistaken notion that the results of three recent studies refute the results of earlier animal tests linking saccharin with cancer. But even the most elaborate of the three new studies was not designed to detect any increase smaller than 15 percent in the incidence of bladder cancer in humans exposed to saccharin. It found no effect at that level, which is not the same as saying there is no effect at all. Earlier evidence that saccharin is a weak carcinogen still stands.

Emmanuel Farber, chairman of the National Academy of Sciences' most recent panel on saccharin, was quoted in Science magazine as saying "the studies do not prove that saccharin is safe, and anyone who says that is giving us a snow job."

It is obviously to the advantage of the saccharin, soft drink and pharmaceutical industries to leave the public with the impression that saccharin is perfectly safe and that animal studies linking it with cancer are invalid. In fact, the Calorie Control Council, an industry organization, has spent hundreds of thousands of dollars since the proposed ban in 1977 to create that impression.

The assumed benefits of saccharin may outweigh its risks. But the Delaney clause of the Food, Drug and Cosmetic Act requires the FDA to ban any substance for which there is evidence that it could cause cancer.

The FDA had no choice but to ban the use of saccharin in processed foods after tests found the sweetener a suspected carcinogen.

Instead of making exceptions to the Delaney clause merely because a particular chemical food additive is popular, Congress should be looking into more flexible regulatory alternatives.

One possibility is to establish two sets of standards: One a standard of usefulness or benefit and the other a standard of safety or tolerable hazard. Against those two standards, the case for and against a particular additive or chemical could be heard in open proceedings.

In that way, such issues as logistics, economics, ethics, and even esthetics also could be considered along with health.

Simply postponing for another year implementation of the ban would be irresponsible.

The Evening Gazette

Worchester, Mass., March 8, 1980

There are no open-and-shut cases in scientific research. One man's carcinogen is another's cancer-free substance.

The good news is that saccharin, an important sugar substitute for diabetics, victims of obesity and others, has been given a new lease on its reputation.

Back in 1977, the U.S. Food and Drug Administration took steps to ban the manufacture and use of saccharin after a study in Canada indicated that the substance caused bladder cancer in laboratory rats.

Unlike the previous bans on suspected carcinogens, this one provoked a hue and cry, especially from those in the general public who needed sugar substitutes. Their congressmen and other officials, as well as many scientists and doctors, said the case against saccharin had not been proved. Implementation of laws to ban it was delayed.

That action sent other scientists to the laboratories for more research and study on saccharin. Now the New England Journal of Medicine has published two studies indicating that, while saccharin may have caused bladder cancer in rats, it does not necessarily do so in human beings.

A third study, published in the American Health Foundation magazine Science, seems to agree.

The New England Journal of Medicine, in an editorial, says:

"After 69 years of scientific study and debate, the issues may be different and the words may be less vivid, but the relative positions in the controversy over saccharin as a food additive seem remarkably similiar.

This leads the media, the legislators, the medical community and the general public to despair that modern science has assisted us little in difficult decisions of national importance."

The Journal editorial then goes on to point out that while a "generation of conflicting laboratory studies raised suspicions of carcinogenicity," continuing study has better defined and refined the information.

As a result, scientists now feel that, while there is confirmation of "the capacity of saccharin itself to initiate cancer," there is also "less po-tency than most other carcinogens." In other words, almost anything can cause cancer, given the right conditions, but those conditions are far more remote with saccharin than with many other substances, even other food additives.

The benefits of saccharin for the diabetic or the overweight middle-aged man prone to heart attacks, stroke or other ailments far outweigh these remote possibilities of it being a carcinogen. On the other hand, the overuse of saccharin in soft drinks and foods consumed by children and pregnant women is to be avoided.

In the cases studied, the scientists report that, while bladder cancer cannot be blamed on saccharin in any appreciable degree, there is further confirmation that heavy smoking does increase the incidence of this type of cancer. That is still another indictment of cigarettes and tobacco.

The studies also indicate that, although researchers may not have all the answers, they are learning all the time.

The Washington Post

Washington, D.C., March 9, 1980

THREE MORE in the seemingly endless stream of saccharin studies have just been published, and the weary and confused consumer would be justified in demanding one final answer: All right, is saccharin dangerous, or isn't it . . . does it or doesn't it cause cancer—*yes or no*? Well, the hoped-for answer is not in these studies. But the scientific facts are at least substantially clearer. Individual and institutional judgments about saccharin use can now be reached on the basis of a combination of science and caution.

There are only two ways to discover whether a substance can cause harm to human beings—and both have severe limitations. The first is by making laboratory studies of inbred animals. While these can reveal a great deal, differences between a particular animal species and humankind do appear—unpredictably—from time to time. Sometimes a drug will have little or no effect on rats but produce terrible effects on people: thalidomide is an example. It also works the other way around. The second method is to use human epidemiological studies, which are afflicted by other weaknesses: genetic differences, variations in dose and length of exposure, inaccurate recollection by subjects, air pollution, occupational exposures and many more. In fact, even when both methods are used, identifying and measuring relatively low-level human health risks is, in the words of one expert in this field, "practically impossible."

Within the limits of these uncertainties, laboratory studies and human studies now indicate that saccharin is a weak carcinogen that does not pose a significantly increased risk of cancer for most people when used moderately. However, the largest human study shows a 60 percent increase in the risk of bladder cancer for heavy users—those who consume the equivalent of four or more dietetic sodas per day. That study also showed a greater risk of bladder cancer for heavy smokers who use a lot of artificial sweeteners than for heavy smokers who don't.

What the studies do not show is almost as important as what they do. Most cancers have very long latencies—the period between exposure to a carcinogen and clinical appearance of disease. Bladder cancers, in particular, have latencies ranging from 30 to 50 years. Since artificial sweeteners came into wide use in the 1960s, the often-mentioned prospective "epidemic" of bladder cancers could be under way but not yet visible. Nor do the studies identify the effects of saccharin on children, who are physiologically different from adults and who receive a much higher dose (per pound of body weight) from a can of diet soda than does an adult. Finally—and perhaps most important—the potentially serious effects on the developing fetus are still unknown.

What all this will mean for government regulators and congressional overseers who are tied up in an emotional (and heavily industry-lobbied) debate over saccharin remains to be seen. However, a prudent course for the individual consumer is relatively clear, and is summarized in this carefully worded advice from Dr. Robert Hoover, who directed the National Cancer Institute's saccharin study: "any use by non-diabetic children or pregnant women, heavy use by young women of childbearing age, and excessive use by anyone are ill-advised and should be actively discouraged by the medical community."

Drive Begun Against 'Junk Food' in Schools

The Kansas City Times

Kansas City, Mo., August 19, 1978

The U.S. Department of Agriculture cites a temporary delay in applying a ban on the sale of so-called junk food at schools until next year. In effect, the buck has slowed down. We hope it hasn't stopped on the side that favors the sale of snack foods and other low-nutritional-value foods at schools.

Schoolchildren might see the move as truly a manifestation of big brother watching too closely. The emphasis is to get schoolchildren to take in foods of a higher nutritional value than snack foods. Congress has given the department authority to prohibit the sale of junk food in schools until the last lunch period is completed. The plan makes sense.

In defense of the schoolchildren, though, school districts will have to be sure the quality of food served in cafeterias does not fall to a level equal to "junk." The problems of taste, quality and appearance can be controlled.

Although the conditioned response of plunking coins into machines or ringing the cash registers with the sale of snack foods is pervasive in America, the schools can do some teaching in nutrition.

Agriculture says it needs more time to draft the guidelines. We hope it doesn't take a generation of malnourished school children to get helpful guidelines on the books.

The Dallas Morning News

Denver, Colo., April 29, 1978

Would the U.S. Department of Agriculture take candy from a school kid? You had better believe it would.

The USDA can't solve the farmers' problems, but it knows how to make American youth eat nutritional, well-balanced meals—by ordering the "junk food" machines unplugged or locked until lunch is over. How can the department do this? By threatening to cut off federal hot-lunch subsidies to schools with a less enlightened view of nutrition, or maybe a loftier view of individual freedom.

Not all students eat federal lunches, to be sure, but for those who don't—as for those who do and nevertheless crave a chocolate caramel dessert—this is tough. The USDA and its resident puritan, Mrs. Carol Tucker Foreman, know what is good for them. Their proposed rules ("proposed" means final, barring the Second Coming) likely go into effect this fall.

We'll see then if nutrition improves, and one hopes it does. Because if not, USDA's next logical step is to lock the cafeteria doors until every morsel is consumed. Ve have vays, my friend, of making you eat spinach.

Los Angeles Times

Los Angeles, Cal., July 5, 1978

The Agriculture Department, we're told, has drawn overwhelming support for its proposal to banish "junk foods" from schools that participate in the national school-lunch program.

"Three cheers," or whatever is said today, was our first reaction. We noted with the maturity that comes with years that school officials, nutritionists, parents, even children approved this idea of stopping sales of candy, sodas, chewing gum and some frozen desserts (not ice cream and yogurt). The ban would last through the last meal period in schools involved in the government's lunch program.

The rationale is quite simple: The kids take their publicly subsidized lunches, dump them virtually uneaten and buy candy, which can rot their teeth. Why not remove the temptation?

We thought about all this, we really did. Then we realized that we might be overprotecting again. We eat junk food. We *love* junk food. Some of us have bad teeth; some don't. Some have pot bellies; some are in the best shape of their lives. But we are adults. We know the virtues of moderation.

Then we remembered our own experience with school-cafeteria food. "Mystery meat," we called it

in college. So we checked in with the neighbors' daughter. "Yukky," came the verdict.

The scales were tilting. You can argue, we decided, the need to curb the advertising of non-nutritious food in the first place over such a persuasive medium as television. But people can do something about junk food in the schools if they don't like it. As we said when the ban was suggested, people shouldn't constantly defer to Washington to act for them.

There are, we're told, Parent-Teacher Assns. If parents think the sale of junk food is inappropriate in a particular school, then the place to take action is through the PTA or the local school board. For example, Milwaukee public schools have banned all food sales except approved school lunches from 8 a.m. to 3:30 p.m.

If there are to be any bans, though, please note a plea from Tina Sims, an eighth-grader in Memphis: "The school lunch is overpriced and raunchy-tasting," she wrote the Agriculture Department. "So we buy potato chips and nutty bars, but it's not by choice. If the Memphis board would get some cooks that could cook, we would eat the food."

The Oregonian

Portland, Ore., August 18, 1978

There is a role for the federal government in sharing in the financial support of local schools and ensuring that national legislation, such as civil rights laws, is observed in local administration of the schools. But there is danger in the exercise of federal bureaucratic power from afar. For example: Decisions on what snack food should be available in the schools should be made locally, not in Washington, D.C.

The Department of Agriculture has authority to ban availability of snack foods until the end of the last school lunch period of the day in schools that participate in the national school lunch program. The department announced earlier this year that, beginning with the new school year, sale of such items as candy, soda water, frozen desserts and chewing gum would be barred until all school lunch periods were at an end. Recently, that order was rescinded because the bureaucracy could not fashion the necessary regulations in time for application this fall. However, a Department of Agriculture spokesman promised that such regulations would go into effect some time in the calendar year of 1979.

There is reason for public concern about what foods are available to pupils during the school day. But the decisions on the subject should be made in local communities and not by federal officials far removed from the schools concerned. Such federal officials have a proper concern with the nutritional value of foods provided with federal funds, but they have no business substituting their judgment for that of local school authorities in matters of policy.

SAN JOSE NEWS

San Jose, Cal., April 28, 1978

The futile tendency to pile regulations atop regulations is manifested in the proposal by Assistant Agriculture Secretary Carol Foreman, made in a talk before the Newspaper Food Editors and Writers Association, to ban "junk food" sales in schools before lunch periods. Schools that fail to go along with the new regulations would lose their lunch subsidy funds.

The intent of the new prohibition is to increase participation in school lunch and breakfast programs, and to halt the waste of nutritious foods by the mass dumping of half-finished meals. But does the end justify the means?

Isn't the Agriculture Department sufficiently preoccupied with other responsibilities to hesitate to act as policeman of the school vending machine or student snack bar? Doesn't it border on regulatory overkill to make pre-lunch sales of candy bars in our schools a federal infraction?

The waste of food in federally subsidized school lunch programs is indeed a national scandal. But is availability of junk foods or the lack of good school lunches the real problem? In an age of open campuses and nearby convenience food outlets, most school cafeterias have keener competition than the candy bar machine. Better meals, not more federal regulations, are the school lunchroom's primary need.

St. Louis Globe-Democrat

St. Louis, Mo., September 8, 1978

The U.S. Department of Agriculture has given Americans food for thought with its proposal for a partial ban on so-called "junk food" in public schools. It's enough to make concerned citizens gag.

And yet for some strange reason the impending rule has drawn some strong support nationwide. According to syndicated columnist James J. Kilpatrick, in a column which appeared in The Globe-Democrat, 82 percent of those responding to the USDA's invitation to comment on what Kilpatrick calls the pending pop, gum and candy decree approved the proposed regulation.

This is, to Kilpatrick's way of thinking, a melancholy situation. He is right. The apparent willingness of some people to let the federal government regulate their lives is depressing.

There is a ray of hope, however, in the attitude of Missouri and St. Louis area school officials toward the USDA proposal. They are not at all anxious for the ban to be imposed.

"It would be a relief to us if nothing comes down," said David R. Page, food services director for St. Louis public schools in reference to speculation that any such decree won't be issued before the end of the year.

"It's a pretty controversial thing," said Wilbert Grannemann, director of food services for the Missouri Department of Elementary and Secondary Education. "School officials are concerned about something that seems to add more restrictions to what they can do on school premises."

Initially, the ban aimed at implementing a 1977 federal statute was scheduled to go into effect in September in thousands of districts that participate in the USDA-monitored $3 billion school lunch program. The new rule would forbid the sale of candy, carbonated beverages, chewing gum and frozen desserts in schools until after the final lunch period of each day.

The theory behind the new federal prohibition law is that if the packaged foods and drinks, which are normally dispensed by vending machines, aren't available to the students during lunch periods, then the students will consume more nutritious foods of the type served by the schools themselves through the federally funded lunch program. The USDA justifies its role of Big Brother on the ground that it is merely trying to save the students from themselves.

This doesn't wash. In practice, if the students want what the USDA chooses to call "junk food" and can't get it at a vending machine in the school, they'll go elsewhere. Noon-time traffic jams between the schools and the nearest drive-ins could become routine.

Page got to the heart of the matter when he said: "We feel that at the high-school level students should have some freedom of choice."

The federal government should leave well enough alone. Let each school decide its own course of action. Nutritious meals should be made available with the schools encouraging greater participation in their lunch programs. Tastier meals would be a big help.

In the meantime, no amount of decrees will change individual eating habits. The USDA's proposed regulations are plainly unpalatable. The pending ban on junk food" should be junked.

Agriculture Department Calls for Ban on 'Junk Food' in Schools

On July 5, the Department of Agriculture announced that it would ban sales of candy, soft drinks and other 'junk food' items in the nation's schools during lunch hours. The regulation was proposed in an effort to promote better eating habits among schoolchildren. The Agriculture Department had sought to ban 'junk food' in schools for a number of years but was blocked by its inability to define 'junk food' satisfactorily. This time, the department reached an acceptable conclusion. The foods it decided to ban had "minimum nutritional value," meaning that one serving or 100 calories contained less than 5% of the department's recommended daily allowance of eight basic nutrients: protein, vitamin A, vitamin C, niacin, riboflavin, thiamin, calcium and iron.

THE LOUISVILLE TIMES

Louisville, Ky., July 12, 1979

Bad news for juvenile junk-food junkies — soon there may be no more candy, gum, ice cream or soda pop in school vending machines. At least not in the morning.

After talking about it for several years, the Agriculture Department has finally come up with a legal definition of junk food, without which, of course, it could not write a regulation banning the stuff. (Parents may have known all along what junk food is, but they're not bureaucrats.)

Now we say "foods of minimum nutritional value," and next year, if all goes well, they won't be sold until after lunch. The government even hopes schools may fill those idle vending machines with real food, such as apples or carrots or peanuts.

Of course we wouldn't want to do anything radical, like totally eliminate candy bars or vending machines. Who knows what might happen to children, or to the junk food industry, if they could eat nothing but lunch during school hours?

Their brains would probably switch off for want of energy. And now if you will excuse us, we'll go get some potato chips before starting our next editorial.

The Washington Post

Washington, D.C., July 7, 1979

SCHOOLCHILDREN should eat lunch every day— there is no doubt about that. Nor is there doubt that many spoil their appetites by stuffing on candy and other junk food before lunch. But is that sufficient reason for the federal government to instruct the principals of 90,000 schools, and the school boards that supervise them, to lock up the vending machines every morning?

The Department of Agriculture thinks it is. It proposed a regulation on Thursday barring schools that accept federal school lunch money from permitting the sale of candy, chewing gum and other foods of "minimum nutritional value" until after lunch. Assistant Secretary Carol Tucker Foreman explained that the federal taxpayers spend about $3 billion a year on those lunches and "have a right to expect them to work well and to contribute to their children's well-being."

The Department of Agriculture tried this same kind of thing last year. Its proposal then was to bar "junk food," but that failed because there was no general agreement on what "junk food" actually is. By changing the wording to "minimum nutritional value," the department thinks it has solved the problem and is on its way to improving the health by changing the living styles of thousands of American students. It also thinks—and it may be right about this—that what it is doing Congress told it to do in 1977 when the legislators gave the department power to regulate the sales of "competitive foods" near school lunchrooms.

The real question, however, has nothing to do with "competitive" or "junk" or "minimum nutritional value" foods. It is whether the federal government has any business telling local school authorities what they can sell in their schools and when they can sell it. Those are questions local school boards are competent to decide without any help at all from Washington or from Uncle Sugar, as the old rascal used to be known.

Wichita, Kans., July 10, 1979

The U.S. Agriculture Department's pending crackdown on the sale of junk food snacks in school is a step in the right direction — the direction of better nutrition.

What effect it will have on the diets of Wichita students remains to be seen. Though it could force the closing down, during morning sessions at least, of the vending machines operated in some schools to raise money for student activities, it also could require the machines' being stocked with more nutritious foods and beverages.

The regulation scheduled to take effect at the beginning of 1980 would ban the sale in schools, prior to lunchtime, of any food not containing at least 5 percent of the recommended daily allowance of any of eight basic nutrients — calcium, niacin, iron, vitamin A, ascorbic acid, thiamine, riboflavin and protein.

Apparently there are foods that fall below so minimal a level — potato chips, for instance, which are rich in fat and carbohydrate content, but almost lacking in vitamin content. Some bottled beverages also fail to meet the standard.

A Class A school cafeteria lunch costs 85 cents in Wichita high schools. A student who lacks 85 cents and who has failed to bring his own lunch from home now may patronize a vending machine, with its "junk food," instead. But the federal regulation may force the vending machine companies to stock them with nutritionally approved foods to keep them from being declared off limits until after the lunch hour.

And that couldn't help but benefit the students. The earlier children can develop good eating habits the more apt they are to have a healthy adulthood.

The Courier-Journal

Louisville, Ky., July 18, 1979

SCHOOLS that hire nutritionists to supervise a quality lunch service have long recognized a glaring inconsistency between this effort and the presence of vending machines and snack bars offering candy, gum and soft drinks in direct competition with the lunchroom.

In 1972, Congress tried to solve the contradiction with a five-year experiment in state and local school regulation of sales of such "competitive foods." But reaction was spotty and slow. Club fund-raisers sold doughnuts and candy bars throughout the school day. And as the vending machines spread through the schools, lunchroom sales sagged proportionately.

This undermined the intent of Congress in appropriating $3 billion in yearly subsidies for school-lunch programs. So, in 1977, the power to regulate food sales in schools getting federal help was restored to the agriculture secretary.

At the same time, Congress was more explicit about goals. School lunches should continue to make their proven contribution to health. In addition, the food service should promote nutrition education in the form of lifelong good eating habits.

This followed the advice of medical authorities who say nutritional ignorance makes a direct contribution to staggering health-care costs. The Gallup Poll also found that two-thirds of parents of children at schools taking part in the school lunch program believe that candy shouldn't be sold there; 65 percent say chewing gum shouldn't be available.

But a new Agriculture Department proposal to ban junk-food sales in school until after lunchtime has drawn criticism. Some term it a scolding from the "National Nanny," and argue that the local school, not a federal regulator, should make the rules. On the other side, Naderites complain that the USDA's proposed rule is too mild. They say that all a candymaker need do is make slight improvements in nutritional content and back his product goes on sale.

This fire from both flanks suggests that the government may have found a sensible compromise. It has identified four categories of snack foods — some candies (spun sugar, for instance), gum, soda drinks and frozen ices — that make virtually no contribution to nutrition.

From this baseline, school authorities can impose stricter rules, as many have done. Vendors relying on "minimally nutritious" products would be encouraged to put more nearly adequate candy bars, fruit drinks, fruits or nuts on sale.

The Department of Agriculture's guideline for junk foods is neither harsh or sweeping. It conforms to the wishes of Congress, both as to immediate food values and the formation of good eating habits. It is only sensible to put junk-food sources off limits during the school day until students have at least had a chance to eat a healthful meal.

Chicago Tribune

Chicago, Ill., July 7, 1979

We're afraid that Carol Tucker Foreman, assistant secretary of agriculture, is more aware than most parents and school administrators of the importance of keeping children from eating so much "junk food" that they have no appetite for the more nutritional food that a growing child needs.

We say "we're afraid" because the responsibility for what our children eat is one that properly belongs in the home and in the school rather than in the Department of Agriculture. As we've learned so many times, often to our sorrow, federal subsidies bring federal controls. Mrs. Foreman has revived the proposal she made last year to restrict the sale of sodas, chewing gum, frozen ices, and many candies in schools that serve federally subsidized lunches—which is to say 98 per cent of our public schools.

Under her proposal, schools would be prohibited from allowing the sale of certain "foods of minimum nutritional value" that fail to meet a government formula until after the school lunchroom has stopped serving lunch. It would take effect Jan. 1 if it survives 60 days of public comment [as it did not last year].

Opposition will no doubt come from soft-drink and candy makers and perhaps from some independent-minded school officials and citizens who don't like Washington to meddle in their affairs.

Unfortunately, there are too many others who think that it is up to Washington to protect us from everything including our own bad judgment. Just last fall, the Office of Technology Assessment warned that bad nutrition "will seriously affect the quality of life" in the future [a proper enough warning] but added that the federal government would have to bear much of the blame.

The federal government is spending up to $100 million a year on research into nutrition and related subjects. Its responsibility is to see that the results of this research are disseminated as widely as possible—and as a result of it, more and more parents and schools have already taken steps themselves to cure the junk food habit. No matter how worthy its motives, we would be sorry to see the government tell schools that they may allow the sale of chocolate bars with nuts, but not chocolate bars without nuts, until after about 1:30 p.m. If Washington can decide what may be put into a pupil's mouth, how long will it be before Washington undertakes to decide what may be put into a pupil's mind?

BUFFALO EVENING NEWS

Buffalo, N.Y., July 9, 1979

It might risk a near revolt in school cafeterias, we suppose, but the U.S. Agriculture Department's proposal to bar the sale of junk foods in school until after lunch still makes good nutritional sense.

In suggesting the ban, to be sure, the department did not use the term "junk food." But that is what is meant by applying the prohibition to foods supplying less than 5 percent of the recommended daily allowance of any one of eight basic nutrients.

Surely no child's health would be injured by removing temptations of soda, chewing gum, frozen ice desserts and candy before noon. Delaying their sale ought to promote better appetites for the school lunch programs, which contain nutritious foods for youngsters in their growth years. Moreover, as Carol Foreman, assistant secretary of agriculture noted, the ban would also help those "inclined to obesity, a significant problem among young Americans."

If finally promulgated, the department would be acting under authority of a 1977 law enacted by Congress and would merely fix minimum standards beyond which states, if they chose, could go. The federal proposal hopefully will command the support of parents, teachers and school officials concerned about the health needs of children for whom the schools are responsible during the noon meal period. With or without a federal nudge, however, curbing the temptations of junk foods for children on school grounds deserves sympathetic consideration from school officials.

The News and Courier

Charleston, S.C., July 17, 1979

The Agriculture Department is moving again to restrict the sale of candy, chewing gum, frozen desserts and soft drinks in schools participating in federally subsidized lunch programs. This time the department is armed with an official definition of "junk food" — or what it prefers to call "foods of minimum nutritional value." A food item is of minimum nutritional value when one serving (or a portion with 100 calories) contains less than five percent of the recommended daily allowance of any one of eight basic nutrients. Having defined the topic of debate, where does Agriculture stand?

About where it stood when the last encounter was broken off. Agriculture is saying taxpayers spending billions a year on lunch programs have a right to expect them to contribute to children's well-being. Such programs can't work well when kids are filling up on "foods of minimum nutritional value" and leaving more nutritious foods on their plates. Vending machine owners oppose the proposed restrictions for all the obvious reasons. Consumer advocates are saying the snack food people will meet the basic requirement and do no more, disregarding sugar content.

No one yet has asked out loud why vending machines that dispense "foods of minimum nutritional value" are considered necessary in schools where everyone can either buy a hot lunch or get one free — and sometimes even breakfast.

The Philadelphia Inquirer

Philadelphia, Pa., July 9, 1979

One trapping of contemporary education is under assault this summer: vending machines that dispense crunchies, sweets and colas to children. For the second time in as many years the U.S. Department of Agriculture is trying to extend the long arm of good nutrition by banning the sale of junk foods until after lunch in schools that serve federally subsidized lunches. The department is soliciting comments on the proposal.

How did the vending machines get into the schools in the first place? They started to proliferate after 1972, when Congress made it legal to sell in the schools foods competitive with subsidized lunches if the proceeds benefited approved school organizations. Not such a tall order for vending machine operators, who could allow a

school organization a rake-off and take home plenty in profits. A couple of years ago Vending Times, a trade magazine, reported that students and faculty were spending $413 million yearly in school vending machines.

But no sooner had the machines appeared than a number of parents, educators and nutritionists started a movement to get them out of the schools, change their contents to more nutritious snacks, or at least restrict their use to after-lunch hours. They asked why taxpayers should subsidize school lunches to the tune of $3 billion a year while making it easy for youngsters to consume foods that could lead to tooth decay and obesity, heart disease and diabetes.

Good question. Obviously, changes were called for. The Agriculture De-

partment tried to ban junk foods last year but was stymied when candy makers and soda producers complained that its definition of low-nutrition foods was vague. Now the department has developed a precise definition involving numbers of calories and recommended daily allowances of nutrients, and it is again seeking comment on a proposal to ban the sale of "foods with minimum nutritional value" until after lunch.

Nutrition is a valid and important federal concern. Even if students (and teachers) are likely to sneak to the corner store to satisfy junk food cravings, it is worthwhile to try in every possible way to encourage good eating habits. The Agriculture Department's proposals deserve endorsement.

DAYTON DAILY NEWS

Dayton, Ohio, July 9, 1979

An award of cola and fries to the U.S. Agriculture Department, which has taken up a desperate, long-shot challenge. The department wants school kids to eat right.

Its assault on the sale of junk food in schools is a worthy one despite the odds. Those odds aren't made better by the fact that even a lot of the youngsters' parents are wrecking themselves by their diets. The parents who do eat sensibly are blessed indeed if they can get their children even to *consider* eating, oh, raisins and nuts — much less sprouts — instead of a candy bar and hot dogs.

The department wants to ban junk food sales in most public schools until the last lunch of the day is served. Actually, some of the junk ought to be banned from schools altogether, but the department doesn't pretend it can run the world and such attempts tend to backfire anyway in the face of human habits and youngsters' immortality complexes.

The Agriculture Department had been holding back on any proposal so it could figure out how to define junk foods. The proposal is that "foods of minimum nutritional value" will be those with a serving or potion with 100 calories and less than 5 percent of the recommended daily allowance of any one of eight basic nutrients.

Even that is a fairly lean definition, but is as practical as any. One can imagine candy and chip manufacturers powdering vitamins into their product enough to get under the wire the same way some cereal makers have added vitamins to their flakes to achieve for their bowl of cereal the same value as a cookie and one vitamin pill.

One can also imagine youngsters simply waiting until the last meal is served so they can get their junk food from the vending machine.

Still, the proposal is modest and worth a try. If by chance the Agriculture Department proves itself able to get America's teenagers to eat properly, this country will have a bona fide, guaranteed, certified miracle on its hands. Even Ayatollah Kohmeini might be awed by it.

The Evening Bulletin

Philadelphia, Pa., July 10, 1979

Those spoil sports at the U.S. Department of Agriculture are at it again; trying to do away with one of the favorite indulgences of the American public — eating junk food.

Actually, the federal nutrition experts just want to make sure that elementary and high school students don't stuff themselves on candy, potato chips and soda before they eat the well-balanced school lunches subsidized by the Federal Government. Officials are proposing that the so-called "junk" foods not be sold in the schools until after lunch is served.

Of course, we too support the *idea* of eating only good, nutritional foods, and curbing our craving for snack foods that are high in calories, salt and sugar — all bad for us, especially if we over-indulge. But we still think the USDA is

fighting a losing battle in trying to keep junk foods away from our youngsters.

For example, what's to keep students from stashing a month's supply of Twinkies in their gym lockers? Or squirreling away a bag of chocolates between the geometry and biology books? What self-respecting teen-ager cares one whit about broccoli, anyway?

And besides, there are loopholes in the proposed regulations that define what junk food is. By the regulations, any food that contains less than five percent of any one of the eight basic nutrients is junk. But any food, including candy, that contains raisins or nuts is considered nutritionally "OK."

Now, all an enterprising young cook needs to discover is how to make potato chips with raisins in them, or soda made from walnuts.

The Oregonian

Portland, Ore., July 8, 1979

"Arright, kid; we saw you sneak a bite from a candy bar."

Can that be the voice of law and order? The FBI? Or maybe special junk food marshals? Not now, perhaps; but in the not too distant future if the U.S. government continues in the direction it is headed.

The U.S. Department of Agriculture is proposing a ban on sales of foods of minimum nutritional value in schools. Its long arm reaches into the cafeterias of almost 98 percent of America's schools through federal support of school lunches, and it doesn't want any competition from junk foods.

"Taxpayers spend about $3 billion a year on federal school lunch programs and have a right to expect them to work well and to contribute to their children's well-being," righteously insists Assistant Secretary of Agriculture Carol Tucker Foreman. We can't argue with that. But we must argue with the proposal to bring the full weight of the federal government into what should continue to be a local prerogative. Federal officials have a proper concern with the nutritional value

of foods provided with federal funds, but they have no business substituting their judgment for that of local school authorities in matters of policy.

Portland's school board has adopted a rule that half the food in vending machines be regulated for nutritional value. That suggests students should make decisions. They should be taught that health and economics both support nutritional choice; but they also should be taught the importance of the right to make even a wrong decision in a free society.

If the federal government is so concerned about tax dollars, it should consider the money it has spent proving the need for the food ban. It should consider the cost of drawing up standards. It should consider the cost of enforcement (a federal training academy for food sleuths?). Most importantly, it should consider the cost of making more decisions for more people in Washington, D.C.

The scales tip from better nutrition to further erosion of local decision-making powers. That's a bad buy.

The News Journal

Wilmington, Del., July 9, 1979

The Department of Agriculture's second attempt to limit the sale of junk foods in schools is sure to draw cries of "foul" from those in the food industry who do a big business selling such things as soft drinks, gum, frozen desserts and candy through vending machines in schools.

This time around the agriculture department's proposed rules are more precise. And the new rules carefully omit use of the words "junk foods." Instead the items that would be limited are termed "foods of minimum nutritional value."

Under the new rules children who want to buy the low nutrition snacks and soft drinks will have to wait until after the day's last lunch is served.

The rules affect those schools which participate in the federally supported school lunch program. Since 98 percent of the nation's school systems participate in the program, the effect of the new rules is virtually universal.

The agriculture department is not acting arbitrarily here. It has the backing of both the president and the Congress in this effort. An amendment to the 1977 Farm Act empowered the secretary of agriculture to regulate the sale of "competitive foods" in or near school lunch rooms.

A year ago the agriculture department withdrew similar regulations after the food industry complained, correctly, that they contained only vague criteria for determining that a given food has nutritional value.

The current set of proposed regulations say that foods fall into the category of those with minimum value if one serving or a portion with 100 calories contains less than five percent of the recommended daily allowance of any one of eight basic nutrients. These include vitamin A, riboflavin, thiamin, iron and calcium.

Obviously the vending machines are in the schools because the students want them there and make sufficient use of them. Having the machines available for an after school snack is fine. But when young people are spending their "lunch money" on foods that aren't nutritious instead of the food prepared under careful supervision for nutrition, then limiting use of the machines seems perfectly justified.

Taxpayers support the federal child nutrition programs to the tune of about $3 billion a year. The programs contribute to the well-being of school youngsters and should be given every opportunity to succeed.

All interested parties have sixty days to comment on the proposed new rules. Certainly the food industry and probably a lot of students will do so. But the new regulations with precise definitions of what constitutes "junk foods" appear reasonable and beneficial. They should be put into effect on schedule next January.

DESERET NEWS

Salt Lake City, Utah, July 9, 1979

Uncle Sam seems determined to infringe on the right of teenagers to eat the kind of food that leads to pimples.

After a year or so of "scientific analysis," the Department of Agriculture has found a definition of junk food. Of course, the department doesn't call it "junk food." The bureaucrats call junk food "food of minimal nutritional value."

But by whatever name, the department intends to ban it from the morning diet of teenagers in school.

A proposed new regulation would forbid schools from allowing kids to buy junk food from vending machines before lunch. No longer could students buy candy, ice cream, soda pop, or other teenage delights, until after lunch

period.

The federal government would cut off subsidy of school lunches to any school that failed to comply with the regulation. About 98 percent of schools take some lunch money from Uncle Sam.

Predictably, this regulation will lead to a boom in business for the candy stores and malt shops located near high schools.

Just as predictably some teenagers will leave campuses in cars, traveling great distances to strike a blow for liberty and tooth decay.

The federal government would do well to attend to its own problems and let teenagers decide for themselves what to eat.

The Burlington Free Press

Burlington, Vt., July 9, 1979

The federal government will take another step toward assuming control over your life if a proposal to ban the sale of so-called "junk food" in schools goes unchallenged.

It would place restrictions on the sales of candy, chewing gum, frozen desserts and sodas in most schools before the day's last lunch is served. The regulation that would take effect Jan. 1 would apply to 98 percent of the schools that serve federally subsidized lunches.

Agriculture Department officials hope that schools and vending machine distributors will offer more fruits, vegetables, fruit juices and nuts to children as snacks.

While the regulation has a noble purpose in attempting to dissuade youngsters from eating junk food, it appears to be just another instance of federal meddling in matters that involve individual freedom of choice and policies that should be set locally. Consumption of junk food at the expense of good nutrition certainly is to be deplored. But it cannot, and should not, be banned by federal regulation.

It should only be discouraged through school programs that stress the importance of a balanced diet.

Arkansas Gazette.

Little Rock, Ark., July 9, 1979

At the behest of Congress, the Agriculture Department has set off once again to banish, or limit, "junk foods" from the nation's public schools that participate in the federal school lunch program. It is not an issue that has concerned us inordinately, for the Republic will surely stand regardless of the outcome.

For many school children, and for almost any adult who will care to remember, school lunches generally call for some highly subjective judgments. Like much institutional food, it often is devoid of flavor and seasonings, even though on the dieticians' charts it may be as nutritious as can be. Given a choice between eating it and going without, plenty of the school folk, young and old, will choose the latter, at least on some days.

This is not a rousing defense of the "junk food" — "foods of minimum nutritional value" in the bureaucratic euphemism — but simply to suggest that there are some areas where individual choices might better be taken into account. The proposed new rule, in any case, is based more on the competitive aspects of cafeteria food v. "junk food" in vending machines than it is on

any other reasoning. That is, schools could not serve such items as sodas, chewing gum, frozen desserts and some candies until after the last cafeteria lunch of the day was served.

A lot of people are very serious about this business of proper nutrition for children and for adults, and we do not belittle that concern in the least. To the contrary, proper nutrition is important to a healthy population and may have more to do than some imagine in heading off debilitating illness that may arise when the deficiencies catch up with the person who overindulges in "junk food" for an extended period. But there's no way, not in American society, to stuff the school lunches down the throats of the unwilling.

School lunches will be competitive with "junk foods" when they become as imaginative and tasty because they already are a big bargain for parents. The Agriculture Department might better spend its time and effort on making school lunches more competitive by simply seeing that a better all-around product is available in the cafeteria line, leaving decisions about the dispensing of "junk foods" to school authorities in the local districts.

THE INDIANAPOLIS STAR
Indianapolis, Ind., July 10, 1979

Big Brother — this time in the guise of the U.S. Department of Agriculture — plans to tell our school-age children what they can and can't eat.

He has the power because he controls the purse strings of about 98 percent of the school lunch programs in the country.

So Big Brother has proposed that after Jan. 1 the kids won't be able to eat "junk" foods until after the last federally-subsidized school lunch is served each day.

That means things like sodas, chewing gum, frozen desserts and some candies are a no-no in the morning.

Looking out for the health of our children appears laudable enough but isn't it just another example of the federal bureaucrats trying to control Americans' lives from cradle to the grave?

ALBUQUERQUE JOURNAL
Albuquerque, N.M., July 9, 1979

The U.S. Department of Agriculture took another long stride in the direction of "Big Brotherism" when it proposed a partial ban on the sale of "junk foods" in the nation's schools.

Thousands of parents, doubtlessly, will bless the USDA for its initiative, but in so doing they will be acknowledging their own failure in enforcing nutritional discipline on their offspring and surrendering one more parental responsibility to officialdom.

For either child or adult, choices of food and eating habits are, and should be, as much a matter of personal choice as the selection of companions, lifestyles, reading material, clothing, music or enjoyment of leisure time. The proposed ban is nothing less than an unwarranted invasion of privacy.

In keeping with its mandate, the Agriculture Department is justifiably concerned with the growing preference of young people for "junk foods" — those delivered to the consumer at excessive perunit cost with little or no nutritional value.

But the USDA has little experience and even less justification in imposing and enforcing a ban of totalitarian propensities. It has extensive experience and an enviable success record in two superior approaches to nutritional problems: education and research.

Through its Extension Service, its vocational education and 4-H Club programs the Agriculture Department has one of the most elaborate and effective networks for public education in government. It is a network geared to family guidance and enlightenment. It has the means of enlightening every man, woman and child — on short notice — of the essentials of an adequate diet and of the dangers inherent in excessive quantities of sugar, starch and synthetic additives.

The USDA's research laboratories have the potential — once committed to an innovative course — to create an entirely new industry in the formulation of nutritional foods that are palatable, relatively inexpensive and conveniently packaged in ready-to-eat form. Why, for example, must liver and spinach — both sources of ever-important iron — be offered exclusively in texture-and-flavor combinations that cause no less than half the nation's population to gag or leave the table?

The proposed ban on junk foods in the schools has all the earmarks of the easy — and, more to the point, the un-American — way out of a dilemma.

The Pittsburgh Press
Pittsburgh, Pa., July 14, 1979

Admittedly, "junk food" is not an appropriate diet for school children. But is it the business of the federal government to police every school around the country to keep kids away from vending machines?

The U.S. Department of Agriculture proposes to bar the sale of candy, chewing gum, frozen desserts, sodas and other foods of "minimum nutritional value" in most American schools until after lunch has been served. The ban would apply to all schools serving federally subsidized lunches, which covers about 90 percent of public schools.

It's another example of Big Daddy in Washington thinking he knows best.

Does the federal government think that parents and local school officials are so dumb or irresponsible that they can't make decisions about lunches and vending machines?

Or have parents and local officials become so inured to federal regulation that they have lost the ability to think for themselves?

The Topeka Daily Capital
Topeka, Kans., July 11, 1979

The federal government is attempting to control too many facets of our private lives these days, but one proposal in the offing has obvious merit.

That proposal is to eliminate junk foods from being sold in schools where a federally subsidized lunch program is offered. If the government has its way — and it will hear comments on the proposal for the next 60 days — by January 1 a student won't be able to grab a candy bar between classes and swish it down with a soft drink. But the student may, if vending machine companies offer it, be able to get an apple and a can of vegetable juice.

The government last year proposed a ban on junk foods but withdrew it because regulations proposed contained only a vague definition of junk foods. Now the government refers to foods to be banished as "foods of minimum nutritional value" and specifies those as ones where a 100-calorie portion contains less than 5 percent of the recommended daily allowance of any one of eight basic nutrients.

The government says taxpayers spend about $3 billion per year on federal school lunch programs and have the right to expect them to contribute to their children's well-being. Last year 80 percent of those who voiced an opinion on the junk foods ban were in favor of the ban. States are free to impose tougher restrictions.

Many if not most children eat too many junk foods now, even when under parental control. Those eating habits continue into adulthood, often causing all sorts of health problems. Students can still get all the junk food they need before and after school. But the school shouldn't foster or help students maintain a habit which is obviously undesirable.

HOUSTON CHRONICLE
Houston, Texas, July 9, 1979

The federal government is going to considerable effort to reduce the competition between vending machines and lunch programs in public schools. A new regulation scheduled to take effect next January has required all sorts of planning, public hearings and such.

The net effect in Houston schools for all this work will be a ban on the sale of soft drinks in vending machines until after the last lunch is served. Somehow it doesn't seem worth the effort. Not many of those students who wanted soft drinks are going to buy milk instead.

The battle of the vending machines has been going on for years. There's no telling what it has cost, in terms of lobbying effort on both sides and regulatory activity on the part of the government (for instance, this time the Agriculture Department is allowing the sale of vending machine goodies if they contain nuts or raisins).

School children are fairly predictable: Most of them gripe about school cafeteria food, but most of them eat there anyway; others wouldn't eat in the cafeteria if the alternative was skipping lunch. How much real competition there is between the vending machines and the cafeteria is debatable. If the cafeteria offers some appealing alternatives to plain vanilla plate lunches and has reasonable service and prices, the students are going to take the bait. The novelty of the vending machines soon wears off.

Even if too many students are abandoning the lunches for the vending machines, the problem belongs to parents and local school boards and schools, not the federal Agriculture Department. The government has enough to worry about without burdening itself with how much "junk food" is being consumed on the school grounds.

The Salt Lake Tribune

Salt Lake City, Utah, July 15, 1979

A controversy rages over keeping so-called "junk food" out of the schoolhouse.

As is common in such skirmishes much of the argument avoids the basic issue.

Not long ago, for example, the Department of Agriculture suggested that the potato chips and candy bars only be sold after each day's lunch period. This, presumably, would keep the kids from filling up on munchies before sitting down to a proper lunch.

Other proposals call for banning sale of all food which does not meet minimal nutritional standards. And so it goes.

Instead of attempting to regulate sale of snack foods or setting nutritional minimums, school officials and others need only face the single question: whether to sell them, period.

If candy and cake and like temptations are deemed detrimental it is better to face up to one unpopular decision and ban them outright rather than quibble over minimum nutrition standards and the hours during which the snacks can be sold.

Actually, what the schools decide may have slight impact on intake of the proscribed goodies. Most schools are flanked by one or more "convenience" store or fast food outlet. Junk food junkies, like all other addicts, will get the stuff one way or another.

Los ANGELES HERALD EXAMINER

Los Angeles, Cal., July 10, 1979

In a long-running battle with the sweet tooth, the Agriculture Department is once again putting forth for approval a plan to limit our schoolchildren's intake of sugar and other questionable foods. The proposal would ban sales of sodas, frozen desserts, chewing gum and some candies until after the *last* lunch of the day had been served in school cafeterias where the lunches have some federal funding (about 98 percent of U.S. public schools).

At first, the plan looked like it might be a good idea, but after some reflection, we decided it was more expedient than wise. An outright government prohibition of free-market sales may be an immediate, strong-arm answer to the problem of sweets consumption, but it's not the long-term strategy we must have to correct the dietary habits that *create* the craving for sweets.

For years, the Agriculture Department has been trying to ban the sale of all those sweets, at all times, from public school cafeterias. The sugar and sweets lobby just wouldn't let them get away with it, so the current proposal is a compromise. But it's a half-baked, unworkable compromise. First of all, the plan sounds vague. Does it mean the last lunch of each individual lunch shift, or, literally, the last-served lunch of the day? If a kid wants to buy a soda, he or she will do so, despite whatever little inconvenience the school puts in the way. Is the only answer the outright ban on sales of sweets? Well, maybe, as a desperate measure, but then the kids might just leave the school grounds and go buy the stuff somewhere else. Moreover, we're always more than just a little bit uncomfortable, as a matter of principle as well as bitter experience, with paternalistic government control.

So let's stop trying to treat the symptom (craving for sweets) and take a look at the deeper problem (failure to provide satisfying eating with non-sweet foods.) To some extent, American kids *and* adults eat a lot of sweets (we've got nothing against a little piece of chocolate now and then ourselves!) because the rest of their diet isn't fulfilling enough.

And no wonder: Remember those cardboard mashed potatoes, suspiciously olive-green French peas, and desicated Salisbury steaks they used to serve up when you went to school? Well, your old friends are all still there in the school cafeterias, just as unsatisfying and non-nutritious as ever. Too many dieticians still aren't convinced by the idea of fresh foods, raw foods, lightly-cooked foods, tasty foods. They stick with the old tried and trues, completely ignoring the well-publicized progress nutritional science has made in the last 10 years.

Rather than go head to head with the sugar industry once again (and there's always a retaliation in this kind of long-running feud), Agriculture could smarten up. The feds should look into their own kitchens and really do a number on menus, food contracts and food preparation methods. No more overcooking vegetables 'til they're like bookbinding; no more meat products plump with preservatives and hormones. Let's see more fresh, colorful meals, colored by nature, not industrial dyes. By setting a good example, the federally-subsidized kitchens can help reeducate palates and eating habits, a much more effective solution than making sugar into a sort of contraband, an action not likely to decrease its attractiveness in children's eyes.

The Boston Globe

Boston, Mass., July 9, 1979

Kids aren't dumb. Many know by now that certain foods are without nutritional value. Many know that too much sugar, too much carbonation, too much artificial flavoring is bad for them. But what all-American child can walk past a candy or soda machine without experiencing a twinge of temptation. Craving the stuff because it's there is simply human nature.

The US Department of Agriculture's proposal to limit availability of foods of minimum nutritional value in schools would certainly make life easier for youthful sweet-tooths. Under rules suggested last Thursday by the USDA's food and consumer affairs office, children in schools participating in the federal school lunch program would have to wait until after the day's last lunch is served to buy low nutrition snacks and soft drinks from vending machines or cafeterias.

The new regulations carefully avoid any reference to "junk foods" — a phrase which has always stuck in the food industry's craw — and define items which would be banned as those in which one serving or portion of 100 calories contains less than five percent of any one of the basic nutrients included in the recommended daily allowance, nutrients such as Vitamin A, protein, ascorbic acid, niacin, thiamine, riboflavin, calcium or iron. Some candy, ice cream and snacks would meet the requirement. Most soft drinks would not.

Some may think that the USDA proposals don't go far enough. But the federal regulations wouldn't prohibit states from enforcing more stringent requirements than those spelled out by the department. In fact twenty five states have some kind of guidelines already in place. Massachusetts, for example, banned all sales of candy and soft drinks in schools way back in 1971.

The USDA proposal makes sense. The federal government is spending $3 billion a year on child nutrition programs and earmarked $26 million for nutrition education two years ago. Failure to curb the availibility of foods of dubious nutritional value would be counterproductive to government efforts to improve the eating habits of American youngsters. And, as any kid will tell you, grown-ups who preach nutrition, should have to put it to practice.

THE KANSAS CITY STAR
Kansas City, Mo., July 10, 1979

It sounds like such a sensible idea, this proposal by the Agriculture Department to strengthen the effectiveness of federally subsidized school lunch programs by removing the physical presence of distracting snacks from the buildings. Under congressional mandate to act, the department has been trying since at least 1976 to do so. The fact that attempts bogged down on definitions illustrates that there is no such thing as a good, simple idea when a powerful industry's pocketbook is being threatened.

Critics, many health authorities and the general public refer to the items in question as junk food. Congress and the Agriculture Department started calling them "competitive food" and in the latest series of proposed regulations, they are "foods of minimum nutritional value." The regulations (to take effect next January after two months of public comment) would prohibit items if one serving or portion with 100 calories or less contains less than 5 percent of the recommended daily allowance of any one of eight basic nutrients. The ban would apply in most schools before the day's last lunch is served. It covers such snacks as candy, chewing gum, frozen desserts and sodas; discussion has stressed that fruit, juices and nuts should be available if children must have snacks.

It's a pretty minimal limitation, leaving the door wide open if manufacturers decide to raise nutritional levels just slightly so products can edge under the line. Even so, it is a positive step if the government doesn't cave in under lobbying.

Ironically, in a preventive health care and economy-conscious era, the public and elected officials wink at the junk pedaled in schools. It is an irresponsible practice to allow the substitution for balanced meals of snacks that are expensive, of little or no nutritional value and in some cases, detrimental to dental and physical health. Where is the wise stewardship of the $3 billion yearly of taxpayer's money spent to subsidize sensible meals when the program is undermined and unchecked?

The effort to improve students' eating habits should be supported.

THE MILWAUKEE JOURNAL

Milwaukee, Wisc., July 14, 1979

The fact that 18 year olds can drink beer is no reason high schools should sell it to students who are of age. The same is true of junk food. Like beer, it has its place — and its place isn't in schools.

Children have enough impediments to learning. They don't need the added temptation to buy candy bars that will supply them with only a rush of energy, followed by a feeling of exhaustion. (Besides, excessive sugar use has been linked to diabetes, obesity, heart disease and tooth decay.)

Happily, the Agriculture Department at last seems well on its way to establishing standards for *all* manner of food that may be sold in schools serving federally subsidized lunches. Congress first told the department to develop standards in 1970; then after extensive lobbying by the vending machine industry, Congress took back the order in 1972, but wisely handed it out again in 1977.

Trouble is, the food industry has taken such big bites out of the originally proposed standards that the revised standards themselves look rather junky. They may be palatable to the food industry, but they don't reflect enough concern for the health and education of the nation's children.

The revised standards would prohibit — until after the final lunch period — the selling of foods that are not of "minimum nutritional value." For sweets, the minimum is met when any product contains a mere fraction of the recommended daily allowance of any one of the eight basic nutrients. That means schools can still sell candy bars with raisins; nuts or peanut butter at 11 a.m. — just in time to ruin a student's appetite for the Type A lunch, which may end up in the garbage while the student ends up dozing through afternoon classes.

Consumer and nutrition groups, even the national PTA, have criticized the Ag Department for backing off. The public has 60 days (until Sept. 6) to comment on the proposed regulations before they are published. Comments are to be sent to Margaret Glavin, Director of School Programs Division, Food and Nutrition Service, US Agriculture Department, Washington, D. C., 20250.

Of the 2,100 comments received last time around, 82% favored the proposals, but still they were watered down. Perhaps the biggest gain for schoolchildren is the lesson offered here in how pressure groups representing proprietary interests can shape public policy.

In Milwaukee, at least, school officials are smarter than that. Except for the lunch program, sale of all foods and beverages is banned in schools until after 3:30 p.m. — an approach other school districts, and even the state as a whole, might well consider adopting.

The Dispatch

Columbus, Ohio, December 21, 1979

OVEREATING IS leading to the malnourishment of many American children in this supposedly enlightned year of 1979.

How can that be, you ask?

Because, say the nutrition experts, kids are substituting too many sugary, salty or fatty snacks and processed foods for traditional food staples.

This is leading to problems of obesity, high blood pressure and even hardening of the arteries.

As many as 20 percent of American children aged six to 11 are overweight and as many as 24 percent have high cholesterol levels — an early warning sign of hardening of the arteries.

Many of the processed foods are high in salt content which is one of the causes of high blood pressure.

The heavy influence of television advertising is cited as one reason children eat so poorly. One estimate puts at 13,000 the number of food product commercials the average child watches during a year's period.

The U.S. Department of Agriculture is deeply concerned about this "overconsumption malnutrition" among children and has begun a $2 million experiment in producing television commercials that will teach kids good nutrition.

This is fine but it seems to us that many parents are remiss in their efforts to teach their children good eating habits and in regulating their television-watching times.

Malnourishment in U.S. children is a very serious problem and certainly deserves comprehensive parental guidance in coping with it.

Pittsburgh Post-Gazette

Pittsburgh, Pa., July 9, 1979

Like their parents, only more so, American children and teen-agers eat not too wisely but too much. And it is hardly news that so-called "junk food" is more popular with children than fruits and vegetables. So why should anyone concerned with the nutrition of children object to a plan by the U.S. Department of Agriculture to require schools to keep low-nutrition snacks out of the hands (and mouths) of children before they have had their lunch?

Well, there is one very good reason — totally consistent with a solicitude for child nutrition — for objecting to proposed "junk food" regulations issued by the department for those public schools (some 90 percent of them) which receive federal school-lunch assistance.

The objection is simply that there seems to be no reason why the federal government, rather than the multiplicity of school boards around the country, should involve itself in the war on spoiled appetites.

In explaining the new regulations, a spokesman for the Agriculture Department insisted that they would simply enforce the homespun wisdom of thousands of mothers who have warned their children to eat moderately. But if that is the case, why not leave the admonitions to Mother or at least to the local school boards which in most cases owe their authority to mothers — and fathers? Certainly there have been circumstances in which state and local authorities, by ignoring a serious problem, have invited a federal approach. But there doesn't seem to be any evidence that local school officials are so unconcerned about nutrition, or so influenced by sinister pressure from the "junk-food" industry, as to be incapable of addressing this problem in their own way.

The fact that the national government subsidizes school lunches provides only a legal basis, not a sound policy reason, for federal intervention. Federal regulation by its very nature is sweeping, general and not very sensitive to the nuances of individual situations. And the ability of the Agriculture Department to make gross, let alone fine, distinctions in this area seems questionable: For example, the junk food regulations would apply with equal force to high school and grade school students, creating a situation in which a 17-year-old high school senior, who is trusted by the law to drive to school, cannot be trusted with a candy machine — at least until after he has had his government-approved lunch.

In schools where students regularly consume junk food to excess, or substitute such food for their regular school meals, there might be good reason to adopt the Agriculture Department's proposal that food sold before lunchtime meet certain nutritional requirements. But there is no evidence that school authorities are incapable of deciding for themselves whether such a scheme is necessary or desirable.

The Agriculture Department, which has the power to revise its sweeping proposed regulations, should do so — in the direction of flexibility and maximum local discretion.

Panel of Nutritionists Discounts Health Danger from Cholesterol

A report issued May 27 by the Food and Nutrition Board took issue with previous findings that excessive cholesterol and fat intake posed a health danger to Americans. The report was the first major study in more than 10 years to contradict the findings of 18 major U.S. health organizations, including the American Heart Association and the National Institute of Health. The Food and Nutrition Board, an arm of the National Academy of Sciences, said its studies had shown no connection between reducing levels of fat and cholesterol and preventing heart attacks. However, it urged Americans to avoid overeating and to limit their salt intake to control high blood pressure.

Controversy over the report arose immediately because several members of the 15-man panel were either employees or consultants in the food industry. Also, basic funding for the report had come from food processors. Critics cited the board's omission of important scientific data, such as population studies that showed a high correlation between cholesterol and fat intake and the risk of heart disease. The composition of the board was criticized on grounds it contained mainly biochemists and nutritionists and lacked heart specialists and public health experts.

The News American

Baltimore, Md., June 12, 1980

You probably read the news yourself: saturated fat and cholesterol aren't so harmful as all that. And you may have scratched your head. The stuff doctors have been saying people should consume less of? It's okay after all? So it seems. The Food and Nutrition Board, an important arm of the distinguished National Academy of Sciences, declared a couple of weeks ago that most Americans needn't curtail their intake of saturated fat and cholesterol — principally in meat and dairy foods.

The truth of the matter is more complicated, and certainly no cause for a resumption of indulgent habits. The majority of U.S. medical and health organizations still insist that the prudent person will consume as little of these substances as a well-balanced diet affords.

The evidence linking high levels of cholesterol and a similar fat in the blood to atherosclerosis and heart disease remains strong — if not conclusive — as does the evidence linking cholesterol and fats in the diet to their presence in the bloodstream.

Why would so respected an institution issue a report that contradicts the best evidence of the day — and without adequately supporting its claim? Your guess is as good as ours. There have been complaints that the consumer point of view on the Food and Nutrition Board has been systematically shut out of deliberations; just a few days ago, in fact, the board's Consumer Liaison Panel resigned en masse in protest of the report.

Then there is the rather telling detail that the board and some of its members have been supported financially by segments of the food industry on whose products they pass judgment — not an especially unusual relationship these days, but no less invidious for being commonplace, and certainly not in keeping with the standard of fairness and objectivity you would expect from the National Academy.

For the consumer, this is a deeply troubling and confusing episode. At a time when people are seeking wise counsel about their health and diet, it reinforces skepticism about scientific authority and undermines the contributions that even responsible scientists can make to the common good.

The Detroit News

Detroit, Mich., June 3, 1980

Deep down, most of us want to believe there is some special diet ingredient that will make us healthy and long-lived — that a magic apple a day will keep the Grim Reaper at bay.

At various points in the past decade, fads (generated by admen, Californians, and authoritative medical councils) have persuaded Americans to embrace or eschew almost everything edible or thought to be edible.

People became certain that health could be achieved by ingesting added amounts of vitamin C, or yogurt, or zinc, or wheat germ — or by removing poisons such as eggs, or salt, or ice cream sundaes. As a result, many a steak-addicted, yogurt-hating heretic has been tormented by fears about the health consequences of his "wrong" diet.

Of all the new food evils, cholesterol has been one of the most consistently and officially condemned. For the past decade, many Americans have conscientiously restricted their intake of eggs and red meat to avoid an early death, or perhaps even a late death, from heart disease.

Now the prestigious Food and Nutrition Board of the National Research Council — the same board that decides national recommended daily allowances of nutrients — states there is no reason for the average healthy American to cut down on his intake of cholesterol.

The board points out that seven major studies of human subjects, whose diets were modified to reduce dietary cholesterol, showed no significant reduction in death rates. It concludes that the evidence linking cholesterol in food to risk of heart attack is too circumstantial to convict dietary cholesterol as a killer. But the American Heart Association, meanwhile, is sticking to its conclusion that cholesterol is too suspicious to be allowed free rein on our plates.

This disagreement among the experts will spur the already passionate public debate. Those for whom diet has become an article of faith, protecting them against everything from cancer to aging, are going to feel confused and angry. Egg, milk, and meat industries will jubilantly proclaim that there is no danger in gorging oneself daily on their products.

Regardless of the cholesterol controversy, we think the board made one very important, general point. We would have made it long ago ourselves — except for an unfortunate timidity when cornered by advocates of vitamin E or the more ardent apostles of vegetarianism.

Said the board: "Sound nutrition is not a panacea. Good food that provides appropriate proportions of nutrients should not be regarded as a poison, a medicine, or a talisman. It should be eaten and enjoyed."

Hear, hear!

T̶ᴴᴱ TENNESSEAN

Nashville, Tenn., June 5, 1980

A NUMBER of scientists and doctors are having a difficult time digesting the conclusions of a report on Americans' diet by the Food and Nutrition Board of the National Academy of Sciences.

The report concluded that, in general, there is no reason for a healthy person to reduce his or her intake of cholesterol and fat. The board said there was not enough evidence available yet to make such general dietary recommendations with the aim of reducing heart disease.

There is evidence, however, that the Food and Nutrition Board has ties with food producers who may have been concerned by previous recommendations of other groups that cholesterol and fat intakes should be moderated. For instance, last February the departments of HEW and Agriculture issued dietary guidelines which recommended that healthy Americans should watch how much cholesterol and fat they ate.

After the Food and Nutrition Board released its report last week, it was learned that the panel's chairman and the author of the study were paid consultants for various food producers. Moreover, the board's basic source of financial support is from the food industry.

What may be more disturbing is that the chairman and author, and a third scientist who reviewed the report, have apparently long had reputations for opposing major dietary changes with regard to cholesterol and fat intake. There were no strong advocates of dietary changes on the panel to balance the viewpoints represented.

With other scientists now rushing forward to dispute the conclusions of this report, it is doubtful it will have much impact on what Americans eat.

But it may cause many more Americans to wonder whom they can believe about what.

TULSA WORLD

Tulsa, Okla., June 13, 1980

SELF-STYLED "consumer representatives" have broken with the National Academy of Sciences because the Academy says more research is needed to determine whether lower fat and cholesterol consumption reduces the risk of cardiovascular disease.

The consumerists say no new evidence is needed and Academy advisers who say otherwise may be guilty of "conflict of interest" because of associations with industry.

The Academy's critics may be right on both points. It may be — although it certainly has not been proved to the satisfaction of all knowledgable scientists — that excessive fat and cholesterol in the diet can contribute to heart disease. It is also true that some people who disagree with this theory happen to include representatives of the meat and dairy industries. So there is some bias.

But speaking of motives, there is hardly a special interest group in America more biased and more inclined to self-serving positions on public issues than the so-called "consumer" groups.

These organizations, even the reliable ones, would go out of business overnight without a steady supply of grievances. A health scare like the cholesterol dispute is the same thing to Ralph Nader that gasoline is to a service station owner.

Can you imagine one of Nader's organizations or a similar group investigating the effects of dairy products (or for that matter any other major industrial product) and finding no fault? It is even less likely than an investigation by the cheese industry concluding that cheese is bad for you.

Bias and conflict of interest? You bet. And consumer organizations contribute more than their fair share.

Rocky Mountain News

A Scripps-Howard Newspaper — Reg. U.S. Pat. Off. — Colorado's First Newspaper—Founded in 1859

Denver, Colo., June 4, 1980

THE Food and Nutrition Board's latest report on cholesterol probably ought to be taken with a grain of, if not salt, at least caution.

The board, a part of the prestigious National Academy of Sciences, concluded that there is no reason for the average healthy American to be overly concerned about cholesterol. It said there is no clear evidence that reducing cholesterol in the blood by dietary changes prevents heart disease.

That will relieve people who have continued their regular intake of fatty foods but worry about whether they're plugging up their arteries.

Or will it? The American Heart Association took vigorous exception to the board's report and said it continues to stand firmly behind its advice to Americans to cut down on consumption of foods high in cholesterol. It says there is a great deal of evidence of a relationship between dietary cholesterol and heart disease.

Naturally, the trade organizations for dairy products, eggs and meat were squarely behind the Food and Nutrition Board's report. And the American Medical Association, contrary to the Heart Association, said it also approved.

Where does that leave the public? About where it is on a large number of controversies — in the middle between scientific and medical experts who can't agree.

More light may be shed on the relationship between cholesterol in the diet and heart disease when two large experiments currently under way are concluded. These studies, involving a total of 16,000 persons, are expected to be finished within a couple of years.

Meanwhile, we wouldn't advise anyone to start wolfing down three eggs every morning and attacking a hog leg every evening. But if you're doing it already and don't intend to quit, you may as well take some comfort in the Food and Nutrition Board's finding and enjoy what you're eating.

CHARLESTON EVENING POST

Charleston, S.C., July 7, 1980

Egg and milk lovers will be disappointed to learn that a scientists' panel studying fat and cholesterol levels apparently was playing with a stacked deck.

After the Food and Nutrition Board of the National Academy of Sciences announced that healthy Americans should bury their fears about fat and cholesterol in their diets, two key panel members were discovered to be paid consultants to the egg and dairy industries.

Panel chairman Dr. Alfred E. Harper, biochemist and chairman of nutritional sciences at the University of Wisconsin, gets 10 percent of his income from consulting for the Pillsbury Co., which makes bakery goodies, and Kraft Inc., the nation's largest cheese merchant.

The author of the main draft of the report, Dr. Robert E. Olsen, biochemist and medical professor at St. Louis University, gets 10 percent of his income as a researcher, spokesman and speaker for the American Egg Board and the Dairy Council of California. And the affliations don't stop there.

Two more panel members have had egg industry research grants. Two others are food industry executives of Hershey Food and McCormick and Co. Three of the board members, including Harper and Olsen, are long-established foes of changes in fat and cholesterol consumption. So is the most important of three scientist-reviewers of the report, Dr. Edward Ahrens of Rockefeller University.

While the preface to the report states that committee members were chosen "with regard for appropriate balance," no strong advocate of dietary change was a member or reviewer.

The U.S. Agriculture Department and the then HEW, recommended last February that Americans eat less fat and cholesterol to cut down the risk of heart disease.

The Food Board strongly disagreed. Now their reasons for disagreeing seem suspect, and more than one panel member has egg on his face.

ARKANSAS DEMOCRAT

Little Rock, Ark., June 14, 1980

People with circulatory ailments can take it as they will the announcement by the American Academy of Sciences that the evidence of the harmful circulatory effects of cholesterol is so uncertain that the academy is content to leave it to the individual to decide whether to avoid cholesterol-rich foods.

That's handsome of the academy, admitting that since it doesn't really know it's not going to pretend to know. Wouldn't it be a wonder if the federal Food and Drug Administration would adopt the same attitude toward, say laetrile, which many cancer patients wish they could get legally but can't because the FDA bans it?

But isn't it predictable that there'd be a dissenting echo about the cholesterol finding from the federal government. Carol Tucker Foreman, assistant secretary of agriculture, says the academy finding is suspect because the food industry put some money into cholesterol research and that she'd rather the study had been done with public money. In one breath, she manages to make the food industry sound like a wilful killer and the American Academy of Sciences a paid tool of greedy interests.

If there are any kept scientists, they work for the federal government. The American Academy of Sciences represents free science. It isn't always brave in speaking out for unhampered research, but we'll accept its finding about cholesterol above any other offered, particularly any produced by the federal government.

ALBUQUERQUE JOURNAL

Albuquerque, N.M., June 10, 1980

For the last decade, most health authorities have warned Americans that foods containing high levels of saturated fat and cholesterol can be hazardous to your health.

Now comes the 15-member National Academy of Sciences Food and Nutrition Board with a highly suspect report to the contrary.

Yet the report is highly suspect because of the conflict of interest found for one-third of the board members. The report's chief writer, Dr. Robert E. Olson of the St. Louis University School of Medicine, works as a researcher, adviser, spokesman and speaker for the American Egg Board and the Dairy Council of California. Dr. Alfred E. Harper, a biochemist at the University of Wisconsin, serves as a consultant for the Pillsbury Company and Kraft Inc., the nation's leading cheese producer. Olson and two other members of the advisory board, Dr. Roslyn B. Alfin-Slater of the University of California at Los Angeles and Dr. Victor Herbert of the Veterans Administration Center at New York, are members of the American Council of Science and Health. The council has been described as being a front for food industry views, an allegation the council denies.

Two other board members are food company executives. The board, which receives some money from the federal government, receives it basic support from the food industry.

No doubt the report has caused confusion for those who love eggs, cheese and red meat and who have been told to reduce consumption of those foods. While the appearance of conflicts of interest for the report writers renders the conclusions suspect, our suggestion to our readers is that they follow the advice of their physicians.

THE RICHMOND NEWS LEADER

Richmond, Va., June 9, 1980

Consider cholesterol, the stuff that clogs human arteries and, supposedly, leads to heart attacks. Studies of cholesterol, it seems, will be keeping hundreds of scientists busy for hundreds of years.

One batch of researchers has just delivered a report saying no hard evidence exists linking cholesterol with heart disease. Eat, and be merry, they say.

Other scientists — *The New York Times* calls them the "better safe than sorry" school — insist cholesterol can be harmful to your health, and criticizes the methodology of the first batch's report.

In this case, better safe than sorry seems the safer course. We're not going to gorge on eggs and red meat. Yet only one certitude exists in the cholesterol debate: It keeps scientists in fat city.

The Des Moines Register

Des Moines, Iowa, May 31, 1980

The Food and Nutrition Board of the National Research Council reported this week that there is no reason for the average healthy American to restrict consumption of cholesterol or fat, except to maintain normal body weight.

The report has been cheered by the egg, dairy and meat industries, but consumers should approach it with caution and skepticism. The conclusions it offers on fat and cholesterol sharply contradict recommendations by some of the world's foremost authorities on disease and nutrition:

● Since 1961, the American Heart Association has advised moderation in the consumption of fat and cholesterol. Its most recent dietary guidelines call for limiting fat consumption to 30 to 35 percent of total caloric intake (the American average is closer to 40 percent). The association recommends that Americans eat less than 300 milligrams of cholesterol per day (present consumption averages 450 milligrams).

● In 1968, the medical boards of Sweden, Norway and Finland advised reduction of fat consumption to 25 to 30 percent of total caloric intake and reduction of sugar consumption.

● In 1977, the Senate Select Committee on Nutrition recommended reduction of fat consumption to 30 percent of caloric intake and of cholesterol to 300 milligrams a day, cutting sugar consumption by 40 percent and salt consumption by up to 85 percent and increased consumption of carbohydrates.

● In February 1980, two federal departments — Agriculture and Health, Education and Welfare — issued a set of dietary guidelines "suggested for most Americans." Among the recommendations was a call to "avoid too much fat, saturated fat and cholesterol." The guidelines noted that, for "the U.S. population as a whole," reduced consumption of such foods "is sensible."

Scientists lack conclusive proof that overconsumption of fat and cholesterol causes heart disease or cancer. But the preponderance of evidence has convinced the groups mentioned above, and many others, that changes in diet are desirable.

The basic argument of the Food and Nutrition Board is that more evidence is needed before the average American should be asked to cut back on cholesterol and fat (except to control weight). This judgment, coming from any scientific panel, would be debatable.

It becomes more questionable when one examines the links between the Food and Nutrition Board and the food industry. As Register Washington Bureau Chief James Risser has reported, the Food and Nutrition Board's study was paid for out of a fund made up largely of contributions from food companies.

The chairman of the study has a long history of working as a consultant for the food industry; another author has lobbied actively on behalf of the egg industry. A person with ties to the egg industry can logically be suspected of taking less than an objective view of the need to cut back on cholesterol.

Nutrition — like cancer and heart disease — is not perfectly understood. More research is needed, and that research may lead to changes in dietary recommendations. For the time being, however, anyone concerned about minimizing the risk of cancer and heart disease would be prudent to follow the dietary guidelines issued by the USDA and HEW earlier this year.

WORCESTER TELEGRAM.

Worcester, Mass., June 6, 1980

After all the gloomy don'ts, be carefuls and watch outs, last week's report by the Food and Nutrition Board is appetizing indeed. The board, part of the National Academy of Sciences, declared that there's no reason for healthy Americans to cut their intake of cholesterol and fat.

"Don't worry, everything's OK," was the report's message. The reassurance contradicts the federal government, the American Heart Association, and many independent researchers, all of whom say there is a connection between the incidence of heart disease and diets high in saturated (solid) fats and cholesterol. They have urged Americans to eat fewer egg yolks, red meat and whole-milk dairy products.

Critics of the report have said that the Food and Nutrition Board's report was funded by 80 food companies, many of which sell foods rich in cholesterol and saturated fats. The board chairman and head of a six-member panel that made the report, Dr. Alfred E. Harper, chairman of nutritional sciences at the University of Wisconsin, derives 10 percent of his income as a paid consultant to food companies including the Pillsbury Co., maker of bakery products and Kraft, Inc., the nation's largest cheese company. Dr. Robert E. Olson, the St. Louis University professor who wrote the report's main draft, is a spokesman and research advisor for the American Egg Board and the Dairy Council of California.

Before the report was written, both Olson and Harper were already outspoken in their opposition to recommending changes in the cholesterol and fat content of the diet. Despite a preface that stated that the board was composed with a fair balance of opinions in mind, there were no cardiologists, epidemiologists or public health officials on the board, and no member had been on record as an advocate of cutting cholesterol and fat.

Furthermore, the Food and Nutrition Board simply reviewed studies that have already been conducted; it didn't sponsor any new ones. The report is a re-reading of the available evidence. Oddly, it warned Americans to lower their salt intake to lessen the risk from hypertension. That is probably good advice, but the case against salt is not ironclad either.

The board and its parent, the National Academy of Sciences, have disputed the contention that they were biased by connections with the food industry. After the report was published, however, the American Heart Association repeated its advice that Americans should watch their intake of saturated fat and cholesterol. The Deputy Assistant Secretary for Health said "the weight of existing evidence" still supports the government's recommendation that Americans cut down on cholesterol and saturated fats.

The report's conclusion that food should be enjoyed, not worried about, cannot be disputed. Eating lots of fruits, grains, vegetables, fish and poultry doesn't mean one is worrying about food, however. In fact, once dietary changes have become new habits, there is peace of mind in eating well. Until there is much stronger and more clearly objective refutation of the evidence against dietary cholesterol and saturated fats, there is less worry in being safe than sorry.

Des Moines Tribune

Des Moines, Iowa, June 10, 1980

The Food and Nutrition Board of the National Research Council stirred controversy the other day with a report that said there is no reason for the average, healthy person to reduce consumption of cholesterol or fat except to maintain normal body weight.

Apart from that question, the report underscored many points made by other experts on diet. Among them:

● Obesity can significantly increase a person's chances of dying of such diseases as high blood pressure, diabetes, heart disease and gall bladder disease. Obesity is the most common form of malnutrition in the Western world.

● Excessive consumption of alcohol can cause not only cirrhosis of the liver but neurological disorders, and can increase a person's chances of getting cancer of the throat and neck. Persons who drink should take no more than the equivalent of three mixed drinks a day.

● The average American consumes about 10 grams of salt a day, many times as much salt as needed, and a potentially dangerous amount. Because of the heavy salt content of processed foods, people should use no salt in cooking or at the table.

Following these recommendations will not guarantee health, but failure to do so will increase one's chances of becoming seriously ill at an early age. Despite the controversy over its recommendations on fat and cholesterol, the report of the Food and Nutrition Board is one more significant warning that millions of Americans are eating and drinking themselves into an early grave.

THE LOUISVILLE TIMES

Louisville, Ky., June 6, 1980

The recent National Academy of Sciences report on fat and cholesterol did not clear up for many Americans doubts about what is or is not safe to eat. But it does prove one thing conclusively: Scientists need to learn what a conflict of interest is.

In the years since the Watergate scandals, politicians and government officials have become aware that it is disreputable to mix public policy with private profit, or even to appear to do so.

Congressmen, for instance, must reveal the nature of their financial holdings. Many candidates for lesser offices now find it politically necessary to make public the sources of their family income.

A similar ethical upheaval is needed among scientists and other experts who often work simultaneously for government, academia and industry.

Their pronouncements about what's safe and what isn't carry considerable weight. They influence public policy, individual behavior and corporate profits. But the scholars in whom we place such faith all too seldom reveal where their own interests lie.

The cholesterol report, which concluded that healthy Americans don't have to worry excessively about their fat intake, made front pages all over the country. It was a dramatic departure from previous findings that certain animal products in the diet contribute to heart disease. Certain segments of the food industry, notably egg producers, found the conclusion very satisfying.

It's entirely likely that the study was as objective as the participants could make it. But not many Americans will think so after reading a few days later that funds for the research came from 80 food companies.

What's more, the author of the report works for the American Egg Board, two of the six study group members have done studies for the board, and another is a consultant to two large food processors.

Such affiliations should at the very least be acknowledged when the results of important research are made public. If scientific investigation is to be credible, researchers must go to some lengths to make sure their study panels are properly balanced. Better yet, they should be untainted by links to industries that stand to profit handsomely from a clean bill of health.

Winnipeg Free Press

Winnipeg, Man., Canada, June 11, 1980

One of the most contentious health arguments has broken out with renewed vigor in the United States, and the two sides are as far apart as ever. The issue is whether a high cholesterol diet makes one more susceptible to heart attacks and cardiovascular diseases.

For many years some medical authorities — including at least 18 organizations in the U.S. — have claimed that it is at least prudent for people to go slow on high-cholesterol foods such as eggs, whole milk, butter, fatty meats, etc. Many doctors, in both the U.S. and Canada, who, while not necessarily subscribing wholly to the theory that a high fat diet leads to trouble, go along with the "better to be safe than sorry" prescription.

Now, however, the Food and Nutrition Board of the National Academy of Sciences, which advises the U.S. administration on the healthiness or otherwise of diets, has come out flatly and said that concern about fat and cholesterol intake is unfounded; that there is no proof that such a diet is harmful. So it has recommended that people should not restrict their cholesterol intake, other than that they should take care not to become too obese.

Naturally, the report has been welcomed by promoters of dairy products. But it has also been approved by the American Medical Association and by some independent authorities who note that, diet nor not, Americans now seem to be pretty healthy and long-lived.

On the other hand, the recommendation has been strongly criticized by those authorities which hold conflicting views, including the American Heart Association. They claim that the report is based on insufficient evidence; that there are no heart or public health experts on the board and that none were consulted. More seriously, the claim is made that two members of the board are food company executives; that other members are paid consultants for food companies, including egg producers; and that the board's basic financial support comes from the food industry. In short, the board's credibility is in question because of these apparent conflicts of interest.

Although the argument is American-based, it concerns Canadians and indeed all people in industrialized nations. Many Canadians, like Americans, in recent years have cut down on their intake of high cholesterol foods and begun exercising more, as a way, they hope, of reducing the risk of heart disease. Some take medication, such as Atromid-S, as a method of reducing their cholesterol count.

It is doubtful, however, if the new report will have a significant effect on dietary habits. Those people who prefer to play it safe will continue to do so. Those who like their food and can see no harm in what they eat, will continue to go for whole milk, steak, lots of butter, and two eggs for breakfast.

The Washington Post

Washington, D.C., June 2, 1980

"TOWARD HEALTHFUL DIETS," the new report of the Food and Nutrition Board of the National Academy of Sciences, not only has increased public confusion over proper diet. It has also soiled the reputation both of the board and of the academy for rendering careful scientific advice.

Its key topic is fat and cholesterol consumption. Offering no new evidence or analysis, the report draws an opposite conclusion—that Americans should *not* try to lower their saturated-fat and cholesterol intake —from that reached by virtually every other major medical and public health organization. Though it is nowhere noted, this contradicts the board's own report of just a few months ago—"Recommended Dietary Allowances"—which urged that total fat intake "be reduced so fat is not more than 35 percent of dietary energy." Dietary energy means calories and, on average, Americans get 40 percent of their calories from fat.

Why the contradictions? Atherosclerosis—thickening of the arteries—and its complications (together known as cardiovascular disease or coronary heart disease) are the leading causes of death in this country. A large body of evidence strongly suggests that high levels of cholesterol and a related type of fat known as LDL in the blood are often associated with atherosclerosis.

It is generally agreed—until this latest report, it was unquestioned—that the amounts of saturated fats (those from animal sources) and cholesterol in the *diet* are related to the levels of cholesterol and LDL in the *blood*, and that reducing the one will lower the other. Experts are puzzled that this report casts doubt on that relationship, or they flatly disagree. Countless patients who have seen their own cholesterol and LDL levels fall as they follow a doctor's prescribed diet are baffled, too.

True, while all the evidence points in one direction, the key link is still not *proven*: whether alterations in the diet will definitely reduce the incidence of atherosclerosis and coronary heart disease. Nevertheless, doctors and government agencies must constantly make recommendations on the basis of just this kind of incomplete but suggestive evidence, and there is a consensus on what to do. Even when the precise cause of a disease is unknown, if a certain change in behavior will statistically lower the risk of it, and if the change does not entail new risks or unacceptable economic costs, it should be recommended.

The Food and Nutrition Board agrees with the general principle: "In our present state of knowledge, sound medical and public health practice should be aimed at reducing the known risk factors to the extent possible." But, inexplicably, in the specific it fails to adhere to its own standard. Worse, it follows a double standard, recommending—on the basis of equally inconclusive evidence—that Americans lower their salt intake because excessive salt is a risk factor for hypertension.

So how many eggs should we eat, and how much salt should we sprinkle on them? Notwithstanding the Food and Nutrition Board, prevailing medical opinion still is that for the average American it is prudent to lower intake of both. Saturated fats and cholesterol (usually found in the same foods) should be lowered so that fat is no more than 35 percent of total calories.

This *moderate* reduction involves no known risks. However, a large increase in polyunsaturated fats, though recommended by some groups, may be risky. Reducing fat consumption is also important because fat has twice as many calories per gram as either protein or carbohydrate, and the commonest form of malnutrition in this country is obesity. Obesity— being 20 percent above proper weight—is in itself a significant risk factor for hypertension, diabetes, gall bladder disease and coronary heart disease.

A final note: heredity plays a major role in determining likelihood of both coronary heart disease and hypertension. But doctors cannot yet predict which individuals are at risk because of their genes. So *particularly* those who have a family history of heart disease, but probably everyone, including children, should have blood cholesterol and fat levels determined at least once in the course of a general physical examination.

NEW YORK POST

New York, N.Y., June 3, 1980

After the celebrations which have greeted the report by the Food and Nutrition Board of the National Academy of Science that found no reason for Americans to reduce their intake of cholesterol and fat, it comes as an anti-climax to learn that two members of the board are food company executives and several others serve as paid consultants to food companies.

Why did they not announce this obvious conflict of interest with their new findings on our diets?

Surely it is stretching credulity for the board chairman to be a paid consultant to Kraft Inc., one of our biggest cheese makers, and for the biochemist who wrote the report to be a paid consultant to the American Egg Board.

Basic recommendations on our health, especially those which carry the imprimatur of the National Academy of Science, should be made by scientists whose salaries come from public funds — not from our cheese and egg producers.

The Providence Journal

Providence, R.I., June 4, 1980

The prestigious National Academy of Sciences, which does not usually engage in the kind of blandishments Americans witnessed last week, may inadvertently have taught the country a lesson.

With much attendant publicity, the Food and Nutrition Board of the NAS on May 27 issued a kind of dietary declaration of independence. It seemed to say that nothing had been found to deter healthy individuals from consuming all the fat and cholesterol they might desire. This finding came despite emphatic warnings to the contrary last February by the Agriculture and the then Health, Education and Welfare Departments. The report ran counter to consistent advice in recent years by the American Heart Association that everyone would be wise to consume less saturated fat and cholesterol. Indeed, over the last 10 years some 18 major organizations have taken a similar stand.

One major problem with the Food and Nutrition Board's pronouncement was that it sounded like an open invitation to abandon all restraint. While it is true that evidence linking high-fat and cholesterol diets with heart attacks is largely circumstantial, the indications are negative and suggest caution. In effect, to countermand all previous advice could be a dangerous disservice to the American public.

That was an initial reaction by some observers, particularly since the American Heart Association did not give ground. "We stand firmly behind our dietary advice to the American public," the association said. "The report questions a whole series of epidemiological studies over a long period of time, yet if you look at the makeup of the board, there's not one epidemiologist on it."

A look at the board's makeup is instructive in other ways, leading to further doubts about its objective judgment. Not only does the board lack epidemiologists. It also lacks cardiologists and public health experts. Moreover, no specialists in these three categories were consulted by the board.

Even more damaging, at least on the surface, are the close ties of several members to the food industry. Two members, including the chairman, derive 10 percent of their income as consultants to egg, dairy and other interests affected by recommendations of reduced cholesterol intake. Two have received research grants from the egg industry. And two more are executives in the food industry.

Said Assistant Secretary of Agriculture Carol Tucker Foreman, referring to the NAS report, "I'd prefer to have such work done by persons whose salaries come from public funds." That certainly is one lesson to be learned from this unfortunate exercise in confusion. The board was neither balanced in terms of expertise and point of view, though it claims to be. Nor was it governed properly by conflict-of-interest rules, though that area also was given lip-service by the academy.

If the merits of various brands of laundry detergent were at stake here, one might readily pass this controversy by. But the risk of heart attack and stroke is not a fit subject for scientific electioneering. Studying the risk of cigarette smoking to health was not left to the tobacco industry (which even now attempts to soft-pedal the dangers). Neither should dietary connections to the dangerous buildup of fatty deposits in the blood vessels be left to those in the pay of egg and cheese producers.

"These scientists are good people, usually," said one knowledgeable observer. "They are just blind to the effect money an have." If that is true, someone should set them straight before any more reports are issued to the effect that so far as they are concerned all's right with the world.

FORT WORTH STAR-TELEGRAM

Fort Worth, Texas, June 4, 1980

The fat's in the fire.

A distinguished group of nutritionists says it's all right for the average healthy person to eat plenty of butter, eggs, cheese and marbled steaks, if he or she can afford them.

That report by the Food and Nutrition Board of the National Academy of Sciences, which states that there is not enough scientific evidence to warrant dietary guidelines such as restrictions on fat and cholesterol intake to prevent heart disease, flies in the face of what was becoming a part of the conventional wisdom on nutrition.

In the belief that too much fat and cholesterol are harmful, Americans by the millions have been reducing their consumption of such dietary ingredients. And last February the U. S. Department of Health Education and Welfare (now Health and Human Services) and the U. S. Department of Agriculture issued a set of dietary guidelines that included the recommendation that Americans do just that.

Now comes this group of nutritionists disputing the justifiability of such guidelines on the grounds that the evidence supporting them is inconclusive and coincidental, not causal. In turn the director of the National Heart, Lung and Blood Institute and other government experts on nutrition challenge the validity of the new report.

The result is public dietary confusion. In cases where experts cannot agree, what's the layman to think and eat? And since both sides of the conflict agree that the evidence is inconclusive about the relationship between fat and cholesterol intake and heart disease it is likely to be a long time before the confusion is cleared up.

But in the interim the advocates of the conventional nutritional wisdom make a cogent point. It is better to be safe than sorry. If persons who are already afflicted by heart disease are advised to abstain from or cut back on fat and cholesterol, might not it be a good idea for those average, healthy Americans who want to stay that way to do so?

Nowhere do the fat and cholesterol apologists say reducing one's consumption of them will hurt you.

And there is this to consider. The Food and Nutrition Board receives most of its funding from the food industry, and some of its members have connections with the American Egg Board, an industry-supported organization that sponsors research and consumer education on eggs.

While there may be no conflict of interest involved, those links to the egg industry make their sunny side up findings about cholesterol a bit hard to swallow.

The Dispatch

Columbus, Ohio, June 14, 1980

CURRENT DEBATE over cholesterol is akin to that involving saccharine — the jury is still out on a positive diagnosis.

A couple of weeks ago, after a decade of recommendations by health and nutrition groups that animal fat intake by humans should be sharply curtailed because of adverse effects of cholesterol on the arterial system, a group of medical scientists flew in the face of conventional wisdom.

The National Academy of Science's 15-member food and nutrition board expressed the opinion that most healthy Americans do not need to decrease consumption of eggs and red meat that are high in fat and cholesterol.

Those scientists said it was their opinion that "the benefit of altering the diet" to lower cholesterol content "has not been established."

The key word is "opinion."

It has been the "opinion" of the U.S. Senate select committee on nutrition, the Departments of Agriculture and of Health and Human Services and the American Heart Association that humans indeed should curtail cholesterol intake to trim the chances of thickening arterial walls which can lead to heart and circulatory disorders.

The Academy of Science board's report caused an immediate stir, none of which has been helpful to the layman on the sidelines who depends on expert advice.

Dr. Robert Levy, a director of the National Institutes of Health, put his finger on the heart of the matter when he noted that the board had issued "another report of opinion rather than any new facts."

And Dr. Samuel Fox of the Georgetown University Medical Center says with reference to his patients, "I tell them the data aren't in but the data as I see it show a reduction of cholesterol is justified."

In other words, until science reaches a definite conclusion, it is better to err on the side of caution.

Nitrites Linked to Cancer; Gradual Phase-Out Ordered

The Food and Drug Administration and the U.S. Department of Agriculture reported in August 1978 that a four-year study had found evidence linking sodium nitrite, a chemical additive used in curing meats, to lymph cancer in laboratory rats. The study was conducted by the Massachusetts Institute of Technology under FDA auspices, and it was the first time that sodium nitrite had been isolated as a carcinogen. Previously, it was thought that nitrites were harmful only when combined with amines to form nitrosamines, which had been definitely linked to cancer and were found in well-cooked bacon.

Banning sodium nitrite posed a problem because the chemical was a prime weapon in fighting the growth of bacteria that caused botulism in preserved foods. In addition, nitrites were used in almost all processed and cured meats, which included most pork products. Nitrites also occurred naturally in many leafy and root vegetables, such as spinach. As a result, the FDA concluded that the hazards posed by botulism were greater than the risk of getting cancer from sodium nitrites, and it decided not to ban the chemical immediately. (Under the 1958 Delaney Amendment to the Food, Drug and Cosmetic Act, the FDA was obliged to ban any edible substance that was linked to cancer.) Instead, the FDA recommended a gradual reduction in the use of sodium nitrite.

After two years of further study, however, the FDA announced in August 1980 that the initial report on nitrite danger was inconclusive. The agency said governmental and independent reviews of the MIT study had not found enough evidence to link nitrites with lymphatic cancer. The FDA and the USDA retracted their call for a ban on nitrites, but they repeated their earlier recommendation of reducing the nitrite level in meats because of the danger of cancer from nitrosamines.

The Providence Journal

Providence, R.I., August 21, 1978

Some favorite American foods — hot dogs, bacon, ham and other processed meats — may never look and taste the same again. New research strongly suggests that nitrites, used in most such products as a preservative, cause cancer. Federal health officials, after years of wrestling with the nitrite question, have decided to phase in a total ban on the chemical in food.

Enough evidence of a nitrite-cancer link has accumulated to justify this sweeping federal action. In experiments at the Massachusetts Institute of Technology, 23.9 percent of the laboratory rats fed nitrites developed lymphatic cancers or pre-cancerous conditions. By inference, a similar risk is present in humans; and although a person might have to eat sizable quantities of bologna and hot dogs to incur the risk, it appears genuine enough to call for nitrites' removal.

Because the chemical protects processed meat against the growth of the deadly botulism bacterium, however, the idea of a total ban has presented health officials with a dilemma. If nitrites are outlawed, argues the meat industry, the risk of botulism will grow.

In order to balance these risks, federal agencies are doing the sensible thing in planning to phase out the use of nitrites over "several years." During that time, the thinking is that the processed-meat industry can develop safer agents for preserving the popular quick meats that Americans consume in such abundance.

This cautious approach indicates that the federal government has learned something from the public clamor that greeted previous warnings suddenly issued for cranberries, swordfish, saccharine and other suspect foods. The proposed nitrite ban has been developed only after long study, and will be effective only in stages. Such a studied approach to a public-health dilemma should convince many people that Washington is weighing risks with more care before stepping in to issue regulations.

Nitrites used only to color food will be banned first, while those used as preservatives will be allowed to remain while processors test new methods — freezing, smoking, salting, refrigeration — of preserving their products. Thereafter, the hot dog or ham you buy is likely to look different, even taste different; and consumers may have to educate themselves in safe methods of handling nitrite-free foods. Yet when one realizes the import of the federal findings — "nitrite has been found to induce cancer" — these inconveniences are trivial.

Wisconsin State Journal

Madison, Wisc., August 23, 1978

The government may be getting ready to phase out the use of nitrite as a meat preservative.

Why? Because recent studies at the Massachusetts Institute of Technology have found that nitrite causes a leukemia-type cancer in laboratory animals.

The controversy over nitrite is nothing new. Earlier research indicated that nitrite can combine with other chemicals under certain conditions to cause cancer. The government already has cut back on the amount of nitrite that processors may add to food.

A ban on nitrite would cause fundamental changes in America's eating habits. Nitrite is used to cure more than 9.1 billion pounds of bacon, hot dogs, luncheon meat and other products each year.

Nitrite not only gives meat, particularly pork, its smoky flavor and appetizing color, it is essential for preventing the deadly food poison botulism.

One of the problems with the banning of nitrite is there are no known alternatives to nitrite as a preservative. Any ban on the use of nitrate would have to be implemented gradually: An immediate ban could lead to many cases of botulism and many deaths. The disease is quickly fatal in one out of every three or four cases.

The risk of death from botulism would be significantly higher without nitrite than the risk of cancer with its continued use.

And, as Paul Roehrig, research director for Oscar Mayer & Co. in Madison, has pointed out, there are risks in practically everything that people eat and drink.

Meat generally accounts for only about 20 percent of the nitrites people consume; 80 percent comes from sources like leafy vegetables and drinking water. Nitrite is present, for example, in human saliva.

The government has done its job in reporting the information it has about nitrites. Having done so, it should press for research into other more satisfactory agents for curing meat and better ways to preserve processed foods.

But a ban on use of nitrites is inadvisable in light of the more overpowering danger of botulism.

Chicago Tribune

Chicago, Ill., August 21, 1978

The problems involved in peanut butter are a hundred times stickier when it comes to nitrite. That's the preservative used to cure meats, particularly pork, to give it a characteristic smoky flavor and appetizing color, and to prevent the growth of deadly botulism.

The Agriculture Department and Food and Drug Administration are working on a plan expected to call for the gradual elimination of nitrite in food. The plan was prompted by studies from the Massachusetts Institute of Technology linking nitrite directly with a leukemia-like cancer in laboratory animals.

Pressure to ban nitrite has been building for years because of earlier evidence that it combines with other chemicals under certain conditions to become carcinogenic. Government regulations already have cut back on the amount of nitrite processors may add to food.

The USDA and FDA are holding off on an outright ban for several reasons. Consumers would surely protest, for the 9.1 billion pounds of bacon, luncheon meat, ham, hot dogs, and other cured products Americans eat annually won't taste or look the same without nitrites. Farmers are worried because 70 per cent of pork production is now processed with nitrite. And there is serious concern that without nitrite as a preservative, deaths from botulism will increase; the disease is quickly fatal in one out of every 3 or 4 cases.

It's also difficult to estimate how great a risk nitrite poses. Meat generally accounts for only about 20 per cent of the nitrites people consume; 80 per cent comes from sources like vegetables and drinking water. Saliva, for example, also contains nitrite. ["I told my son the greatest exposure to nitrite comes from kissing his girl," an FDA expert commented. "He replied he'd rather give up broccoli."]

Fortunately, the government doesn't have to impose an immediate ban. The Delaney Claus is not applied to nitrite in meat, on the ground that nitrite was in wide use before 1958. [It does apply to certain canned pet foods and fish; its application to poultry is being litigated in court.]

Although the use of nitrite is covered by other federal food and drug regulations, these rules are not as absolute as the Delaney Clause and leave more room for weighing benefits against risks. FDA experts hope the phaseout period will provide time to develop other satisfactory curing agents and better ways of preserving processed foods.

This is a much more sensible way to proceed than the outright ban required by the Delaney Clause. If the USDA and FDA, working with food processors, can come up with a sensible plan for safeguarding us against both cancer and botulism while preserving an important part of the American diet, it would make a strong case, indeed, for repealing the overly insensitive Delaney Clause.

The San Diego Union

San Diego, Cal., August 27, 1978

The cancer sleuths keep making it rain on our picnics. First we had to worry about the saccharin in the diet soda. Now it's the nitrite in the hot dogs.

New laboratory findings show a significant statistical link between cancer in test animals and the sodium nitrite widely used for many years as a preservative for bacon, ham, hot dogs and lunch meat. With that bad news comes the good news that the Agriculture Department and the Food and Drug Administration are keeping their bureaucratic cool. They are avoiding the kind of reaction that confuses and frightens the public and deals a low blow to the food industry.

The FDA's proposed ban on saccharin last year caused such a public outcry that Congress ordered its implementation delayed for 18 months. With nitrite coming under the same suspicion as a cancer-causing agent, the government is admitting from the start that it may take several years to deal with the problem.

With that we see federal agencies coming to grips in a more rational manner with data from cancer studies and the resulting issue of risk to the public. The list of substances which have a potential link with cancer is becoming so long that anyone trying to avoid all of them would hesitate to get out of bed in the morning, much less eat breakfast.

Until the action of so-called carcinogens is better understood, it is unrealistic for the government to make zero-risk the goal of regulations controlling their presence in the environment or food supply.

More than a few doctors have said they would rather see a person with a weight problem run the risk of using saccharin as a sugar-substitute than run the clearer risk of being overweight. Where nitrite is concerned, an FDA official admits that if it were banned outright there would be "bodies in the street" — victims of botulism, the poison that can develop in foods not properly stored.

Clearly, if nitrite has to go as a food additive, there must be ample time to find a safer alternative or to overhaul the meat processing and marketing system so that cured meats can reach the family refrigerator without adding preservatives to assure their safety. Not the least of the considerations is that only 20 per cent of the nitrite in the American diet comes from meat products. The rest comes from natural sources, such as spinach.

No one has suggested banning spinach — so far. There are many chemicals found in nature which are exactly the same as those produced in a laboratory and used to enhance the flavor or color of food or to make it possible to market certain food items inexpensively and in abundance. An officer of the Monsanto Chemical Co. argued recently that cancer research is creating the "distorted" view that food additives are invariably dangerous.

"Just because a substance has a tongue-twisting chemical name doesn't automatically make it bad," he said. Popeye would agree with that.

The Courier-Journal & TIMES

Louisville, Ky., August 22, 1978

TWO AGENCIES, the Food and Drug Administration and the Department of Agriculture, reportedly are preparing to announce a gradual phaseout of the suspect nitrites used in processing bacon, ham, hotdogs and a host of other products. This approach seems responsible in terms of human health. Equally important, it appears likely to be reasonably acceptable to a public made suspicious by a progression of scares ranging from cranberries to swine flu to the saccharin controversy.

The nitrite issue is not just a question of getting rid of a dangerous food additive, as in the Red Dye No. 2 and cyclamate cases, for which substitutes are available.

Meat processors use nitrites to prevent the formation of botulism toxin and the growth of undesirable yeasts and molds.

Yet, unlike other preservatives, nitrites do not mask signs of spoilage. No other known substance offers both advantages.

Though such alternate processing methods as drying and freezing could be used, the taste and appearance of such staples as ham and bacon would be altered. Meantime, consumers would have to relearn how to store and prepare these foods.

While a nitrite ban would remove many entree dishes from the American diet for a unknown period of time, it could reach the source of only 20 percent of the nitrosamines in the human stomach. In 1970, tests with animals implicated nitrosamines as potential causes of human cancer. Since then, as a result of food industry and USDA studies, nitrite use has been restricted and traceable nitrosamine reduced.

But the other 80 percent of nitrosamines in the stomach are formed through digestion of natural constituents of certain fresh vegetables, among other foods, together with airborne chemicals.

Thus, even radical action on nitrites would reach only a fraction of dietary sources. Congress has protected the $12.5 billion processed meat industry from the law requiring an immediate ban on any food additive shown to cause cancer. Without such a suspension pending further tests, officials would have had no opportunity to balance the cancer risk against the possibility of food-poisoning deaths associated with an immediate nitrite ban.

The proposed nitrite phaseout calls for an immediate ban on applications related simply to food appearance. Other uses would be banned gradually as new food-handling and preservation methods were found to replace them. It seems a responsible way to go.

Sentinel Star

Orlando, Fla., August 18, 1978

JUST AS we were savoring the news that coffee and fat-rich foods might not be as bad for us as previously thought, and that there might even be a "safer" cigarette, the other shoe was dropped: there is additional evidence that nitrites used in preserving some meats may cause cancer in humans.

A three-year study by the Massachusetts Institute of Technology has shown the common preservative may cause cancer in animals. The additives are used in cured meats, poultry and fish, making it possible to keep them without careful attention to refrigeration.

It is unfortunate that this news comes on the heels of some reversals of previous "bad for us" food news, tending to make the findings less believable on the part of a consumer reluctant to give up any part of the "good life." It also gave false credibility to the meat industry's quick rejection of the problem and helped line up 10 to 20 senators prepared to block any ban of the substance.

True, the Food and Drug Administration has picked up something of a "crying wolf" reputation. In particular its circus-like handling of the cyclamate sweeteners issue several years ago did little to instill public confidence, especially now that further testing indicates it might have been wrong.

But the science of cancer causes is not precise. It takes years, even generations of studies of humans to come close to knowing what is or isn't carcinogenic. The use of shorter-lived animals in testing is the next best method in the effort to address the public's single greatest health fear.

In this instance the FDA acted in a reasonable manner, calmly announcing the results and quickly adding that the risks of use must be carefully weighed against the risks of not using nitrites — an increased chance of botulism.

Had the meat industry reacted in a more responsible manner than it did, it could have gone far in both clearing up the question and bringing respect of the consumer for business back into line. The issue should have been met with a challenge for more research, both into nitrite use and finding a suitable substitute should present fears prove valid.

Congress should not be stampeded into blindly blocking restrictions on the use of a possible carcinogen. The responsible government agencies should maintain their calm approach as they seek more information. The health of the nation demands it.

St. Louis Globe-Democrat

St. Louis, Mo., August 25, 1978

The wonder of the federal government's pending ban on the use of nitrites in the nation's meats is not in the ban itself but in the way officials are going about it. They appear to be shooting first and asking questions later.

Dr. Paul Newberne of Massachusetts Institute of Technology, the scientist who concluded that chemical sodium nitrite causes cancer in rats, has urged a go-slow policy on the part of the government. He sensibly contends his research "definitely" should be confirmed in other animals before an extensive ban goes into effect.

Food and Drug Administration officials, however, say there are no plans for more tests, even though Newberne's report has been in FDA hands since June 5 and, according to the scientist, further animal testing will take "three to four years."

The Newberne report is the result of a $500,000 four-year study commissioned by the FDA. Newberne, a professor of nutrition and food science, found that one rat in eight fed sodium nitrite developed a lymphoma or lymph cancer, and another one in every nine developed a possible pre-cancerous condition.

The findings led the FDA and the U.S. Department of Agriculture to prepare proposed regulations, to be issued this fall, calling for a gradual phaseout over "several years" of all nitrites in foods, beginning sometime in 1979. A joint FDA-USDA "action" plan and summary of the nitrite issue flatly says that the Newberne study "shows that nitrite induces cancer when ingested by laboratory rats."

The federal officials appear to be reading between the lines. An examination of the study—made available by the government only a few days ago—shows it is more tentative.

In the report, Newberne speaks in a summary of "the somewhat less than compelling case that nitrite is lymphanogenic in Sprague-Dowley rats," the strain he used.

He also said: "While these observations require some consideration, the data are only suggestive. . . . There are suggestions, however, of sufficient magnitude . . . to raise questions about the widespread use of relatively high concentrations (of nitrite) in our food supply."

The Newberne report has touched on a gravely serious matter. Since the primary concern of the FDA and the USDA is the public's well-being, no effort should be spared to get the complete picture on nitrites. This does not appear to have been done. Further testing on a broader range of animals seems mandatory to learn the full extent of the nitrite hazard.

OKLAHOMA CITY TIMES

Oklahoma City, Okla., August 30, 1978

IN a now familiar move, the director of the federal Food and Drug Administration has warned Americans that the nitrite preservative found in much of our food supply that we buy at the supermarket may be a cancer-causing agent. But before anyone rushes to the roadside stands to provision the family larder with preservative-free fruits and vegetables, or starts salting down freshly slaughtered meat, it might be well to take a second look at the latest cancer scare.

A study conducted at the Massachusetts Institute of Technology, seeking carcingogens (cancer-causing substances), has found that nitrites can cause cancer in laboratory rats. The coordinator of that study, Dr. Paul Newberne, thinks a ban on the use of nitrites is "unwarranted" without three or four more years of tests, however.

Still, it was the MIT study that prompted Donald Kennedy, the FDA chief, to issue the warning to Americans.

The test rats were fed massive doses of sodium nitrite. A human would have to consume nearly 600 pounds of cured meats a day to ingest an equivalent amount to the dosage given the poor rats.

Several years ago, when a similar massive dosage of cyclamate, an artificial sweetener for those who cannot use sugar, led to a ban on its sale, a noted cardiologist snorted that the FDA was being unrealistic. A human would have to consume 2,500 times the normal intake of sweets per day for some days to develop cancer. "No persons could live long enough to develop cancer on such a regimen," the doctor protested. But that ban is still in force.

A frightening angle to the possible nitrite ban is that it is now our primary protection against botulism. We consume great amounts of prepared foods — canned, frozen, baked, refrigerated, and dehydrated. Most use nitrites to prevent the growth of the source of botulism. Will we be told to trade one unlikely risk for another much more likely.?

Perhaps the nitrite scare will be this summer's re-run of those involving cranberries, saccharin, tuna, cyclamates, and other once-useful things.

THE INDIANAPOLIS NEWS

Indianapolis, Ind., August 16, 1978

In what has to be hailed as a victory for common sense, the Department of Agriculture has decided to leave Sunday morning breakfasts alone.

Since 1973 the USDA has kept its watchful eye on the use of nitrites in bacon. Nitrites, which have been used as a preservative for centuries in the form of saltpeter, are used in bacon to prevent botulism, to provide color to red meat and to aid in curing. Some laboratory tests have shown that the nitrosamines produced when nitrite-cured bacon is cooked can cause cancer.

So in the government tradition which gave celebrity status to saccharin, the laboratory rats moved front and center.

In one German rat study, rats were given 1 milligram per kilogram body weight of nitrosamines and it didn't cause cancer. That is roughly equal to having a human eat 15,400 pounds of bacon fried at high temperatures for 70 years. Eventually researchers did cause cancer in rats by tripling the dosage. In other words, all humans who eat 46,000 pounds of fried bacon per day for 70 years might have cause to worry about cancer.

The USDA, under the direction of Assistant Agriculture Secretary Carol Tucker Foreman, had been considering banning nitrites in bacon altogether. Indiana's large hog farmers, of which there are more than 8,600, did not take kindly to the notion of her crippling this state's $660 million-a-year industry.

Indiana's farmers and their Washington representatives were quick to point out the flimsy evidence upon which the government was considering such drastic action.

Sen. Richard Lugar, R-Ind., for example, cited a Canadian study in which — despite feeding rats a diet of one-quarter bacon — no evidence that nitrite-cured bacon is linked to cancer was found. Lugar warned that a USDA ban could result in bacon prices as high as $4 a pound.

Fortunately, the new regulations on nitrite announced this month by the government are nowhere near the outright ban first proposed.

The immediate regulation's limit on nitrite amounts is already observed by 90 of the major processors. "The decision means," said a spokesman for the Indiana Pork Producers Association, "government has caught up with industry." A proposed future, further reduction is also acceptable to meat processors.

But it was a close call. Before any future shouts of alarm are sounded, we have one last point to make for USDA consumption.

Nitrosamines come from sodium nitrite which comes from sodium nitrate. Sodium nitrate is found naturally in vegetables such as spinach, beets and broccoli. Sodium nitrite is found naturally in human saliva. In fact, more than 80 percent of the nitrite entering the human stomach originates in saliva. We hope the USDA is not thinking about doing something about that.

The News Journal

Wilmington, Vt., August 25, 1978

"In matters of public and personal health, Americans in growing numbers are turning a deaf ear to the pronouncements of public officials and eminent scientists," said a recent New York Times article.

That is unfortunate. But it is not difficult to figure out why this is happening. Much of what we hear and read about health matters is complex and confusing and there are few clear-cut answers about how to avoid risk to health.

Take this month's public health threat — nitrites. Nitrites are widely used to preserve food — they prevent food spoilage and prevent the formation of the deadly botulism toxin. Nitrites also enhance the color and appearance of processed foods. Hot dogs, bacon, ham, smoked fish are some of the common foods in which nitrites are used regularly.

But nitrites have for some years been under suspicion of being a link to cancer, and the Department of Agriculture earlier this year reduced the amount of nitrites that may be added to processed foods. This month, however, the Food and Drug Administration released the results of a study that could lead to the eventual ban of nitrites in food. Please note the word "could" in the preceding sentence. It is crucial and it is part of the unavoidable confusion.

What the latest FDA report showed, based on a three-year study conducted at the Massachusetts Institute of Technology, is that nitrites appear to cause a higher than normal incidence of lymphatic cancer in rats. The obvious concern is that the nitrites may have the same effect on humans.

Under U. S. law, food additives that can cause cancer in animal or man must be removed from the market. If that law were strictly enforced with regard to nitrites, based on this latest M.I.T. study, then there would be chaos in the food processing industry and, even worse, Americans might become exposed to dangerous forms of food poisoning, including botulism.

So, the FDA is working out a gradual reduction in the permitted use of nitrites; in the meantime other, safe preservatives will be sought. That sounds like a reasonable enough approach; and it is certainly a wiser course of action than the abrupt ban of saccharin that the FDA had tried to impose over a year ago.

The cancer connection for saccharin also came out of an animal study as has the current to-do over nitrites. Critics of American law on food additives have long contended that it is not wise to draw conclusions from any single study, however well conducted.

And now we hear from Dr. Paul Newberne, the professor who headed up the MIT study, that he believes that his research should "definitely" be confirmed in other animal experiments before any extensive ban goes into effect. His findings, he says, have raised a "red flag" about nitrites. But since his studies were done on just one strain of rats, he thinks it important that further experimentation proceed on different strains of rats as well as on mice, hamsters and other animals.

Officials at the FDA, however, say that no additional tests are planned.

Is it any wonder that the public is skeptical and turns a deaf ear when decisions on food additives are made as a result of just one study, however solid, that the head researcher himself says should be confirmed by further experimentation?

DAYTON DAILY NEWS

Dayton, Ohio, August 16, 1978

As if killer bees, killer sharks and killer people weren't enough, it seems that to life's worries we must add killer bacon.

For years there has been growing evidence that the nitrites used to cure bacon and other processed meats could be changed by cooking or by interaction in the stomach with other foods into nitrosamines, potent cancer-causers. Because of that, the Agriculture Department is lowering the levels of nitrites allowed. That may not be enough.

A study done for the government by a researcher at the Massachusetts Institute of Technology found that nitrites alone increased the incidence of cancer in rats.

Under the law, called the Delaney Amendment, the Food and Drug Administration must ban most substances found to cause cancer when eaten by animals or humans. It was under that law that the government proposed the banning of saccharin, setting off a political storm that led Congress to delay the ban.

No doubt mindful of that uproar, Joseph Califano, the Secretary of Health, Education and Welfare, has been sitting on the latest nitrite study, apparently trying to devise a strategy for dealing with the screaming that is sure to come from meat packers if nitrite is banned.

HEW and the Agriculture Department say they are trying to decide whether the risks of nitrites outweigh the good they do — mainly the prevention of botulism.

For most substances found to cause cancer, they would not have that choice, but nitrites were grandfathered out of the Delaney Amendment. That does not make them any the less dangerous, however, or make the Delaney approach any less valid.

Rigid as the no-exceptions approach is, it is probably better to live with its shortcomings than to risk cancer on an epidemic scale.

But whether covered under Delaney or not, nitrites could be banned by the Agriculture Department under other laws. If the latest study of their dangers is confirmed, they ought to be.

Some small meat packers have already stopped using nitrites, and there seems no compelling reason why the others should not.

WORCESTER TELEGRAM.

Worcester, Mass., August 22, 1978

The federal government seems to be moving away from its Chicken Little "the sky is falling! the sky is falling!" approach to banning carcinogens.

A more sensible approach is seen in the reaction of the Agriculture Department and the Food and Drug Administration to studies that showed nitrite, the meat preservative, induces cancer.

Instead of banning nitrite outright, the government has decided to weigh the risks against the benefits. That makes sense.

Studies conducted by the Massachusetts Institute of Technology show that nitrite can induce cancer in animals. However, as government agencies pointed out, nitrite also prevents botulin food poisoning and there is no immediately available alternative for preserving the more than 9.1 billion pounds of bacon, hot dogs, lunch meat, cured fish and other products treated with it every year.

There is no instant answer to the nitrite question. A ban on the stuff could lead to botulism and many deaths. Not banning it runs a risk of cancer.

The nitrite question is further complicated by the fact that nitrites in cured meat are only a small part of the nitrites we consume. We also get nitrite in asparagus, spinach, lettuce, celery and even water.

In an editorial the other day, the Wall Street Journal said we can no longer expect "zero risk" in life. The Journal said that it is not reasonable to expect an environment free of every last carcinogen, including those substances that cause cancer "when fed in huge doses to rats specially bred to be susceptible to cancer."

The FDA got burned last year when it announced it would ban saccharin in accordance with the Delaney amendment. That amendment requires the ban of any additive found to induce cancer in man or animal, at any level of consumption. In the saccharin tests, rats consumed the human equivalent of 800 12-ounce cans of diet soft drinks each day. The public outcry caused Congress to reconsider the ban.

Perhaps it was the reaction to the proposed saccharin ban which caused the government to adopt its more reasonable approach to carcinogen bans.

Or perhaps it is the unattractiveness of existing options which sent the federal agencies back for more study. (Cancer or botulism is a tougher either-or than the fatness or cancer possibility in saccharin or the greyness or cancer choice in hair dye.)

Whatever the reasons, the government's more careful weighing of risks of additives versus their benefits, is a step in the right direction.

THE SUN

Baltimore, Md., August 23, 1978

The report last year that Canadian tests with rats indicated that saccharin may cause cancer in humans set off a wave of skepticism toward such tests. The argument was that feeding massive doses of such substances to animals could not possibly provide a basis for extrapolation to humans, who consume far smaller quantities. In fact, when animals are fed massive doses of a substance and subsequently develop higher than normal rates of cancer this generally is a credible indication much smaller doses will cause cancer in some humans.

The latest substances to prove worrisome on the basis of animal tests are the nitrites, simple chemicals used to preserve and enhance the appearance of meat, fish and poultry. Scientists long had known that nitrites could combine with naturally occurring chemicals to produce the cancer-causing substances, nitrosamines. Now Massachusetts Institute of Technology findings show the nitrites to be doubly dangerous; not only can they cause cancer in several organs through the nitrosamine route, they also can cause lymphatic cancers directly.

But nitrites are highly useful substances, far more so than saccharin, which is without nutritional value. Saccharin, however, has proved to be anything but easy to ban, and nitrites no doubt will be harder For one thing, the food industry, even though it knew of the nitrosamine hazard for a decade, did little to develop nitrite substitutes. The alternatives that exist —such as constant refrigeration—are expensive, and improperly preserved food can cause botulism, an extemely hazardous kind of food poisoning.

So the Food and Drug Administration and the U.S. Department of Agriculture must decide if banning nitrites would result in such an upsurge of botulism that the ban would do more harm than good. The decision is complicated by the fact that about 80 per cent of the nitrites in human digestive tracts come from bacterial action on nitrates that occur naturally in leafy vegetables and some drinking water. A nitrite ban thus would eliminate only 20 per cent of the nitrites to which humans are exposed, a factor which certainly must figure large in any decision.

If ever there were a case for careful analysis of both the scientific findings and of the costs and benefits of a ban this is it, and the FDA and the USDA are delaying action on nitrites, probably at least till the end of the year. It seems possible that after the study the agencies will find an immediate ban on nitrites to be impractical. But they clearly need to tell the food industry that it is time to get cracking on development of safe nitrite substitutes. The earlier nitrosamine scare gave the industry ample warning that nitrites were hazardous.

The Seattle Times

Seattle, Wash., May 17, 1978

BACON, hot dogs, apple pie and baloney. These foods are as American as, well, apple pie.

But three of them are under attack for containing suspected cancer-causing chemicals. Can apple pie be regarded as sacrosanct?

For many years, sodium nitrite has been used to preserve and redden processed meats. Nitrites are used in the curing process to inhibit the growth of dangerous micro-organisms, especially those that can cause deadly botulism. Nitrites also give processed meats their pinkish tint and keep them from turning brown when cooked.

But when bacon is cooked at high temperature, particularly when fried crisp the way most people like it, nitrites combine with certain amino acids to form nitrosamines — agents that have caused cancer in laboratory animals.

The Agriculture Department announced this week that the amount of nitrites in bacon must be drastically reduced — to 120 parts per million by June 15 and 40 p.p.m. by next May (compared with 200 p.p.m. today).

The department and the Food and Drug Administration, which share authority over nitrites, have known for several years that these substances are potentially carcinogenic. Why the long delay in government action?

One reason is that there are no documented cases of nitrite-caused cancer in humans. Another is that meat packers and hog farmers have strongly resisted any restrictions.

But the Agriculture Department's new direction seems clear. "We are acting to eliminate (nitrosamines) as quickly as possible," says Assistant Secretary Carol Tucker Foreman.

Nitrites — and their controversial cousins, nitrates — are also present in sausage, salami and sandwich spreads. The outlook for pork futures is guarded, while the traditional American breakfast and lunch may never be quite the same.

Richmond Times-Dispatch

Richmond, Va., August 17, 1978

Perhaps as recently as five years ago a news story headlined "MIT Study Ties Cancer to Nitrites," figuratively would have scared many readers to death. But when it appeared in a recent issue of this newspaper, and under similar headlines in papers throughout the country, it probably caused public concern equal to about a 2 on a scale of 1 to 10.

This is not to belittle the finding of a possible link between nitrites and cancer — far from it. If further studies, or further analyses of studies already made, clearly indicate that nitrites can cause people to contract what many consider the worst of all diseases, then appropriate governmental action to protect us would be completely justified.

But the reason for the probable lack of real concern, at least so far, on the part of the public is that people have simply become numb to cancer warnings, justified or not. The list of probable cancer-causing agents in food and the environment has grown so long in the past few years that many people have just about taken the fatalistic view that *anything* might be hazardous and that there's no use going through life worrying about it.

It's hard for the average layman to assess the importance of the test findings reported from the three-year Massachusetts Institute of Technology study made for the U.S. Food and Drug Administration.

The report shows that almost 13 percent of the test animals giving nitrites contracted lymph system cancer. That sounds alarming; it seems to mean that well over one out of every 10 animals got the dread disease by consuming nitrites, a widely used type of preservative found in many foods eaten by human beings. Do the test results mean that more than one out of every 10 human beings could get cancer from consuming hot dogs, bacon, processed lunch meats and other foods to which nitrites are either added or in which they appear naturally?

A second statistic, however, puts a little different light on the picture, at least for laymen. It is that about 8 percent of the test animals that did *not* receive nitrites also contracted lymph system cancer. But while the difference between 8 percent and 13 percent may not seem highly significant to laymen, the government experts say the "difference is significant statistically and leads us to the concern that nitrite may increase the incidence of human cancer."

Meanwhile, following publication of the MIT report, a Virginia Polytechnic Institute and State University scientist says, in effect, nitrites in food are nothing to worry about.

Dr. Richard V. Lechowich, head of the university's food and technology department and chairman of a task force studying the use of nitrites in meat processing, is quoted as saying the risk is minimal and that it would be "irrational" to ban nitrites.

Dr. Lechowich, and government scientists, point out that nitrites are highly beneficial in foods in retarding the growth of the micro-organisms that cause botulism.

So it all boils down to a balancing of risks and benefits. Which has greater weight: (1) the protection of people from the sometimes fatal disease of botulism, or (2) the danger to people of contracting cancer from nitrites?

Unless the whole problem can be solved by discovery of a harmless substitute preservative, the fate of nitrites as a food additive presumably will hinge on the experts' ultimate answer to the question posed above.

The Pittsburgh Press

Pittsburgh, Pa., September 2, 1978

It has been only a matter of days since the U.S. Food and Drug Administration announced it would begin removing nitrites from meats next year because of a study which indicted the chemical additives as cancer causes in laboratory rats.

So consumers have hardly had time to chew over the idea that the hot dogs, sausage or bacon they buy might look and taste different in the future. Or require much more careful handling.

Now the scientist who directed that study at the Massachusetts Institute of Technology has called for a go-slow approach to the whole matter until his research can be confirmed by further tests with other animals.

The evidence, says Dr. Paul Newberne, is "somewhat less than compelling" that the nitrite additives do cause cancer of the lymph nodes in one strain of rats. "The data are only suggestive."

He agrees there should be a phase-out of sodium nitrite in products where it is used only to enhance appearance and not needed to prevent botulism.

But any "precipitous" action is unwarranted, he says, and a complete ban should be considered only if other methods of preservation can be perfected.

That is no small order. Nitrite has been used for generations, essentially to retard botulism toxins in much processed meat, fish and poultry.

As the anguished meat industry was quick to point out when the FDA announced its plans, there is currently no feasible alternative method of preservation.

In view of the undisputed value of the nitrite additives in preventing botulism, the FDA should reconsider its plans.

Until the evidence linking sodium nitrite to cancer is conclusive, a complete ban on its use could actually place the lives and health of millions of consumers in greater jeopardy from botulism.

ARGUS-LEADER

Sioux Falls, S.D., August 28, 1978

After all these years of eating hot dogs at ballgames, bacon for breakfast and cold cuts at lunch, the government is now telling us that those foods contain a cancer-causing substance.

If that morsel of news leaves you feeling queasy, here's more: The government intends to remove the suspected substance, sodium nitrite, from meats as early as next year. Trouble is, sodium nitrite is put in meat for a good reason—to prevent deadly botulism, which sometimes occurs as a result of bacterial growth.

Given a choice, most people would probably take botulism instead of cancer because it's quicker. That apparently is how the Agriculture Department and the Food and Drug Administration look at it too, since they have put a "high priority" in removing the substance.

To their credit, the two agencies are going to give the food industry some time to find other preservatives, and the substance would probably be phased out over the next few years.

Sodium nitrite has been a cancer causing suspect for years in the scientific community. The FDA, in an attempt to pin down a correlation, commissioned a study by a scientist at the Massachusetts Institute of Technology. The study showed that 12.5 percent of the rats fed sodium nitrite developed cancers of the lymph system and another 24 percent developed pre-cancerous conditions.

The food industry is contesting the results, of course. The American Meat Institute called the study inconclusive. And both a bill and a House resolution have been introduced directing the secretary of agriculture to delay any action until after a study of scientific ability to assess cancer causation is completed next year. That study, incidently, was spurred by the question of whether saccharin causes cancer.

We think the ag department and the FDA should slow down. A full-fledged campaign by the food industry to find replacement additives on the strength of apparently incomplete scientific data will only end up costing the consumer.

The Cleveland Press
Cleveland, Ohio, August 17, 1978

The disquieting news that nitrites, the widely used food additive, may cause cancer has handed the government and public some hard decisions.

Normally, suspicion that a substance is cancer causing is enough to get it pulled off the market but such abrupt action may not be possible or desirable in the current case.

Nitrites are added to some $12.5 billion worth of hot dogs, bacon, ham, sausage, liverwurst, bologna, salami and other processed meats that Americans consume each year. The meat industry says no other substance can be substituted and let its products look, taste and handle the same.

Thus, it argues, a nitrite ban would cause prepared meats to disappear, disrupting the food supply. The hog industry could be decimated, since 70% of U.S. pork ends up in processed meats.

What is more, nitrites have been added to meat for centuries to protect against the poison that causes botulism. Banning nitrites could save, say, 2,000 lives from cancer each year and lose 10,000 to food poisoning.

The facts that present the Food and Drug Administration and the Agriculture Department their dilemma come from a new study done for the FDA at the Massachusetts Institute of Technology. It found that 13% of laboratory rats fed nitrites developed lymph tumors while 8% of rats not fed nitrites got the tumors.

The difference is "statistically significant," FDA and Agriculture said in a joint statement, adding that the study "leads us to the concern that nitrites may increase the incidence of human cancer."

Certain consumer groups are demanding an immediate ban on nitrites. They are going too fast. Before such a blow is delivered to people's eating habits and the meat industry, other scientists should check the MIT findings. And they should weigh the balance of risks: botulism vs. cancer.

No matter what the government eventually decrees, the nitrite question won't go away. Only 20% of the nitrites people eat come from processed meats. The other 80% come from nitrates, a related chemical, naturally present in spinach, radishes, beets, celery, leafy vegetables and drinking water. The body converts these nitrates into nitrites.

Thus the question is not easy: Should nitrites be banned from meats, where they are useful in preventing botulism, when they are unavoidable from other sources?

While the FDA and other experts ponder that riddle, the public can make up its own mind. Knowing that nitrites may be linked to cancer, people can decide how much processed meats they care to consume.

The big winners in the new cancer scare, are children. Unlike unhappy earlier generations, they now have an MIT-approved excuse not to eat spinach.

Roanoke Times & World-News
Roanoke, Va., August 17, 1978

The country has hardly recovered from the confusion caused by revelations that artificial sweeteners — first cyclamates, then saccharin — had been shown to cause cancer in animals. Now comes a three-year, government-commissioned study that indicates nitrite, the most widely used food preservative in the United States, is a carcinogen too.

What happens now? The Food and Drug Administration, which ordered up the nitrite study from the Massachusetts Institute of Technology, isn't sure. A year ago FDA went all out to ban saccharin after laboratory tests implicated the sweetener as a cancer cause in mice. This time the agency says it is faced with "a difficult challenge"; although nitrites may lead to cancers, they also protect consumers against botulism.

Botulism, like cancer, can kill — painfully but much more rapidly. According to *Encyclopedia Britannica*, "Symptoms usually appear within 12 to 36 hours after the toxin is ingested . . . Typical symptoms involving the nervous system are double vision, difficulty in swallowing and in speech, and labored breathing. Death usually results from respiratory paralysis." The affliction is difficult to treat; mortality averages 65 percent.

Cancer, of course, kills many more Americans than botulism. We prevent most food poisoning by cooking and other careful preparation of edibles that must be stored. The practice of adding nitrites to meats is centuries old. As the FDA concedes, there are benefits to nitrite use that pose a balance of risks.

The letter of the law — the Delaney Clause, dating back to the 1950s — may give FDA little choice. That law says, flatly, that the agency must ban any additive shown to cause cancer in animals or humans; it sets no standards for tests and allows no risk-vs.-benefit trade-off. Nor does it allow for the fact that, in this nation's interdependent economy, most people's food supplies come from some distance away and need various additives to protect from spoilage.

In the past, FDA has found ways to waffle or weave around the rigidity of the Delaney Clause. That kind of cynical exercise shouldn't be necessary. Pure Food and Drug legislation should retain its power to shield the public from contamination of these consumer goods. But the law should not force Uncle Sam to the kind of "purification" that, in the end, can make food more imminently dangerous than before.

The Houston Post
Houston, Texas, August 30, 1978

A forthcoming proposal by two federal agencies to ban the use of nitrite as a preservative in meat processing could, if adopted, create a greater danger to the public than the one it is attempting to alleviate. A document prepared jointly by the Department of Agriculture and the Food and Drug Administration outlines a course of action in response to recent findings that nitrite can induce cancer in laboratory animals. That action would be to phase out within a "reasonable time" use of the chemical in such products as bacon and lunch meats. The problem is that we have no known substitute for nitrite, which prevents spoilage that can cause botulism, a deadly form of food poisoning.

The federal agencies should ask for much more information about nitrite and botulism before any action is taken on their proposal. The benefits of using nitrite must be weighed carefully against the dangers of not using it. The issue involves some of this nation's favorite foods — bacon, ham, hot dogs and cured fish. The demand is deep-rooted. Attempts to meet it without use of the traditional preservative or with new processes could create new health hazards. Irradiation, freeze-drying and refrigeration are among alternatives being considered. These methods may require public education on storage in consumers' homes.

As an example of the current risk ratio, researchers concluded that a person eating six pieces of bacon or two slices of lunch meat a day would have one chance in 7,400 of developing cancer from nitrite alone. Though the odds against getting cancer from this source are great, they certainly should be taken seriously. But the odds favoring incidences of botulism in the absence of nitrite is even more frightening. This dilemma must be faced with caution. If nitrite is to be banned, planners should proceed only after exhaustive research points the way. Too little information is available now.

Detroit Free Press

Detroit, Mich., August 19, 1978

THE FEDERAL government's proposed nitrite ban could eventually change not only the taste, smell and shelf life of cured meat and fish, but our whole approach to processed foods. It may take the looming threat of cancer to force a general re-examination of the artificially colored, sweetened, flavored, fortified and pre-served products that dominate our super-market baskets and lives.

Governmental agencies plan to phase in a total ban on nitrites, widely used food addi-tives that appear to cause cancer. The ban, which will be delayed until manufacturers develop other methods of retarding food spoilage, will affect the properties of such foods as bacon, hot dogs, ham and cold cuts.

Though we would be the last to recom-mend a rush to ban substances that do the vital job of combatting food poisoning and spoilage, we can't help feeling there may be something fortuitous in the current ques-tioning of the role of these and other chemi-cal substances.

Manufacturers complain that consumers won't recognize or accept familiar products once preservatives are removed, and that highlights the problem. Consumer demand for products of a uniform color, shape and taste, whether or not those characteristics bear any relationship to the products' natu-ral characteristics, is at an all-time high. It is a little like the American fondness for living in communities filled with identical rows of crackerbox houses, and not too far removed from our obsession with television brand names and fashionable status symbols.

But would white cheese taste any less pungent than orange cheese does? And would it be an irreversible calamity if ham began to taste more like fresh pork or bacon to physically resemble fatback?

Of course, none of these scenarios really need occur. The country ought to have enough scientific expertise to devise nitrite substitutes that avoid drastic changes in familiar products. Still, the question re-mains, so what if such changes do, indeed, occur?

The nitrite controversy may provide us with an unparalled opportunity to examine our priorities and separate the trivial from the real. That could be a contribution as vital as eliminating cancer agents.

St. Louis Globe-Democrat

St. Louis, Mo., August 23, 1978

The joint announcement from the Food and Drug Administration and the Agriculture De-partment that nitrites, which are widely used in pork products, appear to cause cancer presents a difficult problem that calls for a calm, thoughtful response from all concerned—the government, consumer groups, the meat indus-try and, above all, the public. For what is in-volved here is not a substance like saccharin, which is nonessential except for a relatively small percentage of Americans who for medical reasons ought not to consume sugar; nitrites are used in the preparation of bacon, ham, sausages and other cured meat products —foods, in short, that to millions represent part of a healthy, balanced diet.

According to research done at the Massachu-setts Institute of Technology, there is a strong suggestion that nitrites cause lymph cancer in laboratory animals. The additive already had been under suspicion as being an indirect cause of cancer. The question for the government is how to move to prohibit the use of nitrites with-out at the same time dealing a devastating blow to the meat industry, which each years sells some $12.5 billion of cured meat products.

The American Meat Institute has declared that nearly three quarters of all pork is used for processed—or nitrite-added—products. Indus-try officials claim that no other additive achieves the combination of texture, flavor and handling convenience that nitrites provide. Moreover, nitrites are useful in protecting against botulism and in permitting cured meat products to be shipped long distances without —as FDA and Agriculture put it—"careful at-tention to refrigeration." And prohibiting the use of nitrites in meat processing would only eliminate about 20 percent of the nitrites that people consume; the rest is ingested in vegeta-bles and drinking water.

All of this, however, must be set against the government's responsibility to provide the pub-lic with as much protection as possible against substances in food that can cause deadly diseas-es. The fact that an additive has been in use for years is no argument against removing it from the market if new research discloses that it constitutes a severe threat to health. Nor is it much of an argument to contend that since most of the substance consumed comes from natural sources, there would be little gained from pro-hibiting the use of that additive in processed products. That is like saying that if you cannot eliminate the whole danger you need not bother with that portion you can control.

If the risk from nitrites is as great as the MIT study suggests, the government has little choice but to do all it can to remove it from the food Americans eat. Indications are that Wash-ington plans to do that through a phased ban on nitrites. Such a procedure could well take sev-eral years and in the meantime other measures need to be undertaken to protect the public.

Research on nitrite substitutes, perhaps under federal sponsorship, deserves immediate encouragement. A further mandatory reduction in permissible nitrite levels, too, is essential and sensible label warnings should be required as soon as possible. At the very least, Ameri-cans deserve to know the potential risks in the food they eat.

SAN JOSE NEWS

San Jose, Cal., October 10, 1979

IT begins to seem that the complaint "everything I like is either illegal, im-moral or fattening" should be expand-ed to include "carcinogenic" as well.

You can get cancer, we are told, from too much sun, too much sex, too much television too close, too much bacon and, now, too much beer.

A non-profit health and nutrition re-search organization in Washington, the Center for Science in the Public Interest, suggests beer may be 20 times more dan-gerous than bacon.

Ounce for ounce, there are more car-cinogenic nitrosamines in bacon than in beer, but Americans consume far more beer than bacon. In fact, Americans over the age of 14 swilled an average of 237 pints each last year. That's a lot of beer and, presumably, a lot of nitrosamines.

Whether it is also something to worry about in the long run is another matter. As Lord Keynes is said to have observed, in the long run we'll all be dead. And if, in the short run, we fret that every ne-cessity or pleasure holds the potential for disaster we might as well be dead.

Pass the six-pack, John Maynard.

The Des Moines Register

Des Moines, Iowa, August 22, 1980

Consumers who enjoy bacon, hot dogs, other processed meats and fish and poultry will be relieved to learn that these products, all treated with a chemical known as nitrite, will continue to be sold just as before the great nitrite scare.

Nitrite inhibits formation of the toxin that causes botulism, a deadly form of food poisoning. In 1978, Dr. Paul Newberne of the Massachusetts Institute of Technology concluded after a study that nitrite causes cancer in rats, and, by inference, in humans. The Justice Department ruled that, under existing law, nitrite would have to be banned.

This week the Food and Drug Administration and the Agriculture Department announced that two special advisory panels formed to evaluate the Newberne study found that Newberne had not proved his case. The government then announced that it will cease efforts to ban nitrite.

The work done by the two advisory panels was impressive for its thoroughness. Each of the 50,000 slides produced by the Newberne study was evaluated, and, where a diagnosis differed from Newberne's, was re-evaluated by a panel of pathologists.

Dr. Donald Houston, administrator of the Agriculture Department's food safety and quality service, said: "We are not saying that products treated with nitrite are not safe. I eat them myself." Houston added that nitrite has not been given "a fully clean bill of health."

There still is concern about the fact that when bacon treated with nitrite is cooked, nitrosamines are formed. Nitrosamines have been shown to cause cancer. The government and the meat industry have moved aggressively to minimize this danger, partly by reducing the levels of nitrite in bacon.

Houston insists that the nitrosamine problem is "now under control," but the Community Nutrition Institute, which has been critical of nitrite in the past, expressed concern that these actions "have not been sufficient."

Because of lingering questions, it is essential that research into the safety of nitrite continue. As a first step, the government has asked the National Academy of Sciences to review all existing data. The Agriculture Department plans to continue its work to develop an acceptable alternative to nitrite, an effort that so far has been unproductive.

The nitrite episode raises questions about the federal law that governs the safety of food additives. If nitrite had been shown to cause cancer, the law would have required an immediate ban, even though no feasible alternative existed and although the health risk might be greater in no-nitrite meats. Congress ought to decide whether a mandatory total ban on cancer-causing agents is reasonable.

The Times-Picayune
The States-Item

New Orleans, La., August 22, 1980

The latest government flip-flop on an alleged cancer-causing substance will leave consumers wondering whether it is safe or not to eat bacon and other packaged meats preserved with nitrite. After first saying nitrites might cause cancer, the government now is saying they might not.

No doubt many consumers, long since hopelessly confused by often contradictory reports as to which industrial chemicals might cause cancer in humans, have consigned their fates to Providence with the sigh that they have to eat and drink *something.*

It would be far better, however, if consumers (that's all of us) did not have to lean so heavily on Providence, but could count on our government, with all its millions to spend on such things, to get its story straight in the first place.

One problem seems to be a lack of a central authority to serve as a cautiously scientific clearing house for potentially cancer-causing substances. Instead, we have the U.S. Food and Drug Administration, the Environmental Protection Agency and the Department of Agriculture involved in the testing and regulating of innumerable chemicals and substances. Perhaps because each agency tends to attract hard-core constituencies, apart from the general public they are supposed to serve, they are subject to conflicting pressures.

The EPA draws concentrated pressure from private environmental organizations, while the Agriculture Department is subject to pressure from agriculture, manufacturing and marketing interests. This has led, among other things, to the persistent tug-of-war between EPA and Agriculture over which is to be the principal regulator of pesticides and herbicides, with the EPA tending to side with the environmentalists who favor stricter controls and Agriculture tending to support agricultural and chemical interests, which prefer less controls. The result frequently is ambivalent government policies and a confused public.

The conclusion three years ago that sodium nitrite and other nitrites used to preserve packaged meats posed a human cancer risk was based on a $500,000 three-year study done by a researcher with the Massachusetts Institute of Technology for the FDA. The conclusion, based on evidence from tests with rats, "strongly suggested" that nitrite causes lymph cancer in rats and "may increase the incidence of human cancer."

Because of the great importance of nitrites (there are no readily available substitutes) to the meat packing and marketing industries, it was inevitable that the MIT study would be challenged. This week, the other shoe fell when the FDA and the Agriculture Department announced that a study conducted by an independent team of university pathologists cast serious doubt on the conclusions of the original MIT study. There is still concern, however, because nitrites can combine with other chemicals to form substances called nitrosamines, which, it is generally agreed, can cause cancer. For this reason, the FDA and Agriculture said they would continue efforts to reduce nitrites in foods gradually. But for the time being, the pressure is off the meat industry to quit using nitrites; an abrupt ban would be disruptive to the industry and highly costly to dealers and consumers alike.

Meanwhile, the government regulators are asking the National Academy of Science to review all existing data on nitrites. Too bad they were not that thorough three years ago.

The Dallas Morning News

Dallas, Texas, August 21, 1980

There's good news for breakfast: The government has scrapped plans to ban sodium nitrite, which is a preservative in ham, bacon and other meats.

Congratulations should go to the two federal agencies that admitted making a mistake: the Food and Drug Administration and the Department of Agriculture. And the public deserves applause for hooting down the ban in the first place.

The American people have never quite trusted the wisdom of federal agencies that have power to regulate their lives in order to protect them from the hazards of living. That's because federal agencies often apply controls, regulations and bans without sufficient proof and data to back up their actions.

The 1978 study on which they based their actions failed to show conclusively that sodium nitrite causes cancer in humans. The agencies finally admitted insufficient evidence for the ban.

Not only was their decision to impose the ban a poor one. It was dangerous as well. Sodium nitrite long has been used as a preservative that prevents the growth of botulin, a potentially deadly toxin. No satisfactory substitute for the preservative has been developed.

This should be a lesson to the federal agencies that their regulatory actions must be based on sound evidence. Any action short of that becomes one of arrogance.

Richmond Times-Dispatch

Richmond, Va., August 26, 1980

There is good news sometimes. The government now says that the nitrite-cancer scare of a couple of years ago wasn't justified. Nitrite, a preservative widely used in bacon, ham and other processed meats, was indicted as a cancer-causing agent as the result of a study released in 1978 which claimed that the substance caused lymph cancer in rats and that it "may increase the incidence of human cancer." But now the Food and Drug Administration and the Agriculture Department report that a further analysis of the study results reveals that many of the cell abnormalities found in the test rats actually were not cancer. It is true, however, say the experts, that nitrites can combine with other chemicals to form nitrosamines, and these can cause cancer. So efforts will continue to hold nitrites in food to a minimum. Meanwhile, the eating of bacon and other processed meats apparently poses no significant health threat.

The Washington Post

Washington, D.C., August 23, 1980

REMEMBER the big nitrite scare of two years ago? (No more bacon or hot dogs or other cured meats because nitrite additives in the meat "cause cancer.") Well, it now turns out that the study that seemed to show this was incorrect. At the moment there is no evidence that nitrites in the diet cause cancers of the lymphatic system or of any other system.

However—sad to say—that does not mean that the subject is closed, or that there aren't lots of scientists who are still uneasy about nitrites. The reason is that nitrites can be converted during cooking, or by natural processes inside the body, to chemically related substances known as nitrosamines. Nitrosamines *are* known to cause cancer in a number of different types of animals. Though they have not yet been proven to cause cancer in man, it would be unusual if such a potent animal carcinogen were inactive in humans.

It isn't yet known how much of the nitrosamines inside the body originally come from nitrite-treated meats: it may turn out to be a very small proportion. First of all, nitrites are produced in the body by intestinal bacteria that make them from—bear with us—nitrates. Many vegetables have high concentrations of nitrates; so does some drinking water. And there are many other routes of exposure to nitrosamines. Cigarette smoke has a lot, as do agricultural herbicides and many women's cosmetics. Even new car interiors have relatively high levels.

Where does all this leave government regulators? While nitrites do not have an absolutely clean bill of health, they do now seem to rank very low on the long list of toxic chemicals, new drugs, environmental pollutants, food additives and other substances that need investigating. It is therefore unlikely that we will hear anything more about a nitrite ban unless unexpected new evidence turns up.

And where does it leave the bewildered layman—who is accustomed to thinking of scientific research as a slow, but steady march toward the truth but who recently has seen it lurching back and forth in an apparent state of complete confusion? The answer is that science only looks like an orderly process from a distance. Textbooks may make it look as if Pasteur or Curie or Newton went from A to B to C and right ahead to the answer, but the usual progress is more like: E to B to C to R to A. This holds not only for individual experiments, but also for entire fields as they develop. Only after a crucial idea is proposed does a mass of apparently contradictory data all of a sudden make perfect sense. Cancer research and the broader field of toxicology—the study of how substances may harm the body—are in just such an early, messy, confusing stage and are likely to stay that way for some time.

Non-scientists aren't usually privy to all this confusion. But the Freedom of Information Act and post-Watergate supersensitivities about cover-ups face the government regulator with a whole new dilemma. The scientist in him may want to wait for a second study to confirm the first before making any public announcements, but the public servant knows that this is impossible, especially if it's going to take years to get the necessary answers. Our let-it-all-hang-out style of government has its pluses and minuses. This is one of the minuses: the public is going to have to get used to living with a new and unsettling degree of uncertainty—about nitrites and, sooner or later, almost everything else.

Health Warnings on Liquor Bottles Proposed by Sen. Strom Thurmond

With encouragement from the Food and Drug Administration, Sen. Strom Thurmond (R, S.C.) introduced a bill in 1977 to require a health warning on liquor bottles. Under its provisions, any beverage containing more than 24% alcohol would have to carry a label reading: "Caution: consumption of alcoholic beverages may be hazardous to your health and may be habit-forming." Thurmond, a confirmed non-drinker, cited the alarming statistics on the damage done by alcohol abuse each year. He asserted that there was a need for a more direct means of warning individuals against alcohol abuse than federal educational programs. Opponents, principally Sen. Walter Huddleston (D, Ky.), noted that federal health warnings on cigarette packages had done little to stop Americans from smoking.

Thurmond's bill was passed by the Senate May 7, 1979 by a vote of 68-21 and was attached to a measure authorizing $416.5 million for federal alcohol-abuse programs. The House passed a version of the authorization that did not include a provision for health warnings on liquor bottles. The compromise version that was signed into law in January 1980 included a provision to "permit and encourage" health warnings, but it did not take any more concrete steps.

The Oregonian

Portland, Ore., August 24, 1977

President Jimmy Carter and some members of Congress are growing increasingly concerned about the nation's alcohol abuse problems. The problem is they aren't sure what to do about them.

On Capitol Hill, Sen. Strom Thurmond, R-S.C., and others are sponsoring legislation that would require warnings, similar to those now required on cigarette packages, to be printed on the labels of all beverages containing more than 24 per cent alcohol. The apparent rationale behind the 24 per cent cutoff point is that problem drinkers prefer hard liquor to beer or wine.

On the House side, Rep. George E. Brown Jr., D-Cal., wants to eliminate tax deductions for advertising alcoholic beverages. His reasoning is that the liquor industry spends about $315 million a year on advertising while the government spends about the same amount to fight alcohol abuse. Since the two sums nearly cancel each other out, Brown figures the taxpayers' money is being wasted and that the way to stop that is to end the tax writeoffs for the advertising.

The proposal intrigues the National Institute for Alcoholism and Alcohol Abuse, which says there is no evidence that advertising increases alcohol abuse.

Down Pennsylvania Avenue, the President wants to launch a coordinated federal attack on alcohol abuse the first step of which would be consolidation of alcohol abuse programs now spread among 20 different agencies.

On another front, President Carter's Office of Management and Budget has taken the consumer protection approach by asking two agencies to draw up a proposal which would require identification of hidden and potentially harmful ingredients — preservatives, colors, clarifiers and so on — on the labels of alcoholic beverages.

Whether any of the programs actually will be effective in helping curb alcoholism is debatable, for the abuser's addiction is a stubborn adversary. Still, trying something is better than sitting back and ignoring one of the chronic problems of our age.

THE PLAIN DEALER

Cleveland, Ohio, April 18, 1977

Alarming statistics and admonitions about alcohol abuse and alcoholism have had little noticeable impact on curbing or preventing problem drinking, one of the nation's major health concerns and a contributor to crime.

But now, after three years of research and public hearings, a federal task force has recommended a new strategy which it says will produce better results.

The 18-member team suggests changing people's behavior in situations where alcohol is present. The more than nine million alcoholics in the U.S. are an indication that a new approach is needed.

The latest study was prepared for the Department of Health, Education and Welfare as the first step in developing new tactics to combat alcoholism. Among its suggestions are: encouraging other activities besides drinking at social functions; never making drinking the main purpose of a social gathering, and developing a national intolerance toward drunkenness.

This approach could overcome an underlying attitude which contributes to problem drinking in this country — the social acceptability of drinking and polite treatment of alcoholics by many families, friends and associates.

Government, schools, health associations and industry would be urged to cooperate in establishing a new set of standards for drinking behavior and responsible decision-making in regard to alcohol. It is impossible to predict the effect of the new approach, but the public might show more cooperation because of its positive approach.

It would make Americans responsible for their own drinking habits, thereby possibly preventing future government intervention such as increased alcohol taxes or reduced alcohol advertising. President Carter should endorse the task force recommendations and begin their implementation by the National Institute on Alcohol Abuse and Alcoholism.

Sentinel Star

Orlando, Fla., June 2, 1977

THE U.S. Senate has decided "consumption of alcoholic beverages may be hazardous to your health" and agreed that all liquor of more than 24 percent alcohol by volume should be so labeled.

The warning would do violence to the habits of ladies and gentlemen who keep a bottle or two "for medicinal purposes only," but they needn't worry for a while. The measure lacks significant support in Congress as well as from the powerful liquor lobby.

Anyway, when inbibing is overdone, it is not just a hazard to the drinker's health but to the health, welfare and possibly the lives of everyone around him. But how do you warn a sober motorist that the driver of an approaching car is hazardous to his health?

THE ANN ARBOR NEWS

Ann Arbor, Mich., May 29, 1977

A DEBATE which could be fairly called a tempest in a tea-cup, or rather, in a liquor glass, has been stirred up by Sen. Strom Thurmond, R-S.C.

Thurmond, a teetotaler, would like to do something to reduce excessive drinking and alcoholism in this country. So would plenty of other people. Thurmond's idea of doing something is simplistic, to say the least. But the Senate has approved it.

If the House goes along with the idea, all bottles of distilled liquor will carry labels stating: "Consumption of alcoholic beverages may be hazardous to your health."

That phrase would be required on alcoholic beverages containing more than 24 per cent alcohol by volume — basically meaning whiskies, vodka and gin.

By approving this proposal, the Senate has in effect proclaimed there is no likelihood that consumption of beer and wine may be hazardous to health. Both contain well under 24 per cent alcohol by volume.

No one can seriously believe that unrestrained beer or wine drinking is safer than guzzling the stronger stuff. Not for nothing is "wino" a synonym for a down-and-out drunk. If Congress really believes warning labels would deter anyone with an inclination toward alcoholism, the labels should at least be nondiscriminatory. At most, an exemption might be defensible for the 3.2 per cent beer which is the only beer legally sold in West Virginia and Utah, but even that is debatable.

* * *

THE REAL QUESTION is whether such labels would have any useful impact. Certainly they would not substitute, in any degree, for efforts to handle the difficult job of persuading more people to take signs of impending alcoholism in others, or themselves, seriously.

Possibly the warning labels cigarette packs and ads carry have helped some young people resist peer pressure to start smoking, but we know of no clear testimony to that effect. Chances are that the federal ban on televised cigarette ads, and the broadcasting industry's own restrictions on smoking in front of TV cameras, are more important than package labels. Once a person buys a product, he or she intends to use it regardless of warnings on the label.

It's significant that no enthusiasm for Thurmond's simplistic response to a complex question is being shown either by the American Medical Association (which officially but not very vocally favors bottle labels warning pregnant women against the special dangers of alcohol abuse for unborn children), or by Alcoholics Anonymous. Sen. Carl Levin, D-Mich., sensibly voted for an unsuccessful Senate motion that would have killed Thurmond's labels. Sen. Donald W. Riegle, D-Mich., voted with Thurmond against that motion.

San Francisco Chronicle

San Francisco, Cal., May 9, 1977

THE SET-TO IN the Senate was between two gentlemen who don't drink, Republican Senators Strom Thurmond, a fruit-juice devotee from South Carolina, and Mormon Orrin Hatch of Utah, and two from the bourbon country that is Kentucky — Senators Walter Huddleston and Wendell Ford.

When it was over, the non-drinkers had won. An amendment by Thurmond requiring that liquor bottles (beer and wine excepted) bear warnings similar to those on cigaret packages was adopted by voice vote. They would caution that consumption of liquor "may be hazardous" to the purchaser's health.

THURMOND COMES, of course, from tobacco country, and his zeal for retributive justice in the matter of labelling can be understood. Still, one wonders about the efficacy of such caveats. In the case of liquor — unlike tobacco — most people have long been aware of the potential ravages of its unrestrained use. A liquor group dismissed the senate action as both "hasty" and a "simplistic" approach that has been rejected by most experts in the field of alcoholism.

But Thurmond argues that if the label prevents a potential alcoholic from taking his first drink, or dissuades a driver from having "one for the road," it will have been worthwhile. That kind of evangelistic reasoning is hard to counter.

Chicago Tribune

Chicago, Ill., November 28, 1977

Big Brother is at it again. The Food and Drug Administration wants liquor bottles to carry a label warning women that heavy drinking during pregnancy can cause birth defects. It has asked the Treasury Department's Bureau of Alcohol, Tobacco, and Firearms to order this warning placed on every bottle.

The FDA cites a report by the National Institute on Alcohol Abuse and Alcoholism concluding that women who take more than two drinks a day during pregnancy run a higher than normal risk of giving birth to babies who are retarded or deformed.

We don't doubt the accuracy of this report for a minute. It is the sort of thing anybody with 50-proof brains ought to suspect even without the help of a long report. Heavy drinking is also hazardous to the health of motorists, victims of ulcers, tightrope walkers, tree pruners, diabetics, and structural steel workers on skyscrapers.

As for pregnant women, heavy drinking is only one of many practices that can endanger their children. Others include bad or inadequate nutrition, working near radiation, and taking drugs.

Does it follow that each potentially harmful product should carry a label warning each category of user that might be hurt? Should plug-in radios carry a label warning against using them near the bathtub? Should matches carry a warning not to use them near an open gasoline tank?

It is axiomatic that if you treat people like imbeciles, they will act like imbeciles. The more warnings are incorporated into labels, the less attention people will pay to them. How many would-be smokers have been deterred by the warning on cigaret packages?

What's more, if the government assumes the responsibility of seeing that every conceivable hazard of life is warned against on a label, then what about the fellow who loses control of an unlabeled hatchet and chops off a toe? Can he sue the government?

This labeling kick seems to have become a fad of bureaucrats who want to demonstrate that they are "doing something" to earn their comfortable but often superfluous salaries.

Reports like that of the National Institute deserve all the publicity they can get. It is essential that women be kept up to date on all the do's and don'ts of pregnancy. But which pregnant woman isn't intelligent enough to absorb the knowledge thus made available to her, does the FDA really think she will pause to study the label as she grabs for the booze? How many drinkers, incidentally, even see the bottle?

Des Moines Tribune

Des Moines, Iowa, August 17, 1977

Alcohol is by far the most dangerous of drugs used in America, if "dangerous" is measured by how many people's lives are hurt.

Senator Strom Thurmond (Rep., S.C.) and five other senators are sponsoring a bill that would require a health warning on the label of every beverage containing more than 24 per cent alcohol. "Caution: Consumption of alcoholic beverages may be hazardous to your health and may be habit forming."

If anything, that warning is too mild. Consider some statistics on the toll taken by alcohol, gathered from Jack Weiner's 1976 book, "Drinking."

Weiner estimates there are 15 million to 20 million alcoholics in the U.S., including one out of 10 employes in private industry. These alcoholics are annually involved in accidents costing industry some $15 billion.

Because millions of Americans persist in driving after drinking, thousands of people are killed in alcohol-related traffic accidents every year. Alcohol is a factor in half of all homicides and one-third of the suicides in the U.S. It is a major factor in death from choking on food (the sixth leading cause of accidental death in the U.S.). It is often the catalyst of domestic violence.

The warning favored by Thurmond and his colleagues would not put an end to these problems. Similar warnings have been placed on cigarette packages and in cigarette ads for several years without greatly reducing smoking. But the warning at least would be a step toward advising Americans that the "good life" promised by many liquor ads may turn out to be a far-from-good death.

DESERET NEWS

Salt lake City, Utah, March 18, 1977

It's difficult to understand how the Food and Drug Administration can rationalize banning saccharin because it's suspected of causing cancer when taken in large doses, but makes no effort to restrict availability of those proven killers, liquor and tobacco.

The Canadian research on which the proposed ban on sale of saccharin is based involved administering near-killing doses of the drug to laboratory rats. The dosage caused cancer of the bladder in some animals. Saccharin may well prove to be harmful to humans, and it's best to be safe. But how can we be so careful about something like saccharin and so utterly careless about liquor and tobacco?

There no longer is any serious challenge to the fact of their destructive effect on human life. Millions of lives are crippled and cut short by the use of tobacco. Its destructive effects are recognized as a major worldwide health problem. The link between cigarettes and lung cancer is indisputable.

By overwhelming odds, alcohol is the most serious drug-abuse problem in the nation. Its direct toll in wasted lives is incalculable. For example, it's estimated half of all auto accident fatalities are alcohol related. Even more tragic, alcohol kills and cripples thousands who totally avoid its consumption. It adds undeserved burdens to thousands who must tolerate its destructive effect on family members and upon all citizens who must share the cost of its social erosion.

That's why it's important to support all efforts to slow alcohol consumption, which continues to increase. That's why it's important to allow House Bill 77 passed by the Utah Legislature to become law. The bill would require "each state liquor store, package agency and private club" to post a sign in a prominent place warning that consumption of alcoholic beverages "may be hazardous to your health and the safety of others."

Admittedly, placement of the placards would be only a small step in the gargantuan task of bringing alcohol under control. But it is a positive step, a step made more appropriate by the fact that the State of Utah is a monopoly purveyor of alcohol. The state therefore has an extra obligation to warn purchasers of the possible hazardous effects of the stuff it sells.

The Utah Legislature's action has drawn national attention. President William M. Plymat of the American Council on Alcohol Problems cited the Utah bill in a letter to members of Congress. "The Utah Legislature," Plymat wrote, "has just passed, by a wide margin, a bill calling for warning posters on the walls of all state liquor stores, as well as private clubs . . . In addition, they have passed a resolution asking Congress to take warning action on liquor similar to that required in the case of cigarettes."

Plymat is asking Congress to require such warnings be placed in liquor advertising. The Federal Trade Commission, he notes, "is conducting hearings on proposed advertising limitations in the case of over-the-counter drugs, but the drug that is causing more human misery and loss of life than all other drugs combined seems able to be promoted in every aggressive way that the human mind can devise, with no restraints."

The liquor warning placards could help counteract this kind of advertising, and House Bill 77 should become law. There can be no argument about the validity of the warning message. There should be no argument about placing it at every location where liquor is sold.

DAYTON DAILY NEWS

Dayton, Ohio, May 15, 1977

Too much health can go to your head. That is clearly what has led the aged but robust Sen. Strom Thurmond to propose a warning label on bottles of the distiller's gentle art.

What's worse, the Greatest Deliberative Body in the World, the U.S. Senate, has gone along with this scheme, which Sen. Thurmond probably conceived while tripping out on pushups and organic avocados. If the House does not desist and reject this product of a seaweed-seized brain, all liquor bottles will carry a label saying that the U.S. Congress thinks that the contents "may be hazardous to your health."

Another hazard to health may be travel to Lynchburg, Tenn., for a U.S. congressperson who votes for a warning on liquor. Jack Daniels doesn't have much of a sense of humor about such things.

Liquor, of course, may be hazardous. But so may the lack of liquor be, depending on which studies you believe. Some researchers think the stuff is a curse, others a friend when visited in moderation, and still others a major weapon against heart disease if you stay dead drunk long enough. (Which would destroy your liver, but that's a subject for another research project.)

What is sad is that the Senate, if it were going to take up the subject at all, did not aim the warning at pregnant women. Alcohol — as well as other drugs — is almost certainly dangerous to unborn children. And they can't read warning labels.

The Virginian-Pilot

Norfolk, Va., November 28, 1977

The National Institute on Alcohol Abuse and Alcoholism cautioned last summer that women who take more than two drinks a day during pregnancy risk giving birth to retarded or deformed babies. Food and Drug Administration Commissioner Donald Kennedy now regards the link between drinking and birth defects as sufficiently establishd to warrant a warning on alcoholic beverage containers similar to the one on cigarette packages.

But Commissioner Kennedy is not empowered to order the label. Booze is under the jurisdiction of the Bureau of Alcohol, Tobacco, and Firearms, which has agreed to examine the evidence sent to it by the FDA.

Alcohol is a drug. FDA labeling of drugs, listing side effects, is routine. The Bureau of Alcohol, Tobacco, and Firearms needs to adopt the FDA practice in the case of expectant mothers and the drug of alcohol. The FDA recommendation is not an emotional response to Demon Rum. Its evidence is documented; the danger is real. The warning about birth defects ought to appear on liquor bottles.

Rockford Register Star

Rockford, Ill., November 29, 1977

According to the federal Food and Drug Administration (FDA), pregnant women who drink even moderately — maybe as few as two alcoholic drinks a day — may be causing their unborn children grave mental and physical jeopardy.

The FDA thinks the prospect of reduced intelligence and other congenital defects for these babies is sufficiently great to warrant the labeling of alcohol as a dangerous drug during pregnancy.

It is, of course, a dangerous drug at all times.

And perhaps that is the one, clear-cut point on which everyone can agree in what will surely be a sizable debate ahead.

Attempts to ban alcohol would, of course, fail — as they should. But it not a ban being sought, it's a warning label being asked. And as dangers are found in more and more products it is as difficult to object to warning labels as it would be to defend attempts to ban.

The FDA does not have jurisdiction over alcohol. So, it has asked the Treasury Department's Bureau of Alcohol, Tobacco and Firearms to take action on its labeling request.

Such efforts have been resisted by the courts in the past.

And even now experts disagree on just how dangerous alcohol can be to humans, born as well as unborn.

One sure thing, the evidence now available will be reassessed — as it should be.

And, with the FDA's registered concern as a new reminder, thoughtless adults will surely be less inclined to say, "Have another drink. It won't hurt you."

Not only may it hurt, it may hurt those who have not yet taken their first breath of air. That prospect is too serious to dismiss — or to sidetrack in a bureaucratic fight between the FDA and the Bureau of Alcohol, Tobacco and Firearms.

THE ATLANTA CONSTITUTION

Atlanta, GA., November 25, 1977

"Warning. Heavy drinking can be hazardous to your baby's health."

If the Food and Drug Administration has its way, a label like that could appear on liquor bottles. FDA wants labels to warn pregnant women that heavy drinking can lead to birth defects. The FDA proposal was made in a letter to the Bureau of Alcohol, Tobacco and Firearms, the regulator of alcoholic beverages.

The bureau may balk at following FDA's suggestion (FDA has tried to take over regulation of liquor, and ATF officials may see this as a power play) and the liquor industry certainly will resist the labeling. Nevertheless, the proposal seems a reasonable one.

Research does indicate that taking more than two drinks a day during pregnancy exposes the fetus to the risk of mental retardation and physical deformity. FDA and the Center for Disease Control say research indicates infants affected by the so-called alcohol syndrome have IQs that "average 35 to 40 points below normal." However, Dr. Ernest Noble, government expert on alcohol abuse, says, "The best scientific evidence indicates that two drinks a day or less produce no adverse effects."

A label, then, could emphasize the distinction between heavy drinking and moderate drinking.

For some people in the liquor industry a warning label of any kind is not acceptable. One spokesman argues that the labels wouldn't be effective with women who are alcoholics. And he says the evidence on moderate drinkers is not conclusive. So why label?

That argument assumes that every women who drinks is either an alcoholic or a moderate drinker. Every day. That, of course, is not true. Some women likely will have one drink, or two drinks, three or four days a week. Then, on special occasions they will take more than two. Too many of these special occasions, according to research, can be harmful to an unborn baby. A label of warning could cause these women, as well as habitual heavy drinkers, to think twice about pregnancy and drinking.

And those who oppose the labeling because they feel it would be "another imposition of Big Brother's will on a pliable public" should think twice before worrying about that one. One look at the cigarette industry should tell you that a label does not compel people to stop anything. There must be a greater reason. In the case of cigarettes, the motivator sometimes is the threat of cancer or heart disease. With liquor it could be harm to an unborn child.

Portland Press Herald

Portland, Me., May 10, 1979

Requiring health warnings to be printed on liquor bottles is a good way for Congress to pretend it is doing something to fight alcohol abuse without actually doing much of anything at all.

The Senate voted this week to require the following warning on liquor bottles containing more than 24 percent alcohol: "Consumption of alcoholic beverages may be hazardous to your health."

Congress deludes itself if it thinks such a warning will result in even the slightest reduction in alcohol consumption. It has only to look at the ineffectiveness of warning labels on cigarettes.

When the liquor label proposal first surfaced last year, State Sen. Bennett D. Katz of Augusta, who headed an alcoholism study committee for the Education Commission of the States, testified before a U. S. Senate subcommittee that labels would be useless.

A much more effective approach, Katz suggested, would be a comprehensive, community-based effort to educate the public to the dangers of alcohol abuse.

The Senate would have done well to heed this advice, rather than simply indulging in an empty gesture destined to have little or no impact at all on the serious problem of alcoholism in America.

If the U. S. Senate is convinced that liquor bottles should carry warning labels, it should at least insist on a label that conveys important and useful information.

In a surprise action that caused consternation in the Kentucky delegation, the Senate voted to require a label warning imbibers that "consumption of alcoholic beverages may be hazardous to your health."

It's unlikely this vague message will influence fanciers of Bourbon and gin, or youngsters experimenting with booze, to exercise caution.

Moreover, Senator Huddleston, who admittedly had the interests of a large Kentucky industry in mind, was right in pointing out that the Senate should have considered the issue in more detail before acting.

One problem with the bill is that churches, schools, alcoholic rehabilitation programs and even liquor industry advertising have already made most people aware that drinking to excess can damage one's health.

The Louisville Times

Louisville, Ky., May 9, 1979

In addition, Americans have been alerted to so many dangers that the impact of yet another general warning will be slight. It's doubtful that the bland words of caution on cigarette packages deter many smokers from pursuing their habit. If people are smoking less, it is because they have been bombarded with specific information about the diseases linked to tobacco use.

If there is to be a warning on liquor bottles, it should point out that women endanger the health and well-being of their unborn babies when they drink too much during pregnancy.

Studies have clearly established that heavy and even moderate drinking by mothers-to-be can cause fetal alcohol syndrome. Babies afflicted by this condition may have serious physical disabilities. It is a leading cause of congenital mental retardation.

Many women are presumably told about the problem by their doctors. However, the warning may be more or less emphatic, depending on the physician's view of the evidence. Fetal alcohol syndrome has been discussed in news stories, but there's no certainty that the findings have made an impact on the public's habits or attitudes.

A warning label directed specifically at pregnant women, as Sen. Strom Thurmond proposed, could therefore serve a valid purpose. Not only would it spread vital information but might deter women from having one more drink.

There's no question about the need to make the risks more widely known. But the liquor producers, whom Secretary Califano recently praised for their comparatively enlightened public service advertising, should at least have a chance to suggest other ideas for getting the facts to the public.

DESERET NEWS

Salt Lake City, Utah, May 9, 1979

Remember when some members of the Legislature tried two years ago to require that health warning labels be placed on all bottles of liquor sold in Utah?

Remember how they had to settle, instead, for health warnings on placards posted at liquor outlets and how some people consider even this requirement a joke that makes Utah a laughingstock?

Well, maybe someone had better explain that joke to the membership of the United States Congress.

This week the Senate passed and sent to the House a bill that would require bottles of hard liquor to carry the following warning:

"Caution: Consumption of alcoholic beverages may be hazardous to your health."

The idea is that when the government licenses and sells a product, as some states do with liquor, it can convey the impression that its use is safe when it really isn't. The idea is also that while adults may already know the risks involved in drinking, young people often don't — and health warning labels can help get the message across to at least some of them.

But the super-sophisticates, like those who thought it was funny to peddle T-shirts bearing Utah's placard warnings, know better. What a joke this new Senate measure must be to them.

What a joke the proposed warning label must also be to the children born deformed because their mothers drank during pregnancy.

What a joke it must be to those who have seen homes broken and crimes committed because of the nation's most serious drug abuse problem, the one involving alcohol.

What a joke it must be, too, to the families of those 27,000 Americans who die on the highways each year because someone's coordination and judgment were impaired by alcohol.

Some people, like the distillers, shed tears of laughter all the way to the bank. Others simply shed tears all the way to the hospital or cemetery.

Salt Lake City, Utah, November 16, 1979

Since the Surgeon General has seen fit to warn Americans about the health dangers of cigarettes, why not a warning on alcohol?

Alcohol's degenerative influence on health is fully documented. Consumption of alcohol affects practically every major organ in the body. As consumption increases, so do the chances of heart disease, cancer, and nervous disorders.

Cirrhosis of the liver, now the sixth largest cause of death by disease in the United States, would be a relatively rare affliction but for the consumption of alcohol.

Alcohol destroys the early development of the fetus in pregnancy, with damage occurring in the first 85 days. One genetics expert noted recently that "The most susceptible period for detrimental effects of alcohol on the fetus is probably in early pregnancy (the first trimester)." And, she concluded, "no minimum safe level of maternal alcohol consumption can be established at any time during pregnancy."

Then there are the economic losses: $19.6 billion a year in lost production, $12.7 billion in health and medical costs, $5.1 billion in motor vehicle accidents, $2.86 billion in violent crimes, $430 million in fire losses.

Add to that the lives snuffed out in auto accidents. At least half the 50,000 deaths annually on U.S. highways are alcohol-related — many of them the innocent victims of drinkers.

Incalculable, of course, is the cost of alcohol in human misery, broken homes, and the inevitable heartbreak.

What to do? A modest beginning would be a national law requiring warning labels on liquor bottles and in liquor ads. A bill to that effect, HR 4441, has been introduced in the U.S. House and is now in the House Commerce Committee.

But without some strenuous citizen lobbying of their congressional representatives, the bill will probably die. A milder bill applying only to beverages with an alcohol content of 24 percent or more has been re-introduced in the Senate by Sen. Strom Thurmond (R-S.C.) Virtually the same bill has been before the Senate for several years, but the sponsor has been unable to lift it out of committee.

What good is a warning label? For one, it would warn expectant mothers of dangers to their unborn children. For another, it may have some effect on young teenagers and others just trying alcohol for the first time.

No one claims it will have much, if any, effect on alcoholics — they already know from experience what alcohol does. But labels most certainly would add much to the general education of alcohol's ill effects, just as it has done for cigarettes.

Perhaps most important, it will stand as a formal statement that society, through its government, no longer condones the enormous economic and social costs of alcohol.

THE INDIANAPOLIS STAR

Indianapolis, Ind., May 10, 1979

The other day the United States Senate voted 68-21 that a warning label must go on bottles of liquor containing more than 24 percent alcohol — hard liquor.

"Consumption of alcoholic beverages may be hazardous to your health," the label would read if the Senate has its way.

Akin to the familiar warning on cigarette packages, the Senate-approved warning for bottles of liquor hints at a future brightened by all kinds of equally quaint advisories apropos a wide spectrum of other beverages normally harmless but risky if used in excess. A few examples:

"Consumption of pop may lead to obesity."

"Milk, chocolate, cocoa, eggnog, ice-cream soda, kumiss, punch, root beer or sarsaparilla may be dangerously fattening."

"Coffee, tea, chicory, mate or mocha may be injurious to the nervous system."

"Cider, ginger beer, grape juice, lemonade or phosphate may cause excessive accumulations of gas in the abdomen."

"Ingestion of water not boiled for a minimum of 20 minutes may have fatal consequences."

If the ultimate in protection, security, safety and sanctuary from all possible harm is the object, then surely there could be no merit in half measures.

Nonetheless the too-loud crying of "Wolf! Wolf!" can have risks, and the Senate's proposed warning may tend in that direction — possibly to its own undoing.

Most wines, for instance, contain nothing like 24 percent alcohol yet indubitably are "alcoholic beverages." So what does the Senate really mean by its warning? Is it talking about the hard stuff causing the hasty imbiber to grunt or gasp? Is it eyeing some smooth-as-silk wine?

Exactly what does the Senate have in mind that threatens to be so "hazardous to your health"?

Knickerbocker News

Albany, N.Y., May 10, 1979

First it was cigarettes, after the Surgeon General's initial warnings didn't do much good. These days, each pack bears a small message, one that's become so familiar to smokers they don't even see it any more. "Warning: The Surgeon General has determined that cigarette smoking is dangerous to your health."

And now it's liquor. The Senate voted earlier this week to require a health warning label on all bottles of hard liquor, one very similar to the cigarette warning. If passed by the House, the fairly mild caution would say, "Consumption of alcoholic beverages may be hazardous to your health."

It seems there's ample proof, made public in recent years, to believe liquor is addictive, promotes certain diseases and may cause serious birth defects when consumed during pregnancy.

Aren't we taking things a bit too far? When you're served in a bar, will the little cocktail stirrer have the warning printed in tiny type? When will we begin labeling highways, bacon and tap water, all of which have, someplace and in one way or another, been determined to be hazardous to our health? A warning, given without perspective and a massive back-up educational campaign to tell us the dangers in specific terms, is virtually worthless.

Like many other annoyances of life, warnings become familiar by repitition and, therefore, soon lose their effect.

Nagging seldom works; it only irritates.

The Philadelphia Inquirer

Philadelphia, Pa., May 12, 1979

In voting to require a warning label on liquor bottles, the Senate has engaged in an exercise about as useful as filling a drunk with strong coffee: It gives the appearance of helping, but what you really get is a stimulated drunk.

The Senate action was not totally misguided. It grew out of good intentions that have been stressed by Sen. Strom Thurmond (R., S.C.) and others. These senators have been especially concerned about damage that may be done to a fetus when a pregnant woman drinks alcoholic beverages. Senate hearings last year detailed the extent of that damage and raised enough concern on Capitol Hill to spur the lawmakers to look for effective ways to warn the public.

One idea advanced was to require labels on alcoholic beverages to warn specifically that drinking during pregnancy could cause birth defects. The Bureau of Alcohol, Tobacco and Firearms, as well as Congress, has the authority to require such a label but decided instead to mount a widespread public education campaign in cooperation with the alcoholic beverage industry. Industry cooperation and, more important, industry commitment of money for the campaign, would be based on the understanding that labeling would not be required.

If the Senate's action this week jeopardizes industry commitment to an education campaign, it will have done more harm than good. In the first place, the wording agreed on for the warning — "Consumption of alcoholic beverages may be hazardous to your health" — does not even touch the central issue, which is drinking during pregnancy. Also, under the Senate plan beer and wine would be exempt from the label requirement — a silly exemption since the health affects of a standard-size mixed drink are the same as those of a standard glass of wine or can of beer. Finally, the premise that such a label (particularly in the absence of any concurrent national education campaign) would affect *anyone's* drinking habits significantly is questionable.

Actually, one more warning label, in what could be labeled a decade of proliferating warning labels, could turn out to be a more dangerous anesthetic than the booze to which it is affixed. After a while the consumer's eyes may glaze over from the sheer volume of warnings; then what happens when he or she reads a warning on, say, a bottle of barbiturates or amphetamines? Would those more pointed warnings then be more likely to be dismissed?

A sustained public campaign to inform people about the dangers of heavy drinking during pregnancy, and the possible hazards of even moderate drinking, is the most effective way to approach the problem of fetal damage from alcohol. If the threat of mandatory warning labels spurs the alcoholic beverage industry to invest money in such a campaign, this week's Senate action will be to the good. If it does the opposite, it will be worse than a shame. And if the House concurs on the labelling move and that turns out to be the only solution applied, then Congress, like the well-meaning host who pours coffee for an inebriated guest, will be guilty of only making itself look concerned and self-righteous.

Richmond Times-Dispatch

Richmond, Va., May 20, 1979

Congressional liberals do not have a monopoly on that paternalistic philosophy which holds that it is the duty of the federal government to protect people from themselves. An inane manifestation of that philosophy has just come from the congressional right.

Republican Senators Strom Thurmond of South Carolina and Orrin Hatch of Utah have persuaded the Senate to adopt a measure that would require all bottles of beverages containing more than 24 percent alcohol to bear the warning that "Consumption of Alcoholic Beverages May Be Hazardous to Your Health." Both the sponsoring senators reportedly are teetotalers, and they are eager to warn other people of the dangers of strong drink.

It is an inane measure for several reasons.

One is that the potential dangers of alcohol are well known and have been well known for centuries. Telling people that alcoholic beverages *may* be hazardous to health is like telling them that fire may burn their houses down if they allow it to get out of control.

Another reason is that the warning would not be visible to many people who drink, to those who patronize bars. Bars serve alcoholic beverages in glasses, which would bear no warning label.

It might be argued that the label would be helpful as a warning to young people who are just beginning to drink. But the label would not appear on bottles of wine and beer, which are the favorite drinks of the very young.

Indeed, some young imbibers might interpret the government's failure to put warning labels on wine and beer bottles as an indication that the government considers them completely safe. The truth is that the excessive consumption of alcohol in wine and beer would be just as bad as the excessive consumption of alcohol in bourbon or Scotch.

All of which suggests that the Senate's misleading label law, which has been sent to the House of Representatives for its consideration, may be worse than no label law at all. The House should allow it to go down the drain.

Wichita, Kans., May 25, 1979

A recent U.S. Senate vote to require a health warning on liquor bottle labels was a silly one, and there is doubt it ever will be implemented. But if the controversy succeeds in inspiring some fresh thinking about what *might* work to reduce alcohol abuse, some good may be served.

The idea of a label warning — like those printed on cigarette packages — came from Sen. Strom Thurmond, R-S.C. He got it amended onto a bill authorizing a three-year, $669 million extension of federal alcoholism programs.

The House is considering a less expensive one-year extension of such programs, and there is doubt it would go along with the full Senate plan.

Sen. Thurmond's idea is silly because most people recognize already that ingesting too much alcohol can be dangerous to health, and anyone who needs to be reminded of that fact is unlikely to be either a careful label reader or open to persuasion by anything a label might say.

What's needed is the encouragement of moderation, education about the dangers of alcohol abuse and the identification of those who need to be convinced that, for health or psychological reasons, they shouldn't drink at all.

Alcoholism is a major social and health problem. It is estimated that some 10 million adult Americans — about 7 percent — and nearly a fifth of the nation's adolescents have alcohol-related problems. Excessive drinking is a factor in some 200,000 deaths annually, including about half of those resulting from traffic accidents. The economic cost of alcohol abuse may exceed $40 billion a year, if you estimate both productivity loss and medical costs.

The fact that there are many millions of other Americans who do drink with moderation or only occasionally, and who use alcoholic beverages responsibly, does not detract from the fact that the problems of the abusers need to be dealt with. But those problems need to be dealt with intelligently. And label warnings on bottles won't help much.

Incidentally, moderation is a trait that should be practiced by both those who drink on occasion and those who disapprove of the consumption of liquor.

If those who consider it their calling to promote temperance could learn to attack the problems of alcohol abuse from a scientific and realistic point of view instead of a moralistic one, more progress in checking alcohol abuse might be made all the way around.

The State

Columbus, S.C., June 10, 1979

TEETOTALER Strom Thurmond recently got the U.S. Senate to pass an amendment requiring health warnings on the labels of liquor bottles, but few give it much chance of making it all the way through Congress.

The Thurmond amendment to a funding bill for alcohol abuse programs, after being watered down during debate, would require this simple warning: "Consumption of alcoholic beverages may be hazardous to your health." The original version would have included a warning that liquor could be habit-forming and could cause birth defects if consumed by the mother during pregnancy.

No one argues that alcoholism and alcohol abuse are not major social problems in this country. The government estimates that 7 percent of adult Americans and nearly 20 percent of teenage Americans have alcohol-related problems. Some 200,000 deaths annually are attributed to excessive drinking, many in traffic accidents. The total cost to society is put at $43 billion a year.

But there is plenty of room for doubt that a warning on labels will attack this massive problem in any meaningful way. We question whether a similar warning on cigarette labels has prompted many people to stop smoking, although the debate over the 1965 legislation that required it may have helped focus attention on the potential dangers of smoking. Anti-smoking publicity campaigns may have convinced some to quit, but we suspect most people quit because common sense, or a doctor, or a family member persuaded them.

The liquor industry, caught napping at first, predictably has come out in opposition to Thurmond's idea. This opposition caused government and private groups that fight alcohol abuse to become concerned that the Thurmond amendment endangers cooperative efforts by the liquor industry and the government to promote moderation. The industry says it spends millions on advertising and other alcohol education programs.

Perhaps because of this, HEW Secretary Joseph A. Califano Jr., who is promoting a major alcohol abuse campaign, has been silent on labeling. Other health and anti-alcoholism groups haven't given it much support, although the American Medical Association is on record as favoring a warning to pregnant women.

All in all, there are far better ways to fight this problem than putting another government requirement on private industry.

The Virginian-Pilot

Norfolk, Va., May 14, 1979

The Senate in its wisdom decided the other day that some drinkers should be warned off.

A provision for a selective warning on strong drink was agreed upon overwhelmingly, by 68 votes to 21. If the House concurs, drinkers in the future might be cautioned that "Consumption of Alcoholic Beverages May Be Hazardous to Your Health."

The warning didn't escape without a fight. Teetotalers, chief among them Republicans Strom Thurmond of South Carolina and Orrin Hatch of Utah, wanted sterner language. With a fine regard for where their votes come from, Democrats Walter Huddleston and Wendell Ford of Kentucky's bourbon kingdom strove for no labeling at all. The result was a compromise.

The oddity of the booze alert is that it would go on all bottles whose contents are 24 percent or more alcohol—48 proof and up. That discrimination must seem arbitrary to smokers who find no exemption from health-hazard labeling for low-tar cigarettes.

The implication of the potency threshold is that only hard liquor is dangerous. A wide range of lighter tipples, including beer and wine, would escape the government's frown. Alcohol in greater or lesser amounts being the noxious agent in all those categories, the proposed labeling is dangerously misleading. For the immoderate drinker, there are no "safe" or "unsafe" alcoholic beverages, only potions of more or less strength.

It would make sense to label all drink of whatever voltage. An equally persuasive argument can be made, though, that alcohol's potential for evil mockery is sufficiently known to preclude the painting of that lily on Capitol Hill. So no labeling is just as attractive.

Human nature being constant, it isn't probable that a congressional skull-and-crossbones would scare off many users of the hard stuff. The illusion of benignity in unlabeled drink might, however, be the downfall of the unwary. The Senate did ill by trying to do good. The House would be wise to ease it off that proctorial highhorse.

The Idaho STATESMAN

Boise, Idaho, May 11, 1979

A move is afoot in Congress to append warnings to the labels of liquor bottles that caution, "The drinking of alcoholic beverages may be hazardous to your health." Where, we ask, will it all stop?

Without question, alcoholic beverages, consumed intemperately, are hazardous to your health. But there would seem to be more at issue here: Should the government by such action further encourage Americans to suspend individual judgment in deference to governmental wisdom? We say no. As a consequence of such well-meaning government paternalism, more and more Americans are adopting the mistaken expectation that their government will protect them from every harm; the absence of a warning becomes a government stamp of approval. Personal judgment becomes obsolete.

We find both government paternalism and the dependency it cultivates offensive. In such pernicious fashion are the important American traditions of personal responsibility and self-reliance undermined. Innocent though it may seem, this warning on liquor bottles is just another unfortunate federal nannyism, one we could do without.

HOUSTON CHRONICLE

Houston, Texas, October 8, 1979

A Senate bill would require warning labels on all bottles containing liquor stronger than 24 percent, explaining the dangers of alcohol misuse and abuse and the physical and mental deterioration alcoholism can cause. The message would be directed mainly at younger people.

However, the Education Commission of the States is against the idea and it brings some rather impressive facts and figures to its argument.

They were gathered while making a survey for the Department of Health, Education and Welfare on the awareness of 17-year-olds and an older group of the problems connected with alcohol abuse. The conclusion of the commission's final report: "public awareness about alcohol and health is close to saturation levels."

Some 80 percent of the 17-year-olds sampled were aware of the dangers of alcohol abuse and 94 percent of the 26 to 35 group knew about the potential problems associated with drinking. Nor did their awareness appear to be of the superficial kind. They seemed to be expressing genuine recognition that drinking affects driving ability, depresses the body and causes liver and brain damage after prolonged abuse.

The commission went on to say: "We believe the continued emphasis upon warning labels obscures the real need for dealing with alcohol misuse — namely the development of programs that teach and reinforce responsible decision-making behavior about alcohol."

This would seem to us to be the better way to deal with the problem: a program of education about the dangers of alcohol, backed up by a sustained study as to what the real and deep motivating factors in alcoholism really are.

We doubt that very many of the warning labels would be read, either by those for whom the warning might have the most meaning, or by those who have become aware of their message from other sources.

The Globe and Mail

Toronto, Ont., Canada, May 23, 1979

The consumption of alcoholic beverages may be hazardous to your health, and though many would hold this to be a self-evident truth, the United States Senate has voted in favor of placing the warning on all liquor bottles whose alcohol content is more than 24 per cent.

This much can be said for the plan: it is consistent with the precaution printed on each package of cigarets. However, in the case of alcohol, the hazard to one's health could either be a matter of one's liver or one's ability to keep the car from wandering all over the road.

If Canadian law makers are tempted to start nagging us from bottle labels, we can think of more useful messages they might convey than the obvious generality about our health. Many Canadians already know that the official level of driver impairment is established in the Criminal Code at .08 per cent of alcohol in the blood. They may also read from the label on the liquor bottle the proof number indicating the relative strength of the contents.

The problem for many drinker-drivers lies in connecting up the two figures in such a way that a reliable estimate can be made of how much drink would produce a given blood-alcohol level. No reasonable person would expect anything in the nature of a written guarantee, there being many variables at work; but surely something could be offered on the basis of average weight, scaled according to the period of time in which the alcohol was consumed.

Some loose guides have been offered from time to time, one showing for instance that a 150-pound man, after two 12-ounce beers in less than an hour, would register .058 in a breath analysis test. Four beers would take the same man to the critical .08 level, and six would take him to .11. Two hours later, he would return to .05.

Interesting, possibly vital, information — but you won't find it on a bottle. Maybe this would be the best place for it. Unavoidable, accusatory, authoritative, just what the doctor ordered.

Smoking

It was a startled America that received the first Surgeon General's report in 1964 linking smoking with lung cancer, heart disease, chronic bronchitis and emphysema. The cigarette was synonymous with America, ever since Sir Walter Raleigh introduced the Virginian tobacco plant to England in the 17th century. In the 1940s, American cigarettes became a substitute for money in war-torn Europe, and post-war advertising equated smoking with the affluent, carefree lifestyle that all Americans seemed to be enjoying.

The Surgeon General's report changed all that. No one could look upon smoking cigarettes the same way again. Suddenly, pictures of glamorous models with cigarettes in their hands were replaced by X-rays of decaying lungs and the hack of "smokers cough." The grim research plodded on, and Washington created a smoking and health unit in the Chronic Diseases Control Program in January, 1964. Eventually it became the National Clearinghouse for Smoking and Health. In 1978, it was supplemented by the Office on Smoking and Health, an agency of the Department of Health, Education and Welfare. While the National Clearinghouse compiled medical and statistical evidence on smoking and disease, the Office on Smoking and Health disseminated the findings to an increasingly aware, yet largely unaffected, American public.

Tobacco interests aside, few people seriously doubt that smoking is a major cause of lung cancer and other diseases. The problem with OSH's mission lies in its statement of purpose: ". . . providing individuals with information they need to make an informed choice about cigarette smoking." The crux of the matter lies in the word "choice." Warning people of the risks of smoking does not guarantee that they will not smoke.

The limits of government are quite clear. As long as the decision to smoke rests on individual choice, there are individuals who will choose to endanger their health by smoking. Although 30 million people quit smoking since 1964, there are 54 million who still smoke, according to OSH. The agency adds that 340,000 die each year from diseases linked to cigarette smoking. Persuasive though the evidence may be, it still leaves people with the option to smoke. Americans are too well aware of the failure of Prohibition to think that banning cigarettes will be successful.

What happens then, when smoking becomes a danger not to an individual but to a group of people in a restaurant, airplane or theater? Then, it is reasonable to ask that an individual's right be sacrificed to the general welfare. The ring around the public smoker has slowly begun to shrink, as segregated smoking areas have sprung up in public spaces across the nation. It is doubtful that the U.S. will ever ban smoking in public entirely, as has been done in the U.S.S.R. A pragmatic compromise is best, for both physical and political health.

Non-Smokers Combat Cigarettes in Public Places

Research in the late 1970s produced evidence that cigarette smoke was almost as dangerous to non-smokers as to smokers. A widespread campaign started to prohibit or limit smoking in public places. State and local legislatures periodically considered bills to ban smoking entirely in restaurants, theaters, train stations and other public areas. The Civil Aeronautics Board Nov. 22, 1977 voted, 3-1, to consider a permanent ban on cigar and pipe smoke in airplanes, after having issued a requirement that airlines provide seats in non-smoking sections to all passengers who requested them. Since that time, there have been numerous ordinances passed obliging restaurants to set aside certain sections for non-smokers.

Smoking is no longer a matter of individual choice, in view of the evidence that non-smokers are affected by cigarette smoke. The right of an individual to endanger his own health has come face-to-face with the right of a non-smoker to be protected from a health threat. Needless to say, there is plenty of comment on both sides.

CASPER STAR-TRIBUNE

Casper, Wyo., February 2, 1977

Is there no peace for the smoker?

We have become Public Enemy No. 1 simply by carrying on a tradition as old as the Pilgrims.

The public is constantly riddled with anti-smoking messages on radio and television. The habit, which has its virtues, is portrayed as nothing less than leprosy.

Self-proclaimed martyrs parade up and down our city streets boasting of their triumph over the evil weed. We are shunned at parties and ridiculed at barbecues.

Where will it all end? Is there no sanctuary for us who want to do with our lungs what we may? Life is difficult enough and now to be denied an occasional drag, or maybe a pack or two. Have the critics forgotten that many of the world's greatest decisions have been made over a good ole American smoke. Business and Industry could come to a grinding halt without a cigarette in the mouth of every conscientious laborer.

Now Wyoming, as one of the last retreats from the kind of government interference which aims to to control our very souls, is being threatened with legislation which means to ban smokers from the mainstream of public life.

The measure, which received preliminary approval Saturday in the Wyoming House, provides that "no smoking" areas may be established in all places frequented by the public except bars, factories, warehouses or refineries which are usually not public. The measure provides a fine not to exceed $10 if the law is violated.

One of the bill's sponsors, Rep. Alan Simpson, R-Park, said he has no desire to intrude or make the law oppressive on the smoker but he was quick to note, "the rights of the majority who choose not to smoke need to be vigorously protected."

May we remind the Republican from Park County that we have rights too.

The obvious implications of the act is that hordes of otherwise non-violent Wyomingites will force their way into bars, factories and refineries to smoke in exile. This is likely to make alcoholics out of God-fearing men, cause numerous fires in the State's not too-numerous factories, and plague our refineries with explosions. The smoker's life is short enough without having to chance being blown to pieces because he sought out a quiet retreat under the gas pipes.

Our patience is pushed to limit. It's time we let their feelings be known. Smokers Unite! This is our Armagedon. High priced tomatoes, natural gas shortages and drought we can tolerate. Take away our smokes and we will storm the Capital!

The Detroit News
Detroit, Mich., March 30, 1977

With Michigan's new segregated smoking law going into effect tomorrow, it's time to set the record straight — at the risk of being accused of defending sin — about the much-maligned person who enjoys his or her pipe, cigar or cigaret.

First, no smokers of our acquaintance are premeditating the murder of anyone, as nonsmokers whose rights all of a sudden take precedence over lifetime customs would have us believe. It's true that the habit may be annoying to abstainers but there seems little, if any, scientific evidence that merely breathing smoke-saturated air causes cancer or any disease, pulmonary or otherwise.

High-sounding organizations such as GASP (Group Against Smokers Pollution) and ASH (Action on Smoking and Health) have tried to make the smoking populace out to be guilty of enslaving their fellowmen in an ominous scheme to kill off the nonsmokers through thoughtless neglect of their so-called rights.

There is evidence that smoking — at least cigaret smoking — can cause cancer but to imply that smokers are deliberately seeking the demise of nonsmokers is nonsense.

Second, someone once said the function of government is to pass laws protecting the minority. If that be so, then the minority's rights are being abridged because nonsmokers now are reported to outnumber smokers two to one. They just don't talk as loudly, perhaps because smoking has made them hoarse.

Finland has gone so far as to ban smoking in most public places, including the streets. Minnesota segregates smokers in all restaurants, as Michigan's law will do in eateries seating over 50 people, and we are told about a Minnesota restaurant whose seating was confined to back-to-back booths — one for smokers and the other for nonsmokers.

Of course, airlines have segregated smokers and nonsmokers for some time now and although there have been few public complaints about the arrangement, some insist their rights still are being violated at 30,000 feet.

Many public places besides restaurants are covered by Michigan's new segregated smoking law. Overall, we hope the effect will be to satisfy the nonsmokers that the rights of the majority are intact so that the smokers may at least sit back in the privacy of their own homes and enjoy that last stimulating puff before even those sacred precincts are invaded.

Anyway, how many presidents could have been elected without smoke-filled rooms?

Los Angeles Times

Los Angeles, Cal., January 28, 1977

The Tobacco Institute, an organization not always distinguished for the enlightenment of its self-interest, has been in touch with us, seeking our support in defense of a fifth freedom: freedom to smoke.

Its campaign is, shall we say, designed to set a backfire against Civil Aeronautics Board plans to tighten regulations on smoking aboard airliners.

We were complimented, of course. We like to think of ourselves as champions of the downtrodden, advocates of freedom, foes of discrimination. Admittedly, our reaction is not without qualifications: We are almost evenly divided between those who are addicted to the institute's favorite product and those who are not.

The institute has been collecting signatures on petitions at 50 airports to oppose the CAB rules. Its campaign is designed to counter the flood of letters appealing for tighter regulations. At last count, the CAB had 27,000 comments to consider, and hadn't begun reviewing a second round of rebuttals.

Under present regulations, all airlines are required to provide nonsmoking sections aboard all flights. Under proposed regulations, cigars and pipes would be prohibited altogether—we lost two of our colleagues on that one—and rules would be elaborated to assure every nonsmoker a smoke-free seat and firm enforcement of same.

The institute reports "a massive response by travelers in opposition to the rear-of-the-bus syndrome that has developed to resolve a question of mutual social courtesies."

At the institute, there is no confidence in studies that have identified the hazards of ambient smoke to nonsmokers. In fact, the institute continues to refer only to the "asserted dangers" of tobacco, the surgeon general notwithstanding.

The trouble with that, of course, is that it doesn't make it any easier to sort out the "mutual social courtesies." Which must be why the CAB is into this again.

The Washington Star

Washington, D.C., Febrary 11, 1977

All the signs are that smokers face a more and more uncomfortable time practicing their controversial habit. The action of the Montgomery County Council prohibiting smoking in many public places is in keeping with that trend, whether or not the specific legislation survives the doubts expressed by County Executive James Gleason about its enforceability. The anti-smoking campaign — this time aimed not so much at saving smokers from themselves but at saving non-smokers from the smokers' unwelcome and possibly unhealthy exudations — is going strong at the state and national levels as well as the grass (or, rather, tobacco) roots.

Skeptics in the smoking ranks may see the onset of hard times as part of a cycle that later will bring back the relatively unharassed days. This has happened before in the centuries of official wavering toward tobacco.

James I's denunciation of "a custome lothsome to the Eye, hateful to the Nose, harmful to the Braine, dangerous to the Lungs," and fearsome penalties in some countries, gave way to gradual acceptance of the "filthy weed." In the American colonies, Massachusetts banned tobacco while Virginians made it their cash crop. Though there were always qualms about the healthiness of smoking, anti-tobacco reformists were generally unlistened to until the turn of this century. Then, riding piggyback on the temperance movement, they scored some transitory successes. New Hampshire actually outlawed cigarettes in 1901, and Illinois in 1907. The anti-smokers retreated, but came on strong again with Prohibition in the early 1920s. But if modern times and Madison Avenue seemed then to make the world safe for smokers (including women), that calculation did not anticipate the health findings and civil rights assertiveness of the 1960s and 1970s.

The two concerns — health and the rights of a non-smoking majority — are combining powerfully to limit the right of tobacco users to light up at will. Some 30 states have enacted smoking restrictons of varying severity since 1973.

"Clean air" is the watchword for such lawmaking, requiring segregation of smokers and non-smokers in some premises and outright bans of smoking in certain enclosed areas. The Civil Aeronautics Board is considering a complete ban on smoking in commercial passenger planes (separate sections have been required since 1973), and Congressman Drinan of Massachusetts has advocated a sweeping restriction for federal property.

The health argument, that non-smokers are endangered by people indulging the habit nearby, is not as strong as the evidence of what the smokers are doing to themselves. But there is substantial ground for concern among non-smokers about the long list of poisons thrown off by smokers, and there is no question that many people (the AMA says 34 million) are at least discomfited by the smoke.

Debate about what to do has not been without rancor. Smokers don't welcome pariah treatment, and anti-smoking militants are full of horror stories about boorish reactions by smokers to requests for considerate (or merely legal) behavior. But the tales of conflict between smokers and non-smokers, and fears about enforcement problems in new legal bans, seem to be overdrawn.

The overwhelming majority of smokers wish they weren't hooked, and most are fair-minded about the feelings of non-smokers. A Public Health Service survey in 1975 even found 51 per cent of smokers favoring more restrictions on where smoking is allowed. And 35 per cent of the smokers said it annoyed *them* to be near a person smoking cigarettes. Most smoking restrictions, we've observed, are self-enforcing without any need to call in the cops.

So perhaps the nation can endure two-thirds free of tobacco craving and a third enslaved by the insidious weed, provided there is a degree of understanding between the two groups. A major objective of the anti-smokers, after all, is to convert their erring brothers. To the extent this is successful, the problem of non-smokers' rights will solve itself.

THE CHRISTIAN SCIENCE MONITOR

Boston, Mass., February 1, 1977

Anyone who has had the misfortune to sit near a cigar or pipe smoker on an airplane knows how offensive this can be, notwithstanding claims about rapid aircraft ventilation. Cigarettes too can cause discomfort to those nearby.

Some nonsmokers checking in for busy flights have found no more nonsmoking seats were available — or have learned that his or her nonsmoking seat actually was in the smoking section, due to unexpected changes in seating configurations or a misunderstanding at the check-in counter.

One frequent air traveler on the other hand notes a decline in the proportion of seats where smoking is permitted. And not long ago he heard a stewardess direct an announcement to "those of you who still indulge in smoking," almost as if it were going out of style.

Well, now the battle of the puff is really getting under way. After receiving thousands of comments from Americans, many of them doubtless critical, about smoking in airplanes, the Civil Aeronautics Board (CAB) now must decide what further curbs, if any, it should impose. Just so the CAB does not get the impression this is a one-sided argument, the tobacco industry claims 130,000 persons have signed petitions opposing a ban on smoking on commercial airline flights.

For nearly four years, U.S. airlines have been under CAB orders to separate smokers from nonsmokers on domestic flights. The proposal currently under consideration is to prohibit smoking of cigars and/or pipes. A few airlines already have halted this disagreeable practice. And apparently the volume of anti-smoking complaints received by CAB has been heavy enough so that a complete ban on smoking aloft may be among the alternatives considered. This would apply to cigarettes as well. And, in our opinion, it should.

Meanwhile, smoking is not the only questionable practice aloft. CAB and the airlines also need to come to grips soon with the greater problem of excessive drinking in the sky. Smoking can be unpleasant for others; drinking at 35,000 feet can be downright dangerous for everyone in the plane.

The Detroit News

Detroit, Mich., November 25, 1977

The decision of the Civil Aeronautics Board to ban pipe and cigar smoking aboard commercial airliners comes as a rude surprise to many people who thought the restriction was already in effect. Many now know they must not do what they thought they could not do anyway, so the impact should not be too great.

However, the controversial issue of public smoking involves a conflict between two sets of rights. The clean air apostles, who are particularly strident and unreasoning, chorus their claim to pure air. Smokers also have their rights, too, although they have not been as vocal in stating their claims.

One wonders, as this argument progresses, what ever became of ordinary kindness and courtesy. Only the boorish blow smoke into the faces of non-smokers and the considerate do not cause discomfort to their friends and office colleagues.

The Victorians and Edwardians were civilized about all of this. A man did not light his cheroot in the presence of a woman without her permission and it was the custom to withdraw from the dining room to the library for port and cigars.

Rules, it seems, are now required to accomplish what politeness has not. The CAB, banning pipes and cigars from airliners, will also seek to prohibit cigarets and that will involve lengthy public hearings, since the issue is newly introduced while the pipe and cigar issue was raised officially in October of last year.

The anti-smoker lobby has won skirmishes on other fronts, notably the Pentagon. The Defense Department, in a notable capitulation, has proclaimed tough regulations that prohibit smoking in various dining and working areas and in conference rooms. The Army has adopted the rules and the other services are expected to take them up shortly.

The Pentagon has come down with more force on smokers than the Health, Education and Welfare Department, which ought to be the primary source of the rules since health is one of its principal concerns.

There is a danger in all this that the makers of rules may get carried away to the point where they get silly about it. Setting aside nonsmoking areas in airplanes and dining rooms respects the rights of both groups. But prohibition goes too far. It upholds the rights claimed by nonsmokers but tramples all over the rights of the smoker. The desires of both groups can be accommodated without going to that extreme.

DESERET NEWS

Salt Lake City, Utah, December 22, 1977

Freedom from tobacco smoke may soon be more than just a pipedream on U.S. airliners. And why not?

The Civil Aeronautics Board has voted to consider a flat ban on all smoking on commercial aircraft and called for public comment on the proposal.

The possibility of a total ban shows how much thinking has changed. The time was when smoking was so widely accepted that anyone suggesting that non-smokers might have rights to restrict it was hooted down as hopelessly bluenosed.

The tide has turned in response to concerns about health and increasing fastidiousness. A new kind of segregation has evolved, with airliners and restaurants setting aside special sections for smokers and non-smokers.

The movement is so strong that smokers are now complaining about their rights being infringed, and these complaints are bound to be intensified by the proposed CAB ban. But there is ample justification for the prohibition.

An airliner's cabin is a confined space, and some smoke wafts from the smoking sections to the non-smoking seats despite efficient ventilation.

Persons with circulatory impediments, asthma or other breathing problems are trapped in such a situation, as are those otherwise healthy persons who get queasy stomachs while flying.

In this case, one person's pleasure is another's hardship. The CAB should come down firmly on the side of the non-smokers.

The Pittsburgh Press

Pittsburgh, Pa., November 28, 1977

The Civil Aeronautics Board has voted to ban cigar and pipe smoking aboard commercial planes, and it will soon hold hearings on whether to outlaw cigarettes too.

The CAB has been poking at this nettle with a stick for some time, albeit reluctantly. And it continues to be prodded by angry legions of non-smokers who insist that smoking aboard aircraft is bad for their health as well as being just plain offensive.

It is, of course, an imposition on non-smokers who don't want to cough their way to the coast to have to sit beside a cigarette fiend. But that problem has been largely met by dividing passenger cabins into smoking and non-smoking sections.

This isn't a perfect arrangement. But it does satisfy most air travelers—whether they are smokers or not.

Smokers' rights do not extend to injuring the health of non-smokers, of course. But there is no proof this really happens aboard well-ventilated modern aircraft with segregated smoking sections. So why ban all smoking on commercial aircraft?

The crusaders at the CAB should rethink this idea before they fasten yet another dubious rule on our regulation-ridden society.

THE BLADE

Toledo, Ohio, December 5, 1977

FREEDOM from smoke soon may be more than a pipe dream on airliners. And why not?

The Civil Aeronautics Board has voted to consider a flat ban on all smoking on commercial aircraft and called for public comment on the proposal. It has also instructed its staff to draw up final regulations prohibiting airborne pipe and cigar smoking (three airlines already ban pipe smoking).

The possibility of a total ban shows how much American thinking has changed. The time was when smoking was so accepted that anyone suggesting that nonsmokers might have rights to restrict it was hooted down as hopelessly bluenosed.

The tide has turned not for religious or moral reasons but on grounds of health, fastidiousness, and the fact that it now is as fashionable not to smoke as it once was to indulge. A new kind of segregation has evolved, with airliners and restaurants setting aside — by law in an increasing number of states — special sections for each group. In fact, the movement is strong enough that smokers now are complaining, with some justification, that their rights are going up in smoke.

That protest is likely to be used against the proposed CAB ban. But there is more justification for prohibition in this case than in some others. An airliner cabin is a confined space, and some smoke wafts from the smoking sections to the nonsmoking seats despite efficient ventilation. Persons with circulatory impediments, asthma, or other breathing problems are trapped in such a situation, as are those otherwise healthy persons who get queasy stomachs while flying.

In this case, one person's pleasure is another's hardship. The CAB should come down on the side of the non-smokers.

Des Moines Tribune

Des Moines, Iowa, January 19, 1978

Gov. Robert Ray's endorsement of restrictions on where persons may smoke in public is welcome, but the proposal needs strengthening.

The governor's proposal would limit smoking to designated areas in publicly owned buildings, including state, county and municipal buildings and civic arenas. The governor's hope is that the example set in the public sector would be followed in restaurants, movie theaters, etc.

The Iowa Poll recently found that almost two out of three adult Iowans favor restricting smoking to designated areas in such places as restaurants and theaters and that 57 percent favor restrictions for government buildings. Even about half of the adult Iowans who smoke favor such restrictions.

Minnesota has been living for two years with a statute that applies to both private and state-owned facilities used by the public. Secretary of Health, Education and Welfare Joseph Califano Jr. has urged states to adopt clean indoor air laws modeled after the Minnesota law.

A better approach than that suggested by Ray is the bill introduced last week by Senator Joan Orr (Dem., Grinnell) and 24 other senators. The bill would restrict smoking to designated areas in publicly owned buildings and privately owned businesses selling goods or services to the public.

The right to smoke should not include the right to pollute the air of persons who are annoyed by, or allergic to, tobacco smoke.

The Salt Lake Tribune

Salt Lake City, Utah, July 14, 1978

Research may finally be discovering the definite hazards of "second hand" tobacco smoke. If preliminary conclusions can be further authenticated, reason for banning smoking in enclosed public places could be compelling.

Previously, charges that people might contract cancer from breathing cigar, cigarette and pipe smoke others exhaled were debatable. No reputable health or scientific research sources could be relied on for documenting the claim. Now, however, a link between smoke-filled rooms and human impairment has been identified.

Heart disease, not cancer, apparently can be aggravated by lingering tobacco smoke. And not just cumulatively, but instantly.

According to an article in the New England Journal of Medicine, Dr. Wilbert S. Aronow, with information gathered at the Long Beach, Calif., Veterans Administration hospital, found that 10 men suffering from angina, a sometimes crippling chest pain condition, placed in an 11 by 12 foot room for two hours with three people who each smoked five cigarettes, could exercise only half as long as

normal after the test period. Also, the heart rates had increased and blood pressures rose. Three of the men recorded irregular heart beats.

Dr. Aronow concluded that since carbon monoxide in cigarette smoke cuts down oxygen in the blood and nicotine increases the heart's demand for oxygen, a heart with damaged vessels, unable to deliver oxygen at normal rates, could be adversely affected by doses of "second hand" tobacco clouds. He was ready to declare the situation a "health hazard."

If these indications are fully verified, the case for preventing heavy smoking in relatively confined spaces will be made. Commercial airplanes of small and medium size are the most obvious such "offenders."

Until now, smokers could argue that regulations against their habit reflected mostly unsubstantiated bias. Dr. Aronow's findings suggest otherwise. As he observes, millions suffer from angina. If it is effectively proven that concentrations of used tobacco smoke provokes that condition, there will be cause to prevent public smoking in close quarters.

Chicago Tribune

Chicago, Ill., September 2, 1978

This editorial is written by a nonrabid nonsmoker — one who pities smokers as victims of a costly, inconvenient, and unhealthy habit but who is as comfortable in the company of moderate, considerate smokers as in the company of crusading nonsmokers. And one who is content to cope with the normal problems of life without the meddlesome solicitude of a gung-ho bureaucracy.

This brings us to the city ordinance which has been proposed by Ald. Oberman of the 43rd Ward and which would set up smoking rules for every public place and commercial establishment in the city, provided it covers an area of more than 600 square feet [the equivalent of two modest sized rooms]. It would require that smoking be confined to clearly designated areas amounting to no more than half of the area involved and would subject violators — owners as well as smokers — to fines of from $10 to $100 for each offense.

How, in a bank or a ticket office or an optometrist's shop, can it be ordained that the employe a nonsmoking customer wants to see will be in the nonsmoking area, or vice versa? Or will all employes have to be prohibited from smoking — a policy already adopted by some companies on their own initiative? What about O'Hare terminal, where people

are always moving about and sometimes have to wait for hours?

It is hard enough now to enforce the no-smoking rules in elevators and theaters, where they are required by the fire code, and in buses and designated railroad cars, where tobacco smoke can really be objectionable. It would become almost impossible to enforce any such rules if the law were extended to building lobbies, railroad depots, factories, warehouses, restaurants, and other places specifically mentioned in the ordinance — places that are generally large enough so that smokers can be tolerated without undue agony and where the concentration of smoke can hardly be dense enough to endanger anyone's health except the smoker's.

We have often objected to the tobacco industry's glacial reluctance to recognize the no longer disputable dangers of being a smoker. In fairness, we must now share the industry's impatience with the sometimes intolerant demands of nonsmokers, or at least people purporting to speak for them. The proposed ordinance goes far beyond the requirements of health. It would complicate life for everybody, including those for whose comfort it is presumably designed. Which of our foibles will come under regulation next? Chewing bubble gum?

The Evening Telegram

St. John's, Nfld., Canada, February 10, 1978

Strange as it may seem to some people smokers also have rights. Efforts to chivvy them and to close them into their own smoking-allowed corners as if they were pariahs of our society may seem to be justified to some people but there is something very wrong with that approach.

Smoking is a habit, according to some people a bad habit, and is said to be injurious to health, but to attempt to legislate personal habits out of existence is an excessive use of authority. If the city council allows itself to pass bylaws on habits, good and bad, it is going to find itself stomping with hobnailed boots on the personal rights of individuals.

The taking of too much salt on food is said to be bad for the health but we doubt if the medical association is going to ask council to ban the use of salt cellars in dining rooms and restaurants. Not taking frequent baths may not affect the health but can lead to offence to other people. But we can't imagine the city council passing a law requiring

every citizen to have a bath once a day, week or a month, or shepherding those who don't take baths into well ventilated corners of public places.

The Group Against Smokers Pollution, as it calls itself, or GASP for short seems to have a holier-than-thou attitude which is almost as much of an irritant as the smoke it complains about. The council should be nervous of something which has such a touch of self righteousness to it. Certainly the GASP people, have a right to complain but theirs is not the only right at stake.

The proposed bylaw appears to be an infringement on people's rights and for that reason council should steer clear of it. The council should also realize that it will be almost impossible to enforce this law unless it is going to use an army of informers and nosey-parkers.

From our point of view it is something best left alone. Education of the public into good smoking habits is a much better approach, and less of an irritant.

ST. LOUIS POST-DISPATCH

St. Louis, Mo., January 12, 1978

Uncle Sam wants YOU to quit smoking. Not enough, mind you, to abolish price supports for tobacco growers, but enough to spend $23 million next year to offset somewhat the $150 million the tobacco industry spends annually on advertising its product. Though no one but the Tobacco Institute disputes the connection between smoking and lung cancer, there is not much the government can do to end smoking, beyond educational programs, so long as it ruins the health only of the smoker himself.

But if non-smokers are affected by the presence of cigarette smoke in offices, restaurants and other gathering places, as medical evidence now suggests, then the government has an obligation to enlarge its role beyond providing education to that of offering protection. Banning smoking from public buildings and airliners is an exercise of that responsibility, but it is not easy to determine how far to go with such action. To ban cigarettes as a menace to public health would only invite a tobacco counterpart to the bathtub gin and speakeasies of Prohibition. And if the government began paying farmers not to grow tobacco, the price for those who did would go up astronomically and the government would find itself in the position of bidding up its own payments.

The answer apparently is to find a way to make smoking socially unacceptable. That will take many years and there will be many needless cancer deaths before the effort takes hold. Yet in a country committed to the concept of individual choice, that may be the only effective route — along with steps to make the habit more expensive, perhaps. The new anti-smoking campaign is a beginning, and what it lacks in boldness it makes up for in realism.

Arkansas Gazette.

Little Rock, Ark., September 12, 1978

The smokers have launched a counter-attack now in a House agricultural subcommittee, which is moving a parade of witnesses to the stand to testify that smoking in public places doesn't hurt non-smokers' health, either. It appears that the issue is whether smoking should continue to be prohibited in some places and restricted in others. No doubt the evidence on public health will take a while to accumulate, but there is no question that many people find tobacco smoke obnoxious and should be entitled to reasonable protection from it. The day is past when non-smokers had to suffer in silence whilst indoor air was polluted with the burning weed.

ARKANSAS DEMOCRAT

Little Rock, Ark., August 7, 1978

Anti-smoking forces got their constitutional come-uppance in New Orleans the other day when the Fifth Circuit Court of Appeals ruled that no one has a right not to be bothered by other people's smoking. The plaintiffs were trying to halt public smoking in the Superdome as a health threat.

The interesting thing was that these enemies of smoking filed suit under the Civil Rights Act, citing both the First and Fourteenth Amendments—the latter of which smokers would themselves cite in defense of their right to smoke in public. Their argument would be that the state couldn't discriminate against them as a group.

Whether that would hold up against the state's exercise of its police powers in the area of public health is still an open question because neither the state of Louisiana, the City of New Orleans nor the Superdome management has imposed a smoking ban on Superdome patrons.

We don't think they're likely to do that, but the Fifth Circuit made it plain that a ban does lie within their power and that the court would probably have upheld it.

Such bans aren't as yet widespread, but where they do exist smokers observe them and would probably lose a court challenge. But it's a far cry from a state's exercise of its police power to forbid smoking in specified public places to the proposition that non-smokers have a constitutional right not to be bothered by other people's smoke. The court made it plain that no such constitutional right exists. The right is on the side of the smokers.

Portland Press Herald

Portland, Me., September 11, 1978

If tobacco interests are not successful in knocking down some laws and company policies against smoking it will not be for the lack of trying.

The House subcommittee on tobacco which is conducting hearings on local laws and company regulations pertaining to smoking, is chaired by Rep. Walter Jones of North Carolina, the nation's leading tobacco producing state.

Nine other members of Congress appeared at the hearing, all of them from tobacco states but some of them not even members of the parent Agriculture Committee.

Eight persons holding doctorates testified that cigarette smoke is not harmful to nonsmokers and therefore public puffing should not be prohibited.

The subcommittee and its array of impressively credentialed witnesses are overlooking, perhaps intentionally, an argument that deserves consideration.

The scientific world, which rarely is unanimous on any subject, disagrees as to whether second-hand smoke is injurious to the health of a nonsmoker. But there is little argument against the plea that smoke is disagreeable to many nonsmokers. The bind is that nonsmokers have as much right to their comfort as smokers have to their enjoyment of tobacco.

Designating a section of a restaurant for nonsmokers is a mark of consideration that reasonable patrons will appreciate. Designating one area of a public vehicle for smokers is not unreasonable. Passenger trains used to restrict smoking to particular cars. Some coaches were divided to allow for a smoking section on a small train.

Prohibiting smoking in a confined area such as an elevator is entirely defensible. Among the riders may be persons with respiratory ailments, the trips are short and a smoker should be able to get through his elevator journey without suffering denial pains.

The subcommittee should give equal time to smokers and nonsmokers. But in any conclusion it reaches it should not confine its reasoning to disputed claims about health hazards. It should also consider undisputed arguments about comfort.

WORCESTER TELEGRAM.

Worcester, Mass., August 29, 1978

California, which gave anti-tax proponents the example of Proposition 13, may soon do the same for anti-smoking factions with its Proposition 5.

On the ballot in California's general election in November, Proposition 5 would outlaw smoking in virtually all work places and enclosed facilities open to the public. It would impose restrictions on smoking in other public places, such as restaurants and private offices. Violators would be subject to arrest and a fine.

Proposition 5 may sound like a radical approach, but then so was Proposition 13. And anyway, California residents have the reputation — deserved or not — of being in the vanguard of most far-out philosophies, movements, lifestyles, whatever.

The anti-smoking coalition is made up of the California Group Against Smoking, the American Cancer Society, the California Lung Assn., the California PTA, the California Medical Assn. and the Sierra Club.

On the opposing side are labor leaders, a former Republican gubernatorial candidate, an American Civil Liberties Union official, the Democratic State Central Committee, and, obviously, tobacco manufacturers.

The anti-smoking campaign, in this country and abroad, has been generating support in the past few years. Anti-smoking efforts extend into the Soviet Union. And the federal government is fueling anti-smoking sentiment with a campaign budget of $30 million.

Health, Education and Welfare Secretary Joseph A. Califano, a former chain smoker, has called cigarette smoking "slow-motion suicide." Many non-smokers are concerned about studies which show that toxic substances emitted by smoking are inhaled even by people who do not smoke.

Individual tactics by smokers and non-smokers seem to have escalated recently. Nonsmokers are asserting their right to clean air by asking that cigarettes be put out. But smokers are also fighting back. One woman smoker asks with mock concern, "Does this cigarette bother you?" and if she gets an affirmative answer, says, "Then you can move."

It might be said that you can't legislate goodness and niceness, or even basic consideration of the rights of others when it comes to smoking. And, concurrently, that you can't pass a law to force people to act only in such a way that their actions are not harmful to themselves, much less others.

But, the view on whether people could legislate tax cuts was equally pessimistic. And California voters surprised almost everybody.

Proposition 5 may prove to be equally surprising.

The Charlotte Observer

Charlotte, N.C., January 9, 1978

Smoking seems to be on a lot of minds lately, what with HEW Secretary Joseph Califano's vow to make war on cigarettes. Thus it's unsettling to hear of a new employer's regulation that may signal things to come.

The Alexandria, Va., Fire Department recently decided to hire only firefighters who promise not to smoke — on or off the job. Applicants sign a pledge to that effect and are given two weeks to quit smoking or lose the job.

The fire chief says the chief concern is the firemen's health — and pension costs. Firefighters who retire with heart or lung disease get extra pensions, since those ailments are assumed to be job-related. He believes many cases are actually due to smoking.

An asbestos company has adopted a similar rule for similar reasons. Like firefighters, asbestos workers are exposed to special dangers. But does an employer have a right to restrict employees' private behavior?

You don't have to be a smoker to pale at the notion of bosses dictating how employees conduct their lives. If an employer made you pledge to be celibate, for instance, the costs of pregnancy benefits and treatment of venereal disease would be lower, too. Does that mean an employer has a right to limit such private conduct?

THE SACRAMENTO BEE

Sacramento, Cal., September 11, 1978

"Subject to the exceptions set forth in Section 25933, smoking is unlawful in any enclosed public place, in any enclosed place of employment, in any enclosed educational facility, in any enclosed health facility, and in any enclosed clinic. No person shall smoke in any area where smoking is unlawful."

On its face, Proposition 5, the "Clean Indoor Air" initiative, is as straightforward and its objectives as unobjectionable as clean air itself. It is hard to quarrel with the argument that non-smokers have more right to breathe air uncontaminated by the fumes of cigars and cigarettes than smokers' have to foul it. It is equally hard to suggest that smokers have some sort of preemptive right to their bad habits.

Yet Prop. 5 carries those self-evident principles to absurd extremes, converting a humble right into righteous intervention in every place of employment, every school and university, every store, every restaurant, every auditorium, every hotel lobby, every gallery and museum, every elevator, every taxi, and every other public place in the state of California, regardless of whether the place is owned by a private individual, a private corporation or a public agency.

We don't question the right of the owners or operators of such places to prohibit smoking or to restrict it to certain areas — indeed we welcome it — nor do we even challenge the designation of smoking and no-smoking sections on privately owned public conveyances such as buses or airplanes. In such situations, the advantages to the non-smoker far outweigh the inconvenience to the owner and the passenger or customer who smokes.

But in a law as sweeping as this, every factory or office will be subject to state regulation as to smoking areas and non-smoking areas, and every employee will be told where he or she is allowed to sneak a drag. As a consequence, almost every shop and office will be full of twitchy people wondering how long it will be before they can run outside to light up and every employer becomes an arbitrator between the smoking and anti-smoking factions in the office. We can imagine, moreover, a whole state of people debating the uncertain applications of a law that permits smoking at rock concerts but not at performances of pop music, suspiciously eyeing their fellow workers or spectators for evidence of the palmed cigarette, and interpreting their social status, character and general virtue according to whether or not they frequent the area segregated for those who can't break the habit.

What's perhaps most misguided in the Clean Indoor Air Act, however, is the assumption that every moral right can be converted into a legal right, and that every legal right deserves uncompromising state enforcement, regardless of its relative importance. As such it is another expression of an illiberal spirit which, despite all the sanctimonious pieties advanced in its defense, ends, on balance, as a drawback to social health. We believe that smoking is dangerous to those who indulge in it and, at the very least, annoying for those who have to live in other people's smoke. But we are not yet ready to proclaim every person who smokes an enemy of the state.

Public Smoking Bans: Supreme Court, Denver Reject

Rocky Mountain News

Denver, Colo., June 15, 1979

Whether it is a command or a request, "Will you please put that cigarette out" is a phrase woven into the fabric of our times. This week, members of the Denver City Council said no, they wouldn't. We think they made a mistake.

By a 7-to-4 vote, the council defeated a measure which would have banned smoking at McNichols Sports Arena. The arena already has a rule that bans smoking in arena seats but permits it in the lobby-corridor. The no-smoking measure would have given the force of a city ordinance to the rule.

A spokeswoman for the Tobacco Institute (which is forever trying to make us forget that cigarettes kill people) called the measure a "nuisance law." Well, smokers can enjoy their habit in many places besides the seats of the arena. But, in closed public places, it's non-smokers who are subjected to a nuisance when they have to breath the blue clouds from someone else's cigarette.

THE ARIZONA REPUBLIC

Phoenix, Ariz., January 9, 1979

NON-SMOKERS and their allies lost an important round in the U.S. Supreme Court yesterday, one that could affect future regulations to ban smoking in public places.

The high court ruled that non-smokers have no constitutional guarantee to be free from the annoyance and alleged health threats of inhaling tobacco smoke.

The issue involved an appeal from Louisiana , where non-smoking crusaders attempted to have smoking banned from New Orleans' Superdome. But a lower court denied the demand for a smoking ban.

The ruling removes one of the strongest arguments of non-smokers. They contend they have a constitutional right to be free from another person's smoking habits.

One of the first victims of the court's decision could be the Civil Aeronautics Board's announced proposal to consider banning smoking aboard scheduled airliners.

Under current CAB rules, segregated seating must be provided for non-smokers as well as smokers. But a total ban, which the CAB board says it does not necessarily support now, would open the door to sweeping bans on the use of smoking tobacco in virtually every public facility.

Obviously, yesterday's court ruling takes a lot of steam out of that movement.

We still believe that common sense is the best rule for mediating the dispute between smokers and non-smokers. Movie theaters and restaurants pioneered the practice of providing separate and equal facilities for smoking and non-smoking customers— without being compelled by laws.

Without saying it, the Supreme Court indicated its own support for that approach by refusing to put one person's rights above another's

DESERET NEWS

Salt Lake City, Utah, October 12, 1979

Most non-smokers would rather suffer in silence in a smoke-filled room than "raise a fuss" with the smokers. Still, the threat to the nonsmoker's health and well-being could be worse than the smoker's own risk, according to a just-published study.

The study, made by the World Health Organization, shows that "sidestream" smoke from the burning end of a cigarette contains more of tobacco's combustion products than does the "mainstream" smoke inhaled by the smoker.

Specifically, sidestream smoke contains five times more carbon monoxide, three times more tar and nicotine, four times more benzol and 45 times more ammonia.

This means that the non-smoker who breathes the sidestream smoke is getting as big a dose of poisons as the smoker gets.

When there is heavy smoking in small, badly-ventilated spaces such as cars, offices, bars or even homes, carbon monoxide concentrations can reach levels that would not be permitted in, say, an industrial plant. EPA or OSHA would shut it down.

The study shows that high carbon monoxide levels combined with fatigue, alcohol or altitude can cause a reduction in perception and reaction time.

Sufferers from asthma, bronchitis and other respiratory diseases need no expert to tell them their conditions are aggravated by smoke-filled atmospheres. Others who don't have these ailments still notice irritation of the nose, eyes and throat when forced to breathe other people's smoke.

With this kind of information to back them up, non-smokers should be more determined than ever to insist on their right to breathe clean air.

Voters in Miami's Dade County Reject Public Smoking Ban

THE ARIZONA REPUBLIC

Phoenix, Ariz., May 11, 1979

HEADLINE writers around the country undoubtedly are having a field day with that anti-smoking election in Dade County (Miami), Fla., the other day.

"Hopes Turn To Ashes," one headline might read. Or, "Anti-Smoke Crusaders Butt Heads With Tobacco Lobby."

But as punful as the reporting might be, the referendum on whether public gathering places should be segregated to provide equal accommodations for smokers and non-smokers is no laughing matter.

Although only a paltry 27 percent of Dade County's 700,000 registered voters turned out, pro-smoking forces won by only a razor thin margin of 835 votes out of some 192,000 cast.

Thus, victory was by less than 1 percent of the total vote.

This is a signal few public officials can ignore, nor miss its message—anti-smokers are growing in prestige and power, and are demanding more and more rights for themselves, or less for smokers.

More and more local elections are being held to assert those rights. The most celebrated, and costliest, election—in California—ended in defeat for the anti-smokers. In Wisconsin, the antis won.

The economic impact of separate-but-equal treatment for smokers and non-smokers would be substantial for businessmen catering to both classes. It would mean dual facilities in virtually any establishment covered by such a law.

Arizona is a hotbed of anti-smoking sentiment. The state has enacted limited legislation prohibiting smoking in certain public areas. But the Legislature has turned down attempts to erect more rigid barriers in other public and private gathering places.

It would not be surprising to see the anti-smoking movement try its luck at a public vote on the question of segregated facilities in Arizona.

The State

Columbia, S.C., May 17, 1979

A PROPOSAL to restrict smoking in some public areas of Florida's Dade County (Miami) was defeated by a razor-thin margin in a May 8 referendum, but the defeat may actually turn out to be a victory for non-smoking Floridians.

At issue was an ordinance which would have required restaurants and certain other establishments to provide separate areas for smokers and non-smokers. The fact that 95,692 voters supported the proposition (against 96,512 opposed) should carry considerable weight with proprietors concerned with pleasing their patrons.

Our guess is that more and more establishments will voluntarily begin providing separate accommodations for smokers and non-smokers. Furthermore, smokers may themselves realize the magnitude of the resistance and resentment engendered by the public exercise of their habit and become more considerate of their non-smoking colleagues.

The Miami Herald

Miami, Fla., May 10, 1979

THE U.S. Surgeon General's new report on smoking incriminates cigarets far more persuasively than did the first such report in 1964. Its 1,200 pages of research findings reinforce a conclusion already reached by everyone except the tobacco industry:

Smoking kills. Smoking cripples. Smoking harms unborn babies. Smoking costs this nation thousands of lives and billions of dollars in medical bills and lost productivity. Smoking is unsurpassed as a *preventable* contributor to heart disease, arterial disease, lung cancer, emphysema, bronchial disease, and on and on and on.

And yet smoking, like alcoholism and obesity and other vices detrimental to public health, is not something the Government can outlaw. Nor should it; this is still a free country, and that freedom includes the freedom to be a fool in one's choices of private vices.

But there are appropriate measures that governments, Federal and local, can and should take to control smoking. By coincidence, the Surgeon General's report comes as Dade County prepares to hold a special election on an anti-smoking ordinance originated as initiative petitions by GASP, the Group Against Smokers Pollution.

Unfortunately, GASP's proposed ordinance tries to achieve a laudable purpose — protecting nonsmokers' rights to clean air — by intruding government into areas where government has no place. In the name of nonsmokers'

rights, GASP would imperil other, equally valid rights.

GASP's proposal would ban smoking in any enclosed public place or educational or health facility. That is proper, *if* "public place" is defined as a government building. If Dade's voters reject GASP's ordinance, then the Metro Commission itself should ban smoking in governmental, educational, and health facilities.

But in its anti-smoking zeal, GASP would trample on the private rights of businesses to cater to whom they please. It would require restaurants and cafeterias to set aside half their seating space for nonsmokers. That is arbitrary and unjustified.

Granted, private businesses operating as public facilities must accept constraints that somewhat limit pure property rights. But the law cannot force a vegeterian restaurant to serve meat, or a restaurant that requires men to wear coats to admit men in shirtsleeves. To *encourage* restaurants to segregate smokers and nonsmokers is fine. And because most diners don't smoke, market forces alone should make such encouragement succeed. But to *require* segregated seating is to interfere unjustly with the restaurateur's right to attract whatever clientele he wishes.

Moreover, GASP's ordinance stops just short of outright discrimination in other respects. If a concert and a boxing match were held in the same auditorium on the same day, it would ban smoking at the concert but permit it during the

boxing match. It would prohibit individuals from smoking in their own private offices if those offices were used to "meet with members of the public."

In short, the GASP ordinance is extreme, quite possibly unconstitutional in part, and inappropriate as public policy.

IT is too bad that the $400,000 Dade County will spend on the GASP-inspired special election could not be spent educating the public about the findings of the Surgeon General's report. For education is the best hope for stopping smoking among teenagers, among pregnant women, among all citizens who might not start smoking, or who might stop, if the dangers were driven home effectively enough.

The Federal Government ought to use the Surgeon General's findings to make cigarets too costly for Americans to afford. It should end its subsidy of tobacco-growing. It should slap an additional tax of, say, at least $2 on every carton of cigarets, and 25 cents on each pack sold individually, and earmark the receipts for anti-smoking education. It should impose an additional, graduated tax based on tar and nicotine content: the higher these carcinogens, the greater the tax.

The Government has no right to forbid smoking. But it also has the right to make smoking forbiddingly expensive.

Miami, Fla., January 12, 1979

THE GROUP Against Smokers Pollution has made its point. The group's proposed ordinance to restrict public smoking had serious flaws. GASP lacked organization and funds. And it had to counter a sophisticated $1 million ad campaign financed by tobacco interests. Nevertheless, Dade voters came within one percentage point of adopting the GASP proposal.

That is more than a moral victory for one small anti-smoking group. It's a clear mandate for action by both the Metro Dade County Commission and private businesses.

The commissioners sidestepped their responsibility when they blithely passed a bad proposal along to the voters. Now it's time for the commission seriously to address the question of what reasonably can be done to protect the nonsmoker's right to breathe clean air without violating the rights of smokers and businesses.

As a first step, the commission should appoint a committee to examine the question and propose a series of recommendations. No doubt some of those proposals would be for purely voluntary public-education programs, while others

would be mandatory.

Such a committee should include, but not be limited to, representatives from both sides of the referendum battle just past. It will need expertise in a wide variety of fields, including the restaurant business, ventilation systems, and employment practices, among others.

Further, the issue of smokers' pollution should be broken down into separate areas so as to generate a variety of proposed solutions that are appropriate to the respective sectors. For example, a distinction should be made between rules for publicly owned facilities and private property. Work sites also should be considered a separate category.

Cigaret smoking undeniably is a major health hazard. Its dangers are so well documented they no longer need enumerating. Government at every level has a right and a responsibility to discourage the practice in its own house, which includes publicly owned facilities and official meetings and hearings wherever they are held.

A privately owned restaurant, however, is not a "public place" in the same

sense that the courthouse lobby is. There is more leeway and less justification for coercion where attendance is purely voluntary.

In many instances, simple improvements to the ventilation system can make a room usable by smokers and nonsmokers alike. Perhaps the building code or health regulations could address that question for areas where smoking is to be permitted. Very likely there are many potentially helpful techniques that have been obscured by the commotion of the referendum campaign.

All those possibilities now should be explored thoroughly in a good-faith effort to develop rational, fair solutions. No pressure group now should seek a rerun of the election in hope of achieving a total victory that would infringe arbitrarily on others.

Dade County doesn't need another expensive, divisive referendum. It needs sensible solutions, and the referendum's results are the Metro Commission's mandate to provide them.

More Smoking Bans: New York, Maine, Connecticut

Newsday

Long Island, N.Y., May 14, 1979

Many a New York State restaurant is noted for its distinctive atmosphere, but there's nothing distinctive about carbon monoxide, phenol compounds, 3,4-benz-pyrene, nicotine and other toxic constituents of cigarette smoke.

These atmospheric additives will be less of a hazard for restaurant patrons, and many other New Yorkers, if the State Senate passes a bill that recently emerged from the Assembly. The bill generally bars smoking in a number of public places—restaurants, museums, hospitals, theaters, schools and stores—although special smoking areas could be set aside in all of them.

Before the measure passed, Assemblyman George Miller (D-Manhattan) objected that it was "an imposition on my rights as a citizen." That complaint becomes less and less convincing. For one thing, designated smoking sections are provided for in the bill. Beyond that, most people don't claim a "right" to smoke. As the chief sponsor, Assemblyman Alexander Grannis (D-Manhattan) points out, smokers are now a minority. In a Newsday Long Island Poll last February, 36 per cent of the respondents said they smoked cigarettes but 64 per cent said they didn't.

Those figures invite careful attention from leaders and members of the Senate, where there's evidently some skepticism about the bill. The objections apparently reflect the misgivings of businessmen who anticipate inconvenience, expense and damaging effects on patronage.

But voluntary smoking bans are already common in New York—in shops, public buildings and professional offices. And it's rarely wise for businessmen or politicians to overlook what customers or constituents obviously want. The bill deserves early, favorable action by the Senate, even if it has to make its way through a smoke-filled committee room.

The Knickerbocker News

Albany, N.Y., May 2, 1979

Passing a law to regulate smoking in public places is something like trying to legislate a polite "thank you" — courtesy is courtesy and the law is the law and the twain don't meet with very much effectiveness.

There is a proposal for just such a law wafting about the Legislature. The measure would amend the public health law to prohibit smoking in public places and at public meetings except in designated smoking areas.

We certainly agree with the law in philosophy. Everyone, smoker and non-smoker alike, has the right to breathe clean air, free of second-hand smoke and leftover carcinogens. Few of us like to sit next to a smoker in poorly ventilated restaurants or at public meetings where smoke hangs over the hall like a cloud of smelly steam.

One thing we doubt is whether the state can effectively enforce such a law. Who stands over the smoker with a bucket of water and a citation? The restaurant owner? The non-smoker who doesn't want watery eyes and an acrid smell with his dinner? The police?

Another thing we're not sure of is the wisdom of legislating courtesy. It's a free country, and anyone who decides he or she will smoke, in spite of the risk of cancer and all of the other negative aspects of the habit, is entitled to puff away. Most smokers realize their habit is potentially offensive and act accordingly. It is the few who disregard the rights of others the bill is aimed at, something akin to killing a fly with a baseball bat.

Most modern restaurants and some public meeting areas are well ventilated. It would seem more logical to require places where the public gathers to either meet ventilation standards or then and only then provide a separate, clean area for non-smokers desiring one. Or, if a meeting room can't meet the standards, bar smoking in the room completely and allow "smoking breaks."

One particularly bad feature of the proposed bill being considered by the Legislature is the wide-open prohibition of smoking in "the workplace." Smoking would be prohibited "in any place of work or any indoor area open to the public except in designated smoking areas." Most smokers and non-smokers have already come to an acceptable compromise already. If there is a ventilation problem, we see no reason why a calm request by either the smoker or the non-smoker to move a desk, open a window or some such action short of state legislation shouldn't work.

Every non-smoker has the right to breathe air free of another's smoke. Every smoker has the right to pursue his or her habit in peace, short of causing discomfort to others.

Is legislation really the answer?

BUFFALO EVENING NEWS

Buffalo, N.Y., May 12, 1979

By its 80-59 vote for a statewide ban on smoking in most public places, the state Assembly reflected a growing concern for the rights of nonsmokers to breathe air free of another's smoke.

While we fully share this concern, it is something else to write into law regulations that are fair and reasonably enforceable. In this regard, the bill now awaiting an uncertain Senate action serves a desirable objective, but with too many ambiguities and questionable effects to deserve enactment in its present form.

Under the so-called "Clean Indoor Air Act," smoking would be prohibited in all public places except in designated areas. This includes all sizable restaurants, retail stores, public transportation, schools and colleges, hospitals, auditoriums, theaters, arenas and meeting rooms.

The emphasis in the present state health code, making it permissible to light up except where explicitly prohibited, is reversed to prohibit all smoking in establishments having no designated smoking areas. This means that proprietors of affected restaurants must post signs specifying that they accommodate smokers.

What seems to us unsettling about this statutory handiwork is the practical effect of such over-broad restrictions as those lumping some ill-defined private places of work with public places. Some opponents in the closely-split Western New York Assembly delegation question the bill more broadly as to the wisdom of trying to substitute legal compulsion for the voluntary exercise of smoker courtesy. They cite the voluntary efforts by many restaurants and other public places to set aside designated smoking areas or to install ventilation for the protection of non-smokers.

In our view, there is something to be said for using the force of law wherever this can be effective in reinforcing individual restraint against discourtesy or discomfort to others. Thus Erie County's less all-encompassing 1975 ban on smoking in public places, while leading to no arrests and all too often ignored in elevators and other places, has nevertheless had deterrent value in buttressing restrictions in stores and theaters.

Any law that is too immoderate in its reach or that leaves too much to court interpretation, however, risks either becoming a dead-letter law or inviting an offensively capricious type of enforcement.

The hazards of smoking well merit official discouragement in every reasonable way, as in the separate smoking areas required in airline cabins. But this is an area in which government compulsion should be approached with caution and all due regard for fair and feasible enforcement.

EVENING EXPRESS

Portland, Me., June 4, 1979

Harry Truman laid down the political principle years ago:

"If you can't stand the heat, stay out of the kitchen."

The Maine Legislature has its own version of that precept:

"If you can't stand the smoke, stay out of the Senate."

By the narrowest of margins, one vote, the Senate repealed the smoking ban it had imposed only seven weeks earlier. The majority didn't even dignify their action by candor or any expression of consideration for those made uncomfortable by smoke.

Instead, in a manner reminiscent of a small boy groping for an alibi when caught with his hand in the cookie jar, the senators said that the smoking ban was hurting their performance. (So that's what it was?)

"We can't do the job our constituents sent us down here to do," said Sen. Dana Devoe, R-Orono.

That condition had been commented upon by some sources but no one had linked it with nicotine withdrawal symptoms before.

When Sen. Nancy Clark, D-Cumberland, noted that the smoke hurt her eyes, Sen. Ralph Lovell, R-Sanford, suggested that she take off her glasses and maybe it would not hurt her eyes. The Sanford senator thus delivered the coup de grace to whatever vestige of gallantry might have remained in the Senate.

The remark was gratuitously callous in that it suggests complete indifference for what is a very real physical discomfort for many persons caught up in the swirling smoke created by others.

But the senators might have salvaged more respect had they simply said they wanted to smoke and since they were in the majority they intended to smoke.

We doubt that the repeal of the smoking ban will have any benefit for constituents. Sen. Devoe said he had been walking the halls in search of a place to smoke.

Now his nonsmoking colleagues may be walking the halls in search of a breath of fresh air.

The Hartford Courant

Hartford, Conn., October 1, 1979

Smokers will have more reason to smolder, and fewer opportunities to light up in Connecticut, beginning today.

Under a new law, passed earlier this year by the General Assembly and effective today, the number of no-smoking areas are now increased.

Under previous law, smoking is prohibited in any state or municipal building in which a meeting or school or college class is in progress. The new law extends that no-smoking ban to waiting or reception rooms open to the public in those buildings.

Public areas of retail food stores now also are no smoking areas and smoking is prohibited in any public area of a restaurant with seating capacity for 75 or more people, although some of that restaurant space can be reserved for smokers.

Smoking already has been prohibited in health-care institutions, except in designated smoking areas. The new law specifically bans smoking in any diagnostic or treatment rooms and in any health-care waiting area.

The penalty for each violation of the no-smoking area restrictions, and for failing to post signs or for removing them is $5.

It isn't the $5 fine that makes law-breaking difficult. The pressure comes from glares and disapproving remarks from non-smokers. If that doesn't put out the fire, then the non-smokers can put heat on the management of the public facility. The cigarette or cigar usually goes, before the smoker is ordered out.

In addition to the state laws, there are other local and federal regulations, restricting or prohibiting smoking in certain areas of transit vehicles — including aircraft, trains and buses — and in parks and recreation facilities.

It's almost enough to make a smoker want to quit.

Canada Experiments with Public Smoking Bans

The Toronto Star

Toronto, Ont., Canada, April 27, 1979

"Mommy, why is the policeman bothering that man?"

"He's smoking a cigarette dear."

"But, mommy, you smoke cigarettes."

"I know, dear, but this is a public place."

"But mommy, you smoke cigarettes in the street. Isn't that public?"

"Hush, dear, I'll explain it all when we get home."

"Mommy, that policeman sure looks silly. Why isn't he out catching crooks?"

"He's just doing his duty, dear."

"Is it all right if I laugh, mommy? If I don't do it too loud?"

The real danger is the city of Toronto's attempt to pass a new anti-smoking bylaw is that it will make policemen look ridiculous. That's a price too high for any city to pay, even for the benefit of getting rid of slightly used tobacco smoke in stores and offices.

Toronto passed its first no-smoking bylaw in 1977. But the Ontario Supreme Court has declared the bylaw invalid because storekeepers had to enforce it. So the city executive committee has decided to try for a new bylaw that will do pretty much what the old, invalid one tried to do.

The city's lawyers are still trying to figure out how to accomplish this neat trick, but one thing is already clear to them: The police will have to go after smokers. The poor cop on the street will either have to ignore the bylaw or spend a lot of his time hassling smokers and being the butt of smart alec jokes.

Metro's police force already has enough troubles. The police won't be able to hire any new constables this year and won't even be able to bring 42 cadets on to the force.

Toronto City Council should return to exhorting people to quit smoking in public places and give up trying to pass unenforceable bylaws. As it is, the Toronto politicians are making ashes of themselves.

The Montreal Star

Montreal, Que., Canada, August 9, 1979

THE SMOKING BAN war seems to be coming to Quebec. It has travelled around the continent. Two years ago Toronto instituted an anti-smoking bylaw which sat smoldering on the books until a drug store chain challenged the law on constitutional grounds. In April the Ontario Supreme Court quashed the bylaw because it required store owners to enforce it, and the court felt that it was not valid to place such policing authority on the shoulders of the proprietor.

However, it was by no means a coincidence that the drug store chain happens to be owned by the same company which owns Imperial Tobacco. Of all the various anti-smoking devices, the cigarette manufacturers seem to fight the ban with the most vigor. The public ban effectively reduces the number of cigarettes smoked because it makes the act of lighting up more self-conscious, and as any behavioral psychologist will aver, the more one is aware of performing a bad habit the less likely one is to continue.

With every new battle, the smoking ban war becomes more sophisticated. It seems likely that the bill to be presented by Environment Minister Marcel Léger will avoid Toronto's pitfall and leave policing authority in the hands of the police. Nevertheless any ban will be difficult to enforce, and one hates to add an unenforcable law to the books.

The challenge to government is to find a way of making the law useful and meaningful, and to stick to the issue of non-smokers' rights. Second-hand smoke has been clearly enough established as a health hazard to warrant protective legal measures on its own behalf. And there is no justification for using a law simply as a stick to change unhealthy habits.

The London Free Press

London, Ont., Canada, April 25, 1979

The social stigma increasingly attached to smoking and smokers can itself be more powerful than any anti-smoking bylaw passed by a municipality.

That's good. Because restrictive no-smoking bylaws like Toronto's show how government can sometimes be too overbearing. Still, it took two years for someone to challenge the Toronto bylaw before the Ontario Supreme Court.

Top Drug Mart Ltd., owned by a company which also owns Imperial Tobacco Ltd., won its case before a three-member panel of judges which ruled the Toronto no-smoking bylaw invalid, largely because the city went beyond its authority when it turned store owners into policemen to enforce the regulations. The judges also indicated that Toronto probably has the power to restrict smoking (which other municipalities will find reassuring), but the law is vaguely worded.

For two years, the bylaw banned smoking in most stores and places of public assembly and required proprietors to post no-smoking signs. To enforce the bylaw, they were required to refuse service and, if necessary, evict offenders from the premises. Smokers or store owners could be fined up to $1,000.

In some public buildings — city halls, hospitals and courts — a ban on smoking seems appropriate. But in the case of other premises frequented by the public — banks, shops and restaurants — no-smoking regulations should be left to the discretion of proprietors. A local bylaw governing every kind of building defined as a public place is going too far to be practical.

Many restaurants, for example, realize the business advantages to be gained from providing special no-smoking sections. Airlines and railways have also recognized the need to provide sections for both smokers and non-smokers.

But carrying such regulations into a variety or drug store is a little extreme. Perhaps the only surprise is that it took so long for Toronto's bylaw to be challenged. Last year, a hospital and jewelry store were each fined $400 for failing to post no-smoking signs.

The judges said they could imagine the difficulties of a "small, feminine" proprietor of a convenience store attempting to enforce a no-smoking bylaw. In a sense, the onus contained in the bylaw resembles that placed on proprietors of licensed premises to enforce drinking regulations, though drinking establishments are, of course, a specifically controlled business.

There is growing concern over the discomfort and health hazard created by second-hand smoke. But it is a concern best handled through continuing education on the bad effects of smoking and the social pressure placed on the smoker. Both have more clout than a bylaw.

Scientific Study Confirms Danger of Smoke to Non-Smokers

SYRACUSE
HERALD-JOURNAL
Syracuse, N.Y., April 3, 1980

It's official: Smokers not only are rushing a date with the grim reaper, they also are sealing death warrants for those around them.

It's not unusual for a child whose parents smoke at home to develop a "smoker's cough" to rival that of his father or mother.

More recently, a 10-year study conducted by researchers at the University of California at San Diego has established what non-smokers have contended for years, that constant exposure to cigarette smoke — by non-smokers — is a health hazard.

After studying the smoking habits of 2,100 persons for a decade, the researchers concluded "there was no significant difference in the (lung damage) scores of the passive (non-smokers), the smokers who did not inhale and the light smokers."

"Non-smokers who work in a smoky environment have about the same risk of (lung) impairment as do smokers who inhale between one and 10 cigarettes a day."

So please, Mr. Smoker, if a non-smoker — or an ex-smoker — asks you to butt out, do him or her a favor and douse it or leave.

You'll both live longer.

BUFFALO EVENING NEWS

Buffalo, N.Y., April 10, 1980

New scientific evidence indicates that non-smokers can suffer lung damage through breathing other people's smoke. A report in the New England Journal of Medicine revealed that non-smokers who worked in a roomful of smokers suffered scarring and permanent damage to bronchial passages in the lungs. The damage was about the same as that of a moderate smoker — one who smokes 11 cigarettes a day.

The results are not actually surprising, since it is only common sense that polluted air is not good for you. The lung damage done by the smoke could impair lung function and lead to dangerous lung diseases, such as emphysema.

These new findings support the welcome trend toward providing non-smoking areas in restaurants, airliners and other public places. Non-smokers' complaints take on added weight now that tobacco smoke has been shown to be a potential threat to their health.

THE SACRAMENTO BEE

Sacramento, Cal., April 4, 1980

A new report from a team of researchers in San Diego adds urgency to the demand for the regulation or prohibition of smoking in public places. The report, published recently in the New England Journal of Medicine, concludes that "chronic exposure to tobacco smoke in the work environment is deleterious to the non-smoker and significantly reduces small-airways (lung) function."

The results are significant because, as the Journal points out editorially, "until now the case aginst smoking in the general environment has often been anecdotal, based on annoyances, feelings, and sometimes more objective physical reactions such as eye and nose irritation . . . But now, for the first time, we have a quantitative measurement of a physical change (in non-smokers) — a fact that may tip the scales in favor of the non-smokers."

In the general election of 1978, Californians voted against Proposition 5, the so-called Indoor Air Initiative, a measure that would not only have banned or segregated smoking in public places, but also would have applied to private places of work. As such, it would have imposed extremely cumbersome requirements in rearranging shops and offices, was therefore likely to generate as many problems as it solved, and thus, in our opinion, was taking a good idea beyond the bounds of reason.

Obviously, however, the need for a measure to protect non-smokers survived the defeat of the California initiative, a need now reinforced by the conclusions published in the Journal. It has been our hope ever since Proposition 5 was defeated that the Legislature would pass a bill restricting smoking in public buildings and places of public assembly, indeed any place where smokers can be segregated or smoking banned with relative ease. Similarly, it's our hope that private employers and owners of private establishments will, wherever possible, make similar provisions for their workers.

The most compelling argument for Proposition 5 was the right of the non-smoker to clean air — a right that clearly superseded the right of the smoker to maintain his or her habit. There was little clear evidence, however, that otherwise healthy individuals were injured by breathing other people's second-hand tobacco smoke. The report from San Diego indicates that the evidence is now beginning to come in. The case for legislation thus becomes more urgent.

The Kansas City Times

Kansas City, Mo., March 31, 1980

"Don't invade my space by blowing your dirty smoke into it" was once the most rational demand anti-tobaccoists could make of their puffing fellow travelers. Now they can legitimately press the case further and plead, "Don't pollute my lungs with your fallout."

That will be one result of a new study of 21,000 persons showing that non-smokers are affected by fumes from their neighbors' smoking materials. Researchers in a 10-year probe conducted by the University of California at San Diego found that breathing other people's smoke damages the tiny air tubes and sacs in non-smokers' lungs. About the same amount of small airways impairment turned up among non-smokers who worked with smokers as with people who smoke without inhaling or inhale less than 11 cigarettes a day, according to the study. Small airways disease often precedes more dangerous lung diseases such as emphysema.

In typical fashion, the Tobacco Institute denigrates the study evidence as unconvincing, sparse, incomplete. Therefore, people just shouldn't take it seriously. On the other hand, physicians and heads of national health organizations predict it will give non-smokers the scientific arguments they need to demand smoke-free space on the job, in recreational facilities and other public places.

The report should also provoke some examinations of conscience by individual smokers. Does freedom give the right to injure others, even unintentionally? It's one matter to decide to risk one's own health by indulging in the nicotine habit but it is quite another, more sobering decision to damage the lungs of other people.

The Miami Herald

Miami, Fla., March 31, 1980

CIGARET smoke really does damage the lungs of nonsmokers who work in a smoky environment. After years of claims and counterclaims on the subject, there now is hard scientific evidence to support the long-suspected fact that nonsmokers suffer measurable physical damage when subjected to cigaret smoke in closed places.

The 10-year study of 2,100 smokers and nonsmokers is reported in the current issue of *The New England Journal of Medicine*. It has major implications for public-policy makers.

The right of the nonsmoker to clean indoor air now takes on a much stronger claim to protection by law. So long as the dispute was essentially one of conflicting nuisances — the nonsmoker's annoyance versus the tobacco addict's deprivation — public officials understandably tended to duck the whole matter as much as possible. The new evidence, however, tilts the equation far in favor of the nonsmoker.

No reasonable person can claim that his personal addiction to cigarets gives him the right to endanger the health of his nonsmoking co-workers. And an individual who objects to inhaling second-hand smoke no longer must accept the stigma of being a troublemaker or a bluenose. There now is medical evidence to support the objection.

That evidence is almost certain to spawn a new generation of efforts to put legal restrictions on smoking in public accommodations and in places of employment. Employers and proprietors of restaurants shouldn't waste energy in futile resistance to that movement. Instead, they should lead the way to reasonable and cost-effective procedures to protect their nonsmoking employes and customers.

Those measures might include more-efficient ventilation systems as an alternative to segregation, or other steps appropriate to the type of facility and the extent to which it's a public area. Persons who want to maintain their right to smoke are going to have to help find ways to prevent their neighbors from being damaged by the habit. It's as simple as that.

Reno Evening Gazette

Reno, Nev., April 2, 1980

Arguments already have begun over a scientific study which indicates that non-smokers suffer lung damage from just being in the presence of persons who smoke.

The Tobacco Institute (i.e., the smoking industry) questions the validity of the study because it was done in part by physiologist James R. White, who admittedly has an axe to grind. Dr. White, the institute notes, said five years ago that smoking parents should be kept 50 yards from Little Leaguers when they play. Dr. White also headed an unsuccessful attempt two years ago to restrict smoking in California's public buildings.

So White is not what you would call a fan of the tobacco industry. Also, his study is the only one so far to present evidence showing actual injury to non-smokers. This being the case, White's results need to be verified and expanded through other studies, perhaps by more impartial researchers, to gain widespread acceptance.

Nevertheless, the White study was conducted scientifically, as far as we know. It was performed at a reputable institute — the University of California at San Diego. And the number of test subjects — 2,100 middle-aged men and women — was large enough to be significant.

So the study cannot be summarily dismissed, as the Tobacco Institute apparently would wish. It is true that its results do not show that non-smokers will get lung cancer or emphysema from working in offices filled with other people's smoke. But they do show significant harm to air tubes and sacs — in fact, harm to at least 10 percent of the total tubes and sacs. The damage is comparable to that received by a person who smokes heavily without inhaling, or to one who inhales but smokes less than 11 cigarettes per day.

The study affirms the wisdom of the Nevada Legislature when it passed a law outlawing smoking in public buildings and in such places as physicians' offices. And it should give support to concerned persons in other states, such as California, who want to pass similar laws.

The White study also may give non-smokers a little more ammunition to help them when they demand that smokers pursue their habit in their own privacy. This is important, because many non-smokers are too timid to insist that smokers obey the state law and refrain from lighting up in public places. The new evidence may also encourage private business to do more to decrease smoking in offices.

The White study is not the last scientific word on smoking, obviously. But it is an important step in the process of making our interior air more healthy and breathable.

Newsday

Long Island, N.Y., April 6, 1980

A new medical study showing the effects of smoking on nonsmokers is one more good reason for early State Senate approval of a pending public health bill.

The research report, published in the New England Journal of Medicine, concludes that "chronic exposure to tobacco smoke in the work environment is deleterious to the nonsmoker." The bill has bipartisan support and has already cleared the Assembly. It requires that many employers, restaurateurs, bankers and others set aside special areas for smokers.

That would clearly be in the public interest.

Assemb. Alexander Grannis (D,L-Manhattan), co-sponsor of the legislation with Sen. Owen Johnson (R,C-West Babylon), makes an excellent point when he stresses that the bill "does not deal with *whether* people can smoke" but with *where* people can smoke."

It's hard to see how anything fairer could be designed. Smokers may be in the minority, as a Newsday study early last year indicated, but they have rights. Under this new bill, they would be assured indoor public space to use. At the same time, nonsmokers would be much better protected from the kind of lung damage identified in the New England Journal article.

There is nothing radical about the bill. It relates logically to existing state and local laws that forbid or restrict smoking in libraries, hospitals, elevators, shops and other public places.

The measure has the refreshing title of Clean Indoor Air Act. Senate passage now would be as timely as a breath of spring.

SUNDAY TELEGRAM

Worcester, Mass., March 29, 1980

Freedom is being allowed to do what you want as long as it doesn't hurt anybody else, the old saw goes. Cigarette smokers argue that it is their right to smoke, since the only lungs they are risking are their own. It's their body and it's nobody else's business.

They may have coughed slightly this week when the New England Journal of Medicine published a study from California concluding that lungs of non-smokers can be damaged by smoke from other people's cigarettes, cigars and pipes. Another report published last fall showed that children of smokers have impaired lungs, too.

The two studies will be ammunition for non-smokers who don't like other people puffing away near them. Some of the criticism has been neither constructive, considerate or polite.

Smokers, on the other hand, have ridiculed non-smokers as cranks, health nuts and killjoys. Evidence that the "killjoys" have reason to worry for their own health should make smokers rethink that notion. One can't fault those who don't smoke from wanting to be free of the dangers assumed by those who do.

If smokers can't or don't want to quit smoking despite the evidence of its harm to health, it's their right to keep puffing. They owe it to the nonsmokers with whom they share buses, cars, offices, homes and restaurants, however, to try to avoid clouding their air with smoke. It's not just consideration; it's also a matter of health.

"Mind if I smoke?" should be more than a formality tossed in as a match is being struck. "Yes, I do," if said politely, should be accepted as a reasonable reply.

The Knickerbocker News

Albany, N.Y., April 3, 1980

Many non-smokers have always contended the cigarette, cigar and pipe smoke floating freely in the atmosphere contaminates their lungs as well as the lungs of the perpetrators of the stink.

And now, there's scientific proof. It does.

We've known for quite a while that smoking harms the smoker; nevertheless, it's a voluntary habit, and everyone has the right to choose the carcinogens he will consume. But foisting the nauseating stuff off onto his neighbors, particularly now that we know it harms the neighbors' health, is another matter.

This study, published in *The New England Journal of Medicine*, will make the jobe of those who would ban smoking in public places easier. Good.

FTC Seek Stronger Warning on Cigarette Packs

The Federal Trade Commission proposed in July to strengthen anti-smoking warnings on cigarette packs. The agency cited the failure of Americans to cut down on smoking significantly, in spite of health warnings already printed on cigarette packs. The proposed new warning would read: "Cigarette smoking is a major health hazard and may result in your death." The proposal was not put into effect, but it foreshadowed increased government action to combat smoking.

DAYTON DAILY NEWS

Dayton, Ohio, July 25, 1980

Not enough people are quitting cigarettes despite the warnings that they "may be harmful to your health" so the Federal Trade Commission (FTC) is considering something like this:

"Warning: Cigarette smoking is a major health hazard and may result in your death."

The FTC can do that if it likes, but cigarette packages could soon cross the border from warning labels to metaphysical arguments. Driving a car may result in your death. Failing to exercise may result in your death. Breathing near a roadway may kill you.

Something, inevitably, will result in the death of each of our mortal bodies, and who knows which cause is prevalent and if it should have a label? The junk food gorged down by this culture could result in death: Should french fries, candy bars and carbonated soft drinks bear the death labels?

Not a bad idea, really, except that people disagree over what things sustain and what things kill. Smokers smoke without any delusion that it is as healthful as, say, alfalfa sprouts. Any "death" label will likely be dismissed as the "health hazard" labels are because most figure they will get by and somebody else will get the bad news. Either that or all the warnings make people so nervous they smoke more.

The Idaho STATESMAN

Boise, Idaho, July 25, 1980

Now comes the Federal Trade Commission reporting that half of all cigarette smokers still are not convinced smoking is dangerous to their health.

Most alarming in that statistic is not those who refuse to be convinced of the danger, but that half the smokers ARE convinced yet continue puffing away. How do we convince these people to quit? And how do we convince those who do not see the danger to both recognize it and quit, too?

We doubt the answer is to beat people over the head with guilt, as many of the antismoking ads on television do. Those are an automatic turn-off for many smokers, particularly when their children begin repeating the ads each time the parents light up.

Perhaps the answer lies in quietly but persistently posing the alternatives for the smoker. A strengthened warning on cigarette packages is one way of doing this. The present warning makes it appear the health problems with smoking are still a matter of conjecture. They are not.

The risks are personal, and real. If you smoke, you stand a much greater chance of contracting cancer of the lungs. If you smoke you stand a much greater chance of contracting emphysema. If you smoke, chances are you will forfeit X number of days of your life. Now, the choice is yours. Do you choose to trade in those days of your life for the pleasure of smoking?

Sentinel Star

Orlando, Fla., October 20, 1980

POLITICS, big money and the libertarian principle are all mixed up in the proposal that government proclaim a no-smoking day and take other positive action to discourage the use of tobacco.

Just as no Christian is more zealous than a recently converted heathen, the person who has succeeded in shaking tobacco often becomes the most outspoken advocate of its prohibition and limitation. Ex-smoker Joseph Califano, the secretary of Health, Education and Welfare, is considering a number of steps to achieve that purpose, among them: Raising cigarette taxes, giving workers time off to kick the habit, ending government supports to tobacco farmers and indemnifying them with welfare money, and obtaining a Justice Department ruling on how far government can go to control nicotine as an addictive substance. (Wisely, he drew the line at HEW sponsorship of private suits against tobacco companies.)

THERE IS no longer any question, if there ever was one, that cigarette smoking hurts one's health by inducing lung cancer, heart trouble and circulatory ailments. The proper antidote, however, is public education rather than compulsion. When a final test comes of such actions as HEW proposes, the key should continue to be strong and effective warnings of probable health damage. For quite simply it is wrong for government to make choices that should be made by individuals. The ill-fated national experiment with alcoholic prohibition should have taught us that.

Califano Announces Campaign To Curtail Cigarette Smoking

Describing cigarette smoking as "slow-motion suicide," Health, Education and Welfare Secretary Joseph A. Califano Jr. Jan. 11 announced a new government campaign to break the habit among some 53 million Americans. The HEW secretary also hoped, through a more forceful educational program, to discourage children and teenagers from taking up smoking. Califano's proposed anti-smoking package supported the Civil Aeronautics Board proposed ban on cigarette smoking in airliners. It would restrict smoking in public areas of the 10,000 government buildings run by the General Services Administration and would raise, or graduate, the federal excise tax on cigarettes, based on the tar and nicotine content of the product. Califano said a joint HEW-Treasury Department task force would investigate "whether tax policy can influence decisions about smoking."

The HEW project would also target special "high-risk groups" by revising warning labels for persons particularly endangered by smoking. Califano said the Food and Drug Administration was revising labeling requirements for birth control pills to include the warning that users who smoked ran a higher risk of "serious adverse effects on the heart and blood vessels." As part of the consumer education-public interest effort, broadcast networks would be asked to step up the frequency of anti-smoking spot announcements, which had dropped sharply since cigarette advertising was banned from radio and television in 1971. Califano also announced that for fiscal 1979 (beginning Oct. 1), the newly created Office on Smoking and Health would have a total budget of $23 million, $6 million of which would be earmarked for education. The program was announced on the anniversary of the Surgeon General's 1964 Report on Smoking and Health, the document that publicly linked smoking with lung cancer. Since then, 14 million Americans, mostly white males, had given up smoking. But enough teenagers, women and minorities had taken up the habit to keep the number of smokers relatively constant.

Newsday

Garden City, N.Y., January 13, 1978

President Carter was asked a rather frivolous question about a serious subject at yesterday's press conference. Noting that Health, Education and Welfare Secretary Joseph Califano had just put forth a $23 million program to get Americans to stop smoking, a reporter wondered whether Carter would ask his aides to set a national example by giving up tobacco. "No, sir," Carter replied with a smile.

The President knows, as do Califano and millions of other Americans, that smoking is bad for you. He also knows that starting and quitting are personal decisions. It's certainly a good idea to make it more expensive or more difficult to smoke, as Califano's rather modest plan would. But prohibition would only create an enormous and enormously profitable bootlegging industry.

The key question that wasn't asked is why a government that wants to spend $23 million getting people to kick the habit also intends to go on spending some $60 million a year to subsidize the growing of tobacco. Another $36 million or so goes to promote and ship tobacco overseas as part of the Food for Peace program. Attempts to stop both failed in Congress last year in the face of strong lobbying by the tobacco industry and resistance by congressmen from tobacco-growing states. Support from the administration would have been most welcome at this point.

That was not to be, however. White House Press Secretary Jody Powell explained why: "The administration does not feel there is any logic in asking thousands of families and communities to bear the burden of economic ruin which would result if we abolished this part of the farm program because of the habits of an entire nation."

Powell is missing the point. The farmers themselves are not to blame, of course, but the money that now encourages them to produce tobacco would be far better spent as an incentive to plant different crops or even not to plant at all.

Apart from this glaring omission, we wish Califano every success in his venture, not so much for his sake—he's already a reformed smoker—but for the sake of the millions of Americans who are hastening their own deaths by continuing to puff away.

San Jose Mercury

San Jose, Calif., January 13, 1978

Health, Education and Welfare Secretary Joseph Califano made a sizable publicity splash this week when he unveiled a $23 million program to combat smoking in Fiscal 1979.

The goal is laudable enough; 14 years after the initial Surgeon General's report linking smoking to cancer and other diseases, few will question Califano's observation that smoking is "slow-motion suicide."

Nonetheless, it is impossible to believe that the Carter administration is now dedicated singlemindedly to the eradication of the evils of tobacco. The HEW secretary's $23 million program pales in comparison with the $285.1 million in loans and price supports the federal government channeled to tobacco farmers, processors and distributors in Fiscal 1977.

The government needs to cure its schizophrenia in this regard. How can rational men justify such cross-purpose spending?

What is the sense in asking the Civil Aeronautics Board to ban smoking on commercial airliners or requesting the Federal Trade Commission to beef up its label-warning program while, at the same time, the government pays farmers to keep on growing tobacco?

The president should propose an orderly phase-out of the tobacco support program in order to smooth the economic readjustment of the 600,000 families involved it producing and processing this crop.

Smoking is costly, in ruined lives, in inflated medical bills and in ever-rising health insurance premiums. Why should the taxpayers be asked to underwrite the cost of producing the agent of this particular brand of "slow-motion suicide"?

Smoke gets in your eyes

OKLAHOMA CITY TIMES

Oklahoma City, Okla., January 12, 1978

JOE CALIFANO'S new anti-smoking campaign, though well-intended and probably necessary, raises old questions about government inconsistency and the effectiveness of such efforts.

Califano, secretary of health, education and welfare, would spend $23 million of the taxpayers' money in 1979 to help the nation's 54 million smokers kick the habit.

At the same time, the U.S. Department of Agriculture will dispense millions in price supports to encourage tobacco growing. Thus, the USDA seems more concerned about economic health than physical health. But many states, including Oklahoma, which tax cigarettes have to be wary about anti-smoking talk.

The prospective success of Califano's campaign is hard to predict. The U.S. Public Health Service has figures showing the proportion of American adults who smoke cigarettes has decreased in recent years. Yet the American Cancer Society is concerned about increases in smoking among teen-age girls and young women.

Estimates given in connection with Califano's announcement indicate the number of adult smokers (13 or older) has fallen from 42 per cent in 1964 to 34 per cent today. Among men it has dropped from 52 per cent to 39 per cent and among women, from 32 to 29 per cent.

The comparison covers the period since publication of the surgeon-general's report in 1964. It found that cigarette smoking "is a health hazard of sufficient importance in the United States to warrant appropriate remedial action." It emphasized studies that linked cigarette smoking to lung cancer in men but said data for women pointed in the same direction.

Gradually the report has brought about a change in public attitudes about smoking. Reportedly some 30 million Americans have quit the habit. It's obvious, though, that many others have taken it up — annual consumption of cigarettes climbed from 511 billion in 1964 to a record 616 billion in 1976.

The tobacco industry would appear, then, to have little to fear from the Califano campaign. Yet it was worried enough to try to upstage him with a pro-smoking press conference on the eve of the secretary's speech. Tobacco people have their heads in the sand when they try to deny the health hazard in smoking. The scientific evidence is too strong to ignore it.

The Washington Star

Washington, D.C., January 12, 1978

The secretary of Health, Wealth and Happiness, Joseph Califano Jr., has ceremoniously emplaced a brick in the pathway to Utopia. He launched his federal anti-smoking campaign on Wednesday with the department's batteries of heavy public-relations artillery firing salvos intended to echo in every American hamlet.

Secretary Califano is committing $23 million dollars to the crusade against the weed. Many more dollars will follow, we don't doubt. His will be a "vigorous new program" — all new federal programs are "vigorous" and usually "comprehensive." Oh yes, a new federal fiefdom will be created: the Office on Smoking and Health.

A prime focus will be attempting to discourage consumption by teen-agers, particularly young women. Among other thrusts, there will be increased exhortations on TV and radio on health hazards and smoking; a revised label on birth-control pills will warn of the special risk of combining tobacco and birth-control chemicals; and restrictive policies against smoking in federal buildings and facilities will be, as they say, promulgated. An increased excise tax on cigarettes also is being considered.

We don't quarrel particularly with the sumptuary tax, and certainly the educative endeavor of this crusade is appropriate.

What is bemusing in the Califano initiative is its overtones — and omissions. Those who oppose or doubt his notions, Mr. Califano characterizes as a "self-interested minority" — whatever in the world that means. The phrase implies, of course, that those who do not genuflect to his view of rectitude are perverse to a culpable extent and, at some time in the future presumably, are to be treated accordingly. What is presented as a pragmatic assault on smoking appears, on closer examination, to have a tinge of stern moralism, a compound that can be volatile in government policy.

Mr. Califano nimbly avoids two associated areas: He will not "tilt at windmills" about federal agricultural programs for tobacco growers, he mysteriously says. That is a logical focus of anti-smoking fervor, isn't it? And his concern with smoking and health costs, a layman might think, would be a grand opportunity to bring federal influence as visibly against another drug — alcohol — the abuse of which can be as pernicious, or worse, than tobacco's ravages. The secretary has, no doubt, persuasive reasons for omitting those matters.

What Mr. Califano is doing with his anti-smoking hoohah is illustrating further the tilted concept of the feds as parents and the citizenry as recalcitrant and contrary children, to be coerced if they will not heed. This corrosive thesis has become as ubiquitous within federaldom as it is dubious.

Mr. Califano, a reformed three-pack-a-day smoker, says his great leap forward does not involve the "zeal of an ex-smoker who wants to convert the world." Perhaps not. But we fear that one of these days he may decide to abstain, too, from an occasional taste of grape or grain — and mandate a round of celery juice for the boys in the back room.

The Miami Herald

Miami, Fla., January 13, 1978

THE AMBITIOUS antismoking program outlined Wednesday by HEW Secretary Joseph Califano should come as no surprise.

With government now paying an ever-increasing share of medical-care costs, more governmental interest in the prevention of disease is inevitable.

Since the publication 14 years ago of the U.S. Surgeon General's report on smoking and lung cancer, evidence of tobacco's harmful effects has continued to pile up.

Yet despite such evidence and despite antismoking campaigns by the Government and private groups, consumption of tobacco products has continued to grow — especially among the young.

So Secretary Califano's announcement of an escalated Government antismoking effort is both timely and appropriate. Moreover, his multifaceted approach strikes us as more likely to have a chance to succeed than previous tactics.

One key provision is "the most penetrating program of research ever undertaken" to discover what causes people to smoke. More research into smoking's causes is certainly a logical follow-up to the research into smoking's effects.

Eventually, research into what motivates smokers may give Secretary Califano's proposals for an educational campaign a better chance to be effective. Meanwhile, efforts to persuade the young not to start smoking must be intensified.

The Califano proposal also would increase taxes on all cigarets and add a graduated tax on brands with more tar and nicotine.

Those taxes may or may not discourage anyone from smoking, but they would at least force smokers to pay more (and non-smokers less) of the costs the Government incurs because of the widespread use of tobacco.

Non-smokers would also applaud other provisions of the Califano program designed to protect their "right" not to smoke. These provisions would seek an outright ban on smoking aboard commercial airliners, for example, and would designate no-smoking areas in most Federal buildings.

Now, nobody pretends that Secretary Califano's program — even if all its features are implemented — can eradicate the tobacco habit from American society. And as the nation's "noble experiment" with Prohibition demonstrated, there is a limit to what the Government can do. Especially unwise, we believe, would be the creation of a cumbersome bureaucracy to carry the antismoking campaign beyond education and persuasion to coercion.

But as long as the Government is going to be in the health business — and it is — then programs of education, persuasion, taxation, and limited regulation are a reasonable response to a demonstrated problem.

The Courier-Journal

Louisville, Ky., January 13, 1978

IN THE KIND of over-reaction that has characterized the long struggle over smoking, the tobacco industry blindly fired its elephant guns this week at the horrendous beast expected to emerge from the foliage around HEW Secretary Califano's lair. As everybody knows, what escaped this sight-unseen salvo was a modest critter that might well have wondered what all the noise was about.

The industry admittedly had little idea what to expect from Mr. Califano, who had been talking tough about ways to rejuvenate and expand the government's anti-smoking efforts. (Also in the dark was Kentucky's House of Representatives, which without debate rammed through a knee-jerk call for the Secretary's resignation before it heard his message.)

So tobacco spokesmen aimed most of their guns at the Secretary, a former three-pack-a-day man who kicked the habit a couple of years ago. A battery of industry spokesmen depicted him as a born-again zealot, a reformed sinner who wants to force his new-found convictions on everybody else.

If this personal attack was excusable, it's only because the tobacco industry has a weak case in arguing that the government's health agencies shouldn't actively warn the public about the effects of smoking. The overwhelming weight of medical and scientific opinion is against the industry's contentions that smoking (a) isn't a major health hazard or (b) if it is, where's the proof? This stance may be a useful defense against litigation from sufferers of heart disease, emphysema and lung cancer. But it has a problem: Too many confirmed smokers are ready to acknowledge that the doctors probably are right.

Not everyone may agree with government projections that 37 million Americans now living will die prematurely from smoking-related illnesses, nor that the estimated medical bill of $5-to-7 billion yearly for treating these people before death can all be blamed on "the weed." But it's a rare smoker who hasn't seen a picture of the inside of a tar-coated lung; who hasn't thought it might be wise to quit, if only he could find a way; who hasn't become at least mildly sympathetic to those non-smokers who cast annoyed looks in his direction.

Against these numbers and this awareness, the $23 million that Secretary Califano proposed spending on a new Office of Smoking and Health is peanuts. This figure also wouldn't be likely to make much of a showing if it were spent, as the industry suggested, on finding ways to make smoke harmless to the body.

But the actual program that was condemned in advance turned out to be considerably milder than either the tobacco industry or the anti-smoking crusaders expected. Mr. Califano's harsh words about cigarettes aren't likely to be the tipping point in converting many of the nation's 54 million smokers, since most of them have heard equivalent talk from their children, doctors or friends. And many of the measures that may have a long-range impact were either vaguely described or not fully developed.

It's difficult to assess what is meaningful among the long list of measures and proposals Secretary Califano offered at his press conference. In general, however, the measures calling for more and better public education are more impressive than those that run toward coercion of smokers.

It's legitimate, for example, to protect non-smokers on airliners and in other enclosed places from pollution created by smokers. But a ban on all airline smoking, in place of the segregation of smokers and non-smokers that is now enforced, would seem to be aimed more at harassing those afflicted with the smoking habit than at protecting non-smokers.

Efforts to strengthen the government's anti-smoking educational effort are harder to criticize. But that area also is full of pitfalls. Clearly a major effort should be focused on preventing children and teenagers from taking up the habit, since not starting, as Mr. Califano said, is the "only sure way to stop smoking." But old-fashioned anti-smoking sermons, like those against other vices, often are ineffective and even counter-productive, as many of us can recall from our own school days.

Mr. Califano said "penetrating" research is planned on what motivates children and teen-agers to smoke. If the research really penetrates, that will be useful. But it's essential that the effectiveness of anti-smoking education on both young people and adults be carefully monitored.

Meanwhile, it's important that the scientific consensus on smoking hazards be set before the potential smoker in an effective way. That probably warrants a stronger and more explicit warning than cigarette packs and advertising now carry, and it certainly justifies labels for birth control pills that point out that smoking sharply increases the risk of death when the pills are being used.

Mr. Califano was vaguest on his planned efforts to give people incentives for not smoking. The proposal to increase the federal excise tax on cigarettes and graduate it according to tar and nicotine content will have merit if agreement can be reached on how to graduate the tax. One school of thought condemns low-nicotine cigarettes on the ground that they require the nicotine addict to smoke more to get the required satisfaction, thus inhaling more "tar" in the process. On the other hand, a high-nicotine, low-tar cigarette might increase the heart-attack risk.

It's possible to be too skeptical about the prospect of changing habits. While it's striking that after 14 years of ever-stronger warnings, 54 million Americans still smoke (at the rate of 1½ packs a day per smoker), they're a dwindling minority. This suggests that all the warnings haven't fallen on deaf ears. The number of adult smokers has fallen from 42 per cent in 1964 to 34 per cent today. The percentage has dropped for both sexes. The reason has to be concern for health, because people surely haven't grown less self-indulgent or nervous during those years.

What's ahead seems to be more of the same — a gradual trend away from cigarettes that won't suddenly jerk the rug from under the tobacco manufacturer or grower. Secretary Califano wisely steered clear of measures, such as an end to price-support programs, that would needlessly disrupt the industry while having no effect on smoking. But there's no getting away from the fact that tobacco is headed for more trouble, no matter how many elephant guns are fired. Fortunately, there's time to prepare for the change.

The News and Courier
Charleston, S.C., January 15, 1978

Virtually every aspect of a program against tobacco smoking outlined by HEW Secretary Joseph Califano is an invitation to expense, waste and frustration. The secretary's plan to set up an anti-smoking office in HEW with a $23-million budget is only a starter. The rest of his plan runs to high taxes, expense for businessmen, grants for researching what everybody knows already, new burdens on schools, extra legislative time — not to mention what it's all going to cost in terms of penalties to farmers who grow tobacco and those who market it and process it. After all the money is spent, all the new bureaucrats established in place and new bites put on the taxpayers, Mr. Califano's program will produce no results worth mentioning.

For all the above reasons HEW in some way ought to be prevented from undertaking Mr. Califano's crusade against smokers. There are other reasons. The principal one is that the battle between non-smokers and smokers ought to be waged without government dictatorship. Non-smokers may have every reason in the world for complaining about the outrageous habits of their smoking neighbors. The problem, though, is largely self-created. Non-smokers have the notion that somehow good manners compel those who do not like smoke to give first consideration to those who do. When someone asks — as is less often done these days —

whether it is OK to smoke, the response is a smile, though it may be accompanied by an inward shudder. When a smoker lights up without asking, the rule seems to be to grin and bear it. It would be just as easy — and equally polite — to say, "Please, don't." One doesn't necessarily want to put up no-smoking signs around the house, yet nothing stands in the way of removing all the ash trays. Perceptive guests will get the message.

If smokers are going to continue to smoke whether it's good for them or not — as seems likely to be the case — and if non-smokers are going to politely endure the inconvenience, then neither the non-smoker nor the government is going to win the battle against dirty old tobacco.

Our nostrils tingle for those who don't smoke and who have to live in other people's smoke. We're one of those who don't. We are one, we admit, who has greeted such things as non-smoking areas in airplanes with a sigh of relief.

All the same, we have profound reservations about turning the job of policing tobacco smoke over to government agencies. It is more than risky. It's a coward's way out. There are ways within the context of ordinary good manners in which non-smokers ought to be able to defend their interests. At least they ought to try before they cop out and send for Secretary Califano and HEW.

FORT WORTH STAR-TELEGRAM
Fort Worth, Tex., January 15, 1978

"Smoke, smoke, smoke that cigarette," the lyrics of a popular novelty song of a few years ago insisted.

And millions of smokers insisted on continuing to do so, although the lyrics added "...puff, puff, puff it till you smoke yourself to death."

That song was recorded prior to the 1964 surgeon general's report on the health hazards that accompany the smoking habit.

The song suggests that even before the surgeon general's report there was a common sense recognition of the connection between smoking and some terminal ailments.

But the surgeon general's report made the notion that smoking kills official, scientifically supported assertion.

As a result of that report and some of the anti-smoking measures resulting from it millions of Americans have kicked the habit. But millions more have insisted on continuing to smoke, despite the claims that it is a form of slow suicide.

In this 14th anniversary year of the surgeon general's report Health Education and Welfare Secretary Joseph A. Califano has fired up a new anti-smoking campaign aimed at coaxing more American's to quit.

Expectedly Califano already has come under fire from tobacco interests and smokers who would rather fight the odds against lung cancer, emphysema and other deadly ailments than switch to purer air.

They question the propriety of HEW's interfering with the rights of Americans to choose freely whether they want to take the risks involved in smoking or not and raise the spectre of prohibition's failure. At first glance that appears to be a good question, one made more cogent by the fact that other departments of the federal government are at the same time providing supports for the tobacco industry.

But it is a smokescreen. Califano has not really proposed any categorical prohibition against smoking. His measures would extend in two directions — the protection of the rights of non-smokers and the dispensing of information to counteract the activities of smoking pro-

moters.

The proposed banning of smoking on commercial airline flights and further restrictions upon it in government buildings and public places falls into the first category.

The Fort Worth City Council will have to come to grips with this issue, as a result of a smoking restriction ordinance proposed recently by Councilman Jim Bradshaw.

* * *

Califano's proposed intensified anti-smoking educational campaign, including warning labels on birth control pills, is justified.

The tobacco industry is spending millions to portray smoking as a suave, sophisticated, even sexy thing to do.

Although it can't advertise on television and radio anymore, the industry spent $400 million on print media advertising and other promotional efforts last year.

HEW spent $1 million during the same period on anti-smoking information and plans to spend under $6 million next year.

* * *

Although Califano's anti-smoking effort is not prohibitionist, it is possible that it could backfire if the smoking promoters succeed in turning the burning controversy into a civil liberties issue.

The essential point, however, is that smoking is hazardous to the health of both the smokers themselves and the non-smokers they breathe their smoke upon. It is a proper function of the government to go to extraordinary means to emphasize that point in the face of well-financed and orchestrated efforts to gloss it over by those who have a heavy economic stake in keeping a sizable portion of the American population puffing.

Truly, every American should have the right to decide if he wants to smoke or not, but only after being presented with the arguments for and against it.

No one, neither the government through naked coercion nor the tobacco industry through unanswered propaganda, has the right to impose that decision upon anyone.

And likewise, no one who has decided to smoke has the right to exhale his decision upon those who decide otherwise.

The Pittsburgh Press
Pittsburgh, Pa., January 14, 1978

Joseph A. Califano Jr., the U.S. Secretary of Health, Education, and Welfare, is to be commended for launching a new campaign to discourage cigarette smoking.

Mr. Califano is the Cabinet officer charged with looking after the nation's health. And the overwhelming weight of medical evidence supports the thesis that smoking is dangerous to health. Above all, smoking is regarded as a leading cause of lung cancer and a contributing factor in heart disease.

And the government should point all this out to the citizens as often as possible.

* * *

It's true that cigarette sales have remained high in the United States despite all of the previous anti-smoking campaigns. And smoking among women and teen-age girls has increased in recent years.

But it's also true that millions have stopped since the 1964 anti-smoking report was issued by the Surgeon General of the U.S. Public Health Service and more are quitting daily. Had the government been silent on the subject, consumption of cigarettes probably would have risen sharply rather than leveling off in the past 14 years.

Mr. Califano's crusade is, of course, not popular in states where tobacco is grown. In fact, the Kentucky House of Representatives has asked him to resign.

Nor is it popular with the Tobacco Institute, which has accused Mr. Califano, who once smoked three packs of cigarettes a day, of having a "prohibitionist mentality."

Actually, no one is being forced to stop smoking. Such an outright ban couldn't be enforced.

The government's role should be— and is — to inform and educate the citizenry as to the dangers involved in smoking, leaving the individual free to make his own choice.

* * *

The most incongruous aspect of the tobacco picture, however, is that of HEW trumpeting how dangerous cigarettes are and the Agriculture Department at the same time spending $80 million a year on subsidies to tobacco farmers.

President Carter should get this act together and try to get Congress to take the government out of the business of encouraging tobacco production.

ALBUQUERQUE JOURNAL

Albuquerque, N.M., January 13, 1978

There's no one worse than a reformed addict, so far as those hooked on tobacco, alcohol or other habit forming substances contend with some justification.

HEW Secretary Joseph Califano Jr. fills that ogre role to a T with his new anti-smoking campaign that's either going to tax smokers into bankruptcy or ostracize them from government buildings. He wants to protect Americans from their own vile habits.

It figures. Califano was a heavy smoker until he kicked the habit in 1975.

What this country really needs is an agency to protect people from the government that wants to protect them from themselves.

The Virginian-Pilot

Norfolk, Va., January 13, 1978

Joseph A. Califano Jr. probably never heard of the evangelist who catalogued Beelzebub's devices at a revival in a mill-town tabernacle one evening. To the good man's condemnation of picture shows, card-playing, dancing, and bearing false witness across the fence, a little old lady in high-lace shoes shouted "Amen!" When he came down hard on whisky-drinking, playing baseball on Sunday afternoon, and rumble-seat courting, she sang out, "Praise the Lord!" In endorsement of his warnings against rouge, rolled stockings, and bobbed hair, she clapped her hands. But at his mention of snuff-dipping she murmured, "Now he's quit preachin' and gone to meddlin'."

Health, Education, and Welfare Secretary Califano could be relied upon to preach to the people reasonably about the hazards attendant to cranberries, saccharin, hair dye, or even the pill. He doubtless would sermonize about highway slaughter or alcohol's wages with a good grip on his nerves. But in the revival he opened the other day against "Public Health Enemy No. 1" and "slow-motion suicide," which was his way of saying cigarette-smoking, he sounded as shrill as a rooster's

screech in a chicken-thief's ear. The little old lady from the spinning room doubtless recognized the convert's zeal in his homily to the National Interagency Council on Smoking and Health.

The Surgeon General brought smoking under suspicion with the first of a series of reports from his office nearly 20 years ago. Since then the Federal Trade Commission and the Federal Communications Commission have restricted cigarette advertising. Congress has been hauled into the act, but kicking. One President after another has steered clear of the cigarette question. The Agriculture and Commerce Departments meanwhile have supported tobacco production and marketing.

There is, then, no United States Government policy on smoking. Neither the Executive, the Legislative, nor the Judicial Department has taken a definitive, or even a discernible, position. While every pack of cigarettes must bear a warning of smoking's harmfulness, it may be sold and bought as legally as a loaf of bread.

If Mr. Califano's crusade to prevent young people from taking up smoking and to persuade others to follow his

example of quitting the habit is well motivated and, from a medical viewpoint, worthy of success, it nevertheless is personal and idiosyncratic. He is coming close to confusing government by laws with government by men. It is noteworthy that he backed away, in the face of certain defeat, from his intention to oppose the Agriculture Department's tobacco price-support program, and it is a safe bet that his plan for scaling the Federal excise tax on cigarettes to tar and nicotine content, with the idea of pricing the harsher brands out of the market, will never reach Congress' floors'

We make no case for smoking. What the Attorney General says it does to your lungs and heart we believe. We think tobacco taxes should be realistic—that Virginia, for example, is foolish not to collect from cigarette sales the sort of revenue that practically every other state regards as normal. Nevertheless, we think poorly of Mr. Califano's contribution to the history of this, that, and the other Federal agency's setting by preference, prejudice, and whim a tobacco course that the Government itself does not recognize.

WINSTON-SALEM JOURNAL

Winston-Salem, N.C., January 13, 1978

With the righteous zeal of a recent convert, Secretary Joseph A. Califano has marshaled the awesome force of the U. S. Department of Health, Education and Welfare for a crusade against smoking. The battle plan unveiled by Califano in Washington this week calls for spending millions of tax dollars and using the coercive power of the federal bureaucracy to make citizens give up the smoking habit.

Califano used scary language and grim statistics to make the case for the crusade. "Smoking ruins health. Smoking kills," he said. He labeled cigarette smoking as "public health enemy No. 1," and described it as a "major factor" in the deaths of at least 320,000 Americans each year from heart disease, lung cancer and other ailments. Young people are being influenced to smoke, Califano argued, and the government must counteract advertising by cigarette manufacturers through a public education campaign to convince people "that smoking is unhealthy, dangerous, socially expensive, and a leading cause of premature death."

As is often the case with crusades, there is more to admire about the motive than the methods. Public health problems — including alcohol abuse and

obesity, among many others involving personal choice — are a legitimate concern for Califano's department. What remains a serious question is how far the federal government should go in forcing people to do what might be good for them, whether smoking, drinking, or overeating is involved.

No such qualms seemed to bother Califano. He was prepared with a program, drawing on suggestions from an anti-smoking task force, ranging from courses in the public schools to a ban on smoking aboard airliners and in other public places. A proposal to raise the federal excise tax on cigarettes, a request to broadcast networks to run more anti-smoking advertisements, and a suggestion that states adopt "clean indoor air" laws similar to those existing in Minnesota and Alaska were among other items on the list. Califano said the campaign would be conducted through a new HEW Office on Smoking and Health, and the total budget will be $23 million by next September.

Califano timed the announcement of the war on smoking to coincide with the 14th anniversary of the release in 1964 of the first surgeon general's report on smoking and health. Califano himself is a recent convert to the anti-smoking cause. Until a couple of years ago, he

was a three-pack-a-day smoker.

His zeal to break the habit for others seems to have blinded him to the consequences of coercion as a means of reform. The country tried to treat alcohol misuse through legal sanction in the Prohibition era. That sad experience should indicate the dim prospects of success for efforts to force people to stop smoking until they have made the decision for themselves.

A salutary note of caution was voiced by Dr. Peter Bourne, special assistant on health issues to President Carter. Although he applauded the general drift of the Califano anti-smoking program, Dr. Bourne said that the government should take care not to engage in efforts which would "make outcasts of smokers." In the past, he said, a punitive approach involving other health problems has "worked against the development of sound treatment programs."

Further research on the relationship of smoking and health, as well as means to help those who want to stop smoking do so, are quite in order. The role for HEW ought to be one of finding and presenting the facts, as clearly as they can be established, to the public. Califano's zeal to convert smokers is misguided, and a disturbing intrusion by government into the realm of private choice.

"Later on, however, you'll really thank me for this!"

Reprinted by permission of the Los Angeles Times Syndicate.

THE COMMERCIAL APPEAL
Memphis, Tenn., January 13, 1978

SMOKING is a dirty, expensive and harmful habit. People who smoke undoubtedly would be better off physically — and perhaps mentally — if they stopped, never to inhale noxious tobacco fumes again.

But is it necessary for the federal government to become a heavy-handed Big Brother to all the smokers in America, watching over their shoulders, bombarding them with warnings and preachments, and picking their pockets when they wander from the saintly ways of such reformed smokers as Joseph Califano, secretary of health, education and welfare?

Califano, who once smoked three packs a day, has announced a campaign to purify American lungs. His proposals include a ban on smoking in commercial aircraft, smoking restrictions in government buildings and public places, comprehensive antismoking programs in the public schools and a higher federal excise tax on cigarets.

"Smoking ruins health," Califano says. "Smoking kills."

That may be, but as Graham Hemminger wrote in 1915:

"Tobacco is a dirty weed:; I like it.
"It satisfies no normal need; I like it.
"It makes you thin, it makes you lean,
"It takes the hair right off your bean;
"It's the worst darn stuff I've ever seen; I like it."

The HEW secretary has created a new Office on Smoking and Health with a budget of $23 million in 1979. The bureaucrats should be able to quadruple that before the nation's 54 million smokers can strike a match.

Will a Cabinet-level Department of Smoking be next?

Or isn't it possible that the federal government has better things to do? After all, kids still can't read very well, cancer is still a catastrophic disease and HEW still hasn't ended the loss of billions of dollars from mismanagement and fraud in its social welfare programs.

CALIFANO MAY DESERVE a national commendation for kicking the habit, himself.

He could qualify as a charter member of a new legion of merit. But that doesn't entitle him or any federal agency to be the Conscience of American Smokers.

Interestingly enough, an estimated 30 million Americans have stopped smoking since the surgeon general's 1964 report that smoking can be dangerous to health. The number of adult smokers has fallen from 42 per cent to 34 per cent in that time. And those who quit did it without Califano's help.

St. Joseph should find other dragons to fight and let smokers wrestle with their own conscience, which they surely should be able to do without yet one more expensive and meddlesome federal agency.

TULSA WORLD

Tulsa, Okla., January 13, 1978

FEW PEOPLE outside the tobacco industry are likely to quarrel with the purpose of HEW Secretary Joseph Califano's new Government crusade against cigarette smoking.

The evidence that cigarettes are a health hazard is no longer debatable. Reliable statistics show that cancer, emphesema, heart disease and a number of lesser ailments are far more likely to strike smokers than non-smokers.

Health officials are right to point out these risks to Americans and to urge them to quit smoking. But it is quite another thing to use the power of Government to harass adult citizens who choose to accept the risk.

When Secretary Califano says he wants to "help" people to quit smoking he is on solid ground. But when he suggests banning cigarettes from commercial airliners and prohibitions on smoking in Government buildings merely to protect people from their own free choice, then he is meddling in the smoker's personal business.

The truth is that free people just don't always choose to do what is good for them. They sometimes decide to take some risk to do something they enjoy. Some folks like skiing, for example, even though statistics show that it is more dangerous than watching television. Others eat beefsteak despite the warnings of reputable doctors that too much fat in the diet may contribute to heart disease.

Smoking, of course, is much more dangerous than skiing. But the choice should still be left to the individual--not to some all-powerful mother-figure in Washington.

And while it isn't related to the issue of free choice, there is one other flaw in Califano's antismoking campaign. It is the fact that the same Government now pressuring citizens to quit smoking is at the same time subsidizing tobacco and in a way that helps make it more abundant and less costly to the consumer.

The Burlington Free Press

Burlington, Vt., January 19, 1978

IF GOVERNMENT bureaucrats must appoint themselves as missionaries to protect Americans from the consequences of their own vices, at least they should be consistent about it.

The new assault on smoking by Secretary Joseph Califano of the Department of Health, Education and Welfare is a prime example of one interest of the government colliding head-on with another.

Launched with all the customary hoopla that surrounds a bureaucratic excursion into the sublime, the campaign is designed to convince smokers to drop the habit. If the facts about the dangers of smoking are not persuasive enough, Califano has proposed that federal excise taxes on cigarettes be raised, based on the amount of tar and nicotine in the various brands.

What is ludicrous about the new war on smoking is the fact that $23 million will be spent by HEW on the campaign while at the same time the Department of Agriculture will subsidize American tobacco farmers to the tune of $78 million.

It should not be difficult to determine who will have the largest clout in the smoking war.

While there can be little doubt that smoking does serious damage to the health of millions of Americans, the habit simply cannot be curbed by such lukewarm government intervention. All agencies should cooperate in any genuine campaign to cut down the incidence of smoking. The government also might have to demonstrate its willingness to forgo some of the revenue it now derives from tobacco sales.

But the anti-smoking campaign has even deeper implications. The significant question is: How far should the government go in protecting its people from the harm that they inflict on themselves by choice? Is the long arm of the government now to be extended so much that it can pluck cigarettes out of the pockets of Americans who wish to smoke?

If people choose to smoke under conditions that are not offensive to non-smokers, the government simply has no right — by decree or by campaign — to deprive them of their right to choose.

Such is the stuff of which tyranny is made.

The Idaho STATESMAN

Boise, Idaho, January 15, 1978

HEW Secretary Joseph Califano plans to set up a multi-million-dollar bureaucracy to discourage Americans from smoking. The idea stinks.

Americans don't need a federally initiated media blitz, complete with slogans like Califano's "smoking maims, smoking kills," to discourage them from smoking. They've received ample discouragement already, in the form of surgeon general's warnings, anti-smoking ads, abuse from non-smokers, you name it. The only Americans who could possibly be unaware of tobacco's drawbacks are smoking home-grown in the Ozarks.

Aside from that, Califano's new bureuacracy raises the broader question of personal rights. Few will deny that smoking is a costly, dangerous and dirty habit. Even the most adamant smokers, deep down, know they'd be better off if they quit. But is it the proper role of government to entice them to do so?

Americans have always chosen their vices and proceeded to enjoy them, often without regard as to whether they were harmful, dangerous or even illegal. So long as they are not illegal, the government has no business telling them which to embrace and which to forsake.

Government and society tend to alternately champion and trample rights, depending on which happen to be in and out of favor. Ten years ago, discrimination against minorities was not to be tolerated under any circumstance. Today, reverse discrimination is the issue. Ten years ago, cigarette smoking was acceptable, but woe to the poor pot smoker. Now we have an administration that plans to spend more than $20 million a year to discourage tobacco smoking and wants to decriminalize marijuana.

Society determines which vices are fashionable, and society tends to change its mind every few years. Government should stand back and accept that for what it is, not jump in with both feet to criticize the vices that happen to have fallen from grace.

If the administration wants to wipe out smoking, its money would be better spent establishing clinics to help people who want to stop but haven't been able to. And if the administration disapproves so strongly of smoking, why hasn't it canceled federal subsidies to the tobacco industry?

As things now stand, tobacco growers enjoy the security of a guaranteed minimum price. If the market price falls below that, the government — the same government that preaches "smoking maims, smoking kills" — steps in and makes up the difference. It's a nice little arrangement . . . if you happen to be among those who grow the maiming, killing weed.

Califano announced his anti-smoking campaign on the 14th anniversary of the surgeon general's report that said smoking could be hazardous to health. Since that report was issued, 30 million Americans have quit smoking.

They did it without the government beating them over the head with slogans, which is as it should be.

THE LINCOLN STAR

Lincoln, Neb., January 16, 1978

We welcome the intrusion by government into private lives as announced last week by Health, Education and Welfare Secretary Joseph Califano, who will lead a crusade against smoking.

The new program will feature stepped up research, public education efforts and the consideration of various punitive measures such as recommending a graduated increase in the federal excise tax on tobacco depending on the poison content in cigarettes. Califano also urged a ban on smoking on all commercial air flights, said smoking restrictions in HEW buildings will be tightened and invited industry and other government agencies to follow that example.

Califano called smoking "public health enemy No. 1."

It makes sense to us, in that context, that if the federal government spends time and money fighting such things as cancer and swine flu, it should join the battle against a primary cause of health problems which kill hundreds of thousands of people annually.

Understandably, the tobacco industry still maintains, contrary to the weight of evidence, that the link between smoking and health problems is unproven, and it rejects Califano's crusade as an unwarranted intrusion into people's personal habits.

A warning came, too, from President Carter's health advisor, Dr. Peter Bourne. He intimated that the antismoking effort should be sensitive in its treatment of smokers. "The ultimate effort of government," Bourne said, "should be to provide individual citizens knowledge in order for them to make informed decisions. It should not be to make outcasts of smokers. Such efforts are doomed to failure."

That may be, but we can't help but point out that one of the most odious examples of intrusion into private lives is that by smokers into the lives of nonsmokers, who may as well start the habit or resume it for all the good not smoking does them. In today's society, nonsmokers have been the outcasts. The tide is turning however, and the federal government's new anti-smoking crusade is just and deserved retaliation.

Before abandoning the soapbox, we take note of Califano's reluctance to attack the government subsidy for tobacco farmers. The government's spending to fight smoking, with one hand while spending to grow tobacco with the other is a glaring inconsistency. Something has to give.

We are with those who believe that the subsidy should be continued but only temporarily and as an inducement for farmers to make the switch to another crop. That should cut down on the number of tobacco farmers, on the size of the crop and make tobacco profitable enough for those who stay in the business to get by without government support.

Roanoke Times & World-News

Roanoke, Va., January 29, 1978

Our sympathies are with the letter writers who recently expressed astonishment that the federal government would spend more than $23 million on a campaign to harass cigarette smokers. It is possible to agree with the "Warning: The Surgeon General has Determined that Cigarette Smoking is Dangerous to Your Health." But it is sensible, and fair, to agree to some other propositions.

Tobacco is a legal product. Its use and sales contribute heavily to that part of the trade balance which favors the United States. Last year cigarette taxes contributed *six billion dollars* to federal, state and local governments. Those who want to go beyond discouraging smoking to the harassment of smokers have a duty to perform which they are not performing. That is to propose how the loss of dollar exchange is to be overcome, how the six billion dollars are to be replaced.

Cigarette smokers have been corrected for some bad manners in recent years, and that is to the good. But the probability is that tobacco will be around as long as whiskey has been around; and that Carrie Nation tactics will be no more successful against one than the other.

ARKANSAS DEMOCRAT

Little Rock, Ark., January 16, 1978

Smokers probably won't be over-alarmed about HEW Secretary Joe Califano's new crusade against smoking. It's sort of like President Carter's upcoming crusade against inflation — a lot of talk but no action against the untouchable culprit itself.

Sure, Joe gave up cigarettes himself, and you know how converts are. But he can't make anybody quit so long as the weed itself is legal and the government goes on subsidizing the people who grow it. It's an odd thought that, after 370 years, tobacco is about where it was in the beginning — the only American crop sure of a profit. But that's another story.

As for the anti-smoking crusade, there is a threat to raise taxes, which is about all that distinguishes this from earlier crusades. But a Congress that won't raise gasoline taxes to save energy surely won't raise cigarette taxes in the belief that that would save lives. Like the energy crisis, the smoking crisis presents the people with arguments they believe but don't want to hear. Immediate gratification is what counts, and they're willing to take their chances on the future. The most Congress might do is go along with a slogan like "Don't Smoke While You Drive — and vice versa," which amounts to a nod, and no more, to both crises.

Congressmen are politicians and therefore altogether different from the researchers who churn out embargos against drugs, cereal, toys and what-not from those salvationist hives we call regulatory agencies. These fellows are strictly non-political, and though we may not believe what they say we aren't positioned to argue with them, even if we do understand them.

But congressmen know well enough that everybody is aware of the risks of smoking or at least knows that there's a statistical, if not a laboratory, correlation between smoking and lung cancer. Yet, people go right on smoking — and no politician in his right mind will raise cigarette taxes or outlaw the weed itself on the silly presumption that people don't know what's bad for them.

Bureaucrats like Califano, who don't have to answer to the people, don't mind making those assumptions, but they know well enough that they're limited by the political realities — which is why all they mount are crusades and why people will simply blow smoke rings at the Califano Plan.

THE CINCINNATI ENQUIRER

Cincinnati, Ohio, January 22, 1978

HELL, AS everyone knows, has no "fury like a woman scorn'd." Just as furious, however, can be a bureaucrat whose longstanding treaties are similarly scorned.

There was the aura of just such fury surrounding Secretary of Health, Education and Welfare (HEW) Joseph A. Califano's commemoration of the 14th anniversary of the U.S. surgeon general's report citing a causal link between cigarette smoking and cancer.

Secretary Califano was able to rejoice over the growing numbers of nonsmokers among adult Americans and the establishment of nonsmoking areas in many public facilities.

But he also had to face up to the fact that Americans were buying 626 *billion* cigarettes in 1976 and to the sharp increase in the number of teenaged Americans (including a near doubling in the percentage of smokers among teenaged girls).

In the years since the original surgeon general's report, Secretary Califano believes, the case against smoking has, if anything, grown far stronger. Hence, the necessity, in his view, of a wide range of federal activities to arouse the concern of unreconstructed smokers.

He has set forth a multifaceted campaign—at a cost of *$23 million*—to accomplish his goals: He is asking the radio and television networks to increase the time devoted to antismoking announcements; he wants schools to concentrate on teaching the dangers of smoking; he is converting HEW into a nonsmokers' paradise and hoping other government agencies and private industry will follow the example; he is asking the Civil Aeronautics Board to ban all smoking aboard planes; he is proposing federal research into the factors that motivate smoking, particularly among young Americans, and he is exploring with the Treasury Department higher taxes on cigarettes, especially those with higher nicotine, tar and carbon-monoxide content.

It is worth noting that not all of the federal officials concerned with the nation's health share his perception of the smoking menace.

It may be that the health threat posed by cigarette smoking is as grave as Secretary Califano suggests.

But his reinvigorated crusade raises anew the question of how far government can go in protecting the people from themselves.

Cholesterol is also a health threat; so is overeating; so are dozens of other aspects of daily living. Does government's role go beyond putting the facts as it perceives them at the public's disposal? Is there an additional responsibility to make certain that the public embraces its concerns?

Prof. Milton Friedman, the 1976 Nobel laureate in economics, had just such a governmental role in mind when he wrote about "the internal threat coming from men of good intentions and goodwill who wish to reform us.

"Impatient with the slowness of persuasion and example to achieve the great social changes they envision," he wrote, "they are anxious to use the power of the state to achieve their ends and confident of their ability to do so. Yet if they gained the power, they would fail to achieve their immediate aims and, in addition, would produce a collective state from which they would recoil in horror and of which they would be among the first victims. Concentrated power is not rendered harmless by the good intentions of those who create it."

These are thoughts that must haunt all those who have heard Secretary Califano's appeal—even those who share and endorse his objectives.

The Washington Post

Washington, D.C., January 16, 1978

FRANKLY WE DON'T see what the big fuss is about vis-à-vis Mr. Califano, smoking, health and HEW. Despite some characteristically flamboyant and overstated rhetorical flourishes, Mr. Califano was enunciating what seemed to us a modest and sensible enough program. HEW will seek to step up its anti-smoking propaganda; it will stiffen the nonsmoking provisions affecting building space over which it has control; it will seek to tighten up federal regulations and labeling and warning procedures with a view to protecting individuals who smoke and those who don't from various demonstrable hazards of smoke-filled rooms and/or lungs; it will undertake to learn more about the causes of addictive smoking; and it will explore some financial incentives (in the tax and insurance realms, for example) that might encourage people to eschew or kick the habit.

Some critics (who can*not* be dismissed, in Mr. Califano's term, as "self-interested" spokesmen for the tobacco industry) have expressed anxiety that the federal government will, in this campaign, once again be overreaching its authority and busybodying people's lives. That anxiety is not exactly without a foundation in experience and logic, since the federal government, especially in its HEW incarnation, has shown a definite taste for telling everyone what he can or can't or must or mustn't do at each hour of the day. And Mr. Carter's sweeping assertion at his press conference last week that Mr. Califano, who is merely the government's chief health officer, is in fact "responsible for the nation's health," didn't help:

It made it all sound a lot grander and more comprehensive and intrusive than it is.

The point is that, as the government's chief health officer, Mr. Califano surely has taken some steps to fulfill his obligation. The program he has laid out concentrates on diverting the nation's children from taking up the smoking habit and getting others out of harm's way so far as smoking is concerned. It *is* a self-interested gambit for the producers and consumers of tobacco products to dismiss the enormous body of medical research pointing to the terrible effect of smoking on health. At the other pole of the argument, it strikes us as foolish to bewail the fact that the Secretary of HEW did not take on the addictive political and economic aspects of tobacco growing and marketing in this country. If anyone ever takes on those problems frontally it will have to be Congress or the President, and we did not get the impression from Mr. Carter the other day that he was itching for a leadership role in this crusade.

Speaking from our own smoke-filled experience, we would add one cautionary note. It will be madness if the airlines regulators seek to ban smoking altogether on flights of any considerable distance. That way lies cheating, hiding, secret smokes in the lavatories, extinguishing cigarettes in the upholstery—and, in general, fire and danger. We would recommend either some form of the present ghetto system or, possibly, all-smokers flights. The trouble with the latter, of course, is that you wouldn't be able to see the movie screen for the smoke.

THE PLAIN DEALER

Cleveland, Ohio, January 19, 1978

An estimated 53 million to 60 million Americans smoke, each willing to take the risk of eventual and almost inevitable ill effects for the immediate, short-term pleasure of a cigarette.

On Jan. 11, the anniversary of the surgeon general's 1964 report on smoking and health, which fell during National Education Week on Smoking, the federal government struck at the habit. Joseph A. Califano Jr., secretary of health, education and welfare, declared smoking "public health enemy No. 1" and dedicated the government to spreading the word that "smoking maims, smoking kills."

Response was even more immediate than the treacherous pleasures of smoking. In fact, the Tobacco Institute, ever vigilant in its role as defender of the $14-billion-a-year cigarette industry, got into action before Califano issued the accusation, charging him with waging a battle of personal vendetta as a former three-pack-a-day man.

Detractors were not limited to the industry's natural allies. Smoking's enemies also flailed at what they considered his weak approach on the addictive, debilitating habit. They accused Califano of merely walking softly around the beast, tapping it tentatively, rather than making serious, liberal use of the federal government's mammoth arsenal.

To his proposal of a tax increase, even nonsmokers question whether

a user tax is an answer or a punitive measure. His suggestions for smoking bans and segregating smokers trip the argument weighing the freedom of personal choice against the right to clean air.

Bolstering the federal government's antismoking education program by $5 million, bringing it to a $6 million campaign, moved antismokers to wonder how the government can justify $80 million in annual federal support to tobacco farmers while at the same time spending money on antismoking efforts.

A report from the National Clearinghouse for Smoking and Health in Atlanta estimates that nine out of 10 smokers actually want to quit; this is testimony to the severely addictive nature of the habit.

Califano should make greater use of the government's power to discourage smoking. HEW, however, should concentrate on its own system of checks and balances in an effort to suppress the urge to infringe deeply upon individual rights.

And yes, despite all their bad publicity, smokers still have rights. Breaking the tar and nicotine habit is grueling for most people. So, while Califano is right to draw a bead on smoking, his kicking-the-habit campaign will probably produce better results if the pervasive attitude is to help through persuasive education rather than to increasingly punish through taxation and isolation.

THE DALLAS TIMES HERALD

Dallas, Texas, January 16, 1978

IT IS not to argue the demerits or merits of smoking, just to vociferously remind again that the U.S. government, starting with born-again Joseph Califano Jr., has no divine right to inflict punitive measures upon 54 million Americans who just might want to light up a cigarette.

If bureaucrat Califano, the HEW boss who kicked the two-and three-pack-a-day habit a couple of years ago, wants to call a Washington press conference and denounce the evils of tobacco, that is fine.

But, until smoking is declared illegal by the Congress of the United States, Mr. Califano is roaming far off his base in threatening the private lives of individuals with an increase of the federal eight-cent-a-pack excise tax on cigarettes, banning smoking on all airplanes, in federal buildings, etc.

Now, his new Office on Smoking and Health — with an opening budget of $23 million annually — will "coordinate" all of HEW's smoking research and information efforts.

While Califano's busy $23 million army starts scratching for justification of its being by telling citizens how to lead their lives, we have this strange sight of still an-

other U.S. government agency funneling many more millions than that each year into a subsidy for the tobacco industry.

On the one hand is Big Brother Califano telling us we can't do this or that with cigarette in hand; on the other, some of his federal brothers down the street in the Agriculture Department are pumping millions upon millions through subsidy channels to keep those cigarettes and cigars ablazin'!

Califano, in announcing his private war a couple of days ago with research projects he intends to eventually submit to Congress, did not, of course, mention the Agriculture Department's price support programs.

If cigarette smoking eventually proves out, beyond doubt, as extremely hazardous to the health and life of the 54 million puffers now engaged in the practice, definitive action from the Congress would certainly be in order.

But to impose penalties and attempt to regulate the private lives of individual citizens through use of federal power and money is unacceptable.

Warn smokers of hazards? Certainly — just don't threaten them with bureaucratic edicts.

SUNDAY TELEGRAM

Worcester, Mass., January 17, 1978

Declaring that "people who smoke are committing slow-motion suicide," Secretary of Health, Education and Welfare Joseph Califano has declared a holy war on cigarette smoking.

His crusade has all the elements of bureaucratic overkill. How much arm-twisting do American smokers need? And is it any of the business of the United States government if individual Americans, despite all the evidence that cigarettes are dangerous to their health, elect to go on smoking anyway?

Califano, a reformed smoker, is planning to spend $23 million of our money to inform smokers grimly that they are "whistling past the cemetery in their search for a way to rationalize the habit." His program includes education, research, smoking bans in public places, stronger warnings on cigarette packages, increased federal excise taxes on cigarettes, a "graduated tax according to nicotine, carbon monoxide and tar content," and special insurance premiums for nonsmokers. He also wants a new HEW Office on Smoking and Health.

So far he hasn't asked for criminal prosecution of smokers. Nor did he propose to do away with the federal program of tobacco price supports, a move that would be a form of slow-motion political suicide.

The secretary merely hopes to make the 55 million Americans who smoke social outcasts and penalize them for their habit. He is trying to use the full power of his office, the federal tax system and $23 million in public money to accomplish his goal.

Surely there are few persons still unaware of the hazards that go with smoking. The risks involved have been widely publicized and Uncle Sam already sends out the warning on every pack of cigarette sold in this country. Despite all that, cigarette consumption continues to increase. It is still a relatively free country, in which individuals are permitted to make their own mistakes as long as they don't threaten others or society at large.

Prohibition has never succeeded in this country. Califano should tone down his crusade.

The Des Moines Register

Des Moines, Iowa, January 18, 1978

The attack on smoking launched last week by Secretary of Health, Education and Welfare Joseph Califano Jr. is an overdue step toward conquering a major threat to health.

In 1976 more than 50 million Americans purchased more than 600 billion cigarettes. Addiction to tobacco last year was responsible for 220,000 deaths from heart disease, 78,000 deaths from lung cancer and 22,000 deaths from other cancers.

Califano proposes to fight the problem with education, regulations to limit smoking to designated areas in federal buildings and in the nation's largest corporations; and by banning smoking on commercial airliners.

The government also will examine ways to give people added financial incentives to give up smoking, and it will push for "greatly expanded and more comprehensive research into the subject of smoking and health."

The effort will be directed by a new Office on Smoking and Health, which will oversee a $23 million anti-smoking budget in fiscal 1979.

Despite the small amount of money involved, many persons will feel that the decision to smoke is made by individuals, and that government should stay out of it. Americans should continue to be able to decide individually whether to smoke, but a federal government that is charged with protecting the health and welfare of its citizens would be derelict if it overlooked the dangers posed by smoking.

Califano has made an important step toward helping millions of smoking Americans to themselves and their families a favor by giving up tobacco.

The Philadelphia Inquirer

Philadelphia, Pa., January 20, 1978

On Oct. 21, 1975, Joseph A. Califano Jr. gave up cigarets as a birthday present to his 11-year-old son. It "turned out to be one of the hardest things I have ever tried to do."

Now Mr. Califano, Secretary of Health, Education and Welfare, is trying to do a harder thing. He is trying to persuade the approximately 55 million American smokers to stop committing what he so aptly calls "slow-motion suicide."

Is Mr. Califano merely a reformed addict, now a fanatic on the other side? Maybe, but if so, he is a fanatic on the right side. Consider the figures.

Last year, as Mr. Califano pointed out in a news conference, smoking was a major factor in 220,000 deaths from heart disease; 78,000 lung cancer deaths; and 22,000 deaths from other cancers, including cancer of the mouth, of the esophagus, of the pancreas, of the kidney and of the bladder. If people would stop smoking, 85 percent of the deaths from bronchitis, emphysema and other lung disease would not happen. It is a fact — not a surmise — that women who smoke heavily during pregnancy may have stillborn or slow-witted children.

If, say, some new form of influenza were discovered to be the primary cause of some quarter of a million deaths in a year (not to mention up to $7 billion in health care costs and up to $18 billion in lost productivity, wages and absenteeism), the nation would go all out to defeat it.

So the question is whether the HEW campaign goes far enough. A spokesman for one anti-smoking group, Action on Smoking and Health (ASH), says Mr. Califano's department "labored mightily and brought forth a mouse."

The emphasis in the campaign is on education. The broadcasting networks will be asked to step up public-service anti-smoking announcements. Schools will be urged to step up counter-smoking education. Bans will be extended to smoking in public places. A task force is being set up to study making smoking more expensive, by increasing the 8-cents-a-pack federal excise tax. Mr. Califano also hopes more insurance companies will make non-smoking less expensive by offering discounts to non-smokers.

In short, the emphasis is on persuasion, not compulsion. That is just as well. The government can no more force people to stop smoking than it could force them during the Great Experiment to stop drinking alcohol. The government can warn people of the folly of committing "slow-motion suicide" and make it more expensive and inconvenient to do so, but it is up to individuals to kick the habit themselves. Or better, of course, never to acquire it in the first place.

The News American

Baltimore, Md., January 27, 1978

SECRETARY of Health, Education and Welfare Joseph Califano is planning to spend $23 million this year on a campaign to discourage cigarette smoking. Meanwhile, another federal agency a few blocks away from Secretary Califano's Washington offices, the Agriculture Department, will be paying out more of the taxpayers' money as subsidies to tobacco farmers in order to support the price of that nefarious weed.

As Mark Twain said about weather, everybody complains about the dangers of cigarette smoking but nobody seems to be able to stop it. Cigarettes may have been mainly responsible for most of last year's 220,000 deaths from heart disease and 100,000 cancer deaths in America. But what would happen if the federal government tried to put a ban on the sale of cigarettes as it tried to prohibit the sale of alcoholic beverages back in the nineteen twenties?

The black market bootlegging of sky-high priced cigarettes all over the United States would become a national disgrace. Organized criminals would take command of the tobacco industry. As history tells us, no nation that took up tobacco smoking has ever been able to kick the habit. We seem to be stuck with it.

Detroit Free Press

Detroit, Mich, August 21, 1978

THE CONFUSION of voices within the Carter administration over detente, or inflation, or taxes, is as nothing compared to the babel over cigaret smoking.

Here comes HEW Secretary Joseph Califano, waging a $23-million war on smoking; there goes the president down to North Carolina to assure the tobacco farmers there will always be a subsidy. In this corner a government-funded scientist proclaims the advent of the safe cigaret; in the other, a National Institute of Health spokesman warns there's no such thing, Virginia.

The federal government is at once spending money to discourage people from smoking, to find a safe cigaret so they can keep on smoking, and to subsidize a crop that, in the words of the surgeon general, may be harmful to your health. Does it make sense? No; but it's a pretty good reflection of what the American people want.

That the government subsidizes tobacco growers is unfortunate, but neither as simple nor as sinful as it may seem. The subsidy began before the surgeon general put those scary white labels on every cigaret pack and billboard in the land. With the allotment system that controls crop production, it serves as a market stabilizer, and as one of the least costly ventures of the federal government into agriculture, at that. Remove it, and tobacco would still be grown, but the chaos in the market would bankrupt the thousands of small growers who subsist on patches only a few acres in size.

This is not to say that the federal government, over the long term, should not try to extricate itself from the current dilemma, possibly by reducing allotments, encouraging larger growers to switch crops, taxing cigarets based on their tar and nicotine content, continuing the search for a safe smoke, and jawboning, of course, just as Mr. Califano is already doing.

Some would view this as accepting for the duration, if not encouraging, the continued high incidence of lung cancer and emphysema blamed on cigaret smoking. But the Carter administration is at once trying to save the livelihood of 200,000 tobacco producers, and the health of 53 million cigaret smokers, not all of whom want to be saved, anyway, The administration is only playing the conflicting and sometimes impossible roles we insist government play: protect us from economic dislocation, protect us from health damage. Protect us from ourselves. And meanwhile, we'll just go on with the enjoyment of our vices.

AKRON BEACON JOURNAL

Akron, Ohio, January 23, 1978

JOSEPH A. Califano, a reformed three-pack-a-day smoker, has launched a new anti-smoking campaign with a fervor like the religious zeal of a converted atheist.

The secretary of the U. S. Department of Health, Education and Welfare, who quit smoking at the request of his son less than three years ago, says his campaign will be based on public education, regulation and research, backed by higher budgets and, of course, a new government agency — an Office on Smoking and Health to replace the former National Clearinghouse for Smoking and Health.

There's no doubt that smoking, as Mr. Califano points out and as cigaret packages say, "is dangerous to your health." HEW has a responsibility to be concerned with our health, and Mr. Califano's proposals may have some beneficial effect — especially those that ban or limit smoking in public buildings.

He will also name a task force to study the possibility of raising excise taxes on cigarets and will support more research into the effects of smoking on health, factors that lead to dependence on tobacco and ways to overcome that addiction.

So far, so good.

But Mr. Califano also proposes to quintuple funds for anti-smoking education from $1 million to $6 million and to ask all schools to develop anti-smoking programs.

That effort may turn into a puff of smoke from a pipedream. In fact, if past experience is any criterion, tobacco growers should rejoice.

For the last decade most schools have been teaching about the dangers of drugs, alcohol and tobacco, making sex education a part of health courses and to shouldering responsibility for driver education. And what has happened?

The number of girls 13 to 19 who smoke has doubled. Drug and alcohol abuse has increased. The number of teenage pregnancies has risen. And teens continue to account for a disproportionate number of automobile accidents.

It's not that the schools have done a poor job. It's just that there's a limit to what they can do as long as there are permissive parents and freedom of choice in the background.

Mr. Califano's goal is worthy and certain regulations are justifiable. After all, about 53 million — a fourth of the nation's population — still smoke after all these years of being shown why this is unwise.

They have a right to. And a concerned government has a right to try to talk them out of it.

But when the smoke clears in Mr. Califano's new program, you can bet that most of them will still be smoking.

Rockford Register Star

Rockford, Ill., January 20, 1978

It is an irony of ironies that the federal government is spending $23 million to fight cigarette smoking, while spending around $70 million to subsidize tobacco growing.

Setting aside for a moment the good and the bad of smoking cigarettes and other tobacco products, just what is going on?

Joseph A. Califano, U.S. secretary of Health, Education and Welfare, launched his $23 million anti-smoking campaign amid appropriate hoopla. He will, he said, open a new Office on Smoking and Health, ban smoking in new areas of HEW buildings, ask for nationwide media anti-smoking promotion, publish new reports on the dangers of smoking and do a number of other things.

At the same time, another branch of the federal government is spending three times as much taxpayer money for tobacco farm price supports, which keep the growers in business. A White House spokesman, asked about the apparent ideological conflict, replied, "Tobacco growers should not bear the burden of economic ruin" because of efforts to discourage a national habit.

That's a political answer.

Califano's program has little, if anything, to do with politics, and everything to do with health. He said, in fact, that tobacco is the nation's "public health enemy No. 1."

The tragedy is that, in government, health and politics just don't mix.

SAN JOSE NEWS

San Jose, Cal., May 11, 1979

THERE'S no righteous zeal like the righteous zeal of a reformed cigarette smoker, as U.S. Secretary of Health, Education and Welfare Joseph Califano has been demonstrating with a vengeance.

In fact, some of Mr. Califano's anti-smoking strategems have been so extravagantly creative as to prompt speculation within the tobacco industry that he's given up nicotine in favor of more exotic substances.

We don't endorse those suspicions, but the secretary's latest Quixotic foray has done nothing to dispel them.

At a national conference in San Francisco the other day, Smokin' Joe excoriated the tobacco barons for employing advertising to entice young people into the vile habit. He criticized them for using "young, attractive models" in cigarette ads. Then he delivered the capper: the tobacco industry, he said, should spend 10 per cent of its $800-million-a-year advertising budget on messages convincing children and pregnant women not to smoke. The response from the cigarette makers has been an absolutely deafening silence.

One must at least give the secretary credit for originality; never before has a cabinet officer seriously suggested that an industry spend millions of dollars telling people not to buy its products. And if the tobacco industry and Madison Avenue take his suggestions to heart, there should be a welcome upturn in the job market for old, ugly models.

But if the federal government really wants to get serious about discouraging smoking, there are more effective and less illogical ways of doing it — such as, for starters, ending subsidies to tobacco growers.

A further instance of governmental effort to shield us from vice: The U.S. Senate debated several hours Monday before agreeing to order the attachment of the controversial statement, "Consumption of alcoholic beverages may be hazardous to your health," to bottles of booze.

The lawmakers considered an even tougher label stating that alcohol could be habit-forming, but, evidently afraid they would be accused of hysterical exaggeration, rejected it. In any event, a warning label on liquor bottles will be about as powerful a deterrent to alcoholism as a BB gun would be to an ICBM.

The Globe and Mail

Toronto,Ont.,Canada,June 13, 1979

What is this strange fascination which leads people to smoke cigarets? The pleasure of nicotine? The satisfaction of having something to do with their hands? Childhood nostalgia for the smell of burning leaves?

None of the above. Government officials believe people are smoking because the tobacco industry makes it too convenient, and they suggest a few minor changes: putting as few as eight cigarets in a package, for instance, to tax the smoker's patience as well as his pocketbook.

But why stop there? A padlock on the package would do wonders to discourage the casual smoker, cigarets in tin cans would produce an unsightly bulge in jacket pockets, and inch-long cigarets would frustrate the most determined addict. If all else fails, the industry could coat the ends of the cigarets with asbestos. Never a dull moment.

Government officials concede that these modifications are "unlikely in the near future", and perhaps it's all for the best. Ottawa has been trying for years to make it inconvenient to smoke marijuana, and look how popular *that* activity has become.

The Washington Post

Times Herald

Washington, D.C., January 14, 1979

SOMETIMES SCIENTIFIC opinion on health and safety issues reverses itself, so that a product once considered dangerous for human consumption will turn out to have been relatively risk-free . . . and vice versa. But the growing mountain of evidence that smoking cigarettes is bad for you seems to be unbudgeable—and it is getting more so every year as additional evidence is piled on. That is the nub of the matter, and it's what you need to remember as the ashtrays start flying in this year's annual exchange of abuse between the friends and foes of cigarette smoking.

The occasion for the melee was the release the other day of a mammoth new surgeon general's report on smoking and health, which came 15 years after the first report of the surgeon general on this subject, and many thousands of research papers later. For smokers and for the tobacco industry, the news was bad: The evidence grows ever less tentative and ever more demonstrable that cigarette smoking does serious and, all too often, mortal damage to the human body. In effect, this new report, which compiled the work that has been done since the 1964 report was made, was, predictably, subjected to some kind of preemptive attack by the stalwarts at the Tobacco Institute. They disparaged it as a rehash and dwelt on what they called an idiosyncratic excess of zeal on the part of anti-smoker, HEW Secretary Joseph Califano.

Tobacco partisans had already revealed their absolute unwillingness to entertain a conclusion inimical to the industry's interests when they dismissed the bad news in a report of a 14-year, $15-million research project on smoking and health that had been conducted by a committee of the American Medical Association with tobacco-industry funds. They have, in other words, long since debased the currency of their own arguments, so that their assaults on other aspects of the federal government's anti-smoking campaign cannot be taken seriously. We do not conclude from this that the government's effort is wise in every respect, only that the industry and friends have forfeited an important opportunity they might have seized somewhere along the line to help guide that effort in intelligent, prudent ways.

That the government should not remain neutral on the question of cigarette smoking seems self-evident and beyond argument to us. And Mr. Califano, given his particular responsibilities, is surely right in making the health effects of smoking an HEW issue. But the techniques the federal government should employ in trying to discourage cigarette smoking are not self-evident at all. Some extremely delicate questions of government's proper role in the individual's affairs and of economic pressure and dislocation are raised. These, not the propriety of Mr. Califano's concern or the validity of the medical-research results, are what the tobacco industry would be worrying about and addressing itself to—if it were even a little bit serious about trying to resolve this thing in a humane, responsible, public-spirited way.

TULSA WORLD

Tulsa, Okla., October 25, 1979

NO ONE should be surprised that smoking cigarettes is harmful to your health, given the almost unanimous opinion of everyone from anxious parents to sophisticated scientific studies.

But a study released by State Mutual Life Assurance Co. of America, Worcester, Mass., again making the point merits emphasis.

For 15 years, the insurance company has compared mortality rates of smokers and nonsmokers of all ages. Smokers have mortality rates from two to four times as high as nonsmokers, with the rates varying according to the number of cigarettes consumed.

State Mutual has been selling life insurance to non-smokers at lowered rates since 1964, perceiving even before documentation, the added health risks run by smokers.

The toleration of cigarettes, a proven carcinogen also directly linked to heart and circulatory disease, by society is perhaps today's greatest health irony.

Consider that Government spends billions to seek out the smallest pollutant in the atmosphere and food additives that *might* cause cancer while tolerating the widespread sale of cigarettes, a *known* health hazard.

Surely there is something basically wrong with the approach that permits such a skewed result.

The Miami Herald

Miami, Fla., November 2, 1979

CAN IT really be true that the multi-billion-dollar American cigaret industry's refusal to accept the linkage between smoking and disease is running out of breath? That hardly seems possible.

Nevertheless, the industry's own polltaker warns that public belief in the harmfulness of smoke inhaled by nonsmokers is increasing. And that credibility tips the public-health scale in favor of legal measures to control cigarets, the Roper Organization has warned the Tobacco Institute. "Nearly six out of 10 American adults believe that smoking is hazardous to the nonsmokers' health . . . . More than two-thirds of nonsmokers believe it, nearly half of all smokers believe it," according to the report.

While the cigaret industry still was distracted by the vain hope of discovering a "safe" cigaret or of discrediting the overwhelming statistical evidence that smoking causes disease, the public apparently went on to the next step. Once again the public's intelligence has been underestimated by those who hope to profit from the public's gullibility.

The industry pollster's predictions of a "foreboding" future seem a bit overdone, however. The six major American companies sold a record 615.3 billion cigarets last year, and there was only a negligible reduction in the annual consumption per capita.

Still, the poll results are impressive when weighed against the $874 million the big six spent in the advertising and promotion of cigaret-smoking last year. The anti-smoking activists, such as Miami's Group Against Smokers' Pollution (GASP), count their donations in dimes, not dollars. Obviously the anti-smoking message finds fertile ground indeed in the common sense and personal experience of both the smoking and the non-smoking populace.

Elected officials should take their cue from the public. The right of private business to choose its own course must be protected, but there's no excuse for allowing smokers to pollute the air inside government-owned facilities such as the courthouse, the Florida capital, or city hall. Where there is a conflict in a publicly owned meeting place, the right of the nonsmoker to clean air should prevail.

It is premature to sound the death knell for Americans' nasty smoking habit, but public agencies should pull the bellrope whenever they can do so without infringing individual rights.

The News Journal

Wilmington, Del., September 26, 1979

If white males in this country have had the feeling that they are a discredited group, they may have been able to take a little—a very little—encouragement from a news item the other day.

White males, it seems, were the highest scorers last year among people who tried to quit smoking. The National Center for Health Statistics reported that nearly 17 million Americans tried to kick the smoking habit in 1978. Overall one of these in every five succeeded. Of those who made the attempt to quit, however, only one in every 10 blacks and one in every 10 women aged 45 to 64 made it.

An achievement for the white male, perhaps, but the institute's figures don't say much for the efforts of those who have been trying to curb smoking in general.

After years of insisting on labels on cigarette packages telling people that they are taking a risk when they take a puff, there still are 52.3 million smokers aged 17 or over in the United States. The percentage of adults who use the weed has fallen since 1970, from 37 percent to less than 34 percent, but among those the percentage of "heavy" smokers—those who smoke more than 25 cigarettes a day—has risen from 23 to 28 percent.

The institute has a plausible explanation for that last increase: A greater percentage of those who had been smoking only a few cigarettes per day have quit completely, leaving the remainder of the smokers more dominated by the "heavies."

There also are indications that more people are paying attention to the tar content of the cigarettes that they do smoke, possibly in response to all of those warnings that emanate from Washington.

But in general there's no reason to believe that the anti-smoking crusaders have been notably successful.

Probably it is reinforcement of the theory that you can warn people all you want, but you can't legislate morality and you can't impose your notions of sensible behavior on other people. They'll make their own choices.

ST. LOUIS POST-DISPATCH

St. Louis. Mo., May 5, 1979

"It is time to stop preaching against tobacco and to develop economically viable ways to curtail its production," according to Rep. Henry S. Reuss of Wisconsin. And Mr. Reuss backs his sweeping conclusion with examples of how the government might work positively to induce the tobacco farmer to switch to another crop. Instead of repeating Mr. Califano's preface to the surgeon general's report — "there can be no doubt that smoking is truly slow-motion suicide" — Mr. Reuss is speaking in the language the tobacco industry understands — money.

Why, anti-smokers are asking, should the government financially support something that is injurious to people's health? But it is not tobacco per se that agriculture subsidies maintain (though the end result is the same) but the farmer. And small tobacco farmers have few sure options. According to *The Charlotte Observer*, a voice from the heart of tobacco country in North Carolina, one acre of tobacco there earns more than $1,200, an acre of peanuts only $160. Crops that could earn comparable money — strawberries, or sunflowers — don't have a stable market. In South Carolina, soy beans surpassed tobacco by $2 million as the top cash crop, but 1.47 million acres were planted in soy beans and only 71,000 in tobacco.

But back to Mr. Reuss. He wants the government to end its tobacco subsidy, which since 1974 has amounted to more than $180 million in price supports, research and marketing expenses. In place of this, he would finance the conversion of tobacco farms to other crops, just as the government has successfully promoted a switch from opium poppies and other narcotics sources in several foreign countries. The international program has cost the U.S. only $37 million, whereas the domestic tobacco conversion costs would be much higher if small family farms are to be saved. Even though it would be expensive, conversion deserves serious study, especially since direct medical costs from smoking are estimated to be $15 billion annually.

Richmond Times-Dispatch

Roanoke, Va., August 19, 1979

In a letter to the editorial page of *The New York Times* on August 6, James Stewart, who identified himself as president of Smokers United, Inc., made an impassioned plea for the rights of "57 million known American smokers."

With regard to citizens being at liberty to decide whether they shall smoke or not smoke cigarettes, we agree 100 percent with New Yorker Stewart, who stated his organization has no connection with the tobacco industry. Moreover, when he pans anti-smoking zealots like deposed HEW Secretary Joseph Califano, we applaud.

But he weakens his argument when he claims that smoking is of such low-level risk to health that insurance companies do not penalize smokers in their premium schedules, and when he goes on to argue, nonsensically, that jogging is a more serious health menace than smoking and that, therefore, it is the activities of joggers, not smokers, that ought to be discouraged.

The long-standing policy of some 30 life insurance companies is to offer premium discounts to non-smokers because the evidence is that they tend to live longer than smokers. These 10 to 15 percent premium breaks for non-smokers obviously penalize smokers.

Furthermore, according to a survey by *The Washington Post*, several insurance companies have begun offering similar premium discounts to individuals who jog, swim or cycle regularly, in recognition that these active people, too, tend to live longer, healthier lives. One major insurance company, for example, offers a $100,000 annual renewable term policy with a standard annual premium of $309 for a 40-year-old man. If he exercises regularly (and can prove it, if asked, by producing confirmation from a YMCA, YWCA or his physician), the premium drops to $268. If he's abstained from smoking for a year, it drops further to $226.

Mr. Stewart quotes with relish a recent quip by South African heart specialist Christiaan Barnard that "jogging is a dangerous mania" in that highways are "a sewer of noxious gases from car exhaust dragged into your lungs with every straining breath." Jogging is not risk-free. A more serious hazard than breathing fumes is being hit by one of the vehicles emitting the "noxious gases." But it is ridiculous to suppose that the only place to jog is along heavily traveled highways. Joggers should, and most do, find safer avenues for their exercise.

A major study by Dr. Ralph Paffenbarger Jr. at Stanford University found that persons who jog (or engage in other aerobic exercise) for as little as 20 to 30 minutes a day reduce the risk of heart attack by 64 percent. Of course, persons with any pre-existing heart ailment should consult their physician about any strenuous exercise program.

The president of Smokers United was just blowing smoke when he tried to depict the nicotine habit as more healthful than the exercise habit. Rather than fogging the issue, he ought to admit candidly the known risks and base his arguments on the right of informed adults to make their own choices.

—ROBERT G. HOLLAND

THE SACRAMENTO BEE

Sacremento, Cal., May 6, 1979

When cigarette advertising was banned on TV in 1971, the expectations were that fewer people would be lured into smoking and that cigarette consumption in the United States would drop. As it turns out, however, cigarette smoking has increased since the ban. According to the American Enterprise Institute, TV advertising never did very successfully induce people to take up the habit; it mostly influenced their choice of brands. Cutting it out has done nothing so much as save the tobacco industry a fortune in advertising costs.

Worse yet, the ban on cigarette commercials brought with it the end of anti-smoking ads, because the TV stations no longer have to run them under the equal-time doctrine. And the anti-smoking ads apparently were very effective with potential new smokers: Cigarette consumption actually dropped during the three years they were running. It seems that bad new is better than no news at all.

The national attempt to stop smoking — like many individual attempts to quit — has backfired in other ways too. The caution label now required on each pack and each ad seems to have had little effect on smoking — but it has apparently provided the tobacco companies blanket protection from potential liability suits. And the hype about low-tar cigarettes has greatly increased their consumption without profiting anyone so much as the industry. Apparently the low-tar smokers simply buy more cigarettes to reach the same nicotine quotient they've become used to, and since these new cigarettes have about half the tobacco of the old models but sell for the same price, guess who comes out ahead. As any smoker could have told you, it's hard to lose money marketing an addiction.

Rockford Register Star

Rockford, Ill., April 11, 1980

It's enough to make a confirmed nicotine junkie gasp (if his lungs still can gasp): A 10-cent hike in tax cigarette taxes!

After being hit with higher fuel prices, because suplies are short; higher gasoline taxes, because we aren't supposed to drive so much; proposed cuts in public services, because the budget must be balanced; now comes a tax hike on smoking — "because it's not healthy."

The walls appear to be closing in on smokers. Those who escape lung cancer and emphysema are now consigned to the back of the airplane, the back of the bus, and the smoker's section of many restaurants. For all of these privileges it is now proposed that smokers pay a total of 18 cents per pack in federal taxes.

Reason for the tax increase? Smoking isn't good for you!

Stamping out evil in all forms is a commendable goal, but where would the legislature propose to stop? Will we come to a 10-cent tax on double-dip ice cream cones because of the hazards of overweight? Or maybe a 100 percent tax on mountain climbing equipment because the sport is hazardous and there really is no compelling national need to have people standing on top of mountains?

The two congressmen, both reformed smokers, who have proposed the tax-increase legislation say they anticipate opposition from the tobacco growing states. That should be the least of their problems.

If their proposed tax could be related to the problems of smoking — say to provide funding for lung cancer hospitals or emphysema research (or even methods of fire-proofing furniture) — that would be one thing. If a case could be made for the government needing the money and the tax being part of an across-the-board assault on luxury goods, that also could be defensible.

But, to have a tax proposed just because a couple of fussy legislators want to impose their zeal for non-smoking on the public at large goes a little far.

There are plenty of reasons for not smoking without Congress having to get in on the act.

The Des Moines Register

Des Moines, Iowa, April 12, 1980

The federal government's program to support tobacco prices would seem one of the most likely targets for federal budget-cutters. What sense does it make to warn Americans about the dangers of smoking, yet support the tobacco crop?

Senator Henry Bellmon (Rep., Okla.) doesn't think it makes much sense. He tried to get the Senate Budget Committee to eliminate the tobacco program last week, but the committee rejected his proposal.

We think the committee was right. Eliminating the tobacco program isn't the way to get Americans to smoke less. The beneficiaries of the tobacco price support program aren't the giant tobacco companies, but the small farmers who raise the crop.

The support program helps them by stabilizing the price of tobacco through a system of production quotas and crop loans. In fiscal 1979, the government advanced tobacco growers about $229 million, most of which will be recovered as the loans are repaid or the crop is sold by the government.

Robert L. Tarczy, a tobacco program specialist at the U.S. Department of Agriculture, said that the government has lost only $57 million on this loan program since 1933. Price support programs for all farm commodities have cost roughly one thousand times that much.

Eliminating tobacco price supports would do little for the budget but could cause hardship for many of the 250,000 to 300,000 family farmers who rely on the tobacco crop. Tarczy said many small farmers would be forced to get out of tobacco, but few could turn to other crops because their farms are too small.

Unfortunately, forcing them into the cities to look for jobs or go on welfare wouldn't reduce tobacco production. Tarczy said their farms would be taken over by big operators able to withstand swings in prices.

Kicking the small farmers who raise tobacco is not the best way to reduce smoking — or balance the budget. It would make more sense to attack the problem head-on by forcing smokers to pay more: through higher taxes on cigarettes and other tobacco products. This is the approach that Congress should take toward tobacco as it strives to balance the budget.

Driving

Car safety became an issue in 1966, with the publication of Ralph Nader's expose, *Unsafe at Any Speed*. America's love affair with the automobile was not ended by Nader's book, but it entered a new phase. Previously, auto manufacturers were no more interested in stressing safety than tobacco growers were in confronting the health hazards of cigarettes. Advertisers promoted cars as opportunities for freedom, excitement and adventure—not injury and death.

However, with auto deaths exceeding 40,000 a year, Americans could no longer afford to be ignorant about safety. Congress gathered its energies in 1964 and legislated safety standards for auto components. As early as 1962, car makers were installing seat belt hardware as standard front-seat equipment, and by 1967, seat belts were standard equipment in all front seats. The following year, the National Traffic Safety Agency required auto makers to install a number of passive safety devices, such as rupture-resistant fuel tanks, interior padding and headrests.

That seat belts, shoulder harnesses and head rests prevent many accidents from becoming major tragedies has been confirmed by numerous studies. Nevertheless, they depend on the driver's conscious decision to use them. Public service ads remind drivers to "buckle up for safety," but many still do not. Faced with the refusal of drivers to protect themselves, Congress considered the more radical step of protecting the drivers in spite of themselves. Should new car models include automatic seat belts, which lock as soon as the driver sits in the seat, or air bags, which inflate from under the dashboard upon impact in a collision?

Forty thousand deaths a year, billions of dollars in hospital and rehabilitation costs, millions of lost working hours: these are social concerns. They are the other side of the fine line that separates an individual's right to decide whether to protect himself from his responsibility to society. The public is rightfully indignant when auto manufacturers neglect safety. What happens, then, when individuals neglect their own—and others'—safety?

Western States Unite Against 55 MPH Speed Limit

The Wyoming Senate passed Jan. 25 State Senator Cal Taggart's bill raising the speed limit to 65 mph. Legislators had proposed similar moves to raise the speed limit in nine other western states: California, Colorado, Texas, Washington, New Mexico, Nebraska, Nevada, Montana and Oklahoma.

The 55 mph speed limit had been installed as a fuel-conservation measure in 1973. As federal law allowed the Transportation Department to withhold millions in highway funds from states without 55 mph speed limits, most states complied with the measure.

However, western states started in 1978 to coordinate their efforts to raise their states' speed limits, contending the Transportation Department would not cut funds to an entire bloc of states.

Westerners claimed that the 55 mph speed limit was unrealistic in their states' great expanses of open land. They also called the drive to increase the speed limit a motion against the federal government's control over the states.

The Boston Herald American

Boston, Mass., January 30, 1979

There are several sensible reasons for keeping the speed limit at 55 mph — which probably explains why lawmakers in a number of western states want to get rid of it.

A bill raising the limit to 65 mph has already passed one branch of the Wyoming legislature. Similar measures have been filed in Washington, Colorado, Oklahoma and Texas, and the only reason New Mexico hasn't followed suit is that the legislator who plans to submit a bill there hasn't finished writing it.

One problem is that even if all those proposals are passed they will collide with a federal law mandating the lower speed limit, and the states could forfeit their share of government highway funds.

Wyoming, in fact, has been threatened with exactly that if its bill becomes law, and that could mean the loss of $51 million in federal money.

The issue ought not to turn on so crass a consideration, however, because the value of the 55 mph limit has been demonstrated beyond doubt in the five years since it was enacted by Congress.

For one thing, it has saved an average of nine million gallons of gas a day since then. For another, it is credited by Dept. of Transportation officials with being "the single biggest factor" in reducing highway deaths by 36,000 since 1974.

Critics of the 55 mph law may challenge those claims, or attribute them to factors other than a nationally enforced lighter foot on the gas pedal.

But if we're saving lives and energy at 55, why jack up the limit and allow more drivers to kill themselves — and others — at a higher rate of speed?

RENO EVENING GAZETTE

Reno, Nevada, February 4, 1979

Once again, the 55-mile-per-hour speed limit is under attack in the West, where the miles stretch out forever — and so does the time for drivers pushing their way across endless and desolate stretches of landscape.

The issue conjures up states' rights, wasted hours, wasted lives, and wasted gasoline. Like Billy Martin in the televised beer commercial, it is easy to feel strongly both ways.

A number of western states feel strongly one way: they claim the law makes no sense in their wide-open regions. They also feel very strongly that the federal government has no business dictating speed limits to them.

This feeling is especially strong among Nevadans, who never had a state speed limit to contend with before the 1973 oil crisis and the federal law that grew out of it. Nevadans were accustomed to flooring the pedal when they hit the road and getting their long drives over with as quickly as possible. There's no doubt that the law — if obeyed — makes long-distance travel more tedious.

It is also true that federal interference is an especial irritant to Nevadans, who dislike federal ownership of large blocks of land and IRS attempts to collect income tax on tips, to name just two areas of contention.

So many Nevadans will be pleased to see that bills have been introduced in both the Assembly and the Senate to get rid of the 55-mile-per-hour speed limit in this state. AB 252, introduced by Michael Fitzpatrick of Las Vegas, would eliminate all reference to the 55-mile speed limit, and would in effect leave Nevada with no limits at all. SB 176, introduced by Keith Ashworth of Las Vegas, would raise Nevada's state speed to 65 miles per hour.

But despite the joy these proposals will create, there is much to be said for opposition to them.

For one thing, there is no doubt that lower speed limits have increased traffic safety. This is not just an idle statistic, with little relevance to our everyday lives. It relates directly to every person who gets behind the wheel of a car. It means that when you're out of the road, you're a little safer from yourself and a little safer from the other guy. Time is important, but not as important, perhaps, as lives and whole bodies.

Of course, not everyone is driving 55 and under. But even those who exceed the speed limit generally drive slower than they did when there was no limit. If the speed limit is raised, the speeders can be expected to drive even faster; and if there is no limit, there will be a mass return to high and dangerous speeds.

And the accident rate will climb.

Then there's the energy problem. Gasoline remains a once-only commodity. Nobody knows how much fuel is out there under the ground, but it will run out someday. The more we save now, the longer we will have it around. And, as we all know, there is no truly effective alternative power source on the horizon for automobiles.

Also, the deteriorating political situation in the Mideast could lead to another gasoline shortage at any time. This nation could see gas rationing or long lines at service stations, and not enough fuel to go around. Yet Nevadans, like other Americans, have not yet taken to heart the need to conserve.

Any number of national leaders have stressed the need for some sacrifices in the energy area, not only to conserve but to help this nation reduce its burdensome trade deficit and help bolster the dollar internationally. Yet Nevadans, like other Americans, have not yet taken to heart the need to conserve. It is time they did, and one way to do so is to drive more slowly.

So at this point in time, the needs of safety and conservation seem to outweigh states' rights and convenience. The wiser course would be to retain the 55-mile speed limit, at least for the time being.

The Seattle Times

Seattle Wash., February 2, 1979

WASHINGTON is not the only state where legislators are taking shots at the federally mandated 55-mile-an-hour speed limit.

Nine other legislatures, all in Western states, also are considering bills to defy Uncle Sam — either by raising the legal limit to 65 or even 70 miles an hour, or declaring speeding over 55 but under 70 to be an "energy violation" that would not show up on a driver's record.

They include California, Colorado, Texas, Nebraska, Nevada, New Mexico, Montana, Oklahoma and Wyoming.

Responding to an anti-55 slogan that "drivers are bored to death," Wyoming's Senate last week passed a bill fixing the limit at 65.

"Out here," a Wyoming legislator told The Wall Street Journal, "you can drive all day, and maybe see one other car and maybe some jackrabbits and antelope. All we want to do is regulate our own lives."

In Olympia, Governor Ray speculated the other day that "frustration with federal rules and regulations may be a part of the motivation" for the developing trend toward collective resistance to the law that permits a cutoff of federal-aid highway funds to states that don't try to enforce the reduced limit.

The governor has taken no position on raising the limit on Washington's highways. She has said only that as long as 55 m.p.h. is in the law, "it certainly is going to be enforced."

At last report, nearly 62 per cent of this state's motorists were ignoring the limit, a circumstance that helped motivate the State Patrol's "emphasis" enforcement on major freeways.

Despite the unpopularity of the federally prescribed limit, it is hard to argue with the statistics that have been piling up since the law's passage in 1973.

Many may have forgotten the principal purpose: To conserve fuel, an issue frequently overlooked in the debates over state's rights and the fact that "the freeways were built for 70 m.p.h."

This state's Department of Transportation calculates that the widespread defiance of the 55-m.p.h. limit is wasting about 6 million gallons of gasoline a year in Washington alone.

That is an enormous amount of energy.

With this week's news that the turmoil in Iran may compel mandatory allocation of motor fuels (at least two major petroleum companies already have begun to ration supplies to retailers), and the slow-but-sure rise of gasoline prices toward the $1-a-gallon mark, heavy-footed motorists should recognize that the need for energy conservation is real.

State lawmakers should be no less aware of their obligation to provide leadership on conservation issues.

CASPER STAR-TRIBUNE

Casper, Wyo., February 13, 1979

Wyoming competed in an oblique fashion with Taiwan and Russia and the People's Republic of China Monday at President Carter's press conference. The President implied that state legislatures planning to change the 55 mph speed limit are out of step with the times.

Of course, he is right.

Recall that the 55 mph speed limit was established by Congress because of the Arab oil embargo of 1973 - 74. Congress did not insist that the individual states had to follow the 55 mph rule but it did say that those that did not choose to comply then that state would become ineligible for federal highway funds. Not a single state, with the exception of Wyoming, has been willing to forfeit the money - in Wyoming's case $51.7 million annually. The money makes up a major portion of road budgets among all the states.

The original reason for the 55 mph speed limit was the Arab oil embargo. Now, with the new government in Iran, the situation could be as disastrous. The United States has lost its most favored nation status with Iran and even if the situation in that turmoil racked country calmed tomorrow, it would take months for the country to go on full production. Middle East oil, despite the OPEC regulations, has been selling for as high as $20 a barrell since the Iranian crisis.

Driving 55 mph does save gasoline. Federal officials estimate that the 55 mph speed limit saves nine million gallons of gasoline a day. With better enforcement, it is estimated that American drivers could conserve 15 million gallons a day, but most people will readily admit the 55 mph speed limit is minimally enforced.

Another reason why the 55 mph speed limit was adopted is that it saves lives despite claims made to the contrary at the Wyoming legislature that boredom of driving at the speed increases the accident toll.

The first year the speed limit was enforced, 1974, there were 9,000 fewer highway fatalities than the year before. The next year, the total dropped to 44,525. But each year since then the total has been increasing because law enforcement officials have been looking the other way.

The *Arkansas Gazette*, a state where the legislature is also agitating for increasing the speed limit, pointed out to its readers in opposing changing the regulation, quotes the National Safety Council which said that the chances of surviving a highway accident when driving between 51 and 60 mph are 31 to 1. At 70 mph the chances are 1 to 1.

There is no denying that having to drive at 55 mph is monotonous and inconvenient, particularly in a state as large as Wyoming. But considering the alternatives - loss of lives, the fuel crisis, and the loss of $51.7 needed dollars - 55 mph is something we all can live with.

ALBUQUERQUE JOURNAL

Albuquerque, N.M., January 27, 1979

Thousands of unnamed Americans are alive today because of the nationwide highway speed limit of 55 mph, initially imposed on the states in 1973 by the federal government as a fuel conservation measure.

Time and experience have proved the 55 mph speed limit as effective as a lifesaving measure as it is a fuel saver. For this reason the legislatures of New Mexico, Wyoming and every other state should refrain from meddling with the national standard.

Wyoming's Senate, in defiance of the continuing federal threat to cut off federal highway funds, has approved a bill to raise the speed limit to 65 mph. There is now a bill before the New Mexico House to lower the penalty assessment for speeds within 15 miles of the maximum limit from $15 to $5.

Although the New Mexico bill was proposed ostensibly to deprive auto insurance underwriters of access to speeding records, its ultimate effect would be to undercut effective enforcement of the 55 mph standard.

Legislative tampering with the penalty for excessive speeds already has led to a higher toll in lives and blood on New Mexico highways. Legislation setting the penalty assessment at $15 — a nominal sum in this era of inflation, coupled with a means of avoiding the inconvenience of a court appearance — was followed almost immediately by a sharp rise in the death rate on New Mexico highways.

New Mexico and Wyoming have peculiar problems with the 55 mph speed limit. Each has a tourist-oriented economy, a tremendous land area and a small population. With their interstate systems, both serve as wide-open corridors for traffic originating and terminating in other states. Their populations and economies will not afford the police manpower necessary to enforce speed limits rigidly and consistently. It is not surprising that Wyoming has the nation's highest death rate per vehicle mile of travel.

But the answer is not to fight "big brotherism" with suicidal speed limits or nominal speeding penalties. The answer lies in adjustment of the distribution formulae for federal highway funds so that sparsely populated states like New Mexico and Wyoming can enforce the laws foisted upon them by the "big brother who giveth and taketh away."

St. Petersburg Times

St. Petersburg, Fla., January 31, 1979

At Washington's urging, the present 55-mile-per-hour speed limit on the nation's highways was adopted early in 1974, in the wake of the Arab oil embargo, as a way to save gasoline.

It turned out to be a saver of lives as well. Traffic fatalities dropped dramatically, from 55,639 in 1973 to 46,286 in 1974. While this figure has since inched upward — with more automobiles on the road — deaths remain below the level of 50,000-and-up that prevailed from 1966 to 1974.

SPEED LIMITS are established and enforced by the states, not by the federal government. Five years ago, when the gasoline shortage was tangible and painful, the states responded quickly to the Washington initiative, both from patriotic motives and because compliance was tied to the flow of highway construction funds from Washington.

There has always been opposition, most vociferously from truck drivers, who earn less money when their daily driving distances are curtailed. (Tests have disproved the old claim that the big trucks get better gasoline mileage at higher speeds.)

Now a movement is developing in a number of western states, where distances are long and towns far apart, to scrap the national standard and return to legal state limits of 65 or 70 mph.

A TELEGRAM from Transportation Secretary Brock Adams to Wyoming Gov. Ed Herschler, warning that dropping the 55-mile limit would mean a cut in federal highway funds, has further fueled the controversy.

The cry of "blackmail" has been raised in Wyoming and has given impetus to repeal movements in Washington, Colorado, Oklahoma, Texas, Montana and Missouri, where similar moves are being considered.

It is of course not "blackmail," because Adams' warning was in accordance with federal law as well as with the national interest.

Most motorists, including those who do not observe it strictly, favor continuing the 55 mph speed limit. A Gallup Poll last summer found only 21 percent in favor of abolishing it and going back to the traditionally higher limits.

FLORIDA'S Legislature two years ago rejected a proposal to return to a higher speed limit. During the holiday season, the state mounted a special enforcement drive by the Highway Patrol.

This state's example should be followed. It is true that many — perhaps most — motorists feel free to exceed the posted limit by up to 5 miles an hour. But that has always been true.

Speeds in the 55-to-60 mph ran̄ as contrasted with 75 to 80, still sε gasoline and, more importantly, tʰ sands of lives each year.

THE BILLINGS GAZETTE

Billings, Mont., January 30, 1979

Wyoming legislators are living dangerously with their move to up the state's highway speed limit to 65 miles per hour.

We agree that the 65 mph law makes a lot more sense than the pokey 55 mph limit imposed by the nation's Congress in its efforts to save petroleum.

The trouble with the 55 mph law isn't that it is all that slow. No, the trouble is that so few observe it in these wide open spaces that the law becomes a farce.

Worse, all the average law-abiding driver who has been observing the 55 mph limit has to do is decide to keep with the trucks blasting along at 65 to 70 mph. One of Montana's few-and-far-between highway patrolmen spot him on radar and the driver loses all the time he was saving going faster.

Despite trucker arguments to the contrary, driving 55 mph does save fuel. It is a matter of physics. What costs more is the extra driver time on the road at slower speeds.

The 55 mph limit also tends to lower the top speeds on the highways. In the days of Montana's unrestricted speed it was not unusual to have 100 mph and more drivers on the road.

We say that Wyoming legislators are living dangerously, not because of the increased speeds, because their action turned into law could result in Wyoming losing about $52 million in federal highway funds.

Should that happen, the legislators might have to raise the sales tax, impose an income tax and hike property taxes to get enough money to keep their highways fit to drive at 45 mph.

THE CHRISTIAN SCIENCE MONITOR

Boston, Mass., February 8, 1979

Out West, where the deer and the antelope play and drivers have a hard time reining in their cars, some people are getting downright ornery about Uncle Sam telling them how fast they can drive. But before they send their lawmakers to Washington for a showdown over raising the 55 mile-per-hour speed limit to 65, they ought to take another close look at the varmint they're gunning for.

Nationwide that 55 m.p.h. limit has brought a sharp drop in highway fatalities, and Department of Transportation projections show enforcement would save another 31,900 lives over the next 10 years. But there's the rub. Enforcement has been spotty, and the real need is for states to show they mean business by cracking down on violators.

If Westerners remain unconvinced that slower driving is safer in their part of the country, they might give a thought to the 9 million gallons of gas a day federal officials estimate are being saved as a result of the speed limit. With energy officials urging conservation and warning of possible oil shortages, drivers anxious to see the speed limit go up ought not be surprised if motorists in other parts of the country ask to see whose brand is on that extra fuel they'll burn at higher speeds. We're all in this together, pardner.

The Chattanooga Times

Chattanooga, Tenn., February 14, 1979

The state of Wyoming has taken steps to raise the speed limit on its highways to 65 mph instead of the nationwide limit of 55, which Congress enacted some time ago as one way of conserving gasoline. It's not yet clear whether the Wyoming legislature will make the action final, thus forfeiting $51 million annually in highway funds from the federal government. A preliminary move has been turned down.

The 55-mph limit can be a bother, especially as it seems to be so routinely ignored. Certainly, enforcement could be more effective if a uniform limit of 65 were imposed.

The fact is that adherence to the "double nickel" speed limit has proved beneficial. It has saved upwards of 50 million gallons of gasoline. National Safety Council statistics show that the lower speed limit has resulted in fewer highway deaths — nearly 16,000 in the two full years after its passage. As more drivers have started to ignore the 55-mph limit, the highway death rate has begun to increase.

A unilateral decision by Wyoming or any other state would be a mistake. It would open the gates again to a hodgepodge of state limits with all the misunderstandings and disputed arrests that go along with varying levels.

If studies show there should be a higher limit because of, a number of factors — increased voluntary compliance, better enforcement and the suitability of modern highways to greater speeds — then it should come nationally.

The states have a right to do what they will. But if the federal government follows through on its commitment to cut highway funds if the 55 mph limit is bypassed, perhaps it will also distribute the money to other states where it is retained.

THE LOUISVILLE TIMES

Louisville, Ky., February 1, 1979

It's too bad that it took an international oil embargo to get a 55-mile-an-hour speed limit, because pressure to raise the limit has been growing as fast as the supply of gasoline ever since. And saving lives, not fuel, has always been the best reason for the 55-mph limit.

It is under heavier attack now than at any other time in the five years since it became law. Even a new federal law which threatens forfeiture of 10 per cent of highway aid for failure to enforce the limit has not prevented a move to repeal it in half a dozen Western states.

Some legislators in those states are willing to bet that the threat of federal penalties is just as hollow as similar dark threats by the federal government about ignoring federal air and water pollution standards have proved to be. And they complain that the new law is tougher on sparsely-populated Western states than those in the East.

They're right about that — although it certainly is no justification to change the speed limit — and Kentucky is a prime example. Nearly 85 per cent of the motorists checked on rural Interstate mileage during federal surveys last year were speeding, and one of five was going faster than 65 mph — one of the highest speeding rates in the country.

It's hardly surprising, however, in view of official encouragement of speeding on the Interstate system. State police have been instructed not to bother motorists for speeding unless they exceed 60 mph, while the 1976 legislature, at the urging of the governor, eliminated driver penalty points for Interstate speeding convictions below 70 mph. In enacting what has been called "the truckers' relief bill," however, the state retained fines for such convictions. If speed kills — and statistics prove without doubt that it does — Kentucky has granted a license to kill.

With a record as shoddy as this, one might assume that Kentucky would be first in line for that 10 per cent forfeiture of highway funds — amounting to about $15 million a year — under the law that was supposed to toughen enforcement of the 55-mph limit.

Far from it. Kentucky will not only lose no money but is sure to qualify for a highway safety bonus of about $40,000.

Blame geography, plus provisions of the new law which are so loosely-drawn that an 18-wheeler could roar through them.

If fewer than 60 per cent of vehicles surveyed on its federally-aided road system are speeding this year, the state will avoid a forfeiture. If fewer than 50 per cent are speeding, the state qualifies for the bonus. In Kentucky, where most of the federally-aided mileage is in winding, hilly two-lane roads on the state primary and secondary system, passing through many small towns, fewer than a third of motorists speed. That's chiefly because they can't. When they get on wide-open rural Interstate mileage, they really open up, but there isn't enough of it to make a difference in the overall average.

The requirements of the new law are supposed to get progressively tougher, but they are scheduled to do so at such a slow pace that Kentucky should qualify for a bonus for three years without any improvement. And changes in the survey system will make it look even better than it now does.

The new law is a mockery in Kentucky, where it will reward an official policy of evading the 55-mph limit, while at the same time stimulating resistance in Western states because of its geographical discrimination. It must be changed, quickly, and then it must be made to stick, despite unpopularity and political pressures.

Nothing will destroy the 55-mph speed limit — the single most effective highway safety measure we have — more quickly than hypocritical failure by the federal government to enforce a law which is itself supposed to encourage the states to enforce their own laws.

The Morning News

Wilmington, Del., Ferbuary 1, 1979

A movement is developing among legislatures of some states, and among other officials claiming grass roots support, to end, or ignore, the federally imposed 55 mile an hour highway speed limit.

These folks, generally from larger states, want drivers to be able to zip along the roads at 65 or 70.

That's in the face of what seems to be convincing evidence that the 55 mile limit instituted during the 1973-74 oil embargo saves both lives and an estimated 9 million gallons of gasoline every day.

Arguments of people objecting most strenuously to the limit rest basically on the fact that their states are large ones, where great distances are involved.

Oklahoma State Rep. Jim Townsend, for instance, is quoted in a recent Christian Science Monitor survey.

In the East, said Rep. Townsend, highways are "generally more congested" and perhaps "55" is reasonable, but in the West, "distances are great and time is precious" and the limit is not practical or enforceable. "Out here in the open spaces," Rep. Townsend told the Associated Press later, "time is money." In Wyoming, the state's Senate has passed a measure to raise the speed limit to 65 despite federal warnings of withdrawal of highway aid funds. (A Colorado legislator uses the word "blackmail" to describe such a federal warning.)

Wyoming State Sen. Cal Taggert denies that the federal government has any business in setting speed limits in the first place. "That's a state matter," he said.

Perhaps it is. Undoubtedly the feds already are too much involved in details of our lives.

It seems obvious, however, that the feds, like it or not, have a large part of the responsibility for solving energy problems. A saving of 9 million gallons of gasoline a day is a significant one, even ignoring savings in lives and injuries.

The remarks by Oklahoma's Rep. Townsend that in the West "time is precious" and "time means money," are valid, of course. Time is just as precious and time is money to exactly the same extent in the East, and an Eastern motorist has just as many problems on a 500-mile drive, whether or not he crosses some state lines.

The impatience of any motorist embarking on a 500-mile journey may be understood.

For instance, take Wyoming, which seems to be a leader in this faster-is-better movement.

From Carpenter in the southeast corner of that state to Electric Peak in the northwest, or from Aspen in the southwest to Colony in the northwest is a more than 500-mile drive. Presumably Sen. Taggart has frequent occasions to make such trips.

When he averages 65 miles an hour for 500 miles, he requires seven hours, 41 minutes and some seconds for the trip. Averaging 55, he requires nine hours, five minutes and some seconds.

If the senator is transporting a desperately injured person — perhaps a victim of a high-speed highway crash — those 84 minutes and few seconds might make a substantial difference.

But if the traffic stayed at 55 in the first place, the victim might not need help so desperately. The National Safety Council figures there's a 31-1 chance of survival in an accident at 55-60, but a mere even chance of survival at 70.

Even in big states, some officials recognize the stakes. A spokesman for the Department of Public Safety in Texas, where moves are under way to restore a 70 mph limit, says, "We know the death rate would go up if the speed limit was put back at 70."

Forget the fuel saving — for a moment.

It still leaves the question of whether saving those 84 minutes in a 500-mile trip is a matter of life or death to Sen. Taggart.

Newsday

Garden City, N.Y., February 7, 1979

If you're heading for Salt Lake City from Cheyenne, 70 or 80 or even 90 MPH might seem like a reasonable speed for Interstate 80. But you'd be lucky to hit 40 on the same highway from the George Washington Bridge to Hackensack during your average rush hour.

When Congress coerced the states into adopting 55 MPH as the national speed limit in the wake of the Arab oil embargo five years ago, it admittedly picked an arbitrary number. But the previous legal limit on most interstates and reasonably good state highways was an equally arbitrary 70 MPH, and a lot of folks exceeded the speed limit then. They still do, but they've slowed down in the process.

Few drivers, especially long-distance truckers, enjoy the 55-mile limit. It certainly makes you take longer to get wherever you're going—but it saves lives and gasoline in the process.

The drop in traffic fatalities was a startling 17 per cent—from 54,042 in 1973 to 45,196 in 1974, the first year of the lower speed limit. And driving slower saves an estimated 3.6 billion gallons of gasoline a year. That saving becomes all the more important now that Iran's oil exports look to be in doubt for some time to come.

Yet there's a move on in Congress and elsewhere to raise the speed limit by 10 miles per hour or more. Wyoming's state senate already tried, but its lower house wisely shelved the bill.

We hope cooler heads will prevail in Congress as well. The record is encouraging: Last year, in response to similar pressures, Congress voted to force states to crack down on violators instead. That's the right idea; let's stick with the 55 MPH limit, and try to make it stick.

Democrat and Chronicle

Rochester, N.Y., February 13, 1979

WESTERNERS these days are saying they want to throw a rope over the 55 mph speed limit and stamp their own brand on the rate of highway travel.

Up to a point, their frustration is understandable.

Those wide expanses make slow travel irksome.

"Back East," declares Wyoming State Sen. Carl Taggart (R.), "they can drive 35 miles an hour if they want.

"But out here, where we have great distances to travel, we're wasting time, (human) energy, manpower and everything else."

So quite a bit of dust is being raised in the West by those rebelling against the speed limit that has been mandated since 1973 as a means of saving gasoline.

A bill sponsored by Taggart to raise the limit to 65 mph was approved by the Wyoming Senate and considered by the House.

But Washington had one card up its sleeve — the retaliatory cutting off of U.S. highway funds, representing $50 million in federal aid in the case of Wyoming.

Yesterday compromise speed limit legislation died in the Wyoming House, effectively killing the issue for the 1979 legislative session.

But at least eight other states are contemplating giving up the federal aid if need be.

Let's hope, however, that this rebellion doesn't have to be cut off at the pass.

A LITTLE thought should convince Westerners that we're all in the same car together these days and that the kind of shortage threatened by the cutoff of oil from Iran may hit the West even harder than the East.

It's estimated that some 9 million gallons of gasoline are being saved every day by the 55 limit.

And if the West breaks away, so will other sections of the country, with a disastrous drain on reserves that are already inadequate.

The West also has to realize that the 55 limit has saved lives there as well as here. Across the country, some 36,000 people would probably be dead today but for the speed limit.

Nor do Westerners seem to have taken into account the higher cost of chewing up gas at speeds greater than 55.

The real need today is for Western states to get tougher about enforcing the existing law rather than try to repeal it.

Arkansas Gazette.

Little Rock, February 2, 1979

A move is afoot in several state legislatures to scrap the 55 miles an hour speed limit and to substitute a higher limit, usually 65 miles an hour. The impetus comes from the Western states — generally oil-producing states — where there is a good deal of sentiment that the energy crisis is nonsense.

When Congress set a speed limit of 55 mph, in response to the Arab oil embargo of 1973-74, it did not tell the separate states that they had to follow suit. It said, simply, that if any state chose not to comply with the 55 mph limit in its state laws that state would become ineligible for federal highway funds. No state has been willing to forfeit the money, which makes up a major portion of roads budgets among all of them.

One state, Wyoming, now appears ready to defy the federal rule, and there are rumblings in 11 other states, among them Washington, Texas, Oklahoma, Colorado and Kansas. And now, alas, the most recent addition to the list is Arkansas, which saw a bill (SB 311) introduced in the state Senate on Wednesday for a 65 mph speed limit. Wyoming could lose $51.7 million in federal highway funds this year if it makes good on its threat. There is serious talk in Washington state about a joint effort of several states, to dare the federal government to withhold funds by passing state laws setting limits higher than 55 mph.

Well, all we can say is that if these or any other states repeal the 55 mph limit the federal Transportation Department should not hesitate for an instant to withhold funds. It is in the higher national interest that a 55 mph speed limit be on the statute books and enforced a great deal more stringently than is the general rule throughout the country.

There are two prevailing reasons for keeping the 55 mph limit.

One — the original reason for the limit — is that a 55 mph limit can save a lot of gasoline. Exactly how much depends on how closely the speed limit is enforced. At today's level of enforcement — that is, with minimal enforcement — federal officials calculate that the 55 mph limit saves nine million gallons of gasoline a day. With better observation and enforcement the nation could be conserving 15 million gallons a day. Every gallon of gasoline needlessly burned simply means that more dollars will be needlessly flowing out of the country to buy foreign oil.

★ ★ ★

The other reason for keeping the 55 mph limit is that it save lives. The first year the new limit was in effect, in 1974, there were 9,000 fewer highway fatalities than in the year before. The next year, 1975, the total dropped even more, to 44,525. But each year since then, as more motorists have ignored the speed limit and many police agencies have looked the other way, the total has been increasing. If the trend continues, says a Transportation Department spokesman, "we may well see the fatalities back among the 50,000 mark, where they were in 1973." The National Safety Council, for its part, says the chances of surviving a highway accident when driving between 51 and 60 mph are 31 to 1; at 70 mph the chances are 1 to 1.

The fact that many Americans find the 55 mph speed limit inconvenient is not reason enough to abandon it, nor is it reason enough for states to enforce it as little as they feel the federal government will allow. Common sense alone tells us that everyone suffers when drivers exceed 55 mph. What the national interest really calls for is not a relaxation of the 55 mph speed limit but instead uniform observance and enforcement.

History of the Air Bag I: Partial Introduction Suggested

The debate over introducing air bags into U.S. automobiles began in 1976, when consumer advocate Ralph Nader criticized the government for moving too slowly to raise auto-safety standards. He was a strong supporter of the air bag, which did not need to be activated by the driver, in contrast to seat belts. Seat belts, particularly ones with shoulder harnesses, were still considered the ideal automobile safety device, but most car users did not bother to fasten them. They ignored automatic buzzers and dashboard lights that warned them if the seat belt was unlocked, and a proposal to rig the ignition so that it would not start unless the belts were fastened was soon dropped after widespread consumer protests.

Transportation Secretary William T. Coleman acknowledged the air bag's effectiveness in December 1976, but he decided not to require auto manufacturers to include the device in new models. He admitted that little would be accomplished by "forcing on the public an unfamiliar and controversial technology." Instead, he proposed a pilot project calling for 500,000 cars of various makes to be equipped with air bags starting in September 1978. Most of the cost of installing the bags would be borne by the auto companies, and consumers would have to pay only $100 for an air bag that covered the entire front seat or $50 for an air bag that restrained the driver only.

DESERET NEWS

Salt Lake City, Utah; May 2, 1977

If the air bag were installed in all automobiles, it could in the estimation of the U.S. Department of Transportation save upwards of 12,000 lives every year.

Yet U.S. auto makers have been anything but enthusiastic about installing this safety device in their product.

Last December, after agonizing several months over his "final decision," then-Secretary of Transportation William Coleman put off a final decision and refused to order air bags in new models.

Agreeing with the industry, he said the public wasn't ready to accept air bags. Instead, he said he would — and did — persuade Detroit to make air bags optional in some of their models.

One of the first things the new DOT secretary, Brock Adams, promised on taking office was to review Coleman's decision which, he said, "doesn't make sense."

Under the law, as Adams noted, the DOT secretary is not supposed to base his decision on anticipated consumer resistance. Instead, he is supposed to take action if air bags or other passive restraints would save lives and are technologically feasible. On both counts, air bags pass muster.

Following public hearings last week, Adams is expected to follow up with a final decision ordering air bags in 1981 cars.

Since cars are being made lighter and smaller to save fuel, they also need to be made safer.

If Detroit tried selling safety the way it sells style and power, consumers might be persuaded that the air bag makes the highest kind of sense — the difference between life and death.

OKLAHOMA CITY TIMES

Oklahoma City, Okla., February 8, 1977

THE air bag controversy seemed to have been put to rest, at least for a while, in a quite sensible way by former Transportation Secretary William T. Coleman in December.

Pulled from one side by consumer activists and automobile insurance companies and from the other, by economy-conscious car makers, Coleman opted for a limited trial run. He got at least one manufacturer to market some air bag-equipped cars to acquaint the public with them.

His goal was to keep the price at $100 or less for both driver and front-seat passenger and $50 or less for the driver only. Coleman said requiring all cars to be equipped with air bags now could be counter-productive because of adverse public reaction.

Now his successor, Brock Adams, wants to re-examine the situation. He says to improve fuel use and reduce emissions, we need smaller cars, which means requiring built-in safety devices.

There is no guarantee the cost could be held to the Coleman limits. Mandatory use of air bags could put the price of automobiles out of the reach of many American families. And the advantage of air bags over seat belts still has not been established.

ST. LOUIS POST-DISPATCH

St. Louis, Mo., January 22, 1977

By agreeing to equip a number of cars with air bags, the automobile industry has both saved face for former Transportation Secretary Coleman and delayed for at least another five years the day it will be required to include the equipment in all cars. To purchase this valuable time, General Motors Corp. promised to install air bags on a maximum of 300,000 intermediate-sized cars in the 1980 and 1981 model years and Ford Motor Co. promised to equip at most 140,000 compact cars in the same two model years.

Assuming that domestic new car sales will amount to 8,600,000 in each of those two model years (the number sold in calendar 1976), the cars equipped with air bags will represent only 2.6 per cent of the production of 1980 and 1981 models. Two foreign manufacturers, Volkswagen and Mercedes-Benz, will also offer a few cars with passive restraints, so called because the occupant does not have to do anything to gain crash protection from them as he does with seatbelts, which must be locked.

By moving slowly, former Transportation Secretary Coleman said, air bags may eventually gain consumer acceptance. But consumer acceptance is not really the issue, any more than it was with pollution controls, collision-resistant bumpers and seat head rests. What should determine whether air bags should be required is simply whether they work. Late last year, Mr. Coleman concluded that they work very well and would save 12,000 lives a year once all cars on the road were equipped with them. That should have been sufficient for his ordering them installed by manufacturers instead of asking — as he did — for voluntary action by the auto manufacturers.

San Francisco Chronicle

San Francisco, Cal., January 20, 1977

THE SECRETARY of Transportation, William T. Coleman, shortly before leaving office made a decision on the controversial air bag question which once again showed his good sense.

Coleman announced that General Motors and the Ford Motor Company will offer the air bags—safety devices which inflate automatically in the case of a collision—as options on their 1980 and 1981 model cars, at costs ranging from $50 to $100. Volkswagen and Mercedes-Benz, while not under U.S. control, have agreed to participate in the government's demonstration project aimed at generating consumer demand for cars with additional safety equipment.

The incoming Secretary of Transportation, Brock Adams, has not indicated whether he will go along with Coleman's decision. Adams has the right to order air bags installed on all American-made cars once he takes office, Coleman noted.

BUT COLEMAN'S DECISION to leave the choice to the car-buyer appears to be a proper one. The American motorist rebelled at Nader-type controls that would not allow him to start his car without a squawk from an unhooked seat belt. That invasion of individual rights and preferences was quickly squelched. While there is no question that seat belts are a proper safety measure, as are helmets for motorcycle riders, there is something in the American spirit that objects to government-mandated programs that smack of Big Brotherism; to the syndrome of Government Is Smarter Than You Are, So You Must Do What We Say Is Best For You.

Secretary Coleman obviously realized that in the air bag question, and left it to the consumer to make the individual decision. We trust his successor will do the same.

Los Angeles Times

Los Angeles, Cal., January 23, 1977

The U.S. Transportation Department has persuaded General Motors and Ford to offer air bags as an option on 500,000 of their cars beginning in 1980, and that's fine with us. We don't like air bags, and we certainly don't want to see them made mandatory in all cars, but we don't object to having their acceptability tested in the marketplace and their effectiveness tested in an experiment involving a large number of vehicles.

The optional-equipment plan was devised by Transportation Secretary William T. Coleman, who left office last week as the Ford administration ended. Coleman decided last December that air bags shouldn't be made mandatory—though, as he says, that decision could be reversed by Brock Adams, his successor under President Carter. We think that a careful review of the facts ought to convince Adams to go along with Coleman's decision.

Air bags are attractive to some people because, in the jargon of the trade, they are a passive-restraint device, providing some protection in collisions without the need for drivers or passengers to take action on their own. That's what sets them apart from most safety belts, whose use is largely ignored by most of the driving public.

The negative side of the air-bag balance sheet is much longer, however. The bags, unlike safety belts, offer limited protection, being effective only in front-end collisions. They are expensive—the 1980 options will cost $50 for one bag to protect the driver, another $50 to cover the rest of the front seat. Rear-seat passengers would still have to use safety belts. Moreover, air bags can be fired off only once before replacement parts have to be purchased. And, being a lot more complex than safety belts, a lot more things could go wrong with them.

Belts, when used, provide greater protection, at much smaller cost, and with much less chance of dangerous mechanical failure. Experience has proved their value beyond any doubt. The problem is getting people to use them more.

Throwing the belts out in favor of an expensive, unproved device of limited effectiveness is not the way to deal with that problem. Coleman came to that conclusion, and so, we think, should Adams.

The Oregonian

Portland, Ore., February 14, 1977

The American public's resistance to the use of auto safety belts may force vehicle owners to pay the added expense of the installation of the dubious airbags in new cars. The new administration has indicated that airbags are being given a second look after their rejection by William Coleman, the former director of the Department of Transportation.

Brock Adams, the new DOT secretary, has said that he could not "rationalize" Coleman's decision against requiring the airbags. Adams said that airbags might be necessary to make the newer generation of smaller cars safe.

The Oregon Legislature, which has rejected mandatory requirements that safety belts be used by drivers and passengers, has before it a bill called by its sponsor, Rep. Rod Monroe, D-Mult., the Universal Use Safety Belt Bill. He believes passage of this legislation would save more than a hundred Oregon lives each year and prevent more than 2,000 injuries caused by traffic accidents.

Monroe has cited countries like Australia, France, Israel and Russia that have mandatory seat belt laws and have found they reduce traffic deaths. Under Monroe's bill, non-compliance would be a Class D infraction, or misdemeanor.

He said that more than 90 per cent of the motorists killed in the Pacific Northwest in 1975 were not wearing their seat belts.

These are good enough reasons for wearing seat belts. But unless states like Oregon take the initiative, there is a good chance that alternatives to the problem will be sought. These include automatic systems, such as the airbag, that are being considered.

St. Louis Globe-Democrat

St. Louis, Mo., February 2, 1977

Passive restraint systems will be getting an active assist from two of this country's major automakers. It's in the bag—the air bag.

General Motor Corp. and Ford Motor Co. have agreed to a Department of Transportation plan to market a fleet of cars equipped with the automatic safety devices. A German auto producer, Mercedes-Benz, also has agreed to take part in the two-year pilot program, starting in late 1979.

The controversy over air bags, those inflatable devices that cushion the driver when sensors in the front of the car signal a crash is occurring, has been blown up considerably in recent years.

Proponents contend they're needed because the majority of drivers don't use seat belts. Accordingly, there's been a drive to make it mandatory that passenger cars be equipped with air bags or some other passive restraint system that would protect the driver in spite of himself.

Opponents of the plan to mandate the use of air bags claim the system is not foolproof, that the bags could actually contribute to a driving mishap by inflating accidentally. They also cite the cost of the devices—estimated at from $250 to $300—and their resentment of government intrusion.

The plan under which GM and Ford will offer the air bags as an optional safety feature makes far more sense than mandatory usage decreed by Washington. This way the air bags will be given a fair field test by being subjected to everyday driving situations, and drivers will have ample opportunity to acquaint themselves with passive restraint systems. This procedure should result in an intelligent resolution of the air bag debate.

The Detroit News

Detroit, Mich., February 6, 1977

Zealots often harm their own cause by making exaggerated claims. Such a case can be made against the Insurance Institute of Highway Safety in its pursuit of mandatory air bags for automobiles.

William Coleman, President Ford's transportation secretary, was tilted in favor of the air bags, according to inside sources at the department, but he turned cool when he discovered that the institute, a lobbying organization for auto insurers who want air bags, had oversold its case.

Specifically, three accident cases caused Coleman to have doubts. In all three, the institute claimed lives had been saved. However, federal field investigators found out that the three accidents were not nearly as severe as the institute had stated. The institute put the speeds of crashes too high and dramatized the reports far more than was justified by the facts.

In the end, the Coleman report held that air bags which deploy in a crash of 12 m.p.h. or more would save lives and prevent injury. However, Coleman concluded that seat and lap belts would save even more lives if people hooked them up.

So Coleman could not accept the argument that the result would justify the cost of air bags, which would inflate the price of a car by as much as $500. Instead, he persuaded General Motors and Ford to take a loss and install the bags in about 500,000 cars beginning in 1980 to get some practical experience as well as government monitoring of their performance.

There is embarrassment in several quarters over the disclosure the insurance companies overstated their facts. The Journal of American Insurance, when informed that its story on the three accidents was inaccurate, asked the institute — which contributed the material — to explain itself.

The spokesman for American Mutual Insurance Alliance, publisher of the journal, said the alliance supports air bags but "we definitely don't want to destroy our credibility by overstating the case."

It is too late to say that. The damage has already been done.

THE BLADE

Toledo, Ohio, February 9, 1977

THE views of Transportation Secretary Brock Adams on a number of issues involving his department, as outlined in weekend interviews, make a good deal of sense.

Mr. Adams is in favor of opening up the bulging Highway Trust Fund to permit localities to use some of the billions of dollars it holds for uses other than highway building and maintenance, including development of mass transit systems where feasible. He supports continued federal aid to Amtrak in the belief that alternate forms of transportation to cars and planes will become increasingly important. He believes the 55-mph national speed limit should be retained and that efforts to increase the size of trucks ought to be resisted firmly.

It is difficult to disagree with the soundness of Mr. Adams' position in such matters. But there is one area he touched upon where he should move with caution, and that is in taking up the controversial air-bag issue to decide whether the Government should compel auto makers to install the device in new cars.

Mr. Adams said he will review the decision by his predecessor — William Coleman — not to require air-bag installation at this time and to move instead into a voluntary program in which some new models will carry the devices over the next two years. The secretary allows as how he cannot rationalize Mr. Coleman's decision in view of the fact that air bags could supposedly save an estimated 10,000 lives a year.

If Mr. Adams will look further into Mr. Coleman's findings as his predecessor reached his decision late last year, he will discover that Mr. Coleman concluded that seat-belt systems, if used, would be far superior to the air bag both from a safety standpoint and in terms of the cost-benefit factor. Furthermore, he will see that Mr. Coleman also agreed that if motorists used their seat-belt systems, an estimated 16,300 fatalities would be avoided annually and 918,000 injuries would be eliminated or reduced. So the mere fact that air bags might save 10,000 lives — far fewer than seat-belt systems — is no reason to rush to make them mandatory.

Compulsory installation of the controversial air bag would cost American consumers hundreds of millions of dollars. That is a high price to pay for a safety device that is inferior to seatbelt systems in effectiveness — and, in fact, is virtually useless in anything but front-end collisions.

Mr. Adams should tread carefully to avoid being tripped up by the air bag — a pratfall that, for him, could be just as embarrassing as that suffered by those nitwits who attempted to foist off the disastrous ignition-interlock system on the American public.

History of the Air Bag II: A Requirement on 1982 Models

Transportation Secretary Brock Adams June 30 ordered that new automobiles be equipped with air bag safety devices or "passive restraint" seat belts beginning with 1982 models. The air bag is designed to inflate automatically in a crash to keep passengers from being thrown into impact with damaging surfaces. Passive restraint seat belts automatically harness around passengers when the car door is closed.

Adams' order was that one of the two devices must be installed on all standard and luxury size cars beginning with the model year 1982, on intermediate and compact cars beginning with the 1983 models and on subcompact and minisize cars beginning with the 1984 models. "Too many people have needlessly been injured or killed in crashes where passive restraints could have saved them," Adams said, announcing his order at a news conference. "I cannot in good conscience be a party to further, unnecessary delay.... The issue of automobile safety has dragged on too long."

Adams said he had asked the industry to continue an experimental program for trial use of passive restraints in the 1980 and 1981 model years on 500,000 cars. Under legislation enacted in 1974, a mandate from a transportation secretary for installation of passive restraints was subject to rejection by Congress if both houses vetoed it within 60 working days. An air bag resolution was introduced in the House later June 30 by Rep. Bud Shuster (R, Pa.), who said the device would be costly and hard evidence was lacking that it would save lives. Adams had estimated that air bags would add $100 to $300 to the cost of a car and passive seat belts, $25 to $100.

The immediate reaction to Adams' decision was varied. If Congress upheld the decision, a spokesman for General Motors Corp. said June 30, "GM intends to do the best possible job to equip our cars with passive restraints in accordance with the regulations." A Ford Motor Co. spokesman expressed pleasure that Adams had taken into account "lead-time problems" of manufacturing. Chrysler Corp. contended that mandatory use of the current seat belts in cars would save 50% more lives than air bags. Adams' order, it said, would force "the American people to pay triple the cost for a second-best safety system." American Motors Corp. attacked Adams' decision as a "multibillion-dollar gamble with consumers' money." The decision was hailed by United Auto Workers president Douglas Fraser and consumer advocate Ralph Nader, although Nader deplored any delay in implementation.

Des Moines Tribune
Des Moines, Iowa, July 7, 1977

Secretary of Transportation Brock Adams's decision to require installation of air bags or passive seat belts in all new cars by 1984 was necessary because of a grim truth: The vast majority of American drivers, despite countless warnings, refuse to protect themselves by buckling their seat belts before they drive.

Adams reasoned that if drivers won't protect themselves, the government should require installation of devices that will. The logic is sound.

The driver who takes the precaution of "buckling up" before driving reduces his chances of being killed or injured in a collision, but a 1976 study found that fewer than one out of four drivers use both lap and shoulder belts.

There are two alternatives for government action: laws requiring drivers to wear seat belts, or an order making installation of air bags or similar passive protective devices mandatory.

Because seat belts are cheaper and offer more protection than air bags alone in a collision, mandatory seat belt laws that got most drivers to buckle up would be the best of the two alternatives, in theory. But Adams was probably right when he argued that it would be difficult to get such laws passed, and perhaps even more difficult to enforce them.

Adams's ruling will allow automakers to install either air bags, which inflate almost instantly during a crash to cushion a driver against the impact, or passive seat belts, which automatically wrap around the chest and waist of a car occupant when the car door closes behind him.

Passive seat belts may only be feasible on small cars with bucket seats. Other cars would have to be outfitted with air bags as well as lap belts (since air bags do not provide sufficient protection from side collisions or rollovers).

Carrying out Adams's decision could add up to $300 to the sticker price of a car outfitted with air bags, and $100 to the price of a car with passive seat belts. This extra cost should be partially offset by lower car insurance rates. The insurance industry has estimated that it could save up to $2.5 billion a year if air bags were installed in all cars.

Even without the benefit of lower car insurance rates, $300 would be a small price to pay, considering the benefits: as many as 9,000 lives a year could be saved once all cars are outfitted with the devices.

THE BLADE
Toledo, Ohio, July 6, 1977

THE best that can be said for the Transportation Department's order to auto makers to start equipping new cars with air bags or other passive safety devices by the 1982 model year is that it sets a definite schedule that would give the industry sufficient lead time to comply. The bad feature is the department's advocacy of the air bag when the agency's own data show that present belt systems — if used — could save 50 per cent more lives than could these unproven inflatable cushions.

Transportation Secretary Brock Adams has inherited lobbying pressures to put air bags into production. The bag, concealed in the dashboard, would inflate on direct frontal impact but would provide virtually no protection in side or rear collisions, roll-overs, or in multiple-impact accidents. As original equipment, the bag would add up to $300 to a car's price tag, and the cost of replacing the bag after its deployment could be as much as $600.

Mr. Adams properly expressed concern over the 47,000 traffic deaths on the nation's highways each year. His department believes that some type of passive restraint could save an additional 9,000 lives. However, that is no more than a projection drawn from estimates that only 20 to 25 per cent of car passengers use their seat belts— by far the most economical of protective devices.

Congress, of course, has the last word on air bags. It should intervene to countermand the DOT ruling and encourage the development of other less costly and more effective passive restraints.

In the interim, more government officials might acknowledge that the 55-mile-an-hour speed limit has dramatically cut the national traffic death rate even with lackadaisical enforcement. Greater attention to this law would accomplish much toward safer motoring.

The Honolulu Advertiser
Honolulu, Hawaii, July 1, 1977

While President Carter was announcing his B-1 decision yesterday, Transportation Secretary Brock Adams faced up to another issue that involves many thousands of lives each year.

He ordered the installation of airbags or automatic seat belts on all luxury and full-size cars beginning with 1982 models. All autos, including subcompacts, will have to have the safety devices by 1984.

THE DECISION must be upheld in Congress where it will face an uncertain degree of opposition.

On one side, consumer advocate Ralph Nader questioned why it must take longer to have the devices on the smallest cars — especially since they are the ones whose occupants need protection the most.

On the other side, the auto industry is expected to lobby for even more "lead time" before having to install the air bags or safety belts that lock automatically when the door of the car is closed.

Yet the industry should be happy since Adams has given the auto companies a choice between the air bags they opposed and seat belts, whose use they have favored.

One foreign auto maker, Volkswagen, has already introduced the "passive" or automatic seat belts on some models. So it would seem no great task for others to follow soon.

ADAMS MADE the good point that these safety devices could save some 9,000 lives a year which are now lost in accidents. It is an issue that has dragged on much too long due to industry opposition and apathy in Washington.

But, while air bags should be effective life savers in head-on crashes, they won't work in all, including those from the side and rear, and secondary impacts. Real safety calls for both air bags and the automatic seat belts.

That, too, must come some day.

The Morning Union
Springfield, Mass., July 4, 1977

Automatic safety devices in automobiles have been mandated by the Department of Transportation as standard equipment in all cars by the 1984 model year. According to department estimates, up to 9000 lives a year could be saved by the devices, which could be either airbags or automatic seat belts.

Saving lives on the scale would seem worth the effort. But it is likely the mandate will be overruled by Congress because of auto industry opposition and the colossal public indifference to such devices. Only an estimated 20 per cent of American drivers use the seat belts which their cars already have, but which must be buckled in place.

The auto industry has opposed both the airbag and automatic seat belt on the basis of cost, claiming also that the devices are a second-best approach compared to laws requiring the use of existing seat belts. Consumer advocate Ralph Nadar also opposes the ruling, but on grounds its timetable is too slow.

On the other side, the insurance industry supports the ruling, which it says will not only save lives but reduce injuries and hold down the rising cost of auto accidents.

While the reaction from auto industry has not yet been strong, it is expected to pick up with the 60-day period in which Congress can overrule the department's decision. That right was reserved by Congress in 1974, when it nullified the ignition interlock system, which would have forced drivers to buckle up in order to make the ignition work.

That precedent probably won't be broken — at least in the absence of a groundswell of public support for the new ruling.

THE SAGINAW NEWS
Saginaw, Mich., July 5, 1977

Except for some cries of alarm from the No. 3 and No. 4 automakers, it's difficult to detect earth-shaking rumbles in Congress or industrywide over Transportation Secretary Brock Adams' call for passive restraint systems to become standard equipment in all American-made cars by 1984.

Congress has 60 days to review the department's plan and unless it objects, it becomes law.

Congress should not oppose it.

Adams has submitted a reasonable proposal which, if anything, errs on the side of ultimate consideration for the automobile industry. It is softer even than former Transportation Secretary William T. Coleman's last word on the air bag.

Coleman gave the industry two more years to test and develop. Mr. Adams has added even more time to that by calling for phase-in of the passive restraint system beginning with 1982 large size cars and concluding with air bags or passive safety belts in all models by 1984.

The difference is that for the first time an administration has fully committed itself to the passive restraint system and given the auto industry a timetable.

Like so many forces coming together slowly to change the shape and performance of automobiles in times of energy and safety-consciousness, the time has come for the front-seat restraint system designed to minimize death and injury in head-on collisions.

And for a change, a major portion of the auto industry seems willing to go forward under Adams' proposals.

When the day finally arrives, we will have set no records. There's been talk and research and development going on since 1971. There is still another three years for additional refinements before marketing. This is long enough.

Newsday
Garden City, N.Y., July 1, 1977

The Carter administration made another tough decision yesterday, and again it chose the right one. Transportation Secretary Brock Adams reversed his predecessor's stand on airbags and ordered them installed in all cars by 1984.

Trying to get motorists to buy airbags as an option didn't work any better than trying to get them to buckle seatbelts, in part because the cost was comparatively high. But mass production is sure to bring the price of airbags down sharply—and save perhaps 9,000 lives a year.

Within an hour of Adams' announcement, a Pennsylvania congressman introduced a resolution to overturn his decision. We hope a majority of his colleagues show more sense.

THE SACRAMENTO BEE
Sacramento, Calif., July 11, 1977

Air bags or automatic seat restraints wouldn't be necessary if drivers used conventional seat belts. The trouble is, only 20 to 25 per cent of Americans bother to buckle up despite conclusive evidence it can prevent death or injury.

The drawbacks to the devices which Transportation Secretary Brock Adams has ordered installed in new cars, starting with 1982 models, are more than offset by the potential for greater safety. The Transportation Department estimates passive restraints could save 9,000 to 12,000 lives each year and reduce serious injuries by 100,000 to 200,000.

Adams has given auto manufacturers the choice of building in an air bag system or a seat belt harness that automatically covers driver and passenger. Yes, new cars will cost more. And yes, the air bags may be subject to malfunction or American ingenuity may discover a way to disconnect the harness or maybe even the bags. But the positive advantages, which include a prospective lowering of auto insurance rates, should overcome skepticism and opposition to the government's decision.

Under the law, Congress has 60 days to reject Adams' directive by a majority vote in either house. A bill to block the order already has been introduced. It should be defeated and the new highway safety system be allowed to prove itself.

The Burlington Free Press

Burlington, Vt., July 4, 1977

A FEDERAL government order that all automakers start equipping their 1982 models with air bags or other passive safety devices, while laudable, is contradictory in application to the main thrust of energy conservation.

Transportation Secretary Brock Adams ordered that all 1982 standard and luxury-size cars be the first to be equipped. The requirements would be extended to 1983-model intermediate and compact cars and to subcompact and mini-size autos in 1984.

On the one hand the Carter energy policy is aimed at moving Americans into smaller cars instead of the big gas guzzlers. On the other, the Transportation Agency places the smallest cars last in priority for these new safety devices. Theoretically, the largest number of autos on the highways through 1984 will be the most unsafe.

Brock is sincere when he says he could not in good concience delay implementation of the air bags and other devices any longer in light of the 9,000 lives they could save each year. Despite outcries from the auto industry that it cannot meet the deadlines and that the cost will increase the already high cost of cars, Brock's decision basically is correct. However, he should have ruled that, starting in 1982, all cars be equipped with the safety devices. Phasing them in over a six-year period is too long a time. There are too many lives at stake to warrant such a delay.

The Evening Bulletin

Philadelphia, Pa., July 7, 1977

Get ready for another heated national debate about how far the government should go in protecting people against themselves. At the center of this controversy you'll find that most sacred of American institutions — the private automobile.

Secretary of Transportation Brock Adams has ordered that air bags or automatic lap and shoulder belts be installed in all new cars between the 1982 and 1984 model years. The decision follows an eight-year campaign by consumer advocates and the insurance industry to make such passive restraints mandatory.

Mr. Adams's order created a predictable furor. Ralph Nader railed against the delay in implementing the requirement. Automobile manufacuturers groaned at the change, and it is possible they will try to block it in court.

The fact that both sides found something to attack in the decision is one signal that Mr. Adams chose a wise middle ground.

The seat-belt interlock fiasco showed that, left alone, most people will avoid taking simple measures to protect themselves. Carelessness is an inalienable right, some would argue.

That may be; but we can't help but be convinced that the vast majority of the 27,000 automobile occupants who die in crashes each year would rather remain alive. Passive restraints could save an estimated 9,000 of those lives yearly.

Air bags will add $100 to $300 to the price of an automobile; the automatic belts will cost between $25 and $100. Those costs should be offset somewhat by lower insurance costs.

Overall, it is a small price we are being asked to pay to keep people alive. We hope the automobile industry will devote its energy to perfecting the passive restraint systems, not to delaying further these efforts to save people's lives.

Roanoke Times & World-News

Roanoke, Va., July 7, 1977

Transportation Secretary Brock Adams has ordered that U.S. motorists be protected from themselves. Beginning by the fall of 1983, all new automobiles sold in this country must be equipped with air bags (which inflate on collision to cushion driver and front-seat passengers) or passive seat belts (harness-type belts that lock a rider in place when a crash occurs).

Libertarians will contend that, once again, big-nanny government has overstepped its bounds. Washington shouldn't be trying to make decisions that grownups are capable of making for themselves, or taking from them the option of protecting themselves from life's many hazards. A lot of citizens, remembering earlier models' fussy seat-belt interlocks and the buzzing noises that wouldn't let them drive in peace, will agree with that hands-off view.

There's another side to the argument, and it has considerable weight. If no man is an island, neither does the average motorist exist in a vacuum. If he flirts with danger, his actions can affect others. The child, for example, who sits unrestrained beside the driver and unprotected from a crash. Or the family that may be left without the financial support of a motorist who failed to buckle up. Or millions of other vehicle-owners who must pay higher insurance rates because of heedless drivers who will not protect themselves. According to Mr. Adams, use of air bags or passive seat belts on all 10 million autos produced annually could save 9,000 lives a year.

One can assume that these devices would also prevent disabling or other serious injury to about that same number of people each year. That represents a huge saving in life, pain, heartache, expense, lost time and so on and on. In a sense, Mr. Adams' order is more federal meddling, more effort by Uncle Sam to show he knows what's best for the rest of us, and therefore it's objectionable. But the consequences, in this situation, of Uncle's failure to act look worse.

The Wichita Eagle

Wichita, Kans., July 8, 1977

One wonders if it is perversity or penny-pinching greed that inspires opponents of Transportation Secretary Brock Adams' plan to have all new cars equipped with air bags or automatic seat belts by 1984.

Some critics of mandatory protections seem intent on defending drivers' freedom to be injured to the death — other drivers' deaths. The same sort of loud espousal of personal freedom killed off Kansas' mandatory motorcycle helmet law.

Motorcycle helmets can never, of course, guarantee that their wearers will not be injured, or even killed, if an accident is severe enough. But they give a wearer a little more protection than if he is riding bare-headed.

Air bags can never give complete protection — and they may give none if a car is struck from the side. But they give very good protection in the estimated 80 per cent of all serious crashes that involve frontal impact. Furthermore, they give it at the instant of greatest need, then deflate rapidly to leave the driver free to do whatever he needs to do.

Although air bags are more expensive to install than automatic seat belts — actually shoulder harnesses, which would wrap themselves around car occupants when the doors are closed — the instantaneous inflate-deflate operation would be considerably less encumbering.

The results of five years of tests of air bag use in street and highway driving have indicated that the highway fatality toll could be cut two-thirds by the use of such equipment.

Americans are driving more compact cars which, because they are smaller and crowd occupants closer together and closer to the instrument panel and windshield, are potentially more dangerous. Adams wants them equipped with air bags by 1982, other passenger cars by 1984.

Why wait that long? Will you or someone you love be killed because cars were not equipped with automatic safety equipment sooner, or because some congressman who valued "personal freedom" higher than safety managed to block implementation of Adams' order?

ARKANSAS DEMOCRAT
Little Rock, Ark., July 8, 1977

We're on our way to auto air bags, finally — provided Congress doesn't nullify Transportation Secretary Brock Adams' order that installation begin with 1982 cars. Already the right-to-die crowd is ranting against mandatory passive restraints as a violation of individual liberties.

We can't agree with them, and though we don't often agree with Ralph Nader, we're with him in thinking that it's past time that the bags were installed. Sure, they'll cost, but a life is worth $100-$300, isn't, it? The Transportation Department says as many as 12,000 lives a year will be saved and as many as 200,000 serious injuries averted.

But the main congressional argument against bags is libertarian rather than economic. The argument is that government shouldn't force us to save our lives against our will — that we should have a choice of buying or not buying bag-equipped autos.

That sounds good, but it isn't a true libertarian argument. Rights are individual matters, and the argument would be telling only if all cars carried only the driver. But most cars carry more than one person, and if the driver had the option of turning down the bags, he'd be involving the safety of others in his determination to risk his life. It's not as though mothers, wives and babies were to be polled to see whether they shared the individual's decision to take risks.

Government can be awfully intrusive in a lot of matters involving safety. We've seen what OSHA can do, and most of us have sworn a time or two at those buzzer devices that used to remind you that your car wouldn't start unless you buckled up. That was discontinued as the nuisance it was. Besides, nobody can make anybody buckle up — hence the air-bag, passive-restraint system that works whether you think about it or not.

It's good only in head-on collisions, but that's plenty, and it protects all front-seat occupants. For that reason, no one should have the option of playing libertarian loner at the risk of other lives.

BUFFALO EVENING NEWS
Buffalo, N.Y., July 5, 1977

Without awaiting the results of full-scale testing of air bags ordered by his predecessor, Transportation Secretary Brock Adams has now mandated either their installation or that of automatic safety belts in all autos by the 1984 model year.

This latest exercise in "government knows best" compulsion would be more defensible in our view if it followed, rather than preceded, a thorough trial of air bags and alternative "passive restraints" for their effectiveness under actual road conditions.

Even while acknowledging from present data the value of air bags in head-on collisions, former Transportation Secretary Coleman was properly reluctant, pending comprehensive testing in practice, to freeze the auto industry into a costly assembly-line gearing-up for a particular safety device. This could meet with the same public resistance that culminated in congressional rejection of compulsory seat belt-ignition interlock systems.

While appearing resigned to the government's "safety compulsion" barring a congressional overriding of the Adams order, the auto industry cites the persistent unresolved doubts about locking the country into a particular safety-coercion device without a much more reliable basis for evaluating air bag effectiveness under realistic accident conditions.

* * *

That a safety mechanism is technologically feasible is hardly a convincing argument for its universal installation at an additional car-price cost (ranging up to $300) several times that of alternative safety devices. Since instantly inflatable air bags can protect in only frontal collisions, motorists will still need seat belts for protection in side, rollover, rear-end and second collisions.

True, Mr. Adams wants to give the auto industry reasonable time to phase in either air bags or an inflatable belt system. But this is only one of the government marching orders with which Detroit's engineers must comply; they must in about the same time span cut down the remaining pollution emissions and gasoline consumption. And though all of this may be achievable by an industry that has at times needed the pressure of public opinion to shift gears in more economical or safety-conscious directions, the fact remains that the combination of mandates now facing it could well price tomorrow's complex cars beyond the pocketbook of many a family.

* * *

Cost and technical questions aside, though, what the air bag controversy comes down to at base is how far government properly should go in substituting compulsion for individual driver discretion in matters of safety. Certainly public concern about the highway death and injury toll well warrants government rules for motorist safety in areas wherever the individual driver has little or no discretion, as in auto design and highway-safety engineering features.

But it's something else again to carry a "government knows best" philosophy into offensive regulatory reaches, whether by relying on police power to force a buckling of seat belts which prudent motorists should do for their own protection, or by forcing adoption of a complex safety device requiring no motorist action. And in opting for the latter in lieu of a public education campaign to promote a swifter rise in the use of seat belts, is gambling on public acceptance of passive restraints as safety cure-alls without awaiting a properly comprehensive testing of their performance under practical conditions.

The Dispatch
Columbus, Ohio, July 6, 1977

IT IS MORE than a little disturbing to be told by a federal official that the time is near for the government to protect the citizen against himself.

That is the essence of a directive by U.S. Transportation Secretary Brock Adams who has ruled that automakers must equip new cars with air bags or passive devices for the safety of auto occupants.

Discipline imposed by government fiat goes against the grain of fundamental Americanism, for freedom of choice has been a hallmark of this country since its inception.

However, Secretary Adams argues that "too many people have been needlessly injured or killed in crashes where passive restraints could have saved them."

So, he is saying, since they neglected to save themselves, it is imperative the government impose a discipline for public well-being.

Mr. Adams' plan does include an alternative to the controversial air bag. The passive belt-type restraint is activated without human assistance and already is in use in some cars.

The passive restraint would afford protection and allay latent fears among those concerned an air bag could be activated accidentally, obscuring vision, however momentarily, and resulting in an accident itself.

A weak point in the passive restraint system is that it has not yet been perfected to the point where a third front seat occupant is protected.

The fact that automakers are divided in their opinions of the air bag and not all insurance companies are enthusiastic in favor demonstrates the flexibility of both the problem and its solution.

It is a question which cannot be approached as a wholly philosophical matter or one to be judged solely on its safety aspects.

The Adams proposal has merit in that it not only offers alternatives but sufficient lead time — the 1982 auto model year — for the car industry and scientists to perfect both the air bag and passive restraints.

These elements tend to dilute the idea of a government-imposed discipline even though it lurks ominously on the fringes of the controversy.

ALBUQUERQUE JOURNAL
Albuquerque, N.M., July 4, 1977

Transportation Secretary Brock Adams has an exquisite sense of timing. He has ordered automakers to equip all new cars with air bags or other passive restraint safety devices by 1984. That's also the year that George Orwell's satirical Big Brother will begin protecting us from ourselves.

Then again, if the auto lobby maintains its pattern for dodging federal regulations, passive restraints might be staved off until 1990.

And if the petroleum lobby has its way, nobody, not even Big Brother, will be able to afford fuel for those super-safe cars.

DAILY NEWS
New York, N.Y., July 2, 1977

By the august decree of Transportation Secretary Brock Adams, all 1984-model automobiles must be equipped with the controversial air bags or similar "passive" restraints. We can't help wondering if the secretary chose the date, long synonymous with runaway Big Brotherism, deliberately.

Proponents of the devices, which inflate on impact, claim they will save 9,000 to 10,000 lives a year. Foes contend they are nothing but a costly, ineffective nuisance.

The former secretary, William Coleman, wanted to go in a different direction—introducing the air bags gradually and voluntarily in the hope of spurring spontaneous demand from motorists.

With due respect to Adams, we still believe that was the best approach.

HERALD-JOURNAL

Syracuse, N.Y., July 5, 1977

One day, the U.S. Department of Transportation didn't know whether air bags were worth the effort and money but, as a test, persuaded makers to install the automatic restraints in a limited number of cars next year.

The manufacturers had traveled this route once before but took a bath. Few customers bought the air-bag equipped cars because prices had gone up around $200-$300 each.

But the Department of Transportation and its secretary, Brock Adams,

have changed their minds. Air bags are not only nice but necessary and could save up to 9,000 lives a year.

That's the claim.

By governmnent fiat — unless Congress vetoes the order within 60 days — we'll pay another $200 or $300 for our cars starting with the 1982 models to purchase either air bags or automatic restraining harnesses.

Seat belts aren't enough.

The new wisdom arrived with the new secretary.

The Dallas Morning News

Dallas, Tex., July 2, 1977

Gerald Ford's last Transportation secretary, William Coleman, had the good judgment not to order the installation of airbags or passive seatbelt systems in all new cars. Coleman recommended voluntary experiments with the two safety devices.

And how we miss the man! Coleman's Democratic successor, Brock Adams, has steered the voluntary approach into a ditch. Compulsion is the tactic that Adams has embraced. By 1983, he directs, all automobiles shall have either airbags or automatic seatbelts (the latter wrap around the passengers when the door is closed).

No one can fault Adams' intention, which is to save lives. But how far do we go in attempts to force Americans to be safe? Most

drivers presently shun seatbelts and will bitterly resent any attempt by government to oblige their regular use. Airbags are expected to increase car costs by up to $300.

Clearly these things should be available if car buyers want them, but to enforce their use is to go farther than government ought to go. There simply are risks in life from which government cannot protect us without going to extreme lengths and interfering with free choice.

The Adams decision is not final. Congress can reject it within 60 days, and in our view Congress should do just that. Not the compulsory but the voluntary approach should be explored. "Safety First" is an appealing slogan, but in a free society there must always be higher priorities.

THE DALLAS TIMES HERALD

Dallas, Tex., July 3, 1977

ONE MORE TIME — when will protective Big Brother in Washington learn that it cannot spend 24 hours each day babysitting 220 million of us during the waking hours and tucking us into bed each night?

Once again the Washington bureaucracy has decreed that all of us must have air bags or automatic seat belts in our cars, beginning with 1982 models.

No one asked if we, as individual citizens or car owners, wanted them or could be given the right to exercise our own judgments. No, Transportation Secretary Brock Adams, the presiding Big Brother in this instance, merely decreed it and is asking Congress to bang down the rubber stamp.

Congress has 60 days to review the entire plan, which gives precious little time for the citizen to protest if he doesn't want to spend another $100 to $300 for the air bag or just $100 for the automatic seat belts.

If Congress fails to reject the order within the prescribed time, it automatically becomes law. In the present climate of the new Carter administration, it appears that it will receive congressional blessing.

Controversy over the air bag-automatic seat belt systems goes on and on. Automakers and a lot of private citizens feel the individual should make his own decision on

the equipment. Others, including the insurance lobby, insist that it will save lives and is worth the cost. No one challenges the intent of the order — just its actual worth and the thought of having one more federal order shoved down our throats, like it or not. The Chrysler Corp. contends that the order will "force the American people to pay triple the cost for a second best system."

It charged that Sec. Adams is ignoring his own agency's data which shows that the present seat belt system will save 50 per cent more lives than air bags. It is in this scrambling air of uncertainty that we will get, as individual car owners, automatic seat belts that wrap around passengers and lock in place in the event of a crash or balloon-shaped air bags designed to inflate at the instant of collision, keeping passengers from hitting steering wheel, dash or windshield. Or, at least, that is what Big Brother says they will do.

We must agree with American Motors that it is a forced multibillion-dollar gamble with the consumer's money — ordered from Washington. If individual car owners want to pay $300 extra for such devices, it should be their decision — not an order from bureaucrats attempting to shape our lives from sunup to sunup.

TULSA DAILY WORLD

Tulsa, Okla., July 2, 1977

TRANSPORTATION SECRETARY BROCK ADAMS has decided to require mandatory safety restraints for all automobiles, beginning in 1982.

The controversial air bag and automatic seat restraints will be the options available to the American motorists, who have shown little interest in the air bags and downright dislike for seat belts.

The theory of the "passive" restraints is to automatically protect motorists in front-end collisions. The idea of saving 9,000 lives a year, as BROCK predicts, is appealing.

Of course the SECRETARY is on safe ground when he defends such devices in the name of saving even one human life.

But past experience with auto safety indicates that the public doesn't want to pay the extra $100 to $300 that BROCK estimates the air bags or seat restraints will cost.

The likelihood is great that enterprising motorists who have found ways to thwart various devices guaranteeing use of seat belts also will thwart the new passive de-

vices.

Remember the history of the seat belt? Motorists refused to buy them when they were optional equipment and when they were required, they refused to use them.

When warning buzzers were placed in the autos, they were ignored and when a system that made it impossible to start an auto without the seat belts fastened, the public rebelled. Interlock systems were disconnected all over the country and a system featured a return to the buzzer was substituted.

All of this of course cost the public money.

The air bags will do the same. Manufacturers say the cost will be close to $300 and up to $600 for reinstallation in the case of an inflation.

ADAMS' decision on the air bags will not end the controversy. If Congress doesn't overrule him now, there might come a time when the public will. That time could very well be when the buyers start seeing that $300 costs showing up on the stickers of the new cars in 1981.

The Seattle Times

Seattle, Wash., July 5, 1977

SINCE nobody seemed really to have complained (despite the addition of hundreds of dollars to the price of a new car) about seat belts, padded windshield visors, head restraints, and other gadgets mandated the past 10 years or so, the "feds" are preparing to add to the list of compulsory (and costly) auto-safety devices.

This time it's the air bag (or, as an alternative, a belt that will harness drivers to their seats automatically).

Unless Congress overrules him, Transportation Secretary Brock Adams will force the makers of all cars sold in this country to install air bags and the like starting with 1982 models of full-size automobiles.

Reversing the wise course set by his predecessor, which was based on giving car buyers a free choice, Adams said that his order could save up to 9,000 lives a year and that "the issue of automobile safety has dragged on too long."

Although automotive engineers are divided on whether air bags would serve their purpose fully, a large body of opinion (from Ralph Nader to the insurance lobby, and from highway-safety groups to many in the medical profession) is prepared to back up Adams.

The issue as we see it is less

concerned with the technical merits of "passive restraints" in cars than with the philosophy that government will decide what is good for the people, whether the people want it or not.

Innumerable studies have shown that only about 20 per cent of all drivers and passengers regularly use conventional seat belts. Universal seat-belt use would preclude the necessity for the air-bag order, according to federal experts.

Unable to gain compliance with repeated urgings to make wider use of belts, Adams and his cohorts now want to assume the decision-making power for themselves. (At a cost, incidentally, of anywhere from $100 to $300 or more a car, depending on the type of restraint installed.)

Adams cannot be faulted, of course, for his concern for the well-being of American motorists. But the Orwellian denial of free choice needs to be debated fully as Congress weighs ratification of Adams' order during the next 60 days.

The directive assumes that installation in all cars, including subcompacts and mini-sized vehicles, will be completed by the fall of 1983 — that is, for cars marketed as 1984 models.

All things considered, Adams could not have chosen a more appropriate year.

The federal government is once again determined to put big brother in the front seats of private automobiles.

Transportation Secretary Brock Adams has ordered airbags or automatic seatbelts on all luxury and full-size cars beginning with the 1982 model year, and the same devices built into all cars by the 1984 model year.

Such governmental coercion has failed in the past because of strong negative public reaction. We predict it will fail again.

There is little doubt that seatbelts and airbags provide crucial protection in collisons. That is not the point. The point is that while they should be required as available options on new cars, they should not be forced on anyone.

Many motorists resent the federal government dictating such safety measures at their expense. Some have good reasons why they do not or cannot use seatbelts. Others have valid objections to airbags.

It should be an individual decision.

Former Transportation Secretary William Coleman, faced with the same decision, took a wiser approach last year. Coleman chose to push for a voluntary program in hopes that demonstrated results would encourage public acceptance and demand for such restraints.

He recalled the strong negative reaction triggered by federal legisla-tion a few years ago requiring helmets for motorcyclists and pesky interlock systems that kept automobiles from starting until seatbelts were locked.

There is something in the American psyche that rebels at this constant bureaucratic meddling and without public acceptance no program can succeed — nor should it.

MANCHESTER NEW HAMPSHIRE UNION LEADER
Manchester, N.H., July 3, 1977

We sincerely hope everyone in New Hampshire, and the U.S. for that matter, has a safe and healthy Fourth of July weekend. But we're not suggesting that the government order all of us into strait-jackets and padded cells to insure our holiday safety.

If that sounds a bit odd, it's just our way of expressing our strong dis-approval of the Carter Administra-tion's latest governmental meddling into our personal lives.

With all the fuss over state bud-gets and B-1 Bombers, another impor-tant story may have been overlooked last week. Secretary of Transporta-tion Brock Adams has ordered that air bags or automatic seat restraints be installed in all automobiles by 1984.

Mr. Adams, whose order will be-come final if Congress doesn't nix it within 60 days, says the air bags and other compulsory restraints are nec-essary because only 20 to 25 per cent of car riders use seat belts today.

That's precisely our objection to his new order: only one-fourth of the public uses seat belts so the govern-ment will step in and force 75 per cent of the American motoring public to do what it is against.

Mr. Adams conceded that air bags would add $100 to $300 to the price of an automobile, but air bag backers said this cost would be "par-tially offset" by lower insurance costs. (Where have we heard that before and when did it ever happen?)

And that great "consumer advo-cate," Ralph Nader, says nothing about the high cost to the consumer; he's just sorry the order won't be effective sooner.

Congress has negated such Big Brother intrusions in the past — New Hampshire's own Louis Wyman was instrumental in getting rid of the crazy cars which wouldn't start until hope it rejects this one, too.

We urge New Hampshire's pres-ent Congressional delegation to show some real consumer interest and fight this costly, forceful intrusion into our lives. If motorists want to vol-untarily buckle up, more power to them, but the government shouldn't be allowed to order it.

THE CINCINNATI ENQUIRER
Cincinnati, Ohio, July 7, 1977

TRANSPORTATION SECRETARY Brock Adams has made an eminently bad decision in ordering "passive-restraint" safety devices in new cars beginning with the 1982 model year for standard and lux-ury cars and with the 1984 model year for all smaller cars. In so doing he may actu-ally be increasing the risk of injury and death to motorists and their passengers.

Safety experts have long recognized that seat belts and shoulder harnesses, when properly used, are far more effec-tive than air bags. Seat belts work in side-impact crashes where air bags are inef-fective. Seat belts work in rollover crashes for which air bags were not designed.

Yet Secretary Adams is willing to forgo the proven safety of seat belts so the federal government can have the final say in the matter.

Never mind the argument that if peo-ple want to take the risk of riding in a car without seat belts they ought to be free to take that risk.

Never mind the argument that passive-restraint devices will add $112 or $200 or $300 to the cost of a car.

Just look at the simple fact that by changing the rules of his predecessor and requiring air bags or seat belts that auto-matically fold across a driver or passen-ger, Secretary Adams is risking the health and the very lives of the motoring public.

There is no doubt this is a decision that will be hotly contested on Capitol Hill. By law, his ruling is subject to rejec-tion by both the House and the Senate.

Congress has a moral obligation to protect the well-being of drivers and their passengers by striking down the secretary's decision. To do less is to invite the federal government to issue a whole series of edicts that allow a Cabinet offi-cer or a bureaucrat to look important even though their rulings may be wholly contrary to the well being of the Ameri-can people. This is just such a precedent.

The Detroit News
Detroit, Mich., July 4, 1977

If Congress permits Transportation Secretary Brock Adams to have his way — and there is doubt about this — every new American automobile by Sept. 1, 1983, will be equipped with a mandatory "passive restraint" system — either two air bags that inflate in a crash or a safety belt that auto-matically wraps itself around driver and front seat passenger.

Adams said "passive restraints" — protective systems that operate automatically without the motorist doing anything — must go on the luxury and large size cars at the start of the 1982 model year on Sept. 1, 1981, on 1983 model intermediate and compact cars and on 1984 model subcompacts. Thus, the policy would be fully operational by Sept. 1, 1983.

In his own statement, Adams estimates that air bags will add from $100 to $300 to the price of a new car Nothing is said about the cost of reinstall-ing air bags after they inflate. Chrysler Corp says that bill could be as much as $600. The automatic lap and shoulder belt system, as used by Volkswa-gen on a luxury model, would put the price up by $25 to $40 per car.

These figures are controversial. The industry says bags would cost as much as $500 a car and the VW belt system sells in Germany as an extra op-tion for $40, not $25.

Adams says the use of "passive restraint" sys-tems could save 9,000 lives a year. An angry Chrysler spokesman reminded the secretary that Transportation Department files contain study re-ports which say that present manual belt systems would save at least 13,000 lives a year and they are therefore superior. However, that is only so if peo-ple lock them up and other studies show 70 to 80 percent do not.

There are faults in both the air bag and auto-matic belt systems.

Air bags inflate in a crash of 12 miles per hour or greater, cushioning front seat occupants. They do not keep passengers within the car's structure and offer no protection from the sides. Adams says manual lap belts will still be required in cars equipped with bags. Further, the bags cannot readily be installed in small cars because there isn't room for them under the instrument panel.

Automatic belts require reels which are mounted between the front seats — a mechanical feat that is impossible with the popular one-piece American bench seat.

The ruling is already under attack in Congress. Sen. Robert Griffin, R-Mich., and Rep. E.G. "Bud" Shuster, R-Pa., have introduced resolutions to disapprove.

The resolutions will bring both houses of Con-gress back to the vital principle — whether gov-ernment should interfere such an extent in the life of a citizen. Griffin calls the Adams ruling "big brotherism" and rails at the idea that a free American should be deprived of choice.

However, if Congress puts freedom of choice aside and passive restraint systems are going to be ordained, then the Adams report is fair and something of a victory for motorists and industry.

Since automatic belts cost only about one-fourth as much as the bags, the cost-conscious auto indus-try can be expected to go for the belts, even if this means doing away with the traditional bench seat.

However, the Adams ruling is flawed. The trans-portation secretary would begin the program at the wrong end of the car market.

It is well established by a number of studies that the danger of injury or death in a crash is much higher in a smaller car than in a normal sized one. Why, then, start the program by installing the sys-tem in the safest cars? Why not in the more dangerous, smaller models?

THE ANN ARBOR NEWS

Ann Arbor, Mich., June 5, 1977

A CHOICE that really is no choice is being offered by the U.S. Department of Transportation.

The subject, again, is inflatable auto airbags.

The Ford administration wrestled with air bags and finally decided to test them, not in government cars, but by trying to persuade auto-makers to offer the things as options. That begged the question of whether air bags, designed to save lives in head-on crashes, are really safe and worth the $100 or more they would add to a new car's price.

★ ★ ★

THE CARTER administration is considering a pushier approach. According to the White House Council on Wage-Price Stability, car-buyers should be given a choice between air bags, or less costly self-fastening belts.

Some choice.

The belts under consideration would be a step backward from those now installed on cars sold in this country, which involve both shoulder and lap restraints when properly fastened. In place of that sensible arrangement, the proposed system would involve only shoulder belts. These would be held in place by an interlock device (which cannot be required under existing U.S. law), to prevent a car from being started with belts unfastened. In place of lap belts to prevent forward-sliding in a collision, some form of bumpers would be installed in front of motorists' knees.

Even while advocating this so-called choice, the Wage-Price Council acknowledges that motorists in air bag-equipped cars should still wear conventional shoulder-lap belts.

At some point, the Department of Transportation ought to acknowledge that no generally acceptable substitute has been found for existing shoulder-lap belts, or for increased efforts to remind motorists to use them. Instead, DOT Secretary Brock Adams insists that on June 30, he will order installations of either air bags or the new shoulder-only belts in new cars.

If he carries through that threat, it isn't exactly going to do wonders for car sales, or for highway safety.

OKLAHOMA CITY TIMES

Oklahoma City, Okla., April 29, 1977

WHETHER the Department of Transportation's review of the air bag issue will result in another federal mandate to the automobile industry isn't yet known.

But that possibility drew some cogent opposition this week from a spokesman for the American Automobile Association in testimony presented to DOT Secretary Brock Adams. Adams has indicated he will not hesitate to compel installation of the air bag in all cars if the evidence convinces him that it would be in the public interest.

If he heeds the AAA testimony, however, he will let the air bag proposal gather dust.

The AAA testimony pointed out, for example, that with the government embarked on an effort to force U.S. motorists out of their gas guzzlers and into smaller cars, there has been virtually no field testing of air bags in small cars.

Furthermore, the AAA noted there is no proof that the air bags, designed to inflate instantly to protect driver and passengers in a front-end collision, will still function reliably "after years of road use under widely varying conditions."

Beyond that is the high cost of replacing an air bag once it has been inflated, a procedure that could cost more than $600. That would be in addition to the original cost of the device, which even in mass production would add several hundred dollars to the price of a new car.

As the AAA observed, this would more than offset the projected savings from reduced medical payment and personal injury insurance premiums.

Perhaps the best argument against the air bag, though, is the potential hazard from a device that is supposed to be protective. Based on past experience with manufacturer recalls for mechanical defects, it is reasonable to project several thousand faulty air bag assemblies in a total production run of 10 million vehicles a year.

Thus it becomes plausible to argue that unexpected inflation of defective air bags would cause as many or more fatalities and injuries than they were designed to prevent.

A far more sensible approach, concurred in by the AAA, is further refinement of seat and harness belt systems, together with renewed educational emphasis on the importance and benefits of their use.

THE DAILY HERALD

Biloxi, Miss., April 21, 1977

Next week Secretary of Transportation Brock Adams will hold hearings to determine whether the federal government should require passive restraints for the front seats of passenger cars beginning with 1981 model year automobiles.

We suspect the hearings are only a formality in light of President Carter's recent state of energy message.

Adams said he has decided to review the issue of passive restraints, or air bags, because the fuel crisis facing the nation will mean more small cars on America's highways, using less fuel, and these "smaller, lighter cars are not going to be as safe unless you build in safety standards."

It is apparent that the Secretary of Transportation is ready to reverse the decision of his predecessor, William Coleman, who decided last year not to require mandatory installation of automatic restraints in all new cars. Coleman believed that consumers would reject such a mandate unless they first had an opportunity to become familiar with the benefits of air bags. He offered a compromise plan by setting up a demonstration program in which four auto manufacturers would equip about 500,000 cars with air bags and other passive restraints over a two-year period beginning in 1978. The idea was to see if consumers would buy the cars. If the automakers could not sell the first several thousand air bag-equipped cars, they would be released from the program.

The Coleman plan is based not so much on consumer resistance to the idea, as it is on the auto industry's opposition to installing the restraints. At hearings on the matter in August of 1976, consumer advocates and the insurance industry pushed for mandatory installation of air bags. The automakers were just as strongly opposed.

The 1976 hearings produced the following facts:

- Passive restraint systems are technologically feasible.

— They would provide increased motoring protection, saving an estimated 12,000 lives a year and prevent thousands of injuries.

— At full production, the front-seat assembly could be sold for about $100 a car.

Coleman and the auto industry argued that consumers would resist the air bag restraint system just as they did the 1974 ignition interlock safety device — which was later scrapped.

That argument was a weak one by people who should have known better than to try and find cover behind it. The interlock system required physical action by motorists who had to buckle up seat belts before they could start their automobile. The air bag passive restraint system requires NO prior action to be effective.

We favor bags as standard equipment because the need for increased passenger safety will rise proportionately in the near future as the size and weight of automobiles decrease in line with energy conservation policies. Smaller cars mean less vehicle mass and crush distance to help absorb the impact of a collision.

One doesn't have to be on the payroll of an automaker to recognize that principle.

History of the Air Bag III: Congress Confirms It

By refusing to veto the Department of Transportation's order, Congress allowed it to go into effect Oct. 14. Transportation Secretary Brock Adams' requirement that 1982 cars be equipped with air bags as standard equipment was subject to a 60-day review period during which Congress could veto the order. By a vote of 65-31 in the Senate and 16-14 in the House Commerce Committee, the veto resolutions were killed.

THE DALLAS TIMES HERALD

Dallas, Texas, October 8, 1977

ONE MORE push toward forcing the American automobile driver to use airbags, or other "passive restraints," has been accomplished in the U.S. House of Representatives.

It was a sort of shadowy, sneaky approach unworthy of a legislative body representing millions of Americans, but the House Commerce Committee let the airbag controversy float on untouched by simply doing nothing.

Congress has until Oct. 14 to overrule Transportation Secretary Brock Adams' proposal to require the airbags in some 1982 model automobiles and in all models by 1984.

But the House Commerce Committee simply did not meet, claiming the lack of a quorum. It now appears to be too late to take definitive action before the Oct. 14 deadline.

Meanwhile, the Senate Commerce Committee voted 9 to 7 to recommend the Adams position be upheld by the full Senate, which could act as early as Monday. There is almost certain tough opposition ahead in the Senate.

But if the House fails to act at all, the Adams proposal could go merrily on by default. The only chance to pull the airbag proposal back for another look by Congress would come when the new session begins in January.

The American motorist rebelled a few years ago against the interlocking seat belts that had to be used to start the engine. It will do so again against airbags and other restraints forced upon it by the federal government.

The devices should be optional, not forced by bureaucrats who, incidentally, would be raising the price of automobiles $200 to $300.

The Evening Bulletin

Philadelphia, Pa., October 9, 1977

"We won," said Rep. Henry Waxman (D., Calif.), last Thursday.

The victory Rep. Waxman declared is in the battle to save human lives on the highways. Congress has until Oct. 14 to overrule Transportation Secretary Brock Adams' decision to require air bags in automobiles beginning with 1982 models. Rep. Waxman spoke after the House Commerce Committee, of which he is a member, did not act to send a veto resolution to the floor.

"If I can get it to the floor, I can win easily," asserted Rep. Bud Shuster (R., Pa.). We hope he's wrong.

There are about 9,000 excellent reasons for requiring air bags in automobiles. That's the number of lives which the Department of Transportation estimates would be saved every year.

Rep. Shuster says it's just an example of government's "penalizing conscientious citizens by attempting to protect the careless from themselves." So let the "careless" kill themselves? That's like saying the government has no obligation to put stop signs at corners or guard-rails on mountain roads. The air bag is a matter of life and death. Secretary Adams opted for life. So should the Congress.

The Star-Ledger

Newark, N.J., September 9, 1977

History provides abundant and irrefutable proof that safety devices which are activated automatically are far and away more effective than those which demand conscious effort by the driver.

The taillight brake signal is an example of an automatic device. Stepping on the foot brake lights up the red signal at the rear of the vehicle, alerting the motorist in the vehicle immediately behind that brakes have been applied.

Directional signals, on the other hand, require activation by the driver — with results that are frequently misleading and sometimes dangerous. Some motorists give no signals whatever, others are very good about it, and a few flash left turn signals when they intend to go right, and vice versa. Good defensive drivers have learned that direction signals, at best, are not dependable and are to be interpreted with caution.

The conventional seat belt is another example of a safety device that has failed to live up to its potential because motorists are not buckling up, as required. Recent studies show as few as 20 or 30 per cent actually follow through.

With this in mind, Transportation Secretary Brock Adams has issued an order that every new automobile be equipped with a passive restraint system by Sept. 1, 1983. The order gives the industry a choice of installing either air bags that inflate in a crash or a safety belt that automatically wraps itself around driver and front seat passenger when they enter the vehicle.

If Congress approves the Adams directive, passive restraints would be required on 1982 model luxury and large size cars, starting Sept. 1, 1982, on 1983 model medium and compact cars and on 1984 model subcompacts.

The transporation secretary estimates 9,000 lives annually will be saved by implementation of his order. Air bags will increase the cost of new cars by $100 to $300. Automatic safety belts (already successfully used in some Volkswagen models) can be factory installed for $25 to $40.

Air bags were born in controversy and continue to be a subject of bitter debate.

Opponents question their efficacy, citing the possibility of accidental inflation and attacking the safeness of the chemical that does the inflating. They are also unhappy about the high cost of reinstalling air bags after they are activated.

Advocates minimize the risks and emphasize that savings in lives will reduce insurance costs, offsetting the price of air bags. And insurance will reimburse motorists for reinstallation costs.

Air bags and automatic belts are not the last word in vehicle safety. Better devices may be down the road, although not presently in sight. But it is impossible to ignore the 9,000 lives a year that can be saved by passive restraints now — with no further action on the part of the motorist.

Richmond Times-Dispatch

Richmond, Va., October 9, 1977

There have been two interesting developments in the air bag controversy since we editorialized two weeks ago against Transportation Secretary Brock Adams' order making the bags mandatory equipment in future automobiles.

In Harrisonburg, a federal jury heard a case in which a Staunton woman sued General Motors Corp. because of injuries she received when the air bag in her car failed to inflate when she hit a parked truck.

The woman lost the case because the jury decided that GM had not claimed that the bag would work in the kind of crash that occurred. Literature that came with the car said the bag would inflate if the car, traveling at a speed of 11 mph or more, hit "an immovable object," and that it would inflate at a speed of 22 mph or more if the car hit a "comparable vehicle." The woman claimed she was traveling at between 20 and 25 mph when she hit the truck, but one series of GM tests put her speed at 9.6 mph and another series put it at between 11 and 14 mph.

It is significant that a GM attorney said that while this was the first air bag case to go to trial, other cases are pending.

Meanwhile, up on Capitol Hill in Washington, Democratic Rep. Henry Waxman of California resorted to a rare parliamentary maneuver (the *Wall Street Journal* called it a parliamentary "shenanigan") to prevent the House Commerce Committee from voting on a bill which would overturn Secretary Adams' air bag order. Rep. Waxman objected to the committee's meeting while the full House was in session. Committee meetings routinely occur while the House is in session, but a single objection can prevent such a meeting.

And why didn't Rep. Waxman want the committee to vote on the bill? His explanation, according to The Associated Press:

"If it gets to the House floor, the auto industry is going to put enough lobbying pressure on it to defeat the position taken by Secretary Adams."

If Rep. Waxman's action is in accord with the principles of democratic government, then we don't understand those principles.

Secretary Adams' air bag order, which will mean the addition of at least $100 to the cost of future automobiles for a device of questionable value, will automatically become law next Friday unless both houses of Congress vote against it prior to that time. If proponents continue to use such tactics as that employed by Rep. Waxman, the House won't get a chance to vote. Air bags will be a winner, democratic government a loser.

The ♣ State

Columbia, S.C., June 5, 1977

A GREAT deal of debate, complete with conflicting opinions, statistics and estimates, has been aired since Secretary of Transportation Brock Adams announced in June that all cars made for sale or use in the United States must be equipped with "passive restraint systems" after a phase-in period.

This means that they must be equipped with air bags that inflate upon impact or with "passive" seat belts which automatically fasten when a person enters either front seat and closes the door. (Today's regular seat belts are considered "active restraint systems because some action — buckling up — is required on the part of the user before he is afforded any protection.)

Since 1968, all cars have been required to have the lap and shoulder harness, the so-called three-point belt. The trouble is that only 20 per cent of front-seat occupants take the trouble to use them. It was this resistance that prompted the government to seek some automatic protection for these darn fools who won't use the protection they have.

There is no doubt that air bags will save some lives. But after sifting through the conflicting evidence on their effectiveness and talking to S.C. highway safety officials, we have concluded that they should not be required by law, but should remain an option available to car buyers.

A Highway Patrol officer told us air bags would help prevent injuries and deaths — but one would also have to use a lap belt to get full protection.

The air bags inflate only when the car has a frontal crash, which now accounts for about 50 per cent of the fatalities in auto accidents.

The other 50 per cent occur from side impacts, rear accidents or in rollovers. An air bag would provide no protection in these cases while a belt would. A passive seat belt would help, of course, but they can be used only in cars that have bucket seats, and studies have shown that they are generally less effective than fastened three-point belts.

Another concern is that air bags might provide no protection in the case of a secondary crash. Say a car hits an obstacle and the bag inflates, which it does in 1/25th of a second. But it deflates almost as fast and would be useless if the car, after hitting the first obstacle, careened on and struck a second obstacle. The momentarily inflated bag might even impede the driver's ability to regain control of his vehicle and miss the second obstruction.

Since the bags don't deploy at impacts of less than 12 miles per hour, they offer no protection, assuming any is needed, in these low-speed accidents. There have been cases when the bags didn't deploy at all, even in high-speed crashes. And occasionally, the bags have accidentally inflated for no reason at all, which would certainly be a startling and perhaps dangerous experience.

For this limited protection, a new car buyer will have to pay an extra $112 (the government's estimate) or $200 (an auto manufacturer's estimate). The bag can't be reused, and replacement will cost $325, according to the government, or $600, according to the manufacturer.

Secretary Adams' air-bag requirement will become law on October 19 unless Congress overrules him. The matter is now in the hands of the Senate Commerce Committee, where sitteth the Hon. Fritz Hollings. The matter should be sent to the floor for a vote, where, we would hope, the air-bag requirement will be put aside.

The Pittsburgh Press

Pittsburgh, Pa., October 8, 1977

One reason auto manufacturers have been less than enthusiastic about the controversial air-bag safety device is illustrated by a $250,000 damage suit that has just been concluded in Virginia.

Even though the defendant, General Motors, won this round, the case is an indication of what is bound to occur if such air bags become mandatory.

The plaintiff, a real-estate saleswoman who makes extensive use of a car in her work, told a federal court in Harrisonburg, Va., that the air bag in her auto failed to operate one morning when she collided with a parked truck.

She suffered severe injuries, she said, because she was not wearing a seat belt, having been told at the time she bought the car and the $225 air-bag option that she "would never need to use a seat belt again."

General Motors was able to convince the jury that no design failure was involved. The air bag did not inflate simply because the car had been going too slowly at the time of impact to trigger the sensors in the front bumper and instrument panel.

No precedent has been set by this case. But it was the first of a number of pending suits alleging air-bag failure to come to trial.

As such, it is a preview of what will almost inevitably happen should the U.S. government make air bags mandatory on large cars beginning in 1981 and on all cars in 1984, as Transportation Secretary Brock Adams has proposed.

Whether we are talking about air bags, the most likely type of passive restraint, or a seat-belt arrangement that doesn't require the active buckling-up of drivers or passengers, no electrical or mechanical device can be expected to be absolutely dependable always and forever.

Even if the air bag worked 99.9 per cent of the time, in a 10-million car year that would be 10,000 potential failures — and 10,000 potential lawsuits.

Secretary Adams should back up to the position of his predecessor, William T. Coleman, who suggested more extensive field testing of the air bag before requiring Detroit to embark on a mass installation program.

THE ANN ARBOR NEWS

Ann Arbor, Mich., October 10, 1977

CONGRESS never looks worse than on days when some of its members flat-out fail to do their jobs.

The House Commerce Committee is having a series of days like that. They started last Thursday.

That was when the Commerce Committee, headed by Rep. Harley O. Staggers, D-W. Va., was scheduled to vote on the irresponsible order on auto equipment by U.S. Transportation Secretary Brock Adams, issued last June.

Staggers' committee didn't even get a quorum together Thursday, so there was no vote. The committee's next scheduled meeting is Wednesday, which is almost like no meeting at all on this particular subject. Adams' order will take effect Oct. 14 unless majorities in House and Senate stir themselves enough to vote it down.

Congressional inaction will cost car-buyers money, without enhancing their safey.

★ ★ ★

ADAMS' ORDER stipulates that by Sept. 1, 1981, new cars must be equipped either with inflatable air bags, intended to protect the driver and a front-seat passenger in a head-on collision, or else with self-fastening lap belts similar to those in Volkswagens.

No member of Congress can claim ignorance of the arguments against air bags.

They can't be counted on to inflate when needed, as was just proven by a Virginia court case, in which an injured driver unsuccessfully tried to sue General Motors because of non-working air bags. (GM lawyers argued that the injured driver didn't crash hard enough.)

Nor do air bags offer protection against secondary collisions, which they might cause by popping out when not needed, as in a sideways or rear-end collision.

What is needed in all auto accidents is lap/shoulder seat belts, regardless of whether a car is carrying air bags. The self-fastening seat belts of the Volkswagen variety, which Adams wants, don't really qualify. They are only lap belts, without a shoulder belt. And they are a form of interlock device, which is something Congress outlawed a couple years ago, after mistakenly requiring them on 1974-model cars.

Those brief-lived interlock devices cost buyers of cars carrying them about $50 each. Ideally, Congress ought to have refunded the money.

Auto air bags could add something like $300 to the cost of new cars, on top of other cost-boosting factors. Not enough data have been collected about them to justify a decision by Congress to let Adams' order stand, even by default.

Los Angeles Times

Los Angeles, Cal., October 2, 1977

Congress has only until Oct. 19 to reject the Department of Transportation's order for the mandatory installation of air bags on future-model cars, and right now it appears unlikely that this deadline will be met. The Senate may get a chance to vote on an override measure, but signs are that a similar House measure may never get out of committee. If that proves to be the case, we can expect that there will be air bags in our future, like it or not.

We don't like it, and we don't think American motorists will, either, once they realize what they will be paying for, and what they will be getting.

We don't like it because air bags are plainly an unnecessary, expensive and only partly effective safety device, offering limited protection in only a single kind of accident. The installation of air bags, now planned over a three-year period beginning with 1982-model cars, wouldn't eliminate the need for additional interior safety devices. Lap belts, for example, would still be required throughout the car, since air bags protect only front-seat occupants in front-end collisions that occur above certain speeds.

One argument alone has been advanced in behalf of the air bag: It is a passive-restraint device, and as such it is supposed to get around the refusal of most people to use lap and shoulder belts to protect themselves in case of collisions. But how strong is that argument, really?

The air bag is not, by any means, a better device than the belts now required by law on all cars. In fact, the belts, when used, provide equal or greater protection, and they provide that protection in a far greater number of accident situations than does the air bag. The belt system, in short, is safer, cheaper and probably much less susceptible to failure in a crash.

It seems to us foolish in the extreme to abandon such a system in favor of something like the air bag, and Congress will be making a major mistake if that is what it chooses to do in the next few weeks.

TULSA WORLD

Tulsa, Oklahoma, October 10, 1977

OBSERVERS of the workings of Congress probably should not be surprised at the antics of any of the members of that body, but the picture that emerges of House members hiding out from a committee to deny it a quorum somehow is too much.

The supporters of airbags in automobiles are doing just that. Why they are, when it is apparent that Congress is going to go along with the Administration in requiring them in autos, is not clear.

The House Commerce Committee has been unable to make a recommendation on the question because it is unable to get a quorum. The airbag ruling will go into effect Oct. 14 if Congress doesn't overturn it by then.

The Senate Commerce Committee has approved the airbags and sent the measure to the floor for action.

"Hiding in the back room to avoid a quorum is hardly the most honorable way to block the House from expressing itself," charges Rep. E. G. Shuster, (R-Pa.), an opponent of airbags.

Rep. Henry Waxman (D-Calif.) cheerfully admits he's been avoiding the committee. "I have no hesitation in saying it. I was trying to let the time run out on the issue without having a vote take place."

While it is easy to sympathize with either Congressman, depending on your view of airbags, one has the feeling that this is not the way that the Founding Fathers envisioned Congress functioning. And it is doubtful that voters in general would approve of such a devious method of blocking the majority of the House in expressing itself.

The Detroit News

Detroit, Mich., October 11, 1977

The handling of the automotive air bag issue has become nothing less than malodorous. Important evidence against the bags has been hidden from Congress by zealots determined to foist these costly and doubtful things on the public against its will.

Transportation Secretary Brock Adams issued an order mandating "passive restraint" systems on new large cars by 1982 and on all new cars by 1984. Adams gives motorists two choices: air bags that deploy automatically in crashes with a severity greater than 12 miles per hour, or lap and shoulder belts that hook up automatically when a car's front doors close.

Congress has until Friday to act on that order — that is, to kill it. In the absence of congressional action, the order stands.

The air bags have had staunch opponents all along — including, for example, Rep. John Dingell, D-Trenton, who sees the bag system as a doubtful safety device and, more than that, a rip-off of the public.

Dingell contends the bags cost too much. He uses the original installation figure of $200. Some have placed the cost as high as $500. Worse than that, Dingell claims, is the reinstallation charge if the bags accidentally deploy. He says the cost of stuffing the bags back in the instrument panel is $600. Some have placed that figure as high as $700.

The price is bad enough, but mounting evidence indicates that the bags simply do not do their job, or at least are far less effective than a $40 set of passive restraint belts that do not ever need to be stuffed back in the instrument panel at $600 a crack.

The Wall Street Journal points to a Virginia lawsuit in which a woman sought damages from General Motors because the bags in her Cadillac failed to deploy in a crash. She lost the suit. The jury found that GM wasn't liable because GM never promised the things would work.

Would there have been any doubt about whether this woman would have been protected (at much less cost) by a passive restraint belt system? Anyone can see the answer. The belts work.

Now it appears that the National Highway Traffic Safety Administration concealed the bureau's own study on "offset" crash experiments, which showed the bags to be less effective than belts. Previous experiments had involved cars crashing headlight-to-headlight. In an offset crash (90 percent of frontal crashes happen this way) the cars are not lined up perfectly but rather in a driver-to-driver position.

Congressional investigators, checking into the suppression of the report, said the engineer who headed the project, Thomas H. Glenn, was harassed because he had the temerity to put the report on the public docket so that interested persons might read it.

Glenn was threatened with disciplinary action and attacked by Joan Claybrook, head of the NHTSA, the investigators found. The NHTSA evidently wanted to keep the report from Congress during the decision-making process.

The NHTSA in general and Claybrook in particular seem so committed to the air bag system that they have lost sight of fairness and good judgment. Though NHTSA denies this, such is the public's perception of the situation.

On the basis of the Virginia case and the investigation of the suppression of the "offset" study, Congress should kick the whole Brock Adams order out the window.

After that, the issue should to be taken up again, starting from scratch. All the reports, good and bad, about both air bags and passive restraint belts should be fully exposed so that a balanced, reasoned judgment can be made.

The evidence now before the public indicates that passive restraint belts would win, hands down, and the adoption of that system would save consumers billions of dollars without compromising the safety of the individual.

THE BLADE

Toledo, Ohio, October 10, 1977

CONGRESSIONAL proponents of mandatory air bags in autos are pulling out all the stops in an effort to prevent the issue from coming to a vote of the full House and Senate before next Friday. That is the deadline for action by both houses to prevent an administration requirement for passive restraints such as air bags in cars from taking effect.

The longer the matter is delayed, the poorer the chances that Congress will have time to act on it, and this is what air-bag supporters are banking on. The latest gimmick, engineered by Rep. Henry Waxman, California Democrat, was to prevent the House Commerce Committee from meeting to consider the issue while the full House was in session. Such meetings are routinely held at these times but they can be blocked by a single objection, and that is the device that Mr. Waxman seized on.

Backers of the air bag should not be permitted to get away with sleazy tactics of that kind. On as controversial and questionable an issue as the air bag, the full membership of both the House and Senate should have an opportunity to vote one way or the other. The inescapable inference to be drawn from the Waxman maneuver is that, in the face of a considerable body of evidence casting doubt on the effectiveness of the so-called safety device, its backers are afraid they will lose if the requirement does come to floor votes.

At the same time, outside the halls of Congress the Insurance Institute for Highway Safety, which supports Transportation Secretary Brock Adams' proposal to require the air bags, is stepping up its own propaganda campaign. In a cleverly timed statement, the institute announced that its surveys indicate that, despite a widely publicized effort by the auto companies to stimulate the use of seatbelts in the Detroit area, few motorists actually are doing so.

This no doubt is true, but such findings skirt the heart of the matter, which is that seatbelts are installed in cars for the safety of drivers and passengers. If they do not choose to take advantage of them and thus risk serious injury or death, then that is their prerogative; however, they have no one but themselves to blame if something does happen.

But there is no sound reason Big Brother should step in and mandate the installation of costly automatic safety devices such as the notorious ignition-interlock system that cost car manufacturers and buyers millions of dollars before it was dropped and the dubious air bag, which would very likely have the same effect and encounter the same result.

The House and Senate have only a few days left in which to stop this unconscionable rip-off of the car-buying public. They should get at it.

The Honolulu Advertiser

Honolulu, Hawaii, October 13, 1977

Barring a surprise, it appears Congress will not overturn the Carter Administration's order for installation of passive restraints such as air bags in all automobiles between now and 1985.

Both houses would have to vote to overturn the order by Friday, and attempts in the Senate and House were defeated yesterday.

THAT IS GOOD, but it won't end controversy over air bags, or even over the kind of seat belts that go in place automatically which are an acceptable alternative.

Automakers will probably proceed to fight the deadlines, as they have for emission and other standards. Other arguments about safety will arise or continue as air bags become more widely used.

The debate can be beneficial, for there are pros and cons involved, as in almost everything. But indications are now that far more benefits will come from widespread use of air bags — most notably the saving of an estimated 9,000 lives a year or 20 per cent of the number who now die in auto accidents.

Our own feeling is that proper use of seat belts might accomplish much the same end — and they still should be used even when air bags are installed in cars.

Still, the basic fact is that not enough Americans are willing to buckle up voluntarily, and politicians are not going to force them with laws. Polls indicate public acceptance of air bags or other automatic restraints — but also stronger opposition to even a $25 fine for not using seat belts.

MAYBE SOMEDAY educational campaigns will convince enough motorists of the value of using seat belts. But by then air bags seem likely to be overwhelmingly accepted as well.

Since that would amount to double safety, it is not a bad prospect to contemplate.

DESERET NEWS

Salt Lake City, Utah, October 12, 1977

Congress will have to act by Friday if it is going to reject the Department of Transportation's decision mandating air bags or other passive restraints in cars by 1984.

As the lawmakers ponder this decision, they should know there are new studies which raise serious questions about the supposed superiority of air bags over seat belts.

One study involved off-center, head-on crashes — the kind that typically occur when a car veers over the center line and hits a car coming in the other direction.

This study showed that three of the four occupants in cars equipped only with air bags would have been killed or very seriously injured in such crashes. But all occupants in cars equipped with lap and shoulder belts would have survived the same kind of crashes if they had used the belts.

Moreover, air bags don't work at all in accidents involving side impacts, rear end collisions, or rollovers, where nearly half of all fatal accidents occur.

The belts already are installed in 95% of all cars today. Regardless of what Congress does about air bags, lap and shoulder belts will remain the primary passenger-restraint system well into the 1990's.

The trick is to get motorists to use the belts. Indeed, if more Americans buckled up voluntarily, we might never have heard of the air bag. On this score, happily, there's also a new development.

Motorists Information, Inc., a non-profit outfit started by the four major U.S. car makers to conduct education programs on public issues, recently tried a new approach in persuading motorists to use seat belts. Instead of urging drivers to buckle up for their own safety, the new appeal urges them to do it for the sake of their loved ones.

In test areas, the reported use of lap and shoulder belts increased 41% after the new campaign.

Even with air bags, motorists will still need to buckle up to get full protection. If Congress rejects the bags, the lawmakers should make particularly sure they help mount a new campaign to get Americans to use their seat belts.

THE SAGINAW NEWS

Saginaw, Mich., October 14, 1977

The air bag controversy has finally ended with Congress coming down on the side of federally mandated passive systems as standard equipment in all American-made automobiles by 1984.

We're not sorry about this — certainly not as sorry about it as the auto industry in general, Chrysler Corp. in particular and a host of congressmen, including many from our own state, who fought passive restraint almost as if it were a doomsday issue.

Neatly, as it turns out, congressmen won't have to be on record as to how they really stood.

The Senate merely voted to table a resolution disapproving Transportation Secretary Brock Adams' proposal to go to passive restraint systems. And the House Commerce Committee did the same to prevent the full House from voting on it.

The result is that passive restraint systems, whatever form they take, automatically pass into law on Friday. Large cars will have them by 1982, intermediates by 1983 and all passenger vehicles by 1984.

Very honestly, we find ourselves in a strange position on this.

We have generally favored any device within reason that provides a greater degree of life-saving safety in auto crash situations — whether air cushions or automatic seat harnesses which wrap around front seat passengers when the door closes.

But we're not sure we like the way Congress shut off the vote on this. Neither are we very thrilled by 11th hour reports that broke suggesting DOT deliberately withheld test results that found the air bag a lot less than perfect.

Chrysler and Reps. John Dingell, D-Mich., and Bud Shuster, R-Pa., led the way on that charge to deflate air bags.

So we enter the era of passive restraints with a cloud hanging over the true efficiency of air bags, at least, in frontal crashes.

Still, we're not dissuaded about passive restraint systems in cars. And we refuse to believe they are beyond the auto industry to provide at reasonable cost once into mass production. Particularly with General Motors promising to beat the federal deadlines with optional systems.

TULSA WORLD

Tulsa, Okla., October 14, 1977

BELATEDLY, news has leaked out of the Highway Safety Administration that officials of that agency suppressed a scientific report questioning the effectiveness of air bag as a crash protection device in cars.

The director of the Administration, Joan Claybrook, says the report by HSA Researcher Thomas H. Glenn was hidden from the public because the research work "was of poor professional quality."

Well, maybe so. But the report was based on crash tests conducted by a Buffalo, N.Y., firm that has been in the automotive and aircraft safety testing business since 1947. According to the Wall Street Journal, the firm has maintained impressive credentials during those 31 years.

But it makes no difference anyway. Automobile purchasers are going to have to buy airbags at $200 each whether they want them or not.

Ms. Claybrook and other bureaucrats have decided that airbags are good for us, and Congress has refused to override their decision.

THE PLAIN DEALER

Cleveland, Ohio, October 15, 1977

The national debate over the air bag ended Wednesday with the air bag, well, in the driver's seat. Unfortunately, only senators, a handful of members of the House of Representatives and the secretary of transportation had a chance to decide on the issue.

The nation's 100 million drivers were hardly consulted.

But then, there might have been a good reason for not permitting any freedom of choice on this question, at least from Transportation Secretary Brock Adams' point of view. A few years ago when General Motors Corp. offered air bags as an option on some model lines, consumers voted against the bag by the tens of millions by refusing to purchase the things.

Wednesday, the Senate, in effect, purchased air bags for all of us with our own money by refusing to overrule Brock's directive mandating automobile passive restraints for all new cars by the 1984 model year.

Technically, the directive requires only a passive restraint, which might or might not be an air bag. The alternative to the air bag is the automatic seat belt, a device that fits into the car door and encapsulates a driver or passenger when the door is shut. But because the automatic seat belt cannot presently work in conjunction with bench-type seats, Brock's directive spells air bags.

The fact is, as even the Department of Transportation concedes, the combination seat belt-shoulder harness that is now standard equipment in all new cars is superior to the air bag as an injury prevention device.

But seat belt usage is optional and, for a wide variety of reason, most drivers don't buckle up.

Frankly, we think auto occupant restraints, passive or otherwise, should be left to personal preference. But if that is not to be, then a far better case can be made for a mandatory seat belt-shoulder harness use law than for mandatory air bags.

We can only hope, but hardly expect, that sometime before 1984 Congress can devise a solution to this problem that does not involve compelling consumers to purchase air bag systems of limited utility at something like $350 or more per car.

The Case Against Air Bags: Rising Costs, Product Liability

The Houston Post

Houston, Texas, July 1, 1978

At least 19 countries, including Japan and most of Western Europe, as well as the Canadian provinces of Ontario and Quebec, have laws requiring all who drive to fasten their safety belts or risk penalties. The Highway Users Federation reports that adoption of safety belt laws cut traffic deaths 22 percent in France, 25 percent in Australia and 39 percent in Belgium.

In the United States, nine out of 10 motorists do not buckle up, despite massive educational campaigns. The federation calculates that if 70 percent of automobile occupants were strapped in, 12,000 lives could be saved each year. Puerto Rico and the city of Brooklyn, Ohio, are the only two U.S. jurisdictions with laws requiring the use of safety belts. Dr. B. J. Campbell, director of the University of North Carolina Highway Safety Research Center, says, "It's amazing that such a law has not been enacted in the United States when so many people have had so much success with it in almost every country in Western civilization."

Tennessee is the only continental state with any kind of safety belt law, and it applies only to children. Attempts to pass laws requiring proper restraints to protect babies and small children riding in automobiles were defeated in Colorado, Maryland, New Hampshire, Oregon and South Dakota this year. Meanwhile, traffic accidents are the leading cause of death for American children. And we kill 50,000 Americans annually on our highways.

RAPID CITY JOURNAL

Rapid City, S.D., February 6, 1978

The government mandate requiring air bags or other passive restraints on all U.S. cars starting in 1982 is causing concern among auto dealers and auto makers.

In addition to the contention of many involved with auto safety that air bags are not the best way to protect vehicle occupants, manufacturers and dealers are concerned over the question of product liability.

They contend the government, because it is requiring air bags, should come up with some form of liability indemnification that will provide financial protection in cases where airbags inadvertently deploy injuring, or perhaps killing, occupants.

According to the president of the National Automobile Dealers Association, insurance companies are reticent to provide coverage against such mishaps.

The feeling is that if the federal government feels air bags are not dangerous, it should provide manufacturers and dealers with product liability indemnification.

Without getting into air bag effectiveness or the hazard they may present to auto occupants, the problem of product liability appears to be a valid one. We have to wonder whether it even was considered when the government mandated passive restraints in a quest for increased safety.

The Kansas City Times

Kansas City, Mo., September 13, 1978

Air bags, those vehicle safety devices which inflate instantly on crash impact to cushion a car's occupants against striking hard interior surfaces, remain a subject of controversy. But nevertheless the nation's automotive industry, since June 1977, has been heading toward a phased-in, mandatory installation of automatic restraints — either air bags or automatic seat belts which enfold a person as he sits down in the car — beginning in September 1981.

The federal order calls for such restraints in 1982 model full-size cars, in 1983 intermediate and compact cars and in 1984 subcompacts. The lengthy interval between issuance of the standard and its staggered effective dates plainly is intended to allow for more testing of these devices and to give the motoring public a greater familiarity — and acceptance — of them.

Brock Adams, secretary of transportation, believes both these developments are coming along well. The bags and automatic belts are compiling a real-life (as opposed to laboratory) record of saving lives and a survey indicates that at least a majority of drivers endorse their adoption.

In a billion miles of travel by Volkswagen Rabbits fitted with the automatic belts, a fatality rate of .78 per million miles has emerged, compared to 2.34 deaths per million miles in Rabbits with conventional seat belts. In 600 million miles' experience with General Motors air bag cars, mostly 1974 through 1976 models, the death rate of .85 per million miles was about half that of full-size cars with conventional seat belts.

Of course what the bags and automatic belts are all about is the failure of the nation's motorists to buckle up those conventional belts, fewer than 2 percent doing so. Objectors find them uncomfortable, too restrictive, inclined to mess up their clothing or a reminder of possibilities they don't want to think about — any rationale will do. Hence the automatic restraints that require no positive action by the beneficiary, such as hooking them up.

A survey of 2,000 adults found 58 percent strongly or moderately favoring the mandatory restraints order and only 25 to 28 percent opposed. Of course as the sad case of conventional seat belts shows, people's verbal support of motor vehicle safety and their active involvement in it can be two different things.

Many will find the automatic belts ominous and presumptuous and will object to them for the same reasons they rejected the buckle-up variety. Getting popped suddenly in the face with an air bag will be a startling experience (but then so is a crash), and one which will require forethought by a driver to maintain control of his vehicle. The bag at least is not a constant restriction when it is not in operation.

But if in fact such restraints can save 9,000 lives a year and prevent many thousands of injuries, as predicted, they will prove such an asset for survival in the automotive age that reasonable persons should not want to be without them, whatever their disadvantages.

BUFFALO EVENING NEWS

Buffalo, N.Y., July 13, 1978

If Congress needs any additional reason for scrapping its 1977 order forcing every motorist to buy an inflatable air bag for his own protection, let it ponder the cost impact now foreseen by the auto industry.

When the government decreed that Detroit must install bags starting with the 1982 models and put them on all cars by 1984, advocates of the so-called "passive" restraints put down the additional cost factor for car-buyers as no big deal, varying at the most between $112 and $200.

But now the Ford Motor Co. estimates that the bags will add up to $825 in 1982 to the cost of its full-sized cars. And although this projection includes an inflation factor, the same inflation will boost the price tag for all the other pollution-control and fuel-economy refinements that Congress has forced Detroit to put in its car designs.

Even if the auto industry didn't face so many other vexing design challenges in compliance with federal edicts, the air bag mandate would still add up to an overly arbitrary exercise in government-knows-best compulsion.

Certainly motorists should buckle seat belts for their own protection. And certainly government has a perfectly legitimate role in requiring safety measures, as in basic auto and road design, beyond the individual motorist's discretion.

But inflatable bags provide at best a limited and uncertain crash-protection, and recent air-bag crash tests reinforce the claims of critics that they can be extremely hazardous to a child perched on the edge of the seat or otherwise unrestrained or unprotected in a collision.

In any case, we can see no excuse for keeping on the books a government compulsion that supersedes individual motorist choice — at a cost so steep as to keep many a rusted, rattletrap car on the highways long past its normal trade-in time. This is government paternalism gone haywire.

The Detroit News

Detroit, Mich., July 3, 1978

The National Highway Traffic Safety Adminstration (NHTSA), which is trying to push air bags on a skeptical auto industry and an equally skeptical public, has been taken to task by the General Accounting Office (GAO).

The GAO, the congressional watchdog agency, says the "real world" cost of installing an air bag restraint system in a new car runs from $400 to $580, not the $112 estimated by NHTSA.

Thus, if the NHTSA order to install the devices on 1982 regular-size cars is put into effect, that one bureaucratic edict may be responsible for one of the largest automobile price hikes in history.

Nor does the NHTSA order stop there. It demands installation of passive restraints on all intermediate cars in 1983, and all compacts and subcompacts in 1984, with air bag systems favored all the way.

If "passive restraint" systems that operate without any action by the driver or front seat passenger are to be imposed on the public, NHTSA has two choices — bags or belts.

Passive restraint belts are available as an option this year on the General Motors Chevette subcompact. That option is $50 — a long way from the staggering cost of an air bag.

Fortunately, a bipartisan coalition of air bag opponents in Congress is now trying to deny NHTSA the funds needed to enforce its air bag order. Rep. John Dingell, D-Mich., has introduced the appropriate bill that would buy time so Congress can reconsider the issue.

Air bags offer an extremely dubious solution to the highway safety problem. They provide a cushion in a frontal crash, if they deploy. They sometimes fail. Also, they offer no protection in a side crash and NHTSA says belts must continue to be installed even if a car is equipped with an air bag.

The bags present one headache after another. They can burst forth if a car hits a parking lot post at low speed. Restuffing the bags into their recesses would cost about $700, according to the industry.

Air bags are bad news. Belts are better. Belt systems are designed and available, right now, for all sizes of cars. They work and never have to be stuffed back in the dash or steering wheel at $700 a throw.

Why is it, then, that the sensible, practical, cost-efficent, dependable passive belt system is resisted with such passion by the National Highway Traffic Safety Administration? Congress should find out.

Prescribing

As its name implies, the Food & Drug Administration sets standards for the drug industry as well as the food industry. The hundreds of new drugs that are introduced on the American market each year have had to clear an obstacle course of tests on bacteria, animals and volunteer human subjects. The FDA keeps track of the ingredients in all drugs intended for human use and ensures that the drugs produce no serious side effects. In addition, a 1962 amendment to the Food, Drug & Cosmetic Act requires the FDA to determine that a drug is effective, not merely safe. It is this aspect of the FDA's mission that has caused the most controversy in recent years.

The most serious challenge to the FDA's authority has surfaced over the effectiveness of Laetrile, a derivative of apricot pits, as a treatment for cancer. The controversy often takes on an ideological tone. When scientific studies fail to establish Laetrile's worth, its supporters dismiss the findings as part of a conspiracy by the government and the drug companies. To a degree, the attitude of Laetrile supporters reflects an understandable impatience with bureaucratic slowness in approving new drugs. Like most bureaucracies, the FDA can legitimately be criticized for red tape, confusion and failure to implement its own policies effectively.

The medical profession is also to blame for public skepticism toward official reports on new drugs. Disillusionment with high costs and indifferent service in the medical field has produced a bias toward unorthodox drugs like Laetrile. There is a feeling among Americans that any new substance which might be effective but cheaper than current treatments will automatically be opposed by the medical establishment because it undermines doctors' authority.

There is no question that drugs should be subject to regulation. The public may be able to make up its own mind about food and cigarettes, but drugs require special knowledge and training to understand. The FDA must redouble its efforts to restore public confidence in its methods and findings.

Debate Rages Over Laetrile While States Legalize Its Use

Washington June 2 became the seventh state to legalize the sale of laetrile, an alleged cure for cancer. Laetrile can also be sold in Alaska, Florida, Nevada, Indiana, Arizona, and Texas, with the latter three allowing manufacture of the drug as well. The state legislatures voted for legalization despite the federal government's ban on the importation and sale of laetrile which the Food and Drug Administration said May 16 it would continue to enforce. An estimated 50,000 Americans now take laetrile despite the FDA's ruling in 1963 that the drug could not be used because no evidence existed of its efficacy against cancer.

The controversial substance, also known as vitamin B-17 and the chemical amygdalin, occurs naturally in the pits of apricots and peaches, in bitter almonds and other plants. It is available in 26 countries and is being smuggled into the U.S. from Canada and Mexico where it is legal.

Promoters of laetrile use claim that it could prevent and cure cancer. They contend that since there is no evidence of the chemical being harmful, the ban on it should be lifted. However, the FDA noted that laetrile was the most tested of all potential cancer cures and that five studies by the National Cancer Institute alone had indicated that it was therapeutically worthless. (According to the 1962 Kefauver-Harris amendments to the Food, Drug and Cosmetic Act of 1958, drug manufacturers were required to prove not only that a product was safe, but that it was also effective.) Some laetrile advocates maintained that it is a vitamin, not a drug, and should therefore be exempt from the legislation.

THE ARIZONA REPUBLIC
Phoenix, Ariz., May 26, 1977

REASON seems to be dawning, however slowly, on organized medicine and its mindless attitude toward Laetrile.

Two prestigious cancer research organizations agreed yesterday that Laetrile, a bootleg apricot seed derivative with claimed curative powers, should be re-examined in light of growing public pressure.

Clinical tests involving humans may be conducted by the National Cancer Institute and the Memorial Sloan-Kettering Cancer Center.

Scientific fairness did not create this willingness to review Laetrile. What did, however, is the growing American impatience with organized medicine's rigid and ready denunciation of a concoction which, at worst, is simply a harmless source of hope for the incurable, and, at best, is a miracle drug for a very few.

When legislators in Arizona, Nevada, Florida, Indiana and Alaska legalized Laetrile's production and sale within those states, medicine had to review its position. The legislation defies the Food and Drug Administration's ban on Laetrile.

Until this outburst of defiance, the FDA and organized medicine had made criminals out of anyone who chose the use of Laetrile over surgery, chemotherapy or radiation treatment for cancer. Most of those denied Laetrile had been told that organized medicine could not help them, and death was inevitable.

Yet, even when a harmless drug like Laetrile provided the only hope, organized medicine continued to demand that it be denied to the hopeless.

Cancer researchers willing to re-open the Laetrile cases are to be congratulated. Their findings probably will be consistent with past findings — that Laetrile is not an assured source of cure (for that matter, neither is traditional treatment), that there is inconclusive evidence of prolonged life with the use of Laetrile, and that it is not toxic or harmful.

At which point the FDA should get out of the business of prohibiting hopeless cancer victims from using a compound which never harmed anyone at death's door.

ARKANSAS DEMOCRAT
Little Rock, Ark., May 16, 1977

Should the Arkansas legislature follow the lead of such states as Alaska, Florida and Indiana in legalizing use of Laetrile — a supposed "cancer cure" with no established curative powers? Well, why not? The stuff won't hurt you, and cancer patients use it as a last resort anyway.

The U.S. Food and Drug Administration has outlawed interstate movement of Laetrile (vitamin B17 it is called), but the ruling doesn't apply intrastate, and there are people around to swear that laetrile has cured or helped them.

There's no proof of that. This apricot-kernel derivative has been in use since 1920 and has been available in its synthesized state for a quarter century, but in all that time researchers haven't found that it helps cancer at all. The FDA ban is based on fear that people might use Laetrile as a FIRST resort or as a means of saving the expense of standard treatment—and die for lack of treatment.

That's possible, but if Laetrile is so ineffective, it's likely that the best way of discrediting it is to let people use it and see that it's powerless. Meanwhile, people determined to get the thing are risking arrest and jail by smuggling it in, mainly from Mexico, where it's legal.

It says very little for Laetrile that the Canadian Medical Association, the National Cancer Institute and a number of other prestigious medical associations have found Laetrile valueless. But it doesn't say much for our freedoms either that the government is determined to treat us like ninnies by banning the stuff on the ground that it will preempt effective cancer treatment.

The medical fraternity isn't above taking similar approaches. Last week, for example, the National Council on Drugs (a liaison outfit for the American Medical, Dental, Pharmaceutical and related associations) called for classifying Laetrile among "new drugs" instead of as the vitamin it's supposed to be.

Why? Well, in federalese, a new drug has to have a proven effectiveness to pass muster. That is, it must do GOOD and not just "not do bad." We support the council in many of its aims—like revising the Delaney Amendment to exempt saccharin from its current ban—but not in this approach to Laetrile.

The legislature could legalize the stuff either as an across-the-counter or as a prescription drug, and leave it to the individual to decide whether he wants to take it. He or she certainly wouldn't hurt himself taking it and—who knows?—the fact that Laetrile hasn't yet been proved effective isn't certain proof that it isn't. In any case, taking the stuff involves questions of freedom that we don't think the government or the medical profession should deny us.

The Salt Lake Tribune
Salt Lake City, Utah, May 25, 1977

If Laetrile is as worthless in treating cancer as most scientists believe, many patients are being bilked out of their money and perhaps their lives.

If, however, Laetrile is beneficial, then many other patients are being denied a substance that could improve their odds for survival.

Fortunately, there's one point in this controversy on which just about everyone agrees: Taken in normal doses, Laetrile is not harmful.

If this dispute is to be settled on the basis of scientific evidence rather than on the basis of which side can shout the louder, Laetrile should be subjected to carefully monitored field tests.

That's the conclusion to which an increasing number of highly respected scientific organizations are coming, including most recently the National Cancer Institute and the Memorial Sloan-Kettering Cancer Center.

The very existence of field tests may, of course, be taken by some cancer sufferers as an indication that Laetrile is worthwhile.

Morever, even if such tests produce conclusive evidence against the effectiveness of Laetrile, some patients will always be desperate enough to try anything.

But without the tests, there's going to be a growing black market for Laetrile, with all the potential for abuse such operations imply.

Moreover, until the tests are conducted, state legislatures are going to come under increasing pressure to legalize Laetrile even though this is a decision that should be made by scientists, not politicians.

Even though the U.S. Food and Drug Administration has banned the importation and interstate shipment of Laetrile, the drug has been legalized by state legislatures in Alaska, Arizona, Florida, Indiana, and Nevada.

We mention this point because the FDA must give its approval if field tests are to be conducted. Clearly, the Laetrile controversy won't go away merely by trying to ignore it.

Richmond Times-Dispatch
Richmond, Va., May 28, 1977

The medical profession and the federal government can no longer ignore the mushrooming opposition to the Food and Drug Administration's ban on the anticancer agent Laetrile.

Dr. Lewis Thomas, president of the prestigious Memorial Sloan-Kettering Cancer Center in New York, says that human clinical tests of Laetrile should be undertaken. And the National Cancer Institute in Washington reveals that it is "seriously considering" using Laetrile in tests on humans.

In recent months eight states have voted to legalize Laetrile, despite the Food and Drug Administration's ban on the interstate shipment of the substance.

Dr. Thomas wants an epidemiological team to conduct a study of people who claim to have benefited from Laetrile, in an effort to determine if the substance really did have any effect on their cancers.

Many of the state legislators who have voted to legalize Laetrile undoubtedly did so out of the same feelings we have expressed in these columns: that while the preponderance of current medical sentiment is that Laetrile is not an effective anticancer agent, a total ban on the substance denies patients freedom of choice in deciding their own treatment, a freedom they should have, provided the treatment is not harmful per se. Virtually no one contends that Laetrile contains any harmful substances.

There is also the bare possibility that the accepted medical position on Laetrile is in error, just as it was woefully wrong up to about 20 years ago in the widespread use of X-ray for the treatment of acne and other benign conditions — a discredited practice that now has the profession searching for persons who received such treatment, because the radiation has been found responsible for thyroid cancers which some of these patients have developed.

In any event, public sentiment on the Laetrile issue can no longer be ignored by medical authorities. It makes sense for research to be undertaken to try to determine with reasonable certainty if Laetrile has some value or whether it is totally worthless, as most medical opinion now holds.

Los Angeles Times
Los Angeles, Calif., May 30, 1977

Producing Laetrile is only slightly harder than making a pot of coffee from raw beans. Apricot pits are dried and husked; the seed kernel is ground up and cooked with a certain benzene compound that extracts the Laetrile.

But the manufacturing process is the only simple thing about Laetrile, a cyanide-related substance of no known efficacy for which a few cancer patients have claimed amazing curative properties.

Eminent institutions have put Laetrile through cancer tests on rats and mice and found no evidence of health improvement. Researchers have tried without success to substantiate claims of cured human cancer patients. The drug, whose other chemical name is Amygdalin, lacks even a shred of clinically demonstrated worth, except for some evidence that it tends to increase appetite just as other cyanide compounds do.

Laetrile is banned in the United States under the Food and Drug Administration's efficacy standards: No matter how harmless a drug may seem to be, it cannot be used in this country unless someone can show that the substance has some medical value. The National Cancer Institute has just announced that it may launch a new study of Laetrile's value, but that work will take months or years.

As a result, hundreds of desperate American cancer victims troop regularly to Laetrile clinics in Tijuana and elsewhere to get injections, looking to the drug as their only faint hope for recovery. Others spend an estimated $700 to $800 a month for Laetrile made by bootleg manufacturers or smuggled into the country by unscrupulous promoters.

Should the ban on Laetrile be dropped? Many people think so, arguing that basic freedom and plain sympathy demand letting hopelessly sick people use even this costly and medically baseless last resort—if having tried it will ease their sorrow and pain. That is sensible so long as legalizing Laetrile doesn't foster the growth of medical quackery.

Dr. Franz J. Ingelfinger, editor of the New England Journal of Medicine, has urged the legalization of Laetrile even though he considers it "another one of those quack cures that sweep relentlessly through our volatile society."

A cancer patient himself, Ingelfinger said in a recent essay, "Perhaps there are some situations in which rational medical science should yield and make some concessions. If any patient had what I thought was hopelessly advanced cancer, and if he asked for Laetrile, I should like to be able to give the substance to him to assuage his mental anguish . . ."

Continued banishment will only reinforce the Laetrile proponents' zeal as well as their suspicions, Ingelfinger noted. He proposed a two-year trial to assuage those suspicions and also allow the gathering of enough clinical data to give Laetrile a full study.

Already six states have legalized Laetrile, and a bill to allow its use in California is pending in Sacramento. Meanwhile, a bill motivated by the Laetrile controversy is pending in Congress. This sweeping measure would set aside the FDA's entire efficacy standard, allowing *any* drug, including Laetrile, to be marketed so long as tests point to no harmful effects.

We think the federal measure is lacking in caution. No drug is harmless if its easy availability from unethical doctors or distributors diverts a patient from seeking more meaningful therapy in time to save his life. Dismantling the efficacy standard would open the floodgate to all kinds of nostrums and phony cures. Phony cures cause real and unnecessary deaths.

Similarly, California Senate Bill 245—the proposal by Sen. William Campbell (R-Whittier)—is flawed by the paucity of its safeguards against quackery. The bill says a physician may prescribe Laetrile if he has told the patient, in writing, about the risks and reputed benefits of this and other kinds of treatment. The doctor must also urge, but need not require, the patient to see another doctor who is a cancer expert.

We think the restrictions should go further: Laetrile's use should be allowed only for terminal cancer patients who ask for it.

The law has no business denying a citizen's dying wish to grasp at harmless straws. But neither should the law subvert medical care in the name of freedom, lulling patients into thinking they are being treated when they aren't.

The Washington Star
and Daily News

Washington, D.C., May 30, 1977

The possibility that the cancer research establishment — yes, New York's great Sloan-Kettering Center — may test Laetrile on human cancer victims should be welcome news to both schools of thought on the controversial medication. It's obvious that those who believe the apricot pit compound can indeed arrest cancer or ameliorate the condition of people who have the disease would want their claims documented by disinterested research. But those who, like the FDA scientists concerned with cancer drugs, think Laetrile is pure snake oil have reason to want the tests too.

The sad fact is that, as forbidden fruit, Laetrile has an even greater appeal than desperate hope would give it if it were on sale in every drugstore. People in fear of death have resorted to elaborate smuggling devices to get Laetrile into the United States from Mexico, Germany, Hong Kong and other places where it is made. The estimated 50,000 people who take Laetrile will pay any price and go to any difficulty to get it.

They will also believe the latest story supporting the Laetrile mystique. For some, no amount of disproving evidence will dissipate the myth. For many, however, the claims of rationality would outweigh wishful thinking if incontrovertible test results could be shown.

Insofar as any test results can be considered incontrovertible, this means tests involving human beings rather than laboratory animals. While there are strong similarities between the way the animals react and the way humans react, the correlation cannot be considered absolute; there is always a gray area that lets those who want to hope against the preponderance of evidence go on hoping.

The tests the Sloan-Kettering doctors are preparing to undertake are largely a matter of analyzing the cases where the strongest claims of help have been made. If it turns out that other factors produced the cures and remissions, some people with cancer may be won back to more orthodox medical treatment.

Such study will also have a profound effect on state laws having to do with the manufacture and sale of Laetrile. There are now only four states where Laetrile has been legalized, with two more in the process and a couple of dozen legislatures considering the prospect. Even in the states where Laetrile is legal, however, the movement of supplies is hampered by federal regulations keeping it out of interstate commerce.

The probability remains that tests on human cancer victims will tend to debunk Laetrile rather than reinforce its claims. If it happens that way and some people are influenced toward more officially approved medications, fine. If Laetrile turns out to have some of the powers attributed to it, better still. Either way, there can be more informed decision-making on all sides. Which is about the best any of us can wish for ourselves or other people.

Except, of course, the freedom to follow through on an informed judgment once it's been made. And, whether or not the projected tests do anything for Laetrile, the case for a sick person's freedom to use it remains as strong as ever.

Wisconsin 🏛 State Journal
Madison, Wisc., May 16, 1977

With all the legal, lethal pollutants mankind is breathing, drinking, chewing and eating, it seems a little ridiculous to ban something on the grounds that it does not *cure* cancer.

Yet, that is the position of the federal Food and Drug Administration(FDA), which has announced it will continue to prosecute manufacturers of laetrile, a substance derived from apricot pits and thought by some to cure or alleviate the symptons of cancer.

Donald Kennedy the new head of the FDA said the agency will stay "very firm in our position that it should be banned" unless its backers can prove it is effective.

Laetrile most likely is worthless, but so, most likely, are any number of patent medicines on the market. The point is, while it has never been proved *effective*, neither has it been proved *harmful*.

So what's the point in banning it? If it would make the FDA and the medical establishment feel better, perhaps the federal government could require that packages of the substance bear a cigaret-pack style message that no one has proved laetrile *helpful* to human health.

If it would make a terminal cancer patient feel better to eat a little laetrile, what's the matter with that?

It's another example of government wasting valuable time and energy in foolish pursuits.

The Charleston Gazette
Charleston, W.Va., May 22, 1977

Laetrile is a vitamin derived from apricot seeds.

Many cancer sufferers believe it can cure cancer or arrest the dreadful progress of cancer.

But the Food and Drug Administration has pronounced Laetrile worthless as an anticancer agent and has banned its sale in the United States.

As far as we can determine, the FDA does not contend that Laetrile is dangerous. The FDA has given only these reasons for the prohibition against Laetrile:

► It may give cancer patients false hope and induce them to reject conventional treatment.

► It may be used by medical charlatans to make a fast buck.

Since the prohibition, hundreds of U.S. citizens have gone to Mexico to obtain Laetrile. Mexican physicians who recommend it are careful to say it should be used in connection with conventional treatment until more is learned of what causes cancer and how to treat it. It is possible that Mexican physicians, making fortunes as a result of the U.S. ban, offer this conservative approach to preserve an appearance of professionalism.

Is the ban on Laetrile justified?

It is difficult for the layman to present a case for Laetrile without resort to the "last hope" philosophy. This does not mean that the "last hope" philosophy is without merit.

Consider the cancer patient. He undergoes chemotherapy, which, for a brief period thereafter, increases his physical and mental suffering. He undergoes surgery, knowing that in most cases surgery cannot halt the inroads of cancer but merely confirms its presence. His hair falls out. He develops tumors. He becomes skeletonized. He sees death at his shoulder.

Why shouldn't he be allowed a "last hope" of life? Why not Laetrile, which, at least, cannot harm him?

Americans buy and consume tons of vitamins every day against the advice of nutritionists who insist that balanced meals eliminate the need for vitamin tablets. If Laetrile were sold from drugstore counters along with other nonprescription vitamins, no charlatan would be enriched. And what would be the harm?

Before answering, reflect upon some other choices left to lay people without rebuke of any kind from the FDA:

No adult is forbidden to buy cigarettes, although it has been established that smoking tobacco is related to heart disease and lung cancer. Some doctors smoke. Some FDA officials smoke.

Thousands of women must decide daily whether it is better to risk blood clots with oral contraceptives or to risk unwanted pregnancy. The FDA does not interfere in the decision.

Many physicians prescribe drugs they know to be dangerous because no alternative is left to them. Certain steroids can cause bloating, bone deterioration, and intestinal hemorrhaging.

Cancer is a hideous enemy of the human race. Medical science can only guess at cause and cure. Under the circumstances, might not the FDA police action against Laetrile be an unreasonable crusade?

THE SAGINAW NEWS
Saginaw, Mich., May 25, 1977

Again, let us make no claims at all for Laetrile as a cancer curing agent. We know little about it. Only what we've heard and read. And there are sincere and respected medical people who say its worthless.

A funny thing has happened, nonetheless, as the public debate on Laetrile has intensified. States have been moving rather rapidly to legalize its use in this country. And now the National Cancer Institute announces it admits to some second thoughts.

The NCI has announced it is "seriously considering" using Laetrile in tests on humans to determine what effectiveness it has as a cancer treatment.

The institute candidly acknowledges that public insistence on the right of free choice in the use of Laetrile — up to now not known to be harmful — and legislative action that would free for marketing over the counter, not under, is influencing its thinking.

As we've said, that's what the issue is all about. The right of choice. At least until there is any proof that Laetrile can be or is harmful.

And if the NCI should turn the corner and get into study with humans, perhaps it can contribute some useful information. In the meantime we continue to support state legislative measures that would make Laetrile available in Michigan.

THE TENNESSEAN
Nashville, Tenn., May 24, 1977

THE FOOD and Drug Administration seems to be getting a little bit wacky on the subject of Laetrile.

Laetrile is a chemical extracted from apricot kernels which some people believe cures or prevents cancer.

The FDA and most medical authorities say there is not the slightest bit of scientific evidence that Laetrile is an effective cancer medicine.

Furthermore, they say, using it could cause people to delay in seeking conventional cancer treatment. This could prove fatal to patients who might have been helped by early conventional treatment.

Other than this, there does not seem to be any evidence that Laetrile is harmful. But the FDA has banned it as a prescription medicine, and rightfully so. The FDA has a responsibility to see that ineffective as well as harmful drugs are not peddled to the public under false or unproved claims.

However, the FDA is now going beyond the banning of the drug itself and is seizing the apricot kernels from which it is made. The agency is on slippery ground here.

The FDA recently has confiscated two large quantities of apricot kernels, one from Mr. Douglas Heinsohn, a Gatlinburg businessman, and the other from the pharmaceutical house in Wisconsin which produces Laetrile.

Mr. Heinsohn says he has been in the business of buying and selling apricot

kernels for three years and that he makes no claim as to whether they cure or prevent cancer.

In the case of the Wisconsin firm, there can be little doubt that the kernels seized there were intended for the manufacture of Laetrile. However, it seems the FDA should just concentrate on seizing the Laetrile and leave the apricot kernels alone.

Some people claim to eat apricot kernels for food and for their medicinal properties. Whether they do or not, a lot of people do eat various seeds, herbs, roots and other matter to prevent or cure certain diseases.

This doesn't seem to do much harm to many people. It may not do them any good, either, but they think it does and if they think so, maybe it does.

The FDA says apricot kernels contain a poison. This is true. But the poison seems to be chemically bound in such a way that it poses little threat to anyone eating the kernels.

If the FDA sets out to seize apricot kernels because they can be used to make Laetrile, where will it stop? Will it also ban the sale of apricots? Or the planting of apricot trees?

The people must be left some choice in these matters. They should be given the findings of medical science and, where appropriate, warned that popular remedies for serious illness can be dangerous. But the final choice must be left to the individual.

The Cincinnati Post
Cincinnati, Ohio, May 21, 1977

On one side of the Laetrile controversy is the Food and Drug Administration, the American Medical Assn., the National Cancer Institute and the American Cancer Society. They claim the compound is useless in the treatment of cancer and call its promotion a fraud.

On the other side is a hard-core group of patients, their families and others who claim the substance made from peach and apricot pits is an anti-cancer agent that can save lives.

Caught between the two are the general public and many confused cancer patients who have not had access to Laetrile because of a ban on its interstate shipment by the FDA.

That ban appears to be breaking down.

Quantities of Laetrile are being smuggled into the United States from Mexico, and four states have passed legislation legalizing its manufacture and use within their own borders. The Ohio Legislature is considering such legislation now.

Laetrile is already available in Ohio from a growing number of sources. Some doctors will use the drug on their patients but insist that more traditional treatments also be administered.

Is it a hoax or a miracle drug? The question generates more heat than light.

We in no way endorse the use of Laetrile as an anti-cancer agent. Frankly, we are as confused by the claims as everyone else. But at some point in the development of the disease—when conventional treatment has failed—a cancer patient should have the right to choose or reject its use.

The News and Courier
Charleston, S.C., May 26, 1977

The National Cancer Institute will provide a public service if it decides to conduct tests on humans to determine whether laetrile is effective in treating cancer. Results of such tests may not settle the laetrile controversy once and for all, but they should carry enough scientific weight to answer nagging questions in the minds of many. The assumption fairly can be made, it seems to us, that no medical institution would be happier than NCI to be able to announce that clinical trials have proved laetrile beneficial.

Tests on patients who volunteer for experimentation seem to offer the surest means of deciding what was left undecided after a court-ordered hearing in Kansas City earlier this month: Is laetrile a valid substance being suppressed by a conspiracy in the medical establishment, or a product peddled by swindlers who traffic in false hopes?

Legalization of laetrile in five states has increased societal pressures for revocation of a Food and Drug Administration ban. Emotionalism surrounding the issue is heightened by growing public recognition of what cancer patients suffer through.

Consideration the Cancer Institute is giving to clinical tests, and the willingness of the private Sloan-Kittering Cancer Center to help out, suggest that in the months ahead overdue answers will be supplied to some hard questions.

The Cleveland Press
Cleveland, Ohio, May 18, 1977

The emotional controversy over Laetrile, the illegal substance used to combat cancer, continues to grow.

Neighboring Indiana is the latest of three states to legalize this "drug," if that's what it is.

Making a judgment on whether Laetrile should be legalized in Ohio, as State Rep. Patrick Sweeney proposes, is not easy because the issue is not all black and white.

But after examining the arguments for and against, this newspaper concludes that making Laetrile legal in Ohio would do more harm than good.

This position flies in the face of the recommendation of some respected medical men, like Dr. George Crile of Cleveland Clinic. Crile believes if the drug were easily available as a "supplement to standard therapy," then patients would not defer conventional therapy and no harm would be done.

The great danger, it seems to us, is that legalizing Laetrile would be a signal to the unsophisticated, no matter what warning is given, that this substance can be an effective cure.

If a person suspected he had cancer, or if his illness was diagnosed as such, he might immediately turn to Laetrile instead of more conventional treatments which are still the best hope for either a cure or the prolonging of life.

Of course cancer is a dread disease. But it must be stressed that a diagnosis of cancer is not necessarily a death warrant. Early treatment can save a large percentage of patients.

But there is no verifiable scientific evidence that cancer patients can be saved by Laetrile. Stories of Laetrile cures are almost all anecdotal. It is impossible to tell if these cures were sudden unexplainable remissions or the result of treatment the patient previously had taken.

Some wise doctors realize that they themselves, and medical and government institutions, are part of the problem.

Dr. F. J. Ingelfinger, himself a cancer patient, writes in the New England Journal of Medicine:

"An establishment indictment of a popular remedy is one of the best advertisements for that remedy. Thus when the FDA and the AMA . . . inveigh against Laetrile, I suspect they are unintentionally increasing the demand. In essence, the medical profession and the FDA appear to be saying, 'We can't cure your cancer, but don't take that nostrum purveyed by special interest groups and legalized by susceptible and sympathetic legislators.' "

The question has been put to us: "If someone in your family were suffering from cancer and conventional treatment wasn't working, wouldn't you want that person to be able to have Laetrile?"

That is difficult to answer, and the response in that case probably would have to be "yes."

On balance, though, it would be dangerous to pass a law that implied that Laetrile is an effective cancer treatment. For that reason we oppose the approach recommended by Rep. Sweeney.

Chicago Daily News
Chicago, Ill., May 20, 1977

Rep. Aaron Jaffe (D-Skokie) was on target when he told the Illinois House it was "fooling the public and making the Legislature look silly again" with its vote to allow treatment of cancer patients with the controversial drug Laetrile. As long as the drug is banned by the U.S. Food and Drug Administration, it can be used in Illinois only by subterfuge or illegal smuggling, and the bill relieving doctors of liability for administering it still leaves them culpable under other provisions of law.

Nevertheless, the House approved the bill, 130 to 28, and the Senate may follow the same path under the banner of "freedom of choice." Proponents of Laetrile contend that cancer patients should be able to choose their own treatments.

The philosophical argument has appeal, to be sure. Why deny patients stricken by this most dreaded disease anything that might provide hope or mental ease? And there are testimonials that people who have taken Laetrile "miraculously" recovered from cancer.

But the problem is not that simple. Five years of exhaustive testing at the Memorial Sloan-Kettering Cancer Center in New York have failed to show that the drug, which is derived from apricot pits, has any anticancer properties at all. Patients who put their full faith in a useless drug when cancer is first detected, and reject the approved treatments — imperfect and frustrating as they are — may be exercising their freedom of choice to commit suicide. Neither the Legislature nor the FDA should be a party to such a deal.

Allowing the use of Laetrile for terminally ill patients — when all medical hope is gone — is another matter, and one the FDA should consider in weighing its absolute ban and imposition of criminal penalties. If at that stage any drug can provide some peace of mind, why withhold it under threat of prosecution?

In any case, the Laetrile controversy is best dealt with at the federal level, with the benefit of all the medical knowledge that can be brought to bear. The Legislature is no place to practice medicine.

The Laetrile lobby, having failed thus far to budge the FDA, is now working through the states, and Indiana, Florida, Texas and Alaska have already moved to allow use of the drug. Illinois should resist this pressure, and leave the matter in federal hands. If the Senate does not kill the bill, Gov. Thompson should veto it.

San Francisco Chronicle
San Francisco, Calif., May 23, 1977

THE LAETRILE LEGALIZATION bills that have been popping out of state legislatures—the latest our own California senate—represent, it is generally agreed, an expression of public frustration over the regulation of people's lives by government scientists who announce what is good and what is bad medicine for them.

We do not see how it could be rationally contended that government should not have the responsibility for regulating such matters. It is unthinkable that dangerous, harmful, addictive drugs should pass over the counter to anyone asking for them. The Food and Drug Administration generally protects the public from this, and while its rulings now and then chafe, they for the most part are intelligently conceived and scientifically justified. On Laetrile, the FDA verdict is: it's of no use in treating cancer.

While that conclusion is apparently beyond argument for medical scientists, it is totally unsatisfying and unacceptable to citizens belonging to what can only be called a philosophical cult that says if it can't physically hurt the desperate cancer victim, and may psychologically help him, then let us rally around the flag of freedom of choice and legalize the prescription and sale of Laetrile.

SO THAT IS WHERE matters stand in Sacramento. The Assembly now inherits Senator William Campbell's bill making it legal for doctors to prescribe Laetrile, but only on a prescription form that is to give the patient full notice of the risks and benefits of all forms of cancer therapy, Laetrile included. This proviso is intended to disarm critics who say the legalization of Laetrile—its use is currently banned in California as a felony—will discourage "legitimate" treatment for terminal cancer. The bitter fact is of course that some cancers become incurable by any medical means.

Can the terminal patient find psychological relief by putting his faith in the now-forbidden extract of apricot pits? Its advocates strongly urge that he can. Perhaps the issue is, as Senator Arlen Gregorio says, not medicine but political philosophy—what the government should or should not be doing to people. Or, as Governor Brown has put it: "People have a right to participate in decisions affecting their own lives and their own minds and their own bodies."

IF PEOPLE REALLY BELIEVE that there is such a thing as "people's medicine" or "people's science," the rules and terms of which are to be left to them without regard to professional opinions and judgments, they will probably find politicans to accommodate their views. For ourselves, we do not believe that this Birch Society-promoted "freedom of choice" is valid.

A Cancer Society spokesman is convinced that "cancer mortality statistics will start moving upward within two or three years unless this bill is stopped by the Assembly or the governor." Such a consequence of legalizing Laetrile would make "freedom of choice" a tragic delusion.

DAILY ⬛ NEWS
New York, N.Y., June 12, 1977

CEASE AND DESIST, PLEASE

It would be foolish—and potentially dangerous—for the State Legislature to authorize the use of laetrile in the face of unanimous scientific opinion that the substance is worthless for treating cancer.

Lawmaking bodies in seven states have enacted similar laws, swept along on a wave of emotion created by the outcries of doomed cancer victims and their families.

It is understandable that legislators would be moved by the torment and the anguish of the suffering, and feel tempted to give them access to any medication—however worthless. It is hard to deny the desperate and despairing.

That may be a compassionate attitude. But it is not a responsible one.

Politicians are not competent to practice medicine, or to pass on what treatment should be administered to the ill or the dying.

Furthermore, unimaginable chaos would result if each state took it upon itself to usurp the powers of the Food and Drug Administration by arbitrarily sanctioning drugs.

That is not an idle fear. Some of the states which have made laetrile available now are considering applying a similar legislative—

SEAL OF APPROVAL

—on other concoctions just as dubious. The willingness of elected officials to dabble casually in a highly specialized and sensitive field where they have no qualifications whatsoever is frightening.

Don't they give a thought to the harm they can do? If not, it is too bad that someone couldn't whisper into their ears the word Thalidomide.

Thalidomide was a sleeping potion widely prescribed in parts of Europe almost 20 years ago, and deemed safe as well as effective. There was considerable agitation for licensing it in the U.S.

But Dr. Frances Kelsey, a diligent and dedicated FDA scientist who read voluminous reports on Thalidomide, found some data that troubled her. Approval was delayed for further study, while proponents of the drug fumed over the stodginess and the excessive caution of the agency.

In the end, Americans had good reasons to be thankful for the delay. It spared us from the tragedy that struck dozens of families in Britain and West Germany—hideously deformed children born to mothers who had taken Thalidomide during pregnancy.

Laetrile and the other "remedies" which legislatures are so blithely passing on may not be killers or cripplers. Nonetheless, we cannot afford to go by—

AMATEUR JUDGMENTS

—in an area which presents difficult problems in decision-making for the most experienced, conscientious and painstaking professionals.

The process for evaluating drugs is laborious and time-consuming because it requires rigorous, objective scientific study to establish proof of safety and effectiveness.

Many people who grumble about the inefficiency of the FDA do not understand that the exhaustive testing procedures to which drugs are subjected often are established by the scientific community. Nor do they realize that the FDA's seemingly needless, repetitious testing requirements are based on experience.

The FDA is far from flawless. The agency is swamped with work, and its scientists are poorly paid. It lacks the means to establish its own research base.

For all that, it provides the best means we have for determining what drugs should be prescribed. Not even physicians—let alone lawmakers—have the background or knowledge to supersede or overrule the FDA on drug approvals.

DAYTON DAILY NEWS

Dayton, Ohio, May 6, 1977

The People and The Experts are at it again, this time over the cancer drug Laetrile. The struggle over whether to allow the drug to be sold in this country has been on for years, but now it has broken into the open and become an Issue.

The experts — the Food and Drug Administration researchers and the medical establishament — say the drug is worthless. Worse than that, because if cancer patients give up other treatments to try Laetrile, they give up their only real hope of getting well.

The people — cancer patients, health food nuts, and a handful of libertarian ideologues — argue that patients have the right to choose Laetrile for themselves and the government has no right to stop them.

It's easy to feel sympathy for the Laetrile people. When faced with an apparently incurable disease for which orthodox medicine can do little, it's only natural that patients are willing to try anything. It is cruel to prosecute them for smuggling the drug in from Mexico. Maybe they have a right to choose their own treatment in such a situation.

If Laetrile advocates take the issue to court, however, the result could be disastrous. What might be at stake is the whole concept of drug regulation.

Despite its failings and shortcomings, drug regulation is absolutely indispensable, now more than ever, with drugs getting more sophisticated and complicated.

Regulation may in fact stifle some useful drugs or keep them off the market too long. But it also protects patients and doctors from most ineffective and dangerous concoctions.

The FDA is on the spot. It has to decide which is more dangerous: giving in on Laetrile, thus encouraging other groups to push for legalizing other drugs of dubious value, or standing firm and risking a court ruling that could wreck the whole regulation program. In any event, there is more involved in this issue than the simple-seeming argument about a single example.

THE MILWAUKEE JOURNAL

Milwaukee, Wisc., November 11, 1977

The Food and Drug Administration is properly striking at a major facet of the Laetrile problem in a new national poster campaign. "Warning!" the posters proclaim, "Laetrile can be fatal for cancer patients who delay or give up regular medical treatment and take Laetrile instead."

The basic worry is not that the drug is useless, which it may well be. People ingest many useless substances and should be free to do so, within broad limits. Moreover, even if Laetrile has no curative value, it may psychologically ease the final days of terminally ill cancer patients when all else has failed. Little harm is possible in cases of that kind, and the FDA may have been overly zealous when it decided years ago to ban interstate shipment of the drug simply because it had no proven medical worth.

However, it is another matter when Laetrile indirectly causes death by being substituted for therapies that are known to extend useful life. Furthermore, there is now alarming evidence that Laetrile can be a direct cause of death. The FDA attributes at least 16 fatalities to its toxic effects. In view of the direct hazards, as well as the broader problem of patients being tempted to substitute the doubtful product for established treatment, the FDA should forge ahead with its campaign to alert the public.

Meanwhile, until both the hazards and the possible medical value of Laetrile can be researched more thoroughly, the states should be cautious about legalizing its manufacture and distribution. Twelve states have legalized the substance so far and others are under pressure to do so. While there is sense in allowing a physician to provide Laetrile to doomed patients who request it after orthodox treatment has been exhausted, it is important to retain regulations that protect patients from being lured into peril.

The Dallas Morning News

Dallas, Texas, July 29, 1977

Down swooped federal drug agents on the Fort Worth home of Jim Haas. An iniquitous substance was what the agents were looking for; and away they carried it, out of the reach of Haas and his customers. But the substance was nothing so exotic or malignant as heroin. It was in the form of tablets, each manufactured from apricot pits. It was, of course, laetrile.

What an absurdity the federal government's war on laetrile has become! Here is a substance perfectly legal in much of the world, including Western Europe, widely used as a cure for cancer, perfectly harmless to anyone taking it, and the Food and Drug Administration high-handedly forbids Americans to use it.

The FDA's big-brotherism is predicated mainly on the fear that cancer patients will rely on laetrile—which the medical profession considers worthless—instead of on more conventional means of treatment.

Surely this is no excuse for banning laetrile. Since when has a patient forfeited the right to prefer one kind of treatment over another? If laetrile were harmful, that would be one thing, but it is not harmful. That puts it, at the very least, in a class with placebos and faith-healing—maybe helpful, maybe not, but clearly a matter for private, not governmental, decision.

The recent action of 12 states (including Texas) in legalizing the manufacture of laetrile should tell the FDA something—namely, that its bigotry in this matter has become insufferable.

The Texas law takes effect Sept. 1. Perhaps then laetrile dealers like Haas can get their supplies on the intrastate market and thus avoid FDA intervention. This will be good. But better would be for the FDA to climb down from its high horse and drop its ban on laetrile. Life, to be sure, is one of the rights the U.S. government was established to guarantee. And so, we are constrained to note, is liberty.

Richmond Times-Dispatch

Richmond, Va., December 15, 1977

Laetrile may be a worthless drug, as federal health officials and most medical groups contend, but we nevertheless applaud two recent court decisions that held that government bans on the use of Laetrile violate constitutional rights of privacy.

The two courts' decisions dealt specifically with the drug Laetrile, but the basic question involved is of far more significance: How far does government have a right to go in controlling the personal and private actions of the people?

Neither court expressed any opinion as to the effectiveness of Laetrile — that was not the point at issue. What the courts said, in effect, was that a patient has the right to choose his own treatment, provided the treatment has not been found by the government to be harmful in itself. (Up to now, the Food and Drug Administration has banned interstate shipment of Laetrile on the grounds that the drug is ineffective; only recently have Laetrile opponents begun making claims — thus far unverified — that the drug itself can be toxic.)

"It appears uncontrovertible," said the U. S. District Court for Western Oklahoma, "that a patient has the right to refuse cancer treatment altogether, and should he decide to forego conventional treatment does he not possess a further right to enlist such nontoxic treatments, however unconventional, as he finds to be of comfort, particularly where recommended by his physician?"

The choice of Laetrile may be unwise, declared the court, but "to be insensitive to the very fundamental nature of the civil liberties at issue here, and the fact that making the choice, regardless of correctness, is the sole prerogative of the person whose body is being ravaged, is to display slight understanding of the essence of our free society and its constitutional underpinnings."

In the other case, involving California's prohibition against the use of Laetrile, the state's Court of Appeals for the Fourth District wrote:

"The efficacy of Laetrile does not enter into this case. The issue here is human liberty. . . . To [cancer victims] the denial of medical treatment, albeit unorthodox and unapproved by a state agency, must surely take on a Kafkaesque quality. No demonstrated public danger or compelling interest of the state warrants this Orwellian intrusion into the most private zone of privacy."

It is a legitimate function of government, we believe, to protect people from harmful substances, but we don't buy the reasoning that Laetrile is harmful and should be outlawed merely because it may keep cancer patients from undergoing more conventional treatment. There is nothing wrong with government publicizing its findings as to Laetrile's effectiveness or lack of effectiveness. Indeed, patients should be given as much information as possible, pro and con Laetrile and any other drug, so that they can make an informed decision as to the treatment they choose.

THE KANSAS CITY STAR

Kansas City, Mo., August 29, 1977

Few words can strike greater terror than the word "cancer." It stands for a collection of diseases in which treatment often is difficult and cure frequently is elusive. The utter lack of hope cancer inspired in the past is long gone, but its detection, treatment and cure remain at the frontiers of medical science.

Into these regions of doubt and fear has come another word, "Laetrile," the trade name for a substance made of pulverized apricot pits, containing traces of cyanide, and which has been set forth as an effective treatment for cancer. The Food and Drug Administration has banned it in interstate commerce, because it has been proven neither safe nor effective. A dozen states, however, have legalized the use of Laetrile within their borders and efforts are under way to overturn FDA authority in such matters. Various state legislatures have been the scenes of Laetrile blitzes in which public health authorities and the medical profession have awakened to find the stuff legalized against all their counsel.

The usual question is why not? In the case of a hopeless cancer victim with loved ones desperate to try anything, why not Laetrile? What harm could it do?

The answers are that if the bars are let down for ineffective treatment, an inevitable number of cancer victims will delay or eliminate altogether a quest for *effective* treatment; that some Laetrile has been discovered to be impure and harmful, and that for government to fail to oppose the introduction of swindle and quackery into medicine could produce thousands of individual instances of tragedy and dilute the strength of medical science and the practice of medicine in the United States for years to come.

The argument that people should have the freedom of choice to ruin their health or throw their life's savings to charlatans if it makes them happy is erroneous. Everyone has a stake in the advancement of medical science; everybody pays, one way or another, for good medical care or the lack of it.

The most dismaying aspect of Laetrile is the alacrity with which some legislatures and segments of the public have responded to pressure and phony arguments. Some of this no doubt is due to political timidity. But some of it, too, must be a reflection of distrust and dislike of the health industry, its appalling costs and its experts and practitioners who sometimes seem to look down on human illness from a lordly perspective. It is something for doctors, the hospitals, the scientific community and all their satellites to think about, this evidence that public bodies are so willing—even eager—to move against the weight of all medical and scientific testimony to the contrary in the case of the apricot cancer cure.

The Dispatch

Columbus, Ohio, May 31, 1977

REAMS OF conflicting testimony have understandably confused the public in efforts to make rational judgments regarding saccharin, Laetrile and marijuana.

Recently comedian Bob Hope remarked in jest that soon one may buy marijuana over the counter but be forced to go to a pusher for saccharin.

A week ago, the federal Food and Drug Administration held hearings on saccharin, the artificial sweetener which Canadian tests found suspect of containing a cancer causing agent.

Based on those tests, the FDA is expected to restrict the use of saccharin for commercial usage but permit limited use by prescription of the dietary aid discovered 98 years ago.

Yet, Canada has not banned saccharin. In fact, Canada never ruled out cyclamates when this country did.

Legislative hearings presently are underway on the federal and state levels on Laetrile. This is claimed by some to be a cancer-fighting medication. To others, it is a farcical, albeit harmless, drug whose claims for cancer cures are based on emotions.

The Ohio State Medical Association has modified its position on Laetrile while refusing to indorse it.

Its chief fear is some cancer patients will avoid proven medical care in favor of this vitamin supplement. At the same time, it does not want to close the door on a possible cure.

And Congress, studying a criminal code, would eliminate possession of small amounts of marijuana as a federal crime and allow state laws and local ordinances to prevail.

Do saccharin benefits outweigh risks? Does Laetrile actually cure cancer in some cases? Is marijuana dangerous? Does it lead to hard drugs and addiction?

Perhaps the states would be more practical in handling these problems and weighing the alternatives. The FDA has been far too arbitrary and Congress has condoned such latitude.

The Evening Bulletin

Philadelphia, Pa., May 11, 1977

Say the word Laetrile in a crowded room and you just might have a brawl on your hands. The substance—an extract of apricot or peach pits or bitter almonds—is banned from interstate commerce by the United States Food and Drug Administration. But Laetrile has a cadre of vocal backers who claim it cures cancer, and these people are attacking the FDA ban with a vengeance.

First, it should be noted that the respected national cancer authorities, like the National Cancer Institute and the American Cancer Society, reject Laetrile as a cancer treatment. They point out that the drug has flunked tests of effectiveness in the nation's most prestigious laboratories. Desperate people may easily rely on Laetrile and therefore ignore more proven cancer treatments, the experts say. If for no other reason, they contend, Laetrile is dangerous.

Backers of the drug — some of whom are making a great deal of money from selling it on the black market — credit it with miraculous results. Cancer victims claiming remission of the disease and relief of pain have paraded in front of state legislatures to convince lawmakers that the drug should be legalized.

Sad to say, unlike the drug they are pushing, the Laetrile backers' efforts have proved effective. About a dozen state legislatures, including Delaware and New Jersey, have before them bills aimed at loosening restrictions on Laetrile. And Representative Anita P. Kelly, a West Philadelphia Democrat who is chairman of the Pennsylvania House of Representatives' Committee on Health and Welfare, plans hearings this summer on the possibility of legalizing Laetrile in Pennsylvania.

Last year Alaska became the first state to legalize the use of Laetrile. Indiana lawmakers have approved a bill legalizing the manufacture and sale of the drug as well as its use.

All this makes for a chaotic and dangerous situation. Although states have the constitutional right to legalize drugs wholly within their borders, this is the first time such a thing has been done in the face of a federal ban, FDA spokesmen say.

The specter of U.S. citizens hop-scotching the country in search of legal Laetrile treatments is disturbing. If such a precedent is established with Laetrile, it could open the way for states to approve other questionable drugs. What about Gerovital, an alleged "youth serum" approved last week by the Nevada Senate? Will bogus "youth spas" be set up in that state to attract— and soak—the citizens of other states?

The question of which drugs should be allowed on the market in this country requires a kind of scientifically sophisticated decision-making that can best be done by a federal agency, not by state legislatures. When it comes to Laetrile, it appears that state legislators have allowed themselves to be unduly swayed by emotional appeals from ill people and by what seems to be a well-orchestrated campaign.

Of course, decision-makers at the FDA should demonstrate their willingness to listen to those who claim to have benefited from using Laetrile. (In fact, hearings on Laetrile were held in Kansas City last week after the FDA was ordered by a federal judge to compile an administrative record on the drug.)

Further, if the FDA has a good case against Laetrile — and it looks as if it does — the agency should see to it that more people get the facts — facts which presumably would persuade them to agree that Laetrile is a merely a "placebo," a preparation that lulls its users into a totally false sense of security and could thus lead to needless loss of life.

The Providence Journal

Providence, R.I., July 24, 1977

State legislative support for laetrile, the alleged anti-cancer drug, appears to have reached a plateau and in five large states to be waning. Gov. Hugh Carey of New York has said he would veto any legalization bill that reached his desk and in Pennsylvania, Illinois, Michigan and California the movement to approve the manufacture and intrastate distribution of the substance is reported to have stalled.

These developments will be applauded by many thoughtful people who resent the modern version of the oldtime itinerant peddler hawking his "amazing cure." There is nothing amazing about laetrile except the dogged determination of its promoters to exploit that segment of the population most vulnerable to their wiles — terminally ill cancer patients.

Study after study has shown this extract from apricot pits to be worthless, totally without therapeutic value. The federal Food and Drug Administration has banned its interstate sale and distribution. And in a nothing-less-than pathetic appearance before a Senate subcommittee recently the three American leaders of the laetrile movement could not even agree on the chemical composition of the substance. Indeed, they charged that an international conspiracy was preventing the cure of cancer, echoing a line taken by the extreme right-wing John Birch Society.

What is so troubling is not the dispute over the effectiveness of the extract. The scientists have pretty well settled that point. The only research gap is the clinical testing of laetrile in humans which the National Cancer Institute earlier said it would undertake. Now, however, NCI says such tests are virtually impossible because of the inexact nature of the substance and the ethical conflict in administering a compound acknowledged by the scientific world to be worthless.

Hardest to accept is the willingness of 11 states to endorse freedom of choice for a product which the medical-scientific community considers a fraud. Countless federal and state agencies are dedicated to the protection of the consumer against worthless or potentially harmful substances on the market. The sale of tinted water as a treatment for pneumonia, for example, would hardly be tolerated.

Yet so effective are the promoters of laetrile — even more so, it is said, than the earlier sellers of "Krebiozen" who deposited millions of dollars in profits in foreign banks — that the freedom to choose extract from apricot pits is accorded special consideration. Cancer specialists have testified that some patients place so much hope in laetrile that they ignore legitimate medications and treatments that might in fact ameliorate their condition.

Perhaps the message of exploitation and profiteering is getting through. Perhaps that is why some states are having second thoughts about approving a placebo (or worse) which Governor Carey says smacks of cancer quackery. And well they should.

The Chattanooga Times

Chattanooga, Tenn., July 19, 1977

It was unfortunate—but unsurprising—that a Senate subcommittee on the purported anti-cancer drug Laetrile degenerated into a series of "you're another" attacks by rival groups.

On the one hand were the purveyors of the drug, men who have been convicted for dispensing it. Arrayed against them were representatives of the scientific community, the Federal Drug Administration and those who have prosecuted taffickers in the substance.

The latter alleged that Laetrile is, by all standards of scientfic research, utterly useless in the treatment of cancer. Although that is probably true, it does not address the question of why cancer patients, many of them diagnosed as terminally ill, should not be allowed access to Laetrile if they want it. It is undeniably tragic if, as some of the anti-Laetrile witnesses testified, persons vainly turn to Laetrile for an "instant" cure when they could be cured through more conventional means of treatment. But such decisions remain, after all, the sole right of the patients.

Of course, the pro-Laetrile witnesses, the so-called "gurus" of the movement, didn't help their cause when they claimed they were victims of a conspiracy to prevent widespread use of the substance and, therefore, the cure of cancer.

Sounding like some yahoos of the Far Right, they identified the conspirators as the major oil and drug companies, the FDA, the American Medical Association, the National Cancer Institute and the American Cancer Society. Naturally, "the Rockefeller family and some of its business friends" were thrown in for good measure.

Users of Laetrile, it seems to us, are wasting their money and possibly endangering their lives. Some terminally ill patients are understandably desperate for anything that might cure their disease, thus making them potential victims of persons pushing various nostrums.

But the key question remains how far the federal government should go in preventing such patients from exercising a free choice in obtaining a "cure." So far, the government hasn't made an adequate case.

The Wichita
Eagle-Beacon
Wichita, Kan., October 25, 1977

Whether Laetrile actually helps cancer victims is controversial.

The Federal Drug Administration and most medical doctors say it's worthless, but a number of victims swear by it.

The government has taken the position that if the drug is worthless, it should not be sold because it raises false hopes for a cure.

The doctors and the government are overlooking something, we think. That is that the human mind is a powerful instrument that can and does accomplish remarkable things.

Test groups have been given two different kinds of pills — one a powerful drug and the other a plain sugar pill — to determine the effect of the mind in healing.

In many cases similar progress was made when the persons tested did not know which pills they were taking. In other words the sugar pills worked as well as the drug, indicating that the patient's mind convinced him that he was benefiting from a drug he wasn't getting.

It is a matter of believing.

So if a cancer victim believes he can be helped by Laetrile, who can say he is wrong?

If he is helped because he believes in the drug rather than because it is effective, he still is helped isn't he? The aim should be to relieve suffering and to sustain hope.

No definite cure for cancer exists, though some drugs and treatments can slow its progress. All most treatments can do is give the victim hope for a few additional years of life.

Laetrile often is requested by cancer sufferers only after other remedies have been tried without success. So, to prescribe Laetrile would not deprive the victim of some other, more effective therapy.

Therefore if the doctor is willing to prescribe it and if Laetrile gives the patient hope, it should not be kept from him.

For these reasons we support a prefiled bill to legalize the use of Laetrile by doctor's prescription in Kansas.

The Miami Herald
Miami, Fla., December 10, 1977

MEDICINE is at least as much art as science, and often this subjective art — including the patient's faith in his therapy — accomplishes results that the objective science cannot explain. So it is with laetrile, the apricot-pit drug that science says is ineffective but that some cancer patients insist is their only hope.

A federal judge in Oklahoma has ruled unconstitutional the Food and Drug Administration's ban on interstate laetrile shipments. That ban had kept laetrile from legal channels even in the 13 states that permit it to be dispensed. If Judge Luther Bohanon's ruling stands, cancer victims whose laetrile was available only via smugglers will be able eventually to get it by prescription from their druggist.

The laetrile debate involves two fundamental questions, one medical, one philosophical.

On the medical question — Does laetrile work, or doesn't it? — no one has the definitive answer. Not the FDA. Not medical science. Not the cancer victims who, judged incurable by their doctors, are betting their lives on laetrile.

Since the medical question is unanswerable, the pivotal issue becomes philosophical: Should not an individual have the right to choose therapy, albeit unconventional and unproved, that he believes will help when conventional therapy will not?

Our answer is yes. Thus we endorse Judge Bohanon's ruling, despite its pitfalls, because we deem it a reasonable response to an issue involving fundamental rights.

We anticipate a deluge of protests from doctors who will think we are endorsing quackery. Not so. Our stand is not anti-doctor; it is pro-patient. The distinction is of paramount importance.

Cancer is the scourge of Western man. And despite the billions spent on research, its key unknowns — Is it viral? Genetic? What starts it? Stops it? — defy solution. Advances in therapy have improved survival rates for some types of cancer, but therapy itself sometimes leaves patients wan, nauseous, bald, barely functioning.

Enter laetrile and its growing cult of true believers. Denied access to laetrile whose purity and strength the FDA could control, they turn to smugglers and pay heavily for laetrile of unknown quality manufactured under unknown conditions in Mexico.

Judge Bohanon deemed this a "needless hardship and expense" for cancer patients. It is, as well, a shameful denial of the individual's right to the treatment of his choice. The patient's right to reject all treatment implies, we believe, a corollary right to treatment that may help simply because he believes it will help.

Moreover, FDA policy only increases laetrile's appeal as forbidden fruit. It drives laetrile users away from their physicians and prevents the gathering of scientific data, based on clinical trials, that could establish laetrile's therapeutic value.

Laetrile may prove to be nothing but hope. Yet in the art of medicine, hope is a potent ally.

The Washington Post
Washington, D.C., May 22, 1977

A GREAT MANY people believe that Laetrile, a substance made from apricot pits, relieves the symptoms and slows the pace of cancer, though it does not cure it. But decades of tests (on animals) have led a virtually unanimous medical and scientific community to conclude that Laetrile has no such effects. This is the basis of the national argument raging over whether Laetrile, long available in Mexico, should be licensed here. Three states have done so; others are considering it. The Food and Drug Administration is waging an uphill battle to block legalization of Laetrile by the courts, and a "Medical Freedom of Choice" bill has been introduced that, while not described as a Laetrile bill, would remove the major obstacle—a requirement for proof of efficacy—to its general marketing.

The professionals' and bureaucrats' reluctance to approve a "drug" (friends of Laetrile insist it is not a drug but a natural food substance not requiring license) that has not been proven effective and that might distract terminal patients from other treatment is understandable. But as the suits and bills show, the matter is already out of their control. The cancer dread, anti-establishment sentiment and perhaps the "forbidden fruit" aura have kindled a popular fire. It has heated up the claim—a reasonable one, in our view—that since what is involved is personal relief from a killing disease far from fully understood by medical men, the state has scant right or interest in denying a terminal cancer patient his choice of what in fact may be nothing more than a placebo—as long as the patient has been offered no false hopes to the contrary. The popular force behind Laetrile is a political fact.

This dictates a political solution. It means, first of all, that Laetrile should not be left to the courts. Nor should the issue be dealt with, variously, by state legislatures. It is, necessarily, a national political concern. The "Medical Freedom of Choice" bill recognizes this but, frankly, it scares us. It is being advanced in the emotional atmosphere generated by Laetrile, and it would strike down the effectiveness standard, leaving just the question of safety for *all* new drugs. Would it not be better to legislate strictly on Laetrile? As long as the door is opening anyway, the federal government had best be the doorkeeper. Legislation could contain requirements 1) for disclosure, to warn buyers they were getting a drug not proven effective, 2) for clinical trial, and 3) for close and continuing review. This would satisfy the craving of terminal cancer patients for the treatment of their choice, and it would protect the government's long-term interest in caring for the public health.

The Boston Globe

Boston, Mass., May 29, 1977

A nationwide effort to lift the Federal ban on Laetrile, an apparently useless drug with an unearned reputation for curing cancer, has touched down in the Massachusetts Legislature, where a bill to allow its use is before the Committee on Health Care.

The ban seeks to protect the public—particularly the most vulnerable among us, those who are ill with cancer—from fraudulent medical practises. Ideally, there should be some middle ground between the outright prohibition of an apparently harmless substance and legalization, with its implied endorsement of a nostrum that is ineffective and that may turn patients away from real cures.

Laetrile is an extract of apricot pits whose main active ingredient seems to be cyanide. It was prohibited from interstate shipment in 1963 by the US Food and Drug Administration, which is mandated by Congress to ensure that drugs marketed in America for therapeutic use are not only safe, but effective. The FDA has concluded that the substance is indeed safe but that it is also ineffective.

The entire medical establishment, minus a handful of individual physicians, concurs. Yet a number of doctors, including Dr. Franz Inglefinger of the Harvard Medical School, feel that so long as they are not expected to prescribe the drug, so long as it is harmless, and so long as it gives mental comfort to terminally ill patients, Laetrile should not be denied to cancer victims any more than you would deny a terminally ill person the comfort of some favorite food or drink.

The deeper concern of many physicians is that Laetrile, which is now being touted as a prevention as well as a cure, will be used as a substitute for surgery, radiation or chemotherapy. Some Laetrile advocates insist that Laetrile treatment is incompatible with any other. Yet conventional medical treatments have increased the five-year survival rates in cancer patients from one in five in 1930, to one in four in 1950, and to one in three cancer victims in 1970. And experts argue that one of every two cancer victims could be saved if today's advanced techniques are applied from the outset while new victims will surely die of cancer if they rely solely on Laetrile.

If it were possible to make Laetrile available without any appearance of endorsement, if legalization could be conditioned on selling the substance at cost to prevent profiteering, if it required labeling with an FDA disclaimer regarding its effectiveness as a treatment for cancer, if it carried stiff penalties for false advertising, if its use could be restricted to last-resort status, then perhaps the public interest would be protected.

Such comprehensive legislation would be hard to write and still more difficult to enforce. For that reason and because Laetrile might not be considered harmless if it holds out fraudulent hope and interferes with the positive treatment, the FDA, and not the state legislatures, has been given the mandate to act as guardian in such public health measures.

The FDA has asserted there is no medical evidence of Laetrile's effectiveness. Unless this finding is overturned in a 10th series of tests, called for last week by the National Cancer Institute, Laetrile can only be regarded as a quack device for gulling the innocent, the naive or the desperate. Yet Laetrile is available in 23 countries and five states have acted to legalize its use. An estimated 50,000 Americans are taking the substance, available illegally in a thriving black market and legally in Alaska, Arizona, Florida, Indiana and Nevada.

The Massachusetts Legislature will hold June 27, on a bill to prevent health facilities or the Massachusetts Medical Society from taking action against doctors who administer Laetrile at the request of a patient. The measure would contradict the FDA ban and would also mean that neither hospitals nor the Society would have any power to control Laetrile treatment in this state. And Massachusetts, with its worldwide reputation for medical excellence, should not support the legislation.

THE BLADE

Toledo, Ohio, July 16, 1977

A bill to legalize the controversial drug laetrile is now wending its way through the Ohio General Assembly. It was approved overwhelmingly last week by the House and seems to be headed for probable approval by the Senate and Governor Rhodes.

The Blade supports efforts to legalize this supposed anti-cancer substance. But we do so reluctantly and with a sense of bitterness that matches the acrid taste of the apricot kernels from which laetrile is manufactured. For although laetrile itself represents a special case, its legalization carries implications of a growing anti-science sentiment that can only work to the detriment of the health of Americans everywhere.

Laetrile, like so many other fads, is a product of California — specificially of a father-son team of physicians who in 1952 turned the substance into a lucrative business on an international scale.

Numerous studies since then have failed to show that the substance has any promising anti-cancer effect, a fact that laetrile advocates brush off with talk of a "conspiracy" between the medical profession and the Federal Government to suppress laetrile.

Not long ago, the U.S. Food and Drug Administration asked Dr. Ernesto Contreras, a Mexican physician who is one of the best-known laetrile advocates, to submit case histories of his most dramatic successes with the substance. Of the nine case histories that American authorities could review, six of the patients had died from cancer; one had died from another disease after cancer surgery, and the other was under conventional medical treatment.

So far as can be determined today, laetrile is not an effective anti-cancer drug. Laetrile, however, is relatively nontoxic when properly used. And, for many terminal cancer victims, this apricot-based substance also represents a last, desperate hope for life.

Spontaneous regression of cancer does occur for reasons beyond the grasp of contemporary science. So if laetrile can be the instrument of such "psychological miracles" in some terminal cancer patients, it should be available — if only to give terminal patients the consolation of knowing that they have tried every possible treatment.

Caution, however, will be needed to insure that the substance is not used by other cancer victims in situations in which it could discourage or delay their seeking the best available medical treatment.

The probable legalization of laetrile in Ohio, like its legalization in 11 other states, however, remains distastefully upsetting because it represents a major victory for health-food faddists, anti-fluoridationists, and other opponents of the rational application of scientific procedures who have joined the laetrile backers.

Future movements of this ragtag group will warrant close scrutiny.

National Cancer Institute Considers Testing Laetrile on Humans

Dr. Guy Newell, director of the National Cancer Institute, said May 23 that clinical testing of laetrile was being "seriously considered" in light of the controversy over its effectiveness as a cancer treatment. Laetrile had been tested on animals, and those tests had not shown any positive results. However, widespread skepticism about the early findings lead a number of experts to believe that tests on humans might solve the controversy at last.

THE ⛰ SUN

Baltimore, Md., June 1, 1977

The National Cancer Institute's consideration of a plan for human tests of Laetrile, a drug touted by some as a cancer cure or reliever of cancer-caused pain, is obviously a response to popular pressures. Four major cancer research centers report that Laetrile was shown to have no effect on cancer in animal tests. It has been banned from interstate commerce by the federal Food and Drug Administration.

But passage of bills to legalize Laetrile for intrastate use in seven states indicates that many people believe the FDA's Laetrile ban is a product either of callous bureaucracy or of an arrogant medical establishment. It appears that the only way to put this popular myth to rest is through tests on humans. Though they probably will produce the same results the animal tests did, the time for the human tests has come.

ST. LOUIS POST-DISPATCH

St. Louis, Mo., August 26, 1977

In the message accompanying the veto of legislation that would have legalized the use of laetrile by terminally ill cancer patients in Illinois, Gov. James R. Thompson refuted the two principal contentions of that drug's promoters. On the matter of efficiency Mr. Thompson noted, "Although forms of laetrile have been around for more than 50 years, it has never been shown to be effective against cancer in any reputable clinical study." And on freedom of choice, he said, "Freedom of choice in a democracy always depends on accurate knowledge about the choices available."

The federal Food and Drug Administration, which has banned laetrile, requires that a drug be proven effective in laboratory tests on animals before it is tried on humans. And all controlled clinical tests of laetrile have shown that substance to be ineffective in the treatment of cancer in animals. But the proponents of laetrile have discounted the laboratory tests—conducted by such reputable organizations as the National Cancer Institute and the Memorial Sloan-Kettering Cancer Center—and have relied on patient testimonials to promote their drug.

The problem with patients' statements lies in the nature of the disease. Cancer is not an ailment that continues at a set rate of development; its advance fluctuates, it goes into unexpected remissions and may sometimes disappear. So some improvements claimed by patients may have been the normal course of their illness. In some cases of purported cures, pathological reports do not exist to prove the person ever had cancer; in some, patients had used recognized cancer treatment along with laetrile so the effectiveness of laetrile could not be ascertained; some later died of cancer. But those who have improved credit laetrile despite a complete lack of medical data to substantiate such claims.

One of the points that must be considered is the placebo effect of laetrile. Placebos, substances without pharmaceutical effect usually given to patients who want medication and believe the substance to be such, have been shown to reduce pain or to help effect cures, because of the patient's belief in them. So if laetrile does not harm the person, and may bring some relief because of faith in its effects, what is the harm in permitting its use? The harm lies in the fact that laetrile has never been shown to act against cancer, and other treatments have. To permit the use of laetrile increases the possibility that persons will avoid proven treatments that often have undesirable side effects. And during the time a person tries the easy treatment, the cancer may well progress to the point at which proven methods are no longer effective.

Both sides in the laetrile controversy have promised to act on the results of tests on humans, and for this reason there has been a strong push to have such trials conducted. The National Cancer Institute is considering doing the testing, but has yet to resolve ethical problems. Can a doctor responsibly administer a substance to a cancer patient, even a volunteer, for which no scientific evidence is available to demonstrate effectiveness in curing or preventing cancer? And to break the rules of the FDA and allow tests on humans without a showing of laboratory effectiveness would open the door to every peddler of purported cures who could garner sufficient political support and would greatly weaken the protection provided to consumers of medical products by the Federal Government.

Until proponents can show scientific proof of effectiveness, they have only one way to get laetrile on the market and that is the acceptance of "freedom of choice" in medications. But, as Mr. Thompson noted, free choice depends upon informed choice. The argument that persons should not be protected from themselves, when applied to the drug field, would have meant permission for thalidomide to enter the U.S., would reopen the door to many discredited patent medicines and unscrupulous quacks. Laetrile has failed every reputable test to date. Until there is clinical evidence that it may possibly help in the treatment of cancer, it should not be available to interfere with methods that have been proven effective.

DAYTON DAILY NEWS

Dayton, Ohio, May 26, 1977

The nation might as well go ahead and test laetrile, the controversial cancer drug, on people — if their conditions cannot be helped by conventional treatment and if they agree. But no one should expect the outcome to settle the issue.

The results of medical research, particularly into complicated diseases like cancer, are often ambiguous or at least arguable. Cancer sometimes goes away for a time or permanently for no apparent reason. If the patient has been swilling, say, Dr. Pepper before this happens, he may believe that was what cured him.

And many of the laetrile backers are the victims of their own fears and hopes and paranoias and perhaps a slick con job by the folks who push the drug. Part of the bit is that organized medicine opposes laetrile because it likes the money it gets giving people ineffective treatment — a neat reversal of what others believe may be true about the laetrile promoters.

If people will believe that about organized medicine, they are not likely to trust new research any more than they trust old research that found the drug to be worthless.

But more tests ought to at least give the rest of us — legislators particularly — more information on which to base public policy regarding the drug. In the meantime, state legislatures ought to hold off on "legalizing" the drug. The present state of the evidence indicates strongly that the stuff is worthless. Worse, really, because it may prompt patients to give up the only treatments that might help them.

The Virginian-Pilot

Norfolk, Va., December 19, 1977

A cancer "cure" called Krebiozen turned out to be a cruel hoax and disappeared. Now there is Laetrile, which most scientists and the Food and Drug Administration label worthless for treating cancer but which refuses to go away. Whatever the eventual outcome of the Laetrile controversy may be, even if it is relegated to a shelf of medical curiosities, it has seriously challenged the scientific establishment and set some legal precedents.

Those precedents come from Oklahoma, where Glen Rutherford, ill with cancer, last year brought suit against the FDA claiming the right to decide for himself whether to take Laetrile. He said he could not wait through a lengthy drug-testing process, that he might be dead before it was over. Federal Judge Luther Bohanon agreed, and in so doing set terminally ill patients apart from others, at least in regard to untested drugs. Later on Judge Bohannon went even further, ordering the FDA not to interfere with the importation or use of Laetrile in Oklahoma. The agency is expected to appeal.

Cancer has become big business as well as a dreaded ailment, more than $10 billion having been spent on its research in the past 20 years. That money has created a scientific bureaucracy under incredible pressure to find a cure. Laetrile, made from ground apricot pits, is a back-door attempt at a cure. Used in conjunction with vitamins and an enzyme, it is a nutritional approach to disease, a method increasingly popular but running counter to the traditional search for drugs and vaccines.

There has been no rush to test it. In fact, the only tests have been on animals, and have been inconclusive. Laetrile proponents say medicines based on nutrition need to be tried out on people—mice won't do. Good scientific methodology discourages experiment on human beings, especially when animal tests are negative.

But some 75,000 Americans are reported to be taking Laetrile. Thirteen states have legalized its use, although the FDA bans interstate shipments. There would be no dearth of volunteers for monitored tests. Responding to pressure, which lately has come from a few prominent scientists and some Congressmen, the National Cancer Institute has begun to look for Laetrile case records. It says if it finds evidence of cancer remissions it will consider clinical trials.

Cancer claims 380,000 lives a year. Any approach to it, offering even faint hope, needs to be pondered. Chances are considerable that Laetrile is only an illusion grasped at by desperately ill people. But the medical and scientific establishment needs to make sure. Definitive tests are in order. Laetrile should be labeled accurately.

Rockford Register Star

Rockford, Ill., June 21, 1977

As scientists for New York's prestigious Memorial Sloan-Kettering Cancer Center seemed to sense, their studies and papers are not the last chapter of the controversial drug, laetrile.

What the Sloan-Kettering researchers found, using mice for their tests, was that laetrile had no effect whatever in the control or cure of cancer.

Yet, the ranks of those who believe in laetrile are so numerous and so frustrated in their search for a solution to cancer, that seven states have legalized this component of apricot pits at their request.

They talk about laetrile's help to them personally. They say it lessens pain. And they resent those who would deny them a substance they believe in while offering no ready solution to the illness that plagues them.

They will pay whatever price is asked to obtain laetrile from whatever source necessary, despite how dubious that source may be.

It is in this context that scientists, whatever their deductions from mice, must proceed. They must test laetrile on consenting humans so the preliminary findings on efficacy can be confirmed or refuted or given a "maybe."

This seems to be a reluctant course for some doctors and researchers who believe the laetrile controversy is much ado about nothing.

Such scientists may know their way around a laboratory, but they do not sense the human equation which is much more complex if less precise.

Medical research, despite heroic efforts and strides, has not found a solution to cancer.

Recent testimony before Congress in Washington has hinted that science is nearing a breakthrough, not with a simple answer but with a combination of surgery and chemo-therapy.

To many, this course will still seem radical.

They will seek a less drastic course. Many will do this against the advice of their doctors. But they will do it.

In making their choice, these patients should know precisely the risks they are taking. They should know whether laetrile, a failure in the laboratory, offers them a viable alternative based on carefully documented research.

Ultimately, as it must be, the patient will make his own decision and chart his own course. But he should be able to do this in an enlightened and informed manner.

That's why the Sloan-Kettering research should continue with all due haste so that medical science, if it does not have the answer to cancer, at least has the answer to laetrile.

Detroit Free Press

Detroit, Mich., July 14, 1977

LAETRILE, the controversial alleged cancer cure, is being laid on the line.

Both backers and detractors of the substance, which is extracted from apricot pits and which is at the center of a massive medical tug-of-war to either legalize or completely ban it, have agreed to a scientific showdown. Laetrile will be tested on humans by the federal government.

If the tests show the substance to be effective in treating cancer, Sen. Edward Kennedy has pledged that he will lead efforts to legalize it nationally. If the tests prove it to be a useless palliative—as U.S. officials and some of the research completed thus far indicate—then the boosters of Laetrile will stop pushing it publicly.

Given the vindictiveness and vilification being brought into play by both sides in the dispute, this compromise, worked out by Sen. Kennedy, is a real coup.

Perhaps now both tempers and public relations campaigns will quiet. And the American people will find out what, if anything, is the real worth of Laetrile.

The Houston Post

Houston, Texas, July 21, 1977

Laetrile is more of an idea and a *cause celebre* than a specific drug. The term covers a wide variation in potencies and doses, and up to now has been without standards or safeguards in this country. In the heated, sometimes ugly controversy, therefore, proponents and opponents have been arguing about a material that has no precise definition. All this makes the new plan for clinical trials doubly important.

Both advocates and opponents of Laetrile have agreed to a showdown. Sen. Edward M. Kennedy, D-Mass., as chairman of a Senate health and scientific research subcommittee, proposed a federally conducted series of clinical tests and promised that if the controversial substance proves to benefit human cancer, he will move in the Senate that Laetrile be legalized nationally. But he wrung from Laetrile's supporters and opponents a promise that they will abide by the findings of the clinical tests, whatever the outcome.

This may not end the controversy. Diehards tend to die hard. But the federal tests will be useful in giving the general public and state legislatures a basis upon which to make objective decisions. Furthermore, if Laetrile proves effective, these tests should lead to standardization. Several state legislatures, including that of Texas, have made it legal for Laetrile to be manufactured and administered within the state. Cancer patients reaching for this last grasp of hope deserve protection against uncertain substances and untested dosage.

The Evening Gazette

Worcester, Mass., July 16, 1977

It seemed like a great idea, as first reported by the radio and television wire services. Sen. Edward M. Kennedy, chairman of the Senate health and scientific research subcommittee, had proposed a "winner-take-all clinical showdown" to determine, once and for all, whether Laetrile fights cancer.

First accounts said both sides had agreed to abide by the results of an impartial, scientific test. But it was too good to be true. Follow-up stories revealed that neither side trusted the other. Each wanted to set the ground rules. Dr. John A. Richardson, author of a book claiming many remarkable cancer cures from laetrile, could not even agree with Dr. Donald Kennedy, head of the Food and Drug Administration, as to the chemical composition of laetrile. As Dr. Kennedy said, a test would be impossible "if we don't know what's in it."

Another pro-laetrile spokesman said that "orthodox medicine was not qualified" to evaluate any test.

We're all for settling the controversy by any means short of a duel. But anyone who has heard the emotional arguments from both sides will doubt that reason will ever rule the field. For one thing, the pro-laetrile side keeps talking darkly about "conspiracies" to keep laetrile off the market. There is an element of paranoia present. It would be nice if heated arguments could be settled by decisive tests, but it just doesn't happen very often.

The Pittsburgh Press

Pittsburgh, Pa., May 31, 1977

A disease such as cancer often breeds desperation in its victims and their loved ones.

And from that desperation has come a wildfire growth of demand for legalization of the drug laetrile in the United States. Laetrile is made from apricot pits in Mexico and West Germany but is banned by the U.S. Food and Drug Administration (FDA).

Because laetrile has not been scientifically proven as effective, the FDA is adamant in its stand and insists that patients should not be steered away from approved cancer treatments.

However, the pressure for laetrile has resulted in passage of bills legalizing its use in five states. And similar bills are pending in 28 other states.

Yielding to this public pressure, the federal government's National Cancer Institute very likely will test laetrile on several hundred human cancer victims in a number of treatment centers.

Laetrile has never been used in controlled human tests. The time has come to do this, so that the claims and counterclaims surrounding laetrile can be cleared away.

There are some stumbling blocks.

The first is that believers in the efficacy of laetrile fear the National Cancer Institute, as well as the FDA, is convinced the drug is a fraud—and thus the tests will be biased.

Another problem is that it may be difficult to recruit appropriate patients to take part in the laetrile tests. At best, only persons who are near death from cancer may be willing to cooperate, thus giving proponents of laetrile grounds to complain that the tests are invalid because the drug wasn't given soon enough.

But the tests should be made, under the best scientific conditions. Otherwise, the controversy will continue — to the possible detriment of the public's health.

The State

Columbia, S.C., July 18, 1977

As SERIOUS as the argument is over the merits of Laetrile in treating cancer, the tone lately has been that of petulant children doggedly insisting on contradicting one another.

Thanks to U.S. Sen. Edward Kennedy, the Laetrile argument may not become endless. At a hearing before his subcommittee on health and scientific research, the Massachusetts senator announced that he would abide by a new government-sponsored research to determine Laetrile's effectiveness against cancer. The senator challenged supporters of the drug to also accept the results — whatever they may be.

Pro-Laetrile spokesman for the Committee for Freedom of Choice in Cancer Therapy accepted the senator's challenge. They even agreed to supply the researchers with samples of the drug, data and research personnel to help in the tests.

Perhaps the issue can be settled finally on a scientific basis now that contestants agree to abide by the findings. The public, and particularly those cancer patients who are looking for effective treatment, have a right to know the true value of Laetrile.

Tulsa World

Tulsa, Okla., August 3, 1977

A FEDERAL decision to allow testing of the controversial cancer medication, laetrile, has run into a snag.

The Director of the National Cancer Institute says doctors are reluctant to use the drug in tests on human beings, knowing that other medication or treatment might do some good.

The ethical questions are not easily resolved.

Many cancer patients are obviously eager, even desperate, to try the unproved laetrile. The orthodox medical establishment considers it harmless but worthless as a cancer cure. So the Federal decision seemed to offer a way out for everyone.

Patients who wanted to try the drug could do so under experimental conditions. It would be voluntary, of course. Doctors would then accumulate the clinical evidence to say with some certainty whether laetrile does or does not have an effect on cancer.

But Dr. Arthur C. Upton, Institute director, says physicians face tough ethical questions when they give an unproven drug to a patient when a proven drug is available.

The tests that were supposed to clear the air on laetrile now seem to raise more questions than they answer.

The Oregonian

Portland, Ore., December 7, 1977

The nationwide controversy over Laetrile, used by some cancer patients, will be heated up by a U. S. District Court judge's issuance of a permanent injunction against enforcement of the U. S. Food and Drug Administration's prohibition of interstate movement of the substance.

Judge Luther Bohanon, in Oklahoma City, said the FDA order was arbitrary and capricious and places a "needless hardship and expense" on its users. Some of these have been bringing Laetrile from Mexico.

The FDA and much of the country's medical establishment contend that there is no proof of the effectiveness of such usage. The FDA is expected to appeal Judge Bohanon's ruling.

Although some of its users say they have been helped, there has been no professional proof that Laetrile is a cancer cure. There is some evidence that its use could be dangerous if not controlled. A 10-month-old daughter of a cancer patient in Buffalo, N.Y., recently died of cyanide poisoning after swallowing an unknown number of her father's Laetrile pills.

Despite the questions about Laetrile, a trademark for a derivation from the chemical amygdalin, found naturally in the pits of apricots and peaches and in bitter almonds, 13 states, including Oregon and Washington, have legalized its use.

Thomas Caton, executive secretary of the Oregon Board of Pharmacy, has said that Laetrile will be sold in Oregon only if it is manufactured in Oregon and derived from products produced in the state.

There is a certain logic in giving cancer patients the freedom to choose their own treatment, even though it involves taking what many physicians and the FDA think is no more than a placebo. Earlier this year, a Harris poll indicated that a 53-to-23 majority of the American people opposed the FDA's ban against interstate transportion of the substance.

But the legalization and manufacture of Laetrile within a state, such as Oregon or Washington, imposes the responsibility on the state to control distribution and identification of the product so as to prevent, if possible, any harmful effects from its use.

Some of the energy devoted to the debate of Laetrile should be devoted to reliable experiments and records of its use. At this stage, it apparently stands higher in public opinion than does the FDA. But the real tests must be scientific, not popularity contests.

The Birmingham News

Birmingham, Ala., May 30, 1977

A good many Americans are convinced that the drug laetrile has a beneficial effect in the treatment of cancer. Despite a ban on importation of the drug by the federal Food and Drug Administration, five states have legalized it and legislation to the same effect has passed in two other states and is waiting approval by governors.

The position of the FDA is that laetrile is worthless in the treatment of cancer and that it gives cancer patients false hopes, plus luring them away from proven, orthodox treatment methods.

Those opposed to the laetrile ban include those who swear that the drug does help cancer patients and others who simply argue that the federal government has no business denying any treatment to persons who believe in it and are willing to pay for it.

Now the National Cancer Institute says it is "seriously considering" using laetrile in tests on human beings to find out if it is an effective cancer treatment. The president of Memorial Sloan-Kettering Cancer Center in New York, Dr. Lewis Thomas, has said his cancer center would be willing to carry out the tests if asked to do so by the institute.

It seems only reasonable for scientific inquiry to be made into the effectiveness of laetrile. To date we have had only animal studies, which scientists say have shown no positive effects of laetrile, and personal testimonies by numerous patients who say they have been helped.

All seem to agree that laetrile is not toxic, that it causes no harm. But there is that scarcity of information about whether it does any good or not. The information gap should be filled with some solid facts, one way or another. It is to be hoped that the National Cancer Institute will decide to carry out the tests.

The Evening Bulletin

Philadelphia, Pa., June 15, 1977

The Food and Drug Administration is fighting a losing battle against Laetrile. The apricot-pit extract, touted as a cancer cure, is now legal in eight states, and it probably will soon be legal in others, including Delaware, Pennsylvania and New Jersey.

The rush by individual states to legalize a substance banned from interstate commerce is setting a dangerous precedent. Some states are approving other substances in a challenge to federal regulation.

Do states really have the resources and know-how to maintain safety standards for such substances?

Would it be good for our society to return to the day of the roadside medicine man and his bottled remedies?

Beyond those questions is the more poignant one, particularly appropriate in the case of Laetrile: Will some people who might otherwise have lived, die because they used a do-nothing treatment?

The FDA and members of the medical establishment have tried to convince state legislators that Laetrile is worthless. But the results of numerous animal studies showing the drug's ineffectiveness have not proved as convincing as emotional testimony from people who claim to have used the drug successfully.

Now the National Cancer Institute has informally proposed that Laetrile be tested on humans. It is time for such a test, which would require FDA approval, to be undertaken.

Already large numbers of Americans are taking Laetrile. The drug has been available on the black market for some time, and under a recent federal court order terminally ill patients may obtain Laetrile.

Perhaps some of the people already taking Laetrile would be willing to participate in a National Cancer Institute study of its effects. Maybe a scientific study based on human experience would help stem the pro-Laetrile drive—a movement whose success so far has undermined what should be an orderly and safe approach to the use of drugs.

Studies Reveal Danger of Poisoning from Laetrile

The Detroit News
Detroit, Mich., June 2, 1978

In view of the growing mass of medical evidence casting doubt on both the safety and effectiveness of Laetrile, the public should receive with skepticism a Michigan legislative report which suggests that the drug, properly administered, is as safe as aspirin.

Laetrile, a concoction of mashed apricot pits promoted as an "anti-cancer" drug, has been banned from interstate commerce as a dangerous health problem and labeled useless by most medical and scientific organizations.

Georgetown researchers reported last year that they had watched cancer patients develop adverse reactions from Laetrile. "The main purpose of the report," they said, "is to alert the medical profession and the public that this material may not be safe."

Only a few days ago, a group of University of California researchers said Laetrile can be a fatal poison if users eat certain common foods. They wrote in the Journal of the American Medical Association: "Our studies suggest that some patients . . . will take Laetrile and will suffer acute toxic effects and perhaps even die."

And now a spokesman for the U.S. Food and Drug Administration has told the Michigan House Public Health Committee flatly that using Laetrile to treat cancer is "a major medical fraud of the 20th century."

Dr. Thomas Anderson asserted last week: "Laetrile is not in our view a safe drug. It is a serious public health problem in this country because many people opt for Laetrile rather than other known therapies."

Several bills to legalize Laetrile are pending before the House Public Health Committee. Apparently the issue will come before the full House sometime this year. If it does, legislators will be sorely tempted to pose as the dispensers of holy water to desperate people searching for magical cures. The issue will severely test the honesty and good sense of those who make our state laws.

We urge the Legislature to reject any effort to legalize Laetrile in Michigan. If the Legislature does pass such a bill, Gov. William G. Milliken should veto it.

RAPID CITY JOURNAL—
Rapid City, S.D., March 17, 1978

The principal argument of those who think cancer patients should have access to Laetrile is "freedom of choice." They maintain that even though research indicates Laetrile is not effective in combatting cancer, its use should not be restricted by government.

Laetrile supporters contend that even if the substance is not effective in treating cancer, its consumption "can't hurt."

Now, however, scientists at the University of California at Davis say cancer patients taking Laetrile and eating certain fresh or uncooked foods are running an increased risk of poisoning themselves with hydrogen cyanide.

The scientists studied the effects of oral Laetrile consumption with fresh almonds on 10 mongrel dogs. The almonds contain an enzyme found in many salad foods such as mushrooms, lettuce and celery, as well as in other nuts, beans and fresh fruit.

Six of the 10 dogs died of acute hydrogen cyanide poisoning from about 20 minutes to three hours after feeding. All the animals showed evidence and the effects of the poisoning.

Dogs were used in the studies because they have a physiology similar to humans. Unlike Laetrile, all of the more than 50 cancer drugs currently sold have been proven to have some degree of medical effectiveness in dogs before they were marketed.

The California study indicates that cancer patients who exercise their freedom of choice and take Laetrile would be well advised to also be choosy about what they eat.

The Des Moines Register
Des Moines, Iowa, March 14, 1978

Laetrile advocates argue that even if the controversial compound is worthless as a cancer cure, it won't harm anyone. There is growing evidence that the argument is worthless, too.

Cyanide poisoning is one risk of taking Laetrile that health authorities have recognized for some time. The main chemical ingredient in Laetrile, which is made from the pits of apricots and other fruits, is amygdalin, which contains cyanide. Several recent deaths from cyanide poisoning have been linked to overdoses of Laetrile.

Now the Journal of the American Medical Association has published reports of research showing that Laetrile, when combined with certain foods, produces deadly amounts of hydrogen cyanide in the body. Sixteen mongrel dogs used in the research project died or became severely ill after they were given Laetrile and sweet almonds. The almonds contain enzymes common to many fresh fruits and vegetables.

Doctors in the University of California research program warned that older patients weakened by cancer would take critical risks if they ate fresh fruits and vegetables while taking Laetrile orally.

The research should prompt questions about the advisability of state legislatures rushing to legalize the sale and manufacture of Laetrile in defiance of federal regulations against it. The Food and Drug Administration has called Laetrile a "cruel hoax" and has banned its shipment in interstate commerce.

Fourteen states have legalized Laetrile and several others, including Iowa, have Laetrile bills under consideration this year. The Iowa bill would make the State Health Department responsible for setting standards for manufacturing, prescribing and selling Laetrile in the state.

The federal government has methods of determining the safety and effectiveness of prescription drugs. The federal system is not without flaw, but states are not equipped to make these judgments. The report in the Journal of the American Medical Association shows why it is reckless for states to authorize distribution of chemical substances before their safety and value are established.

Laetrile Use Approved for Terminally Ill Patients

BUFFALO EVENING NEWS

Buffalo, N.Y., July 17, 1978

Laetrile may be utterly worthless as a treatment for cancer patients, and certainly any claim to the contrary well merits the appropriate concern of the medical profession.

Even so, we think a U.S. Court of Appeals in an Oklahoma case made a defensible distinction in upholding a ruling that "safety" and "effectiveness" as used by the federal Food and Drug Administration, in banning laetrile, have no meaning in the context of persons who are terminally ill.

In barring the FDA from attempting to stop the use of the substance when administered by a licensed medical practitioner to persons certified to be terminally ill of cancer, the appeals court declared: "What can be 'generally recognized' as 'safe' and 'effective', mean to such persons who are so fatally stricken with a disease for which there is no known cure?"

The issue here is not whether laetrile has any value, but whether government should go beyond reasonable precautions, in the form of proper warnings and reasonable requirements for certification that all medically-accepted therapies have been exhausted — in short, whether it should superimpose its judgment over the right of the desperately ill to make possibly unwise choices.

THE DAILY HERALD

Biloxi, Miss., July 13, 1978

Terminally ill patients may take some small comfort from a federal court's ruling this week allowing them to have Laetrile injections.

The ruling was long overdue. The U.S. Court of Appeals in Denver correctly noted that the federal government is wrong to apply normal drug standards of safety and effectiveness to Laetrile.

The court said safety means nothing to persons afflicted from incurable, terminal diseases like cancer.

It is the latest acknowledgment that American government and medicine must do more to ease the final days and hours of pain-wracked patients.

The Carter administration — and particularly the Food and Drug Administration — have vocally opposed the use of Laetrile.

That opposition has forced cancer victims to circumvent the law. Some sought the drug abroad, often in Mexico. Others smuggled it in.

The drug itself is extracted from apricot pits. The federal court noted that Laetrile is regarded by some to be more of a folk medicine than anything else. That's not for us to judge.

Groups like the American Cancer Society, the FDA and the Mississippi State Medical Society have said much worse.

They termed it "dangerous and ineffective" earlier this year when the legislature considered legalizing its use in Mississippi. It is precisely that reasoning when applied to the dying which the federal court criticized this week.

The Mississippi proposal was eventually killed, but several states have approved the use of Laetrile.

We don't profess to be a medical expert on Laetrile. But we do think that Laetrile — or any other treatment which can ease physical and emotional suffering of dying patients — ought to be available.

The ultimate decision to use such treatments should be made by the doctor and patient. Whether a drug eases physical pain or sets the mind at ease, government should not deny a dying person these small comforts.

Meanwhile, both government and private researchers should press ahead in the development of other drugs and therapies to help the dying. It must be recognized that relief from pain is often more important to dying patients than the dangers of drug addiction.

In addition, the development of hospices — places offering treatment and comfort for the terminally ill — should be encouraged.

Des Moines Tribune

Des Moines, Iowa, July 18, 1978

Three federal judges at Denver further muddled the confused controversy over Laetrile when they ruled that injections of the drug can be given legally to terminal cancer patients. The ruling disrupts a Food and Drug Administration bar against interstate shipments of Laetrile, which the government lists as an unproven drug.

The three-judge panel ordered the FDA to set guidelines "with all due dispatch" to enable cancer patients to receive Laetrile injections. The ruling does not apply to restrictions against Laetrile in capsules or tablets.

Leading medical authorities have called Laetrile a worthless compound. So the judges are saying in effect that the government should not try to prevent the dying from buying a hoax. That is something quite different than letting pain-wracked patients have an unlimited amount of pain-killers.

Deciding when a cancer patient reaches the "terminal" stage is often guesswork. Some patients who have been told that they have only a few months to live have lived for years.

As FDA Commissioner Donald Kennedy observed, the judges are taking away from the terminally ill the protections given to other persons under terms of food and drug laws, especially the requirement that all medications must be both safe and effective. Waiving those safeguards for the dying is a curious way of showing kindness.

THE DENVER POST

Denver, Colo., July 19, 1978

SHOULD A PERSON whose doctor says he is dying of cancer be denied the use of a drug he believes might be helpful?

Many believe Laetrile, an extract of apricot pits, is effective in control of cancer. However, the Federal Drug Administration has a long-standing ban on its use on the grounds that its "safety" and "effectiveness" are unproven.

In 1976 a suit was filed in Oklahoma to prohibit the FDA from enforcing its Laetrile ban. In response a Federal District Court issued an injunction against FDA. Last week the 10th U.S. Circuit Court of Appeals sitting in Denver upheld that injunction.

The appeals court ruled that the law requiring the FDA to pass on the safety and effectiveness of a drug has "no reasonable application to terminally ill cancer patients."

While releasing Laetrile for use, the Court limited it to "intravenous injections administered by a licensed medical practitioner" to patients who are certified to be terminally ill of cancer. Making the medical profession a part of the Laetrile treatment process will help reduce the possibility of quackery, which many feared.

The court's decision is humane and compassionate.

It continues to be distressing that medical science is unable to cure many forms of cancer. If a physician in his expert judgment determines he can do no more for a cancer patient, no law should prevent that patient from a receiving a drug he believes may be efficacious even though there may be no scientific evidence to support that belief.

If medical science admits a cancer patient is beyond help, what harm is there in making other treatment—even though it may be only folk medicine—available to him if he believes it brings him comfort?

Laetrile Treatment for Chad Green Disputed

The parents of Chad Green, a three-year-old boy suffering from leukemia, were ordered by the Massachusetts Appeals Court Jan. 30 to stop treating him with Laetrile, a controversial substance derived from the pits of apricots, peaches or bitter almonds. Laetrile (amygdalin) was said to release cyanide when metabolized by the body and had never been approved as a drug in the U.S. Despite a federal ban on shipment of the substance, its manufacture, sale and use had been legalized in 17 states.

The appeals court order on Chad's treatment upheld a Jan. 23 ruling by the Massachusetts Superior Court after court-ordered laboratory tests had found evidence of cyanide poison in the child's blood. (Several deaths had been reported from overuse of Laetrile, mostly among cancer patients who believed in its curative value.)

In defiance of the courts' rulings, Gerald and Diane Green fled Massachusetts Jan. 25 with Chad and checked the boy into a Laetrile clinic in Tiajuana, Mexico.

The U.S. Supreme Court was planning to review the case to determine whether laetrile should be an exception to the Food and Drug Administration's rule that drugs on the U.S. market must be proved both safe and effective.

The snake oil salesman still lives

In separate actions last week, the US Supreme Court agreed to hear arguments on the federal government's right to ban the use of laetrile for terminally-ill cancer patients. And a Plymouth Superior Court judge in Massachusetts ordered the parents of 3-year-old Chad Green to stop giving him laetrile, Vitamin A and enzym enemas in addition to medically-prescribed chemotherapy. Both cases raise the troubling question of the state's jurisdictional interests in the health of its citizens.

The argument has been a thorny one for a long time. In fact it was discussed by Plato and Socrates, who agreed that science should not intervene to prolong the lives of the mortally ill.

But the question becomes immeasurably complicated when the state—in this case, the court—is asked to distinguish between a mortal illness and a curable one, to arbitrate between areas of privacy and protection, and to decide whether one treatment or another is likely to be medically beneficial.

It seems inevitable that the US Supreme Court will be drawn into the question of trying to define mortal illness in reviewing the lower court finding that "terminally ill cancer patients" must be allowed to use laetrile. And that is as murky a region as the question of when life begins, which the court faced in its 1973 abortion ruling. The answer, whatever it may be, will probably satisfy no one.

But Chad Green, by all the evidence, has not been mortally ill. With early and sustained conventional treatment, doctors a year ago gave him an 80 percent chance to be permanently cured. Those chances will have been lessened if his parents, who took the boy to Mexico last Thursday, are allowed to discontinue chemotherapy in favor of their preferred metabolic program, a program which has already raised the cyanide level in his body to six times above normal and his Vitamin A levels to 10 times above normal.

The Greens, like many others before them, are acting out of love and conscience. But they are making a life-and-death decision for a boy who cannot decide for himself, and it is a decision that contradicts the widest and best knowledge available, however imperfect. In the case of competent adults, the state by and large does not intervene. But it has intervened, and must, where the rights of a child or helpless adult are involved. Surely the right to life outweighs the right to privacy here.

In the Supreme Court case, the FDA will argue that, even for terminally-ill patients, legal sanction of laetrile would undermine the FDA's mandate to protect the public from harmful drugs and from ineffective ones. That is a very valid concern. There is increasing evidence that laetrile is harmful as well as ineffective against cancer, but some will not listen. Ours is still a gullible society and it needs some protection against the salesman of snake oil.

The Evening Bulletin
*Philadelphia, Pa.,
February 1, 1979*

Last week, Gerald and Diane Green fled from their Massachusetts home with their son Chad, three. The boy suffers from leukemia, and the Greens fled the state to escape a judge's order that Chad not be given the drug Laetrile in treatment.

Was the Greens's action that of desperate parents trying to save the life of their critically ill child? Certainly. Was it foolish? Probably. Could it have hurt Chad more than it helped him — even endangered his life? Quite possibly.

Mounds of evidence already indicate that Laetrile, a substance made from apricot pits, is useless as a treatment for cancer. Nevertheless, thousands of cancer patients throughout the country who attest to Laetrile's supposed curative powers have been successful in getting the manufacture, sale and use of the substance made legal in 17 states — including New Jersey and Delaware. State legislators evidently have been swayed by the argument that there is no harm in allowing cancer patients, often hopelessly ill, to take a drug that probably won't hurt and just might help.

But scientific reports increasingly show that Laetrile is not entirely harmless; under certain conditions it can release hydrogen cyanide — a poison that can kill human beings. Also, there is a risk that cancer patients who take Laetrile will stop having chemotherapy — a cancer treatment which can be painful, but which is known to be beneficial.

Because of the controversy surrounding Laetrile, we look forward to the results of a study by the National Cancer Institute, which last year started testing the drug on human beings. That report may permanently put to rest the medical concerns about the drug's effectiveness and safety.

We look forward also to a forthcoming decision by the U.S. Supreme Court, which will determine whether Laetrile is exempt from federal laws requiring drugs to be safe and effective. A lower court earlier ruled that because Laetrile is administered primarily to cancer patients who have no hope of being cured by other means, the drug's effectiveness and safety are not relevant.

In our view, it is cruel to offer false hope to terminally ill people, and that would be the case if Laetrile is proven to be of no medical value. If it is solidly established that Laetrile can be a fatal poison, then even those doomed to die of cancer — should not be allowed to take it. To recognize that there is no solution is the hardest challenge for all.

THE DENVER POST

Denver, Colo., February 2, 1979

CHAD GREEN is the 3-year-old leukemia patient whose parents took him to Mexico because a Massachusetts court ordered them to stop giving him Laetrile. Widespread publicity has made it appear Chad is a victim of cruel official intransigence.

However, the facts show the case is not nearly as simple as it may appear. It isn't as though the controversial drug, made from apricot pits, is the last hope of a dying boy and his desperate parents.

Chad isn't dying, a spokesman for Massachusetts General Hospital in Boston where the boy was being treated, told us. He has a relatively common type of leukemia, acute lymphatic leukemia, which has yielded increasingly in recent years to treatment with conventional drugs.

Chad's cancer flared up after his parents stopped giving him his prescribed pills. It went back into remission after chemotherapy was resumed at Massachusetts General, the hospital spokesman said. To all outward appearances, he is a robust, healthy child, although doctors think the disease probably is still lurking in his bloodstream.

The hospital says there is at least a two-in-three chance for survival if patients are kept on the chemotherapy regimen for three years—a striking change from 10 years ago, when the disease meant almost certain death.

Chad's parents have been described as very loving and well-meaning. They fled because they felt the chemotherapy was painful and turned their son into "a wild animal." They said the boy was "wonderful... happy now" at the Centro Medico del Mar in Tijuana, where he was getting chemotherapy along with Laetrile.

The hospital contends Chad has had only minor, short-lived side effects from chemotherapy. But Laetrile, which the parents apparently started in April, is blamed for low-grade cyanide poisoning which showed up in recent tests on Chad.

Medical researchers have theorized that hydrogen cyanide, a deadly poison which attacks the heart and central nervous system, is produced when Laetrile comes into contact with certain fruits and vegetables containing hydrolytic enzymes.

The pro-Laetrile theory is that this poison attacks primarily the cancer cells, interfering with their reproduction while leaving normal cells alone.

The 10th U.S. Circuit Court of Appeals in Denver six months ago told the federal Food and Drug Administration that its Laetrile ban, based on concern for the drug's "safety" and "effectiveness," had "no application" to terminally ill cancer patients.

The court suggested the FDA issue new regulations allowing the use of Laetrile if it is limited to intravenous injections administered by licensed medical practitioners to patients certified as terminally ill from some form of cancer.

The FDA didn't change the rule. It appealed to the U.S. Supreme Court, which has agreed to review the case.

There are two very different sets of circumstances here. We can see no reason to deny a person who is dying of cancer the comfort of one last hope. If chemicals and surgery and radiation haven't worked, and if the patient is fully aware that Laetrile's efficacy is, to say the least, in doubt, then it appears extremely unlikely the cyanide in the drug would accumulate enough to do serious harm. But Chad Green, thankfully, doesn't seem to be in danger of imminent death, and there is evidence Laetrile is poisoning him. His case is unique. It shouldn't be made, by an excess of oversimplified publicity, the final test for the success or failure of Laetrile.

St. Petersburg Times

St. Petersburg, Fla., January 28, 1979

It is a poignant case: parents losing and then regaining custody over their 3-year-old boy as his cancer ebbs and flows. Diana and Gerald Green had been treating their son with Laetrile and vitamins; a judge had ordered chemotherapy as well.

After six months with chemotherapy, the leukemia is in remission; so far little Chad's evidence of cyanide poisoning (presumably from the Laetrile) is as bad as would be found in an adult smoker. The judge ordered the parents to stop giving him Laetrile and large doses of vitamins.

But as soon as he returned Chad to their custody, the Greens ran away with him. They left a note implying that a sort of sinister Big Brotherism interfered with their freedom — the freedom to give him the Laetrile, no matter how much harm it might do.

LAETRILE IS a substance derived from apricot pits or other fruits. It is sold as a treatment for cancer. The medical profession says it has no known curative value and that its use may encourage delay in life-saving medical treatment.

Its involvement in the case of Chad Green points up one of Laetrile's problems. It is that anxious relatives of cancer patients, not just the patients themselves, encourage (or in this case force) its use.

The well-meaning relatives would rather believe in a miraculous "control" — not realizing it can cause the patient more medical problems — than turn their loved ones over to effective but unpleasant therapy.

SOME OF THEM have been convinced by Laetrile boosters that the government, doctors and drug companies are conspiring to cover up Laetrile.

These true believers, who work to widen their circle, persuade patients and their relatives that the "medical establishment" would rather perpetuate cancer than cure it. They cloud the subject by making Laetrile an issue of individual liberty.

And a tangle of legal confusion makes it possible for distraught parents, wives, husbands and children to obtain and use a substance that may have no medical value at all. Locally, that confusion helps keep in business a clinic where some patients say they have been put on Laetrile treatment costing up to $100 a day.

SO WE'RE glad to see that the U.S. Supreme Court has agreed to take up the issue. A group of cancer patients sued the government in 1975, claiming that its ban on interstate shipments of Laetrile violated their right to privacy by preventing them from buying it.

A District Court agreed, and a Circuit Court of Appeals ruled that terminally ill patients could obtain Laetrile, even though the Food and Drug Administration (FDA) says there is no evidence of its effectiveness.

NO ONE would want to keep a useful drug from a sick person and certainly not from one who is dying. But as the Green case illustrates, it is not always dying patients who voluntarily choose Laetrile — or who are forced into taking it.

Three-year-old Chad Green has leukemia, a kind of cancer that in some of its forms can be cured.

UNLESS THE FDA uncovers evidence that Laetrile does control cancer, no one should be fooled into taking it.

The placebo that eases the mind of one dying cancer victim can take the life of another who might have lived years with real cancer therapy.

The Hartford Courant

Hartford, Conn., January 28, 1979

Chad Green doesn't have to die to prove a point.

The 3-year-old Massachusetts child has been at the center of a year-long battle between his parents and doctors over how best to treat his leukemia.

Gerald and Diane Green have expressed lack of faith in the traditional chemotherapy treatment for their son, and have fought a long legal battle to stop the drug therapy and use their preferred means of treatment. The courts have ruled against them, and they have now fled with their son to Mexico to partake of the laetrile clinics available to them there.

If this case involved only a debate on the merits of the unproven cancer drug laetrile, perhaps Mr. and Mrs. Green's actions could be justified. If this case involved only an academic debate over parental discretion, perhaps Mr. and Mrs. Green might merit some sympathy. But in fact, the end result of this case will be the life or death of Chad Green.

And if the Greens persist in avoiding a reasonably successful chemotherapy program, in favor of apricot pits in a Mexico clinic, their son is going to die, and they will face a well-deserved manslaughter charge.

Mr. and Mrs. Green may well be distressed by the unpleasant side affects that often accompany chemotherapy treatments, but the alternatives they have found are saddening. The Greens have fed their son limburger cheese, his grandmother's chicken soup, heavy doses of vitamins, laetrile and a host of other remedies that suit their fancy at any particular moment. Their latest laetrile and vitamin treatment has apparently contributed to a mild poisoning of Chad's body.

If Chad Green were near death from a terminal illness, with no medical treatment available to him, this last-gasp chicken soup and cheese therapy might have some sad justification. But Chad Green can be saved. There is a treatment that offers him reasonable hope for cure, or at least significant years of good health. To deny him that right is inexcusable.

The Philadelphia Inquirer

Philadelphia, Pa., January 27, 1979

The story of young Chad Green wrenches the heart. The three-year-old has leukemia, and for months his parents have been wrangling with the state of Massachusetts over his treatment. They want to give him Laetrile and vitamin therapy, but the state has maintained that he should have conventional cancer treatments such as chemotherapy.

For a while Chad was given both kinds of treatment. Now a court has ordered that the Laetrile and vitamin treatments cease. The reason? State officials contend that Chad is suffering from cyanide poisoning from the Laetrile as well as from Vitamin A poisoning. His parents, who vow to fight the order all the way to the U.S. Supreme Court, have taken the child into hiding to avoid the court directive. At present, Chad's life-threatening disease is in remission.

The drama revolving around this small blond boy raises all the important questions in the Laetrile dispute, questions the Supreme Court apparently will try to settle. The court agreed this week to decide whether the federal government has the authority to ban use of Laetrile, a substance derived from apricot pits. The court will be reviewing a U.S. Court of Appeals decision that allows terminally ill patients to import Laetrile for their personal use.

The central legal issue in the Supreme Court case is fairly clear: Should Laetrile be an exception to the Food and Drug Administration's 1962 rule that drugs marketed in this country must be proved both safe and effective? (FDA contends Laetrile has been proved neither.) Litigants say a grandfather clause in the 1962 legislation setting up the "safe and effective" rule exempts Laetrile along with other drugs on the market at the time.

The human issue is less clear: Under a constitutional right to privacy, should cancer patients, and presumably persons who are terminally ill from other diseases, be allowed to use any drug they choose?

We hope that in deciding this case the Supreme Court won't do damage to the concept that the FDA may require drugs marketed here to be safe and effective. To undermine that rule would be to open the door to quacks and fast-buck artists, some of whom already are making a substantial penny on the Laetrile trade.

If Laetrile, which has been used by an estimated 70,000 Americans, is ruled an exception, its use should be allowed only under strictly controlled circumstances. Perhaps it could be provided only to terminally ill patients who sign an affidavit attesting to their understanding that almost all respected medical authorities view Laetrile as worthless and possibly even harmful.

On that last point: The National Cancer Institute is proceeding with plans to test Laetrile on humans, tests so far having been limited, as is customary, to animals. Its plan for the tests on several hundred informed cancer patients were presented to the FDA in December, and at present discussions are underway to reach agreement on procedures. Both agencies should proceed speedily on this. It is a matter of life and death.

AKRON BEACON JOURNAL

Akron, Ohio, January 25, 1979

THE DECISION of the U. S. Supreme Court last week on a Pennsylvania abortion law seemed a particularly wise one for two reasons:

It signaled the reluctance of the court to get itself involved in the practice of medicine, and it protected the right of a woman and her physician to make an important health decision, regardless of how others may view the morality of the decision.

That same reasoning could be just as wisely applied in suits involving use of Laetrile, a controversial substance believed by some to be effective in treating cancer.

Probably the most famous suit involves Chad Green, a three-year-old Massachusetts boy whose parents were ordered by lower courts to stop giving him Laetrile. The court earlier had given custody of the boy to the state so he could receive chemotherapy, after which, doctors at Massachusetts General Hospital said, there was a remission in Chad's leukemia.

Now the Supreme Court has agreed to hear a suit brought by a group of cancer patients seeking to determine whether the federal government has the authority to ban the use of Laetrile for terminally ill cancer patients.

The Food and Drug Administration has for years effectively prevented patients from getting Laetrile by banning interstate distribution of it. The FDA based its decision on research by some of the nation's most prestigious cancer research centers that indicated Laetrile has no value in treating malignancies. Furthermore, some now contend that, given in large doses, it may cause cyanide poisoning.

Nevertheless, a federal appeals court in Denver ruled last July that concepts of safety and effectiveness are essentially meaningless when applied to terminally ill cancer patients.

The Justice Department asked for the Supreme Court review on the basis that there is no way of distinguishing accurately between "terminal" cancer patients and those who may respond to conventional therapy.

The logic of that argument would be hard to deny.

Few if any physicians faced with prescribing the best treatment for a cancer patient would say with certainty that the disease is terminal. They might suggest that the chances for survival are not good, but not that recovery is impossible.

At that point, the type of treatment to be followed is a matter for competent physicians, not judicial experts.

Furthermore, it is the patient's right to choose his physician. If, in the face of all scientific evidence to the contrary, a patient of legal age believes that Laetrile will help him, and if he is able to find a physician willing to administer it, does the court have the right to deny him such treatment?

That is the difficult question before the Supreme Court, and it is one in which an individual's rights may well override the best intentions of the Food and Drug Administration.

The San Diego Union

San Diego, Calif., January 30, 1979

All the cruel dilemmas — legal, philosophical, and moral — bound up in the national debate over the use of Laetrile as a cancer treatment are exemplified in the sad case of 3-year-old Chad Green.

The boy suffers from leukemia. His parents believe his treatment should include Laetrile doses administered in conjunction with a high-nutrition, natural diet. Courts in the Greens' home state of Massachusetts have forbidden Chad's Laetrile treatments. In apparent violation of a court order, Chad's parents have brought him to Tijuana, where Laetrile treatments are legal.

Reportedly, Chad will undergo limited chemotherapy augmented by his special diet and Laetrile.

It is difficult to review this case without feeling sympathy for the conflicting positions of both Chad's parents and Massachusetts officialdom.

Massachusetts courts, including the commonwealth's supreme court, believe that conventional chemotherapy is the only treatment that offers Chad any hope for survival. Thus the state's statutory interest in Chad's welfare coupled with medical testimony that the Laetrile doses and Vitamin A supplements had produced a buildup of cyanide left the courts little choice but to mandate exclusive reliance on chemotherapy.

And yet, what parent could condemn the Greens for objecting to chemotherapy's ravaging side effects and seeking an alternate treatment regimen they believe provides Chad the best chance for life?

We can offer no easy resolution of this agonizing conflict.

But we continue to believe that the predicament of Chad and his parents, as well as that of tens of thousands of cancer victims, underscores the need for an exhaustive study of Laetrile, its chemical components, and the ways in which these components may effect cancer cells. Indeed, while Laetrile remains rightly controversial as an anti-cancer agent, the reported discovery in Japan of a scientifically acceptable explanation of the way Laetrile may work against cancer is precisely the kind of lead that American cancer researchers ought to pursue with all deliberate speed.

A noted biologist, Andrew A. Benson of the Scripps Institution of Oceanography, cites the Japanese evidence as cause for intensive investigation.

We think Chad Green's parents and the judges in Massachusetts would find themselves in complete agreement on the need for a maximum-priority study by both the American Cancer Society and the National Institute of Health.

The Boston Herald American

Boston, Mass., January 27, 1979

The dilemma created by the medical, legal, and parental conflicts in the Chad Green case is, simply and tragically, this:

Everyone involved has been driven by a desire to do only what is right for the three-year-old Scituate boy — but what they have done has turned out all wrong.

Surely the doctors at the Mass. General Hospital wanted what was best for him by overriding the objections of his parents and insisting on the chemotherapy they say gives him a fighting chance to survive the leukemia that otherwise could kill him.

Certainly Superior Court Judge Guy Volterra was concerned with Chad's well-being when he transferred custody of the child from Jerry and Diana Green to the state to make sure he would get the treatment they oppose.

And unquestionably the judge had the same high motive a few days ago with his second ruling in the case. Not only did he reject the parents' plea for return of Chad's custody to them, but he ordered them to stop giving him Laetrile and large doses of Vitamin A as supplements to the chemotherapy.

But Jerry and Diana Green claim nobody has been more closely linked to Chad's life than they — and nobody has been more worried about his welfare.

Rather than comply with an order they felt had unjustly deprived them of any shred of parental right to supervise the medical care of their son; rather than submit him any longer to a course of treatment they were convinced was worse than the disease; they fled with him to Mexico. There he, and they, are beyond the reach of Massachusetts law.

Now Chad will continue to get the Laetrile and nutritional treatment which doctors said — and court testimony supported — had introduced a high level of cyanide and Vitamin A poisoning to his system.

But he presumably will *not* continue the chemotherapy which his parents, after study, are certain filled his small body with toxic, life-destroying substances.

And who could lose, ultimately, by this seeming inability of those who care deeply and sincerely for Chad Green to somehow strike a compromise on their differences, difficult though that may be?

Who else but little Chad?

Chad Green Dies of Leukemia; Laetrile Dispute Continues

Chad Green, 3, died Oct. 12, 1979 of leukemia in Tijuana, Mexico. He had been the center of a dispute over the merits of Laetrile in the treatment of cancer. Chad's parents fled to Mexico following a court order Jan. 23 that directed discontinuance of Laetrile in his case after laboratory tests found evidence of cyanide, attributed to the Laetrile, in the boy's blood. The parents had continued him on chemotherapy until sometime in mid-August when they elected to take him off the treatment—against the advice of Mexican doctors—in favor of a strict Laetrile treatment combined with a vegetarian diet. At that time, Chad's leukemia was in "complete remission" and the parents apparently believed their son had been "cured."

An autopsy reported Oct. 21 was said to have indicated that Chad "had a relapse in his leukemia and he died of it." The parents still faced legal charges in Massachusetts for flouting the court's authority in their fight to treat Chad with Laetrile.

The Star-Ledger
Newark, N.J., November 3, 1979

The death of Chad Green in the third year of his life is a sorrow shared by millions of Americans who became aware of his terminal illness as a result of the controversy precipitated by the type of treatment which compelled his parents to defy the courts.

Rather than submit their child to court-ordered conventional chemotherapy for leukemia, Mr. and Mrs. Green chose to flee the jurisdiction of the courts and take their son to Mexico for treatment with an unproved cancer drug — laetrile.

There is no question that the parents believed they had acted in the best interests of their boy . . . a love that was evident "amid the pain of hard decisions," as a cleric noted in services for Chad.

Whether the youngster could have reached a state of remission through medically approved chemotherapy is conjectural at this stage. But it would be a reasonable assumption that this course of treatment — at the very least — has a certifiable degree of success; certainly more than can be said for laetrile.

Although 20 states, including New Jersey, have laws permitting the manufacture and distribution of laetrile within their borders, the Supreme Court last summer upheld the authority of the federal government to ban distribution of the purported cancer cure.

The court rejected the belief that terminal illness is not a proper concern of government, that it was beyond regulatory power.

It may be small solace for his bereaved parents, but Chad Green's premature passing should graphically underscore the inherent hazards of foregoing conventional cancer therapy for the still unproved laetrile treatment.

THE ATLANTA CONSTITUTION
Atlanta, Ga., October 16, 1979

Thousands of people, including children who've hardly begun to live, die daily. Most of us, except for the famous, die in obscurity, mourned only by family and close friends. Sometimes, someone emerges from mass humanity to catch national attention briefly before he dies; usually that someone is a child and usually the child catches national attention because of the way he or she is dying.

Chad Green was such a child. A leukemia victim, Chad died last Friday afternoon at age 3.

Chad died in Tijuana, Mexico, where his parents — Diana and Gerald Green — had fled with him last January from Massachusetts where authorities had refused to permit the boy to be treated with Laetrile, which is a derivative made from the pits of apricots, peaches and bitter almonds. There is a great deal of controversy over Laetrile; federal laws forbid its use, and most medical experts say it's useless against cancer.

But there are those who think otherwise. The Greens, faced with an agonizing choice, believed Laetrile helped Chad — and so took their son and fled to Mexico where Laetrile treatment is available.

The Greens continued chemotherapy treatment for Chad also. But then two months ago, they apparently thought Chad had been cured — or was at least well enough — to stop the chemotherapy. Chemotherapy is a standard treatment for many cancers, but it also has unpleasant side effects.

Whatever, Chad began declining and died Friday afternoon. Reports say that moments before death, Chad said, "Mommy, look out the window. There's a bright light out there, and I have to go to it. Please let me go."

Now, there are hard cases who might smile, even joke, about Chad's statement and its implications. But not us. And there are persons who might rage with anger at the Greens for choosing their own counsel about Laetrile and not the majority view of doctors and scientists. But not us.

Medical indications are that Laetrile is quack medicine. But one can believe that and still identify with the terrible, hard choices that the Greens were faced with, and not decry them for the choices they made. Especially persons who are mothers and fathers can understand.

THE INDIANAPOLIS STAR
Indianapolis, Ind., November 1, 1979

Apparently, no one ever told Massachusetts Attorney General Jonathan Brant that justice should be tempered with mercy.

He still wants to prosecute the parents of Chad Green for contempt of court.

Three-year-old Chad was suffering from leukemia. His doctors were giving him the accepted treatment, chemotherapy. So far as his parents could observe, it was doing him no good.

In desperation, they sought to have Chad treated with Laetrile, a derivative of apricot, peach and bitter almond pits.

The court refused to countenance this, because the American medical profession considers Laetrile treatments simple quackery.

In defiance of a court order, Chad's parents fled with him to Mexico, where Laetrile treatments are legal. There Chad died.

Misguided as Chad's parents might have been, what they did they did for love of him. He was suffering and they were suffering with him.

They did what they did because they wanted him to live, knowing they were risking jail. They are now deep in grief, penniless and in debt.

If the law has any humanity, it should leave them alone.

FORT WORTH STAR-TELEGRAM

Fort Worth, Texas, October 22, 1979

A parent can love a child in many ways. And sometimes that love is so strong that it hurts.

Chad Green was loved. In his three short years he probably received more parental love than most children do in their lifetime. Chad was different. He had leukemia.

It was because he had leukemia that Chad's parents acted as they did, in defiance of the law. They took their child to Mexico, against a court order, so that he could be treated with laetrile, a controversial drug that some say is a cancer cure.

For nine months the Greens had been living in Mexico, far from their Massachusetts home, clinging to the hope that one day their boy would be healthy.

Chad died recently. Whether it was because of or in spite of laetrile, or because chemotherapy was stopped, perhaps we will never know.

Whether the court was correct and the parents wrong is not important. What is important is that Gerald and Diane Green loved their son and they did what they believed was right.

A contempt charge against the Greens is pending. But a court cannot bring back young Chad. It cannot change the love of his parents. The court is superfluous. Gerald and Diane Green are guilty of having loved their child. And that is not a crime.

SAN JOSE NEWS

San Jose, Calif., October 16, 1979

CHAD Green died of leukemia on Friday. He was three years old.

Chad was "the Laetrile boy." His parents wanted to treat his cancer with Laetrile and nutritional therapy instead of chemotherapy. His doctors protested, saying that Laetrile was ineffective and potentially dangerous. A Massachusetts court ordered the Greens to stop giving their son the controversial drug.

In January, the Greens fled to a clinic in Tijuana, Mexico, where doctors prescribed both Laetrile and chemotherapy. Chad seemed to be doing well. Then, against the advice of his new doctors, the Greens decided he had been cured and ended the chemotherapy. In two months Chad was dead.

For most of his brief life, Chad Green was a symbol, an issue, a controversy. Can Laetrile cure cancer? Is it safe? Should its use be legalized even if its effectiveness is disputed? Does chemotherapy cause children unnecessary suffering? Do parents have the right to substitute their judgment for conventional medical wisdom? Should the courts become involved in medical decisions?

Now Laetrile's true believers and the medical establishment will debate whether the withdrawal of chemotherapy caused Chad's death. The controversy will outlive its most visible symbol.

But the death of Chad Green reminds

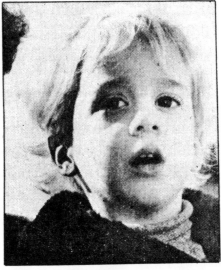

Chad Green

us that he was more than a symbol. The "Laetrile boy" was a real person, a little boy who missed his grandparents and his puppy and wanted to go home. That fact got lost in the legal and medical wrangling, so it's worth repeating. Chad Green was a real little boy who was with us for a short while and isn't anymore.

The Courier-Journal

Louisville, Ky., October 16, 1979

CHAD GREEN was one year old when doctors at the University of Nebraska Medical Center told his parents that he had leukemia. Last week, in Tijuana, Mexico, he died at the age of three.

He lived amid legal and emotional conflict between parental and state rights. His parents asserted their right to decide what kind of medical treatment was best for him. The state acted to protect the child from harm caused by that decision.

Early in Chad's story, he was placed under the care of a Boston specialist. His condition improved. But the side-effects of the chemical injections, his parents said, caused him to act "like a wild animal."

They stopped hospital treatments, and were given pills for home use. The leukemia soon returned. The Greens admitted substituting laetrile pills.

That started a court battle. After a year, a judge ruled that the laetrile was causing cyanide poisoning. He ordered the Greens to resume conventional cancer therapy and to stop using laetrile.

At this, his parents took Chad to Mexico, telling relatives they wished to try *both* courses of treatment. Meantime, a higher Massachusetts court upheld the ruling that laetrile was actually harmful.

In Mexico, the leukemia once again appeared in remission. Believing him cured, his parents took Chad off chemotherapy. They did so in violation of the Massachusetts order and against the advice of doctors at Tijuana's internationally known center of laetrile use, the Clinica Del Mar.

Dr. Julio Edgar Selva, the Tijuana doctor who had been treating Chad, said, after the child's death, "If the boy had remained on chemotherapy, he would still be alive today."

Massachusetts authorities do not intend to prosecute the parents. There seems no reason to doubt that their decisions, however legally or medically questionable, were made out of loving concern.

But cancer specialists note that 40 percent of cancer victims who receive conventional treatment, however unpleasant, do survive. No one, they claim, has offered scientific, impartial studies showing that laetrile confers any benefits.

Until long-promised federal studies of laetrile are completed, such child-custody cases will be settled by convincing individual judges that the medical argument is correct and that the state must protect the children involved. It is high time federal officials took an interest in accelerating the studies, in order to give the courts a source of more reliable information in this difficult controversy.

The Morning News

Wilmington, Del., October 17, 1979

Chad Green is dead. He was the three-year-old from Massachusetts whose parents objected to the chemotherapy doctors had prescribed to control his leukemia. Mr. and Mrs. Green believed that the "right" diet and laetrile were all the cure their son needed. When the courts in Massachusetts, on advice of physicians, ruled that chemotherapy was necessary to preserve Chad's life, his parents chose to leave the country. They took their son to Tijuana, in Mexico, where laetrile is big business; and it was in Tijuana that their son died.

Chad's parents loved their son. They gave up their home in Massachusetts and they broke the law—just for him. But in so doing they put their untutored judgment ahead of that of skilled physicians. Those physicians were as certain as humans can be that Chad's best chance for survival and for a normal life lay in the treatments that had been shown successful in similar leukemia cases. The Greens, however, worried about the immediate side effects from the treatment; they did not want their little son to suffer. And so

they chose the painless laetrile route, which led to death.

Who knows how long and well Chad would have survived on chemotherapy? Since he had done well on his initial course of chemotherapy, one can conjecture that he might be chipper today. There is no certainty. But at least the best that medical science can offer would have been tried.

Now it is too late. The Greens have lost their son. On the scale of human misfortune, that is punishment enough. The Commonwealth of Massachusetts, which still could bring action against the Greens, should show compassion and drop all charges. No purpose could be served by further legal action. The child cannot be brought back to life and harassing the Greens, however justifiable legally, would contribute nothing to the public welfare or the rule of law.

Let this case be buried with little Chad as far as court action goes. But let the sad story of laetrile's uselessness for little Chad be told to anyone willing to listen.

The Boston Globe

Boston, Mass., October 16, 1979

There is no simple moral to the story of Chad Green, the 3-year-old leukemia victim who died in Mexico last week. As John Truman of the Massachusetts General Hospital, who treated him, said Sunday, the youngster's death was essentially a tragedy "because it didn't have to happen."

But it happened and it happened in large measure because Chad Green's parents' fear of the cure was as great, if not greater, than their fear of the disease itself. And this fear fostered a distrust of the medical establishment and made the Greens particularly susceptible to the claims of those who advocate laetrile and vitamin therapy as a painless, sure-fire cure for cancer.

The Greens, acting from the love and concern that motivates all parents, refused to accept widespread medical evidence that chemotherapy has a particularly effective track record in fighting the type of cancer Chad had, a form of cancer considered to be among the most curable of all malignancies. They feared the side effects of the treatment and could not believe in its power to restore their young son to full health.

Yet chemotherapy had twice proven effective in Chad's case. He was in remission at the time the Greens initially abandoned the treatment in November 1977 and again after the court ordered that the treatment be resumed in February of 1978. Doctors gave him anywhere from a 50- to 80-percent chance of a permanent cure if the treatment was sustained.

Even the weight of the legal arguments made on their little boy's behalf didn't convince them. The Supreme Judicial Court decided in July 1978 that Chad's best chance for survival rested in drug therapy, that it offered him a substantial hope for cure, and that the state had the right to intervene because parents do not have "life and death authority" over their children. But the Green's whisked Chad off to Mexico in January to avoid the court order.

Fear won and, in the end, Gerry and Diana Green have to face the daily reality of life without their little boy. Their anguish and pain will be great and, for that reason, the state should drop all charges against them.

Doubtless, many will struggle to find some greater good in Chad Green's death. Some will say the case defined children's rights, parental limitations and the state's responsibility on such matters. Some will say it may work to sensitize a medical profession that is perceived, rightly or wrongly, to be too cold and too sure of itself. Some will say it raises the level of awareness about the different kinds of cancer and the success of different cancer treatments. Some will say it raises the level of public skepticism about laetrile and other unorthodox cures that prey on our fears.

Although we have all sympathized with the desperation of those who will grasp at any straw rather than face the facts, members of our cancer-fearing society are victimized as often as not by false hopes that there is some easy cure for the disease. Too often, valuable time is lost when conventional therapy is rejected in favor of quackery. We forget that only one in five persons survived cancer in the 1930s compared with one in three today. Cancer is grim; it is not always fatal.

Critic Susan Sontag has written that our fear of cancer is often worse than the disease itself and clearly she's right. The very word is whispered and we are terror struck. Perhaps Chad Green's story ultimately forces us to confront that fear and piece out how we can best allay it.

CHARLESTON EVENING POST

Charleston, S.C., October 18, 1979

We all know that we cannot endanger Chad's life and comply with the court order that would not allow us to give him nutritional support. It is clear that the politics involved would take our son's life, lost in stride, as we are to be made public examples. — the parents of Chad Green, Jan., 1979.

Chad Green had leukemia and was receiving chemotherapy treatments, but his parents said the treatments turned him into "a wild animal." They stopped them, and started giving him laetrile, a drug derived from the pits of apricots and peaches. The state of Massachusetts intervened, declared Chad a ward of the state, and ordered his parents to stop the laetrile and resume the chemotherapy. His parents moved to Mexico, where laetrile is legal.

The Greens saw themselves as pioneers. In their departing note they likened their stance to that taken by their forefathers, who were "free thinking," not hemmed in by the dogma of the day.

Now Chad Green is dead. His parents have agreed to an autopsy of their child, and said they hope that something can be learned from his death.

The Chad Green story is the stuff of which tragedies are made, a primitive drama in some ways, and more complex in others. What rights does the government have in the parent-child relationship? Should we accept, as the Greens saw it, "a system that forces a child into exile"? Should parents be allowed to refuse medical treatment of their children which they find disagreeable? (Bear in mind that throughout much of human history "the best medical opinion" supported practices now universally regarded as rank quackery.)

Who is really responsible for the death of Chad Green?

The Hartford Courant

Hartford, Conn., October 16, 1979

Chad Green no longer needs legal protection; he is dead.

But there are other children who may well face a similar life-threatening family situation, and the state of Massachusetts should pursue the Green case, for the sake of those youngsters whose parents choose to act in an irresponsible manner.

Gerald and Diana Green chose to treat their child's leukemia with faith, good food and unproven laetrile. At various times, the couple accepted, rejected and contradicted themselves about the value of the chemotherapy that was designed to keep their child alive.

Doctors, and eventually a Massachusetts judge, sought to protect Chad from such emotional and potentially destructive behavior, but the Greens escaped to Mexico, and that is where Chad died.

Even at their most willful and premeditated, they appeared to be more confused and immature than wantonly malicious. But their son is dead, and he deserved a better chance to live.

In children of Chad Green's age, with the kind of leukemia from which he suffered, the disease does not necessarily lead to the kind of inevitable death so often associated with cancer. The allure of magic cures must be discouraged by a society that is committed to protecting its members from inadvertent harm.

If the autopsy on Chad indicates that the quixotic vision of his parents was responsible for his death, then Gerald and Diana Green should be prosecuted, if they return to the United States.

Legal action would not be a vindictive blow against the parents, but an act of love for children who have not yet fallen victim to the fantasies, however well-meaning of their guardians.

The Evening Bulletin

Philadelphia, Pa., October 16, 1979

In his short life, Chad Green was a charming child who touched the hearts of all who knew or heard of him. In his death, little Chad has become the tragic symbol of a medical controversy that may invoke memories of him for years to come.

Chad, just three, had leukemia, an acute blood disorder most often treated by chemotherapy. His parents, however, chose to put their faith in Laetrile, a substance made from apricot pits that has been deemed by medical authorities thus far to be worthless in treating cancer. In spite of being banned from interstate commerce in the U.S., Laetrile is legal in 17 states — including New Jersey and Delaware — and many desperate cancer patients attest to its curative powers.

When a Massachusetts judge ordered Chad's parents to stop treating him with Laetrile early this year, the Greens fled to Mexico, where Chad underwent Laetrile and chemotherapy treatments at a clinic. Three months ago, they stopped the chemotherapy. On Friday Chad closed his eyes and died.

The exact cause of Chad's death will be determined by an autopsy, but the boy's Mexican doctor has stated that Chad would still be alive had his parents not stopped the chemotherapy. In fact, that is the prime reason U.S. medical experts think Laetrile is dangerous: Although it has no known value as a treatment, cancer patients who take it often give up on chemotherapy, which is known to be beneficial to many of those suffering from the disease.

It is hard to fault Chad's parents for doing what they honestly believed was best for their son. The fact is that they still face contempt of court charges in Massachusetts. But what law, what punishment will ever match the heartache, the emptiness they will feel the rest of their lives?

We hope and pray that the death of Chad Green will not have been in vain, and that it illustrates to believers in Laetrile that the substance is hardly the "miracle cure" many of them think it is.

The Providence Journal

Providence, R.I., December 2, 1979

There is something terribly wrong in the latest chapter of the Chad Green story. For a year, Americans followed news accounts of the 3-year-old boy's battle with leukemia and his parents' battle with the courts.

Many read approaching tragedy in Diana and Gerald Green's efforts to treat their son's often fatal disease with a special diet and the drug laetrile, a substance made from extract of apricot pits which is banned for general use by the federal Food and Drug Administration. The Greens' confidence that their way was best despite medical opinion and their determination to wrest the final decision on medical treatment from the doctors and the courts by taking Chad to Mexico struck many as appalling at best.

The child's death on Oct. 12, following the parents' reported decision to end the chemotherapy treatment he was receiving in a Tijuana clinic, seemed to conclude this tragic sequence of events. But it hasn't. The story continues as the couple carries on their fight to legalize laetrile. It continues despite that discredited drug's failure to help Chad and the unaltered position of the medical and scientific community that, so far as has been determined, laetrile is worthless and sometimes harmful.

The Greens now are promoting a freedom-of-choice referendum in California as part of the drive for legalization of laetrile. Mr. Green has agreed to serve as national chairman and ads are running in pro-laetrile publications announcing that he is available for speaking engagements.

Meanwhile, the Greens have been besieged by agents bidding on the book and movie rights to Chad Green's story. The *Boston Sunday Globe* last week quoted the couple as saying they turned down a $100,000 offer from one publisher because "it's worth a million." But Mr. Green called the report "a bunch of garbage . . . As far as we're concerned, we're not interested in any money. We want Chad's story to be told because we think it is important to the public."

The issue, then, is not laetrile but freedom of choice. "Whether laetrile works or not is not the question," said a leader of the California movement. "I prophesy that the role of laetrile is the key pin in the freedom-of-choice battle. And it will include the right to put children on laetrile. We expect Gerry Green will lead the fight for us."

What the Greens and their supporters are fighting for is the return of that period ended many years ago when quacks and itinerant peddlers could foist upon an uninformed and often unsuspecting public any phony nostrum — worthless or harmful — that seemed to offer some element of hope. Should they succeed, government efforts to protect consumers from profiteers and charlatans would be ended. The Food and Drug Administration and Federal Trade Commission could be abolished. The "good old days" when Americans judged a bottle of colored water by the huckster's pitch and dropped their money in the flim-flam artists' bag would be with us again.

And in the bargain, more Chad Greens would die.

If Chad's story is worth a million, the legalization of laetrile would be worth that amount countless times over even though the scientists and their professional organizations say the drug does no good and may cause harm.

Anyone who buys the freedom-of-choice argument as it applies to medicine is living in a dream world built by those unscrupulous operators who would exploit the fear and lack of sophistication of helpless people. Why do they do it? There's big money to be made out there and "a sucker's born every minute."

Supreme Court Upholds FDA Ban on Laetrile

The Birmingham News

Birmingham, Ala., July 25, 1979

The continuing fight by the federal Food and Drug Administration to keep laetrile, that disputed cancer-curing miracle, out of the hands of an unwary public has about as much to do with the proper functioning of government as a Huey Long election speech.

The FDA recently won a suit before the U.S. Supreme Court which bans laetrile from interstate commerce. Now it is seeking to close a loophole, which the Supreme Court left open, that allows cancer patients, certified as terminal by a physician's affidavit, to import the drug for personal use.

For our money, it seems the FDA could save a lot of time and expense by sticking to the job its supposed to do, instead of entering protracted crusades. For a fact, reputable research suggests that laetrile does no more than weight the pockets of those who sell it. But, on the other hand, it would seem that the FDA's proper role is to advise us on what we *should* or *should not* take rather than telling us what we *can't* take.

If a terminally ill cancer patient wants to take laetrile despite that advice, more power to him. The Constitution guarantees us the right to be wrong.

The Star-Ledger

Newark, N.J., June 26, 1979

The ruling by the Supreme Court that the federal government has the authority to ban the distribution of laetrile is certain to revive the emotional controversy over the purported cancer cure drug.

In overturning an appellate decision, the high court held that no exception to the federal Food, Drug and Cosmetic Act — the basis for government authority — could be made for medication for the terminally ill.

This was the reasoning behind the decision by the U.S. Court of Appeals, that the requirements of federal law for a drug to be safe and effective have "no reasonable application" for patients in terminal stages.

The Supreme Court's unanimous decision rejects a humane interpretation that terminal illness can stand outside government regulation. It was the statutory intention of Congress, Justice Thurgood Marshall wrote for the court, to shield patients with fatal illness from "fraudulent cures . . . the vast range of self-styled panaceas that inventive minds can devise."

New Jersey and a number of other states have enacted laws that permit the manufacture and distribution of laetrile. These statutes may have little meaning inasmuch as laetrile cannot be transported in interstate commerce.

Thousands of Americans are using laetrile despite medical documentation that it is ineffectual in reversing or curing this malignant disease. It has stirred strong feelings, pro and con, a controversy with a poignant emotionalism, the desperate final resort for persons with terminal cancer.

One of the most potent arguments against the legalization of laetrile is that it would deflect cancer patients from advanced medical treatment, such as chemotherapy that in a significant number has arrested this disease. That could well be a greater tragic consequence than denying terminally ill cancer victims laetrile.

The Evening Bulletin

Philadelphia, Pa., June 20, 1979

The U.S. Supreme Court's ruling that the drug Laetrile can't be distributed in interstate commerce upheld the integrity of federal drug laws, which make no exceptions for using unproven drugs to treat terminally ill persons. That should prompt the 17 states, including New Jersey and Delaware, that have legalized Laetrile within their borders to reconsider the value of their Laetrile laws.

The court ruling puts the state laws out of step and in the position, we think, of holding out false hopes to cancer patients.

Laetrile, a substance made from apricot pits, has not been found to be a safe and effective cancer treatment by the Food and Drug Administration or by any cancer research institute. Some studies indicate that the drug, which contains small amounts of cyanide, can even be fatal in some circumstances. Nonetheless, thousands of cancer patients believe in Laetrile's powers.

Now the Supreme Court has held that Congress passed the Food, Drug and Comestic Act to protect all Americans, including those who may be dying from incurable diseases. There is no warrant for using Laetrile to treat cancer, Justice Thurgood Marshall wrote in a unanimous decision, except in closely supervised experimental situations.

That means the drug cannot be taken across state lines to be sold, and that federal agents can prosecute interstate distributors. Since nearly all the Laetrile in this country is imported from Mexico and West Germany, it's now virtually a contraband drug.

The Supreme Court's ruling overturned two lower courts that placed terminal cancer patients in a separate category from other sick people. We think the high court acted properly in standing behind the federal law, and not inviting a situation in which terminally ill persons could become prey to all sorts of "cures."

We hope federal agents act aggressively to prevent the spread of a "black market" in Laetrile. That would be easier if the states that have passed laws legalizing the drug rescinded them.

For cancer patients who need good, sensitive care, Laetrile is akin to a prescription for disappointment.

ST. LOUIS POST-DISPATCH

St. Louis, Mo., June 19, 1979

The Supreme Court decision upholding the Food and Drug Administration's authority to ban from interstate commerce drugs whose safety and effectiveness have not been demonstrated is a victory for consumers. In the unanimous decision in a case concerning Laetrile, the controversial treatment that some promote as a cancer cure, Justice Marshall noted that during debate on the controlling legislation, "Congress expressed concern that individuals with fatal illness, such as cancer, should be shielded from fraudulent cures." So they should.

This ruling overturned a lower court decision that said a terminally ill person had a right of privacy to choose whatever type of treatment he or she wanted. But the type of treatment does matter. For one thing, a doctor, at some point, has to determine that "conventional" treatments will have no effect. After this jolt, the patient is given hope by the Laetrile promoters that the apricot-pit-based treatment will cure cancer. But no set of clinical tests by respected scientists in this country has supported the claims that Laetrile cures. The cancer patient who turns to Laetrile is doubly a victim — of the disease and of a cruel hoax.

The Laetrile controversy is far from over with the Supreme Court decision, though contention is now firmly placed in the federal arena. None of the 17 states that have legalized the use of Laetrile grows the raw materials for the substance, so the federal ban on Laetrile in interstate commerce will stop its legal availability. Meanwhile the promoters will continue to push for federal legalization, and researchers will try to find any evidence of benefit. Unless that is available, the federal government ought to hold firm on its ban.

THE INDIANAPOLIS NEWS

Indianapolis, Ind., June 21, 1979

When the Indiana General Assembly was considering several years ago whether to legalize Laetrile, it provoked some of the hottest debate this state has seen in years.

It was to be expected. Matters of life and death, after all, touch upon the most private feelings of us all. So any discussion over treatment provided to the terminally ill is automatically beyond the realm of academia.

Laetrile was developed in 1926 and ever since, the compound derived from apricot and peach pits has been the subject of controversy. Some claim it to be effective against cancer; the government disagrees. In 1963, the Food and Drug Administration (FDA), saying that Laetrile's safety and efficacy were unproven, banned its importation and interstate shipment. Because it is often the last resort of the hopeless, Laetrile became a black market item with many seeking treatment in other countries where its use is legal.

Federal authority over drugs comes into play when the item is for sale or distribution in inter-state commerce. In 1977, Indiana's General Assembly eventually legalized Laetrile here, over Gov. Bowen's veto. The state believed it could legalize the drug for use, sale and manufacture for within the state. It would have to prove, however, that no part needed for the drug's manufacture came from out of state. Shortly thereafter a Federal judge began allowing terminal cancer patients to import Laetrile, saying FDA authority did not cover the terminally ill. So the state's law has not really made a difference.

Well, it might make a difference today. The Supreme Court has just ruled the FDA does indeed have authority to bar the use of Laetrile for the terminally ill. The court ruled that the Food, Drug and Cosmetic Act cannot be interpreted in such a way as to prevent the FDA from denying to the terminally ill any drug that hasn't been shown to be "safe and effective."

We're sure the Supreme Court is more qualified than we are to interpret the FDA's charter. But we are not sure that use of Laetrile can be regulated based on that argument alone. All the high court has done is to clarify FDA authority to protect the terminally ill from possible fraud.

But there are greater authorities than those of the FDA. A District Court that had upheld use of Laetrile ruled that by denying cancer patients the right to use Laetrile, the FDA infringed on constitutionally protected privacy interests.

And that is how we perceive the Laetrile debate: As one concerning freedom of choice. When the Supreme Court ruled it also told the lower courts to consider the privacy argument. It had been upheld by the District Court but hadn't been addressed by the Appeals Court.

We urge that consideration as quickly as possible. We cannot vouch for the medical value of Laetrile, except to say it has done some good for some people. We can, however, defend the terminal patient's right to choose his own treatment. The government has gone to excess in telling us how to live; it has no right to tell us how to die.

THE ARIZONA REPUBLIC

Phoenix, Ariz., June 22, 1979

LAETRILE is a medical substance made from apricot pits. Many cancer patients have sworn that it helped them. Most doctors say it does no good. So far no one has proved the use of Laetrile to be physically harmful.

The Food and Drug Administration long ago banned the use of Laetrile. Arizona is one of 20 states that have since legalized its use.

The Supreme Court has now come down on the side of FDA. That means Laetrile, or the products from which it is made, cannot legally be moved in interstate traffic. However, the renewed ban by the Supreme Court will not take effect until some legal technicalities have been attended to.

The Supreme Court ruling is in accordance with the law. A lower court had ruled that the FDA ban could not be applied to terminally ill cancer victims. The Supreme Court, which decided unanimously but with some reluctance, held that the FDA authority covered all drugs, whether intended for the terminally ill or not.

So long as no one can prove that Laetrile hurts anyone, it seems both dangerous and nonsensical to ban it. But that will be the result of existing law which allows the FDA to outlaw any drug not proved to be "safe and effective."

At one time or another every medical doctor has prescribed a placebo for a patient. It is usually made of sugar and water. It frequently works wonders with the mental attitude of sick persons who think they are getting a powerful drug.

At the very worst, Laetrile is a placebo. At the best it may nullify or reduce the ravages of cancer. Until someone can prove that Laterile is harmful, its use should be permitted under federal as well as state regulations. If the Supreme Court can't do that, Congress should. ☐

FDA Approves Laetrile Tests; Human Studies to Follow Rabbits'

The Food and Drug Administration gave tentative approval Jan. 3 to the National Cancer Institute to conduct the first clinical study of the effects of Laetrile on humans. The institute, the federal government's main cancer-fighting agency, would first have to repeat a Laetrile test on rabbits. Then it would have to conduct a three-month toxicity study on six patients to make sure that they did not ingest excessive cyanide from Laetrile, while on a "metabolic" diet during the treatment. The institute trial was expected to take a year and would involve 200 to 300 advanced cancer patients who had volunteered for the Laetrile treatment.

Four cancer research centers were to participate in the study: Mayo Clinic in Rochester, Minn., the University of California at Los Angeles, the University of Arizona at Tucson and the Memorial Sloan-Kettering Cancer Center in New York. FDA approval of the cancer institute study had reportedly been stalled for more than a year over the debate on testing an allegedly ineffective drug.

Richmond Times-Dispatch
Richmond, Va., January 8, 1980

It is good that the Food and Drug Administration has finally gotten around to giving permission for the first clinical trial of Laetrile on cancer patients.

Despite the fact that Laetrile's use, under certain conditions, has been authorized by several states, that some judges have granted permission for its use in specific cases, and that thousands of Americans go outside the country to get it, the federal government had refused even to permit testing of the alleged anti-cancer substance. The National Cancer Institute had been trying for more than a year to get the FDA's permission for the testing before the agency announced last week that conditional approval had been given.

The conditions are, first, that before the substance can be given to people, a test must be run on rabbits. Then, prior to the full-scale testing, a three-month toxicity study must be conducted on six patients to determine if there is any danger from the ingestion of too much cyanide from Laetrile while on the special diet that is also part of the Laetrile treatment program.

If the preliminary testing does not militate against it, the full-scale trial will involve 200 to 300 patients for about a year. The patients will be those who have advanced cancers and who volunteer. Four prestigious cancer research centers will participate.

The medical establishment of this country is almost 100 percent of the opinion that Laetrile is worthless as a cancer fighter, and the substance cannot be legally prescribed in most places. To many people, the legal ban seems to approach the point of cruelty when it denies Laetrile to terminally ill patients who have tried every other treatment without success and who, in desperation, want to resort to Laetrile. The government's ban has been predicated on the theory that Laetrile is harmful in that its use could prevent a patient from submitting to other types of accepted treatments that might do him some good. It has been only recently that Laetrile opponents have been emphasizing that the substance itself might be harmful.

On the basis of all the literature we have read on the subject — some pro and some con — we incline toward the belief that Laetrile has no therapeutic value, other than that which any treatment might have if a patient *thinks* it is going to help him. Medical authorities may be, and probably are, right in their view of Laetrile's worthlessness, but they have fought too long against putting the substance to a real test in clinical trials. The FDA's recent decision should finally put to rest any reasonable doubts as to whether Laetrile is a useful drug or a hoax.

Des Moines Tribune
Des Moines, Iowa, January 10, 1980

Confusion about the curative powers of Laetrile may be cleared up by clinical tests that have been given conditional approval by the Food and Drug Administration. The tests would be performed on human volunteers, possibly as many as 300, on whom conventional cancer treatments have been either ineffective or impossible.

Four cancer research institutions, including the Mayo Clinic at Rochester, Minn., have agreed to take part in the tests, which will be carried out under standards set by the National Cancer Institute. The institute will repeat tests on rabbits before proceeding with the Laetrile treatments on cancer patients.

Previous research with animals produced unfavorable results that led to a government bar against interstate shipment of Laetrile, which the Food and Drug Administration classed as an unproven drug. Numerous medical authorities called it a "cruel hoax" and warned of its danger, because a key ingredient of the apricot-pit compound is amygdalin, which contains cyanide. Several deaths from cyanide poisoning in recent years were linked to Laetrile overdoses.

Widespread dread of cancer coupled with a growing anti-intellectual antagonism toward scientific inquiry provided fertile ground for public confusion. An emotion-charged controversy followed when Laetrile advocates tried to circumvent federal restraints by pressing courts and state legislatures to let terminal cancer patients obtain the drug.

Now that the public controversy has subsided, it is an opportune time for the clinical research proposed by the National Cancer Institute. It probably can be done free of the pro-and-con fervor that might have prejudiced such research a few years ago.

THE MILWAUKEE JOURNAL
Milwaukee, Wisc., January 4, 1980

The most ardent supporters of Laetrile probably will keep regarding it as a magic drug, even if it is proven entirely worthless. However, there are some less dogmatic people who would be impressed by scientific findings on the subject.

Therefore, it is good that the Food and Drug Administration has approved a full-scale scientific study of the drug's effectiveness (or noneffectiveness) in the treatment of cancer. On the basis of what has been learned so far, we doubt that the drug will be found to have much curative value, but we'd be delighted to be proven wrong.

If nothing else, the go-ahead for research deprives Laetrile zealots of a favorite argument — namely, that a conspiracy between the government and the medical profession has kept the drug from getting a fair trial. Although the charge seemed spurious on its face, it persisted as long as the government blocked extensive Laetrile research.

The Evening Bulletin
Philadelphia, Pa., January 7, 1980

We hope the federal Food and Drug Administration (FDA) carries through on its tentative intention of testing the effectiveness of Laetrile on human beings. Such testing could prove, once and for all, whether the controversial substance is useful in treating cancer or a worthless placebo.

The FDA has contended that Laetrile, a substance made from apricot pits and almonds, is valueless as a cancer treatment — potentially even dangerous. However, several thousand cancer patients nationwide take Laetrile, pinning their hopes for being cured on its reputed powers. Laetrile has been banned from interstate commerce, but its use is legal within 17 states, including New Jersey and Delaware.

Laetrile should either be legalized nationally or banned altogether. Letting states sanction it individually is no answer.

We're glad the FDA has decided to ease off from its previous opposition to testing Laetrile on humans because we'd like to see the Laetrile debate come to a definitive close in the next few years. The dispute at times has been hot and very often sad, as in the case of Chad Green. The three-year-old eukemia patient was whisked to Mexico by his parents when a Massachusetts judge ordered them to stop giving their son Laetrile. The boy received both Laetrile and chemotherapy treatments for his disease for awhile in Mexico, and then his parents stopped the chemotherapy. Three months later, little Chad died.

Laetrile's opponents point out that it may not be merely worthless, but dangerous because cancer patients, like young Chad, may drop conventional chemotherapy treatments, which have been shown to have value as cancer fighters. Others add that Laetrile also can release enzymes that break down into cyanide, which is fatal to humans.

The FDA is asking the National Cancer Institute first to find out whether cyanide is produced when cancer victims combine Laetrile with the vegetarian diet that Laetrile proponents recommend. Later, some 200 volunteer cancer patients in four clinics will participate in Laetrile testing that is to last about a year.

To offer false hope is cruel. Cancer victims deserve to know whether the money and hope they invest in Laetrile is worth it, or merely wasted. We hope this testing will accomplish that.

Newsday
Garden City, N.Y., January 7, 1980

It's extremely doubtful that a full-scale federal study of Laetrile will offer much hope to Americans who have cancer.

But the results of such research may help control some of the malignant quacks who peddle cancer "cures."

That's one modest hope from the news that the U.S. Food and Drug Administration is finally prepared to authorize a major scientific test of Laetrile by respected hospitals, including New York's Memorial Sloan-Kettering Cancer Center and the Mayo Clinic in Minnesota.

That many cancer-stricken people and their agonized families earnestly believe Laetrile may help in some way is a fact of life today. The substantial lack of any real medical basis for these hopes is just as evident; that's why the federal government and states like New York have refused to legalize Laetrile treatment.

But this responsible policy will always be open to tortured questioning from persons with cancer and will continue to be exploited, by both the vicious and the ill-informed, as long as Laetrile has not been given a thorough, comprehensive, controlled test. The medical quack trades in ignorance and doubt. The projected study can help reduce both.

There are presumably enough cancer patients willing to participate so that a valid inquiry can be made. It will almost certainly confirm what other responsible researchers have already found in more limited studies: that Laetrile is not helpful. But the federal investigation may produce other data about cancer and those afflicted with it that will be genuinely useful in treatment. This hope may be frail, but it alone is enough to justify the FDA's decision.

The Times-Picayune
New Orleans, La., January 7, 1980

The Food and Drug Administration has finally approved the testing of Laetrile on humans. Announcements of the approval indicated that the FDA took the action "reluctantly."

This is puzzling indeed, because some expert testing of the drug by prestigious cancer research centers is long overdue. Failure to prove the effectiveness or ineffectiveness of Laetrile has led to unnecessary controversies over an individual's right to choose certain treatments and over the possible toxicity of the drug.

The FDA has been steadfast in maintaining that all the data to date suggest that Laetrile has no effect on cancer. But the proponents of Laetrile have been equally steadfast in their contention that the drug, made from the pits of apricots, almonds and other foods that contain cyanide, is a cancer cure.

These proponents claim that 50,000 to 75,000 Americans have used Laetrile and 20 states have legalized its use within their borders. But the FDA has banned interstate shipments of Laetrile and is fighting an affidavit import system set up by a federal judge in Oklahoma in 1977.

In such a situation, the average person, especially one who is suffering with cancer, does not know whom to believe. And although many advances have been made in cancer treatment, victims of that most dread disease are often easily convinced to try any cure.

The lack of some definitive word on the effectiveness of Laetrile as a cancer drug for humans has meant that many people have abandoned traditional treatment in favor of the controversial drug. The FDA has limited the testing to patients for whom conventional therapy has failed or whose cancer has no proven method of treatment.

After considering the request for more than a year, the FDA gave its approval for the experiments on humans on the condition that it not prove toxic in a repeat test on rabbits and a three-month study of the drug and the accompanying "metabolic" diet on humans. If these pan out, a 12-month clinical trial of the drug will begin on 200 to 300 patients at four major cancer research centers.

We hope the tests prove conclusive, so that we may either rejoice that a new and effective cancer drug has been found or accept the fact that we will have to depend upon conventional treatment and future scientific advances.

ST. LOUIS POST-DISPATCH
St. Louis, Mo., January 4, 1980

Laetrile is but the latest in a long line of heavily promoted but unproven cancer treatments. It has been so heavily promoted, in fact, that it has attracted a large following and become a national issue. Yet it is still devoid of scientific evidence proving it to be an efficacious drug for treating cancer. And that's why a report that the Food and Drug Administration has conditionally approved a study of its effectiveness on cancer patients is welcome news.

The FDA has steadfastly refused to approve Laetrile for use as a cancer treatment, maintaining that there is no evidence to show it as safe or effective. That position was backed up by a four-year study by the Memorial Sloan-Kettering Cancer Center, which showed no statistically significant evidence that Laetrile has preventive or curative benefits.

Still, proponents have continued to clamor for approval, arguing that freedom of choice ought to prevail in this instance, evidence or not. That, however, defeats the purpose of government regulation to protect consumers. A really free choice is an informed choice. Citizens have no way to effectively test Laetrile. The government does. And that is why it has the responsibility of making the decision. If freedom of choice is the issue, why not approve the sale of chalk dust as a cancer cure? The government has kept Laetrile off the market because it is responsible for protecting consumers from fraud. Now that the FDA has approved a new study, perhaps the controversy will soon end.

The Wichita Eagle
Wichita, Kans., January 9, 1980

It's encouraging that the Food and Drug Administration had decided to begin preliminary testing of the drug Laetrile. It is hoped that many of the questions surrounding the anticancer effects of this apricot pit derivative finally will be answered.

Equally as important, there now should be an end in sight to the traumatic emotional struggles and legal battles that have been experienced by many cancer victims and their families. The continuing controversy has caused pain and consternation in the lives of people at a time when stress and strain can be least tolerated.

If no harmful effects are found during the upcoming testing, then less rigid restrictions should be placed on use of Laetrile. This is especially true in the case of the individual suffering from terminal cancer who has exhausted all other forms of treatment.

Barring any negative physical aspects of Laetrile, the most positive physical benefit may reside in the belief of a cancer patient that the drug actually works. No one fully understands the ability of the human mind to aid in the prevention or cure of disease. If Laetrile can provide the psychological lift of giving a person badly needed peace of mind during the most trying period of his or her life, that in itself means a great deal.

The Boston Herald American
Boston, Mass., January 19, 1980

For nearly 25 years, Laetrile's defenders have insisted that this extract of apricots pits and bitter almonds is a useful agent in combating human cancers. Its detractors, including the bulk of the medical and scientific community, contend that Laetrile is worthless in treating cancer or anything else.

In the absence of conclusive testing and medical studies, the debate would probably continue indefinitely. Meanwhile, cancer patients who use Laetrile as well as those who don't might never know whether their treatment regimens were accordingly enhanced or compromised.

The logical way to resolve the Laetrile debate is so obvious we can only wonder why it has taken a quarter of a century for the U. S. Food and Drug Administration and the National Cancer Institute to agree on a comprehensive program of tests.

Both have rejected all past claims made on Laetrile's behalf. But neither the FDA's ban on the importation or interstate shipment of Laetrile nor the National Cancer Institute's official skepticism has prevented tens of thousands of cancer patients from obtaining the substance abroad or through a network of sympathetic physicians in this country. And, in just the last few years, the pro-Laetrile lobby has persuaded the legislatures of 20 states to legalize use of Laetrile as a "dietary supplement."

The few independent studies of Laetrile and its effects on cancer patients have either proved inconclusive or are disputed by one side or the other.

The comprehensive clinical tests sanctioned recently by the FDA will involve four of the nation's most prestigious cancer research institutions: the Mayo Clinic, UCLA Medical Center, the University of Arizona, and the Sloan-Kettering Institute for Cancer Research.

The results of these tests may not persuade everyone, but they will undoubtedly shed much additional light on a question that could and should have been resolved years ago.

The Hartford Courant

Hartford, Conn., January 12, 1980

The National Cancer Institute has won approval from the Food and Drug Administration for testing in hopes of settling whether Laetrile is an effective drug against cancer or is a particularly cruel hoax, offering hope where there is none.

Only persons who have advanced cancer, for whom traditional treatment proved fruitless, will be involved in the tests. Laetrile, generically known as amygdalin made from apricot pits and other foods, contains cyanide and the FDA contends that it can be poisonous.

Proof of Laetrile's bane or benefit has been difficult to pinpoint because it invariably is used by so-called "hopeless cases." That same situation prevails in the tests.

However, every effort will be made to make the findings as scientifically sound as possible, according to the cancer institute. First, there must be repeated tests with rabbits, followed by a three-month toxicity study involving six advanced-cancer patients whose conventional treatment failed. When safety levels are judged, up to 300 human volunteer patients will participate at Mayo Clinic in Rochester, Minn., the University of California at Los Angeles, the University of Arizona at Tucson and the Memorial Sloan-Kettering Cancer Center in New York.

While the tests are proceeding, officials caution that patients outside the study must continue to follow accepted treatment as prescribed by their physicians. Nothing yet has been proved, but at least the FDA finally recognizes the need to try to answer questions about Laetrile through careful research.

Lincoln Journal

Lincoln, Neb., January 7, 1980

At the request of the Food and Drug Administration, the National Cancer Institute is going to test Laetrile as a cancer-arresting substance. Experiments are to be conducted on 200 to 300 patients — with their prior approval, of course.

This must be regarded as a forward step, considering the national controversy over Laetrile. (The Nebraska Legislature is to resume debate on a Laetrile-legalizing bill in a matter of days.)

If the stuff is as worthless as the established medical community claims, the upcoming controlled tests should provide a higher and more convincing level of demonstrated proof. On the other hand, the results could be surprising. Nothing is lost, and a considerable much is to be gained either way, in making the research effort.

Coincident with the FDA's common sense decision about testing Laetrile comes health-related news of a different sort. The FDA has sanctioned the experimental use of an artificial blood substitute called Fluosol. Only for patients who have exhausted all conventional medical treatments may it be prescribed.

This is of particularly special interest to people who are Jehovah's Witnesses. Their religious belief prevents them participating in or even approving any blood transfusions — a belief which when implemented always produces an intense personal drama and sometimes a human drama of national interest.

Dr. Ron Lapin of Santa Ana, Calif., has done two of the three transfusions so far recorded utilizing the blood substitute. He is wisely cautious. Still, he suspects that the substance could prolong the lives of patients who might otherwise bleed to death, refusing transfusions.

Especially with the Jehovah's Witnesses in mind, the California doctor reportedly is trying to develop what he calls bloodless surgery. That involves electric cautery techniques. Backstopping it may be Fluosol.

This strikes us as another medical research area that the FDA should probe more extensively. It could be that a scientific development keyed to solve the unique medical problems of a specific religious sect may have therapeutic application for all peoples.

Chicago Tribune

Chicago, Ill., January 26, 1980

The Food and Drug Administration has given a conditional go-ahead for clinical tests, on humans, of the controversial cancer drug Laetrile. In view of the FDA's long and inflexible opposition to Laetrile—which has kept the drug from being manufactured in the United States or shipped in interstate commerce—this seems a startling about-face. Has the FDA all along been less certain than it seemed that Laetrile was worthless? Is it, in fact, now admitting that it might have been wrong and that the drug may have cancer-fighting capabilities after all?

Well, not exactly. The decision to let the National Cancer Institute begin tests had been long expected, and is based less on medical reasons than psychological ones. Laetrile just isn't going to go away, no matter what the FDA says. So it might as well have the facts established as impartially and convincingly as possible, and let them speak for themselves.

The decision makes sense. Faith in Laetrile is hard to uproot because so many people want desperately to believe in it. Understandably, cancer victims and their families seize on whatever evidence they can find for Laetrile and discount all the evidence against it. Pressure from the believers has made some states ease the restrictions on it.

But if the drug really is ineffective against cancer, this confidence in it can have tragic results—as it did in the case of Chad Green, the 3-year-old leukemia victim whose parents last year defied court orders to stop treating him with Laetrile. They took him to a Laetrile clinic in Mexico and triumphantly pronounced him cured; two months later, Chad was dead of leukemia. [Laetrile's defenders promptly claimed, as they always do, that the system of treatment was at fault, not the drug.]

One of Laetrile's effects, moreover, is to release a high concentration of cyanide into the bloodstream. For that reason, the FDA made its approval of the tests conditional on a three-month toxicity study on six patients.

The FDA expects, as do we, that the tests will prove Laetrile ineffective. It cannot realistically hope that the proof will convince believers that they've been wrong, but it should help keep to a minimum a tragic traffic in misplaced hopes.

This step is so sensible, in fact, that it brings up a final question: Why didn't the FDA approve these tests earlier? That's easy: The FDA is a Washington bureaucracy, which means that any decision it takes, sensible or other, requires at least a year to put into effect.

EVENING EXPRESS

Portland, Me., January 7, 1980

After years of controversy and legal battles, the drug Laetrile finally is going to be thoroughly tested in four highly reputable American medical centers.

It's a welcome decision. It should establish once and for all whether the drug, refined from apricot pits, really is useful in the treatment of cancer. If it is, certainly it should be made available. If it is not, let the sentence be pronounced conclusively and with finality and perhaps save thousands from false hopes and unnecessary expenditures.

Preliminary tests on six cancer patients at the Mayo Clinic in Rochester, Minn., established that at least Laetrile could be tested more extensively without endangering anyone.

For years the National Cancer Institute, the American Cancer Society and the Food and Drug Administration have argued that Laetrile has no therapeutic value in the treatment of cancer. The FDA prohibited interstate shipment of it. Many have been prosecuted for violating that prohibition. Thousands of cancer victims have gone to Mexico for treatment and 21 states have legalized it.

Some authorities condemned its use as quackery which diverted cancer patients away from therapy which might have been effective. Nevertheless, an estimated 70,000 Americans have resorted to it in seeking relief from the dread disease.

Now it will be tried on 200 to 300 persons with advanced cancer. That may be challenged by those who will suggest that it should be tried at an earlier stage of the disease. But the counter claim is that in its earlier stages, cancer will respond to established methods of treatment.

The insistence on use of Laetrile by so many sufferers persuaded the Cancer Institute to authorize the tests. Results won't be known for another two years. But if nothing more, the extensive experiment should take the controversy out of Laetrile.

The San Diego Union

San Diego, Cal., January 7, 1980

For nearly 25 years, Laetrile's defenders have insisted that this extract of apricot pits and bitter almonds is a useful agent in combating human cancers. Its detractors, including the bulk of the medical and scientific community, contend that Laetrile is worthless in treating cancer or anything else.

In the absence of conclusive testing and medical studies, the debate would probably continue indefinitely. Meanwhile, cancer patients who use Laetrile as well as those who don't might never know whether their treatment regimens were accordingly enhanced or compromised.

The logical way to resolve the Laetrile debate is so obvious we can only wonder why it has taken a quarter of a century for the U.S. Food and Drug Administration and the National Cancer Institute to agree on a comprehensive program of tests.

Both have rejected all past claims made on Laetrile's behalf. But neither the FDA's ban on the importation or interstate shipment of Laetrile nor the National Cancer Institute's official skepticism has prevented tens of thousands of cancer patients from obtaining the substance abroad or through a network of sympathetic physicians in this country. And, in just the last few years, the pro-Laetrile lobby has persuaded the legislatures of 20 states to legalize use of Laetrile as a "dietary supplement."

The few independent studies of Laetrile and its effects on cancer patients have either proved inconclusive or are disputed by one side or the other.

The comprehensive clinical tests sanctioned last week by the FDA will involve four of the nation's most prestigious cancer research institutions; the Mayo Clinic, UCLA Medical Center, the University of Arizona, and the Sloan-Kettering Institute for Cancer Research.

The results of these tests may not persuade everyone, but they will undoubtedly shed much additional light on a question that could and should have been resolved years ago.

Reno Evening Gazette

Reno, Nev., January 21, 1980

The federal Food and Drug Administration is taking a much-needed step in ordering clinical tests of Laetrile.

Despite emphatic opinions both pro and con, there has been no definitive verdict on whether the substance is an effective cancer treatment or a sham. Considering the growing popularity of Laetrile, this lack of information is creating unnecessary difficulties for doctors, patients and the friends and loved ones of sick persons.

It would be in the best interests of everyone for the controversy to be resolved quickly one way or the other. For if the drug is effective, the FDA ban against it is cheating many individuals out of helpful medical aid. On the other hand, if it is ineffective, the substance is cheating those who manage to obtain it despite the ban — cheating them of their money and, in some cases, of better treatment.

As long as no one knows for sure, terminally ill cancer patients will continue to seek it out, hoping it will provide the miracle that modern science cannot. But neither they nor their loved ones will know for certain if their efforts are a waste of time and money, or an opportunity for a new lease on life.

For this reason alone — to provide a much-needed answer — a complete study is advisable. But the study is also advisable to halt the growing stream of contraband and to protect dying persons from being forced into unsettling tangles with the law or exhausting and costly trips to other nations such as Mexico.

At present, unless a person can afford a foreign trip, he will probably have to break the law to obtain Laetrile. That is true even in Nevada and many of the 16 other states which have legalized the substance in some form or another. For in June the U.S. Supreme Court upheld the law banning Laetrile from interstate commerce.

This ruling meant that, if Laetrile cannot not be produced inside a given state, it can be obtained only through illegal means after the existing supply runs out. Production of Laetrile requires apricot orchards, because the substance is derived from the pits of this fruit. And at the time of the high court ruling, Nevada Health Officer John Carr said Nevada had no orchards for Laetrile production, nor did he think it was financially feasible to plant them. So, for Nevadans, the only route to Laetrile is outside the country or outside the law.

Even if the drug is found to be useless, of course, there is no guarantee that sick persons will not continue to evade the law, at great personal effort and expense. But a reliable report indicating the substance has no value should reduce this number considerably.

But will the FDA tests be conclusive enough to convince people one way or the other?

One would hope so. The tests will be conducted by the National Cancer Institute on as many as 300 volunteers in advanced stages of illness. The tests will be held at four prestigious research centers, including the University of California at Los Angeles. If the tests indicate Laetrile is effective as an anti-cancer agent, more extensive tests will be ordered.

These procedures appear satisfactory. So an answer should be forthcoming.

And then a great many minds will be eased, one way or the other. And that will be a good thing both for the medical community and its patients.

The Philadelphia Inquirer

Philadelphia, Pa., January 8, 1980

The Food and Drug Administration has given tentative approval to the National Cancer Institute for clinical tests of Laetrile, a drug, made of apricot seeds, which is supposed to cure cancer. The FDA's decision, a reversal of its long-standing opposition to such tests, should do no harm and may do some good.

The likelihood that Laetrile will turn out to be effective is at best remote. Until now, the FDA has opposed clinical tests on humans on the ground that the drug (which contains cyanide) is not only ineffective but unsafe. It has banned it from being shipped in interstate commerce, and the U.S. Supreme Court has unanimously upheld its authority to do so. The medical profession is virtually unanimous in agreeing with the FDA. Tests of Laetrile have been made many times on animals. Invariably, they have turned out negative.

Why, then, has the FDA reversed itself? "Because," an FDA spokesman explains, "there's a legitimate public question about the safety and effectiveness of Laetrile."

To put it another way, there are quite a few people who, notwithstanding the evidence — or rather, lack of evidence — to prove Laetrile's worth still believe in it. They are themselves suffering from cancer. Their cases may be terminal. Nothing else has worked. They are desperate. They want to believe.

Yet, as the longshoreman-philosopher Eric Hoffer once observed, "It is startling to realize how much unbelief is necessary to make belief possible." Those who believe in Laetrile do not believe their government, of which the FDA is a part. They do not believe in organized medicine, which they accuse — contrary to all rationality — of wanting to stifle a cure for cancer.

Will such people be persuaded by the results of the clinical tests if these, to be conducted at four prestigious cancer research centers, turn out to be negative? Sadly, it must be expected that some will not.

Many others, however, should be persuaded by the clinical tests, and perhaps the possibility that Laetrile is not a quack cure should be left open at this time. Neither the cure for cancer nor the cure for credulity has been discovered, but every feasible effort to find them should be explored.

The Star-Ledger

Newark, N.J., July 15, 1980

Having successfully completed preliminary safety screening, the controversial drug laetrile is now being given to cancer patients participating in government-sponsored tests.

The National Cancer Institute authorized the testing after a limited two-month trial in which six cancer patients at Mayo Clinic were given the drug, five of whom experienced no ill effects. A sixth patient had problems only after eating a large number of almonds. When the almonds were eliminated from the diet, the problem disappeared.

Government officials have long contended that laetrile — made from apricot pits and other fruit kernels — is worthless against cancer but some 70,000 Americans have used the drug, despite a federal Food and Drug Administration ban on interstate shipping and American Cancer Society pronouncements that there is no evidence that laetrile is effective.

Many users have been desperate persons who have not responded to accepted forms of treatment, and their desperation has led to the legalization of the substance in 19 states, including New Jersey.

Significantly, the government-sponsored tests will be restricted to patients who have not been helped by conventional medical procedures.

Participants, 200 in number, will be given laetrile in oral or intravenous form. They will also be required to maintain largely vegetarian diets, which laetrile advocates say is essential for those using the drug.

Under the present timetable, results of the tests at the four medical centers are not expected to be known for two years. Considering the years of controversy, however, that is a short time to wait.

In the initial announcement of the testing, the National Cancer Institute said the trial should determine "once and for all" whether laetrile is effective in the treatment of advanced cases of cancer.

A definitive answer would be worth the waiting.

The Courier-Journal

Louisville, Ky., October 24, 1980

THE SUPREME COURT has wisely rejected the argument that terminally ill cancer patients wanting to use laetrile have a constitutional right that overrides the government's interest in protecting the public against medical quackery.

The final verdict on laetrile, made from apricot pits, is still pending. Some doctors support its use, or at least defend the right of the terminally ill to grasp any straw. Others say it's a fraud on the gullible, and this view has prevailed. The Food and Drug Administration has banned interstate sale or distribution of the product until its worth is proven to the satisfaction of medical authorities.

Past court rulings have protected a patient's right to refuse medical treatment on religious or other grounds. But the Supreme Court has effectively modified this right by upholding a lower court ruling on laetrile. Without changing the right of refusal, it says the selection of a particular treatment or medication is within the area of government responsibility to protect public health.

Part of that government responsibility is being discharged through the long-delayed tests of laetrile being sponsored by the National Cancer Institute at four major cancer clinics. If the product works, then obviously federal authorities would have to change their tune.

It may seem inconsistent for the Supreme Court to place protection from quackery ahead of the asserted privacy-right of dying cancer patients to choose any medicine they can afford. But the money being made in the laetrile trade offers some evidence that a completely unregulated public-health marketplace would be full of exploiters and dupes.

About $300,000 worth of laetrile a month, enough to supply some 4,000 cancer patients, has been entering the country legally under an import permit that is likely to dry up in the wake of the Supreme Court action. All told, an estimated 70,000 Americans are using laetrile, most of them with supplies smuggled from Mexico.

Throughout the history of this product, the normal disciplines for medical experiment and drug-testing have been open to laetrile practitioners. But both laetrile patients and doctors have been unusually skeptical of the good will of scientific medicine. This skepticism and refusal to cooperate in scientific testing, in turn, have strengthened the suspicion that the profit motive is the chief engine of laetrile promotion.

Perhaps so: the results of the National Cancer Institute tests, which are due in about a year, could do much to clear the air. Meantime, a drawback of the Supreme Court's action is that the laetrile "underground" may go further into hiding. And no one can be sure that negative findings would be accepted by laetrile's advocates.

The wealthy, at least, can always find succor, such as the $10,000-a-month course of "holistic" care being received by cancer-stricken actor Steve McQueen in Mexico. And only a fool would argue with those who say that faith in a "cure" may sometimes be the ideal medicine.

But one purpose of government is to protect society against those who fraudulently prey on its fears for personal profit. Today's wild eccentric or even "quack" may be tomorrow's Nobel Prize winner. But first he must show results extending beyond his own wallet.

THE INDIANAPOLIS NEWS

Indianapolis, Ind., April 9, 1980

American medical research may not deserve the bum rap it has received over laetrile, but it has done little so far to erase it.

In spite of growing numbers of personal testimonies supporting laetrile in treating cancer, the medical profession has scoffed at the claims of "cured" patients and has denounced laetrile as worthless.

Now, the pendulum may be swinging; the first phase of a major study on the effects of laetrile has begun at the Mayo Clinic in Rochester, Minn.

About a week ago the first patient began receiving laetrile and five more will be receiving it soon. Three patients will receive oral laetrile and three will receive it intravenously. Each patient must receive laetrile for from seven to 21 days in a test of possible toxicity demanded by the National Cancer Institute, which is sponsoring the study. The patients are volunteers for whom standard cancer therapy has failed.

After the first phase has been completed, the cancer institute will evaluate the results and probably continue into a planned second phase in which 250 patients will be treated at Mayo, the University of California at Los Angeles, the University of Arizona at Tucson and Memorial Sloan-Kettering Cancer Center at New York.

Laetrile is a substance that develops naturally in the pits of apricots and other fruits and is given in connection with a special enzyme and vitamin diet. It has been a subject of intense controversy within the American medical profession and the Food and Drug Administration. Both groups have ridiculed the claims of hundreds of Americans who say that they have been cured or their cancers arrested by journeying to Mexico.

These pressure groups have managed to have laetrile banned from interstate shipment, but many states, including Indiana, have declared it to be a legal substance. Scores of Indiana cancer-sufferers make regular pilgrimages to Mexico to obtain their laetrile and to consult their Mexican doctors.

Now, at an inexcusably tardy hour, Americans should learn from unbiased American researchers and doctors if laetrile is worthwhile or worthless.

Los Angeles Times

Los Angeles, Cal., April 15, 1980

Cancer is an enigma; Laetrile is not. Despite millions of dollars spent on research, scientists still haven't found the answers on the cause and treatment of cancer. But one thing that all the distinguished authorities on treating cancer do know is that Laetrile is worthless, possibly even harmful. For that reason, the Food and Drug Administration has banned the substance, made from apricot pits, from interstate commerce.

Even in the face of scientific evidence that Laetrile does nothing to help cancer patients, the drumbeat on the back of the snake-oil wagon goes on. Step right up, folks, get your legislature to legislate what your doctor won't prescribe. Yes sir, folks, it's happening right up there in river city, right up there in Sacramento.

The Senate Health and Welfare Committee has sent on to the Senate Finance Committee a bill, sponsored by Senate Republican leader William Campbell of Whittier, that would legalize Laetrile for the treatment of seriously ill cancer patients. There are some safeguards in the bill, in that patients would have to be given consent forms explaining the risks and benefits of Laetrile as well as those of conventional forms of treatment such as chemotherapy, radiation and surgery. The forms would encourage patients to consult a second doctor who specializes in conventional treatment.

That is not enough for the American Cancer Society or the California Medical Assn., and it is not enough for us. There is no scientific evidence that Laetrile does anything for anybody, and there are some signs that it is not innocuous, because it contains cyanide. Even though Campbell's measure specifies that Laetrile be legalized only for use by terminally ill patients, we don't think in practice that that limit would be successful. We fear the effect on patients whose cancers are potentially curable but who might turn to Laetrile because it appears less debilitating than chemotherapy or surgery. Even for the terminally ill, Laetrile could be a cruel hoax, leading them to spend money on something that is worthless.

During committee discussions, Campbell agreed to let the legislation expire Jan. 1, 1985, to allow the Legislature time to reconsider the law once the National Cancer Institute has completed studies now under way on Laetrile's safety and effectiveness. We think this approach is somewhat backward —that is, the state should wait to act on Laetrile until after it learns whether scientists, not politicians, consider it safe.

Campbell views the issue as "human liberties versus paternalistic big government." We think that there is nothing wrong, and everything right, with government following the concept that any father or mother would follow: offering protection from medical and financial harm.

This is a question not of free choice but of bad choice. The state of California should not raise false hopes by putting what amounts to a stamp of approval on this snake-oil solution. □

ST. LOUIS POST-DISPATCH

St. Louis, Mo., October 24, 1980

The recent Supreme Court action upholding the Food and Drug Administration's control over laetrile leaves the future of the controversial substance up to scientific proof of usefulness, as it should be. In the case before the court, a cancer patient had asserted a right of privacy to make his own medical choice as to what treatment to follow. The high court affirmed a lower court ruling that said, "The decision...whether to have treatment or not is a protected right, but his selection of a particular treatment, or at least a medication, is within the area of government interest in protecting public health."

Numerous tests have so far failed to demonstrate any effectiveness for laetrile. But the FDA has not been unresponsive to the lobbying of laetrile proponents, and four clinical tests are now taking place. What the FDA requires is not a showing that laetrile is a 100 percent effective cure for cancer, but that it is useful in treating some form of the disease. If that basic requirement is not met, and it has not been yet, the use of laetrile ought not to be permitted, for it is a cruel hoax on patients who may be helped by other, more painful, treatments.

The right to privacy argument may appeal to the public's belief in individual liberty, but in this case it cannot prevail over the government's responsibility to ensure that drugs sanctioned for use in this country meet safety and effectiveness standards. Laetrile's real day in court will come with the test results from the laboratory.

THE SACRAMENTO BEE

Sacremento, Cal., October 3, 1980

Add the following to the lists of things we don't completely understand: In Washington, the Food and Drug Administration, under pressure from consumer groups, agrees to order the removal from the market of some 3,000 medicines whose effectiveness has not been demonstrated. The largest seller of those medicines, which must be removed from the market within four years — assuming the order is not reversed — is Dimetapp, a cough syrup and decongestant that is fed routinely every day to thousands of children with hacks and runny noses. In Sacramento, meanwhile, the Legislature passes, and the governor signs, a bill legalizing the limited use of Laetrile in the treatment of cancer, a substance whose effectiveness has not been proven either.

Since we approved of the Legislature's action on Laetrile we feel that consistency demands that we disapprove of what the FDA is doing; yet we're not entirely comfortable with that position. In part, we can explain the apparent paradox by saying that while the government ought not to prevent desperately ill people from receiving a form of treatment in which they passionately believe, it ought to do its best to protect the casual consumer from spending a lot of money on worthless drugs even if they are prescribed by doctors. Further, we might also say that there hasn't been nearly as much of an opportunity to test the effectiveness of Laetrile as there has to test Dimetapp and many of the other preparations the FDA wants removed from the market.

Still, we acknowledge the paradox, and while we suspect that no one is as passionate about Dimetapp as some people are about Laetrile — certainly not the 5-year-olds who have to drink the stuff — that does not resolve the inconsistency. Thus, there remains the suspicion that it is political clout which is removing Dimetapp, etc., from the market and political clout which is putting Laetrile on it. That conclusion could easily justify a thorough re-examination of all government policy about the licensing of drugs. If a preparation is safe, after all, why not allow it to be sold, even if it hasn't been proven effective, provided only that it is so labeled? Caution, the label might say, this stuff probably won't hurt you, but it probably won't help you either.

Such an examination, particularly given the current mood of deregulation, might be worthwhile in any case. Why should the government interfere with the free market decisions of consumers who, knowing the doubtful effectiveness of something or other, want to buy it anyway? Indeed, if the government got out of what appears to be the business of blessing the effectiveness of the drugs it licenses, all consumers of medication might be more cautious about what they ingest and more searching in the questions they ask their doctors. They might even take more responsibility, as the government often suggests, for their own health.

Yet here again, we feel some hesitation, some caution about how this might all work in the real world. If it were certain that deregulated drugs would be honestly labeled and not advertised as capable of effecting cures that they cannot effect — something that even now seems difficult to enforce — then we might be more comfortable. As it is, maybe we'd rather live with the inconsistency.

Drug Firms Sued over DES, Synthetic Hormone Linked to Cancer

Between 1947 and 1964, more than one million American women had taken diethylstilbestrol, an artificial hormone, to lessen the risk of miscarriage during pregnancy. By 1971, doctors were warning of the risks of vaginal cancer to daughters born to women who had taken DES. Studies carried out between 1977 and 1978 indicated no direct link between DES and vaginal cancer, but a number of women whose mothers had taken the drug sued the manufacturers and were awarded large amounts in damages. By early 1980, new research pointed to an increase in miscarriages and premature births among the daughters of women who had taken DES. The drug could still be used to treat symptoms of menopause and cancer of the breasts and prostate. The Food and Drug Administration had banned its use as a growth stimulant for cattle and sheep in 1979.

The Washington Star

Washington, D.C., April 6, 1978

Which of us, stumbling over a chair in the dark, hasn't had an impulse to kick the chair? Whenever anything unfortunate happens, we all want to blame somebody or something.

There are, of course, times when somebody *is* to blame. These days, though, law and social custom operate more and more on the assumption that there is no bad luck of any kind that can't be explained by the evil-doing of prosperous villains. When in doubt, sue.

Item: A New Jersey drug company that manufactured a hormone used to prevent miscarriages has just agreed to pay damages to a cancer victim whose mother took the hormone 25 years ago. The hormone is now believed to cause vaginal cancer in a small number of women whose mothers took it.

A connoisseur of logic would not, perhaps, call the evidence any more compelling than the data that says laetrile is worthless or the coincidences suggesting that cigarettes and whiskey may be bad for people. Just enough to sue on.

The successful lawsuit against a manufacturer of diethylstilbestrol, or DES, as the hormone is commonly called, claims that the drug company was negligent in testing it. It's a claim that presents some first-class mind-bogglers.

Where does responsibility begin and end in selling any product? Twenty-five years ago, when this medicament came on the market, there was considerably less awareness of side effects than there is now — among doctors and pharmaceutical manufacturers as well as among non-professional citizens. How fair is it to hold them responsible for that a quarter of a century later?

Since the alleged effects of this drug take a generation to appear, it is possible to imagine that seemingly reasonable checking on the soundness of the product would fail to identify the hazard. Particularly since human guinea pigs are hard to find in meaningful numbers for drug testing and we know that the laboratory kind can't tell us all there is to know.

We have reason to suspect that trusting laboratory animals has led to some overblown panics on other products anyway. How many soft drinks a day was it that a human being would have to consume for how many years to fall victim to saccharin?

And then there are the ironies. The traffic in contraband laetrile. Prosperity in the tobacco and alcohol industries. And, apparently, no woman who's been dying her hair is going to let the prospect of cancer scare her away from having more fun as a blond.

Does the out-of-court settlement in the Canrick Laboratories case tell us about changing ideas of justice and responsibility? Or simply about changing estimates of what the threat of bad publicity can pry out of a drug company in an era of militant consumerism?

The Canrick case is one of the first DES lawsuits to be settled. Undoubtedly, it will set a precedent through which other cancer victims will collect from other drug companies manufacturing the hormone during the 1940s and '50s. Undoubtedly, too, the net result will be wider testing of pharmaceuticals. Think of the way malpractice suits have caused doctors to increase the number of tests they give so nobody can say in court that they didn't. Sure it's expensive, but the insurance pays.

The prospect is for an upward spiral on drug prices and on government regulations delaying the release of new products when it doesn't outlaw them altogether. How the cost/benefit balance will come out for the consumer is a good deal less certain.

Nobody wants to defend the cynical snake oil vendors of yesteryear. Or, for that matter, the cynical snake oil vendors who, in one form or another, survive today. But *ex post facto* judgments on the research inadequacies of a quarter of a century ago seem to us to deny that risk is as inescapable an element in medication as the promise of betterment. The quest for total safety can become self-defeating. The more bans and barriers and testing requirements pile up, the brisker the trade in laetrile.

ST. LOUIS POST-DISPATCH

St. Louis, Mo., September 26, 1978

Federal Food and Drug Administration proceedings leading toward a possible ban of DES, a cancer-causing hormone used to stimulate cattle growth, are moving, after six years, toward a conclusion. The process of reaching a final decision has been slowed by the federal courts' insistence on providing due process for a suspected hazardous chemical before its use can be banned as a threat to human health.

The FDA first banned DES as an additive in animal feed in 1972 and as an animal implant in 1973. But a U.S. appeals court overturned the bans in 1974 because the FDA had not held a hearing. Hearings have now been held. And FDA Administrative Law Judge Daniel Davidson has just recommended a ban after ruling that the existence of DES residues in food has been "sufficiently established" and there isn't any known level below which it doesn't cause human or animal cancer. FDA Commissioner Donald Kennedy can now issue a final ruling following a 50-day comment period.

Although meat production had gotten along for years without the use of DES, this artificial substance, introduced without adequate knowledge of its safety, suddenly acquired legal rights because its manufacturers wanted to sell it and cattle producers wanted to use it in order to hasten growth and reduce feed costs. Judge Davidson has found, however, that the economic benefits don't outweigh the risks to health.

An issue of public safety should not have to hinge on years of legal wrangling over due process for a chemical. Rather, the rule should be that a product may not be put on the market until its makers have demonstrated by thorough testing that it is safe. Most consumers undoubtedly would rather pay an extra cost, necessitated by animal feeding, than to be subjected to a cancer-causing substance that they only find out about years after they have been exposed to it.

ST. LOUIS POST-DISPATCH

St. Louis, Mo., December 14, 1979

The Michigan Court of Appeals has handed down a decision that should make drug manufacturers a little more cautious about what they put on the market. Reversing a circuit court judge's ruling, the appellate court held that women who risk health problems because their mothers took the synthetic hormone, DES, can sue all manufacturers that distributed it in Michigan at the time. The circuit court had held that the women had to be able to identify which manufacturer made the DES their mothers took.

In Michigan 165 women and 17 of their husbands had sued 16 makers of the drug in that state, claiming that all of the women whose mothers took DES to prevent miscarriages have cancer or precancerous lesions. The suit contends that most women have no way of knowing which company made the DES prescribed for their mothers. What the appellate ruling apparently does, therefore, is to divide the liability in the event that the ultimate decision is against the manufacturers.

If liability is eventually upheld, the decision could have wide consequences, since the drug was made by more than 300 firms and it was taken by an estimated 6 million women over two decades. One of the defenses advanced in behalf of the manufacturers is that DES was approved by the Food and Drug Administration in 1947 for treating threatened miscarriage. The question now — after the drug has been found to be both dangerous and of doubtful effectiveness — is whether the makers should be relieved of responsibility because an understaffed and often pliant federal agency allowed a product to be used without adequate testing. Should not rigid testing be an obligation of manufacturers that want to produce and make a profit from a new product?

Chicago Tribune

Chicago, Ill., September 3, 1979

It's easy to sympathize with the young Chicago woman who last week was awarded $800,000 in damages from White Laboratories of New Jersey by a federal district court jury. Anne Needham, 26, charged that the vaginal cancer she suffered was caused by diethylstilbesterol [DES] taken by her mother to prevent miscarriage before her birth in 1953.

But the award, which White Laboratories says it will appeal, raises troublesome questions about the legal and moral liability of pharmaceutical companies when products which seem safe and useful turn out — perhaps decades later — to have unforeseeable side effects.

DES was considered to be an urgently needed, potent, inexpensive, synthetic estrogen when first produced in 1938. It was approved by the Food and Drug Administration [FDA] in 1947 for treating threatened miscarriage.

Studies by respected researchers in medical journals cited the apparent effectiveness of DES. Not a patented drug, it was manufactured as a generic product by more than 300 pharmaceutical companies and taken by an estimated 6 million pregnant women over more than two decades. The question of damage to unborn babies wasn't considered. Until the thalidomide tragedy in 1961, doctors believed no harmful substances could cross the placenta from the mother's body to reach the unborn infant.

Some doubts were raised about the effectivness of DES in preventing miscarriage late in the 1950s and use of the drug dropped off. But it wasn't until 1971 that physicians linked a rare form of vaginal cancer in adolescent girls with the DES their mothers had taken years earlier during pregnancy.

As physicians began locating and checking daughters of DES-treated mothers, they were dismayed to find one-third had an abnormality called adenosis. Doctors feared it might be a forerunner of cancer and that an epidemic of vaginal cancer was about to occur.

So far, the worst of these fears have not been realized. About 350 cases of vaginal cancer have been found in the United States [about one-third in women with no known exposure to DES]. Doctors think most can be cured if caught early. And encouragingly, studies are beginning to show that adenosis does not develop into cancer, but tends to disappear spontaneously when these young women reach their late 20s.

Even so, serious problems remain. Young women exposed to DES prenatally need to be located and checked periodically for possible cancer. Many insurance companies are denying them insurance or cancelling their policies. And recent studies show that male offspring of DES-treated mothers may have some increased risk of genital tract abnormalities and impaired fertility.

The legal questions are even more complicated. Is it fair to hold the pharmaceutical companies responsible for producing a drug the FDA approved as safe and doctors said they needed? [Eli Lilly and Co., one DES manufacturer, already faces lawsuits seeking more than 1,000 times its total gross sales of DES for pregnancy use between 1947 and 1971.] Is the inconvenience of adenosis and fear of cancer sufficient reason to win legal damages? [Fewer than 10 per cent of 480 plaintiffs suing Lilly have cancer; the rest are other DES daughters, mothers, fathers, husbands, or sons.]

Holding the companies liable for unanticipated consequences that occur decades later may seriously curtail their willingness to take the financial risk of developing new medications — which would be a serious loss to us all.

Should the federal government pick up the tab for DES-related problems? It has already set up a DES registry to collect data and do research. But DES volunteer groups are pushing for a federal law similar to one passed in New York state which would finance a national education campaign, a screening program, follow-up care, and treatment — and prohibit the cancellation of insurance. But this humane solution does carry the hazard of uncontrollable cost.

There well may be some risks individuals simply have to assume for themselves and their children.

SUNDAY TELEGRAM

Worcester, Mass., September 7, 1979

A young Chicago woman, Anne Needham, has been awarded $800,000 in damages from White Laboratories of New Jersey by a federal district court jury.

The woman sued because she had vaginal cancer, allegedly caused by diethylstilbesterol (DES), taken by her mother to prevent miscarriage before her birth in 1953.

The case, which will be appealed, raises a host of questions.

In the first place, did Anne Needham sue the guilty party? The Food and Drug Administration (FDA) had certified the drug in 1947 for treatment of threatened miscarriage. Several drug companies were manufacturing and selling DES, in those days considered a wonder drug.

It was not until the thalidomide tragedy of 1961 that doctors and scientists realized that harmful substances could cross the placenta from the mother's body to reach the unborn infant. It was not until 1971 that a rare form of vaginal cancer in young girls was linked to the DES their mothers had taken years before.

Although fears were expressed that an epidemic of this rare form of cancer was in the offing, so far only 350 cases have been identified. About a third of those are in women with no known exposure to DES.

There has been an epidemic of litigation, however. Eli Lilly and Co., one DES manufacturer, is facing hundreds of lawsuits, many of them from husbands and relatives of those affected. If the company is found liable for millions of dollars in damages, what will that mean for the future development of drugs to prevent diseases? All new drugs pose risks, no matter how thoroughly tested in laboratories on animals.

Is the federal government liable in any way? The FDA has set up a register for DES problems, but so far is restricting its actions to research.

This is a devilishly complex and painful subject, made worse by the legal ramifications.

It is ironic to consider that, if Anne Needham's mother's doctor had not prescribed DES back there in 1953, the result might have been a miscarriage and no Anne Needham to bring a damage suit today.

But would the doctor have been subject to a lawsuit then, on the ground that he failed to prescribe a certified and widely recommended drug to prevent miscarriages?

At some point in matters like these, common sense must be brought to bear. Legal maneuvering is not enough.

THE SACRAMENTO BEE

Sacremento, Cal., March 30, 1980

Between 1947 and 1971, as many as 3 million pregnant women in the United States took diethylstilbesterol (DES), an artificial estrogen drug that was supposed to prevent miscarriages, and one generation later it is coming back to haunt them and their offspring. In disproportionate numbers, their daughters are suffering from vaginal and cervical cancers which require radical surgery and from dangerous precancerous growths that must be regularly monitored.

Not surprisingly, several DES daughters have sued the drug companies which manufactured DES. They have asked for compensatory and punitive damages for themselves; on behalf of other victims, they want the drug companies ordered to publicize the DES situation and to pay for screening clinics. So far, they have lost almost every case.

One can legitimately question whether the drug companies should be held responsible for the damage done to DES daughters. The daughters claim that the drug companies knew — or should have known — the dangers of DES, that they failed to adequately test and monitor the drug and that they did not inform patients and doctors of its experimental status. The drug companies argue that there was no good reason at the time to conclude that DES caused cancer and that they couldn't forewarn about this particular DES risk because they couldn't foresee it.

However, this is not the issue on which the cases have been lost. Indeed, in the only two cases in which this real dispute between the daughters and the drug companies has been resolved, the DES daughters won. Every other DES case was dismissed because the women involved couldn't prove which of the 200 or so drug companies that manufactured DES made the particular pills that their mothers took 20 or more years ago. Although about 90 percent of the DES sold in the United States was produced by only six or seven companies, no company could be held responsible for any one woman's injury when it was as likely as not that some other company caused it.

It was, thus, a major breakthrough for the DES daughters when the California Supreme Court recently decided that they need not identify the particular company that manufactured the particular pills their mothers took. If this information is unavailable, the court ruled, a daughter can sue those companies that manufactured "a substantial share of the DES which her mother might have taken." And if she wins her suit, each of those companies will have to pay a proportion of the settlement based on its share of the DES market.

The new rule is fairer to the DES victims, who will now get their day in court, and it more realistically reflects today's world in which drug side-effects can show up generations later, in which prescriptions are often for generic rather than brand-name drugs and in which drug testing and labeling are essentially uniform throughout the industry.

But as it was written, the decision is unnecessarily broad. The court has thrown open a new door to lawsuits against manufacturers, without imposing adequate protections against abuse. It did not specify how big a share of the market manufacturers would have to have before they could be sued as a group, didn't indicate what effort would have to be made to determine the actual manufacturer of a faulty product before the court would allow a whole industry to be sued, and didn't decide how similar the conduct of several manufacturers would have to be before they could be found proportionally liable.

The laws governing a manufacturer's liability for the injuries its products cause is already tricky. It requires the courts to tread a very fine line between assigning blame according to actual negligence and assigning responsibility for accidents to the party most able to bear it. The court's decision to remove the artificial barrier that had prevented consideration of the DES cases need not have upset the balance between these two principles, But the court's vagueness in describing its new rule has provided too many opportunities to penalize companies simply because they can afford to pay damages. It will have to be refined.

The Wichita
Eagle-Beacon

Wichita, Kans., April 9, 1980

The growing flap over the illegal implantation of a cancer-causing growth stimulant in feedlot cattle shows signs of boiling down to a case of "failure to communicate." The drug, diethylstilbestrol, more commonly known as DES, was not to have been sold after July 12, 1979, and not to have been implanted in beef cattle or sheep after Nov. 1, 1979.

Investigations by USDA and FDA officials however, have revealed that perhaps as many as 200,000 head of cattle now being fattened in feed yards for slaughter have been administered DES to speed their weight gain. Forty-five feedlots have been banned from selling DES-treated cattle for slaughter, and nearly half of that number are located in Western Kansas.

Both the feedlot operators and the supply companies that provided the DES to them claim they never received formal notification of the cutoff dates that applied to them. It is hard to believe, following the massive publicity on the carcinogenic effects of DES, and the government's moves to get it out of the food production chain, that the only people who weren't aware of those steps were the ones most directly affected by the curtailment.

But it is altogether possible that formal notification from an appropriate government agency wasn't forthcoming, as they claim. Certainly, the government shouldn't rely on word of mouth or media accounts to advise meat producers of such a major policy action. The investigators, who are continuing to check into the DES situation, should not shrink from pointing a likewise accusatory finger at the government if it did, in fact, fail to properly notify the makers, sellers and users of DES of the deadlines.

If the government is found culpable in that respect, it should share in the financial losses that a mandated delay in slaughtering cattle will produce. Once DES implants have been removed from the affected cattle's ears by approved veterinarians, the animals cannot be sold for 35 days — 63 days if their liver or kidneys are destined for human consumption — under the restrictions imposed. That will give the cattle time to eliminate the DES from their systems before they are slaughtered.

Obviously, the DES problem may have a stunning impact on the cattle industry, if the situation is as widespread as many believe. With beef prices already poor, such a turn of events promises only to make a bad situation even worse.

But, even though the use of DES as a cattle growth stimulant was commonplace for more than 25 years and scientists say that DES is a cancer threat only after an extended period of accumulation in the body, the government is right to show that it means business in putting an end to the substance's use as an artificial cattle fattening agent.

We only hope the government will be as enthusiastic and willing to share the blame if it turns out that it muffed the job of getting the word out on the harmful effects of DES.

THE DAILY OKLAHOMAN

Oklahoma City, Okla., May 2, 1980

CONTROVERSY over the 22-year-old Delaney amendment has been rekindled by the disclosure that 116 feedlots in 16 states, including 13 in Oklahoma, may have violated the federal ban on use of DES implants in livestock.

DES (diethylstilbestrol) was used to speed cattle growth on less feed until it was banned last year by the Food and Drug Administration. Before that, DES was used to prevent miscarriages and also as a "morning after" contraceptive.

Medical use of DES was halted after research indicated a higher than normal incidence of vaginal cancer in the daughters of women who had received DES during their pregnancies. Its manufacture was outlawed, and livestock implants were forbidden last Nov. 1.

The catalyst was the Delaney amendment to the food and drug act. It prohibits the addition to food of any substance found to cause cancer in either test animals or humans.

This law prompted the ban of the artificial sweetener, cyclamate, and caused the ongoing ruckus over the attempt to outlaw saccharin.

Few would quarrel with prohibiting any food additive that has been proved carcinogenic in humans. But many researchers question the validity of extrapolating huge dosages of test chemicals fed to animals into findings of cancer risk to humans.

The House Agriculture Committee has urged the FDA to recommend changes in the amendment. And FDA Commissioner Dr. Jere Goyan agrees that the law's "zero tolerance" should be reconsidered.

Livestock growers are gaining scientific support of their contention that outlawing DES implants in livestock will increase food costs and reduce meat production without making any real contribution to health protection.

Nutritionist Thomas Jukes at the University of California calculates the risk of cancer from eating DES-treated beef at about one case in 10,000 years. He notes that DES residue has never been detected in the muscle tissue of slaughtered beef and only miniscule amounts were found in livers or kidneys.

He estimated a human would have to eat more than 5,000 cattle livers and kidneys daily to get the amount of one DES pill formerly used by women. It recalls the cyclamate case, where a human would have to consume several hundred cans of diet soft drink every day to equal the dosage that caused bladder tumors in some laboratory rats.

This should comfort those who fear they might develop cancer from beef consumed before DES was banned. It also suggests that some relaxation of the Delaney amendment may be in the public interest.

'Miracle Drug' DMSO Wins FDA Approval for Limited Prescription Use

The Seattle Times

Seattle, Wash., March 28, 1978

DMSO, the controversial "wonder drug" that has an extraordinary ability to penetrate the unbroken skin and be absorbed into the body, has finally won the U.S. Food and Drug Administration's approval for commercial distribution and human use.

The F.D.A. approved DMSO use only for a particular bladder ailment, but most experts predicted that it would be prescribed for many other health problems as well.

DMSO (dimethyl sulfoxide) is made by the Research Industries Corp. of Salt Lake City, which has a license from the patent holder, the Crown Zellerbach Corp. A byproduct of paper production, it was discovered in Russia in the 19th Century.

In the early 1960s, Dr. Stanley W. Jacob, a University of Oregon Medical School surgeon, discovered its remarkable medical qualities. Studies have found that the drug can help relieve bursitis, rheumatism, warts, eczema, burns, gum disease, ear infection, whiplash, and cataracts. There are also indications that it may be helpful in treating spinal-cord and head injuries, heart disease, and strokes.

In the United States, DMSO has been legal only for animals — it is used widely to relieve stiff joints in race horses, for instance. But it has been available for years in Canada, Japan, Austria, Great Britain, Germany and Russia. The Oregon Legislature last year legalized its sale in that state, but there were no DMSO manufacturers in Oregon and it could not be imported from other states without breaking federal law.

The F.D.A.'s reluctance in granting approval apparently was based on fears that DMSO might become "another thalidomide" and cause birth defects or other harmful side effects. The hesitation also may be attributable to the facts that DMSO fits no existing category of drugs, is made for treating no specific disease, and most doctors aren't sure exactly how it works.

DMSO's remarkable properties may help relieve pain or other problems in many individuals. The long wait for F.D.A. approval — based more on bureaucratic delay than scientific evidence — hardly seems justified.

The Oregonian

Portland, Ore., March 22, 1978

In 1963, when Dr. Stanley W. Jacob of the University of Oregon Medical School ascribed certain medical properties to the forest industry byproduct "dimethyl sulfoxide," his discovery was hailed as "a major medical breakthrough comparable to the discovery of aspirin, insulin, the sulfa drugs, penicillin and cortisone."

Those may have been overly enthusiastic terms to describe the new wonder drug that came to be known as DMSO, but the U.S. Food and Drug Administration never gave the nation's medical schools or laboratories an opportunity to prove Dr. Jacob right or wrong, because within two years, the FDA had peremptorily ordered all experimentation stopped.

DMSO, which has the ability to be absorbed directly into the system, carries some of its own healing properties, but also can serve as a vehicle for other medication. It had been found to be of considerable value in treatment of muscular conditions, providing relief to sufferers of rheumatism, bursitis, arthritis, burns, sprains — even fractures.

Much experimentation was being carried out worldwide when from England came the news that "adverse effects" on the eyes of some test animals had been reported. Forthwith, the FDA banned further experimentation in this country and effectively stopped a research program that by now might have developed far broader fields than has been possible under the regulations imposed — relaxed though they have been to some extent, with some animal research and use permitted.

Monday's FDA blessing of the "wonder drug" still is relatively half-hearted, restricting the drug to use in treatment of a bladder ailment, but as one FDA official said, "Once a drug has been approved for any use, then the burden is on the practitioner to use it how he wants." Other nations, Russia, Germany, Japan, Canada, Austria, among them, have previously approved the drug.

The Oregonian has never been able to fathom the workings of the bureaucratic mind of the type that called off research into DMSO in the first place, and has said so many times. Probably, we should congratulate the agency for its decision; instead, an "It's about time" seems more in order.

Oregon Journal

Portland, Ore, March 23, 1978

At last, DMSO has been approved as a prescription drug for a specific disease. It is to be hoped that this first step toward fuller approval will be followed by others in orderly fashion.

Admittedly, the drug has been widely used by people to treat their own aches and pains after obtaining it illegally. Its reputation for reducing inflammation and promoting healing of broken bones and muscular strains is too widely known to be ignored. It is available in a form for use by veterinarians, which is not considered sufficiently pure for human treatment.

The long, frustrating examination of DMSO by the Food and Drug Administration probably has done as much to contribute to the illegal use of DMSO as its availability in what is an unsuitable but usable form. People suffering pain are not so much concerned with niceties like legality as they are with obtaining relief from that pain.

One of the difficulties of studying the effect of DMSO is that the usual "double blind" experiment is not appropriate to testing it. An unmistakable odor accompanies use of the drug.

A property of DMSO is its ability to penetrate the body directly through the skin, either alone or carrying with it another drug needed for treatment. Its value as a remarkable transfer agent may prove to be its greatest worth. Still another quality of DMSO is to increase the effectiveness of some of the other drugs used to treat illnesses.

It must be gratifying to Dr. Stanley Jacob and Robert J. Herschler, who uncovered the unusual properties of DMSO in 1962, to see a solid step forward. Dimethyl sulfoxide, to give DMSO its full name, had been known to exist for years previously, but had never been appreciated for its unique value.

Now, in the name of people who still endure unremitting pain and who suffer from maladies which may be in the province of DMSO to be treated, we must hope that the Food and Drug Administration will continue to move expeditiously toward further permissions to physicians to use this medicine.

FDA Approves Sale of Anti-Epilepsy Drug

The Food and Drug Administration Feb. 28 approved the use of sodium valproate in the treatment of epilepsy. The anti-convulsant drug would be marketed under the name Depakene by Abbott Laboratories, which had done the research leading to the FDA approval. Valproate had been widely used in Europe during the 1970s, and U.S. experts and epilepsy foundations had pressured the FDA to permit its use in the U.S. In an unusual move, the FDA advised Abbott Laboratories to request marketing approval, which was granted in much shorter time than normal. Under the terms of the FDA approval, Depakene could be prescribed for both minor epileptic seizures, which involved a brief loss of consciousness ("petit mal"), and for serious seizures, which were accompanied by convulsions. It was estimated that 300,000 of the two million epileptics in the U.S. could benefit from using the drug.

The Birmingham News

Birmingham, Ala., March 6, 1978

The U. S. Food and Drug Administration is to be commended for bowing to pressure from thousands suffering from epilepsy by approving the drug valproate.

According to information gathered by the Epilepsy Foundation of America and other groups, over 100,000 Americans will use the drug to control their tendency toward brief epileptic seizures known as *petit mal* and 750,000 may use it to control other forms of epilepsy.

An estimated 200,000 Europeans had been using the drug over the past 10 years, and many American parents of epileptic children have been illegally smuggling the drug into the country. The FDA's announcement said further evidence supporting valproate was submitted, to the agency's satisfaction that the drug should be licensed.

Caution on the part of the FDA is to be admired, but being overly-cautious on a drug that had been so widely used for 10 years borders on the ridiculous. And that over-cautiousness has given the FDA an image that suggests hampering rather than protecting.

And it is hoped a lesson was learned by FDA officials as well as those with epilepsy who discovered that proper protest pays off with action.

THE BLADE

Toledo, Ohio, March 7, 1978

THE continuing saga of the U.S. Food and Drug Administration's perversity in regulating the introduction of new drugs into medical practice in America took a surprising twist last week when the agency summarily gave its approval to a new drug for the treatment of epilepsy.

Like so many other promising new drugs, sodium valproate was developed in Europe, where it has been in wide use for fully 10 years. The drug has a reputation as a safe and effective medicine that helps certain patients who cannot be managed with other anti-epileptic medications.

Yet, the drug remained generally unavailable to American doctors and their patients — even though estimates suggested that it could help 500,000 epileptics here, some of whom are incapacitated by seizures.

From the events of recent years, one might reasonably conclude from these facts that sodium valproate was unavailable in the United States because the FDA dragged its bureaucratic feet for years and refused to approve its marketing — just another manifestation of the agency's restrictive attitude toward the introduction of new drugs.

Indeed, these policies have created the much-discussed "drug lag," reducing the number of beneficial new medicines available to treat sickness. Pharmaceutical houses that wish to sell a new medicine in the United States now face the prospect of spending more than five years and well over $12 million to gain the FDA's approval.

As a result, drug companies tend to introduce their new medications in Europe first, and patients there often benefit from them — with fewer side effects, for example — for years before Americans can obtain them. This sad state of affairs has generated numerous cries for the reform of America's drug regulatory process. And the case of sodium valproate doubly reinforces those cries — even though the drug was not kept off the U.S. market by the FDA.

The fact is that no U.S. drug manufacturer asked FDA for permission to market sodium valproate until last September when Abbott Laboratories took that step at the FDA's urging, a full year ahead of its planned schedule.

At a time when approval of new drugs, even those with the best safety and efficacy records abroad, is measured in years, FDA took a total of only 160 days to approve sodium valproate. The quick approval came during a period of such intense lobbying by the Epilepsy Foundation of America, epilepsy patients, and physicians who treat the disease that it leaves the unmistakable impression that the drug-regulatory process in this nation is on the verge of becoming politicized.

When one puts aside all the benefits sodium valproate promises certain epilepsy patients, plus its safety and efficacy record, the impression remains that drugs now apparently are being approved more quickly on the basis of appeals and demands from consumer groups.

No matter how good the aims of the Epilepsy Foundation were in this specific case, the prospect of drug approval based upon consumer pressure and lobbying carries such a great potential for abuse that it must never happen again.

America's drug-regulatory process clearly needs reform. Congress and the executive offices involved should move ahead with this task as rapidly as possible.

The Times-Picayune / The States-Item

New Orleans, La., March 2, 1978

Petit mal epilepsy, a brain disorder occurring most usually in children, is characterized by transient losses of consciousness, tiny blackouts which may occur as often as several hundred times a day. The afflicted child is severely handicapped in learning, in play, in all the business of living.

An anti-convulsive drug, valproic acid, has just been approved by the Federal Drug Administration to combat this disorder and other forms of epilepsy in which it has been found effective. The Epilepsy Foundation of America says 560,000 young patients can benefit; it is recognized as safe and valuable.

So far, so good. But why has valproic acid, or sodium valproate, been available to epilepsy sufferers in Europe for ten years, so that some of our most law-abiding doctors have actually had to smuggle it in? Why is it only now approved for manufacture here?

One reason is that the FDA was demanding further clinical documentation. It has only now been satisfied. A second reason is that nine of ten U.S. pharmaceutical houses offered the drug's patent by its French manufacturer turned it down: costs of winning FDA approval, they said, were too high, especially for a drug with a fairly limited clientele. Finally Abbott Laboratories agreed to market it.

Now that the FDA is satisfied, the drug will be available as soon as supplies can reach druggists' shelves. But the ten-year wait dramatizes weak spots in the system. Is the FDA hamstrung by scientific safeguards? Responsible citizens from the medical community and other professions have charged time and again that because of the FDA's hyper-timidity, valuable new drugs are regularly delayed for months or years in reaching the market. Obviously, the FDA's bible of regulations needs a thorough going-over by competent medical and scientific people who can revise it.

FDA Criticized for Being Too Slow to Approve New Drugs

The controversy over Laetrile eventually turned public attention to the Food and Drug Administration's procedures for evaluating new medication. Doctors and public health groups had criticized the agency for a number of years for being too slow to approve new drugs. In early 1978, the Carter Administration proposed to overhaul the agency, streamline its decision-making processes and give it more power over the sale of medicine in the U.S. Despite the general consensus that the FDA needed change, the proposals were opposed on grounds they gave too much power to the regulatory agency and would actually aggravate the problems they were intended to solve. The proposals included making it easier to market generic, rather than brand-name drugs, giving patients more information about drugs and their side effects, requiring manufacturers to reveal more data about the drugs they produced and changing the approval process for new drugs. Drug manufacturers argued that the rules would require disclosure of trade secrets and would increase the government's authority in the drug field.

In June 1979, the General Accounting Office officially reported what many medical experts had said for years: the FDA actually hampered the development of new drugs in the U.S. In testimony before a House subcommittee, a GAO spokesman said the average approval time for 132 new drug applications in 1975 was 20 months. He said some of the drugs approved by the FDA between July 1975 and February 1978 had been available in Europe for as long as 12 years. The FDA was criticized for unclear guidelines, delays in processing applications and failure to act quickly to resolve disagreements with the drug industry. The GAO findings were compiled from two years' worth of interviews with FDA and drug company officials and with drug firms and government agencies in Canada and Europe.

NEW YORK POST

New York, N.Y., March 7, 1977

A pharmaceutical analysis just offered the Federal Trade Commission by the Health Research Group contends there is a gross lack of data on whether certain non-prescription cold and cough remedies are either safe or effective. Many Americans might breathe easier if they had the facts.

But the Food and Drug Administration apparently doesn't yet have them. Nevertheless the agency has permitted advertising and sale of several familiar over-the-counter drugs before establishing their merit.

In the face of the Nader unit's attack, the FDA and the manufacturers reply, as phrased by one agency official, that it is "not fair to impugn the reputation of a product while efforts to establish its safety and effectiveness are still continuing."

True. It does not follow, however, that such a drug should be prematurely offered for sale and aggressively advertised when its "safety and effectiveness" remain to be demonstrated. Many Americans confidently assume the FDA is now protecting them from such risks. Perhaps Dr. Donald Kennedy, the new Commissioner-designate of the agency, can proceed after confirmation to put the public's trust on a more credible basis.

THE SUN

Baltimore, Md., October 8, 1977

Only once has the federal government declared a prescription drug an "imminent hazard" and summarily banned it. The oral anti-diabetic drug, phenformin, was removed in this fashion in July because it was shown sometimes to cause a fatal condition, lactic acidosis. Perhaps such a ban has been imposed only once because prescription drugs are so thoroughly tested before going on the market that one rarely proves to be such a threat as phenformin.

But medical knowledge changes, and sometimes drugs once approved later need to have their uses circumscribed. Unfortunately, the federal Food and Drug Administration often lacks tools more precise than the imminent hazard bludgeon—tools that would permit actions short of outright bans for drugs in need of some restrictions on their use. Among the options FDA needs are the right to restrict drugs to hospital use and to prohibit some, but not all, use of particular drugs. It also should be able to ban suspect drugs temporarily while they are being investigated. Paradoxically, the absence of such a range of options often makes it difficult to get FDA approval for *new* drugs. Knowing that it may be well-nigh impossible to limit their uses later, FDA officials put proposed new drugs over such high hurdles that approval can take years. Too often, useful drugs are kept off the market.

Joseph A. Califano, secretary of health, education and welfare, has proposed sweeping reforms of U.S. drug laws aimed at overcoming these and other problems. He recommends legislation to require more careful monitoring of adverse drug reactions and temporary bans of suspect drugs. At the same time, approval of new drugs would be accelerated. Mr. Califano also wishes to increase public participation in choices about drugs. He recommends making public the results of the now-secret data drug companies use in support of new drug applications. He also proposes providing patients with detailed brochures, in simple language, describing the assets and liabilities of drugs they are prescribed.

These worthy proposals deserve a sympathetic hearing from Congress. We suggest one caveat, however. New drug approval must be accelerated, but not to the point where insufficiently tested drugs might be approved. Those high FDA hurdles kept off the U.S. market a drug, Thalidomide, later proved to cause birth defects in Europe. The hurdles must not be lowered to the point where a latter-day Thalidomide might get across them.

THE RICHMOND NEWS LEADER
Richmond, Va., May 26, 1977

In 1962, Congress amended the Food, Drug, and Cosmetic Act to provide strict regulations for the testing and marketing of new drugs. The amendments were intended to protect Americans from the harsh side effects of inadequately tested drugs, such as thalidomide.

That intent was a laudable one, but in the ensuing years the new regulations may have had a less salutary result by inhibiting the marketing of new drugs that could have alleviated pain and suffering. In fact, some doctors contend that the U.S. now is well behind many foreign nations with less stringent laws in the development of new drugs.

Dr. Richard Spark, professor of medicine at Harvard Medical School, says that the exorbitant costs of meeting the exacting U.S. requirements are restricting drug development here. He says:

In 1962, a single new drug could be developed for $1.2 million in the United States and around $900,000 overseas (United Kingdom, Holland, Sweden, France, and Germany). By 1972, the cost of developing a new drug in the United States increased to $11.5 million, while the comparable overseas figure was $7.5 million. Projections are that in 1977 the development of a single new drug in this country will cost $40 million.

Dr. Spark is not alone in his fears that over-regulation is putting the drug industry in a straitjacket. Writing in the *New England Journal of Medicine*, Drs. William Franklin and Francis Lowell contend:

The public does not fully appreciate that stringent drug regulation for society as a whole limits therapeutic choice by the individual physician, who is better able to judge the risks and benefits for the patients. . . . The introduction of new drugs has become extremely expensive, preventing development of drugs for less common indications. Because smaller companies cannot afford to spend several million dollars for the cost of a [Food and Drug Administration] review, large companies gain a monopolistic position and can maintain high prices.

Several scientifically reliable studies have projected the loss of lives in the thousands owing to overly restrictive reins on the U.S. drug industry. The cost in needless pain suffered by patients is incalculable. Meanwhile, the development of many beneficial drugs has been delayed or postponed — perhaps even for some diseases now thought incurable.

No one can argue that the drug industry should be given a completely free hand in marketing drugs before they are tested to meet minimum safety requirements. But the drug lag that Drs. Spark, Franklin, and Lowell cite is ample evidence that Congress ought to consider modifying the law, with a view toward stimulating drug development instead of handicapping it.

Rocky Mountain News
Denver, Colo., December 24, 1977

LIKE MOST regulatory agencies, the Food and Drug Administration suffers from a certain amount of bureaucratic inertia. Promising new drugs are kept off the market. Older, less reliable drugs often stay in circulation for years.

The FDA has tried to speed up its procedures in recent months by giving special priority to new drugs with "unusual potential." But the agency still is hamstrung by the law itself, which discourages initiative and puts a premium on following the rules.

In short, there's an obvious need to rewrite and simplify the laws under which the FDA operates – and the Carter administration now proposes to do just that in 1978.

Being passed around Capitol Hill is a rough draft of legislation that would give the FDA authority to approve new drugs and recall risky drugs much more quickly than present law permits.

The proposed legislation would require that printed precautions and directions be included with most drugs – something the FDA has had a difficult time doing under present law.

It also would permit the limited distribution of a promising new drug – only in hospitals, for example – while the drug still was being tested for general use.

In extreme situations, where a patient was dying or disabled, potent new drugs could be tried even though their impact had not been fully tested under controlled conditions.

Of course, no one is suggesting that we return to the days of the patent medicine man, who sold quack remedies for "roomytism and tired blud" from the back of a prairie schooner.

But there isn't much sense in investing millions of dollars in drug research if we're too encrusted in regulatory red tape to make timely use of the knowledge we've gained.

DESERET NEWS
Salt Lake City, Utah, October 7, 1977

The people at the U.S. Food and Drug Administration must have cringed this week when they heard the latest prescription for what ails the agency.

So should any consumers who care about getting newly-developed medicines as expeditiously as is consistent with assuring the drugs' safety.

The prescription comes from HEW Secretary Joseph A. Califano Jr., and it largely consists of just another dose of what already ails the FDA — namely, more red tape including disclosure of the tests that various manufacturers conduct on new drugs to assure their safety.

This requirement would involve forcing private drug firms to disclose trade secrets to their competitors, much like requiring Ford to reveal its new-car plans to General Motors.

Moreover, Califano's reforms fall considerably short of his demand for a "top-to-bottom overhaul" of the way Washington regulates drugs.

If such reforms are to be complete, Congress should start by reining in its own proclivities to hunt headlines at the FDA's expense.

Whenever a controversy over a new drug has been resolved by its approval, the FDA has often found itself under investigation by Congress. But when such controversies have been resolved by disapproving the drug, there usually has been no inquiry.

The message from Capitol Hill to the FDA, then, has been to the effect that it should always go slow on new drugs. This despite the fact that delaying approval of an important new drug can be just as harmful to public health as okaying a potentially bad drug.

The FDA, moreover, gets bogged down not just because it's too cautious but because it's understaffed, underfinanced, and over-worked. When most agencies formulate their budgets, they start by listing their responsibilities and then figuring out a price tag. The FDA, however, is first told how much it can spend, and then must figure out how it can stretch that allotment the farthest.

Then there's a 1962 law that ought to be rescinded or modified if the FDA is to do its job more expeditiously and effectively.

Originally, the FDA was required to do no more than ascertain that new drugs are safe. The 1962 law requires that agency to make sure the drugs are also effective.

Never mind that most consumers are quite capable of determining for themselves whether a particular drug actually does what its manufacturer says it will. Never mind that a free market could deal effectively with medical products that don't deliver what's promised.

The point is that this extra requirement adds long delays in the distribution of drugs that could be saving many lives. Before the 1962 law, it took only seven months to get FDA action on a new drug; now the process takes four to nine years.

These delays, according to a study by Professor Sam Peltzman of the Chicago Graduate School of Business, cost Americans $250 million to $350 million a year in deferred economic benefits alone.

The same red tape also exacts a cruel cost in human suffering. If pre-1962 drugs for tuberculosis and severe mental disorders had been subjected to the same delays now required, thousands of patients would have died or endured needless hospitalization.

All progress entails some risk. But the FDA has been too intent on avoiding even the slightest risk and too insensitive to the potential gains. What the agency needs now is less red tape — not new encumbrances.

The Courier-Journal

Louisville, Ky., March 31, 1978

CRITICS have called the Food and Drug Administration weak-kneed in combatting pharmaceutical industry pressures, slow in clearing life-saving products for marketing, technically inadequate, and ineffective in protecting Americans from hazardous reactions brought on by new drugs. But while recent FDA chiefs have tried to mend those faults, the job is too big to be done effectively without the help of Congress.

So it's fortunate that cooperative efforts by Senate and House members, teamed with administration experts, have now produced what could be the first major revision of federal drug laws since the thalidomide scare of 1962. The proposal follows 10 years of controversy between drug companies and consumer advocates and publication of 20 volumes of Senate health subcommittee hearings on drug regulation problems.

Still, because of the strength of the drug lobby, the job won't be easy. Some firms in the $16 billion-a-year industry reportedly have been saving up "political action" contributions to give to congressmen who will vote on the FDA bill.

Pharmaceutical companies mostly oppose the bill, despite the fact that it addresses many of their regulatory and marketing concerns. They say the provisions for making test information available — to assure the sometimes questioned integrity of pre-market research — could compromise trade secrets. The industry also calls the bill's consumer-involvement and hearings procedures a waste of time. Research, drug lobbyists say, would have to be conducted overseas lest rivals obtain key information prematurely.

Among the main aims of sponsors of the massive bill, which took up 27 pages of fine print in the *Congressional Record*, are these: Consumers should have fuller information on effectiveness and health risks. New drugs should become available earlier, with some critical drugs freed for sale before completion of testing. Many regulations which have caused complaints about a U. S. "drug lag" should be lifted. The FDA's powers to take dangerous drugs off the market should be strengthened. Duplicative drug formulations should be curbed, and generic-naming and price-posting measures should help reduce the cost of prescription drugs.

Could reduce company costs

In the licensing area, a plan to preempt the states' authority to authorize intrastate use of such questionable products as laetrile is sure to raise a flap.

Overall, the fact that the measure already has been tailored to meet many industry complaints about FDA regulation should impress Congress, despite the tendency to disparage "consumer" legislation as perfectionist and expensive. In fact, the FDA reform bill contains many provisions that would reduce pharmaceutical company costs in introducing new drugs. And the industry could hardly complain about new efforts to reform the "detail man" system, within which salesmen have given some doctors gifts as inducements to prescribe their products, and other anti-competitive practices.

Clearly, it's time for Congress to make sense of drug regulation. The new spirit of cooperation between the administration and congressional critics of the FDA in anticipating most industry criticism augurs well for this year's effort.

The Salt Lake Tribune

Salt Lake City, Utah, March 21, 1978

An overhaul of federal pharmaceutical laws is needed, as Secretary of Health, Education and Welfare Joseph A. Califano Jr. says. But it is by no means certain that the HEW-prescribed changes are what the doctor ordered.

With some notable exceptions the new regulations proposed by the Carter administration would further inhibit an industry whose lifeblood is innovation.

The new rules expand upon the basic misconception of 1962 amendments which resulted in a substantial decrease in development of new drugs. That misconception is the assumption that the ethical drug industry thinks it can prosper by turning out ineffective, even dangerous products which a gullible public and irresponsible physicians will accept like so many sheep.

Useless pharmaceutical products are in fact produced. But they don't rack up the large profits that have drawn consumer attention to the industry. It is the effective, needed and safe drugs that brings in the money. The others are usually short-lived because they are soon shunned by physicians and their patients.

In attempting to prevent introduction of some products that the consumer will quickly doom anyway, the government's myriad regulations, those of 1962 and the latest proposals, discourage development of new medicines which could save lives and significantly cut health care costs.

Existing rules are denying Americans the benefits of certain drugs that have proven their values in long use abroad. That is because of the inordinately long and expensive testing that each new product must undergo to secure Food and Drug Administration approval. The HEW proposals, to their credit, seem aimed at reducing this time lag.

A degree of regulation is necessary for public safety. But the point has been reached where official interference in development of new products is actually reducing safety by denying the public medicines it needs.

Too much well intentioned interference in development and marketing of drugs can have the same negative effect as too little official intervention. Some of the latest HEW proposals are an extension of the excess interference trend.

NEW YORK POST

New York, N.Y., March 18, 1978

The Carter Administration's limited new proposals for reforming 40-year-old federal regulations of pharmaceutical drugs are long overdue.

The legislation would enable the public consumer to be heard in the testing of new drugs—a provision the drug companies have long resisted. It will get drugs onto the market more quickly, and get them off more quickly too if there is evidence of danger.

But when it comes to consumer protection, the program stops short of the bold, broad legislation pioneered by New York State. The federal government would provide doctors with the capacity to prescribe lower-cost generic drugs rather than the more expensive advertised brand names.

Unfortunately it would not take the extra step of encouraging the sale of the lower-priced drugs—the breakthrough New York has achieved.

It is a minimal, faltering forward step.

The Chattanooga Times

Chattanooga, Tenn., March 28, 1978

When HEW Secretary Joseph Califano announced the administration's plan to revise drastically the regulation of prescription and over-the-counter drugs in this country, he called it "the most important piece of legislation in the health field in many years."

Only hours later, however, C. Joseph Stetler, president of the Pharmaceutical Manufacturers Association, denounced the legislation, saying that "if we had to say the administration bill or none at all — we'd say none."

Given those two positions, you might say that there's no hope of a reconciliation between HEW and the PMA. In fact, however, there is something in the bill of benefit to the drug-consuming public and the producers of those drugs. With some cooperation, Congress and the PMA could come to an agreement that gives each something of what it wants.

As presently written, the bill would enable pharmaceutical companies to put new drugs on the market faster. Conversely, the Food and Drug Administration would be empowered to remove dangerous drugs from pharmacists' shelves faster in case a problem develops. Finally, the bill also requires that consumers be given more information than is now available about various drugs' side effects, and provides that drugs be sold by their generic name instead of only by the pharmaceutical companies' designations.

Since, for example, the bill would cut the red tape that slows a new drug's availability to the market, why does the PMA object so vociferously?

One reason is the disclosure provision, which Mr. Stetler says would unfairly expose drug makers' trade secrets to competitors. Moreover, if the requirements for disclosure of test data on safety and effectiveness are retained, many drug houses say they would test and introduce their drugs overseas, thus withholding needed new medicines from consumers in this country.

The concern is legitimate, and it has even prompted Sen. Edward Kennedy, a frequent health industry critic, to promise he would "look long and hard at whether this legislation provides sufficient incentives to maintain and stimulate the private research capability of the industry . . ."

Other than that point, the bill appears fairly balanced, making it easier for manufacturers to put new products on the market, while — taking into consideration that no drug is always absolutely safe — giving the FDA new authority in case a drug is shown to have unforeseen side effects. This balance of increased availability and greater safety assurances should withstand most of the amendments sure to come.

ST. LOUIS POST-DISPATCH

St. Louis, Mo., July 22, 1978

Unless committee work is completed quickly on the Carter administration's Drug Regulatory Reform Act, time may run out on a chance for its passage this year. That would be unfortunate, for the measure is basically sound, would increase the protection and information given to drug consumers and thus deserves passage after just a little strengthening.

This bill would be the first major change in drug regulations since 1962. It contains several revisions that ought to cut the costly, time-consuming requirements now imposed on the drug industry. And this, naturally enough, the drug industry applauds. But in the course of drafting legislation designed to help both the pharmaceutical industry and consumers, the administration added safeguards that the producers claim will cancel out the benefits. Because of additional discretionary powers given to the Food and Drug Administration, because of data release requirements and because of what is seen as too much regulation of research, the Pharmaceutical Manufacturers Association is opposing the bill.

If drug manufacturers were infallible and if drugs did not have a potential for harm as well as for good, strict regulations would not be needed. Such is not the case. The example has been used many times but it is so relevant to drug control that a reminder is valid: No firm would consciously have marketed a drug that deformed babies, but Thalidomide was produced and sold.

Federal controls on research may be resented by the industry, but some are needed. For example, there have been recent reports of inaccurate data turned in on drug safety experiments done for industry. Standardizing tests as much as possible would aid the FDA in checking such things as well as other data. Complete standardization cannot be required, however, because of the different characteristics of various drugs. But where controls are appropriate, they should be instituted.

Also because of these differences, Congress would be hard put to write strict scientific regulations to cover every situation. Counting each brand, there are approximately 60,000 prescription drugs and 200,000 others. The discretionary powers given to the FDA would thus seem to be a more positive response to the problems of the drug industry than would congressional rule-making. In addition to having problems with the FDA's proposed power increase, the industry is resisting data disclosure, saying it will dampen innovation. However, the legislation provides for a protected period in which the developer of the new drug ought to be able to recoup the cost of development. With strong enough provisions here, innovation in the drug industry ought not to be impaired.

A past president of the Pharmaceutical Manufacturers Association, after finding many things wrong with the proposed legislation, called for "the most painstaking care in the construction of those provisions that impact research, reinforced by a legislative record that clearly states the intent of Congress that the end result be a regulatory process that is fair, efficient and supportive of innovation." An effective regulatory process has to have power and has to be able to monitor and control the regulator; it cannot be a rubber stamp for the producers. The administration's proposal seems to have been constructed with that kind of care—with a mind toward fairness for the industry and for the consumer. Congress should expedite drug regulatory reform.

The News American

Baltimore, Md., April 23, 1978

SEN. Edward M. Kennedy is pushing a bill in Congress that would give the federal government tight controls on prescriptions of medical drugs. Recently Kennedy made a speech at a convention of druggists complaining because doctors are allowed complete freedom in prescribing drugs and amounts of drug doses for their patients.

"Drugs may be used for any purpose that the doctor wishes," Kennedy said in his protest. "The current system allows individual doctors to substitute their judgment for that of the Food and Drug Administration."

What's wrong with that? Certainly a doctor knows more about his patient's medical needs than a federal regulatory agency in Washington knows about how that particular case should be treated.

Putting the prescription of medical drugs under tight government supervision would be a menace, not a protection, for the patient and, also, for the practice of medicine.

THE INDIANAPOLIS NEWS

Indianapolis, Ind., March 15, 1978

The Carter administration will soon be sending Congress a major bill affecting the pharmaceutical industry — the first major reform in drug legislation since the Food and Drug Act of 1906.

The bill is already in its second draft and probably won't please either consumers or the industry entirely But its basic premise is a good one and long overdue: Making it faster and easier for the Food and Drug Administration to approve a new drug or remove a bad one from drugstore shelves.

According to the *New York Times*, new drug marketing applications to the FDA average 34 volumes in length and take years to process. Valuable drugs are not in use in the United States because of the FDA's long and costly approval procedure.

An example is sodium valproate. The drug is an anti-convulsant helpful to some victims of epilepsy. Sodium valproate has been on sale outside the U.S. for a decade. But not until 1974 did a pharmaceutical company in the U.S. agree to take on the expensive chore of getting the drug approved. For sodium valproate is a so-called "orphan" drug — nobody wants to manufacture it because of the limited market for the drug. So those who need it wait.

The proposed reform legislation is sweeping in scope. Just a few examples:

•a section allowing "breakthrough" drugs to be marketed before testing is completed;

•a section allowing the FDA to impose civil penalties of up to $10,000 a day against companies that disobey drug laws;

•a section forbidding drug companies from giving doctors free samples or gifts worth $5 or more;

•a section requiring easy to read consumer information packaged with prescription drugs.

Pharmaceutical companies object most strongly to those portions of the bill requiring them to reveal trade secrets and manufacturing information on new drugs to FDA committees. While there would be criminal penalties for revealing such information, some companies feel that such information could easily fall into the hands of competitors.

At present, many provisions of the bill need work. But drug regulation is an area long and unnecessarily overrun by redtape. Drastic reform is needed. Life-saving drugs must be sheperded out of the research stage and into use where they're needed most. The letter of the current, cumbersome law isn't worth lives.

THE SACRAMENTO BEE

Sacremento, Cal., March 13, 1978

The White House, in collaboration with members of the House and Senate, is preparing a major bill to revise the regulation of prescription and over-the-counter drugs. The bill, known as the Drug Regulatory Reform Act of 1978, requires pharmacies to provide buyers of prescription drugs with information about their effects and side effects; speeds the process by which certain "breakthrough" medications are approved and brought to market; opens up the drug licensing procedures of the Food and Drug Administration to public scrutiny; makes it easier for the FDA to order hazardous or ineffective drugs off the market, and revises the rules and procedures under which experimental drugs are tested.

Although the bill, which will be formally submitted to Congress this month, is subject to further revisions and although it contains provisions which deserve serious scrutiny before they become law, the act represents a significant step in opening up and demystifying the licensing and use of prescription drugs in America. In the past, the process by which the FDA approved new drugs was usually a closed and cozy exercise whose only participants were FDA officials, FDA consultants, and representatives of the manufacturer. The research data on which approval was theoretically based were also regarded as confidential. As a consequence, the FDA was often charged with buckling under to industry pressure, of ignoring reports of dangerous side effects and of generally being more responsive to the manufacturers than to the public interest.

Under the new procedures, studies of drug safety and efficacy, as well as the licensing process itself, will be open to consumer groups and independent health organizations.

Equally significant are provisions which will make it possible for manufacturers to bring important new drugs to market more quickly. Physicians and drug industry officials have often complained that a preparation which could save lives, and which is in use abroad, is arbitrarily held off the U.S. market to satisfy cumbersome licensing procedures. Under the bill, the FDA can give provisional approval for such "breakthrough" drugs pending completion of all required studies. Such drugs would be subject to continuing review until all requirements had been met.

Most important, perhaps, is the bill's requirement that pharmacists provide each client with a printed slip describing the effects and hazards of the medication dispensed. In theory, physicians give their patients such information when they prescribe. In practice, they often do not. Sometimes, indeed, the physician himself is unaware of the drug's side effects; as a result, patient and physician alike frequently attribute those effects — which can include anything from headaches to fatal illnesses — to the disease rather than the remedy.

Giving the patient such information will not eliminate that problem, but it should reduce it. It should also reduce sometimes irresistible patient demands for "miracle" drugs that promise instant cures. Anyone who has ever read the FDA-required descriptions of the effects of drugs that manufacturers give physicians will almost certainly become more cautious about what he expects of his medication.

The Drug Regulatory Reform Act contains some dubious provisions, among them one creating a National Center for Clinical Pharmacology within the Department of Health, Education and Welfare. The functions of that center, still subject to review, will be to foster education and research on the use of prescription drugs, a function which may just as easily be performed by existing agencies, either through FDA or the National Institutes of Health.

Despite such drawbacks, however, the act is a major step in demystifying drugs and drug use and in making the patient and general public greater participants in health care. In the past, the medical profession and the drug industry have often treated the whole process as a complex, arcane secret beyond the comprehension of ordinary people. The new act will not abolish medical mystification, but it will let a little more light into the darkness.

The News Journal

Wilmington, Del., April 8, 1978

When monitoring pharmaceuticals, the Food and Drug Administration has to perform a delicate balancing act. On the one hand, the agency must make certain that the drugs it allows to be marketed are effective and do no harm. At the same time, the FDA must also bear in mind that drug manufacturers can develop new drugs and keep on producing well-established drugs only as long as there is an orderly, efficient process for approving these drugs, so that there is some profit in the business.

In both aspects of its work, the FDA has been hampered by outdated laws that make the drug approval process cumbersome and the withdrawal of undesirable drugs almost impossible. And present laws have in some instances not provided enough protection or relevant information for drug consumers.

A new pharmaceutical act, on which the Senate health committee is going to hold hearings soon, would bring the handling of pharmaceuticals more in line with today's needs.

Drug manufacturers and drug users would benefit from a new category of "breakthrough drugs" that would make possible quick, conditional FDA approval of a new drug if it is needed for the treatment of "life threatening diseases." Along similar lines, the proposed law would permit limited distribution of some drugs — say by hospitals — if those drugs are not yet ready for general approval but are urgently needed by some patients. The potential advantage of these changes — assuming the new drug works — is clear as far as patients are concerned.

Manufacturers too would benefit from the data they could gather from the use of these still experimental drugs and from being able to market their products a bit earlier under circumscribed conditions. At the same time the normal drug testing process, which is lengthy, tedious and costly, would not be diluted, because the instances cited above would be clearly identified as exceptions.

Another desirable feature of the pharmaceutical bill is that it would require drug companies to monitor the effects of their new drugs for five years. This would be done through contacts with hospitals, doctors and pharmacists. Such monitoring would provide data not only on drug effectiveness but also could offer clues on undesirable side effects. The crippling effects of Thalidomide, for instance, might have been uncovered a lot sooner with that kind of monitoring process.

In line with today's greater involvement of patients in their health care, the law would require patient-information leaflets to be included with drug packets. Prices of common drugs would have to be posted in pharmacies. And free samples to physicians, or gifts to doctors from drug companies, would be ruled out.

When the pharmaceutical law was drafted last fall, it required the drug companies to make extensive scientific disclosures when marketing approval is first sought. Since getting such approval takes several years, there was fear that this disclosure requirement would make too much information available to competitors too early in the game. In the present bill, these disclosure requirements have been modified and manufacturers' proprietary interests are better protected. Nevertheless, with the proposed law requiring input from advisory committees and some public hearings, pharmaceutical companies still fear that too much "secret" information will leak out.

These concerns have some merit and further tightening may be called for. While scientific experts and consumer representatives working in the public's behalf have a right and a need to know much about new drugs, the manufacturer, who is investing large resources in the new product, must be able to protect his position on the market place.

The new law has some excellent features for making needed medicines available faster and for giving drug users better protection and more information. But in doing so, let us make sure that we do not cripple the manufacturer. Else there may be no new drugs to test.

THE BLADE

Toledo, Ohio, March 28, 1978

AFTER years of intense criticism from physicians, pharmaceutical companies, consumer groups, and others, the Federal Government finally has proposed a sweeping revision of its system for regulating the introduction of valuable new drugs into medical practice in the United States.

Health, Education, and Welfare Secretary Joseph Califano, explaining provisions of the proposed Drug Regulation Reform Act, noted that it would represent the most complete overhaul of federal drug-regulation laws since the 1938 amendments to the Pure Food and Drug Act of 1906.

Nothing less than that would be acceptable, considering the changes that have occurred in the pharmaceutical sciences over the last 40 years and the tumult in recent years over the Government's foot-dragging attitude toward the approval of potentially life-saving new drugs.

By moving too slowly and applying unrealistic safety standards, the U.S. Food and Drug Administration has been roundly criticized for creating a "drug lag" in this country and for stifling the development of new drugs by the American pharmaceutical industry.

It now takes more than five years and costs more than $12 million for a drug company to produce the 34 thick volumes of scientific data necessary to satisfy FDA's demands for the issuance of a license to sell a new drug. Beneficial new medicines tend to be available to European doctors and their patients years before they are available in the United States.

The Administration's proposed legislation is designed specifically to speed the introduction of new medicines without sacrificing safety requirements At long last, the point is explicitly emphasized to the FDA that its demands for virtually absolute safety in new drugs are unreasonable. Sensibly, the new law would state that there always is a risk in taking any drug — that safety is a relative matter. A new drug would be considered safe if its health benefits outweighed its risks.

For example, is a drug "safe" if, as a side effect, it lowers a patient's resistance to infection? The answer

under the proposed law might be "yes" if the drug in question were intended to treat some devastating disease such as cancer It might be "no" if the drug were proposed as a minor pain reliever

Drug manufacturers would be required to undertake formal programs of "postmarketing surveillance," monitoring and reporting side effects of new drugs for long periods of time after initial marketing.

Such a requirement is wise in light of the many changes that have occurred in the use of prescription drugs. Years ago, drugs typically were prescribed for a few days or at most a few weeks to treat infections and other acute illnesses. But today drugs more and more frequently are prescribed for relatively healthy people to take over long periods of time for conditions such as high blood pressure.

The Administration's bill also would take steps to stimulate research on new drugs by American firms. And it would provide consumers with potentially helpful information on drugs and prices.

One distinctly misguided provision of the bill, however, stipulates that consumers be provided with "package inserts" and other information on drug side effects. Indeed, some medications could be dispensed only after patients signed an "informed consent" form attesting to their understanding of a drug's hazards.

Such provisions carry consumerism to the point of absurdity, promising only to overwhelm, confuse, and frighten many patients with technical and statistical data that they, as laymen, simply are not prepared to consider knowledgeably. The benefits and risks of any drug must be weighed by the physician who decides whether to prescribe it for a given patient.

We trust that these sections of the legislation will be among those modified or dropped during congressional hearings. The lawmakers also will have to deal with various other objections expressed by pharmaceutical houses and consumer groups.

Congress should, however, make every possible effort to insure that the broad goals of this long-overdue legislation remain intact.

DAYTON DAILY NEWS

Dayton, Ohio, March 28, 1978

The nation's prescription drug laws aren't doing the jobs they are supposed to, but the prognosis is not good for the Carter administration's effort to overhaul those laws. It has taken major scandals and public outrage to get Congress motivated to undertake drug law revisions in the past, and no scandal is evident now.

Nonetheless, the effort ought to be made.

Both the drug industry and consumer groups are dissatisfied with the present laws, and rightly so. The industry has to deal with cumbersome and slow drug approval processes that sometimes delay good and effective drugs from being sold.

But some of that delay is desirable because the Food and Drug Administration has such limited powers to stop the sale of drugs that turn out to be ineffective or harmful. Once a drug is approved, it's hard to withdraw approval. That naturally and properly leads to caution in granting approvals.

The administration bill would streamline the approval procedure a bit and make it easier for the FDA to pull bad drugs off the market. It would allow breakthrough drugs onto the market even more quickly on a conditonal basis — but only for major health problems such as cancer.

Industry, consumer groups and legislators who specialize in health matters all have reams of other proposals at the ready and will try to tack them onto the administration bill. Some of them sound like good ideas. One, for instance, would set up a board to evaluate test data provided by drug companies, because there is evidence that at least some of it is sloppy or even fraudulent.

Perhaps the biggest point of conflict in the bill is its provision for increasing the amount of test data made available to the public. Consumer groups say it still is not enough, while drug companies say it is so much it would destroy competition. It will be a hard balance to achieve.

But one thing is sure. The worst thing that could happen would be a new law speeding up the approval process without a compensating increase in the speed of the withdrawal process and without increasing the amount of information made available to patients.

That's what will happen if the drug companies have their way. And in the past, they often have.

The Washington Post

Washington, D.C., March 22, 1978

WHEN HEW SECRETARY Joseph A. Califano Jr. unveiled the administration's drug-regulation bill the other day, he described it as "the most important piece of legislation in the health field to be sent up in many years." The usual hardsell, we note—but he could be right. The bill contains a complete overhaul of the law governing the ways in which drugs are tested and sold. If Congress passes it in anything like its present form, pharmaceutical companies will have fewer hurdles to surmount in putting new drugs on the market; the Food and Drug Administration will have more power to take dangerous drugs off the market, and consumers will have access to more information about the side effects of the drugs they take.

Given the fact that each of those aims is something the group benefitting from it has been seeking for years, you might think the bill would be regarded as a wondrous example of consensus legislation. And, HEW and FDA in fact tried hard to make it just that: The first draft, which grew out of a blue-ribbon commission study, was subjected to hearings, and efforts were made to reconcile objections to it. But the conflict between different parties in the drug field is so great that reconciliation was not possible. Thus, some drug companies and consumer groups have already denounced various aspects of the legislation and some legislators who will sponsor it on Capitol Hill intend to introduce major amendments.

Two basic facts account for the trouble. One is that no drug, not even aspirin, is absolutely, 100 percent safe; the other is that the development and testing of a new drug can be extremely expensive. Those who focus on safety want to make the pre-market testing of drugs as rigorous as possible; those who manufacture the drugs argue that if the testing procedure gets too rigorous, the rising costs will discourage the development of new drugs, and the protracted time involved will deny the benefits of new drugs to patients in need. Add to that the disclosures of the past decade concerning phony testing, weak law enforcement and deceptive advertising techniques, and the stage is set for a king-sized battle in Congress.

Our own impression of Mr. Califano's proposal is that it balances the competing interests quite carefully. The easier road to the market for the drug companies, for example, would be offset by the increased authority of the FDA to act if a drug's safety were to be called into question. Other aspects of the bill reflect other trade-offs. Some adjustments here and there may be necessary once all sides of the arguments have been fully presented. But it seems to us that the outline is there for a new law—an improved law that will keep the essential new drugs coming while giving the public the necessary reasonable assurance of safety.

THE  SUN

Baltimore, Md., March 29, 1978

No one seems satisfied with the Carter administration's proposals to change the way drugs are regulated by the Food and Drug Administration. Consumer groups say, for instance, that the reforms do not go nearly far enough in requiring public disclosure of the data drug companies use to back up safety and efficacy claims for new drugs. But drug companies are claiming that it requires disclosure of *too much* data—enough, they say, to mean loss of valuable trade secrets to competitors. Senator Edward M. Kennedy suggests he may agree with them.

Implicit in the dispute over data release is the question of whether the FDA can be trusted to evaluate confidential data honestly. A blue ribbon panel that recently completed a 27-month study says the FDA's procedures are "fundamentally sound." But there have been recent reports of fraud in drug testing by some companies, and though fraud probably is not widespread, public access to drug company data might allay public fears. However, the disclosure requirement is given virtually no chance for adoption.

Other almost as controversial features of the administration bill may stand a better chance. Clearly in the public interest are two proposals, one of which would speed up and simplify the processing of new drug applications, and another which would expand the FDA's authority to recall drugs when there is "unreasonable and substantial risk of illness or injury." Also needed are the bill's curbs on misleading advertising and on gifts from drug companies to doctors—as well as its provision for giving patients information on drug side effects.

Passage of the administration bill will not satisfy consumer groups, which want not only full data disclosure, but also curbs on drug company profits, federal testing of new drugs and other far-reaching changes. Yet this represents a reasonable approach, one that, minus the data disclosure requirements, probably has the most realistic chance of passage.

ST. LOUIS POST-DISPATCH

St. Louis, Mo., April 8, 1978

Though the Carter administration's proposal to change the country's drug laws should help drug manufacturers and consumers as well as regulators, both user and producer are being skeptical. Yet on the whole, this is a well thought out, balanced set of improvements that should eventually be adopted by the Congress, with only a few modifications. We say eventually, because the drug manufacturers are already amassing a war chest with which to combat the changes, and their money is sure to carry several votes.

The major complaint of the producers concerns requirements for data disclosure that the Pharmaceutical Manufacturers Association claims would destroy the incentive to develop new drugs because trade secrets would be available to competitors. The administration's proposal, however, bans any manufacturer but the originator of a new drug from using disclosed data commercially for five years. This data would consist of a "scientific summary" when the manufacturer first applies for marketing approval, and safety and effectiveness data two to three months before the public hearing. The disclosure is not all inclusive; for instance, manufacturing processes would not be available to the public. But the information should help public scrutiny to guard against fraudulent tests and, therefore, harmful drugs.

The new system would use a "monograph" of each generic drug containing a descriptive standard. Once the Food and Drug Administration accepts the standards in the monograph, manufacturers would be licensed to produce brand-name drugs under those guidelines. Once a monograph is set, subsequent drugs, produced after the five-year protection period, would have to conform to the monograph standards, and would not need costly and duplicative testing. This should ensure uniform quality at the same time that it eases the burdens now placed on drug companies.

The Food and Drug Administration currently demands so much pre-market testing partially because of the difficulty it has doing anything to a drug after it is approved. The Carter changes would enable the secretary of Health, Education and Welfare to amend or revoke the monograph at any time in response to new data on the drug. This aspect is essential to passage of the whole package that reduces the pre-marketing load on the manufacturer, revisions that would also aid the consumer by decreasing the time it takes to market a new drug.

Congress should make sure that sufficient safeguards remain when drugs are tested on humans, and should mandate careful monitoring and control of the use of the so-called breakthrough drugs—those of such importance that they are allowed to be produced prior to completion of all the normal tests. The Carter proposal, as it now stands, would be a definite improvement over current drug law; but the protections it provides could be strengthened. The pressure from the drug industry, pressure backed with campaign money, will be to do the opposite. But, when dealing with drugs, Congress would be more responsible to be overcautious, rather than lenient.

The Evening Bulletin

Philadelphia, Pa., March 21, 1978

A sweeping new health proposal backed by the Carter Administration was introduced in Congress last week. It calls for the overhaul of the nation's drug laws, and many of the reforms, we believe, are past due.

Basically, the measure would involve the Federal Government more directly in both prescription and non-prescription drugs. At a time when Americans are spending $16 billion annually on drugs, such involvement could prove to have an important impact on our pocketbooks as well as on our health.

Specifically, the Carter-backed legislation would, among other things, require that patients be informed of drug side effects, make it easier to prescribe drugs by their lower-cost generic names rather than their trade names, and allow more public access to information about drug testing. It would also seek to end excesses in promotion of drugs by, for example, limiting gifts that drug companies may offer doctors.

The Pharmaceutical Manufacturers Association opposes the proposed legislation. Drug companies worry that too much disclosure of test procedures could tip off competitors. They also object to a provision in the bill which would create a National Center for Clinical Pharmacology to help train pharmacologists and to work on developing certain drugs, such as those used against what have come to be known as Third World diseases. The drug companies say this would amount to an invasion of the drug industry, and they may be right.

We like to think that many of the provisions would benefit the individual American, who pays for — and presumably takes — an average of seven prescriptions a year.

Since the last major enactment of drug laws 40 years ago, many changes have occurred in the way Americans use, and abuse, drugs. In our view it makes sense that some changes are also due in the rules the Federal Government imposes to regulate the flow of drugs on the American market.

TULSA WORLD
Tulsa, Oklahoma, June 9, 1980

FROM 1973 to 1977, U. S. scientists led the world in discovering new medicines and drugs with 74. But it was able to get only 18 of those medicines through the cumbersome Government approval process to make them available to the public.

Caution in the introduction of new medicines certainly is necessary. One has only to remember the tragic thalidomide cases to see the wisdom of going slow.

The statistics from other advanced nations shows they are able to get the new drugs into the hands of the public without undue risk. In France, researchers found 57 new drugs and the Government introduced 57 in the 1973-77 period. West Germany found 49, introduced 40; Japan, found 32, introduced 34; and Switzerland's numbers were 26 and 21.

If officials in those countries have the same concern for safety as U. S. officials, and few would argue that they don't, the statistics suggest the U. S. needs to consider changes in the procedures used to approve drugs.

Delays caused by procedures to insure safety are not the issue. Excessive regulation, slow approval process and archaic patent laws are the culprits.

Unfortunately, Federal agencies regulating drug research and introduction have too often gotten away with confusing genuine safety concerns with bureaucratic inertia.

Roanoke Times & World-News
Roanoke, Va., August 26, 1980

Channel 15 recently showed the television program "On Giant's Shoulders," which our Jeff DeBell praised for its depiction of a thalidomide victim and the English couple that adopted him.

Thalidomide was in use in England in the 1960s when its manufacturer was plugging for a government OK here. The Food and Drug Administration refused — and held out against strong pressure. FDA's stand was vindicated when the expectant mothers who'd taken the drug began bearing children with grotesquely deformed limbs. There were many pitiful stories; "Remember thalidomide!" became the battle cry for those who wanted the drug testing and approval program to be long and thorough.

Thalidomide ought not be forgotten. People should be protected against careless introduction of drugs that could be harmful or ineffective. The other side of the coin is that drugs with curative potential can be withheld from use too long by federal officials.

That is what a number of observers, including economist Milton Friedman, have contended. Their view is bolstered by a recent report from Congress' investigative arm, the General Accounting Office. GAO examined a period of 4½ years wherein it found that the average time to approve a drug application was 20 months, 17 of which the FDA was responsible for. The report added:

In many cases, FDA takes about as long to approve important new drugs as it does to approve [unimportant] drugs . . . The lengthy approval process delays the therapeutic advantages of important new drugs to the public and, according to industry officials, adds substantially to the cost of developing new drugs. One industry source advised us that, for each month a drug firm is awaiting approval of a drug, about $200,000 is incurred for clinical studies.

A number of foreign countries, FDA noted, give approval in less time without sacrificing safety. No responsible party would urge rushing a new drug into use without adequate testing. But indications are that screening takes an unnecessarily long time in the United States, and that in itself, this extra time buys no added security.

FDA already is moving to streamline its procedures; GAO's report suggests other means that the agency and Congress could consider to shorten the process still more and to encourage useful innovations in drug therapy. Regulation is needed — the guinea pigs should be in the laboratory, not in sickbeds — but delay shouldn't always be equated with safety. It can hurt more people than it helps.

The Idaho STATESMAN
Boise, Idaho, June 10, 1980

A recent report by the General Accounting Office indicates the federal Food and Drug Administration takes an inordinate amount of time to evaluate new therapeutic drugs proposed for sale in the United States. The report points up an area in which government red tape and gobbledygook stifle society.

The GAO report, ordered after years of criticism of the FDA by pharmaceutical companies and others, says the legal requirement for action within 180 days on new drug applications is rarely met. The average approval time is actually about 20 months, and often longer, the report says.

The FDA's performance stands in contrast to comparatively quick approval processes in other Western countries. The delay in the U.S. often deprives Americans of the benefits of new drugs developed elsewhere, notably Europe. For example, Propranolol, a drug termed a "most important" advance in the treatment of high blood pressure, was approved for use in England seven years before the FDA saw fit to allow its use in the U.S. Somatrotropin, a drug used to promote growth in children who lack a specific growth hormone, was approved in 1971 in Sweden and Switzerland and in 1972 in Great Britain — but not until 1976 in the U.S.

Dr. William M. Wardell, who is credited with coining the term "drug lag," says the FDA process is a "desperately complicated system that . . . is getting worse. Right now there are very fascinating drugs available from German and Swiss companies that aren't marketable here."

Every drug developed in Europe shouldn't be rushed onto the market in the U.S. There are risks associated with the taking of any drug — even aspirin — and the potential harm of a given pharmaceutical should be weighed carefully in relation to its possible benefits. But the confusion and delays outlined in the GAO report on the FDA approval process sound familiar to anyone who has dealt with a bureaucracy. Steps should be taken to speed up the process and make it more rational.

DESERET NEWS
Salt Lake City, Utah, February 25, 1980

Those who try to get government approval for new drugs in America have a bitter joke: aspirin, they say, would not receive federal approval if it were a new drug.

It turns out the joke isn't a joke.

In 1969, E.R Squibb and Sons, a drug manufacturer wanted to conduct a study to see if aspirin in normal doses might be useful in preventing future heart attacks in patients who had already had heart attacks.

The federal Food and Drug Administration (FDA) refused to allow the study. Indeed, the feds threatened to shut down all of Squibb's clinical research program if the company went ahead with the study.

Squibb cancelled the research.

In 1974, the National Institute of Health began a $16 million, government-financed study to investigate the same possible effects of aspirin. Final results of the study aren't in, but it appears aspirin may indeed help some heart patients.

The American people have had some experience with aspirin. In normal doses, it may often be taken without harmful side effects. Under a physician's care, normal doses of aspirin would seem unlikely to do serious harm to most patients.

Yet many Americans may have suffered heart attacks that could have been prevented if the FDA had not set research back five years.

The problem is not limited to aspirin.

A group headed by pharmacologist William Wardell at the University of Rochester looked into the development of new drugs and their regulation in the United States and other countries. Some of their findings are:

—Important new drugs are regularly held up for years in America while they are used in other nations. Even drugs developed by United States firms and later proven safe and effective are often approved in foreign countries before the federal government will allow them to be used in the United States.

—The average time required to test and gain government approval for a new drug is nine years in the United States. This time is getting longer. And only one in ten proposed new drugs is finally approved for use

—The most ominous finding of all is that, faced with this regulatory burden, U.S. drug companies are developing fewer new drugs. The number of new chemical entities—entirely new drugs rather than adaptations of old drugs—tested by American companies has fallen since 1964, and may have fallen as much as 40 percent between 1974 and 1976. Increasingly, American firms are adapting foreign drugs, and introducing their own drugs first in foreign countries where the regulatory burden is less onerous.

Americans need federal regulation of drugs to assure that they are safe. But there are costs in overregulating as well as in allowing unsafe drugs on the market.

St. Petersburg Times

St. Petersburg, Fla., January 14, 1980

Do pregnant women who drink more than five or six cups of coffee a day run the risk of giving birth to a deformed baby?

Maybe.

Do children who play on swings, slides, monkey bars and seesaws stalled over a hard surface run the risk of suffering a terrible head injury should they fall off?

Almost certainly.

Do consumers have a right to be told of such risks so they can make informed choices about how much coffee they drink or where they install playground equipment?

Of course.

All else being equal, prudence suggests that it would be wise to require warning labels on products that are thought to be dangerous. Then consumers could at least decide whether they want to risk using the product. Unfortunately, all else is seldom equal in such matters.

TWO FEDERAL agencies — the Food and Drug Administration (FDA) and the Consumer Product Safety Commission (CPSC) — are now wrestling with the question of whether warning labels should be required on caffeine-containing foods and playground equipment.

Seemingly, the decisions should be easy to make. But they aren't, at least not for politicians and government regulators.

Although indirect evidence has been accumulating for years that caffeine may cause cleft palates and other birth defects when consumed in fairly large quantities by pregnant women, the federal regulators are still reluctant to require warning labels on caffeine-containing products.

That's not to say the regulators just don't care about the health and safety of the public they are supposed to serve. There is much agonizing in Washington these days over what to do about caffeine, in particular.

Two reasons for the agonizing are that politicians are worried about making an unpopular decision that will hurt their chances of re-election and that regulators are worried about losing credibility should evidence be proven wrong.

The necessity of rule makers to evaluate conflicting scientific studies is another reason. Like politicians, scientists often disagree. The evidence on the dangers of caffeine is open to debate. Many, *but not all*, of the studies on rats, mice and rabbits show a link to birth defects.

Evidence about potential dangers of playground equipment is more conclusive. At least 50,000 people require hospital treatment every year for injuries related to swings, seesaws, slides and monkey bars. Four out of five injuries reported are suffered by children under 10.

Cuts and bruises are the most common playground injuries. However some of the most serious result from falls, especially if the equipment has been installed over concrete, asphalt or packed earth. Of the head injuries suffered, 62 percent occurred in children under 5, the age group where falls are most common.

BUT WHEN is the evidence on caffeine, playground equipment and other products thought to be dangerous sufficient enough to require a warning label? Sufficient enough to justify any economic consequences that might result? Sufficient enough to jeopardize campaign contributions from businessmen irritated by government overregulation?

The drawn-out delays in decision making often come from trying to answers questions such as these, questions that are more of a political nature than a safety issue.

Regulatory agencies should seek the answers to such questions. But there is no justification for the search to delay action for years when the possibility exists that a product really is hazardous.

Nothing would be lost by putting warning labels on products as soon as any evidence of potential danger is discovered. If scientists later agree that the danger is nonexistent, that's fine. The warning labels could be immediately removed.

On the other hand, a lot would be gained by swift regulatory action on suspected hazardous products. Warning labels would certainly be worthwhile if they prevented even one woman from giving birth to a deformed baby or they prevented even one child from suffering a horrible head injury.

Dying

Death was a forbidden topic in America until recently. Now, however, that organ transplants have become a routine medical procedure, many people have begun to consider using their own deaths to help the living. This new development calls for a legal definition of death, so that organs can be ready for transplant in time to do the most good. A number of states have established "brain death," the ceasing of brain waves, as the legal definition of death. Cessation of brain activity, although other organs may still be functioning, is irreversible. Once the brain has stopped, a person has no hope of recovering any semblance of a normal life. He must go on as a vegetable, being kept alive solely by machines.

The prospect of such a fate has moved many people to prepare "living wills" in which they specify what is to be done to them if they are injured beyond hope of recovery. This has created deep legal and moral dilemmas. Who should be legally responsible for making the fateful decision that a person is beyond all hope of recovery? Furthermore, does any individual have the moral right to end his own life, rather than letting nature take its course? Suicide is considered a crime in Western society, but in Eastern tradition, suicide is often considered honorable. If it is accepted that people should have control over their own lives, it would seem to follow that they should be allowed to choose to die.

Chicago Tribune

Chicago, Ill., March 18, 1978

Two front page stories in Tuesday's Tribune illustrated the moral and legal difficulties posed in dealing with people whose remaining days are short and likely to be painful. Here in metropolitan Chicago, Craig Sieck's parents asked Loyola University Medical Center to turn off the machinery keeping their son's heart going after his brain wave activity had ended. In England, Derek Humphry has told on television how he assisted the 1975 suicide of his wife, afflicted by an advanced stage of bone cancer. If he is brought to trial, he says he will "plead guilty and ask for the mercy of the court."

Except for capital punishment and war, society views deliberate homicide as a heinous crime, and few sensitive persons wish for increased toleration of homicide. Yet technological advance has enabled hospitals to prolong life under conditions that only recently would have been decisively fatal. There is general recognition that under some circumstances death is a merciful release, to be welcomed rather than deplored.

Do health care institutions and personnel have either a moral or a legal obligation to postpone that release as long as is technically possible? Few persons would claim there is a moral obligation. The legal situation is less clear.

Loyola Medical Center administrators were at first unsure of their legal position in dealing with the request of Mr. and Mrs. Wayne Sieck. Only after Dr. Frank P. Stuart of the University of Chicago School of Medicine had assured them that the Illinois brain death law of 1975 clearly authorized disconnection of life-support systems to retrieve donated organs did they unplug the respirator. Had the Siecks been unwilling for organs to be donated, Dr. Stuart said "there could be some confusion." And the Cook County state's attorney's office

reviewed the case before announcing it would not bring charges against the hospital or the Siecks.

Now that machines can keep hearts beating after the brain has died, is it not desirable to clarify further Illinois' legal definition of death? Should doctors' freedom to disconnect respirators depend on families' willingness to donate organs for transplanting? Should there be any basis left for contending that life [and homicide] are defined in terms of only one organ, the heart? Legal definitions of death need revision in the context of modern technology.

The problem posed by Mr. Humphry is a more difficult one. In practice, a lengthening series of defendants on criminal charges have been found not guilty on the basis of extenuating circumstances acceptable to juries rather than of demonstrated noninvolvement in another's death. The thought of giving legal sanction to mercy killing [euthanasia], though, provokes grave misgivings, both theoretical and practical. If the theoretical obstacles to making an exception of euthanasia are overcome, the practical problem of recognizing in specific instances the difference between euthanasia and culpable homicide remains. Mr. Humphry agrees that motivation is critical. He thinks that his own action, which he calls "a supreme act of love," should not be prosecuted, but that aiding suicide for reasons of malice or greed should be. Juries after hearing evidence about a particular act are better judges of motivation than statutes written before the event can be.

That Mr. and Mrs. Wayne Sieck and Mr. Derek Humphry are entitled to universal sympathy is clear. Their tragic circumstances deserve whatever lightening of their great personal burdens society can find the compassion and ingenuity to provide.

Pittsburgh Post-Gazette

Pittsburgh, Pa., September 12, 1978

With the Karen Quinlan case in New Jersey, national attention focused on the question of "brain death."

Because technology now can prolong breathing and heartbeat long after the cessation of virtually all functioning of the brain, new questions have been posed as to how long life support systems should be continued. At least 18 states—not including Pennsylvania—have now enacted legislation recognizing "brain death" as well as the traditional common law definitions of death as "an absence of spontaneous respiratory and cardiac function."

Now the National Conference of Commissioners on Uniform State Laws has drafted a Uniform Brain Death Act, with the hopes that all state legislatures will adopt it.

The proposal recognizes that "for legal and medical purposes, an individual with irreversible cessation of all functioning of the brain, including the brain stem, is dead." "Determinations of death" would be made "in accordance with reasonable medical standards." But the act expresses "community approval of withdrawing extraordinary life-support systems when the whole brain has irreversibly ceased to work."

The act is short and purposely narrow. It does not deal with such problems as: medical criteria for establishing death; the effect of the time of death on legal rights; "living wills"; euthanasia; rules on death certificates; "death with dignity"; use of technology to maintain breathing and heartbeat after brain death in pregnant women or prospective organ donors; and protections for bodies.

In the case of Karen Quinlan, who suffered "brain death" after a drug overdose, the young woman continued to live even after her parents prayerfully agreed to remove life-support systems. The proposed law couldn't answer that dilemma.

But it could be immensely helpful for hospitals, physicians and families in similar instances. Pennsylvania should pass the NCCUSL's Uniform Brain Death Act.

Richmond Times-Dispatch

Richmond, Va., August, 16, 1978

A Florida judge on July 11 ruled that a 73-year-old man who was being kept alive, against his will, by a mechanical respirator had the right to order the treatment stopped.

The circuit court judge said that the man, who was mentally aware of the nature and consequences of his request to end use of the respirator to sustain his "miserable, wretched life," had attempted to remove the respirator but was prevented from doing so by hospital personnel. The respirator was connected to a breathing hole in the man's trachea.

"Neither the medical profession nor the courts should substitute their judgment for his [the patient's], even though such attempted substitution is undoubtedly well motivated," declared the court. "The court finds as a matter of fact and law that no state or medical interest is sufficient to upset this patient's decision to decline any further life-prolonging treatment by extraordinary means and that his right to privacy and his self-

determination as to the course of his remaining natural life is entitled to enforcement by this court."

The judge said that the death that would result from removal of the respirator would not be homicide or suicide, but would be from natural causes. And no one who assisted the patient in the exercise of his right to privacy would be committing an unlawful act, the judge added.

It is important to note that the judge's decision related to the specific circumstances in this particular case, involving a patient who was terminally ill, who was suffering great pain, who was being kept alive by a machine, and who himself was pleading that the machine be disconnected. Obviously, the court's decision could be viewed as being dangerously broad and as involving grave moral questions if it were interpreted to mean that any patient, at any time, should have the right to order discontinuance of treatment involving use of medical

devices that were keeping him alive.

The question of a suffering, terminally ill person's "right to die" is one of the most awesome and agonizing ones that ever confront patients, their families and physicians. The feeling has grown in recent years that it is not an act of mercy — indeed, some feel it is more an act of cruelty — to keep a dying person breathing and suffering a few additional days or weeks against his will when there is no remote possibility for any improvement in his condition.

Most people will feel, we believe, that the Florida judge's decision in this particular case was in the spirit of compassion. However, compassion does not necessarily speed up the slow-moving processes of justice, and as of yesterday, the patient was still connected to the respirator and, presumably, still suffering while the matter awaits consideration by an appeals court.

The Miami Herald

Miami, Fla., June 30, 1980

LIFE and death used to be relatively simple concepts, and the line between the two states was, until recent years, fairly easy for the typical person to discern.

Not so today. Modern medical miracles have the power to become nightmares of tubes and respirators that can make a human life seem to be a repugnant, artificial thing lacking in dignity and essential humanity. How to extricate oneself or one's loved one from that artifice has been the subject of innumerable court cases and painful attempts at legislation.

By consensus, Americans seem to have agreed that there is a point beyond which it is not necessary to continue with extraordinary mechanical means to prolong life. But the laws that rightly put the highest social priority on the protection of life are ill-equipped to let a patient die whose human life might be prolonged yet a little while. There is a reasonable fear of abuse of any license to kill, no matter how lofty the motive or how eager the victim.

Into this cacophony of vague public opinion and frantic judicial confusion has come a welcome voice, a voice that is the more comforting to laymen because of its undisputed commitment to the protection of human life. The Roman Catholic Church's opposition to euthanasia, or "mercy killing," is historic and well-known. For that reason, any person who sympathizes with the "death with dignity" cause should welcome the church's recent elaboration of its view that some modern medical treatments simply are not worth the burdens they impose on the patient and his family.

The distinction between killing, even for merciful motives, and simply permitting a natural illness to exact its final toll is useful. To turn off a respirator, for example, is simply yielding to the illness or injury that has destroyed the patient's own capacity to breathe. In contrast, the removal of intravenous feeding tubes would cause death by the unnatural means of starvation. The law should not deny the former to a comatose, terminal patient. But the latter is not acceptable.

In its new "Declaration on Euthanasia," the Vatican has summed up the problem with classic simplicity. "Life is a gift of God and, on the other hand, death is unavoidable. It is necessary, therefore, that we, without in any way hastening the hour of death, should be able to accept it with full responsibility and dignity."

Civil law should continue to protect the lives and rights of the sick and the dying. But it should not rob a terminally ill patient of a responsible, dignified death.

The Evening Gazette

Worcester, Mass., April 10, 1980

Earle Spring's peaceful death Sunday mercifully took from his family, doctors and the courts the burden of deciding whether or not his life-sustaining kidney treatments should be stopped. Dilemmas like theirs, however, will continue to burden society for years to come.

Every day, doctors must decide how aggressively they should treat very old, terminally ill or senile patients. These quiet decisions are sometimes just as difficult and morally challenging as the publicized courtroom deliberations over Karen Quinlan or Earle Spring.

Science has raced far ahead of the capacity of our religious and ethical systems to adjust. "Am I my brother's keeper?" takes on new meaning for families bearing the cost and anguish of caring for relatives who are only technically alive. Old rules about right and wrong and life and death just don't match up with the tools science has provided. As a last resort, we thrust questions of life and death onto the courts, to be argued by lawyers and doctors who have no more moral answers than anyone else.

The ethics time lag affects other issues besides the "right to die." Religious tenets on fertility, marriage and childbearing were created before conception could take place in a test tube and the world was overpopulated. Religious leaders try to fit old ethical systems into the new reality, but it isn't easy. New questions present themselves faster than new answers can be phrased.

Perhaps in time, ethical systems will adapt and adjust to help modern men and women make better decisions about life and death. Until then, one can only hope that the decisions made in court and hospital rooms will be made soberly, responsibly and mercifully.

The Toronto Star

Toronto, Ont., Canada, June 30, 1980

By affirming the right of individuals and doctors to turn off machines that keep dying people breathing and their hearts pumping, Pope John Paul II has added his voice to the solution of what has become a serious legal and moral problem in today's society.

Not unexpectedly, the Pope has made a clear distinction between mercy killing — where death is directly caused through an act of intervention or omission — and allowing an individual to die in peace and with dignity by not using sophisticated medical machinery to unduly prolong agony.

In the wake of the Pope's statement, it should be easier for public policy-makers, at Queen's Park and in Ottawa, to write new legislation giving people the clear legal — as distinct from moral — right to refuse artificial means of life support.

Less than a year ago, the Ontario Advisory Council on Senior Citizens recommended that the provincial government adopt a law permitting a person, while still fully competent, to specify in writing that he or she does not want artificial means used to prolong life when there's no hope of recovery from a fatal illness. Such a "living will," as it's called, would be binding on medical personnel and on relatives.

Indeed, as early as 1977, the Ontario Legislature gave approval in principle to a private member's bill incorporating the advisory committee's recommendation. But the bill died on the order paper when its proponent, Lorne Maeck (PC—Parry Sound) was appointed to the cabinet.

Maeck's remarks when introducing his bill are given increased validity in light of Pope John Paul's statement.

Maeck said: "Many people don't think about (whether machines should be kept hooked up when patients are no longer unable to communicate) until someone in their family has a stroke or something and can't speak. It then becomes a matter for the family and the doctor to decide.

"But I don't believe it should be up to the family and the doctor. I feel that as an adult the individual should have the right to make that choice. I want to relieve my family and my doctor of that responsibility."

Last summer, the Law Reform Commission of Canada published a working paper that also addressed the issue of the use of artificial life-support systems. The paper recommended that uniform legislation clearly defining when death occurs be adopted by both Parliament and the provincial legislatures.

Essentially, the working paper argued for a definition that death occurs when the brain has ceased to function even though breathing and heartbeat are maintained mechanically.

Such a definition is needed to resolve moral dilemmas for families of dying patients reluctant to make decisions to turn off machines. It's also needed to resolve legal complications for doctors intending to do organ transplants and who keep heart-lung machines going to keep organs healthy after brain death has occurred in the donor-patient.

These laws are needed. Pope John Paul's declaration should help give our legislators the necessary courage to proceed with them.

The Boston Herald American

Boston, Mass., June 21, 1980

There is a temptation to romanticize the death-by-choice of New York artist Jo Roman, to clothe it with a robe of nobility and rationalize it as an act of courage.

But was it, really?

That most difficult question gives rise to others equally as hard, in which moral standards and the very human fear of physical pain are intermixed.

For example, was suicide Roman's right — or an abuse of the gift of life? Was choosing it courageous — or cowardly?

Was it an answer — or an escape?

Was it a rational act — or a selfish one?

For those who missed the televised documentary of the Roman case, it evolved from her decision to end her life painlessly, at a time of her own choosing, rather than endure the hopeless agony of what she

thought — mistakenly — was terminal breast cancer.

The program dealt with the dispassionate way she went about it, and the laid-back way her husband and friends accepted it. It was all very trendy — and sterile. Mostly, though, it was terribly troubling, in that it tended to paint surrender in the false colors of victory. In fact, said Dr. Bruce Danto, it might have been enough to "nudge some suicidal individuals beyond the point of ambivalent feelings," to persuade them that killing themselves is laudable and sensible answer to whatever torments them.

Dr. Danto is a Detroit psychiatrist who is also immediate past president of the American Ass'n of Suicidology, an organization which studies death-by-choice in the hope of deterring people from resorting to it. What he said of the program

might also, we think, be said of Roman's decision.

"It turns death into a carnival affair," he declared. "It glorifies something that should not be glorified. It dehumanizes death and gives honor to suicide . . .

"It isn't that suicide is more acceptable. It's that life has become less acceptable. People either have never learned or are losing the art of coping . . .

"The danger of suicide promotion, which is what this program is, is that it is a permanent solution to a temporary problem."

Not only permanent but in the Roman case, tragically unsound, for after she died by her own hand, an autopsy was performed which showed that the cancer she thought was "terminal" was treatable, susceptible to therapy.

In short, she could have lived.

The Globe and Mail

Toronto, Ont., Canada, August 13, 1980

Exit's guide to suicide will, mercifully, not be published. Lawyers for the British society for euthanasia say its executives could be charged with "aiding and abetting" a suicide, and that professionals who helped draft the pamphlet could lose the right to practice. So, under protest, the society has bowed out of the field.

And none too soon. Exit's draft handbook outlined four bloodless methods of suicide; it warned against steps which might prove unusually slow or painful; it removed a major deterrent for people considering suicide — that it might fail, or hurt terribly. What Exit's pamphlet sold was suicide without tears.

In defending its right to distribute the literature, Exit cited case histories which presented the option of suicide in its best light. It pointed to New York artist Jo Roman who, on learning in 1978 that she had breast cancer and had no more than five painful years to live, decided to kill herself. She organized a farewell party, toasted her guests with champagne and swallowed an overdose of sleeping pills.

But hers was an exceptional case. As the head of Toronto East General Hospital's crisis intervention unit, Diane Syer, noted last year, there are occasions "where suicide does not seem unreasonable... If someone is confronted with certain knowledge that he or she is going to die a painful, undignified death through terminal illness, then suicide can be a viable option." But most potential suicides "are bowled over by emotion and they over-react to stress, without being able to see that there are other ways of coping with their problems." Their judgment is impaired, and — with a book like Exit's available to them — the decision to take their lives becomes that much easier.

Nicholas Reed, secretary-general of Exit, made a giant leap from a logical assertion — that dying easily is preferable to a "long, slow, painful death" — to

an assertion that "we're simply helping in the fight for another human right: the right to die." Publishing a do-it-yourself suicide manual draws no line between the person suffering a painful terminal illness and the person seeking a quick end to a life which isn't working out as planned. It just lays the weapons out on the table; anyone can take his pick. A.J. Levinson, executive director of the U.S. educational council Concern for Dying, said Exit's pamphlet might even make people "feel obligated to commit suicide if they're terminally ill." And if society accepts suicide as an alternative to coping with life, she said, there is a danger that it "won't work as hard to take care of its dying and suffering people."

The question Exit appeared not to have faced was this: would the victim have killed himself on his own? Suicidal tendencies are frequently the product of illness; the pamphlet, said the British Medical Association, "may discourage people who are suffering from depression from seeking help." Paul Whitehead, chairman of the sociology department at the University of Western Ontario, noted last year that people often get the idea of committing suicide from others. "What we want," he said, "is to have less people think it's an option, not more."

Unfortunately, no sooner had Exit cancelled its plans than an organization called Hemlock, based in California, announced plans for a similar, less clinical, pamphlet. It is making noises similar to Exit — "we are not," said its director, "into advising people to die" — and says it directs its message specifically at the terminally ill. It ignores the possibility that many readers might previously have considered suicide as nothing more than a whim. And that, in California as well as Britain, is only a stone's throw from aiding and abetting; if Hemlock's conscience will not dissuade it from publishing, perhaps the law will.

The Houston Post

Houston, Texas, July 13, 1980

Most of us like to live. Most people have an instinctive urge to survive whether threatened by a heart attack, cancer, a speeding automobile or a handgun. But few want to be kept alive for months when all consciousness or awareness has vanished, or when death would surely come without the machines. There comes a time when a dying person needs to die just as a sleepy person needs to sleep.

Texas is one of perhaps 10 states in the country that has provided by law a directive to physicians asking that life not be prolonged artificially. Passed under the leadership of Sen. Ray Farabee of Wichita Falls, the Texas law has been endorsed by the Texas Medical Association. Anyone age 18 or over may sign this directive before two witnesses who are not relatives and, once it is notarized, expect it to be respected whenever needed in the future.

Made by persons of sound mind, willfully and voluntarily, the document states: "If at any time I should have an incurable condition caused by injury, disease or illness certified to be a terminal condition by two physicians, and where the application of life-sustaining procedures would serve only to artificially prolong the moment of my death and where my attending physician determines that my death is imminent whether or not life-sustaining procedures are utilized, I direct that such procedures be withheld or withdrawn, and that I be permitted to die naturally."

The signer asks that "this directive shall be honored by my family and physicians as the final expression of my legal right to refuse medical or surgical treatment and accept the consequences of such refusal."

Such a directive is a great act of kindness and generosity. It frees the doctor and loving family of having to make the decision to let the patient die. Anyone who signs such a directive has the reassuring thought that he will not lie in a hospital bed, with pipes and tubes and electric wires providing an artificial life to a body long ready to free the spirit. Copies may be obtained from the Texas Medical Association, 1801 North Lamar Blvd., Austin 78701.

Des Moines Tribune

Des Moines, Iowa, June 10, 1980

It's easy to regard suicide as an irrational act, because that view softens its implicit challenge to some fundamental assumptions. Conceiving of it as rational, even positive, behavior is difficult or impossible for many people.

That's why Jo Roman, a New York City artist who elaborately planned and coolly executed her suicide a year ago, wanted people to understand why she did it. To foster that understanding, she left a manuscript and 19 hours of videotape. A one-hour television documentary about her suicide will be offered to public television stations for broadcast on June 16. (It is scheduled to be shown on the Iowa Public Broadcasting Network.)

Although the documentary's maker denies that the film advocates suicide, it apparently suggests that a case can be made for it. That case won't be made, however, on 16 public TV stations in Maine, Connecticut and Mississippi. Public TV representatives in those states said the program won't be shown because it is one-sided and potentially dangerous.

We don't question the motives of those who made that decision, or the legitimacy of their editorial authority. We do question their judgment and their dedication to the principle of free expression.

There is some reason for their fear that the documentary may lead people who are contemplating suicide to make the attempt. (That's not to say that canceling it will save any lives.) Tragic as those deaths would be, is that the basis by which the suitability of a TV program (or a film, book or article) ought to be judged — the potential of danger?

If so, many shows probably would have to be banned, because many kinds of ideas and behavior can lead people into trouble. Where is the line to be drawn? How is the potential for danger to be measured? Does the medium matter? Is a TV show more potent than a book?

The most troubling aspect of this decision is that an idea is being deemed unfit for public consumption. The idea of rational suicide may be anathema to many people — and they, of course, wouldn't have to watch. But it isn't an idea so insubstantial that it doesn't deserve a hearing.

Freedom of expression means little if it applies only to the kinds of ideas we are comfortable with.

Richmond Times-Dispatch

Richmond, Va., April 11, 1980

A recent court case gives further evidence of the growing realization that keeping terminally ill patients alive by extraordinary measures often is the antithesis of compassion.

It is true, said the appellate division of the New York Supreme Court, that the state has a responsibility to protect life. But, the court went on, the patient in a permanent vegetative coma has no hope of recovery and merely lies, trapped in a technological limbo, awaiting the inevitable. The fact, declared the court, is that such a patient has no health, and in the true sense, no life for the state to protect.

In the case in question, a proceeding was begun to obtain judicial permission for the withdrawal of the respirator from a patient who lay terminally ill in what was described as a chronic "vegetable coma." The patient died shortly after the case was filed, but the court proceeded to deal with the issues raised.

The court said that a competent terminally ill patient would have the right to refuse extraordinary medical treatment not only as an exercise of his bodily self-determination, but also pursuant to his constitutional right to privacy. It is both logical and morally right, then, the court reasoned, that an incompetent terminally ill patient be granted the same right, to be exercised by others in his behalf. Under New York law, the withdrawal of life-sustaining measures can only be done by court order.

More and more people, having undergone the agonizing experience of watching terminally ill loved ones suffer needlessly, have instructed their own doctors not to use extraordinary measures to prolong their lives — or, more aptly, their dying — in the event of a terminal illness. Among those who have given such instructions are doctors themselves.

The Boston Globe

Boston, Mass., June 17, 1980

Many people were appalled when the bizarre details of Jo Roman's death were made public a year ago. The 62-year-old artist, a New Yorker, gathered friends and family around in the months prior to her death to discuss her decision. She videotaped their conversations, had her suicide plans notarized, her obituary notice drawn up and dispatched to the local papers. She toasted her husband, a psychologist and professor of psychiatry, with champagne, took a shower, put on her favorite pink nightgown. Then she swallowed 35 Seconals.

At the time Roman, who had planned her death after learning she had breast cancer, sounded like a woman hell-bent on attaining immortality regardless of the cost; her so-called "self-termination" an act of supreme ego; her determination to defy life's uncertainty by choosing the precise hour of her death more selfish, personal indulgence than self-controlling statement.

But "Choosing Suicide," a documentary edited from Roman's videotape and shown on Channel 2 last night, helps us see her gesture as one made by an ordinary mortal, an artist all right, but not someone deluded by abstract theories or aesthetic principles about killing herself. As she tells the camera, "I don't want one day of pain, one minute of pain." She is shown as a woman struggling to find meaning in life and death, sure of herself even though many of those who are close to her can't and won't accept her decision, a woman who very simply doesn't want to give up her life to cancer, to medical treatment, to suffering.

We tend to think of suicide — jumping off a bridge, slitting the wrists, shutting the garage door and turning on the engine — as an act of desperation, a step taken by those who can't cope with their lives, by those who may wish to punish relatives and friends whom they feel haven't understood them or loved them enough. But this program helps us see that in some individual cases suicide can be an an act of affirmation.

The program makes a strangely compelling case. It doesn't advocate suicide but it forces you to consider the alternatives, to contemplate your own life and your own inevitable death. You may disagree with Jo Roman's reasoning, but you can't help but wonder what you would do in her place.

THE MILWAUKEE JOURNAL

Milwaukee, Wisc., October 10, 1980

Doctors, lawmakers and religious leaders have failed to grapple sufficiently with the enormously complex issue of death with dignity. It might help if they would listen carefully to the thoughts of one dying doctor.

Frederick Stenn, 71, an internist from Highland Park, Ill., died of cancer shortly after writing an eloquent letter to a medical journal, stating: "Man chooses how to live. Let him choose how to die. Let man choose when to depart, where and under what circumstances the harsh winds that blow over the terminus of life must be subdued."

As an internist, Stenn must have faced countless other people's deaths and must have had a thorough understanding of the terminal illness within him. Such experience added significance to his plea:

"As one . . . whose days are limited by a rapidly growing, highly malignant sacroma of the peritoneum; whose hours, days and nights are racked by intractable pain, discomfort and insomnia; whose mind is often beclouded and disoriented by soporific drugs and whose body is assaulted by needles and tubes that can have little effect on the prognosis — I urge medical, legal, religious and social support for a program of voluntary euthanasia with dignity."

There have been perplexing cases in Wisconsin — for example, the 83 year old mother who recently helped her crippled 53 year old daughter commit suicide. But there has not been an appropriate, helpful, open discussion of the many anguishing issues involved. Is society afraid to face those issues of death, just as individuals usually fear death itself? In both cases, an honest examination of reality would be beneficial.

TULSA WORLD

Tulsa, Okla., October 15, 1980

THE ISSUE raised by the "assisted suicide" broadcast on "60 Minutes" this week is a troublesome one. It is a question with no single answer, no ready solution — and so it should remain.

On one hand, groups in England and the U.S. are calling for the right of terminally sick individuals to commit suicide, helped if necessary by a friend or family member.

The euthanasia supporters want to take the law of the "right to die" a step further, making it legal for the dying person to enlist the help of another in ending life. These groups want to counsel patients on how to end their lives quietly and painlessly.

On the other hand, there are our cultural, religious and legal prohibitions against killing — even in mercy. Although attempted suicide is no longer a crime in Britain or the U.S., aiding and abetting a suicide is still illegal.

Might this personal decision of how and when to die become an obligation to die? Would the elderly person feel a need to relieve the family of the burden of caring for him longer? Would some begin making decisions for others?

There is the potential here for much wrong to be done in the name of right and mercy.

Dying does not need help from organizations. It needs only heavy doses of compassion and understanding among those dying and those suffering with them.

St. Louis ✠ Review

St. Louis, Mo., July 4, 1980

The Second Vatican Council in its pastoral constitution "Gaudium at Spes" condemned such crimes against life as murder, genocide, abortion, euthanasia and willfull suicide. Recently the Doctrinal Congregation elaborated on the Church's teaching on euthanasia. One of the main problems discussed is the obligation of using extraordinary means to maintain life in those who are in danger of death.

This most recent document maintains and develops the ideas put forth by Pius XII as early as 1947. Indeed moral theologians have been discussing this problem of extraordinary means since the turn of the century when it was disputed whether serious surgery could be put in this category or not.

The problem today is that what was once extraordinary is no longer considered to be that. Medical science has developed new techniques which now need to be evaluated with regard to their necessity or advisability.

First let it be stated that nowhere does the document discuss the problem of legal death — whether it be cessation of the vital signs of heart and pluse or cessation of brain waves. Some secular commentators have mistakenly taken it to endorse the brain death theory.

What it does do very clearly is state that one cannot impose on anyone the obligation to have recourse to a technique which is already in use but which carries a risk or is burdensome.

It also states that when death is inevitable and imminent it is permitted in conscience to make the decision to refuse forms of treatment that would only secure a precarious and burdensome prolongation of life, so long as the normal care due to the sick person is not interrupted.

This latest document from the Doctrinal Congregation not only condemns euthanasia but it is an exceptionally firm statement which reaffirms that nothing or no one can in any way permit the killing of an innocent human being, whether a fetus or an embryo, an infant or an adult, an old person or one suffering from an incurable disease or a person who is dying.

The Church's teaching authority is ready for the pro-euthanasia groups as well as for the pro-abortion groups. The most fundamental of all rights is at stake — the right to life.

—*Msgr. John T. Byrne*

ST. LOUIS POST-DISPATCH

St. Louis, Mo., June 27, 1980

The Vatican's new document on euthanasia strongly restates the opposition of the Roman Catholic Church to mercy killings, or any action or omission that permits the killing of innocent human beings. What is new in the document are guidelines allowing doctors or the desperately ill to renounce artificial life support where, in medical judgment, death is inevitable.

This is an effort by the church to apply its traditional principles to cases that have developed because of the advances of science. Where death is imminent in spite of the means used to prevent or delay it, the document indicates, conscience would permit the refusal of treatment that "would only secure a burdensome and precarious prolongation of life."

The statement could have practical results in many states, including Missouri. For some years the Legislature has refused to pass legislation adapting the law to the problems raised by new life support systems. The legislation would add to the old definition of death, which depends on cessation of respiration and circulation, the cessation of brain functions. Support systems, after all, can sometimes maintain respiration long after the patient has lost any prospect of the restoration of mental capacity. Yet physicians take a legal risk in suspending the life support systems, even when there is a possibility of using organ transplants to save the lives of others.

True, a number of states have adopted modernized definitions of death, as advocated by much of the medical profession and proposed by the National Conference of Commissioners on Uniform State Laws. In Missouri, though, there are still some legislators who say the proposed definition would condone murder. It would not, of course, and the Vatican document might help persuade them to change their minds.

BUFFALO EVENING NEWS

Buffalo, N.Y., July 2, 1980

The searching questions that have surfaced with the stunning advances in medical science have drawn a careful new statement of the Catholic Church's teachings to distinguish between euthanasia and exceptional circumstances permitting rejection of artificial support systems for the terminally ill.

While reaffirming the Vatican's condemnation of mercy killings, the Sacred Congregation for the Doctrine declared that a decision to refuse or interrupt sophisticated life-support systems is "permitted in conscience" when these would only secure "a precarious and burdensome prolongation of life" for the dying.

In such circumstances, the Vatican said, "the doctor has no reason to reproach himself with failing to help the person in danger." The church was careful, however, to couple the patient's consent with the exercise of the doctor's judgment as to whether the investment in life-prolonging instruments is "disproportionate to the results foreseen" and whether such techniques "impose on the patient strain or suffering out of proportion with the benefits" foreseen.

The case of Karen Ann Quinlan, the New Jersey woman who has remained in a coma despite the disconnecting of a life-sustaining mechanism in 1976, underscored the need for resolving the legal and moral questions thrust forward by the power of medical science to keep the incurably ill indefinitely lingering in a twilight between life and death.

In giving compassionate weight to these questions, the church declaration properly left for legal determination such issues as those relating to definitions of when death occurs and the need for multiple medical opinion in authenticating a patient's irreversible illness.

The church's primary concern remains a respect for the sanctity of life that forbids any "action or an omission which of itself or by intention causes death in order that all suffering may in this way be eliminated." At the same time, the statement holds that a desperately ill patient's refusal to accept extraordinary life-sustaining measures "is not the equivalent of suicide" but rather an acceptance of death as a "human condition."

The Vatican document is a timely statement that offers valuable general guidance in coping with the perplexing new questions prompted by the advances of modern medicine.

The Virginian-Pilot

Norfolk, Va., June 29, 1980

The Vatican has issued a new communique which may be a blessing for families who agonize over their moral responsibility when a loved one's life is being prolonged only by life-support machinery.

Fortunately there are few Karen Ann Quinlans who in the prime of youth fall into a coma from which there appears no hope of emerging.

But there are numbers of families with older members whose natural lives have about run their course, but whose failing conditions might be sustained by modern medical technology. In the best of circumstances this has to be one of the worst of all of life's dilemmas.

"When inevitable death is imminent in spite of the means used," says the Roman Catholic Church, "it is permitted in conscience to take the decision to refuse forms of treatment that would only secure a precarious and burdensome prolongation of life, so long as the normal care due to the sick person in similar cases is not interrupted."

Ever since the Quinlan case, which went to court when doctors refused to unplug the girl's equipment without a court order, many such cases have gone to a judge to decide. The Vatican statement may relieve the medical profession, for it says: "In such circumstances the doctor has no reason to reproach himself with failing to help the person in danger."

The Rev. Richard McCormick of the Kennedy Institute for Bioethics, a leading Catholic thinker in this field, expressed hope that it would counter "the overinvolvement of the courts in the management of the dying." That would be one of the more welcome results.

More important, it should help counter any sense of guilt on the part of survivors who consent to withdrawing respirators and other devices when doctors have given up all hope of recovery.

And while many folks today don't think of themselves as religious, even for most of them there remains an inescapable mystique about death. For the humanistic there is at least an ethical issue.

The church's statement is unyielding in its opposition to euthanasia, of course, and to abortion, suicide, or killing of an innocent human being of any age.

For the devout at least, it also attempts to put into spiritual context the meaning of suffering, especially during the last moments of life, as having a special place in God's saving plan. "It is," declares the Vatican, "a sharing in Christ's passion and a union with the redeeming sacrifice which He offered."

The statement, approved by Pope John Paul II, is welcome.

Appendix

The spiraling cost of medical care has motivated a number of people to suggest that doctors advertise their fees and services. The logic behind doctor advertising is pure free enterprise: if doctors were obliged to publicize their fees in advance, people would automatically choose cheaper doctors. Doctors themselves are horrified by the suggestion. They warn that incompetents and cheats could ensnare a gullible public with slick ad campaigns and special "introductory" offers. Despite their protests, the Federal Trade Commission ordered the American Medical Association to end its official ban on doctor advertising. However, there is little indication that doctors are rushing to reserve space in local newspapers.

If an individual can choose his own doctor, why not allow him to control his own medical records? Hospital records containing the most intimate personal data are routinely provided to law enforcement agencies. As a result, it seems that once a person enters a hospital he becomes its property. If one's bank account is off-limits to routine inspection, why should one's body be open to public scrutiny?

FTC Orders End to Ban on Doctors' Advertising

The Federal Trade Commission issued an order Oct. 24 charging the American Medical Association with unlawfully restricting competition among doctors and directed it to end its restrictions on advertising or solicitation of patients by physicians. (In contrast to the decision, the commission said it would permit the nation's largest organization of doctors to adopt "reasonable ethical guidelines" for advertising.) Any member organization violating the order was to be expelled, the commission directed. The order also barred any disciplinary action against physicians for participation in a health-maintenance organization.

The AMA said it would appeal the FTC's ruling and took issue with the FTC contention that the AMA had restricted competition or prevented physicians from disseminating information on services or prices.

THE COMMERCIAL APPEAL
Memphis, Tenn., October 27, 1979

THE FEDERAL GOVERNMENT wrote its latest prescription for healthier competition among the nation's professionals Wednesday when the Federal Trade Commission ordered the American Medical Association to lift its curbs on advertising by doctors.

AMA rules restrict most forms of advertising and ban price advertising. But the FTC complained that such regulations violate federal antitrust laws and encourage spiraling health-care costs.

Another part of the order, which stops the 200,000-member association from taking disciplinary action against a physician who participates in a health-maintenance organization, or HMO, is also aimed at economy. HMOs are seen as a way to cut back on costs not only because the groups' doctors are paid salaries instead of fees but also because HMOs are designed to deliver preventive as well as emergency care.

It remains to be seen whether the FTC is right in its prognosis that these moves will help hold down the soaring cost of medical services. After all, patients in the market for a doctor are as concerned about the quality of care as they are about what the care will cost. Doctors are only *allowed* to advertise; they aren't being told to do so.

And an advertised fee — even for such routine services as check-ups and immunizations — cannot preclude possible complications or the need for tests or further examination.

The AMA has already said it will appeal the ruling in federal court, but the order has given the association an important opportunity. The AMA has been asked to come up with "reasonable ethical guidelines" for advertising.

THOSE GUIDELINES can be drawn to ensure that the public is informed of professional competence at the lowest possible cost. And once the rules are in place, the AMA can also make sure that any false or deceptive claims are brought to the attention of state licensing agencies along with its own disciplinary boards.

The AMA and other professional organizations have a duty to set standards for admission to their fraternities, which they willingly accept. Yet they also have a history of reluctance when it comes to policing those who are already members.

Now that doctors can advertise, the AMA has the chance to uphold its standards and show its responsibility for the welfare of patients and physicians alike.

TULSA WORLD
Tulsa, Okla., October 26, 1979

THE FEDERAL Trade Commission says the American Medical Association's restraints on advertising by doctors inhibits competition and deprives consumers of needed information.

But doctors who oppose advertising in their profession need not worry too much. If highly competitive, aggressive advertising ever takes hold in the medical business, the Federal Trade Commission will surely step in and call a halt.

A World editorial last Tuesday described FTC's five-year campaign against a national supermarket chain's price-cutting ads. One objection was that the supermarket was able to get promotional discounts that allowed its customers to pay less for some items than they would have had to pay in competing stores.

The FTC believes in advertising as a principle, but discourages it every day with nitpicking rules.

The Providence Journal
Providence, R.I., October 31, 1979

Throughout the 20th century virtually all American physicians have abided by a code of professional ethics that prohibits advertising beyond simple announcements of a new practice or change of address. That code, strictly enforced by the 200,000-member American Medical Association, was declared to be in restraint of trade last week by the Federal Trade Commission, and few outside the profession will regret that finding.

At a time when high health care costs have sensitized a broad segment of the population to the lack of traditional market restraints in the medical profession, the public's inability to compare price and service is an extraordinary anachronism. One by one the anti-competitive codes long enforced for lawyers, eyeglass manufacturers and pharmacists have given way to compelling legal argument that these professions possess no a priori right to police their members in a way that is contrary to the best interests of consumers.

The practitioner who is prohibited from disseminating information about his services — costs, types of services performed, office hours, and so on — need have little fear of the usual competitive forces. With an uninformed clientele, for example, he lacks the usual motivation to maintain fee schedules at the lowest possible level. Indeed, as others raise their fees, the natural inclination is to follow the trend.

The FTC decision, written by Commissioner David A. Clanton, declares, "The evidence indicates that specific fee information is important to consumers, that consumers lack access to fee and other information necessary to make an informed choice of a physician, and that information obtained by word of mouth does not fulfill this need."

It is still uncertain whether the AMA will appeal the ruling in the courts, as well it may. But to its credit the Rhode Island Medical Society is unenthusiastic about fighting the inevitable. The society's president, Dr. Charles Hill, said he thinks advertising by doctors is "a good idea." And the same might be said for Dr. Hill's proposal that a board be created on a voluntary basis to oversee physician advertising. Such a panel, he suggested, might include consumers, media representatives and physicians.

Obviously, there would be some risk in an "anything goes" policy. That fact was recognized by the FTC, which said the AMA could adopt guidelines for physician advertising. It said the association can play a "valuable and unique role" in preventing false and deceptive advertising.

Holding health care costs down ought to be a top priority in the fight against inflation. One important way to help achieve that goal is to bring doctors — indeed, the entire health care industry — into the 20th century by allowing the market to function as it does for virtually all other enterprises in this country. The hour is late.

THE DAILY HERALD
Biloxi, Miss., October 26, 1979

The Daily Herald's sampling of physicians' opinions about advertising confirms what nearly everyone expected: advertising by doctors will be more infrequent than advertising by attorneys.

The Federal Trade Commission's ruling that the American Medical Association had illegally restrained physicians by restricting their advertising was greeted on the Coast with a ho-hum by the doctors we contacted. The ho-hum was followed by declarations of adherence to the long-standing policy of not advertising.

When the advertising option was opened recently for attorneys, the number exercising it in this area was minimal.

The value of the FTC's ruling, from the patients' viewpoint, is that advertising will be permitted. Many Coast residents are unaware of medical services that are available in the area and can learn of their existence only through word of mouth, a limited method of communication. New doctors coming into the area will now be able to do more than hang a shingle over their door. That will be an improvement.

As for competitive advertising, it's difficult to disagree with the consensus that local doctors will disdain it. The FTC can rule to permit competition but the ruling won't, and shouldn't, mandate it.

ST. LOUIS POST-DISPATCH
St. Louis, Mo., October 26, 1979

Some of the nation's medical associations and physicians who have expressed disapproval of a recent Federal Trade Commission order that allows doctors to advertise no doubt genuinely fear that the profession will never be the same. And they probably have some basis for expecting a certain amount of unflattering commercialism that they feel will tarnish the profession's image. But apart from a blow to the profession's image of itself, the FTC ruling is not likely to wreak the havoc predicted and could prove a boon for consumers. Doctors will still be judged on their competence, and the public now will have the advantage of price comparisons on routine services. In addition, the ruling ordered the American Medical Association not to interfere with doctors' ability to work for low-cost group health plans by branding such as "unethical."

The AMA, however, will still be allowed to regulate deceptive ads, and can impose ethical guidelines on the advertising. Certainly maintenance of high standards is vital for the sake of all concerned, but the standards that the AMA settles upon ought to be watched carefully to see that they do not encourage monopolistic practices and are not unduly restrictive.

"They're not supposed to advertise, but he gave me a special rate for promising to show it to everyone!"

The State
Columbia, S.C., October 29, 1979

Arguments by the Federal Trade Commission that advertising by physicians will lower doctor bills are not very persuasive. But neither are the physicians' claims that their profession will be harmed.

The FTC, striking down certain restrictions that medical societies place on advertising, said lack of public notice about physicians' fees and services have kept costs up. It is difficult to see how.

Medical treatment is costly, indeed, for various reasons. Lack of advertising is not one of them. Doctors don't have to charge high fees, and some of them don't. The fees are high because physicians either expect them, demand them or must have them to handle the costs of doing business.

On the other hand, some physicians, especially those speaking for professional organizations such as the American Medical Association, have exaggerated fears of a deterioration in medical care related to advertising.

Professional medical spokesmen say the public might be harmed by false or misleading ads placed by a few physicians. Such public harm is questionable, since most people are not in a position to make solid judgments about the quality of a physician anyway.

Competency has been mostly up to the doctors themselves, or the government. The somewhat closed system of peer review through which physicians police themselves has worked well, although by no means perfectly. It has also helped to reduce the length of patients' hospitalization.

In connection with peer review, there might even be some positive results of open advertisements. Few physicians are likely to take advantage of advertising, but, if a doctor does exceed the bounds of propriety, his peers will quickly know who to put under the microscope for an ethical examination.

Most doctors probably will not advertise at all, even if given the ethical freedom to do so. As several Columbia physicians said in reaction to the FTC's ruling, there is no need to advertise. They have as many patients or more than they can see. Competition is not now a major factor in the medical profession.

The prospect of saving sick people billions of dollars because of advertising, as the FTC claims, is not probable. The government should concern itself with high medical costs, but advertising — or the lack of it — is not a promising place for important results.

The Idaho STATESMAN
Boise, Idaho, October 26, 1979

The Federal Trade Commission's ruling on medical advertising is a victory for competition in a field where competition traditionally has been limited.

The FTC has ordered the American Medical Association to end its restrictions on advertising and certain other means of attracting patients. The commission maintains that restrictions have kept medical bills unnecessarily high.

The ruling met with a progressive response from the Idaho Medical Association president, who said it is "perfectly appropriate for physicians to advertise ... their type of practice, professional background and qualifications, office hours, participation in prepaid health plans, languages spoken other than English, and fees, or range of fees, which are being charged."

Appropriate indeed. Advertising would do much to enlighten people on a topic about which the average person knows precious little. In the view of the typical consumer, the medical profession is somewhat intimidating. In most cases, the doctor is better educated than the patient. He makes more money, he moves in different social circles. Many patients are afraid to ask questions concerning fees or professional qualifications for fear of appearing either miserly or ignorant. Advertising can remove a barrier and stimulate a needed flow of information.

As the FTC points out, advertising could provide another valuable public service by bringing about lower fees paid for medical treatment. If Dr. X reads that Dr. Y charges less for office calls, he might think about revising his own fee schedule.

Opinion is divided on decorum in medical advertising. Physicians understandably would be appalled to read about a weekend "special" on appendectomies.

Medical advertising should be tasteful, truthful and provide enough information to allow the patient to make an educated choice.

Under the FTC ruling, the AMA would be allowed to regulate deceptive claims and certain types of personal solicitation. Since the AMA is appealing the ruling, it obviously believes that this is not enough.

Not having seen the actual text of the ruling, we won't comment on that aspect. It is our opinion, however, that the AMA would best serve the public by exercising its power to end deceptive advertising and not by restraining legitimate competition. That's what the ruling is all about.

St. Petersburg Times
St. Petersburg, Fla., October 26, 1979

For most people, shopping for doctors is like choosing a telephone company. There's no competition.

Sure, the Yellow Pages are full of them. But the actual choice is limited to guesswork, aided on occasion by praise or blame from patients one happens to know.

That's because doctors don't advertise. The American Medical Association (AMA) wouldn't let them.

FOR MOST of this century, the AMA and its state and local affiliates forbade all advertising except for the occasional discreet notice that a practice had begun or had moved its location.

State laws and regulations, dictated by the profession, gave the force of law to the prohibition.

Advertising, the doctors said, would be "unethical."

IT WAS NONSENSE. Selfish, hypocritical nonsense.

The rule certainly didn't purge the profession of incompetents and quacks, did it?

What it did do was to make price competition an act of futility. It would serve no purpose except conscience for a doctor to keep fees low. Who else would know?

Two years ago, the U.S. Supreme Court struck down a similar prohibition against advertising by lawyers, and most state medical boards, Florida's included, followed suit. Even the AMA and its state affiliates changed their codes to permit some advertising, though the efficacy of the change is open to debate.

MEDICAL advertising remained so rare as to be remarkable, largely because the medical profession continued to intimidate itself through tradition, peer pressure and other subtle influences.

Thus three cheers are due for the Federal Trade Commission (FTC), which ruled this week that it is an illegal restraint of trade for the AMA to inhibit doctors from advertising fees and services.

Quite properly, the FTC said that the AMA could differentiate between ethical and unethical forms of advertising, such as to prohibit that which is dishonest or unscientific.

But it isn't dishonest or misleading for doctors to advertise their fees, their specialties, their office hours and other matters that are factual — such as, one would hope, their willingness to make house calls. From that, the public can only gain. And the profession itself, before long, will gain from an infusion of new public respect.

REGRETTABLY, the AMA is appealing the decision. A profession whose members so often preach free enterprise is strangely unwilling to see them practice it.

Another obstacle to the public obtaining the full benefits of the FTC decision is the fear many doctors will feel that if they advertise, punishment will be dealt in subtle ways — such as denial of hospital staff privileges or loss of patient referrals.

These are reasons why the FTC should keep the health industry under investigation and pressure. What about doctors who send patients to pharmacies and to hospitals which these same doctors own? What about hospital boards that grant or deny staff membership in such ways as to keep troublemakers in line? The FTC clearly has work left to do.

And the public can help by keeping the Congress under pressure to reauthorize the FTC without such hobbles as a one-house veto of FTC rules and blanket exemptions for certain special interests.

Take two aspirin, Doc.

And more power to the FTC!

The Times-Picayune
New Orleans, La., October 26, 1979

We usually think of large corporations when we think of antitrust cases, but lately antitrust officials have been focusing on antitrust abuses by professionals — optometrists, druggists, engineers, lawyers and now doctors.

This week the Federal Trade Commission told the American Medical Association that it must end its curbs on doctors' advertising because such curbs violated federal antitrust law. The FTC claimed that the AMA rules — restricting most forms of advertising, including price advertising and the solicitation of patients — had restrained competition among its 200,000 members

The AMA has claimed that its restrictions were "ethical" ones that did not proscribe advertising but "did prohibit false and misleading advertising that may adversely affect quality care to patients." But the FTC ruling will not prevent the AMA from regulating deceptive claims. In fact, the commissioners noted that the association can play a valuable role in preventing deceptive ads.

After a June 1977 U.S. Supreme Court ruling struck down the AMA's restriction on advertising, the association revised its code of ethics, but the FTC said its order was needed to prevent a recurrence of practices cited in the 1975 complaint that started the case.

The FTC ruling also banned AMA action to interfere with doctors' ability to work for low-cost, fee-for-service group health plans. The federal agency sees such health plans, increased competition among doctors and public awareness of fees as a means of keeping down ever spiraling health costs.

The majority of people may still base their choice of a doctor on recommendations of other physicians or friends, but advertising should give the average citizen another means of choosing a health care provider. And, as consumerism enters the medical field, more patients may find the courage to shop around for a new doctor if the one they have subjects them to long waits or condescending treatment.

The Virginian-Pilot

Norfolk, Va., October 28, 1979

Ralph Nader must have cheered.

The Federal Trade Commission ruled this week that doctors have a right to advertise their fees and compete for patients.

"It is especially important that price advertising remain as unfettered as possible," said the FTC. The American Medical Association, which had branded doctor advertising unethical, was accused by the FTC of causing the public "substantial injury."

What's it all mean? New price competition? An end to spiraling health costs? Consumerism in the saddle? No more exorbitant doctors' fees?

The ruling probably will have little immediate effect. To be sure, California newspapers have been sprinkled with ads from cosmetic surgeons. But most physicians still regard the practice as "undignified."

We entertain misgivings. Professional service—whether doctoring, dentristy, lawyering, or engineering—strikes us as different from the making of widgets. Consumers might think twice about running to a doctor who needs newspaper ads to bring patients to his door.

We wonder how much there is about medicine that can safely be classified routine and thus subject to competitive price. Just what is a "routine checkup," for example? What tests and opportunity for consultation would it include? Suppose the physician detects in the course of a checkup something suggesting investigation beyond that included in the advertised "routine" price. Many a patient who entered a physician's office at one price may leave to his chagrin at something else.

Professional advertising can over time alter the climate of professional service. There is some danger that aggressive advertising and a new spirit of solicitation could attract more patients to unnecessary surgery and care.

In a free enterprise society, it is foolish to think that public price competition won't have benefits. Yet in its rush to professional advertising, society has overlooked some real costs.

The Washington Post

Washington, D.C., October 26, 1979

NO, YOU'RE NOT LIKELY to see ads offering "Cut-rate surgery! Prices slashed!" or "Today Only: 2-for-1 Special on Major Operations!" This week's ruling by the Federal Trade Commission ordering the American Medical Association to let its member doctors advertise fees and compete for patients is no carte blanche for grubby or deceptive hawking by physicians. The AMA remains free to write its own prescription for medical advertising and to enforce "reasonable ethical guidelines" to prevent deceptive or unsubstantiated claims. So why not let doctors tell people what goods and services are available at what prices?

We do confess to a certain special affection for advertising—it supports newspapers. But there is also a potential benefit to be realized by the public: safe and reasonable competition with a consequent lowering of medical fees, and a better chance for people to do some informed comparison shopping. That seems to be the case with lawyers, who have been advertising in increasing numbers since the Supreme Court upheld their constitutional right to advertise. Prices of certain routine legal services—uncontested divorces and writing of wills, for example—have declined.

When people don't know what the going rates are, they may be timid about inquiring—and therefore may avoid medical or legal protection they need and could afford. This doesn't mean that they will be fooled by ads offering absurdly low prices for complicated work. Most people know that quality and price do have some relationship. Adding a little competition to the mix won't hurt, either. It may even be good for business. Surely there's some additional medical work that will be done when people can find out more readily where to get it at a price they can afford.

Incidentally, who *does* still make house calls—and how much are they?

SUNDAY TELEGRAM

Worcester, Mass., October 29, 1979

Back in the "good old days," when medicine was part hucksterism and quackery, it was standard for doctors to advertise miracle cures for all sorts of ailments.

So it was no wonder that the various medical associations and societies came to see that restraint in advertising was called for. For many years, the American Medical Association has forbidden its members to advertise or promote themselves.

Specifically frowned on was any advertising of fees. The AMA has been very tough on that point.

But a few days ago the AMA was overruled. The Federal Trade Commission, following the lead of an administrative law judge last year, has told the AMA that it must let doctors advertise their fees and compete for patients.

Does this mean a return to cancer quacks and miracle nostrums? We think not.

Although the controversies over Laetrile and krebiozen may seem to indicate otherwise, the public today is far more discriminating than it was 100 years ago. And medical treatment is far superior.

Allowing a limited amount of competition into the field of medical service won't be hurtful. The FTC stipulated that the AMA may set "reasonable ethical guidelines" to prevent "deceptive" or "unsubstantiated" claims. That should provide the needed protection.

The AMA, over the years, has constantly striven to maintain high standards of medical treatment in this country, for which we all can be grateful.

But the AMA has also sometimes seemed to be overly concerned with the effects of competition. It resisted the growth of health maintenance organizations. At times it opened itself to the charge that it was more concerned about the fee-for-service concept than it was about the health of patients.

The new FTC decision is comparable to the U.S. Supreme Court's decision two years ago striking down the American Bar Association's restrictions on advertising by lawyers. The change has not hurt the legal profession. Neither will the new ruling hurt the medical profession.

The great majority of people will continue to select their doctors in the traditional way, especially for serious illnesses. But there's no harm in a little competition.

Doctors' Advertising, Continued: FTC Charges AMA with 'Conspiracy'

AKRON BEACON JOURNAL

Akron, Ohio, December 1, 1978

A FEDERAL Trade Commission judge has ordered the American Medical Association to end its ban on advertising by physicians. AMA officials say they will appeal the order, even to the point of seeking a congressional remedy, if necessary.

And both defend their positions on the basis of what they contend is best for those who need medical care.

But it's difficult to accept that argument from the AMA, partly because the ban on advertising, in effect since the early 1900s, has not and cannot guarantee patients protection against incompetence and quackery as it was designed to do. Furthermore, it deprives those in a particular professional group freedom of expression, a basic right of all citizens.

The battle against restrictions on advertising is one that the American Bar Association faced and lost in 1977 in the U. S. Supreme Court. The ABA is not particularly happy about the ruling, nor is the Akron association, but, in this area at least, it has not resulted in a sudden deluge of legal ads or in a rash of blatantly irresponsible or fraudulent advertising.

But it can and it has in other states, according to a lawyer who offered as evidence advertisements from California guaranteeing results in, for instance, divorce or drunk driving suits or giving misleading data on fees.

Unfortunately, no profession is immune from scoundrels. If they were, there would be no cause to argue about whether advertising by physicians is good or bad, for they have already vowed in their Hippocratic oath to abstain from corruption and deleterious and mischievous conduct.

The judge's position, similar to that in rulings in recent years that have given lawyers, engineers and druggists the right to advertise, is that the AMA ban constitutes a restraint of trade that discourages competition and deprives consumers of pertinent information.

The lack of competition, federal officials contend, makes it more difficult to hold down rapidly rising health care costs. That may be so.

But, in issuing his ruling, which still must be approved by the entire commission, the judge went one step too far. His decision would require the AMA to get federal approval for a professional code of ethics, including guidelines for advertising.

Trustees of the AMA are justifiably incensed at that provision, which, they say, is without precedent in the United States. Certainly those trained and practiced in the area of medicine are more qualified to determine what constitutes ethical practice and honest advertising than is any group of laymen.

No doubt many of the most talented physicians and skillful surgeons, like highly qualified lawyers, will choose not to advertise. That is their right. If they choose to advertise their services and fees, that should also be their right. It is hard to see how such advertising — by members of a profession that takes seriously its obligation to police itself — can adversely affect the health of medical care consumers.

The Washington Star

Washington, D.C., December 1, 1978

If you start with the view of the learned professions that seems increasingly to sway federal judges and regulators — that professions are, essentially, an arm of trade — you come out just where Judge Ernest G. Barnes of the Federal Trade Commission did this week.

In a ruling that could drastically reshape the ethos of American medicine, Judge Barnes found that the American Medical Association's ethical rules on advertising by doctors amount to a "conspiracy" restraining trade. They must be scrapped says Judge Barnes or, at least, rewritten to the FTC's liking. His ruling is subject to full FTC approval, which is expected, and, beyond that, to a court test that is inevitable and would surely be warranted.

The thrust of Judge Barnes' decision, three years in the making, is to dissolve important philosophical and ethical distinctions that set medical practice apart from, say, auto repair and the ministrations of massage parlors. It follows a more guarded Supreme Court decision of June 1977 relaxing the traditional ban on lawyers' advertising.

Let us admit, before examining the legal and philosophical implications of the decision, that there *is* some "restraint of trade" in certain AMA activities and those of local member societies. In those activities the AMA (and its political arm, AM-PAC) have probably invited the trouble they get when a federal administrative judge assails their professional mystique.

Pure greed sometimes flourishes behind the decorous veil of professionalism; so does the obstruction of innovations in styles of medical practice that pose no threat to ethical standards. Legal and other forms of learned professionalism, moreover, are not engraved on stone tablets. Every student of medical history knows that surgery began in barber shops, and that quackery is perennial at the fringes.

These, however, are peripheral issues. The important issue is whether some abuses justify the debasement of a profession, in FTC eyes, to the level of a commercial trade. Such debasement is implicit in Judge Barnes' decision, and in the law and philosophy with which he justifies it.

His decision cites "the free flow of commercial information" as its legal basis. The notion, basically, is that the utilitarian rules of a commercial society — competition, comparative shopping, etc. — are in some sense superior to the ancient self-restraints of the professions:

the values that set them apart from the marketplace and the shop window. This is "consumerism" run wild. Judge Barnes, revealingly, calls those who seek medical services "consumers," not patients.

This decision not only strips medical professionalism of much ethical meaning; it also sets up the government, once again, as the all-wise arbiter of the private as well as the public interest.

It is to be expected that the FTC will supplant the AMA and its member societies as final judge of what is "ethical" in medical advertising and maybe, by extension, in medical practice as well. The FTC has been given, or assumed, sweeping powers over advertising in the trades, from razors to soaps. This is its first major sally into professional advertising and it is sweeping. Judge Barnes gestures in the direction of encouraging medicine to continue self-regulation. But if the FTC seizes plenary oversight (if, as Judge Barnes puts it, "the FTC . . . has the organizational flexibility and knowhow to . . . assure that such guidelines as are approved are in the public interest") it isn't hard to guess who'll be calling the shots.

And with what result? Professional advertising is a tricky business, of uncertain effect. The Supreme Court, permitting it for lawyers, spoke glibly of "routine" legal services, while seeming to reserve some control in more complicated questions to the bar.

But what, to think in parallel, is a "routine" medical service? What about an appendectomy with dangerous complications? Would it be ethically misleading for a doctor to advertise *any* service, beyond a simple checkup, as "routine"? Who should decide? What qualifies the FTC to usurp the ethical sense of the doctors themselves?

We aren't arguing that the law should countenance everything that organized medicine does in the name of professionalism. We *are* arguing that Judge Barnes has intruded regulation dangerously far into an area long reserved, for reasons that aren't frivolous, to private discretion. We *are* arguing that his decision, in the name of correcting some recognized abuses hidden beneath the mantle of professional ethics, threatens to shred the garment itself. We *are* arguing, finally, that the FTC should rethink this sordid commercialization of medical ethics or, failing that, the courts.

THE LOUISVILLE TIMES

Louisville, Ky., August 30, 1978

What one would think is the basic right of a person to see his medical records is by no means assured. In most states, including Kentucky, doctors are under no obligation either to tell a patient anything or to share with him the documents in his files. Nor are physicians required to send a patient's file to another doctor should he choose to go elsewhere for care.

Thus, it's virtually impossible for the discerning or dissatisfied consumer of health care to be fully informed or to exercise freedom of choice.

The rights of property collide head-on when a patient demands to see his medical records, and the traditions of law favor the physician. Courts have generally viewed a physician's record of his patients as his personal property. It becomes a part of his estate which may be sold or destroyed.

Clearly, this is an archaic view, particularly in a time when more and more people are interested in not only understanding illness, but in preventing it.

"Patient-access" bills introduced in several state legislatures have not been successful. In California and Wisconsin, bills to allow patients copies of their physicians' and hospital records, respectively, failed to get out of committee.

Kentucky should seriously consider a law giving every citizen the right to view his own medical records. The 1980 General Assembly should draft a comprehensive "bill of rights" for all forms of health care — including that provided by physicians, dentists and hospitals.

"A complete medical record may contain more intimate details about an individual than could be found in any single document," says the executive director of the American Medical Association in an excellent new report of the Public Citizen's Health Research Group, part of the Ralph Nader organization.

Unfortunately, he may never see this amazingly intimate document, even though it is available to health insurance companies, law enforcement investigators, schools, researchers, credit bureaus and employers.

If a patient hopes to become an informed consumer of health care, and that seems one solution to the dizzying escalation of medical costs in this country, he must be better informed about his condition.

The Nader Group has discovered that doctors who conscientiously inform their patients about their conditions are pleased with the results.

"I make my patients be their own doctors," one Indiana physician says in the report. "Once a patient understands the alternatives he has available for his illness, he can make his own decision and plan his own cure. The good things we doctors accomplish with patients are accomplished only with their entire assistance."

In contrast, incompetent physicians may be most likely to refuse patients who want to read their own files. "Many doctors may, in fact, hold up the specter of incomprehensibly technical records," the report concludes, "because they would prefer not to have other doctors to whom the patients show the records reading and commenting on their possibly sloppily compiled memoranda."

As always happens, the callous attitudes of some doctors are contrasted with the enlightened attitudes of others. In this community many excellent physicians share the belief of the Indiana doctor who informs his patients completely about their conditions.

But in other situations, the results are depressing. Unfortunately, the least educated patient is perhaps the easiest to keep uninformed. He is also the person who may be least able to afford the expense of medical care and the one who would most profit from informed decision-making.

Information about one's health is the most basic kind of knowledge. Healers must understand, and cooperate, with the patient who seeks to help himself by learning what his health problems are — and how to correct them.

THE ☼ SUN

Baltimore, Md., January 15, 1977

A new study sponsored by the National Bureau of Standards shows that personal medical information is widely disseminated to government agencies and private organizations which have no right to it. While computerized medical data banks pose a potential problem of even larger-scale misuse of medical data, current abuses appear to derive more from non-computerized systems. It is still easier to get information from filing cabinets than from computers.

The principle that most medical records should be kept in strictest confidence scarcely can be questioned. The only exceptions should be cases, such as gunshot wounds or communicable diseases, where law enforcement agencies or public health officials have a clear legitimate public interest. The individual's right to privacy alone is enough to support the principle, but there are other reasons as well. One is the fact that medicine is an inexact science in which the same raw data may permit several different interpretations. This is particularly true in psychiatry, where a half dozen schools of thought contend, and where the potential for abuse is large if information gets into the wrong hands. One example is the frequency with which alcoholism produces bizarre symptoms that until recently sometimes were misdiagnosed as severe mental illness. The symptoms disappear when the alcoholics quit drinking, but the diagnoses often remain in their records.

A related issue explored by the study is the extent to which patients should have access to their own files. Ironically these files often are available to outsiders—prospective employers or insurance companies, for instance—but not to the patients themselves. With a few exceptions, such as in certain psychiatric disorders, patients should have an unquestioned right to learn all they wish to learn about their own illnesses and their physicians' diagnoses.

The new study recommends that safeguards against misuse of medical information be erected now, before the potential for abuse grows larger with more computerization. The safeguards recommended by the study include requiring explicit patient consent any time medical records are released to outsiders; excluding the release of information in which the recipient has no legitimate interest; and providing patients with exact copies of requested information before it is released. Congress should act to give such safeguards the force of law before abuses become even more widespread.

The Seattle Times

Seattle, Wash., January 14, 1977

THE most recent of the horror stories now in vogue about computer-engineered invasion of citizens' privacy concerns the field of medicine. Therein are ample grounds for concern.

A $130,000, two-year study, financed by the National Bureau of Standards, found that individual medical records commonly circulate from doctors' offices, clinics, and hospitals to the files of insurance companies, employers, credit bureaus, police, government agencies, and elsewhere.

Alan F. Westin, a Columbia University professor who headed the study, says Americans "have simply lost control over the flow of medical information about them in our society."

"It is this loss of control," Westin adds, "that is the heart of the privacy issue."

The study showed federal and state laws to be altogether inadequate in protecting the privacy of the individual.

An incident in this state last spring illustrates what can and should be done. At the insistence of County Executive John Spellman and other King County officials, the state dropped a demand for identification of persons screened for involuntary mental-health commitment.

But that was only one victory in what appears to be a losing war against "big brotherism." The heavy artillery, in the form of computerized data-processing technology, is on Big Brother's side.

As Columbia's Westin says, "securing individual rights in the increasingly computerized world of health care is a job that has barely begun."

WORCESTER TELEGRAM.

Worcester, Mass., March 8, 1978

Should patients have access to their medical records?

That is a question facing the Massachusetts Board of Registration and Discipline in Medicine. A proposed regulation would require doctors to let patients see summaries of their medical records unless the doctor believes such information would adversely affect the patient's health.

Some doctors are reluctant to grant this kind of access, maintaining that it would damage the doctor-patient relationship.

Massachusetts is one of a few states which grants patients the right to inspect medical records — but only those kept by hospitals. The new proposal would add records kept by physicians.

Although the Massachusetts law giving patients the right to hospital records was enacted more than 30 years ago, two recent studies have shown that hospitals do not always comply. A 1973 study by the Center for Law and Health Sciences of Boston University Law School claimed that nine out of 10 major Boston hospitals denied patient requests for information. A 1975 study by the Massachusetts Public Interest Research Group claimed that only three out of 28 hospitals examined were in compliance.

In the past, medical records were used only by the physicians and the hospital. But today, these records are extensively used by health insurance companies, law enforcement agencies, welfare departments and others.

Thus, it becomes important for the patient to be able to see the records and correct any mistakes that could affect education, government benefits or career advancement.

Testimony before the medical board indicated that problems feared by doctors did not materialize in a two-year experiment at Beth Israel Hospital in Boston.

Ruth Fischbach, a nurse-practitioner at the hospital, said that the experiment in the outpatient department showed that free access to records has made the doctor-patient relationship "more collaborative."

Some physicians, however, argue that full access to records may not always be in the best interests of the patient. The American Medical Association holds to that view. The overwhelming majority of health professionals oppose full access because they believe it is the doctors' right and duty to withhold information in circumstances in which the information would be harmful to the patient.

The access question points out the changing doctor-patient relationship. There is the trend in some courts to view the relationship as a decision-making partnership rather than a medical monopoly. There is increasing emphasis on telling the patient enough about the medical treatment recommended by the doctor and about its risks. In this way, the patient can better decide whether to accept the doctor's recommendation.

In the consumer theory of health care, the doctor is seen as an agent hired by the patient to exercise professional skills and judgment. But, under this theory, it is also necessary for the doctor to make full disclosure if the patient demands it.

From the physician's viewpoint, however, there are some cogent reasons for denying full access to records. The records are usually written in technical terms difficult for the layman to understand. And doctors would have to write notes and observations in a way that would be diplomatic when read by the patient, but perhaps in a way that is less direct and less clear.

Doctors might also be tempted to leave out speculative and hypothetical comments they now make to help themselves and other professionals who may consult the medical record. Such defensive practices might make the records less valuable for medical research, review of care and other purposes.

To counteract these negative effects, some have recommended a dual system of medical records. The first part would consist of all personal information about the patient: social and family history, complaints, tests and examination results; diagnoses; treatment summaries, medication programs and payment information. This would be the official record and the patient would have full access to it.

The second part would include any sensitive judgments about a patient's emotional or psychological condition. It also would include speculative and tentative hypotheses that a doctor wanted to save for personal use or for others sharing in the patient's primary care. This information, like doctors' notes now, could be subpoenaed by the patient in a malpractice suit. Thus, the doctor, then as now, would find it unsafe or unwise to record certain kinds of information permanently.

The notion of dual records has been endorsed by some diverse groups. They include the American Society of Internal Medicine, the American Civil Liberties Union and the IBM Medical Department.

Some health professionals will probably continue to oppose patient access to medical records. But with changes in the health delivery system — more automation, more computerization and more group practice — changes are inevitable. Patients are going to demand — and get — more information from doctors than they ever got before.

The Providence Journal

Providence, R.I., March 6, 1978

As the nation's health care system moves more and more into the public domain, with government attempting to hold down rapidly escalating costs and to insure that all citizens have access to medical care and treatment, concern is rising over the confidentiality of medical records. With good reason.

The individual is increasingly vulnerable to the data-bank syndrome; that is to say his privacy runs greater risk of infringement as health insurance programs in both the public and private sector become more sophisticated and all-encompassing.

In states like Rhode Island, which lacks legislation to protect the confidentiality of medical records, the risk is greatest of all. Although a bill to provide strong safeguards in this sensitive area was introduced last year with strong backing, it failed to pass. Instead, the bill's sponsor, Rep. Victoria S. Lederberg, D-Providence, was named to head a Special Legislative Commission to Study the Confidentiality of Health Care Information.

On Thursday, Mrs. Lederberg reintroduced her proposal with this valid observation: "At the present time in Rhode Island, lawyers and their clients enjoy an absolute privilege, which means that an attorney must keep strictly confidential any information supplied with that understanding. To some extent, a similar privilege is allowed to a clergyman and a member of his congregation. But no such privilege exists in law between a doctor and a patient."

Again the proposal has strong backing — from the Rhode Island Medical Society and in principle from the Rhode Island Mental Health Coalition Properly, the bill would exempt government regulatory agencies that would be allowed access to records for cost and quality control. Likewise, in certain medical emergencies, in some court cases and when the public health might be involved, exceptions would be made.

Privacy is no longer something the individual can take for granted. It is under assault from all sides with advanced computer technology serving as the mechanized vehicle. Under the circumstances, there should be no question in the mind of any legislator how to vote on this one. By rights it ought to be enacted by acclamation.

Index

PASSIVE Restraints—*see AIR Bags*
PHARMACEUTICALS—*see DRUGS*
PREGNANCY
   Saccharin risks cited—17–24
PRESCRIBING—*see DRUGS*
PRIVACY
   Use of medical records scored—179–180

R

ROMAN, Jo
   Suicide decision aired on TV—166–171

S

SACCHARIN
   FDA sets ban; modifies; Congress postpones; cancer risk doubted—2–24
SAFETY Regulations—*see AUTOMOBILES, TRANSPORTATION, U.S. Department of*
SEAT Belts
   'Passive restraint' system ordered—100–106
SENATE—*see CONGRESS*
SHERWIN–Williams Co.
   Saccharin ban opposed—2–7
SMOKING
   Saccharin risk to smokers seen—17–24
   Alcohol health warnings proposed—50–58

   Danger seen to non-smokers; public bans sought—60–74
   Govt seeks stronger anti-smoking effort—75–90
SMOKING & Health, Office on
   Califano creates—76
SODIUM Valproate
   Approved for epileptics—154
SOFT Drinks—*see BEVERAGES*
SPEED Limits—*see AUTOMOBILES*
SUGAR Substitutes—*see SACCHARIN*
SUICIDE
   Artist's TV suicide—166–171
SUPREME Court
   Rejects public smoking ban—66
   Upholds FDA Laetrile ban—140–141
SWEETENERS, Artificial—*see SACCHARIN*

T

TAGGART, Cal
   Wyoming raises speed limit—92–96
TEENAGERS
   Smoking increase noted—76
TELEVISION—*see MEDIA*
TEXAS
   55–mph speed limit opposed—92–96
   Laetrile legalized—116–125
THALIDOMIDE
   FDA procedures criticized—155–164
THURMOND, Sen. Strom (R, S.C.)
   Seeks health warning on liquor bottles—50–58

TOBACCO—*see SMOKING*
TRANSPORTATION—*see AUTOMOBILES*
TRANSPORTATION, U.S. Department of
   55–mph speed limit opposed—92–96
   Air bag controversy—97–114

U

UNITED Auto Workers
   Praises air bag plan—100–106

V

VITAMIN B-17—*see LAETRILE*

W

WASHINGTON
   55–mph speed limit opposed—92–96
   Laetrile legalized—116–125
WOMEN
   Saccharin held pregnancy danger—17–24
   Smoking increase noted—76–90
   DES linked to cancer—149–152
WYOMING
   Auto speed limit raised—92–96